6th Edition

North American Indian Artifacts

A Collector's Identification & Value Guide

Lar Hothem

Published by

krause publications

700 E. State Street • Iola, WI 54990-0001
Telephone: 715/445-2214

Please call or write for our free catalog.
Our toll-free number to place an order or obtain a free catalog is 800-258-0929
or please use our regular business telephone 715-445-2214
for editorial comment and further information.

Library of Congress Catalog Number: 98-84635
ISBN: 0-87341-554-X

Printed in the United States of America

Some product names in this book are trademarks of their respective companies
The Child's Blanket™

Featured on the front cover:
Zia pot, 9-3/8 in. high and 11-1/4 in. in diameter. Courtesy John W. Barry, Davis, California.
Cochiti pueblo Storyteller figure, 10-1/2 in. high. Courtesy Charles F. and Susan Wood, Ohio.
Featured on the back cover:
"Slave-killer" axe, 14-in. long, ca. AD 800-1200. Rainbow Traders, Godfrey, Illinois.

DEDICATION

To the North American Indian artisans of whatever time and place—and to the collectors of today who value what they made.

Indian on horseback, pulling crossed-stick travois with traveling bundle; photo taken in Montana, unknown date, probably late 1800s.

Photographer Roland Reed; Courtesy Photography Collection, Suzzallo Library, University of Washington

AUTHOR'S NOTE: This book is intended as a guide to many kinds of artifacts in a variety of value ranges. It is for general education and information purposes only. Neither the author nor the publisher will be responsible for any transactions based on the values listed herein. This includes profits, losses, and trades.

ACKNOWLEDGMENTS

It is the usual practice for a writer to thank those for without whose help the book could not have been completed.

For this project, the writer acknowledges over fifty persons, without whose assistance and encouragement the book would not have gone beyond the early stages of research.

This is not the definitive book on all American Indian collectibles and their values, for such will never be compiled by anyone. It is, however, as comprehensive as possible, including many examples which are both common and rare.

The book is also authoritative, for many of the contributors are highly knowledgeable and experienced in their respective fields—as will be obvious on even a casual reading. The book, in short, goes far beyond single-individual approach and comprehension.

The persons who provided photographs from private collections are thanked, and their photographs and valuations appear throughout the book. They are, in each case, credited to the sender. The extent of individual contributions, and my thanks, will be evident.

However, there were some who made available photographs that were outstanding in both quantity and quality. They are: John W. Barry, Tom Browner, H. Jackson Clark, Kenneth R. Canfield, Marguerite Kernaghan, Harvey and Rose King, Wayne Parker, Bill Post, and Summers Redick.

Thanks also to Howard Popkie and Robert C. Calvert, for an extended look at some scarce Canadian artifacts. In some cases, collectors and dealers had professionals photograph items, and thanks for that fine work.

A number of institutional or governmental sources were drawn upon for excellent photographs of historic significance. These illustrate a variety of scenes, from contemporary activities to prehistoric ruins. They are:

- Florida Division of Tourism
- National Photography Collection, Public Archives of Canada
- Nebraska State Historical Society, John A. Anderson Collection
- South Dakota State Historical Society
- Photography Collection, Suzzallo Library, University of Washington
- U.S. Department of the Interior, National Park Service
- Utah State Historical Society, Collection of Smithsonian Institution

Thanks are due, very much so, to the various Indian art galleries and dealers that kindly permitted reprinting. This was of descriptions and prices of selected artifacts and artworks from their catalogs and listings. They are:

- W.J. Crawford, The Americana Galleries, Phoenix, Arizona
- James O. Aplan, Midland, South Dakota
- Sherman Holbert, Fort Mille Lacs, Onamia, Minnesota
- Pierre and Sylvia Bovis, Winona Indiana Trading Post, Santa Fe, New Mexico
- Kenneth R. Canfield, Plains Indian Art, Kansas City, Missouri
- Barry Hardin, Crazy Crow Trading Post, Denison, Texas
- Hyde's, Santa Fe, New Mexico
- Sam and Nancy Johnson, Caddo Trading Company and Gallery, Murfreesboro, Arkansas
- Manitou Gallery, Cheyenne, Wyoming
- Armand Ortega, Indian Ruins Trading Post, Sanders, Arizona
- R.G. Munn, Whispering Pines Gallery, La Mesa, California

Other specialty listings were used, and are noted and credited throughout the book.

Thanks are due to auction houses which allowed item descriptions from catalogs and results from bid-sheets. Appreciation to:

- Col. Doug Allard, St. Ignatius, Montana
- Tom King and Tom Porter, Garth's Auctions, Inc., Stratford Road, Delaware, Ohio
- Jan Sorgenfrei, Old Barn Auctions, Findlay, Ohio
- Rod Sauvageau, Trade Winds West Auction Gallery, Portland, Oregon

Various private collectors sent thorough descriptions of items, placing a fair market value on some of their prize specimens. Very special thanks, also, to those who went considerably out of their way to provide detailed chapter introductions, namely: Tom Browner (Bannerstones), Dick Weatherford (Baskets), and John Barry (Pottery).

Respects to several gentlemen who contributed literature and all possible help on the Federal level. Robert G. Hart, General Manager, Indian Arts and Crafts Board, U.S. Department of the Interior, Washington, D.C., gave personal help and literature. Also, Charles Dailey, Museum Director, Institute of American Indian Arts (Bureau of Indian Affairs, U.S. Department of the Interior), Santa Fe, New Mexico, for pertinent literature and personal help. Further, to Lloyd New, former Director of the Institute of American Indian Arts, for his excellent summary regarding the state of Indian Art.

Acknowledgment goes to the Executive Director of the Indian Arts and Crafts Association, this in two directions. First for the literature and reprint permission, and second, for personal correspondence that aided greatly in an area of sensitive coverage.

Ultimate gratitude to Sue McClurg Hothem, who assisted in suggestions, paperwork, and fine moral support throughout. And the same to Adena and Hopewell, for understanding. Deep thanks to Ronald E. Hothem, Attorney-at-Law, San Francisco, for legal counsel in several areas of importance.

Lar Hothem

Today, American Indian art rides at the pinnacle of appreciation. Works which only a decade or two ago were viewed generally as the curious output of America's aboriginal wagon train raiders have suddenly been accorded super-status. This phenomenal rise in acceptance is manifest in the virtual craze on the part of the public for Indian arts and crafts today, not only in traditional modes, but in innovative styles as well. Indian arts and crafts are now treated within the same elitist exhibition and marketing channels as those previously reserved for the finest art from other sources throughout the world.

From *One With The Earth*, catalog of the Traveling Exhibit; by Lloyd New, Director, Institute of American Indian Arts, Bureau of Indian Affairs, Santa Fe, New Mexico.

TABLE OF CONTENTS

INTRODUCTION

Fascination with things American Indian is deeply ingrained in our culture. It began with childhood games, such as Cowboys and Indians. It is continually reinforced by advertising symbols, company names, movies, television, everyday conversation.

No American needs to ask the meaning of these phrases: "Burying the hatchet"; "Smoke the peacepipe"; "Indian Summer." And how many low-ranking military personnel have complained about "Too many chiefs, not enough Indians"? The American Indian or Amerind presence is everywhere, and a healthy part of our national existence.

This partly explains the present fascination with objects made by Indians. There are today probably well over two-and-a-half million persons who collect Indian goods or are involved in other ways in the vast area.

There are certain characteristics of Amerind collectibles. One is that they are almost always made from natural materials and substances, whether plant, animal, or mineral. Another is that all, or almost all, of the work required to complete the object is done by hand, slowly and carefully.

Yet another characteristic is workstyle, with the object being shaped into a form familiar to the Amerind lifeways. It is decorated, if at all, with designs that have their origin in the timeless North American past.

The essence of the Amerind art form—be it utensil, tool, weapon, ornament, whatever—is uniqueness. For all authentic pieces there was, and is, no such "improvement" as assembly-line mass production. And no two objects are ever totally alike, no matter how much they may resemble one another. The pieces are as varied as the individuals that made them; each is a sole creation.

Perhaps still another hallmark of Amerind works, and one that appeals highly to collectors, is the "utility-plus" factor. A great percentage of Amerind objects were made far better than necessary to merely complete a task. Much loving skill and attention to detail were added.

Amerind art and artifacts have long been admired and collected in European countries and elsewhere. Americans, pioneer and recent, have largely failed to understand or appreciate the field. Only within the last few years has there been a broad groundswell of interest and attention, but Americans have now begun to accept good Amerind material as good art.

Native American art, sometimes primitive, sometimes amazingly sophisticated, has gone (in regard to marketability) far beyond the flash and fad stages. It has become a major field to be in, a heritage to be knowledgeable about, the collectibles to have.

Some preliminary explanations and comments are in order. There are terms used throughout this guide that are important. "Prehistoric" means before writing, or the arrival of Europeans to record events. Prehistoric also means cultural items designed by Amerinds alone, without ideological contamination from European sources. Generally this means all human-occupied North American time before about AD 1500.

"Historic," as used here, means heavy cultural contact with Europeans and Russians, in a time zone broadly ranging from AD 1500. "Recent" is here considered to be from 1900 to 1980. "Contemporary" indicates years from 1980 to the present. These time-zones are open to debate, but if the meaning is clear they remain sufficient and descriptive.

This book is a guide to American Indian collectibles and their values. It identifies and describes major collecting areas available today. Representative prices, or close price ranges, are accurately given.

It should be noted that the listed value—whether for item description or photograph—is not an ultimate valuation. It does not usually constitute an offer to sell. It does not represent an appraisal. Instead, it is judged by the possessor to be a fair market value. Information is given for the sake of knowledge.

To a certain extent, the chapter lengths reflect the quantity of that sort of American Indian material available to the collector. It is to a degree a guide to the amount of material on the market.

For example, for every, say, presentation-grade pipe tomahawk, there are many thousand flint projectile points. For every Plains Indian beaded dress in ultra-fine condition, there are hundreds of other beaded clothing items, more available and less expensive.

Don't be upset by what may seem to be high prices; don't feel that American Indian items are beyond your financial reach. A major and long-term effort has been made to secure listings and photographs of some of the top collector pieces in North America for this book. They are here for your study.

These are very good examples, for the most part, of material you will see and have the opportunity to purchase. Bargains can still be picked up at auctions, flea markets, and antique shops, providing you know what you are looking at and have some idea of the market value.

And while the guide should be a general help in acquiring good pieces at reasonable prices, there is no substitute for personal knowledge and experience. The more you know about what you decide to collect, the better your Amerind collection will be.

Key letters preceding price figures: The source
- A) Auction   D) Dealer
- C) Collector   G) Gallery

Consider the advantage of knowing Indian Collectibles' values:

A rancher finds a prehistoric flint artifact which a neighbor tells him is incomplete because it does not have notches. The rancher sells it for $10, which is about what the neighbor tells him it is worth. Later, the rare Paleo-period fluted-base point is sold for $175.

A box of old costume jewelry in an antique shop attracts the attention of a buyer at $12.50. Among the items is a heavy trade-era silver beaver-shaped pendant and a handful of glass trade beads. Once a necklace, the set is now insured at $500.

A man at a Midwestern farm auction pays a few dollars for what the auctioneer called "an old hatchet." It is that and more. The collector who now owns the late-1700s pipe-tomahawk with original handle has twice refused offers of $600 or over.

A "musty old leather thing" is donated to a charitable organization and passes through several hands. The last owner refuses to part with the piece; it is a fine Plains Indian pipebag with exquisite bead and quillwork designs. It is valued, conservatively, at $950, because there was also a genuine two-piece pipe inside.

An old Indian weaving is obtained for a nominal sum at a flea market. A knowledgeable dealer and collector is intrigued; he flies halfway across the country to take a look. He obtains the item, a fine late-phase Chief's blanket worth many thousands of dollars.

ALLARD AUCTION — IX

Col. Doug Allard, Flathead Indian and well-known auctioneer of American Indian material, presided over a recent auction featuring 1,520 fine Indian-related lots. (The Allard catalogs alone have become not only solid reference sources, but collector items as well.) Some 100 listings and eleven photographs (by Jeanine Allard) are reprinted here, by permission of the Allards. This three-day auction took place March 13–15, 1998, in Phoenix, Arizona, and was known as the Phoenix Million Dollar IX auction.

In-depth coverage is accorded these objects for several reasons. One is the high quality of the items, most being in the advanced-collector category. Another is the great range of artifacts, from many tribes, geographic regions and time-periods. This provides a broad-spectrum look at American Indian art and artifacts. Criteria used to select objects for inclusion here included: Types collectors will likely encounter, unusual pieces, and those which, due to rarity, are not covered elsewhere in this book. All listings included here would of course carry the "A" designation.

My sincere thanks to Col. Allard for permission to include selected auction results from this event. For those wishing further information, the address is: Allard Auctions, Inc., P.O. Box 460, St. Ignatius, Montana, 59865-0460. The phone number is (406) 745-2951, and toll-free, (800) 821-3318; FAX is (406) 745-2961.

Cree jacket, large tanned moosehide jacket with floral beadwork on front, sleeves, and shoulders, large size, ca. 1920. $375

Curtis photogravure, limited edition of a 1905 Edward Curtis photograph, "Sioux Chiefs," 12 x 16 in., year 1904. $215

Cornhusk bag, Nez Perce bag in excellent condition, ex-Goodman collection tag, 10 x 13 in., late 19th century. $500

Arapaho knife sheath, sinew-sewn beaded knife case with long beaded drop, decorated with tin cones, included is a Green River trade knife; sheath is 2-1/2 x 10 in., 20th century. $325

Pueblo necklace, exquisitely carved seven strand fetish necklace with multiple colored birds and animals, 26 in., contemporary. $200

Two Grey Hills rug, fine Navajo rug by famous weaver Daisy Toughlechee, in top condition, 15-1/2 x 25 in., ca. 1940s. $600

Apache saddle bags, old throwover rawhide and buckskin saddle bags decorated with red and blue trade cloth and long fringe, 15 x 80 in., ca. 1920s. $1,600

Plains doll, fully costumed Plains beaded buckskin doll, 9 in. high, ca. 1920s. $500

Yosemite basketry, rare cradleboard, beaded tassels on woven hood, woven strap, excellent condition, 13-1/2 x 22 in., ca. 1958. $1,050

Horsehair basket, miniature Pima/Papago coiled horsehair basket with double snake design, diameter 4 in., ca. 1985. $500

Comanche moccasins, rare and unusually decorated ceremonial moccasins with fully beaded uppers and trim, 4 x 13 in., ca. 1900. $3,250

Photograph courtesy Allard Auction

Comanche boots, full-length buckskin and hard soles with beaded flap on green ochred background, with conchos and twist fringe top, height 21 in., ca. 1900. $1,700

Photograph courtesy Allard Auction

Osage skirt, rare Osage ribbonwork skirt on blue wool trade cloth, decorated with silver conchos, ca. 1900. $500

Kachina figure, handcarved cottonwood root kachina with large Mana, height 12 in., post-1880. $325

Eskimo pipe, handmade fossil ivory with scrimshaw in archaic style, 7-1/2 in. long, 19th century. $225

Buffalo lance, long Pueblo lance with 14-inch handwrought 18th century Spanish iron blade, with documentation, 58 in. long, 18th-19th centuries. $400

Bird rattle, finely carved Northwest Coast rattle with classic ceremonial figures, 5 x 15 in., contemporary. $375

Dance mask, working Northwest Coast eagle ceremonial mask, 22 x 24 in., contemporary. $400

Catlinite pipe, old carved Sioux pipe head with stylized horse figure, 5 x 7-1/2 in., ca. 1910. $685

Chevron beads, old classic red/white/blue beads, extra-length strand at 36 in., ca. 1840. $175

Plateau pommel bag, early full contour beaded Cayuse flap on early hand-tooled pommel bag, 9 x 13 in., ca. 1870. $2,950

Great Lakes bandolier, fine Anishinabe fully beaded bandolier bag in original, excellent condition; with documentation, 13-1/2 x 36 in., 19th century. $1,750

Plains quillwork, antelope hide "Medicine Bundle" with

twelve rows of dyed quills and six quill and horsehair drops, 35 x 42 in., ca. 1890.   **$1,500**

Anasazi jar, corrugated pottery, gray ware with incised and indented design pattern, 11 x 13-1/2 in., prehistoric.   **$600**

Plateau bag, semi-contour beaded bag with floral motif on white ground, mint condition, 11 x 13 in., ca. 1900. **$500**

Eskimo doll, rare old doll of sealskin with some beading; seal fur, excellent condition, height 15 in.   **$375**

Knife sheath, fully tacked heavy leather with Green River trade knife, sheath 4 x 11 in., 19th century.   **$400**

Pawn earrings, older turquoise/silver cluster style earrings with inlaid cut turquoise triangular stone and drops, 1 x 2 in., ca. 1950.   **$200**

Hand drum, large Northwest Coast (Tlingit) painted drum, diameter 23 in., 20th century.   **$425**

Pomo basket, classic shaped basket with open bottom stair-step design, 3 x 6 in., ca. 1920.   **$700**

Panamint basket, beautiful rim-ticked polychrome shoulder olla with rattlesnake, cross designs, and five human "Friendship" figures, 4 x 5 in., ca. 1920.   **$2,500**

Salish basket, choice large embricated basketry tray with large polychrome butterfly, 12 x 17 in., ca. 1910.   **$250**

Courting flute, old Arapaho carved loon-headed flute, 23 in. long, ca. 1890.   **$1,000**

Plains hide-scraper, old scraper made of elkhorn with rawhide-wrapped blade, 14 in. long, ca. 1860.   **$200**

Navajo rug, fine all vegetal dye wool Crystal weaving, 45 x 65 in., ca. 1975.   **$450**

Parfleche bonnet case, Northern Plains painted elk parfleche cylinder, 20th century.   **$375**

Blackfoot bag, old fully beaded dispatch case of elk hide with long fringe, 7 x 27 in., ca. 1920.   **$750**

Cheyenne pipe bag, old tabbed top, beaded on ochred antelope hide with long twisted fringe and tin cones with deer hair, size 4-1/4 x 29 in., ca. 1910.   **$1,400**

Pima basketry tray, finely woven early basket with whirlwind design, fifteen stitches per inch, mint condition, size 2 x 7-1/2 in., ca. 1950.   **$800**

Plateau vest, choice fully beaded panel vest with striking outlined floral designs, medium size, ca. 1900.   **$1,200**

Blackfoot parfleche, rare painted container with quill-wrapped rattle filled with original medicine contents, with documentation, 8 x 11 in., ca. 1860.   **$3,250**

Sioux dance stick, old handcarved and painted cottonwood horse dance stick, length 29-1/2 in., ca. 1920.   **$1,400**

Lakota telescope case, rare sinew-sewn fully beaded telescope case with original Civil War period telescope, size 2-1/2 x 8-1/2 in., ca. 1880.   **$3,000**

Blackfoot leggings, classic panels with white background fully beaded in geometric design, 9 x 11 in., ca. 1900.   **$700**

Kiowa pouch, full contour beaded Kiowa mirror bag on ochred antelope, with fine twisted fringe terminated with old U.S. silver coins, ca. 1900.   **$750**

Assiniboine parfleche case, old mineral-painted designs on elk hide, all original, 12 x 26 in., ca. 1890.   **$625**

Southern Plains jacket, early buffalo hide jacket with loom-beaded strips and shoulder cutouts, large size, ca. 1900. $2,400

Photograph courtesy Allard Auction

Iroquois cornhusk mask, False Face Society, braided and coiled husk face with medicine ball, 11 x 11 in., historic. $800

Pima basket, classic deep coiled basketry bowl with swirling line design, 6 x 18 in., ca. 1950. $475

Apache basket, fine-weave coiled basketry bowl with striking geometric design, 3 x 11 in., ca. 1930. $1,400

Nez Perce dress, beaded yoke front and back interspersed with elk teeth on buckskin, all original, 42 x 49 in., ca. 1885. $4,500

Kiowa beadwork, child's hightop moccasins with twisted fringe and small conchos, height 10-1/2 in., 20th century. $650

Plateau bag, round-bottom beaded bag with contour beaded front on red trade cloth, buckskin fringe, and a navy cloth back, 10-1/2 x 20 in., ca. 1890. $800

Sioux teepee bag, sinew-sewn buffalo hide "Possible" bag, canvas back and striking geometric beaded panel design, 14 x 24 in., ca. 1890. $2,250

Sioux horn cup, classic buffalo horn cup with quilled decoration and tin cones, 4 x 10 in., ca. 1880. $1,000

Ojibway bandolier, dramatic bandolier bag, floral, partially curvilinear, trade cloth, and bugle beads, outstanding example, 14 x 44 in., ca. 1900. $1,250

Crow awl case, sinew-sewn on buffalo with elaborate drop, beads, and cones, ca. 1880. $650

Hunkpapa Sioux tobacco bag, rare old Ghost Dance bag, antelope hide, sinew-sewn, design and beads are on both sides, length 18 in., ca. 1890. $675

Cheyenne pouch, rare early tobacco pouch, sinew with green pigment. Various beaded elements are on both sides, 7-1/2 x 16 in., ca. 1870s. $2,000

Gros Ventre shot pouch, classic fully beaded front with beaded flap backed by beaded outline, length 4-1/2 in., 19th century. $325

Paiute basket, fully beaded coiled basket with top and with birds and arrows, by Dora Clifford; Emporium (Carson City, Nevada) documentation # 1062, 7 x 7 in., ca. 1929. $2,500

Washo basket, coiled basketry bowl with geometric designs, said to be by famous maker Dot-So-Lo-Lee, 5-1/2 x 8-1/2 in., ca. 1920. $3,750

Sioux beaded bag, old Fort Peck Sioux bag fully beaded on buckskin with fringe, 5-1/2 x 12-1/2 in., ca. 1920. $400

Quapaw pot, rare polychrome red and white ornate sunfish bowl, Mississippi County, Arkansas; ex-collection Fowler, with documentation, diameter 7-1/2 in., ca. AD 1100. $675

Ute tab pouch, sinew-sewn tabbed whetstone pouch on mountain sheep hide, all original, museum quality, ca. 1880. $500

Navajo bracelet, heavy hand-hammered silver bracelet with eleven choice coral stones, signed H.S.B., 1-1/2 x 7 in., contemporary. $425

Eskimo cribbage board, finely polished ivory board with full story scrimshaw on bottom, 2-1/2 x 17 in., ca. 1930. $225

Navajo concho belt, medium-size hand-stamped and shaped all silver belt with eleven conchos and butterfly buckle, 3 x 42 in., ca. 1940. $750

Sioux child's dress, fully beaded front and back on buckskin. Sioux made at Fort Peck Reservation, Montana, size 34 x 38 in., 20th century. $2,400

Plains necklace, carved horn "Bear Claw" necklace with beaver, ermine, trade beads, and an otter drop, 4 x 44 in., 20th century. $2,500

Southern Cheyenne moccasins, rare fully beaded on buckskin with rose top and leaping deer figures around sides, 3 x 8 in., ca. 1890. $400

Osage blanket, Osage navy trade cloth ribbon blanket with beaded and appliquéd "Friendship" hands, 58 x 70 in., ca. 1920. $1,500

Cheyenne breastplate, three-row bone and bead breastplate with brass beads and bell, woven cloth, and leather neck strap, 12 x 16 in., ca. 1890. $600

Blackfoot medicine bag, rare ochred hide medicine bag with many small medicine bags and ermine skins, 11 x 15 in., various ages. $1,250

Apache headdress, mountain lion head hat with bead trim, brass eyes and topped with feathers, 6 x 12 in., ca. 1900. $1,750

Nez Perce bag, large cornhusk bag with bright colorful geometric designs on each side, 14 x 21 in., ca. 1950. $1,300

Photograph courtesy Allard Auction

Crow bow case and quiver, sinew-sewn hide bow case and quiver with geometric beaded designs and line-quilled decoration, 5 x 50 in., ca. 1890. $2,000

Ute strike-a-lite pouch, seed-beaded strike-a-lite bag sinew-sewn on old leather, fully beaded both sides and flap, 3-3/4 x 6 in., 19th century. $650

Zuni bracelet, classic sculptured inlay, multi-stone and silver Eagle Dancer, bracelet 3 x 4 in., ca. 1930. $400

Pima basket, woven black and white horsehair in fantastic squash blossom design, diameter 6 in., ca. 1985. $700

Northwest Coast carving, cedar and abalone inlaid Loon Mother and Child feast dish/bowl with removable top, by Otterlifter, size 28 x 11 x 16 in., ca. 1990. $500

Maria San Ildefonso bowl, one of the best "Marie" artworks, pristine condition large shallow bowl with geometric design, black on black, 3 x 12 in., collected in 1929. $5,000

Nez Perce pouch, fully beaded belt pouch on saddle leather with colorful floral design, 6 x 6 in., ca. 1910. $650

Sioux moccasins, sinew-sewn fully beaded with beaded tongue and outstanding geometric design; ex-collection Lesard, 4 x 11 in., ca. 1890. $1,600

Apache saddle drape, classic hide and trade cloth drape with cutouts, fringe and hawk bells, 11 x 43 in., ca. 1890. $2,000

Sioux rifle case, elaborate hide case with long fringe and American Flag beaded decoration, 7 x 50 in., ca. 1920. $1,450

Eskimo knife, old slate knife with bone handle attached with hide cord, 11 x 12 in., ca. 1840. $250

Sioux arm bands, early fully quilled arm bands on painted parfleche with quilled balls and drops, rare, 1 x 36 in., ca. 1890. $900

Peace medal, James Monroe U.S. Indian peace medal in original Sioux buckskin bag, two pieces, dated 1817. $610

Sioux leggings, large sinew-sewn woman's hide leggings with fully beaded geometric designs, each 9 x 17 in., ca. 1920. $500

Apache basket, tightly coiled basketry bowl with star in center, dogs and human figures, 1-1/2 x 7 in., ca. 1920. $1,050

Cheyenne painting, outstanding tempera of Eagle

Sioux bow case and quiver, sinew-sewn buffalo hide bow case and quiver with beaded crosses, American flags and long fringe, choice set, 4 x 44 in., ca. 1890. $1,350

Photograph courtesy Allard Auction

Maidu basket, coiled storage basket with redbud connecting triangular motif, rare, 13 x 20 in., ca. 1920. $2,750

Photograph courtesy Allard Auction

Dancer with much detail; artist (Archie Black) deceased, 12 x 14 in., ca. 1940. $325

Flathead drum, huge stretched rawhide drum with green and red designs on both sides, 10 x 24 in., ca. 1920. $300

Crooked knife, old carved hardwood handle and forged knife blade, Penobscot, 1 x 9 in., ca. 1900. $155

Haida hat, twined basketry Haida rain hat with inside headband, 8 x 11 in., ca. 1890. $425

Northwest Coast mask, White Face Cannibal mask with shell teeth, nasal bone, and hammered copper brows, 8-1/2 x 15 in., ca. 1930. $800

Navajo blouse, green velvet blouse with concho beads and ribbon trimwork, 19 x 50 in., ca. 1940. $225

Taos drum, tall drum of hollowed cottonwood and stretched rawhide, painted in traditional Pueblo colors, 14 x 18 in., ca. 1920. $650

Athabascan quilled belt, one of the finest existing rolled quillwork pieces, one-of-a-kind, 3 x 38 in., ca. 1900. $2,000

Zuni fetishes, group of choice Zuni hand-carved animal fetishes, five pieces, contemporary. $125

Plains pipe-tomahawk, old, with heart cutout and tacked wooden handle/stem, 9 x 19 in., ca. 1870. $800

Tlingit spoon, carved wooden spoon with original Cook Inlet museum collection tag, 2 x 7 in., 19th century. $250

Hohokam pottery, unusual red on buff bowl with sun and bird designs, 4 x 10 in., prehistoric. $350

Papago horsehair plaque, classic woven miniature black and white basketry plaque, diameter 4 in., ca. 1980. $150

Navajo concho belt, old stamped silver concho belt with butterfly buckle and turquoise dot centers, 2 x 46 in., ca. 1930. $600

Sioux pipe, black stone with pewter inlay and carved oak puzzle stem, 3 x 31 in., ca. 1940. $275

Pottery jar, signed Lucy McKelvey, huge flat jar with intricate designs, rare, 7 x 15 in., ca. 1990. $2,000

Photograph courtesy Allard Auction

A young Ute warrior and his dog, with bow and iron-tipped arrows. Note the attractive necklace and full-length leggings. Picture taken in the Uintah Valley, on the eastern slope of the Wasatch Mountain, in Utah.

Photo by John K. Hillers, 1873-1874

CHAPTER I

ARROWHEADS AND PROJECTILE POINTS

The small chipped points of ancient times are among the most collectible of Amerind artifacts. They exist in one form or another over all of North America, and many types are still very reasonably priced.

Projectile points—the term means both arrowheads and lanceheads—are often the earliest signs of humans on the land. It has long been agreed that people came from Asia, via the Bering Straits, more than 20,000 years ago.

Some of the flint artifacts, including those found by archaeologists along the Alaskan Pipeline right-of-way, may be even older. Such chipped tools and weapons may well be the oldest cultural debris in The Americas.

The much-admired fluted-base points are up to 11,000 years old, though related varieties were made until about 5000 or 6000 BC. Points were chipped until the coming of European Whites, the Metal People, when iron and steel points were either traded or made from White-supplied materials.

Until about 500 AD, the chief weapon in North America was the Atl-atl, a hand-held wooden lance thrower, a very rare item today. It acted as an extension of the human arm, providing leverage to fling the lance or javelin further and harder. Many of the existing prehistoric lances had a short and thin foreshaft. This was apparently left in the target animal, and the valuable feather-vaned main shaft was retrieved.

It is not always easy to tell the difference between a lancehead and an arrowhead. One guideline is that most lanceheads average about 2 inches (50mm) in length, and 1/2 inch (12mm) between basal notches. Arrowheads tend to be closer to 1 inch (25mm) or slightly longer, and about 1/4 inch (7mm) between basal notches. Arrowheads are also proportionately thinner and much lighter in weight than the typical Atl-atl point.

Projectile points were made by various chipping processes, by controlled blows that flaked off unwanted material. Bone and antler chipping rods and billets were used. Hammerstones helped create the rough blank. Then, percussion flaking worked the material into a preform, similar in size and shape to the finished artifact.

The preform was further reduced by a process called pressure flaking, which added basal notches, and retouched and evened all edges. Final steps may have included basal grinding, when sharp lower edges were dulled. This was probably done so that binding thongs of sinew were not cut through.

Many different types of material could be chipped, most of them being classed as "crypto-crystalline quartz." This includes the common names: flint, chalcedony, chert, jasper, and so on, many with regional names. Obsidian—natural volcanic glass—was widely used, especially in Western areas.

Other materials were used: petrified wood (Southwest), agatized coral (Southeast), and many types of quartz (Eastern). Even though it is brittle, the better grades of material are extremely hard. Many varieties will actually scratch plate glass.

Determinants of point value to both dealer and collector involve over half a dozen factors. Size is important, with a larger point being worth comparatively more than a smaller point, other factors assumed equal. Material is a key element; dull and coarse quartzes are less admired than higher, more nearly pure grades. Color is important, with some collectors preferring bold or subtle hues.

Workstyle means the manner in which any one projectile point was fashioned. Desirable qualities would be the thinness and uniformity of the finished point, plus the number and regularity of pressure-chipping scars. Workstyles range from poor to superb, with an infinite number of in-between grades.

Condition of the point refers to any damage sustained by the piece, no matter when such damage occurred. For example, many points being picked up today show the typical sharp-edged breaks caused by agricultural equipment and construction machinery.

Even minor damage can detract greatly from point value, though each instance is of course judged by itself. Perfect specimens are the most avidly sought and command the higher values.

Point-type—there are more than 1000 regional main and sub-group point varieties in North America—is a determinate of value, with many collectors willing to pay more for a variety that they admire. One key factor here could be called "intricacy," meaning the delicate and accurate chipping skill evidenced by the point. Examples might be an obsidian fluted Paleo point from the Pacific Northwest, or the rare Midwestern fractured-base point. The last, by the way, refers to a manufacturing technique, not damage.

The final two value determinants are related. One is the "mirror-image" examination, and simply means how much the point obverse resembles the reverse. Or, are both point sides or faces pretty much the same? If there are startling differences in chipping patterns or one side has areas "bare" of chipping (from the original crypto-crystalline material from which the point was made) this lowers the value. Both faces, in short, should show extensive, similar, and good workmanship.

Symmetry, as the writer uses the term, means the degree to which one face on one side of the point resembles the other. Looking at either the left or right side; there should be visual "balance."

All the determinants add up to a quality that can be called aesthetics—how pleasing the point is in an artistic sense. While collectors will place different weight on the various determinants, all or most will be considered in regard to collector desirability, hence value.

Fakes are a real problem today. And the person who believes that only the ancients could chip flint well is likely to be surprised at the skill with which modern points are being turned out. There are many ways to tell good (original) points from bad, but the beginner is advised to purchase only from reputable dealers or collectors with authentic material. And if a price appears too good to be true, it very possibly is.

Most importantly, talk with knowledgeable people. Learn as much as possible about authentic specimens, and study broken points to see how they were made. Before long, modern-made points will begin to stand out.

EASTERN POINTS

Folsom-type fluted point, 1-7/8 in. long, found on New York ocean beach Paleo site. Well-fluted both sides, nearly to tip. All edge treatment extremely well done, with minute chipping. An out-of-state, dark flint material. C-$175

Arrowheads from Connecticut, average 2 in. long. D-$4-7 each

Beveled-edge arrowhead, fine white 1 in., undoubtedly made in post-AD 500 era, apparently from the tip of an Archaic beveled-edge blade. Portion of base missing. Unusual. C-$12

Florida gempoint made of translucent material called agatized coral. Stemmed point is 1-3/4 in. long and 3/4 in. wide at sloped shoulders. High colors, fine chipping. C-$80

Arrowheads and projectile points, frame of twenty-four, from James River, Virginia area. D-$90

Cahokia gempoint, Illinois, 1-3/8 in. long, amber and white flint. Notched on sides and at base center; very delicately chipped. Mississippian period. C-$65

Paleo points, set of three, from near Hartford, Connecticut. D-$70

Projectile point, stemmed, 2-1/2 in. long, chipped from white flint from Virginia. Wide stem has the base bifurcated; that is, deeply incurvate in base center. D-$15

Wide and shallow-notched point or blade, Alabama, 2-1/2 in. long, possibly Woodland period. Black flint, low grade. D-$13

Folsom-type fluted point, unusual Paleo, 1-7/8 in. long, but channel-fluted to tip on both sides. Found near Mississippi River, in state of that name. Perfect condition.C-$175

Triangular point, Alabama, 1-1/4 in. long and made of a gray chert material. Perfect condition. D-$7

Arrowhead, common flint, late prehistoric, 1 in. long, stemmed, of white low-grade material. Chipping haphazard and uneven, and foreign inclusion makes part much thicker. One notch smaller than the other. C-$2

Point, triangular flint, 1-1/4 in. wide at base. Very thin. Made of black and pink flint, unknown origin. Found in North Carolina and may have been traded there. Base has bottom edges ground, very unusual for the type. C-$20

Pentagonal point or blade, 2 in. long, pink and cream high-quality flint. Comer-notched, 1/4 in. of tip missing, also one base corner. (Perfect condition would have been a $20 point.) With damage and as-is, valued less. C-$14

Side-notched Archaic point, 1-1/4 in. long and 1/2 in. wide, gray-brown flint. Chipping average–good, no major damage. C-$10

Triangular arrowhead, 1-1/4 in. long and point is 5/8

in. wide at straight base, late prehistoric, found in New York state. C-$5

Arrowhead, 1-1/8 in. long, small quartzite, "sugar" or opaque white type, from near Washington, D.C. Corner notches are wide and shallow. C-$5

Corner-notched point, New Jersey, made of a rough material, collected (according to accompanying card) on an archaeological survey as a university project. Point broken near tip. C-$4

Projectile points or arrowheads, four small of sugar quartz, average about 1-1/2 in. long, from coastal Virginia. No damage, but workmanship about average. D-$2 each

Hardin barbed point, small white flint, 2-1/4 in. long and 1-1/4 in. wide; Illinois. G-$55

Quartzite stemmed point, 1-3/4 in. long, thick, with short sturdy stem; from Maine coastal site and probably Archaic period. Rough-chipped due to nature of material. C-$2

Hopewellian point or blade, 3 in. long, notching fine and medium-depth. Damage to one shoulder tip and one corner of base but very minor. Excellent chipping. A-$20

Corner-notched serrated-edge point, 1-1/2 in. long, probably Archaic, glossy black flint, from Indiana. Well-notched. C-$22

Point or blade made of black flint, 3 in. long and 1-1/4 in. wide at shoulders. Serrated edges are still sharp; piece was found in south central Tennessee. C-$50

Photo courtesy of Jim Northcutt, Jr., Corinth, Mississippi

Blade or projectile point, 2-1/2 in. long and 1-1/4 in. wide, found in Prentis County, Mississippi. A Benton type point, it has good symmetry.C-$30

Photo courtesy of Tracy Northcutt, Corinth, Mississippi

Hardin barbed point, found in Adams County, Illinois; Burton Creek area. It is 2-3/4 in. long and 1-1/2 in. wide at shoulders. From Early Archaic times, approx. 7500 BC. The unique characteristic of this point is that the serrations point forward instead of backward or out to sides.   C-$195

Photo courtesy of Pat Humphrey, west central Illinois

Paleo period projectile points from West Texas surface sites, Edwards Plateau flint. Points are 1 in. to 4 in. in length, of following types:

Top row: Clovis, Fishtail Yuma, Fishtail Yuma, Yuma, Yuma.
Middle: Hell Gap, Clovis, Meserve, Plainview, Agate Basin.
Bottom: Folsom, Folsom, Sandia, Sandia, Sandia. $75-550

Private collection

Hopewellian projectile points, showing an interesting range of size and styles. The two specimens on right are both of high grade Flintridge material. Values, from left to right:

C-1st point	$6
2nd point	$15
3rd point	$30
4th point	$11

Private collection

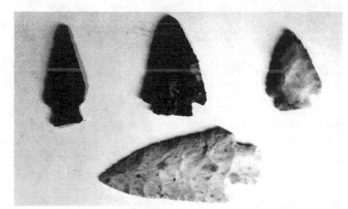

Top row, left to right:

Ashtabula-type point, dark gray flint.   C-$7
Corner-notched point on blade, black and cream flint.   C-$75
Corner-notched point from Indiana Archaic period site, of translucent pinkish material. Flintridge.   C-$7
Large white chert knife, blade from Kansas: stemmed variety, 4-1/4 in. long.   C-$14

Private collection

Stemmed point of blade, well-flaked and thin, of Quitaque flint quarried in the Texas Panhandle. Found in New Mexico. Piece would be more valuable if not for missing portion on right side above shoulder. Point is 2-3/4 in. long.   C-$50

Photo courtesy of Ralph W. White, Oklahoma

Stemmed lanceolate point or blade, Late Paleo period ca. 8000 BC, made of brownish flint. Boone County, Arkansas. $200

Kenneth Hamilton collection, Harrison, Arkansas

Dalton point or blade in rare gem-grade material, Knife River flint. It is dark-amber in color, translucent, and with small white clouds. Early chipped artifacts of Knife River have been found over much of the central U.S. but only sparingly. Rare piece. Johnson County, Arkansas. $1,250

Kenneth Hamilton collection, Harrison, Arkansas

Fluted-base Paleo point, perhaps Clovis-related, made of brown high-grade flint. It was a surface-find in Boone County, Arkansas. $200

Kenneth Hamilton collection, Harrison, Arkansas

Quad point, Late Paleo and ca. 8000 BC, 2-1/2 in. long. This is a scarce early point type, and this example is made of Fort Payne chert. Humphreys County, Tennessee. $575

C. H. Baggerley collection, Nicholson, Georgia

Dalton points or blades, Late Paleo period. These examples are heavily resharpened and each was originally nearly twice as long. Boone County, Arkansas.

Top:	$100
Bottom:	$75

Kenneth Hamilton collection, Harrison, Arkansas

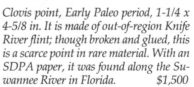

Clovis point, fluted obverse face, 2-5/8 in. long. Clovis points are a distinctive type, found across North America. This specimen is made of Florida chert and came from the Suwannee River area, Florida. $1,000

Scott Young, Port St. Lucie, Florida

Clovis point, Early Paleo period, 1-1/4 x 4-5/8 in. It is made of out-of-region Knife River flint; though broken and glued, this is a scarce point in rare material. With an SDPA paper, it was found along the Suwannee River in Florida. $1,500

Scott Young, Port St. Lucie, Florida

Cumberland fluted point, Late Paleo period, 7/8 x 3-1/2 in. long. Made of hornstone, this piece has authentication papers and was found in Barren County, Kentucky. $1,000

Scott Young, Port St. Lucie, Florida

Eastern U.S. Clovis points, 9000-12,000 BC, left example 3 in. long, all left to right:

Clovis, white glossy chert, Marion County, Illinois. $800
Clovis, fully fluted, so possibly a Redstone, Fort Payne chert, Ohio. $600
Clovis, glossy gray mottled Indiana hornstone, Harrison County, Indiana. $400
Clovis, fluted, brown flint or chert, Tennessee. $300

Collection of, and photograph by, Michael M. Hough, California

Archaic point, about 2 in. long; unusual prehistoric salvage work. Made of black flint and has typical corner notches and serrated edges. Obverse shows fine percussion and pressure flaking. Reverse has a long channel, averaging 1/2 in. wide, running from basal base to tip. Without doubt, one of the early Paleo-period fluted points was found much later by an Archaic Indian and reworked to present form. Double worked. C-$65

Side-notched point, 2-3/4 in. long and 1 in. wide. Thin Illinois, Kramer type, of white flint. G-$16

Small "birdpoint" arrowhead, 7/8 in. long and 1/2 in. wide. Late Woodland or Mississippian period, with crisp and well-done basal notches. C-$6

WESTERN POINTS

Dalton-type point, Arkansas, 1-7/8 in. long, deeply basal-notched, edges heavily serrated, perfect condition. Very well proportioned and balanced; basal grinding. C-$70

Northwest coast arrowhead; point is 7/8 in. long, notched from bottom, with wide stem; very delicate. Translucent red and orange gem point. Shoulders drop below stem base. Point almost resembles swallow in flight. Excavated find, state of Washington. D-$50

Frio point from Texas, 2-1/4 in. long and 3/4 in. wide, of pinkish white material. G-$8

Columbia River gem point, 2-1/16 in. long and perfectly symmetrical; shoulders barbed with tips that extend 1/8 in. below stem. Extra-delicate triangular form, reddish translucent chalcedony, square-stemmed; also equally attractive obverse and reverse. Perfect condition. C-$175

Steuben point, 2-3/4 in. long and 3/8 in. wide. Made of good gray flint, classic shape. G-$14

Oregon arrowhead, 1 in. long, chipped from petrified wood, red and yellow striped colors, stemmed and barbed. Very well chipped. C-$22

Arkansas Dalton, 2 in. long and 3/4 in. wide. Small, slightly damaged, white and pink material. G-$13

Epps point from Missouri, 2 in. long and 1 in. wide. Small, classic type, and made of gray flint. G-$10

Agate arrowhead from Columbia River Valley, 1-1/2 in. long; beautiful reddish color and translucent material. C-$65

Red gem point, Oregon, 1-1/8 in. long, stemmed, down-swept shoulders reach same distance as stem base. Very balanced. C-$45

Sandia-type point, found by New Mexican rancher in dry cave near arroyo. Exactly 2 in. long, rough-made in classic Sandia-II form; heavy-duty and notched on only one side. C-$135

Alba-type Caddo points, two nice ones averaging 1 in. length; white and gray flint. G-$15

Obsidian point, 1-7/8 in. long and just over 1 in. wide at tangs. Ornate black; base deeply indented to "V" shape, high side notches, base ends form curved tangs. Very symmetrical and perfect condition. C-$50

Godar-type point from Arkansas, 2-3/4 in. long and 1-1/2 in. wide. Side notched and made of pink flint. G-$25

Dalton point from Arkansas, 1-3/4 in. long and 3/4 in. wide. White and very nice. G-$25

Archaic period point, 2 in. long, corner-notched; about 1/8 in. of tip gone. Bifurcated-base, reddish obsidian. C-$10

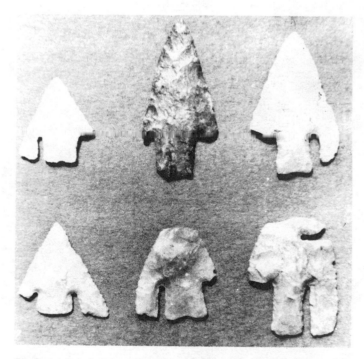

Six flint points from a surface site in West Texas, showing long barbs. They are 2 in. to 3 in. long. These are similar to the Calf-Creek points, but have not been named or classified yet in Texas. Archaic period. Five of the points are of Edwards Plateau flint, while middle point, top row, is made of Tecovas jasper. C-$55-80

Photo courtesy of Wayne Parker, Texas

Small Scottsbluff Paleo point, made of brown petrified wood. Material has black streaks and black specks throughout. Artifact has nice form, is of unusual material; 2-1/8 in. long, from Oklahoma.   C-$60-70

Photo courtesy of Ralph W. White

Reverse of a fine Dalton-type point, found in Adams County, Illinois. Of high-grade white flint, the point is nearly 3 in. long and in perfect condition. Point probably dates to the early Archaic, and has lasted thousands of years. Age: 7000 BC to about 5000 BC.   C-$175

Photo courtesy of Pat Humphrey westcentral Illinois

Flint Darl points, average length 2-1/4 in. These were surface finds in central Texas, and are made of Edwards Plateau flint. The points all have right side bevels, and are from the Archaic period.   C-$40 each

Photo courtesy of Wayne Parker, Texas

Arrowheads, late prehistoric era, longest example 1-1/2 in. All are of the stemmed form, are made of black obsidian, and were surface finds in the El Rito Mountains of New Mexico.   Group, $25

Jack Baker collection, Ozark, Missouri; David Capon photograph

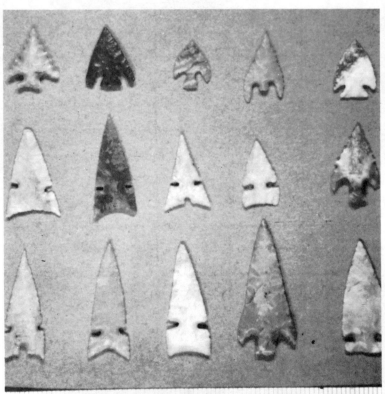

Small arrowpoints from West Texas Surface sites. These are the more common types found in the Panhandle and West Texas. Late prehistoric, they are classified as Scallorn, Harrell, Bonham, Perdiz and Rockwall.   C-$35-85

Photo courtesy of Wayne Parker, Texas

Plainview point, Late Paleo period, made of river-stained Foreacre chert. The fine piece is 4-1/2 in. long. This exceptional Plainview in size, workstyle, and condition was found by the owner in January of 1998.   Museum quality

Joe Waffle collection, Kansas; Daniel Fox photograph

Knives and projectile points, Paleo and Archaic periods, 3/4 to 1-3/4 in. long. Various materials are represented and all were surface finds in northeastern Colorado. Each, $50-200

Collection of Eugene and Marcille Wing

Knives and projectile points, Paleo and Archaic periods, 3/4 to 3 in. long. These are made of Alibates flint and petrified wood and were all surface finds in northeastern Colorado. The fine Folsom point just right of the large central corner-notched blade is exceptional. Each, $75-400

Collection of Eugene and Marcille Wing

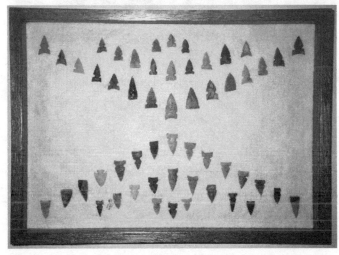

Small projectile points, late prehistoric periods, 3/4 to 1-1/2 in. long. They are made of Alibates flint and were surface finds by Eugene Wing in Kansas. Each, $50-100

Collection of Eugene and Marcille Wing

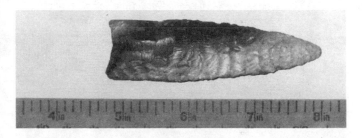

Plainview point, Late Paleo period and ca. 8000 BC, 3-3/8 in. long. The material is Florence chert and the point has pronounced basal thinning that is flute-like. It was found by the owner in 1997 in Kansas. $800-1,200

Joe Waffle collection, Kansas; Daniel Fox photograph

Side-notched arrowhead, gempoint, late prehistoric times, 1/2 x 1-3/4 in. long. This beautiful point is made of moss agate and was a surface find by Vicki Wing in 1965 in northeastern Colorado. $100-150

Collection of Eugene and Marcille Wing; photo courtesy of Vicki (Wing) Mildenberger

Clovis fluted point, Early Paleo period and ca. 9500 BC, made of tan and pink flint. It measures 3-1/2 in. long, with obverse basal flute 1-1/2 in. and reverse flute 1-1/4 in. This is a superb early example of a hard-hitting lance or spear point used for big game hunting. The Clovis came from near Portales, New Mexico. $1,350

Jack Baker collection, Ozark, Missouri; David Capon photograph

Agate Basin point, Late Paleo period, 4 in. long. This is a superb example, made of pink and white agate-like flint. Points of this quality are rarely found in undamaged condition. It was picked up near Santa Rosa, New Mexico. $750

Jack Baker collection, Ozark, Missouri; David Capon photograph

Agate Basin (?) type point with oblique parallel flaking, 3 in. long. This is a scarce point with rare chipping technique, made of glossy black flint. It was found in the Abiquiu Mountains region of New Mexico. Museum quality

Jack Baker collection, Ozark, Missouri; David Capon photograph

Birdpoints, true arrowheads from late prehistoric times, these chipped from a variety of colorful and high-grade materials. Also referred to as gempoints, all came from near Sandia Park, New Mexico. Each, $5-20

Jack Baker collection, Ozark, Missouri; David Capon photograph

Folsom point, Late Paleo period, 2-3/4 in. long. Fully fluted to the tip as is characteristic for type, these delicate points are usually found in broken or damaged condition. Material is brown and gray flint and the artifact was found near Melrose, New Mexico. $600

Jack Baker collection, Ozark, Missouri; David Capon photograph

Plainview(?) point or blade, 3/4 x 4-1/2 in. long, 1/4 in. thick. This longer-than-usual artifact is made from quality gray flint and is undamaged; the rare find came from the El Rito Mountain region of New Mexico. $850

Jack Baker collection, Ozark, Missouri; David Capon photograph

Arrowheads, late prehistoric period, all done in light-colored gem-quality flints. These came from the Santa Fe area of New Mexico. Each, $10-45

Jack Baker collection, Ozark, Missouri; David Capon photograph

Late Paleo point, probably an Agate Basin, 3 in. long. It is made of rose-colored flint with a white band, and was found while surface-hunting near Tucumcari, New Mexico. $300

Jack Baker collection, Ozark, Missouri; David Capon photograph

Birdpoints or small true arrowheads, all made of obsidian or dark natural glass from volcanic activity. These came from the El Rito Mountain region of New Mexico. Each, $5-20

Jack Baker collection, Ozark, Missouri; David Capon photograph

Arrowheads, Pueblo area and late prehistoric period, all in various gem quality flints. Of interest are the unusual multiple-notched points, with additional notching on one upper side. The arrowheads were found in the San Jose region of New Mexico. Each, $5-45

Jack Baker collection, Ozark, Missouri; David Capon photograph

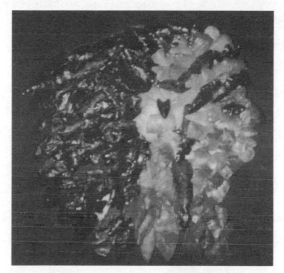

Frame of arrowheads and other projectile points, made in the design of a Plains Indian. Light and dark flints were used, both whole and broken, and frame size is 12 x 16 in. The artifacts were found in many places, all in the state of New Mexico. Unlisted

Jack Baker collection, Ozark, Missouri; David Capon photograph

Clovis fluted point, Early Paleo period, 1-1/8 x 3 in. long. It is made of high-quality red jasper and is a fine example of a Western Clovis. This was a surface find by Marcille Wing in 1966, northeastern Colorado. Museum quality

Collection of Eugene and Marcille Wing

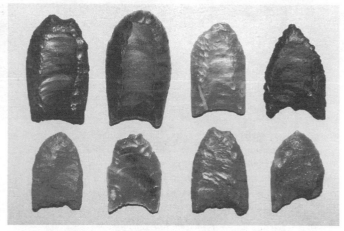

Folsom points, all rare, Late Paleo and ca. 7000-10,000 BP. Top row (top left example 1-1/2 in.) left to right:

Yellow moss jasper, patinated red, impact fracture on tip, Grants, New Mexico. $1,000
Flat-top chalcedony (found by K. Glasscock), Morgan County, Colorado. $1,500
Translucent gray Edwards flint, very thin, Gaines County, Texas. $800
Brown jasper, Deming area, New Mexico. $800

Bottom row, left example 1 in. Left to right:

Pink chert, Dona Ana County, New Mexico. $600
Translucent Edward flint, tip impact fracture, Curry County, New Mexico. $400
Brown speckled jasper, tip damage, Chaves County, New Mexico. $400
Tan quartzite, missing ear, Harding County, New Mexico. $400

Collection of, and photograph by, Michael W. Hough, California

Midland points and blades, 10,400-10,700 Before Present (BP), rare Late Paleo artifacts with left example 1-3/4 in. long. Top row, left to right:

Gray and green Edwards flint, Gaines County, Texas. $350
Gray and green Edwards flint, Midland County, Texas. $800
Light gray Edwards flint, Hale County, Texas. $400
Light gray Edwards flint, Andrews County, Texas. $300

Bottom row, left example 1-1/8 in. Left to right:

Gray Edwards flint, Midland County, Texas. $500
Gray Edwards flint, Gaines County, Texas. $300
Brown jasper, patinated yellow on reverse, Colorado. $500
Mottled red and white jasper, Las Vegas area, New Mexico. $800

Collection of, and photograph by, Michael W. Hough, California

Scottsbluff point, Late Paleo period, in dark gray flint with a brown tip. It carries a typical median ridge on both faces. North Platte area, Nebraska. $375

Larry Lantz, First Mesa, Indiana

Hohokam arrowhead from Arizona, 2-7/8 in. long, made from a white flint. Very narrow, with three deep indentations along lower base sides. Condition perfect, fine chipping. Scarce. C-$95

Hohokam point, 1-1/2 in. long, very narrow, edges deeply serrated and undamaged. C-$70

Dalton-type point, 1-1/2 in. long, perfect, from Louisiana. Serrated edges; ground base sides and bottom. C-$40

Clovis-type point, 3 in. long, found in Minnesota. Made of a regional chert; fluted both sides. C-$100

Flint point, Paleo-period from prehistoric lake (now dried) in Nevada; 2 in. long and made of a dull chert. Has rounded base, excurvate sides. No damage, but not too artistic. C-$22

Fluted-base Clovis-like point, found in Montana, 2-3/8 in. long. Material is a colorful, quality chert. Chipping very

distinct, flute-channels deep. Said to have come from a "buffalo jump" site. C-$120

Gem point, found in Nevada, 2-7/8 in. long. Made of black obsidian; corner-notched and bifurcated base. Piece is translucent; probably Archaic. D-$60

Obsidian arrowhead, 3/4 in. long and 3/8 in. wide at base. Small, triangular form with no notches. C-$8

Projectile point, Texas, 2-3/4 in. long and 1-1/4 in. wide. Deep-notch and of gray flint. G-$16

Obsidian point, from northern California, 2 in. long, side-notched and brownish in color. C-$19

Evans point from Yell County, Arkansas, 3 in. long and 1-1/4 in. wide. Pink color, double notches. G-$18

Arrowheads, frame of all fine obsidian point from Nevada. They (twenty-five) range in length from 1/2 in. to 2 in. G-$125

Texas "birdpoint," 1 in. long and very thin. Decorative white flint serrated edges, small squared notches, base very concave. Made of a glossy red flint with superb chipping. D-$50

Arrowheads, frame size 8 x 10 in. There are thirty fine obsidian points, with six damaged. Range in length from 1/2 in. to 2-1/2 in. G-$70

Crystal quartz arrowhead, rare, Arkansas; 3/4 in. long and 1/4 in. wide. G-$50

Caddo arrow points, three of them, average length 3/4 in. Two are made of novaculite; one of brown chert. G-$18

Leaf-shaped arrowheads, frame of twenty, from near Twin Falls, Idaho. D-$90

Arrowheads, frame, range from 1 in. to 2-1/4 in. long. All obsidian and twenty-one points. Several styles, and most are perfect. G-$125

Western U.S. Late Paleo points or blades, left example 2-3/4 in., all left to right:

Goshen, 9000-10,000 BP, caramel petrified wood, oblique transverse flaking, Colorado. $800
Plainview, 9000-10,000 BP, orange-brown translucent agate or chalcedony, New Mexico. $650
Plainview, 9000-10,000 BP, Barren Fork chert, McIntosh County, Oklahoma. $350
Plainview, 9000-10,000 BP, brown translucent Novaculite, Gregg County, Texas. $350

Collection of, and photograph by, Michael W. Hough, California

Western U.S. Late Paleo points or blades, left example 2-5/8 in., all left to right:

Firstview, 7000-9000 BP, mottled Edwards flint, Winkler County, Texas. $1,000
Eden, 7000-9500 BP, red quartzite, Lincoln County, Colorado. $500
Eden, translucent white chalcedony, Lincoln County, Colorado. $400
Eden, white chalcedony, Curry County, New Mexico. $300
Eden, patinated red and white agate, El Paso County, Colorado. $200

Collection of, and photograph by, Michael W. Hough, California

Clovis-type fluted point, from New Mexico 2-7/8 in. long. Made of high-quality translucent agate-flint, gray and green, unusual. Has two opposite small nicks on sides, probably from being wired to a frame by early collector. Well-fluted both sides, a very attractive piece.   D-$375

Beveled-edge shouldered point, from Iowa, 2-1/2 in. long and 1-1/2 in. wide.   G-$30

Fluted Clovis-type point, Oregon, 3 in. long. Obsidian, fluted on only one side and very thin. Perfect.   C-$130

Chalcedony point or blade, Washington state coastal-site, 2-1/4 in. long. Black obsidian, perfectly symmetrical. Shoulder tips even with flatish base, diagonally bottom notched. Regular chipping with very tiny flakes removed.   C-$95

CANADIAN POINTS

Arrowheads, frame of nine, from central Canada. Range from 1-1/8 in. to 2-1/2 in. in length. Most are chipped from a gray flint; all in perfect condition. There are seven notched types and two triangular forms, all probably Woodland and later in time.   C-$70

Side-notched point, central Canada, 2-1/8 in. in length. Gray flint; Archaic period.   C-$19

Triangular point, from British Columbia, 1-1/2 in. long. Chipped from argillite; blackish in color.   C-$8

Projectile point, from Saskatchewan, Canada; 2-3/8 in. long. Paleo period. Small, unfluted, has concave base and good chipping.   C-$60

Small-notched point, New Brunswick, Canada; 2 in. long. Made from a white material; edges are lightly serrated.   C-$14

Suggested Reading

Bell (& Perino), *Guide to the Identification of Certain American Indian Projectile Points*, Special Bulletins No. 1-4; Oklahoma Anthropological Society, Oklahoma City, Oklahoma.

Folsom, Franklin. *America's Ancient Treasures*. Albuquerque: University of New Mexico Press, 1983.

Basic Clovis-type projectile point, a Paleo variety often found around Debert in Nova Scotia. In the opinion of a Canadian researcher, this point would be about 11,000 years old; it may have been picked up and modified by later Amerinds, as the edge serrations help make this a unique point. Piece is 2-1/4 in. long, and less than 1/4 in. thick.   C-$120

Photo courtesy of Howard Popkie, Arnprior, Ontario, Canada

Fine Folsom point, 2-1/4 in. long and 7/8 in. wide. Very nicely chipped artifact, as are most Folsoms. From an old Canadian collection in Canada. Folsom points are generally found on the High Plains of Alberta.   C-$120

Photo courtesy of Howard Popkie, Arnprior, Ontario, Canada

Canadian projectile point, found at Woodstock, Ontario. Piece is 1-3/4 in. long, and is a side-notched variety somewhat resembling U.S. Woodland-era points.   C-$8

Photo courtesy of Howard Popkie, Arnprior, Ontario, Canada

Canadian projectile point, found near Dundas, Ontario. Point is 1-1/2 in. long and is probably an Archaic variety. Made of a green flint.   C-$9

Photo courtesy of Howard Popkie, Arnprior, Ontario, Canada

Canadian point or blade, believed to be Archaic but possibly Paleo era, and picked up near Moose Jaw, Susk. Artifact is 2-1/2 in. long, and made of a brown flint or chert.   C-$10

Photo courtesy of Howard Popkie, Arnprior, Ontario, Canada

Frame of prehistoric points and blades, plus a design of shell beads. All from Ontario, Canada. Longest piece is just over 3 in. Material priced without frame.   C-$450-650

Photo courtesy Robert C. Calvert, London, Ontario, Canada

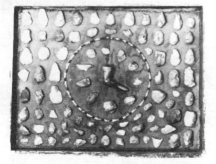

Frame of artifacts, with small flaked tools and scrapers from prehistoric times, plus clay pipe and fine strand of trade beads. Material priced without frame.   C-$150-175

Photo courtesy of Robert C. Calvert, London, Ontario, Canada

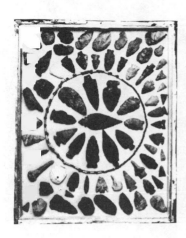

Fine frame of artifacts, containing prehistoric points and blades, plus French trade beads. Age of chipped artifacts range from Paleo to late Woodland and Mississippian times, and cover some 10,000 years. Material priced without frame.   C-$600-800

Photo courtesy Robert C. Calvert, London, Ontario, Canada

Rare Cumberland points, pictured elsewhere in book. The left example is Kentucky blue flint and was found in Steward County, Tennessee. $400-600

Right: Ft. Payne chert, from Montgomery County, Tennessee. $300-450

John M. Maurer collection, Ft. Campbell, Kentucky; photograph by Dan Privett

Top: very thin blade with long base, possibly an Adena Waubesa type. It is 2-15/16 in. long, from Benton County, Tennessee, and made of Dover flint. Ex-coll. Mark Clark. $35-55

Bottom: Adena point or blade, with tapered stem, very thin and well made from Dover flint. From Benton County, Tennessee, and ex-coll. Mark Clark. $225-300

John M. Maurer collection, Ft. Campbell, Kentucky; photograph by Dan Privett

This Clovis point is known as the "Red Cedar Clovis" and is made of oolitic hematite of Canadian origin. It is 1 x 3-1/8 in. and is from Barron County, Wisconsin. Until 1987, there was no known Early Paleo material from the county; as a first, this piece has attracted considerable attention. $650

Mert Cowley collection, Chetek, Wisconsin

Clovis point (Early Paleo), museum quality piece, made of brown jasper. It is from Bladen County, North Carolina. $950

Rodney M. Peck collection, Harrisburg, North Carolina

Lanceolate, Late Paleo, from Tuscarawas County, Ohio. Length is 5-3/4 in. and material is Coshocton flint. This lance has fine parallel percussion flaking and is in fine condition. $400-500

Alvin Lee Moreland, Corpus Christi, Texas

Cumberland point, from the Mammoth Cave region, Kentucky, made of Dover flint. This rare early artifact is 3-1/2 in. long. $1,200-1,400

Rodney M. Peck collection, Harrisburg, North Carolina

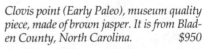

Clovis (Early Paleo) points, all from North Carolina and made from silicified shale. Each, $200-350

Rodney M. Peck collection, Harrisburg, North Carolina

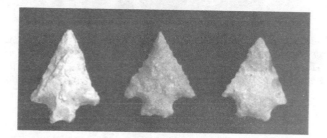

Stanly points or blades, from North Carolina and Virginia. Materials are quartzite and silicified shale. Each, $7

Rodney M. Peck collection, Harrisburg, North Carolina

Wisconsin chipped artifacts in colorful materials. Various time periods are represented. Collection, $250-400

Robert D. Lund collection, Watertown, Wisconsin

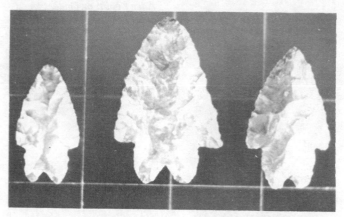

Bifurcated or split-base blades, Early Archaic period, all Ohio. Material is Upper Mercer in several shades of blue. One inch background grid gives scale.

Left: $15-20
Center: $35-45
Right: $20-25

Private collection, Ohio

Agate Basin, Late Paleo/Early Archaic, from Pike County, Illinois. This exceptional point or blade is 5-3/4 in. long and very well-made. $1,000

L.M. Abbott, Jr. collection, Texas

Woodland point or blade, possibly a Hopewell variant, 1-1/2 in. long. From Vinton County, Ohio, material is jewel amber-colored translucent Flintridge. $30

Private collection, Ohio

Adena point or blade, translucent Flintridge, from Washington County, Ohio. At 1-1/2 x 2-1/16 in., the relatively short length for basal size indicates extensive prehistoric resharpening. $40

Private collection, Ohio

Quad point or blade, Late Paleo/Early Archaic, 3-1/8 in. long. It is made of tan flint, is thin, with heavily ground hafting region. From middle Tennessee, it is ex-colls. Clark and Ransford. $325

John M. Maurer collection, Ft. Campbell, Kentucky; photography by Dan Privett

Fluted points, Paleo period.

Left: Redstone fully fluted, dark patinated Dover flint, found by Adrien Boudoin in Todd County, Kentucky. $600+
Right: Redstone-like fluted point, found by Dennis Drugman in Christian County, Kentucky. The missing ear was salvaged in that area after prehistoric damage. $150

John. M. Maurer collection, Ft. Campbell, Kentucky; photograph by Dan Privett

Lanceolate point, Late Paleo, from Hancock County, Ohio. It is made from Upper Mercer flint, Coshocton variety, in white, gray, blue-black, and with reddish spotting. Size, 1-3/8 x 6-3/16 in.; G.I.R.S. authentication number C88-27. One of the largest and finest lances to be found in the state. $1,250+

Collection of David G. & Barbara J. Shirley

Paleo points, various types.

Left two: multiple flutes, 2-1/4 in., found by Geoff Ransford in Christian County, Kentucky. Each, $150
Next: Montgomery County, Tennessee, ex-coll. Clark. $175
Right: unfluted Clovis from Logan County, Kentucky. $50

John M. Maurer collection, Ft. Campbell, Kentucky; photograph by Dan Privett

Late Paleo/Early Archaic point, a Dalton-Colbert, 2-1/2 in. long. From Benton County, Tennessee, it is thin with heavy basal grinding and with basal thinning. Ex-coll. Mark Clark, this piece is lightly serrated. $175

John M. Maurer collection, Ft. Campbell, Kentucky; photograph by Dan Privett

Points or blades from the Coles Creek culture, Mississippi/Louisiana state line region. These are very high quality artifacts. Each, $20-150

Wilfred A. Dick collection, Magnolia, Mississippi

Late Archaic/Early Woodland point or blade, white Hixton quartzite, from Dunn County, Wisconsin. Size is 1-1/16 x 1-5/8 in. and type is Durst-stemmed. $15-18

Mert Cowley collection, Chetek, Wisconsin

Cumberland points, Late Paleo period.

Left: small fluted point from Todd County, Kentucky; found by owner. $50
Next: Kentucky blue flint, Steward County, Tennessee, ex-coll. Mark Clark. $400-600
Next (center): Ft. Payne chart, Montgomery County, Tennessee, ex-coll. Boudoin. $300-450
Next: unfluted Cumberland, Kentucky blue flint, western Kentucky, ex-coll. Clark. $150-225
Right: thin and fully fluted. $50-100

John M. Maurer collection, Ft. Campbell, Kentucky; photograph by Dan Privett

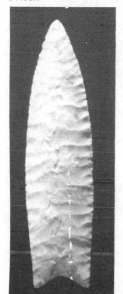

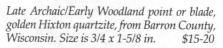

Late Archaic/Early Woodland point or blade, golden Hixton quartzite, from Barron County, Wisconsin. Size is 3/4 x 1-5/8 in. $15-20

Mert Cowley collection, Chetek, Wisconsin

Dalton point or blade, Pike County, Illinois. At 5-1/2 in., it is made of gray-tan high quality chert. Late Paleo/Early Archaic, this piece has very fine flaking. $600-800

Alvin Lee, Moreland, Corpus Christi, Texas

Known as "The Glacial Lake Scottsbluff," this fine Late Paleo lanceolate has been pictured in the "Creme de la Creme" section of Indian Artifact Magazine. This piece is made of chert with crystalline inclusions and was found in northern Wisconsin, rare for the region. Size, 1-1/4 x 4-3/16 in. $450-500

Mert Cowley collection, Chetek, Wisconsin

Expanded-stem point or blade, golden Hixton quartzite, from Barron County, Wisconsin. It is 3/4 x 1-3/16 in. long. $20-25

Mert Cowley collection, Chetek, Wisconsin

Paleo period points and blades. Top to bottom, rows left to right: Clovis, Dover chart, from Tennessee, 5 in., $650; Clovis, McIntosh County, Oklahoma, 3-3/4 in., $300; Clovis, Illinois, 3-3/4 in., $375; Clovis, Taney County, Missouri, 3-3/4 in., $425; Midland point, Midland, Texas, 2 in., $200; cast replica of Folsom, Custer County, Oklahoma, Edwards Plateau chart, 2-1/4 in., original point, $550; Folsom, quartzite, Blain County, Oklahoma, 1-5/8 in., $550; Clovis, 2-3/4 in., St. Clair, Illinois, $225; Clovis, McIntosh County, Oklahoma, 2-1/2 in., Boone chart, $200; Center, St. Louis type Clovis, 5-3/4 in., Hickman County, Kentucky, Indiana hornstone; $775. Folsom, 1-1/4 in., jasper from Arnold County, Nebraska, $300; Clovis, 3-3/4 in., Boone County, Illinois, Knife River flint, $800; Cumberland, Hamilton County, Tennessee, 3-1/4 in., $425; Clovis, Flintridge flint, 2-7/8 in., Tuscarawas County, Ohio, $425; Clovis, 3-1/4 in., Alibates flint, $300; Quad type, Morgan County, Alabama, Fort Payne chart, 2-3/8 in., shown in Story in Stone, $200; Clovis, 2 in., $125; Clovis, Miami, Texas, 5 in., $625; Clovis, St. Clair, Illinois, 4-1/2 in., $300; Ross County type Clovis, Callaway County, Missouri. $400

Larry Merriam collection, Oklahoma City, Oklahoma

Harrell point, late prehistoric Caddoan, and a classic example. It is from Runnels County, Texas, and 1-1/2 in. long. $75-100

Grady McCrea collection, Miles, Texas

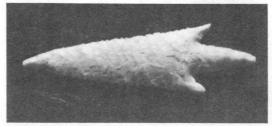

Perdiz point or blade, very thin and with fine flaking. The classic Texas example is 2-3/4 in. long. $125

Grady McCrea collection, Miles, Texas

Washita point, late prehistoric Caddoan, found in Runnels County, Texas. Made of translucent gemgrade flint, this piece is 1-1/4 in. long. $65

Grady McCrea collection, Miles, Texas

Angostura point or blade, Texas, made of Edwards Plateau flint. This very rare specimen has the remains of the original flint nodule or cortex at the base bottom. It is 4 in. long. $400-750

Grady McCrea collection, Miles, Texas

Dalton points or blades, Late Paleo/Early Archaic period.

Left side top to bottom: Northeast Arkansas, 6-1/2 in., Cherry Hill Style, $650; Adams County, Illinois, 6 in., $450; Benton County, Arkansas, 6-1/4 in., $475; Jefferson County, Missouri, 5 in., $275. Center: Howard County, Missouri, 6-3/4 in. $650
Lower center: Cherry Hill Dalton, 5 in. $250
Right side, top to bottom: Pike county, Arkansas, 6-1/8 in., $325; Boone County, Missouri, 6 in., $300; Ripley County, Missouri, 6-3/4 in., $650; Saline County, Missouri, 5 in. $350

Larry Merriam collection, Oklahoma City, Oklahoma

Perdiz point, late prehistoric period, from Runnels County, Texas. This specimen is 1-1/2 in. long. $35

Grady McCrea collection, Miles, Texas

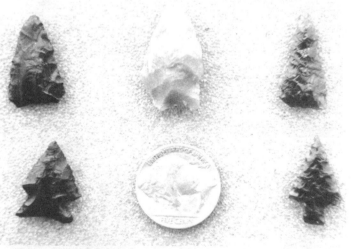

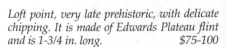

Loft point, very late prehistoric, with delicate chipping. It is made of Edwards Plateau flint and is 1-3/4 in. long. $75-100

Grady McCrea collection, Miles, Texas

Obsidian and quartz points, all from Box Elder County, Utah. The small size of these artifacts suggests they may be true arrowheads of later prehistoric times, except for the top center piece which may be older.   Group, $30

Randall Olsen collection, Cache County, Utah

Meserve point, from Polk County, Texas, 4-1/4 in. long.　　　　　　　　　　$275

L.M. Abbott, Jr. collection, Texas

Darl dart or lance point, Edwards Plateau chart, from Coryell County, Texas. It is 4 in. long.　　$80

L.M. Abbott, Jr. collection, Texas

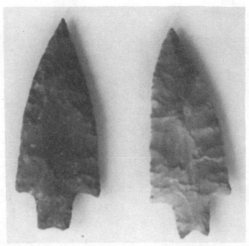

Pedernales points, Late Archaic, both made from Edwards Plateau chert. Each is 4-1/4 in. long.　　　　　　　　　Each, $125

L.M. Abbott, Jr. collection, Texas

Pedernales, made of Edwards Plateau flint, from Coryell County, Texas. A good type example, it is 4-1/4 in. long.　　　　　　$150

L.M. Abbott, Jr. collection, Texas

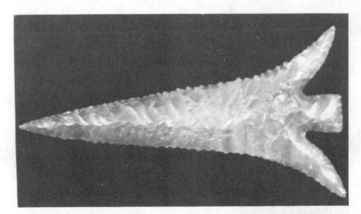

Gunther point, 1 x 1-7/8 in., made of Oregon gem material. It is from the Columbia River area, Washington. This is one of the finer Northwest Coast gempoints.　　　　　　$235

Larry Lantz, First Mesa, South Bend, Indiana

Barber point, Early Archaic, made of unknown material. It is from Upshur County, Texas.　　　　　　　　　　$250

L.M. Abbott, Jr. collection, Texas

Pontchartrain points made of an unusual material, petrified wood. They are from Angelina County, Texas.

Right: 3 in.　　　　　　　　$65

Left: 3-1/2 in.　　　　　　　$80

L.M. Abbott, Jr. collection, Texas

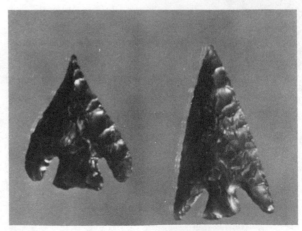

Points or blades from North Dakota, found by Steve Childress and made of Knife River flint. These are high-grade pieces made of a gem material.　　　　Each, $65

Larry G. Merriam collection, Oklahoma City, Oklahoma

Point or blade, Agate Basin of Late Paleo/Early Archaic period. It is made of brown jasper and is 4-1/2 in. long. It came from Platte County, Wyoming. $375

Steven D. Kitch collection, Pueblo, Colorado

Folsom (Late Paleo) points.

Left: from Cedar Creek, Oklahoma, a personal find of the owner. It is 1-3/8 in. and made of Edwards chert; found in two pieces. $350

Right: Folsom variant with slight side-notches (may be a newly recognized type), 1-3/8 in. and also found by owner. The material (white) is unknown. $450

Larry G. Merriam collection, Oklahoma City, Oklahoma

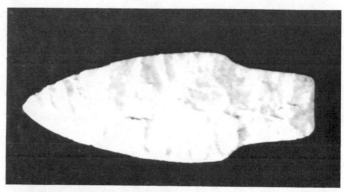

Point, Hell Gap, Late Paleo/Early Archaic, made of highly patinated Knife River flint. It is 3-1/2 in. long and from Pueblo County, Colorado. $275

Steven D. Kitch collection, Pueblo, Colorado

Texas points and blades, high-quality flints and cherts, with half a dozen different types represented. There are 192 pieces in the frame.

Individual: $25-200
Total: $6,000

Larry G. Merriam collection, Oklahoma City, Oklahoma

Agate Basin point, Late Paleo/Early Archaic period, made of a gem material, dendritic (branching minerals) jasper. It is 3-1/8 in. long and from Saguache County, Colorado. $560

Steven D. Kitch collection, Pueblo, Colorado

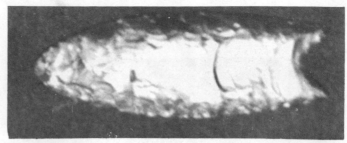

Clovis point or blade, Early Paleo period, from the Council Bluffs area, Iowa. At 3-1/2 in. long, the piece is made from Knife River flint, amber with white cloudy inclusions. It is fluted on both faces, 1/2 and 2/3 length, respectively. $450-600

Alvin Lee Moreland, Corpus Christi, Texas

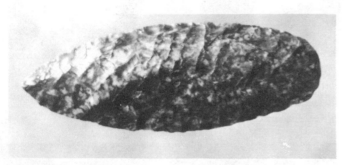

Eden point or blade, Late Paleo/Early Archaic, made of a fine translucent amber-brown flint. It has parallel flaking and no damage. This is a scarce type, from Texas. $400

Alvin Lee Moreland, Corpus Christi, Texas

Agate Basin point or blade, Alibates flint, from Baca County, Colorado. Late Paleo/Early Archaic, this fine piece is 3-1/8 in. long. $400

Steven D. Kitch collection, Pueblo, Colorado

Scottsbluff point or blade, late Paleo/Early Archaic, Zafala County, Texas. At 4-1/2 in. long, material is a glossy blue-green to gray flint. Flaking is parallel to collateral. $550

Alvin Lee Moreland, Corpus Christi, Texas

Scottsbluff point or blade, Late Paleo/Early Archaic, from Texas. Material is a brown translucent flint. It has collateral flaking and highly unusual hafting residue. $400-550

Alvin Lee Moreland, Corpus Christi, Texas

Scottsbluff point or blade, Late Paleo/Early Archaic, from southern Texas. It is 4-3/16 inches long and material is pink, cream and red chert. This is a fine piece with oblique and transverse flaking. $250-350

Alvin Lee Moreland, Corpus Christi, Texas

A fine collection of artifacts from Ontario, Canada. Included are two birdstones (Late Archaic), three pipes, two gorgets, several knives, and a pendant. *Unlisted*

Robert C. Calvert, London, Ontario, Canada

Collection of artifacts from Ontario, Canada, very high quality pieces. Included are three birdstones, a humped adz (top right), a pipe, a gorget, a hafted blade, and two Early Paleo Clovis or Clovis-like points. *Unlisted*

Robert C. Calvert, London, Ontario, Canada

Far View Ruins, foreground; background, Pipe Shrine House. Both are on the canyon rim in Mesa Verde National Park, Colorado. Many of the early ruins (including those shown) have been carefully preserved and stabilized to protect them. Both of the ruins shown are Developmental Pueblo period.

Lar Hothem photo

CHAPTER II

CHIPPED ARTIFACTS

Chipping was the first of the three great prehistoric and early historic tool-shaping methods.

In Chapter I, projectile points were arbitrarily grouped as about 3 inches (75 mm) or under in length. There is some debate in the area, and undoubtedly some of the artifacts listed were actually blades or small knives.

In general, the various other chipped artifacts were made of the same crypto-crystalline materials as were the projectile points. The two requirements seem to have been that the flint or chert chipped well, and that it had few foreign inclusions—bad spots—to interfere with that chipping.

Some of the value factors for the projectile points are relevant here, like the emphasis on quality material, work-style, size, and condition. There is the added factor of a rare class. There have never been many notched hoes, for example, so an artifact in that category is more highly valued than, say, a crude chopper.

Here, other chipped artifacts are described and listed; there are a number of them, so rather than attempt to introduce and list them all, each sub-group has a brief preface.

Knives or blades are usually medium to large-size chipped tools, apparently used as cutting instruments. They are in many shapes, and no one definition covers them all. If there is a generalization, it is that blade edges were more important than the tip; these areas often show minor work-breaks and heavy wear.

Some blades had serrated or saw-tooth edges, while others were sharply angled or beveled. Others had nondescript edge treatment, and may have been multi-purpose knives. The base is usually fairly sturdy, and the distance between notches, or the width of the basal stem, may be an inch (10 cm) or so on average. Other blades do not show specific chipping for hafting, and it is unknown how the handle, if any, was attached.

All of the valuation factors mentioned for projectile points apply to symmetrical blades. Length is of special importance, and large authentic pieces command much collector attention. Condition is vital, for larger artifacts are difficult to locate in absolutely perfect form.

EASTERN CHIPPED BLADES

Base-notched translucent blade, Florida; point is 3 in. long and perfect in all details, of a high-quality light-transmitting flint; notches thin and well-made.   C-$95

Cache blade, Indiana, 5-1/4 in. long and 3 in. wide. Oval-shaped, unfinished, gray flint; probably Woodland. D-$24

Osceola blade, Illinois, nearly 6 in. long and about 2-1/4 in. wide. Made of a reddish and white high-grade flint. Colors form artistic pattern. Only slight original wear shows on blade sides; base fully ground. No damage.   D-$550

Side-notched blade, 4-1/2 in. long, probably Archaic. Small, but deep, notches put in about 1/2 inch from base bottom. Sides are almost straight, and then incurvate to tip.   A-$80

Bifurcated-base blade, 3-1/2 in. long and 1-1/2 in. wide, Archaic. Blue-gray flint. Base bottom is indented to same degree as corner notches. Small side serrations.   A-$40

Dovetail or St. Charles blade, just under 5 in. Large, damage to one corner of base, otherwise fine condition and a good specimen for restoration.   A-$165

Dovetail of Carter Cave flint, Kentucky, 5 in. long and 1-1/4 in. wide.   G-$90

Blade or knife, 6-1/4 in. long, uncertain period, may be Archaic. Large, base-stemmed, with base bottom slightly incurvate. Blade sides are slightly excurvate, serrated edges.   A-$265

Quartzite blade, Pennsylvania, 7 in. long.   D-$55

Triangular blade, 3-1/2 in. long and 1-1/2 in. wide at base. This is a very thin piece, only 3/16 in. Other artifacts found on the same site include a fluted point and an Atl-atl weight. Found in southern Tennessee.   C-$60

Photo courtesy of Jim Northcutt, Jr., Corinth, Mississippi

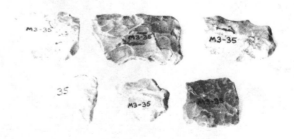

Problematical artifacts, from Prentis County, Mississippi. Largest piece in photos is 1 x 2 in. Over 100 have been found on just one village site, and have been associated with Benton points. These seem to have once been blades or points, were broken, and then were smoothed on all sides and faces. These are not water-worn, but abrasion or smoothing was intentional.   C-No value listed

Photo courtesy Jim Northcutt, Jr., Corinth, Mississippi

Serrated edge blade, 1-1/2 in. wide and 3 in. long, Mississippian period and found in south-central Tennessee. Base with missing corner has been ground smooth and cutting edges clearly show re-touching or resharpening.   C-$18

Photo courtesy Retha D. Northcutt, Corinth, Mississippi

Scottsbluff or stemmed lanceolate, Alibates flint. This is 1-1/3 x 3-7/8 in., ca. 7500-6500 BC, and a rare point for the region where found. In unused condition, high-quality material, it also has horizontal transverse flaking on both faces. Important for such major pieces , it has authentication papers from Perino and Rogers, and was a 1997 find in central Louisiana.   Museum quality

Collection of, and photograph by, Steve Granger, Hallsville, Texas

Five flint cores, the portion remaining after thin flake knives have been knocked off. Highest grade Ohio Flintridge material, very color-ful and glossy. Per each   C-$10-15

Private collection

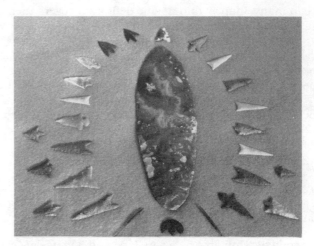

Frame of Caddoan flint, Mississippian period, Early to Late Caddo. Shown are various arrowhead types plus a large blade which measures 2 x 8 in. The longest point is 1-1/4 x 1-3/4 in. Materials used include: Novaculite, rock crystal, green chert, green jasper, agatized wood, Ogallala chert, and Edwards Plateau chert. This is a very high-grade grouping of artifacts, which were found in Arkansas and Texas.   Museum quality

Collection of, and photograph by, Steve Granger, Hallsville, Texas

Dovetail blade, Early Archaic period, 1-1/4 x 2-3/8 in. and 3/16 in. thick. It is made of blue-gray flint or chert that has faded to a light gray due to time and weathering. It was found in Alabama. $150

Tom Fouts collection, Kansas

Left to right: rough-chipped flint celt, age unknown. Midwestern; about 6 in. high.   C-$20

Rough-chipped flint axe, age unknown. Midwestern; about 7 in. high. Some collectors feel these may be of Paleo origin, but proof is lacking.   C-$25

Private collection

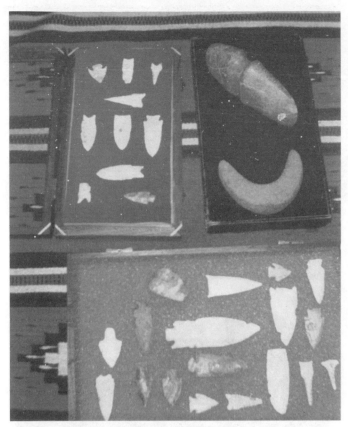

Grouping of Midwestern points, blades and stone artifacts, mainly Archaic era, all found on one major prehistoric site in Randolph County, Illinois.

Top right: grooved axe. $300
Top lower right: crescent bannerstone, quality hardstone. $1,400
Other points and blades. Each, $5-200

Rainbow Traders, Godfrey, Illinois

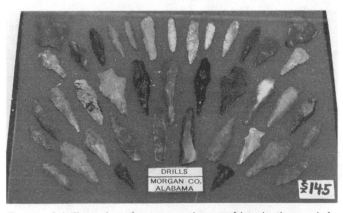

Frame of drills and perforators, various prehistoric time-periods, made of various flints and cherts. All are from Morgan County, Alabama. $145

Larry Garvin, Back to Earth, Ohio

Middle to Late Archaic points and blades, Big Sandy type, many probably well-used knives that have been reduced to shorter forms. These are ca. 3500 BC. All are from Barren County, Kentucky. $170

Larry Garvin, Back to Earth, Ohio

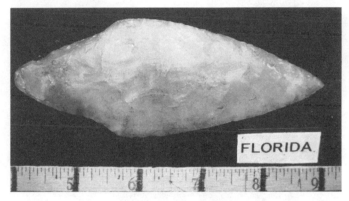

Stemmed blade, probably made of translucent agatized coral which is a favored Florida material for high-grade points and knives. This fine specimen is from Jackson County, Florida. $265

Larry Garvin, Back to Earth, Ohio

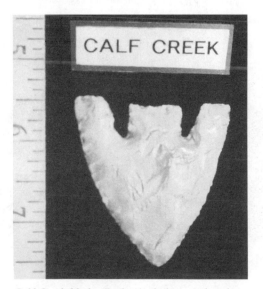

Calf Creek blade, Early Archaic period and ca. 7000 BC. The material is a high-grade salmon-pink flint and artifact is 2-1/8 in. long. This scarce example (due both to the type, and long, delicate shoulders being intact) is from Poinsette County, Arkansas. $195

Larry Garvin, Back to Earth, Ohio

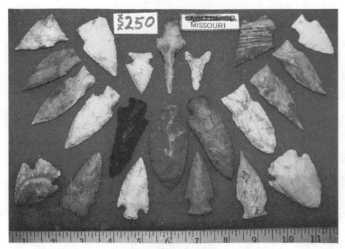

Points, blades (knives) and drills from three major prehistoric periods, Paleo, Archaic and Woodland. A wide variety of regional materials was used for these artifacts from Missouri. $250

Larry Garvin, Back to Earth, Ohio

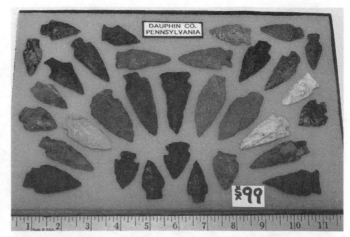

Points and blades, notched and stemmed forms from the Late Archaic/Early Woodland timespan. Notice the use of dark Pennsylvania cherts and flints. $99

Larry Garvin, Back to Earth, Ohio

4 1/8" BENTON

Benton blade, Archaic period, 4-1/8 in. long. It is made of gray and purple-tan flint and is from Humphries County, Tennessee. $195

Larry Garvin, Back to Earth, Ohio

Points and blades, stemmed and notched varieties, made of various regional flint and chert materials. Most appear to be Archaic in origin. Dauphin County, Pennsylvania. $135

Larry Garvin, Back to Earth, Ohio

Two large Archaic blades, both from Alabama.

Top: stemmed, 4-5/8 in. long, Coffee County. $125
Bottom: Benton type, corner notches, 5-1/8 in. long, Colbert County. $235

Larry Garvin, Back to Earth, Ohio

Large knives with drills or perforators, Paleo through Woodland times, various flints and cherts. All are from DeKalb County, Tennessee. $155

Larry Garvin, Back to Earth, Ohio

Archaic and Woodland period points and blades, with several Mississippian triangular forms. Made of various area cherts and flints, all are from Fentress County, Tennessee. $95

Larry Garvin, Back to Earth, Ohio

Frame of points and blades, mostly from the Archaic period (ca. 8000-1000 BC), done in dark cherts and flints. Fentress County, Tennessee. $199

Larry Garvin, Back to Earth, Ohio

Frame of Archaic and Woodland points and blades, side and corner notched plus stemmed examples. Most are made of regional cherts and flints. York County, Pennsylvania. $89

Larry Garvin, Back to Earth, Ohio

Jakie stemmed blade, remains of serrations or saw-edge chipping on the lower sides, honey-colored flint. These knives are Middle Archaic and ca. 6000-4000 BC. Boone County, Arkansas. $100

Kenneth Hamilton collection, Harrison, Arkansas

Chipped points and blades, mainly Archaic and Woodland periods, various regional flints and cherts. Clay County, Arkansas. $120

Larry Garvin, Back to Earth, Ohio

Late Paleo/Early Archaic artifacts, both evidencing knife use. Example on left is shortened and has an angled blade. Example on right is shortened and has worn-down serrations. Arkansas. Each, $60-75

Kenneth Hamilton collection, Harrison, Arkansas

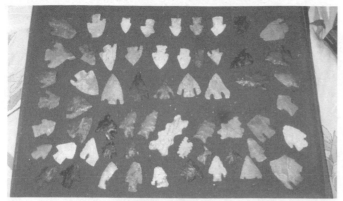

Calf Creek blade display with several other types. Calf Creeks are not common and examples shown illustrate varying degrees of use-damage and resharpening. It is unusual for both shoulders to remain on the piece. Arkansas.   Unlisted

Kenneth Hamilton collection, Harrison, Arkansas

Dalton and other early knife and point types, size range 2 to 3-1/2 in. A variety of materials is represented for these artifacts, Late Paleo into Early Archaic times. Arkansas.   Each, $35-250

Kenneth Hamilton collection, Harrison, Arkansas

Western blades or knives, all left to right:

Knife, 3000-5000 BP, 6-1/2 in., banded black obsidian, Modoc County, California. $350
Knife, 3000-5000 BP, 7-3/8 in., banded black obsidian, Modoc County, California. $300
Knife, 800-2000 BP, 6-3/4 in., mottled red/black obsidian, California. $250
Knife, 500-1500 BP, 6-5/8 in., gray Alesian chert with red veins, California. $350
Knife, 800-2000 BP, 5-3/4 in., red with black obsidian, Humboldt County, California. $200

Collection of, and photograph by, Michael W. Hough, California

Dovetail or St. Charles blade, small-base variety, blue and mauve near-gem quality Flintridge material. This is an Early Archaic piece, ca. 7500-7000 BC, and is ex-collections Meador and Weidner. It measures 2 x 4-1/16 in. and is valued according to high color, good size and fine workmanship. With authentication papers, this Dovetail is a good old piece that came from Delaware County, Ohio. $2,000-2,500

Collection of Linda Granger; photograph by Steve Granger, Hallsville, Texas

Knife, Late Paleo to Early Archaic period, in glossy amber-brown flint. The blade is slightly angled to the left, typical of some knives. Boone County, Arkansas. $100

Kenneth Hamilton collection, Harrison, Arkansas

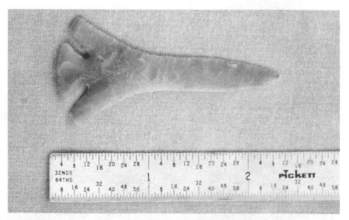

Agee point, bat-wing sub-type, a true arrowhead type dating ca. AD 700-1000 (see Perino, Selected Preforms, Points and Knives of the North American Indians, Vol. 1). This is a superb example, found by Glen Kizzia who remarked that this is the biggest and best of the type he ever found. Size of this piece is 1-1/8 x 2-1/4 in., and it is made of orange translucent novaculite. Arkansas.   Museum quality

Collection of, and photograph by, Steve Granger, Hallsville, Texas

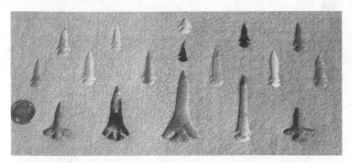

Frame of Agee points, with large central example shown elsewhere in book. The largest example is 2-1/4 in. long and materials are novaculite in different colors and high-grade brown chert. All were found in Arkansas. *Museum quality*

Collection of, and photograph by, Steve Granger, Hallsville, Texas

Frame of Agee points, with large central example shown elsewhere in book. These are late Coles Creek culture and the material is novaculite in various colors. This is an excellent frame of Agees. Arkansas. *Museum quality*

Collection of, and photograph by, Steve Granger, Hallsville, Texas

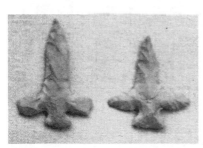

Agee variant points, ca. AD 700-1000, true arrowheads made of high-grade brown chert. Left example, 13/16 x 1-1/4 in.; right, 7/8 x 1 in. Both were found by Glen Kizzia in Miller County, Arkansas.
Museum quality

Collection of, and photograph by, Steve Granger, Hallsville, Texas

Cotaco Creek point or blade, Archaic period, 1-11/16 x 3-1/16 in., 5/16 in. thick. Made of yellowish-orange river chert, it has age spots and encrustations. This piece was found in Alabama. $50

Private collection

Cumberland point, Late Paleo period, 1 x 4-3/8 in. and 3/8 in. thick. The material is blue-black flint and the piece is fluted on both lower faces. The obverse flute is 1-7/8 in. and the reverse flute measures 2-3/4 in. long. There are age encrustations on one face of this superb example of a scarce point type. Alabama. $2,500+

Private collection

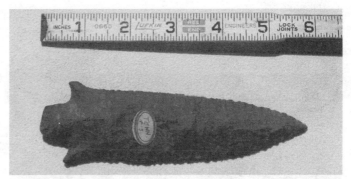

Etley point or blade, 1-3/4 x 5-3/4 in., 5/16 in. thick. This piece has well-done chipping and good symmetry, with edge serrations. Material is gray-brown flint or chert with soil staining. Formerly in the Terry Allen collection, this artifact came from Tennessee. $450

Tom Fouts collection, Kansas

Western points and blades, all in black obsidian, all left to right:

Knife, 6 in., translucent, 3000-5000 BP, Nevada. $250
Eden-type point, 8000-9500 BP, 5 in., translucent banded, Nevada. $300
Sierra knife, 800-1500 BP, 4-3/8 in., translucent, Kern County, California.   Unlisted
Parman, 7500-8500 BP, 5-1/4 in., black, large for type, Oregon. $200

Collection of, and photograph by, Michael W. Hough, California

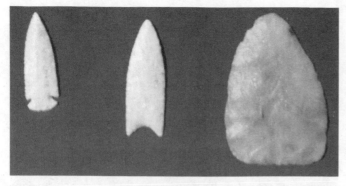

Midwestern prehistoric artifacts, all top-grade specimens, and all from Jersey County, Illinois.

Left: Dovetail, Early Archaic, 3-1/4 in. long, Burlington chert. $250

Center: Clovis point, Early Paleo period, 3-7/8 in., Burlington chert. $1,900

Right: preform blade, unknown period, unusual material (sugar quartz). $100

Rainbow Traders, Godfrey, Illinois

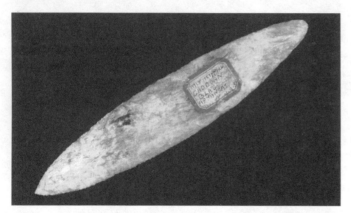

Knife, large Mississippian (Caddoan) blade in waxy marble-like flint with gray, cream, blue, and milky quartz areas. Unusually fine, this 9-in. specimen is from the Arkansas River area, Arkansas. $1,500

Larry Lantz, First Mesa, Indiana

Calf Creek blade, a basal-notched type from the Early Archaic and ca. 7500-6500 BC. This example is in nearly worn-out or "exhausted" condition; when discarded in prehistoric times the shoulders were about ready to be resharpened off. Arkansas. Museum quality

Kenneth Hamilton collection, Harrison, Arkansas

Greenbrier Dalton, Late Paleo/Early Archaic period, 3-1/5 in. long. This serrated-edge blade has been considerably resharpened from the original, larger form. It is made of Fort Payne chert and came from the Florence area of Alabama. $750

C.H. Baggerley collection, Nicholson, Georgia

Newnan point or blade, Archaic and ca. 3500 BC, 1-1/2 x 2-1/4 in. long. It is made of colorful fossil coral and came from near Plant City, Florida. $175

Scott Young, Port St. Lucie, Florida

Late Paleo lanceolate point or blade, 1-1/8 x 2-3/4 in. It is made of river-stained chert and is from Florida. $250

Scott Young, Port St. Lucie, Florida

Citrus points or blades, Woodland period, large and fine type examples, all made of Florida materials and from Florida. Left to right:

Citrus, 3-1/8 in., very pointed tip. $500
Citrus, 4-1/8 in., one of the best from the state. $1,500
Citrus, about 3 in. long. $100

Scott Young, Port St. Lucie, Florida

Eastern U.S. Late Paleo points or bludes, middle example 3 7/8 in., all left to right:

Holland, 7000-9500 BP, Burlington chert, ex-Weidner, Midwest. $700
Holland, 7000-9500 BP, mottled gray-white chert, Pike County, Indiana. $650
Plainview, 9000-10,000 BP, Burlington chert, Calhoun County, Illinois. $500

Collection of, and photograph by, Michael W. Hough, California

Eastern U.S. Lost Lake blades, Early Archaic and ca. 9000-7500 BC, left to right:

Lost Lake, 4-1/4 in., nicely balanced, hornstone, Harrison County, Indiana. $4,000
Lost Lake, 3-3/4 in., Fort Payne flint, Trigg County, Kentucky. $2,500
Lost Lake, 3-1/4 in., hornstone, Lincoln County, Kentucky. $2,500

Brad MacKenzie collection, San Francisco, California; Michael W. Hough photograph

Eastern U.S. Early Archaic blades or knives, all left to right:

Lost Lake variant, 3-1/2 in., Sonora flint, Monroe County, Kentucky. $3,000
Lost Lake, 3-1/2 in. long, Fort Payne flint, Hardin County, Tennessee. $2,500
Lost Lake, 3-3/4 in. long, Fort Payne flint, Lawrence County, Tennessee. $3,500

Brad MacKenzie collection, San Francisco, California; Michael W. Hough photograph

Eastern U.S. Lost Lake (Sunfish; from side profile) blades, ca. 9000-7500 BC, all left to right:

Lost Lake, (Sunfish), 3-3/4 in., Sonora flint, Jefferson County, Kentucky. $4,000
Lost Lake, (Sunfish), 3-3/8 in., hornstone, Picket County, Tennessee. $3,500
Lost Lake, (Sunfish), 3-1/4 in., hornstone, Daviess County, Kentucky. $3,000

Brad MacKenzie collection, San Francisco, California; Michael W. Hough photograph

Early Archaic Lost Lake (Sunfish) blade, ca. 9000-7500 BC, one of the better large blades from the eastern U.S. With edge-serrations, this artifact was chipped in Fort Payne flint, measures 4-1/2 in. long, and is from Mason County, Kentucky. $6,000

Brad MacKenzie collection, San Francisco, California; Michael W. Hough photograph

Eastern U.S. Pine Tree blades, pre-6000 BC, all left to right:

Pine Tree, 2 in. long, gray hornstone, Stewart County, Tennessee.$300
Pine Tree, 2-5/8 in., red Carter Cave flint, eastern Midwest. $750
Pine Tree, 2-3/4 in., tan hornstone, Stewart County, Tennessee. $2,000
Pine Tree, 2 in. long, dark hornstone, Barren County, Kentucky. $300
Pine Tree, 2 in. long, glossy hornstone, Swan Landing, Indiana. $175

Brad MacKenzie collection, San Francisco, California; Michael W. Hough photograph

Hardin point or blade, Early Archaic and ca. 7000 BC, this example with excurvate edges showing little resharpening. It is 3-2/5 in. long, is made of Burlington chert, and came from Union County, Illinois. $550

C.H. Baggerley collection, Nicholson, Georgia

Hardin Barb point or blade, Early Archaic period, 3-1/2 in. long. This long-stemmed subtype is made of Burlington chert and came from St. Clair County, Illinois. $450

C. H. Baggerley collection, Nicholson, Georgia

Pine Tree blades or knives, Early Archaic period and pre-6000 BC, all varieties of corner-notched blades. A nearly similar variety is known as the Charleston; all left to right:

Pine Tree, 2-3/4 in., angled blade, brown flint, Barren County, Kentucky. $350
Pine Tree, 2-1/2 in., Bangor chert, classic form, northern Kentucky. $400
Pine Tree, 2-5/8 in., regional chert, northern Kentucky. $200
Pine Tree, 2-1/4 in., regional chert, Stewart County, Tennessee. $300
Pine Tree, 1-3/4 in., resharpened, bicolor hornstone, Kentucky. $450

Brad MacKenzie collection, San Francisco, California; Michael W. Hough photograph

Abbey point or blade, Archaic period, 3-1/3 in. long. This example is made of river-stained chert and came from Lee County, Georgia. $400

C. H. Baggerley collection, Nicholson, Georgia

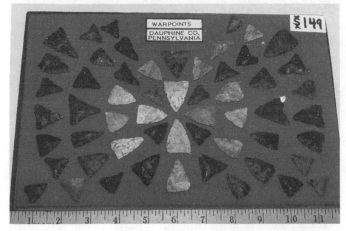

Mississippian period triangular points, illustrated examples are true arrowheads. These were made of regional flints and cherts and are in the typical size range. Dauphine County, Pennsylvania. $149

Larry Garvin, Back to Earth, Ohio

Serrated blade, found in Ohio near West Lafayette in 1953 on site that produced Archaic and Woodland periods material. Piece is 3-1/8 in. long, wide-stemmed, thin, of red and white flint. Extremely fine chipping, glossy surface, no wear.   C-$95

Pentagonal blade, 3-1/4 in. long, made of Ohio Flintridge multicolored material. Small section missing from one barbed shoulder, hardly noticeable.   D-$30

Hopewellian point or blade, Kentucky, 3-7/8 in. long and 2-1/8 in. wide, of a glossy black flint. Perfect. D-$95

Adena blade, Woodland period, made of a fine light-colored flint, 5-1/2 in. long and 2-1/8 in. wide at shoulders; large and well-stemmed. Slight damage to one corner of stem, small nick from one side halfway to point tip, possible equipment strike.   A-$120

Blade, Alabama, 3-1/2 in. long. Barb-shouldered and of high quality. Probably Archaic, and found on site that has produced such artifacts; perfect condition.   C-$40

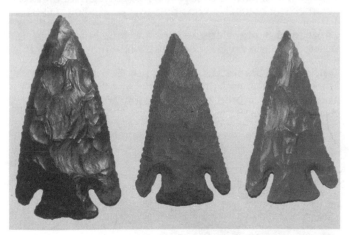

Eastern U.S. Lost Lake blades, Early Archaic and ca. 9000-7500 BC, all examples from Kentucky and all left to right:

Lost Lake, 4 in., few signs of resharpening, Indiana hornstone. $3,000
Lost Lake, 3-3/8 in., Dover chert, Benton County. $2,500
Lost Lake, 3-1/2 in., striated hornstone, Allen County. $2,000

Brad MacKenzie collection, San Francisco, California; Michael W. Hough photograph

Beveled-edge blade, 4-1/2 in. long, Archaic. Symmetrical, of a mixed dark and light brown flint in pleasing bands. Notches deep and regular, base well-notched and edges ground. Perfect.   A-$250

Adena cache blade, leaf-shaped, about 6 in. long and 3 in. wide.; made of translucent Flintridge material.   A-$225

Ashtabula-type blade, Indiana, 4-7/8 in. long. Made of a gray, nondescript flint.   C-$85

Expanded-notch or E-notch blade, Illinois, 3-1/8 in. long, perfect. Edges worn but overall good lines.   C-$75

Blade, Alabama, 5-1/4 in. long; whitish chert, side-notched. Shaped solely by percussion flaking, no edge retouch.   C-$45

Dovetail or St. Charles blade, 5-3/4 in. long and 3 in. wide. Exceptional piece; large and perfect. No damage anywhere. Basal notches deep, base edges ground. Made of translucent multi-hued Flintridge material; from an old collection.   A-$500

Blade, New Jersey, 4 in. long. Chipped from black chert and leaf-shaped. No edge retouch; average workstyle.   C-$14

Beveled-edge blade, 5-3/4 in. long. Archaic; finely chipped base with deep notches, and surface is nicely patinated to a pale cream. Damage: About 1/2 inch missing from tip, exposing lighter-colored interior. As is, a superb example of prehistoric flint-knapping. Easily restored.   C-$255

Clovis-like blade, Florida; point is 3-3/8 in. long. Made from a black high-grade material. Deeply fluted both sides, perfect, ground basal edges.   C-$150

Large Turkey-tail blade, found in West Virginia; 5-1/8 in. long. Light gray shade of Indiana hornstone flint. Large blade may have once been part of cache or underground deposit of artifacts, as accompanying card in old-style handwriting states "1 of 13."   C-$225

Tennessee blade, 5-1/4 in. long. Triangular, beveled edges, no stem or notches.   A-$90

Fluted point from lower Michigan; 4-1/8 in. long. Made of black Coshocton County (Ohio) flint. Average wear on all sides, base not ground, no damage. Fluting channels extend for approximately 2 in. up both base sides.   D-$375

WESTERN CHIPPED BLADES

Corner-notched blade, Iowa; 3-1/2 in. long, well balanced. Both sides or faces equally good, base excurvate and well-ground, sides deeply serrated. Archaic period.   A-$115

Shouldered blade Arkansas, 3-1/2 in. long; blue-white flint.   G-$15

Chipped Obsidian blade, Santa Catalina Island, southern California cultural area; 4-1/8 in. long. Leafshaped and undamaged; unusual locale.   C-$90

Flint blade, Kansas, 2-15/16 in. long; unusual form. Large side notches halfway between tip and base; base bottom deeply indented (bifurcated) which gives blade a tri-notched appearance. Minor damage to one side near tip.   C-$55

Angular knife, left, 2-1/4 in. (5.5 cm) by 4-1/2 in. (11.5 cm). Archaic period. Flint is blue-black and condition is perfect. C-$15

Dovetail blade, right, 1-3/8 in. (3.5 cm) by 2-1/2 in. (6.0 cm) long Archaic period, with heavy basal grinding. Blue-black flint with white and gray mottling; Dovetails are increasingly rare finds. C-$95

Photo courtesy of Mark Hersman, Lucas, Ohio

Unusual blade, Paleolithic period, found in Oklahoma in 1972 by a camper. Point is 3-3/8 in. long, and expands from a forked base about 1 in. wide and very thin. Non-fluted piece of a superior flint, origin unknown. Chipping, especially pressure retouch, is regular and excellent. Type not mentioned in any of the standard reference works; may be regional sub-variant.　C-$275

Corner-tang blade from Oklahoma Panhandle region; 4-1/8 in. long. Lower blade slightly excurvate, larger than usual for type. Notching is deep, remaining section forms triangular stem, yellowish flint of unknown quarry site.　D-$250

Eden-type blade, found in a wind-erosion "blowout," Nebraska, in 1951; 4-1/8 in. long, evidencing parallel flaking, gray flint. Perfect condition, flint high grade, well made.　C-$450

Sedalia-type blade, Missouri, 8-1/8 in. long; widest measurement is 2-1/4 in. from the tip. Squared base, excurvate sides tapering to very sharp tip. Pale white chertish material, and excellent chipping overall. Perfect condition.　C-$400

Concave-convex sided blade, Plains-Midwestern (?); 7-1/4 in. long and 1-3/8 in. wide at squared base, resembling a dagger. Shaft area incurvate; working edges excurvate. This type of flint artifact is not often found intact due to size and brittle nature of flint. Perfect condition.　C-$575

Leaf-shaped blade, Woodland period, 5-1/2 in. long. Made of mottled white and dark flint. Not notched or stemmed. Base casually rounded, blade presents an ovate appearance.　A-$140

Point or blade, exactly 3 in. long. Wide-shoulder and wide stem, whitish flint, possibly Woodland and resembles Snyder type.　C-$45

Chumash point or blade, southern California, site on coast, excavated find; 3-1/2 in. long, diamond-shaped. Made of a low-grade material.　D-$20

Pedernales-type blade, central Texas; 3-1/4 in. long. Sharply indented base and sharply barbed shoulders; edges finely serrated. Perfect condition.　C-$145

Large obsidian blade, 9-1/4 in. long and 2-1/8 in. wide at base near small corner notches. Backside of knife straight-edge, working edge convex and mild wear shows authenticity. Excavated from early Colorado site.　D-$245

Lanceolate blade, late Paleo, Colorado; 4-7/8 in. long. Made of chert; good form, but material not of best quality.　A-$27

Cache blade, large, 6 in. Ovate, rough, found in northern Georgia and made of gray Indiana hornstone. Part of a deposit of more than fifty blades said to have been found by a fisherman along a river.　C-$50

Novaculite blade, Arkansas; 3-1/4 in. long, pink. G-$32

Obsidian blade, Washington state; exactly 4-1/2 in. long. Excurvate sides with ends nearly identical, duo-tipped.　A-$38

Base-notched point or blade, Missouri, 7-1/4 in. long. It is 2-1/4 in. wide at shoulder tips, same measurement at expanded sides near tip. White flint, finely chipped, with flake removal regular and consistent. Perfect.　C-$650

Large flint blade, extreme western Midwest, 6-3/8 in. long, notches deep and perfectly matching. Resembles a cross between Godar and Gravel Kame types. Inside of notching heavily ground, bottom of base not. Unknown period but probably Archaic because of fine edge retouching and basal grinding and serrated edges.C-$775

Large duo-tipped blade, Oregon, 9-5/8 in. long. Obsidian of a reddish hue, and surface find from beach area that has produced late Paleo and early Archaic materials. Rather thick, but good chipping.　C-$235

Black obsidian blade, Nevada; 4-1/2 in. long and 1 in. wide at mid-length. Concave base, side-notched, and very symmetrical blade. Notches narrow and shallow.　C-$125

Large and wide blade, 3-1/2 in. long and 1-3/4 in. wide. Ovate, no notches or stem, well-chipped.　C-$20

Dalton-type blade, Missouri, 3-1/4 in. long. White flint, smooth edges. One minor chip from blade edge; easily and quickly restored with minimum of detraction from form.　D-$45

Cache blade, top, 3-1/2 in. (9.0 cm) in length, made of black flint with gray flecks; probably a Woodland-era piece. C-$20

Double-fluted Paleo point, 3-1/8 in. (8.0 cm) long, made of brown-black flint and with lateral grinding. Basal section broken. C-$25

Photo courtesy of Mark Hersman, Lucas, Ohio

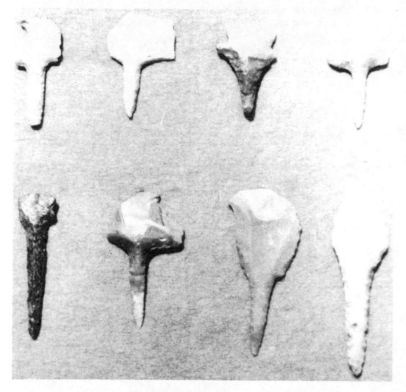

Stemmed knife or blade, beveled edges, late prehistoric period. It is 5 in. long and resharpening created beveled or sharply angled edges with a left-hand twist. In 1997 this was found by the owner in Kansas. $400-600

Joe Waffle collection, Kansas; Daniel Fox photograph

Eight flint drills, from different sections of Texas. Archaic and late prehistoric. They range in length from 1-1/4 in. to 3 in.   C-$35-65 each

Photo courtesy of Wayne Parker, Texas

Plainview point or blade, Late Paleo period, 4 in. long. It is made of Foreacre chert and has oblique flaking across the face. This was a 1997 surface find of the owner in Kansas. $600-1,000

Joe Waffle collection, Kansas; Daniel Fox photograph

Three Midwestern blades.

Left: Heavy-duty blade 3-1/4 in. long, of black Coshocton flint, one minor area of damage in left side, otherwise fine.   C-$55
Center: Large blade, probably Woodland and late prehistoric, perfect, edges worn.   C-$55
Right: Midwestern bevel-edge blade, quality gray flint, serrated edges. One tip of left shoulder missing, minor damage, could be restored. Basal area heavily ground.   C-$75

Private collection

Meserve Dalton knife, Early Archaic period, made of Foreacre chert. It measures 3-1/2 in. long and the resharpened edge is steeply beveled to the right. It was a 1997 personal find by the owner in Kansas. $400-500

Joe Waffle collection, Kansas; Daniel Fox photograph

Very fine and classic Clovis point, made of Edwards Plateau flint. Point is 3-1/2 in. long, and dates from early Paleo times. 10,000 to 15,000 BC.   C-$650

Photo courtesy of Wayne Parker collection

Harahey or four-way beveled blade, late prehistoric and ca. AD 1500. This is an above-average example in colorful Alibates flint, and was a surface find in Pratt County, Kansas. $400-500

Collection of Eugene and Marcille Wing

Corner-tang knife, Late Archaic period, length 3 in. The long cutting edge opposite the tang is steeply beveled from repeated resharpening. The owner found this knife in 1997 in Kansas. $500-600

Joe Waffle collection, Kansas; Daniel Fox photograph

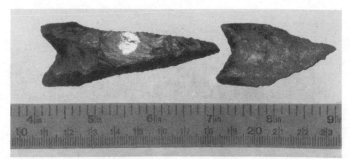

Left: Dalton Meserve, Bailey chert, 1 x 3 in. $200
Right: Dalton in classic form, Florence chert, 1 x 2 in. $45
Both were found by the owner and are Late Paleo/Early Archaic in time. Kansas.

Found by Daniel Fox; photo by Caroline Fox, Manhattan, Kansas

Stemmed lanceolate point or blade, Late Paleo/Early Archaic, made of Florence chert. It measures 5/8 x 3-1/2 in. and was retrieved by the owner on the Kansas River in 1997. Wabaunsee County, Kansas. $200

Daniel Fox collection; photo by Caroline Fox, Manhattan, Kansas

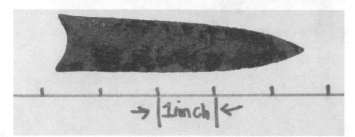

Plainview point, Late Paleo/Early Archaic, ca. 7500 BC, made of river-stained Florence chert. It is 4-3/8 in. long and was found by J. Waffle on the Republican River in 1998. Chipped artifacts of this size, condition, and rarity are very difficult to find. Museum quality

Collection of Daniel Fox; photo by Caroline Fox, Manhattan, Kansas

Lanceolate point or blade, Late Paleo period, made of Florence chert. This piece measures 1 x 3-1/4 in. and was found by the owner on the Republican River in 1998. Geary County, Kansas. $150

Daniel Fox collection; photo by Caroline Fox, Manhattan, Kansas

Alberta point or blade, Late Paleo/Early Archaic period. The type was named after examples found in Alberta, Canada, but examples are also scattered across the northern U.S. This piece is made of Foreacre chert and measures 7/8 x 3 in. It was a find made by the owner along the Kansas River in 1997. Potowatomi County, Kansas. $600

Found by Daniel Fox; photo by Caroline Fox, Manhattan, Kansas

Hemphill blade or knife, Archaic period and ca. 3000 BC, made of stained Florence chert. It is 3-1/2 in. long and was found along the Kansas River in 1997. Potowatomi County, Kansas. $500

Found by Daniel Fox; photo by Caroline Fox, Manhattan, Kansas

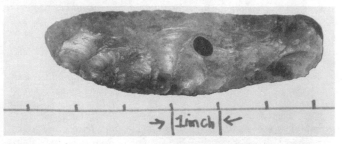

Munker's Creek knife, Late Archaic and ca. 2300 BC, made of Florence chert with darker inclusions. This blade, about 6 in. long, was picked up by the owner on the Kansas River in 1997. Riley County, Kansas. $200

Found by Daniel Fox; photo by Caroline Fox, Manhattan, Kansas

Jimmy Allen type point, Transitional Paleo to Early Archaic period, made of Foreacre chert. This beautiful artifact is 4-1/2 in. long and has delicate ribbon-like flaking plus fluting or large flakes removed from the basal face. This was a personal find of the owner in October of 1997 on the Kansas River. Riley County, Kansas. Museum quality

Found by Daniel Fox; photo by Caroline Fox, Manhattan, Kansas

Early knife form, possibly a Brown's Valley, Late Paleo period. It is nearly 3 in. long and material of manufacture is Florence chert. This was a personal find of the owner in 1997. Kansas. $150

Found by Daniel Fox; photo by Caroline Fox, Manhattan, Kansas

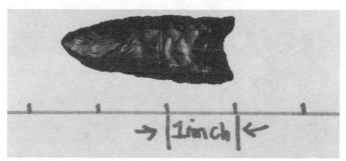

Clovis point, fluted, Early Archaic period and one of the oldest chipped artifacts that can be found in North America. It is 7/8 x 2-5/8 in. and was picked up along the Republican River by K. Reeser. Geary County, Kansas. $500

Collection of Daniel Fox; photo by Caroline Fox, Manhattan, Kansas

Obsidian points, made of black volcanic glass, center example 3 in. long. Illustrated is a variety of types to either side of the long knife blade. All came from the Abiquiu Mountain region of New Mexico. Each, $10-50

Jack Baker collection, Ozark, Missouri; David Capon photograph

A wide selection of points and blades or knives, illustrating what a dedicated surface-hunter can still find. Note the variety of shapes and materials. All were found by the owner in one year, 1997. Unlisted

Found by Daniel Fox; photo by Caroline Fox, Manhattan, Kansas

Dalton point or blade, Late Paleo/Early Archaic period, gray and tan Missouri flint. This fine specimen measures 4-1/2 in. long and has extra-distinctive edge serrations for type. It came from Webster County, Missouri. $700

Jack Baker collection, Ozark, Missouri; David Capon photograph

Helton knife, Archaic period, made of an unknown chert. It measures 2-7/8 in. long and was a personal find by the owner on Wild Cat Creek in 1996. Riley County, Kansas. $150

Collection of Daniel Fox; photo by Caroline Fox, Manhattan, Kansas

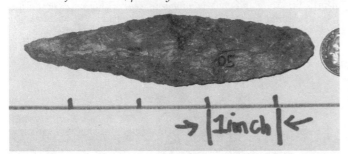

Harahey knife, late prehistoric period ca. 1300-1700 AD. Also known as four-way bevels, these unusual blades have four cutting edges and can be turned or reversed to use any one edge. Made of Florence chert, this piece is a little over 4 in. long. It was found by the owner on an island in the Kansas River in 1997. Riley County, Kansas. $200

Found by Daniel Fox; photo by Caroline Fox, Manhattan, Kansas

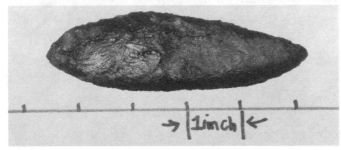

Beveled knife blade, late occupation period, this artifact made of Niobria jasper or Smokey Hill jasper. It measures 4-7/8 in. long and was a personal find by the owner on the Kansas River in 1998. Riley County, Kansas. $200

Found by Daniel Fox; photo by Caroline Fox, Manhattan, Kansas

San Patrice or Pelican point or blade, Late Paleo period, this example made of Florence chert. It is 2-1/2 in. long and was found by S. Umscheid in 1997 along the Kansas River. Kansas. $500

Daniel Fox collection; photo by Caroline Fox, Manhattan, Kansas

Plainview or Jimmy Allen point, Late Paleo/Early Archaic, made of banded and river-stained Florence chert. It is 2-3/4 in. long and a fine example of an early piece. It was picked up by the owner along the Kansas River in 1997. Potowatomi County, Kansas. $500

Found by Daniel Fox; photo by Caroline Fox, Manhattan, Kansas

Frame of Pacific Northwest points, Rogue River and Molly types, ca. AD 1200-1800. The longest point shown is 1-1/8 x 1-5/8 in. long, and the center point is shown in Who's Who in Indian Relics No. 9, p 146. Other points are ex-collection G. Perino. Materials for these top examples include jasper, dacite, agatized wood, and agate, and all points are from Oregon.   Museum quality

Collection of, and photograph by, Steve Granger, Hallsville, Texas

Stemmed lanceolate point or blade, Late Paleo/Early Archaic, 5/8 x 3-1/4 in. long. The material is Florence chert and the artifact was a personal find of the owner on the Republican River in 1997. Geary County, Kansas. $200

Found by Daniel Fox; photo by Caroline Fox, Manhattan, Kansas

Nebo Hill point or blade, Late Archaic and ca. 1750 BC, made of Florence chert. This artifact is 3/4 x 3-3/8 in. long and was found by the owner on the Blue River in 1997. Nebo Hills greatly resemble some of the Late Paleo lanceolate points but both are different and distinct in time. Kansas. $250

Found by Daniel Fox; photo by Caroline Fox, Manhattan, Kansas

Frame of chipped artifacts, 12 x 18 in., with material being various flints and cherts of different grades. Many of the artifacts shown are from the Archaic period, and most were personal surface finds made by the owner. Kansas. $500-600

Tom Fouts collection, Kansas

Left: Darl point or blade, 15/16 x 3-3/4 in., dark gray chert. Greenfield, Missouri. $110

Top right: corner-notched Archaic point, dark red flint. This was a personal find by the owner in Cherokee County, Kansas. $35

Bottom right: corner-notched Archaic blade, 1-7/16 x 2-3/4 in. It has three shaft-scrapers opposite the cutting edge. A personal find by the owner, it came from Cherokee County, Kansas. $35

Tom Fouts collection, Kansas

Stilwell blade, 1-1/4 x 3-1/8 in., 1/4 in. thick. It is made of pinkish-gray flint with encrustations on one face. This is well-made, with fine and uniform serrations and delicate notching. The blade was found by LTC Floyd Lyerla in Cherokee County, Kansas. $300

Tom Fouts collection, Kansas

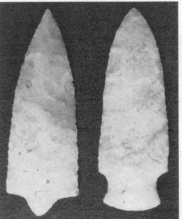

Left, Morrow Mountain blade, pink heat-treated flint, 1-5/16 x 3-3/4 in., 1/4 in. thick. It has fossil inclusions plus age deposits and encrustations. Cherokee County, Kansas. $90

Right, Benton blade, 1-1/4 x 3-1/2 in., 5/16 in. thick. Material is pink heat-treated flint and the artifact has excellent workstyle and oblique flaking. Cherokee County, Kansas. $100

Tom Fouts collection, Kansas

Points and blades plus several perforators, mainly stemmed varieties in regional flints and cherts. Kaufman County, Texas. $85

Larry Garvin, Back to Earth, Ohio

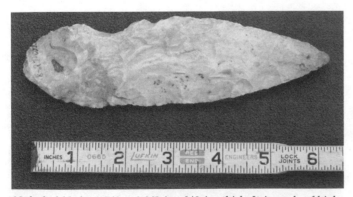

Unhafted blade, 1-7/8 x 6-3/8 in., 3/8 in. thick. It is made of high-quality glossy grayish-white flint or chert and has age-spotting and encrustations. An old ink find date of 8-22-1902 is on the base. One edge (here, top) has two different-sized concave shaft-scrapers. The origin of this piece is unknown, but it may be from west of the Mississippi River. $300

Tom Fouts collection, Kansas

Grand point or blade, Middle Woodland period, made of dark mottled Florence chert. This piece is 3 in. long and was found at the confluence of the Smokey Hill and Republican Rivers, which form the Kansas River. This was picked up 5-14-97 by the owner. Also found with the Grand was an engraved bone pin. Kansas. $250

Found by Daniel Fox; photo by Caroline Fox, Manhattan, Kansas

Kay blade, Early Caddoan of the Mississippian period, made of stained Florence chert. It is 2-3/4 in. long and was found by the owner on the Kansas River in 1997. The blade or knife was associated with a fine bone pin. Kansas. $175

Found by Daniel Fox; photo by Caroline Fox, Manhattan, Kansas

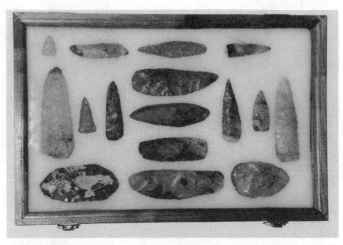

A large frame of knives, various prehistoric time-periods. All were found in 1997 by the owner except two which were picked up in 1998. Note the wide range of sizes, shapes, and materials which is typical of surface-found authentic artifacts. Kansas.   Unlisted

Found by Daniel Fox; photo by Caroline Fox, Manhattan, Kansas

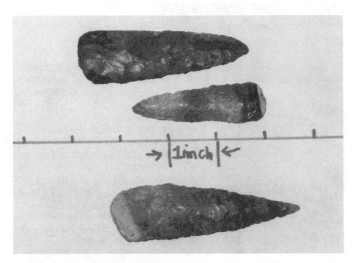

Asymmetrical unhafted blades or knives, dark flints, and cherts. Sometimes the lighter (or at least another color) portion of the material is at the base because this might have been of inferior cutting capability. The ancient knapper worked the form so that this would not be on a cutting edge; in fact, this material positioning is often seen on such artifact types as the eastern U.S. Turkeytail. Kansas.   Each, $75-100

Found by Daniel Fox; photo by Caroline Fox, Manhattan, Kansas

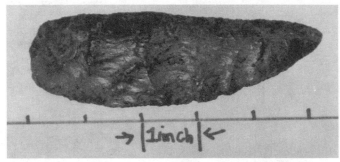

Knife, Late Plains culture, made of dark Florence chert. It is 5-1/4 in. long and is well-chipped and nicely finished. The large blade was found by the owner on the Kansas River in 1997. Riley County, Kansas. $400

Found by Daniel Fox; photo by Caroline Fox, Manhattan, Kansas

A large frame of broken pieces, the condition in which the majority of surface-found artifacts are picked up. All of these were found in just one year by the owner. Kansas.   Unlisted

Found by Daniel Fox; photo by Caroline Fox, Manhattan, Kansas

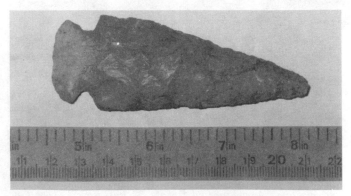

Gibson knife, Middle Woodland period, ca. AD 300. It is made of Florence chert and measures 1-1/2 x 3-1/2 in. In 1998 this was a find by the owner on the Republican River in Geary County, Kansas. $250

Found by Daniel Fox; photo by Caroline Fox, Manhattan, Kansas

Ensor knife, 1 x 3 in., ca. 500 BC. The material is Florence chert for this example, picked up by the owner in 1998 on the Kansas River. Geary County, Kansas. $150

Found by Daniel Fox; photo by Caroline Fox, Manhattan, Kansas

Knife made of chert, late prehistoric, very unusual in still having asphaltum on the base for handle attachment. Often such blades had long wooden hafts. This example measures 7-1/2 in., is made of Monterey chert, and came from California. $4,000

Private collection

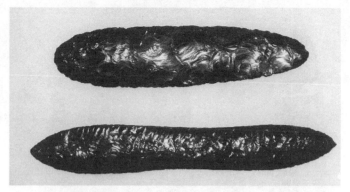

Late prehistoric Wealth Blades, both from Humboldt County, California, and both from the Dr. H.H. Stuart collection. These fine and rare blades are ca. 800-200 BP.

Top: #149, red and black obsidian, 11-1/4 in long. $2,500
Bottom: black obsidian, double-pointed, 13-1/2 in. long. $3,500

Collection of, and photograph by, Michael W. Hough, California

Leaf-shaped blades, all 1000-2000 BP. They are made of black obsidian and each once had a handle, probably of wood or bone. These came from Marin County, California. Left to right:

Leaf-blade, 5 in., bluntly-pointed base. $200
Leaf-blade, 4-1/2 in., bluntly-pointed base. $175
Leaf-blade, 4 in., rounded base. $175
Leaf-blade, 3-7/8 in., narrow configuration. $150
Leaf-blade, 3-5/8 in., expanded lower blade section. $150
Leaf-blade, 3-5/8 in., widest at blade base. $125
Leaf-blade, 3 in. long, about same form as #3 from left. $75

Collection of, and photograph by, Michael W. Hough, California

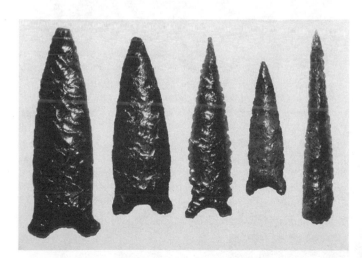

Western blades or knives, all left to right:

Sierra Eared knife, 1500-3000 BP, 4 in., black obsidian, California. $400
Sierra Eared knife, 1500-3000 BP, 3-1/4 in., black obsidian, California. $300
Humboldt Expanded Base, 3000-6000 BP, green-black obsidian, Oregon. $200
Humboldt Expanded Base, 3000-6000 BP, brown w/ black obsidian, Oregon. $100
Eden, 7500-9500 BP, 3-5/8 in., translucent banded obsidian, Nevada. $100

Collection of, and photograph by, Michael W. Hough, California

Osceola point or blade, Archaic period, 1-3/16 x 4-3/8 in., 3/8 in. thick. This artifact is made of white heat-treated flint or chert with a red lightning-line across the face. The finely made artifact was obtained from the family of a 5th grade student who took it to school for show-and-tell. It was found by the student near the Marmaton River in Bourbon County, Kansas. $200

Tom Fouts collection, Kansas

Western blades or knives, all left to right:

Humboldt Expanded Base, 3000-6000 BP, 2-3/4 in., black obsidian, Nevada. $150

Humboldt Constricted Base, 4000-6000 BP, banded black obsidian, Nevada. Unlisted

Bat Cave (rare), 8000-9000 BP, black obsidian, Churchill County, Nevada. $200

Plainview, 7000-10,000 BP, banded black obsidian, Humboldt County, Nevada. Unlisted

Humboldt Expanded Base, 3000-6000 BP, 2-1/8 in., black obsidian, Nevada. $100

Collection of, and photograph by, Michael W. Hough, California

Frame of Columbia River points, ca. AD 1200-1800, all ex-collection Greg Perino. Mr. Perino remarked that the point second from the left in the top row was the finest point he had ever owned. It is made of Biggs Picture jasper and has some of the most delicate chipping known. Other points in the frame are made of materials that include carnelian agate, agatized wood, moss agate, and plum agate. Points no. 2 and 4 in the top row and point no. 3 in the bottom row (all from left) are pictured in Who's Who in Indian Relics No. 4, p 206. All points in this frame have a solid, authentic pedigree. Museum quality

Collection of, and photograph by, Steve Granger, Hallsville, Texas

Blade, 1-7/8 x 2 in., 5/16 inch thick. Made of gray-white flint or chert, this is probably an exhausted or worn-out blade that received use as a special tool of some sort. It was found in Cherokee County, Kansas. $30

Tom Fouts collection, Kansas

Stockton blades or knives, 1000-2500 BP, black obsidian and ex-collection Johnson. These came from Contra Costa County, California. Left to right:

Blade, 2-3/4 in., fully serrated with some worn off. $200

Blade, 1-7/8 in., serrated toward base. $100

Blade, 2-3/8 in., large serrations. $175

Blade, 2-1/8 in., two-thirds serrated. $150

Blade, 2-7/16 in., fully serrated. $150

Collection of, and photograph by, Michael W. Hough, California

Stockton blades or knives, 1000-2500 BP, black obsidian, ex-collection Johnson. All are from Contra Costa County, California. Left to right:

Blade, 3 in. long, worn serrations in several places. $200

Blade, 1-7/8 in., small and/or worn serrations. $100

Blade, 2-3/8 in., nicely balanced serration extensions. $200

Blade, 1-7/8 in., with 'double' or notched serrations. $150

Blade, 2-1/2 in., even-sized serrations for most of length. $175

Collection of, and photograph by, Michael W. Hough, California

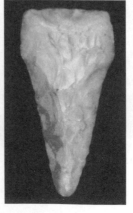

Triangular blade, 3-1/2 in. long, made of mottled tan and gold material. This Archaic knife has a beveled edge due to resharpening. Baca County, Colorado. $145

Larry Lantz, First Mesa, Indiana

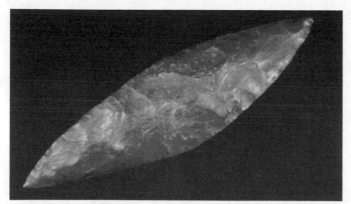

Knife, Harahey from late prehistoric times, 5 in. long. This four-bevel blade is made of glossy black flint with tiny brown dots. It is from the North Platte area of Nebraska. $295

Larry Lantz, First Mesa, Indiana

Western blades, both from Texas, left example 4 in. long, left to right:

Base-tang knife, 2000-4000 BP, brown Edwards flint, Coryell County. $300
Harahey beveled knife, in little-used condition, brown Edwards flint, Williamson County. $450

Collection of, and photograph by, Michael W. Hough, California

Abbey point or blade, Archaic period, 4-1/2 in. long. It is made of river-stained white coral and is one of the finest known to exist, being very rare in this size and condition plus type. Brooks County, Georgia. Museum quality

Bruce Butts collection, Winterville, Georgia

Darl point or blade, medium gray flint, 15-16 x 3 in., 5/16 in. thick. The material has attractive white streaks and the piece is from Cherokee County, Kansas. $75

Tom Fouts collection, Kansas

Western U.S. Late Paleo points or blades, left example 3-3/8 in. long, all left to right:

Eden, 7000-9500 BP, tan Edwards flint, classic form, Gaines County, Texas. $1,000
Eden, 7000-9500 BP, tan quartzite, median ridge on one face, Wyoming. $800
Plainview, 9000-10,000 BP, yellow-tan quartzite, collateral flaking, Colorado. $600
Goshen, yellow silicified sandstone, oblique transverse flaking, New Mexico. $800

Collection of, and photograph by, Michael W. Hough, California

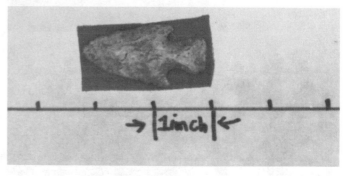

Cupp point, found on the Kansas River by Dan Fox in 1997. Material unknown. Unlisted

Found by Daniel Fox; photo by Caroline Fox, Manhattan, Kansas

A nice frame of projectile points, ranging in length from 1 in. to 2-1/4 in. These range in time from Archaic to Mississippian times, although long point or blade in center may be late Paleo. All found in Pennsylvania; material is flint, rhyolite, jasper, quartz and chalcedony.C-$250 frame

Photo courtesy of Jonas Yoder, Jr., McVeytown, Pennsylvania

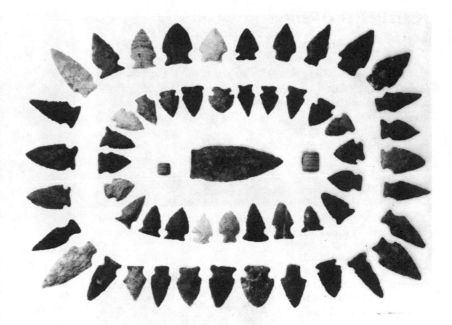

Base-notched blade, Oregon, 3-1/2 in. long. Reddish flint of good quality. Notches 1/4 in. deep.   D-$20

CANADIAN CHIPPED BLADES

Obsidian blade found in British Columbia, Canada; 4-7/8 in. long and 1-3/8 in. wide. Leaf-shaped. Perfect.   C-$85

Diamond-shaped blade, Canada's Great Slave Lake region. Blade is 3-5/8 in. long. Made of pinkish chert and believed to be very early, possibly Paleo. Edges worn and were never resharpened (rechipped).   C-$12

Large argillite blade, western Canada; 7-1/2 in. long. Made of the black material that can be both carved and chipped.   C-$35

Flaked blade, British Columbia, Canada; blade is 7-3/4 in. long. Made of a light chert-like material and leaf-shaped.   C-$75

Chalcedony blade, found in southwestern British Columbia, Canada; 3-3/8 in. long. Basal notched; gem quality.   C-$145

Knife blade, Nova Scotia, Canada; 4-1/4 in. long, made from quartzite. Found on coastal site, middle Archaic period. Rough-chipped but with good overall form.   C-$18

Fluted Paleo point or blade, from central Canada near Regina; 4-1/8 in. long, perfect, with flutes extending more than 1 in. (25mm) on both base sides. Made of fine-grained quartz. Good form, but rough due to average-quality material.   C-$90

Agate Basin type Paleo point, found in Adams County, Illinois, in 1975. Piece is 4-1/4 in. long and 7/8 in. wide, and evidences very fine flaking and good basal grinding. C-$500-700

Photo courtesy of John P. Grotte, Illinois

Projectile point, 1-1/4 in. wide and 3 in. long, from Tennessee. Point is probably a Benton type, and 1000-2000 BC. Perfect condition.C-$30-45

Photo courtesy Flint Na Mingo Northcutt, Corinth, Mississippi.

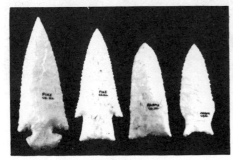

Four blades or points, all from Illinois. Left to right:

Dovetail (St. Charles) blade. C-$400-600 Hardin barb with fine serrated edges. C-$300 Plainview variant. C-$100 Dalton point. C-$125

Photo courtesy of Pat Humphrey, westcentral Illinois

Projectile point or blade, 3-1/4 in. long and 1 in. wide. Very detailed chipping, dark red and white early Archaic. Found in Tishomingo County, Mississippi near the (future) Tennessee-Tombigbee Waterway.   C-$30

Fine Hardin barbed point or blade, found in Pike County, Illinois. Note the fine and regular serrations on both edges, and the excellent symmetry.   C-$295

Photo courtesy of Pat Humphrey, westcentral Illinois

A very fine corner-tang knife of blade, found in Texas County, Oklahoma. It was made from a blue-gray Alibates flint and is larger than average for the type. The blade is 3-3/4 in. long.   C-$550

Photo courtesy of Ralph W. White, Oklahomae

CHIPPED DRILLS

Drills have been used in North America for at least 10,000 years, and fine specimens have been found on many Late Paleo sites. They range in length from 1/2 in. to specimens more than 4 in., though the longer types are rare.

This particular tool was used to make holes in bone, shell, hard-stone, banded slate, wood, and rock crystal. Drills were turned with fingers, attached to a rod, twirled between the palms, and secured below the flywheel of the bowturned drill-set. Because they are long and slender, they are fairly fragile and perfect artifacts of this type command a premium.

Small drill, Maine; 1-1/4 in. Side-notched and chipped from a white flint. Perfect condition. C-$15

Large ceremonial drill, 4-1/4 in. long. "T"-shaped top, said to have been a mound recovery in northern Kentucky. Adena or Hopewell periods. Made of a black, glossy flint with thin "lightning" streaks of white. No signs of wear or use. C-$500

Cylindrical drill southern Canada; 2-1/4 in. long, made from a brown flint. Tip worn from use, but perfect. C-$20

Flint drill, American southwest, 1-1/2 in. long. Made of a good flint; perfect condition, base notched. D-$18

Flint drill, 3 in. long. Wide base and drill-shaft thin and very well chipped. Pink-white material, glossy. C-$65

Drill, Missouri; 2-7/8 in. long. Oval base with flaring barbs. G-$13

Fine flint drill, 3-1/2 in. long. "T"-shaped top, dark flint of good quality. Found in Illinois. C-$40

Miniature flint drill, Oklahoma; just under 1 in. long, with notched base. A-$9

Fine drill, 3-5/8 in. long. Made of multi-colored Flintridge material, translucent. Very fine chipping, no damage. D-$150

Rounded-top drill, 2-3/8 in. long; well-chipped. C-$17

Flint drill, just 3 in. (75mm) long. Made from an earlier Paleo point, with basal flute still extending on both sides of drill base. Rare. Yellow-white material, perfect. C-$90

Small flint drill, 1-1/2 in. long. Cylindrical form; tip shows considerable wear. C-$13

Drill, 2-1/8 in. long; wide-notched base, perfect. C-$15

Drill, found in central Indiana; 1-7/8 in. long, with wide base. Kentucky Carter Cave flint; possibly Woodland-era. C-$30

Quartzite drill, North Carolina, 1-3/4 in. long. Probably Archaic; roughly notched at base. D-$9

Early drill, found in southern Michigan on site that has produced Aqua-Plano material, about 7000-8000 BC. Drill is 3-5/8 in., with a narrow, 3/8 in. wide "T"-shaped top. Exceptionally fine chipping; extremely smooth and glossy surface. Balanced. C-$295

OTHER CHIPPED ARTIFACTS

Scrapers, for hide preparation; perforators, for piercing materials; and gravers, for scoring bone, are all frequent finds on early Amerind sites. There is, however, not much market activity for such artifacts, and most would fall in the $5 range or below. They are, none-the-less, excellent examples of the daily prehistoric lifeway; tools reflect the times.

Hafted scrapers, end-scrapers with basal notches or stems, mainly from Archaic and Woodland periods. Many began as full-size knives or points and were later "adjusted" into this tool form. Trimble County, Kentucky. $75

Larry Garvin, Back to Earth, Ohio

Tennessee swords, Mississippian period, 7 to 9-1/2 in. long. These are classic examples, made of Dover flint. They were found in Humphreys, Stewart and Davidson Counties, Tennessee. Group, $4,000

Bruce Butts collection, Winterville, Georgia

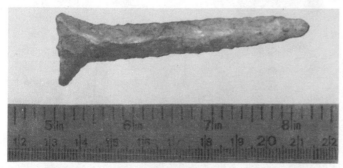

Drill, Archaic period, 3-1/4 in. long. It is chipped in Florence chert and was a 1995 find by D. Ince in Kansas. $250-350

Joe Waffle collection, Kansas; Daniel Fox photograph

Point or blade, Hardaway-Dalton and Late Paleo/Early Archaic. It is made of silicified shale and is a scarce very early type. This piece is from Moore County, North Carolina. $250

Rodney M. Peck collection, Harrisburg, North Carolina

Waller knife, Early Archaic period, 1-7/8 x 3-5/8 in.. A scarce knife form, this example in Florida chert was found near the Suwannee River, Florida. $125

Scott Young, Port St. Lucie, Florida

Crescent artifacts, 6000-9000 BP, 1-3/16 to 2-7/8 in. long. These are scarce objects and examples shown are made of agates, jaspers, conglomerates and obsidian. The exact use of these artifacts is unknown, though the longest (usually slightly incurvate) side appears to be a working edge. These Crescents are from Oregon and Nevada. Each, $35-150

Collection of, and photograph by, Michael W. Hough, California

CHIPPED SPADES

Generally large artifacts, spades typically have a smaller, often squared end and a larger, heavier end with the semblance of a digging blade. Other than traditional value factors such as size, shape, and material, collectors value more highly spades with heavy use-polish on the working blade edge. The better the polish, the more desired is the object—at least to many Midwestern collectors. Most spades and hoes are from this region.

Unfluted Clovis-type Paleo point, made of a fine quality brown flint; a purple stripe runs from near the base almost to the tip. Piece is 4-1/2 in. long and 1 3/8 in. wide at shoulders. A very colorful point, it was found in Pike County, Illinois. C-$550

Photo courtesy John P. Grotte, Illinois

Spade, 8 in. long and 5 in. wide, with outstanding bit polish; fine example. D-$300

Illinois spade, St. Clair County, Illinois; 1-1/4 in. long and 4-1/4 in. wide. G-$475

Spade, Schuyler County, Illinois; 1-1/2 in. long and 4-1/2 in. wide. G-$400

Spade, 8-1/2 in. long and 5-1/2 in. wide. Unusual shovel-nose type with well-shaped bit and heavy polish. G-$325

Spade, Jefferson County, Missouri; more than 7 in. long. D-$165

Spade, 13 in. long and 5-3/4 in. wide at curved bit. Large and fine flint; good polish in blade region. Some small damage to spade base in handle attachment region, minor. D-$425

Paleo-period point converted in prehistoric times to a beveled-edge knife. Blade is made of blue banded Alibates flint, and is from the neo-American period, 900-1300 AD. Blade is 3-1/2 in. long and well-chipped. C-$90

Photo courtesy of Wayne Parker collection

Beveled blade, four edges and in diamond shape. It is of a reddish Alibates (?) flint, and large for the type. Blade is 6 in. long, while average size is closer to 2-1/2 in. or 3 in. Found in Texas County, Oklahoma. One shoulder has some battering, but minor. C-$300

Photo courtesy Ralph W. White, Oklahoma

Large Clovis-type point or blade, made of a light gray quartzite, fine-grained material. Beautifully flaked point is 4-5/8 in. long, and from New Mexico. Basal edges are heavily ground as is common for the type.   C-$550

Agate Basin type Paleo point, found in Adams County, Illinois, in 1974. It is 4-3/16 in. long and 1 in. wide, and displays superb workmanship and fine flint-knapping. It would be from the late Paleo or Early Archaic period.   C-$600

Private collection

Eight beveled knives, from South Texas Plains region, and from 3-1/2 x 4-1/2 in. long. Left column, all of Edwards Plateau flint. Right column, top to bottom: Alibates flint, Alibates flint, Tecovas jasper, Edwards Plateau flint. All were surface finds, from late prehistoric times.   C-$225-450

Photo courtesy of Wayne Parker, Texas

Four beveled-edge knives from Texas, and 4 in. to 6 in. long. These date from AD 900-1300, and came from a Panhandle Pueblo site.   C-$200-400

Photo courtesy of Wayne Parker, Texas

Spade, chipped flint, Mississippian period, 9-1/2 in. long. Material is Dover flint and the artifact was found in Benton County, Tennessee. $500

Bruce Butts collection, Winterville, Georgia

Spade, in classic Mill Creek chert, high blade polish from use, 13-1/8 in. long. Illinois. $350

Native American Artifacts, Victor, New York

Spade, Mississippian period, made of high-quality white chert or flint that has weathered gray. This above-average example, 1-1/8 x 4-3/16 x 7 in. has high use-polish and came from Labette County, Kansas. $95

Tom Fouts collection, Kansas

Good Arkansas spade, 9 in. long and 5-1/4 in. wide. Made from a brown chert and has a polished bit.　　G-$250

Spade, found in Hickman County, Kentucky; 12 in. long and 4-5/8 in. wide. Very fine with extra-heavy polished bit.　　G-$650

Oval-type spade, 8-1/4 in. long and 5-1/2 in. wide. Good polish, fine condition.　　G-$245

Flint spade, 9-1/4 in. long and 5 in. (12.5 cm) wide. Very thin, with good polish.　　G-$350

Polished flint spade, Missouri, 7-1/4 in. long and 4-1/4 in. wide. Not too thin, but nice.　　G-$125

Spade, eastern Missouri; 14 in. long. Extra-long, un-notched flint. Very thin, fine chipping, good polish. C-$550

Shovel-nose spade, Missouri, 7-1/2 in. long and just under 5 in. wide. Heavily used; some breaks on working edge.　　C-$115

CHIPPED HOES

Compared to spades, hoes tend to be smaller. Many varieties have notched bases for a right-angle handle attachment. Bit polish adds to value, as does blade thinness and traditional factors of size, workstyle, and quality of material. Hoes are late prehistoric, and generally used with the development of agriculture and permanent village sites.

Small hoe (?), eastern Ohio, 4-1/4 in. wide and 3-1/2 in. high, with no prominent notches. Fine-grade blue-white flint, made from a very large flake. Well pressure flaked around all four sides and edges.　　C-$30

Large notched hoe, Tennessee, 7-1/2 in. long and 5-1/2 in. wide.　　G-$2,200

Square-back hoe, Arkansas, 5-1/2 in. long and 2-1/2 in. wide; made from a pink chert.　　G-$75

Fine-notched flint hoe, Missouri; 6 in. long and 3-7/8 in. wide. Highly polished blade area. Made from a pink and brown glossy flint; thin, good workstyle.　　C-$250

Hoe, with polished working edge, 5-1/4 in. long and 4-1/4 in. wide. Good quality black flint; notched at base. C-$125

Brown flint hoe, Midwestern; 5-1/8 in. long and 3-1/4 in. wide. Not notched, but upper portions are narrowed.　　C-$110

Ornate white flint hoe, 5-1/2 in. long. Well made, with use-polish on bit. Strangely notched, with two shallow notches at top sides, one at top center.　　C-$350

OTHER CHIPPED TOOLS

Flint spud (sharp, narrow spade), Union County, Illinois; 9 in. long and 4 in. wide. Classic shape with wide flaring bit, much polish.　　G-$600

Flaked celt (ungrooved axe), Arkansas; 3-1/2 in. long, good shape.　　G-$35

Duo-bladed flint axe, 6 in. long. Blades semi-circular with nice curves, flint unremarkable. Percussion chip-

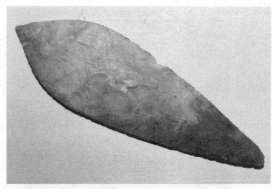

Aztec knife, 500-2000 BP, 7-3/16 in. long. This is a fine large late prehistoric blade, made of white translucent chert. The dark area to lower right may be where the original handle was secured; made of organic material, it has now disappeared. This knife was found near Teotihuacan, Mexico.　　$800

Collection of, and photograph by, Michael W. Hough, California

ping average; large notches in sides, no blade polish. Unknown period.　　C-$40

Digging tools, cache of fifteen; average length 3-1/2 in. All made of white and gray flint.　　D-$80

Unusual eccentric flint, 1 in. long and 1/2 in. wide; authentic. Chipped in the form of a half moon.　　G-$18

Spud, Johnson County, Illinois; 8 in. long and 3-1/2 in. wide. Made of fine polish white flint. It has the flared bit and polished for entire length.　　G-$750

Cache of Mississippian tools, three artifacts found together made of chert and Dover flint. All are from Benton County, Tennessee. Left to right:

Chisel, highly polished small bit, 7 in. long.
Adz, 8-1/2 in. long, polished blade area.
Chisel, 6-3/4 in. long, polished bit. The three, $1,000

Bruce Butts collection, Winterville, Georgia

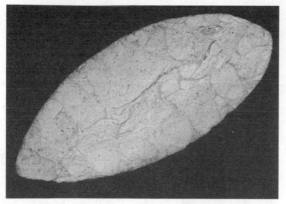

Ovate knife, late prehistoric, speckled tan-white flint, thin for size of 4 in. long. Lafayette County, Wisconsin. $145

Larry Lantz, First Mesa, Indiana

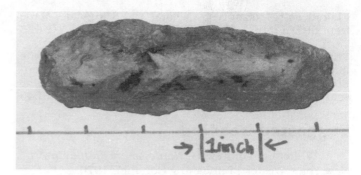

Adz or celt, Late Plains culture, chipped in Florence chert. This unusual artifact, found by the owner, measures 2-1/4 x 5 in. Kansas. $75

Found by Daniel Fox; photo by Caroline Fox, Manhattan, Kansas

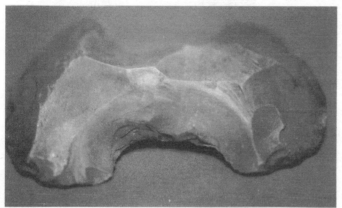

Chipped axe made of dark yellow flint, 2-1/2 x 4-1/2 in. Such pieces can be difficult to date but despite the appearance of great age, this axe probably came from fairly late in prehistory, during pottery-producing times. It was found near Tucumcari, New Mexico. $50

Jack Baker collection, Ozark, Missouri; David Capon photograph

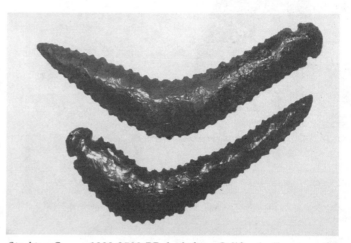

Stockton Curve, 1000-2500 BP, both from California. Exact use for these very unusual artifacts is not known, but it has been speculated that they might be for two very different purposes, harvesting or fighting. The owner of these Stocktons notes that authentic pieces are very rare.

Top: 4-1/8 in., black obsidian, San Joaquin County, California. $350
Bottom: 3-5/8 in., black obsidian, Contra Costa County, California. $350

Collection of, and photograph by, Michael W. Hough, California

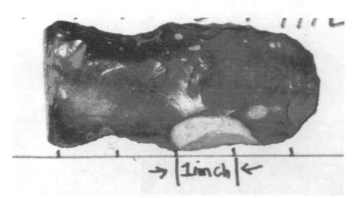

Hafted chipped axe with groove, Late Plains people. The dark material with lighter inclusions is Kay County chert. The axe measures 2-1/4 x 4-1/2 in. and was found by the owner on the Kansas River in 1997. Kansas. $150

Found by Daniel Fox; photo by Caroline Fox, Manhattan, Kansas

Spade or hand-chopper, white chert or flint with orange-pink cast due to heat treatment, 2-1/2 x 3-7/8 in., 7/8 in. thick. The surface has age deposits and the material has weathered to a yellowish-gray. A personal find of the owner, it is from Cherokee County, Kansas. $75

Tom Fouts collection, Kansas

Flaked celt, Missouri; 5 in. long and 3 in. wide. Made from brown flint.　　　　　　　　　　　　G-$33

Flint celt, 5 in. long and 2-1/8 in. wide. Made of white flint; very good lines and no damage. Polish over the entire surface that has largely obliterated original chipping scars.　　　　　　　　　　　　C-$245

Suggested Reading

Whiteford, Andrew H. *North American Indian Arts.* New York: Western Publishing Co., Inc., 1970.

Drill, chipped from black flint, and 3 in. long, and 1-1/4 in. wide at notch protrusions. This would be late prehistoric, probably Woodland. Found in Mifflin County, Pennsylvania. C-$110

Photo courtesy of Jonas Yoder, Jr., McVeytown, Pennsylvania

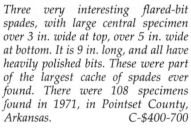

Three very interesting flared-bit spades, with large central specimen over 3 in. wide at top, over 5 in. wide at bottom. It is 9 in. long, and all have heavily polished bits. These were part of the largest cache of spades ever found. There were 108 specimens found in 1971, in Pointset County, Arkansas.　　C-$400-700

Photo courtesy of Pat Humphrey, westcentral Illinois

Oval-bit spade of tabular flint, with markings indicating Muskatine County, Iowa, as the source. It is Mississippian culture, and found rather far north for the type. Heavy use polish on rounded blade.　C-$150-200

Photo courtesy of Pat Humphrey, westcentral Illinois

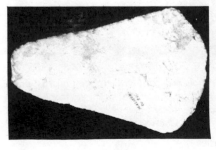

Flared-bit spade, made of brown Mill Creek tabular flint. It is 8-3/8 in. long and 5-3/8 in. wide at bit. Found in Madison County, Illinois, it may be Cahokian, from the Mississippian period.　　　C-$550

Photo courtesy of John P. Grofte, Illinois

Large flint spade, made of a brown Mill Creek tabular flint, and is from the Mississippian culture and period. Piece is 11-1/2 in. long and 4-3/4 in. wide; it was found in Madison County, Illinois.　　C-$125-200

Photo courtesy of John P. Grotte, Illinois

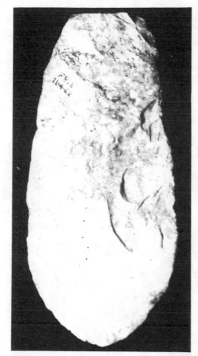

Fine spade or hoe, 8-3/4 in. long and 4 in. greatest width. From the Mississippian culture, it is highly polished for nearly half of length. Spade is made of a conglomerate that is pink, gray and yellow in color.   C-$150-225

Photo courtesy of Jim Northcutt, Jr., Corinth, Mississippi

Sandstone spade or agricultural implement, 8-1/2 in. long and 4-1/2 in. wide. Piece was rough-flaked into form; found in Mifflin County, Pennsylvania. This may be a Woodland-era object. C-$35

Photo courtesy of Jonas Yoder, Jr., McVeytown, Pennsylvania

Two polished hoes, each 3-1/4 x 7-1/2 in. in size. Example on left contains a visible seashell fossil at the top right and center of back side.   C-$175-250

Photo courtesy of Bob Brand collection, Pennsburg, Pennsylvania

Paleo points and blades, Late Paleo period.

Top row, tips downward, left to right: Pike county type, 4-1/4 in., $325; Agate Basin, 4 in., Maury County, Tennessee, $350; Plainview, from Kansas, 3 5/8 in., $300; Allen, colorful material, High Plains region, 3-3/8 in., $475; Eden made of Knife River flint, Cody, Wyoming, 3-1/2 in., $325; Beaver Lake, 3-1/2 in., from Illinois, $350.

Second, semicircular row, tips upward, left to right: Holland type, from Missouri, 3-3/4 in., $300; Agate Basin, 4-1/8 in., Illinois, $275; Scottsbluff, from Missouri, 5-1/4 in., $350; Agate Basin, from Illinois, 5-7/8 in., $550; Paleo knife, 6-3/4 in., St. Charles county, Missouri, $400; Scottsbluff,

Pike County, Illinois, 5-1/2 in., $475; Eden, from McIntosh County, Oklahoma, 5-1/2 in., $625; Eden, 5 in., from Cherokee County, Oklahoma, $450; Eden, 4-1/2 in., from the Arkansas-Louisiana-Texas region, nice piece, $600.

Bottom center piece, Agate Basin or Eastern lanceolate, Marion County, Ohio, 4-3/4 in. $450.

Larry Merriam collection, Oklahoma City, Oklahoma

Dovetail or St. Charles blades, mainly Midwestern. Three points or blades upper left corner, lower left to upper right: Black flint, provenance unknown, $700; chert, from Tennessee, 5 in., $350; light material, from Howard County, Missouri, 3-3/4 in. $225

Lower left corner, left to right: Small-base or button-tang Dovetail, Putnam County, Indiana, $900; Kentucky, 5-1/4 in., $375; St. Clair County, Illinois, $575. Upper right corner three blades, left to right: Flintridge, Ross County, Ohio, 3-3/8 in., $400; chert, 4-1/4 in., Callaway County, Missouri, unlisted; beveled-edge blade, 4-7/8 in., Kentucky $400

Lower right corner, top to bottom: Chert Dovetail from Tennessee, 6-7/8 in., $900; Clark County, Arkansas, 4-3/4 in., $325; Greene County, Missouri, 4-1/8 in. $350

Five blades, clockwise from top center: Cooper County, Missouri, 3 in., $200; Schuyler County, Illinois, 4-3/8 in., $450; Pike County, Missouri, 3-1/2 in., $325; St. Louis County, Missouri, 4 in., $375; Upper Mercer flint, Ross County, Ohio, 4-1/4 in. $450

Larry Merriam collection, Oklahoma City, Oklahoma

Early Archaic Dovetail or St. Charles blade, large-base type, made of very colorful Flintridge material. It is from Ohio and 5 in. long. Dovetails have long been one of the most collectible of early flint types.   Museum quality

Bill & Margie Koup collection, Albuquerque, New Mexico; Bill Koup photograph

Very early type points and blades.

Daltons are from Missouri, Illinois, Kentucky, Tennessee and Florida.   Each, $75-400

Decatur, top center, Kentucky. $225
Greenbriar, second from top on right, Tennessee. $150
Scale, bottom center 4 in.

Pocotopaug Trading Post, South Windsor, Connecticut

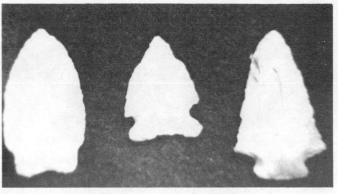

Early Woodland blades, various regions, all left to right:

Cresap Adena, Union County, Ohio. $140
Robbins blade, Upper Mercer material, Meigs County, Ohio. $225
Robbins, Delaware County, Ohio. $225
Waubesa Adena, Shuyler County, Illinois. $600
Marion, agatized coral, central Florida, 6-3/8 in. $900

Pocotopaug Trading Post, South Windsor, Connecticut

Flint blades, all Eastern Midwest, the three in lighter shades of material. Example on left is about 2-1/2 in. long.   The three, $35-55

Private collection

Alamance point or blade, Late Paleo/Early Archaic period, made of silicified shale. It is from Alamance County, North Carolina. $275

Rodney M. Peck collection, Harrisburg, North Carolina

Hardaway side-notched point or blade, Late Paleo/Early Archaic period, from Union County, North Carolina. It is made of silicified shale. $100

Rodney M. Peck collection, Harrisburg, North Carolina

Morrow Mountain point or blade, Middle Archaic period, from Virginia. $150-200

Rodney M. Peck collection, Harrisburg, North Carolina

Hardaway-Dalton point or blade, Late Paleo/Early Archaic, from Stanly County, North Carolina. It is made of silicified shale. $135

Rodney M. Peck collection, Harrisburg, North Carolina

Point or blade, Hardaway-Dalton and Late Paleo/Early Archaic. It is made of silicified shale and is a scarce, very early type. This piece is from Moore County, North Carolina. $250

Rodney M. Peck collection, Harrisburg, North Carolina

Dovetail or St. Charles blade with probable shoulder notching, from Ohio. Material is an attractive Flintridge in gray translucent chalcedony with dark blue tip and blue streak. Size is 1-3/8 x 3-3/4 in., exceptionally thin, G.I.R.S. authentication number C889-19. $900

Collection of David G. & Barbara J. Shirley

Turkeytail or Red Ochre blade from the Early Woodland, black to dark gray and tan Indiana hornstone. It is very thin and measures 1-3/4 x 4-13/16 in. It is ex-coll. Dean Driskill. $1,800

Collection of David G. & Barbara J. Shirley

Dovetail or St. Charles blade, from Montgomery County, Ohio. It is made of Coshocton flint in gray, tan and black and is 1-11/16 x 4-5/8 in. Ex-coll. Wachtel, it has G.I.R.S authentication number C88-17. $1,100

Collection of David G. & Barbara J. Shirley

Archaic blade, concave-base corner-notch type, 3-1/8 in. long. Made of caramel and blue Upper Mercer, the piece is from Perry County, Ohio. $85

Private collection, Ohio

Turkeytail (Red Ochre) blade from the Early Woodland, 1-3/4 x 5-1/16 in. long. Made of blue Indiana or Kentucky hornstone, this came from Marion County, Indiana. This is a very fine piece, with all Turkeytail characteristics desired. Ex-colls. Cline and Cameron Parks. $550

Private collection, Ohio

Woodland-era point or blade, from the Eastern Midwest, 2-1/2 in. long. Material is a yellow-tan chert or flint; narrowness of the blade portion suggests heavy prehistoric resharpening. $15

Private collection, Ohio

Archaic side-notch blade, 4-7/8 in. long. Material is a high-grade mixed brown flint of unknown origin. This exceptional early piece is from Licking County, Ohio. $225

Private collection, Ohio

Hopewell (Middle Woodland) blade, from Licking County, Ohio. It is made of translucent gray Flintridge, a typical high-quality Hopewellian material. Size, 2-5/8 in. $55

Private collection, Ohio

Archaic corner-notch blade, material an unknown gray banded flint. From Fairfield County, Ohio, size is 2-1/2 in. long. In many ways this is a typical Archaic piece. $25

Private collection, Ohio

Archaic side-notch, from Licking County, Ohio. Material is a medium blue Upper Mercer and the artifact is 3 in. long. This blade has a balanced mix of percussion and pressure flaking typical of the Archaic. $50

Private collection, Ohio

Early Archaic blade, deep-notch beveled type, 2-1/2 in. long. It came from Fairfield County, Ohio, and is made of a cream translucent material that is either Upper Mercer or Flintridge. Nice specimen. $75

Private collection, Ohio

Dovetail or St. Charles blade, blue Upper Mercer flint, from Vinton County, Ohio. At 1-3/4 x 4-5/8 in., this artifact evidences the rough usage (edge wear and chipping) typical of knives. $250

Private collection, Ohio

Morrow County lanceolate, Late Paleo, 1-1/2 x 3-5/8 in. This type has a definite stem but no shoulders, expanding gradually to greatest width near mid-length. Material is blue Upper Mercer flint and the stem sides and base are ground. This is a good type specimen, from Morrow County, Ohio. $350

Private collection, Ohio

Indented-base Archaic beveled blade, material is a dark blue Upper Mercer flint with many brown inclusions and several small lightning lines or quartz veins. From Coshocton County, Ohio, size is 1-3/4 x 3-1/2 in. $325

Private collection, Ohio

Base-notch, Early Archaic period, a fine long blade in mottled blue Upper Mercer flint. From Licking County, Ohio, it measures 1-5/8 x 4-7/16 in. A far-above-average specimen. $325

Private collection, Ohio

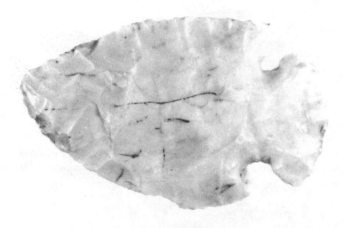

Thebes family Archaic bevel made of translucent jewel Flintridge. From Licking County, Ohio, size is 1-3/4 x 2-5/8 in. $55

Private collection, Ohio

Big Sandy type points or blades, Middle/Late Archaic period. Example on far right is from Montgomery County, Tennessee, while the others are from Christian County, Kentucky. This is a good type grouping. Group, $150

John M. Maurer collection, Ft. Campbell, Kentucky; photograph by Dan Privett

Ledbetter points or blades, Early Woodland period, from Benton County, Tennessee. These are ex-coll. Mark Clark; longest piece here is 4-3/8 in. Group, $225

John M. Maurer collection, Ft. Campbell, Kentucky; photograph by Dan Privett

Thebes family Archaic upswept notch style blade, 2-1/2 in. long. Material is a fine caramel and green Flintridge variety; from Fairfield County, Ohio. $55

Private collection, Ohio

Benton points or blades, all four made of Dover flint. These examples are from western to central Tennessee. $25-95 each

John M. Maurer collection, Ft. Campbell, Kentucky; photograph by Dan Privett

Early Archaic notched-base made of blue Upper mercer material, 1-1/2 x 2-7/8 in. long. From Licking County, Ohio, it has very large serrations (sawtooth edging) for size. This was a personal find by the owner in 1980. $165

Larry Garvin collection, Ohio

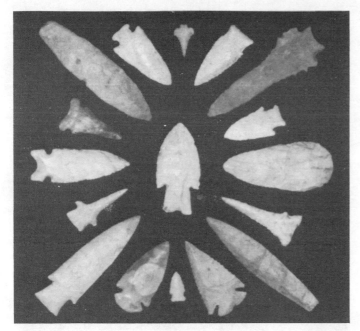

A fine flint collection, Late Paleo through Archaic times. These are from Illinois, Missouri, and Tennessee. For scale, the numbered boxes are one inch square. The small Fox Valley at 12 o'clock was gift to the owner while serving in Saudi Arabia during Operation Desert Storm.   Group, $2,800+

John M. Maurer collection, Ft. Campbell, Kentucky; photograph by Dan Privett

Archaic blade, deep corner-notch type, made of blue Upper Mercer flint. It measures 2 x 3-1/8 in., and is very thin for size. It was found in Muskingum County, Ohio. $200

Larry Garvin collection, Ohio

Dovetail or St. Charles blade, from Indiana and made of Indiana hornstone. It is gray and light tan, and 1-7/16 x 4-5/8 in. This is an excellent Early Archaic piece. $425

Collection of David G. & Barbara J. Shirley

Early Archaic notched-base made of blue Upper Mercer flint, 1-5/8 x 3 in. long. The type may be related to Dovetails (St. Charles) but is a distinct type. From Licking County, Ohio. $185

Larry Garvin collection, Ohio

Adena stemmed blade, from St. Joseph County, Michigan. Material is gray/tan Flintridge and size is 2 x 5-5/8 in. This superb artifact bears G.I.R.S authentication number C88-21. $1,000

Collection of David G. & Barbara J. Shirley

Hopewell (Middle Woodland) blade, made of gray translucent Flintridge chalcedony. Possibly from Ohio, it measures 2-1/16 x 4-3/16 in. $600

Collection of David G. & Barbara J. Shirley

Hopewellian (Middle Woodland) blade or knife, found in northeastern Ohio in the 1960s. Made of multi-colored high-grade Flintridge, this piece is thin and very well-made. It is 5-1/2 in. long. $700+

Private collection; photograph by Rick Foster

Dovetail or St. Charles blade, Early Archaic and ca. 7500 BC, from Ohio. Material is Flintridge in creams, yellows, tans, and pinks. Length is 4-3/8 in. A crystal quartz eye appears on both faces. Slight basal damage. $625

Alvin Lee Moreland, Corpus Christi, Texas

Cache blades, from Michigan. A photo of these artifacts appeared in Moorehead's Prehistoric Implements, p. 23, when they were in the Mitchell collection. Each, $150

Wilfred A. Dick collection, Magnolia, Mississippi

Prehistoric blades, various regions, all left to right:

Hopewell(?), Knife River flint, Ross county, Ohio. $140
Corner-notch, Livingston County, New York. $175
Hopewell, Middle Woodland, 3-3/8 in., Illinois. $275
Motley cache blade, 4-1/4 in., from Kentucky. $450

Pocotopaug Trading Post, South Windsor, Connecticut

Hardin-barbed, Early Archaic, from Illinois. It is 7-1/8 in. long and made of white to cream chert with red inclusions and a reddish base with a red stripe. This is large for a Hardin and the piece has fine flaking. $1,200

Alvin Lee Moreland, Corpus Christi, Texas

Fluted points, Early Paleo period.

Top left: Clovis, 3-1/4 in., agatized coral, from Columbia County, Florida. $350

Top right: Redstone, Coshocton flint, from Ross County, Ohio, tip restored, 3-1/4 in. $200

Bottom row, left to right: Clovis, Hixton quartzite, Wisconsin. $350
Clovis, 4 in., Dover flint, Tennessee. $600
Clovis, 4-3/4 in., hornstone, Kentucky. $1,000
Clovis, gem hornstone, 4-1/8 in., Kentucky. $750
Clovis, Harrison County, Kentucky, 3-5/8 in. $350

Pocotopaug Trading Post, South Windsor, Connecticut

Dovetail, Early Archaic and ca. 7500 BC, from Ohio. Material is Flintridge in multicolored hues; this piece has gem-quality material and fine overall flaking obverse. $800

Alvin Lee Moreland, Corpus Christi, Texas

Late Paleo points and blades, various regions.

Top left: stemmed lanceolate, Ford County, Illinois, 3 in., collateral flaking. $125

Top right: Plainview, jasper, transverse flaking, Wyoming, 3 in. $350

Lower, left to right:

Eastern Scottsbluff or stemmed lanceolate, 3-1/4 in., Warsaw, Ohio. $145

Angostura, Cooper County, Missouri, heat-treated Burlington chert, oblique transverse flaking, 4 1/8 in. $425

Lind Coulee, oblique transverse flaking, red and black jasper, southeastern Washington, 3-7/8 in., rare piece. $650

Plainview, oblique transverse flaking, red Alibates flint, Moore County, Texas, 4-1/4 in. $350

Scottsbluff, Missouri, collateral flaking, 3-5/8 in., fine piece. $525

Pocotopaug Trading Post, South Windsor, Connecticut

Very early points and blades, various regions.

Upper left: Folsom, Cheyenne County, Colorado. $525

Upper right: Beaver Lake, Henderson, Kentucky. $150

Semi-circle of artifacts, left to right:

Clovis, Boyle chert, Boyle County, Kentucky, 2-1/2 in. $160
Clovis, Morrow County, Ohio, 2-1/2 in. $135
Clovis, Allen County, Ohio, 2-5/8 in. $225
Beaver Lake, Hannibal, Missouri, ex-coll. Payne. $425
Unfluted Cumberland, near Louisville, Kentucky, Ft. Payne chert. $400
Clovis, Marion County, Ohio, 2-1/4 in. $175
Clovis, Henderson County, Kentucky, 2-1/2 in. $275
Clovis, Burlington chart, Missouri, 2-3/4 in. $225
Bottom center: obsidian crescent from Texas, 5-1/4 in. long. $400

Pocotopaug Trading Post, South Windsor, Connecticut

Alabama blade types, made of colorful flints and cherts. This is a very good regional collection. Individual, $8-40.   Total, $625

Larry G. Merriam collection, Oklahoma City, Oklahoma

Dovetail, reverse shown, Early Archaic, from Ohio. This is a fine, large blade. $725

Alvin Lee Moreland, Corpus Christi, Texas

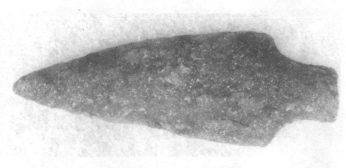

This stemmed Late Archaic/Early Woodland point or blade is made of golden Hixton quartzite and came from Barron County, Wisconsin. Size is 1-3/16 x 2-1/4 in. This material is sometimes referred to as "brown sugar" quartzite. $20-25

Mert Cowley collection, Chetek. Wisconsin

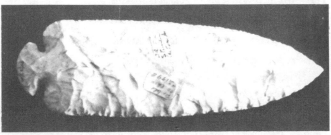

Button-base or small-base Dovetail (St. Charles) blade, Early Archaic and ca. 7500 BC. Length is 5 in., from Preble County, Ohio; material is pink and cream Flintridge with pink stripes. $800

Alvin Lee Moreland, Corpus Christi, Texas

Preble County, Ohio, Dovetail (reverse view). Made of jewel-grade Flintridge from Ohio's Licking County, this is an exceptional early blade. $800

Alvin Lee Moreland, Corpus Christi, Texas

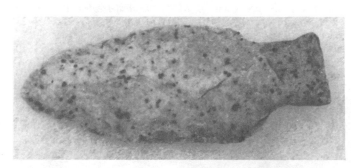

Woodland blade or point, made of oolitic chert, from Dunn County, Wisconsin. It measures 1-5/16 x 2-7/16 in. $25-30

Mert Cowley collection, Chetek, Wisconsin

Waubesa point or blade, contracting stem, Early Woodland period. It is 1-1/16 x 2-3/8 in., and is made of cream/tan flint. From Barron County, Wisconsin, this comes from a verified Early Woodland site that is 150 miles further north than any previous Early Woodland sites registered in the state. $90

Mert Cowley collection, Chetek, Wisconsin

Sloan Dalton, Illinois, 11-plus in. long. Made of high-grade translucent white flint, transverse flaking is present. This is an important Late Paleo/Early Archaic piece, very rare. $15,000-20,000

Alvin Lee Moreland, Corpus Christi, Texas

Late Paleo points and blades; Left, top to bottom:

Sloan Dalton, Worland, Missouri, 4-3/4 in. $350
Holland point, McIntosh County, Oklahoma, 3 in. long. $255
Sloan Dalton, Clark County, Arkansas, Burlington chert, 4-3/4 in. $295

Second row from left, top to bottom:

Dalton, 2-1/2 in., McIntosh County, Oklahoma, white Boone chert. $200
Paleo knife, unknown type, 6-1/4 in., Greene County, Illinois. $325
Dalton variant, Boone chert, McIntosh County, Oklahoma, 2-1/4 in. $75

Center column, top to bottom:

Cherryhill Dalton variety, Arkansas novaculite, Pike County, Arkansas, 2 in. $145
Dalton variant, Burlington chert, Poplar Bluff, Missouri, 3-3/4 in. $295
Dalton, 2 in. long, McIntosh County, Oklahoma. $145

Second column from right, top to bottom:

Dalton, McIntosh County, Oklahoma, very thin, 2-1/2 in. long. $195
Dalton knife, 5-3/4 in., Crescent chert, St. Charles County, Missouri. $575
Dalton, Crescent chert, from Missouri, 2-1/2 in., left-hand bevel. $195

Right-hand column, top to bottom:

Sloan Dalton from Arkansas, 4-3/4 in. $250
Dalton, Burlington chert, McIntosh County, Oklahoma, 2-7/8 in. $195
Sloan Dalton, Stuttgart, Arkansas, 5-5/8 in. $350

Larry G. Merriam collection, Oklahoma City, Oklahoma

A superb frame of flint, time-period ranging from the Early Paleo into the Archaic. Shown are point or blade examples of the following types: Daltons, Allen, Eden, Pike County, Agate Basin, Clovis, Alberta and unnamed types. Examples shown are from the states of Colorado, Missouri, Illinois, Arkansas and Montana. The value range here is from $25 to $800.

Larry Merriam collection, Oklahoma City, Oklahoma

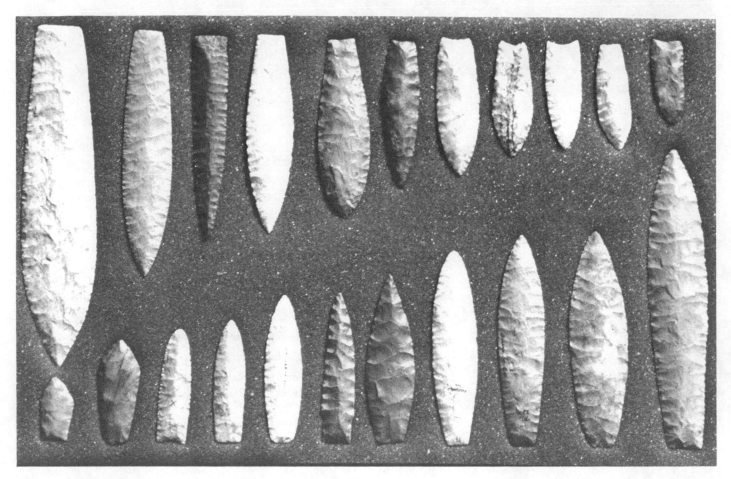

Lanceolates, mainly Late Paleo, superb frame, upper row left to right:

Wadlow knife, 8-1/4 in., fine large blade, from Missouri.	$500
Agate Basin, from North Dakota, 6 in. long, excellent chipping.	$425
Eden, Knife River flint from Wyoming, 5 in. long.	$650
Sedalia/Nebo Hill from Marion County, Missouri, 4-7/8 in.	$475
Point resembling a Hell Gap, 4-1/2 in. long, Adams County, Illinois.	$225
Angostura, from Texas, 3-7/8 in. long.	$225
Agate Basin, Late Paleo, 3-1/2 in., from Pike County, Missouri.	$200
Unknown type, Alibates flint, northwestern Oklahoma, 3 in. long.	$200
Plainview, from Missouri, 2-7/8 in.	$195
Agate Basin, rather rough, from Missouri, 2-3/4 in.	$95
Plainview, made from petrified wood, Maverick County, Texas, 2-1/4 in.	$90

Bottom row, left to right:

Agate Basin, exhausted condition, Edwards chert, Texas, 1-1/2 in.	$75
Possible Lake Mojave point, 2-1/2 in., from Southwest U.S.	$150
Plainview, banded Florence chart, 2-3/4 in., Howard County, Missouri.	$175
Agate Basin, 2-7/8 in., from southwestern Missouri.	$175
Agate Basin, 3-1/2 in., from Schuyler County, Illinois.	$265
Texas Eden, 3-1/2 in. long, made from Edwards Plateau chert.	$265
Eastern lanceolate, 4 in. long, from Kentucky.	$300
Agate Basin, extremely fine, 4-5/8 in., Fulton County, Illinois.	$450
Agate Basin, from Greene County, Arkansas, 5 in. long.	$450
Agate Basin, southeastern Colorado, 5-1/4 in. long.	$375
Agate Basin, Cass County, Missouri, 7-1/8 in. long.	$400

Larry G. Merriam collection, Oklahoma City, Oklahoma

This fine blade was found by an archaeologist near Durango, Colorado. Very well-chipped, it is 5-1/8 in. long.   Museum quality

Grady McCrea collection, Miles, Texas

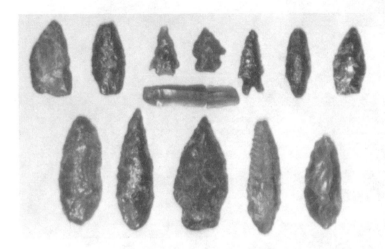

Knives and blades, black obsidian, 1-1/4 to 3-1/4 in. They are from the Western U.S.   *Group, $150*

Pat & Dave Summers, Native American Artifacts, Victor, New York

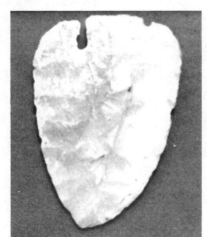

Sloan Dalton, Illinois, 11-plus in. long, reverse view. (See other photo for obverse.) This superb blade has a slight reddish-orange cast from soil contact and iron oxide deposits. This artifact is extremely rare.   *$15,000-20,000*

Alvin Lee Moreland, Corpus Christi, Texas

Base-tang knife or blade, found in Runnels County, Texas. This piece is quite thin, with excellent flaking overall.   *$400*

Grady McCrea collection, Miles, Texas

Texas chipped artifacts, all material various grades of Edwards Plateau flints.

Three blades far left, top to bottom: San Saba, dark material, 6 in. long, Medina County, Texas, $350; Pedernales, 4-3/8 in., light-colored material, $325; Montell, 4-1/8 in., light-colored, Coryell County.   *$325*
Second row left top piece: base-tang knife, curved blade, tan chert, Waco, Texas, 6-1/4 in.   *Unlisted*
Second row left second piece from top: 3 in., Bandy Creek (?), Bandera County, Texas.   *$225*
Center row top to bottom: Base-notched ovate blade, central Texas, 4-1/2 in., $365; corner-tang knife, 4-1/2 in., $495; untanged corner-tang (bottom middle), 6-1/4 in., unusual, use-marks and beveled, central Texas.   *$475*
Second row from right, top piece: Knife, heavy white patina on one side with lighter material on opposite, 5-1/4 in., central Texas.   *$250*
Second row from right, middle piece, Uvalde, 3-1/4 in., thin with heavy patina, from Gillespie County, Texas.   *$200*
Far right row, top to bottom: Base-notched-knife, 6-1/2 in., Bandera County, Texas, $475; Montell, 4-1/2 in., nice thin piece from near Temple, Texas, $300; Castroville, 4 in., from central Texas.   *$325*

Overall, this is a fine representative selection of large and superior Texas blades.

Larry Merriam collection, Oklahoma City, Oklahoma

An extremely fine frame of points and blades from the Central United States region, most being Dalton cluster pieces plus related subtypes. These are from the states Arkansas, Texas, Oklahoma, Louisiana, Missouri, Illinois, and Ohio. The San Patrice points or blades (some with bifurcated bases and serrated edges) are from Texas, Arkansas, Missouri, and Oklahoma.

The frame examples show a wide variety of styles, sizes and materials. The value range per each is from $35 to $395, depending on size, material, the workmanship quality, and overall appearance.

Larry Merriam collection, Oklahoma City, Oklahoma

Corner-tang knife, white Georgetown flint, Coryell County, Texas. The color, size, shape, workstyle and condition make this a very rare piece, and a very expensive one.   Museum quality

L.M. Abbott, Jr. collection, Texas

Prehistoric artifacts, all Texas

Left: Ouachita (related to the Little River), Calf Creek top center, and small Plainview to right. Bottom center: a White River. Bottom right: a Barber (Clovis-related).   Group, $1,300

Willie Fields collection, Hallsville, Texas

Base-tang knife, from Bell County, Texas, 3 x 5-3/4 in. Material is a cream Edwards Plateau chert or flint. $850

L.M. Abbott, Jr. collection, Texas

Early Paleo and Early Archaic pieces.

Left: Ross County Clovis, Gregg County, Texas. $275
Right: Calf Creek with shoulder missing, probably removed during resharpening, Gregg County, Texas. $195

Willie Fields collection, Hallsville, Texas

Angostura blade or knife, ca. 7000 BC, Edwards Plateau chert, from Comanche County, Texas. Size is 2-3/8 x 6-1/4 in. $550

L.M. Abbott, Jr. collection, Texas

High Plains knife, found in 1991 in Box Elder County, Utah. Material is unknown, while the type is probably ca. 3000 BC. This is a fine, large blade at 2 x 5 in. $200

Randall Olsen collection, Cache County, Utah

Large Caddo blade, late prehistoric, from Henderson County, Texas. This fine piece is 6-3/4 in. long. $850

L.M. Abbott, Jr. collection, Texas

Double-pointed blade, Georgetown flint, from Bell County, Texas. This is a large and fine piece, measuring 4-1/2 x 9 in. $1,400

L.M. Abbott, Jr. collection, Texas

Gahagan blade or knife, Edwards Plateau chert, from Hamilton County, Texas. Size is 4-1/4 in. long. $350

L.M. Abbott, Jr. collection, Texas

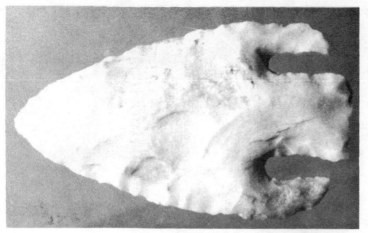

Late Paleo knife, Chillicothe, Missouri. It is made of tan and brown flint and is 1-3/32 x 5-1/32 in. This exceptional piece has G.I.R.S. authentication number C89-40. $1,300

Collection of David G. & Barbara J. Shirley

Calf Creek type blade, 3-1/2 in. long, found by C.W. Womack in Pontotoc County, Oklahoma. This is ca. 7000 BC and is made of Frisco chert in creamy white. (A cast replica is available from Peter Bostrom, Troy, Illinois.) $350

Courtesy C.W. Womack collection

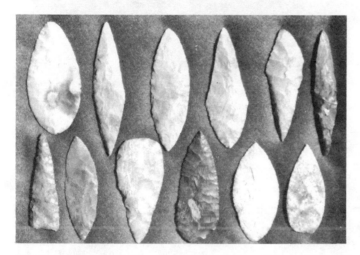

Knife, Harahey, made of weathered quartzite. This is an attractive piece with good workstyle, 6-1/2 in. long. It is from Elberl County, Colorado. $350

Steven D. Kitch collection, Pueblo, Colorado

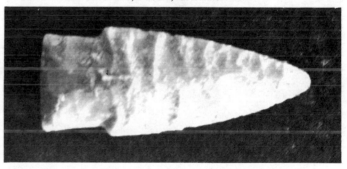

Harahey knives, Neo-Indian period or very late prehistoric period, all found in Runnels County, Texas. This is a fine selection showing the type in different stages of being resharpened, wide to narrow. Each, $100-400

Grady McCrea collection, Miles, Texas

Scottsbluff point or blade, Late Paleo/Early Archaic, found in Cheyenne County, Colorado. It is made of Knife River flint and is 3 in. long. $300

Steven D. Kitch collection, Pueblo, Colorado

Corner-tang blade or knife, 3-3/8 in. long and very thin. This scarce type is Late Archaic and is widely distributed in Texas. $400

Grady McCrea collection, Miles, Texas

Eden point or blade, Late Paleo/Early Archaic period, from Pueblo County, Colorado. It is made of an unusual material, petrified bone. This scarce artifact is 4 in. long. $425

Steven D. Kitch collection, Pueblo, Colorado

Hell Gap point or blade, found in Crowley County, Colorado. It is 3 in. long and is made of purple quartzite. $225

Steven D. Kitch collection, Pueblo, Colorado

Hell Gap point or blade, from Pueblo County, Colorado. It is made of black basalt and is 4-1/4 in. long. $400

Steven D. Kitch collection, Pueblo, Colorado

Plainview point or blade, Early Archaic and ca. 7500 BC. This fine artifact was found near Lander, Wyoming and has a Perino paper of authentication. Length is 2 in. $150

Steven D. Kitch collection, Pueblo, Colorado

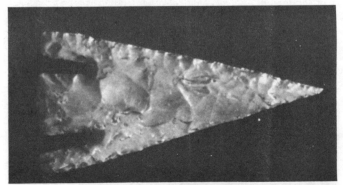

Castroville, Late Archaic period, from Dimmit County, Texas. It is made of Edwards Plateau flint in browns and tans, 4-1/8 in. long. This is the scarce squared-barb type with needle tip. It has random flaking and deep notches. $400-500

Alvin Lee Moreland, Corpus Christi, Texas

San Saba base-tang drill, made of Edwards Plateau chert, from Coryell County, Texas. This superb piece is 4-3/4 in. long. $750

L.M. Abbott, Jr. collection, Texas

Triangular blade, probably Woodland and a possible cache piece, from Licking County, Ohio. It is made of translucent gray Flintridge and is 2-3/8 in. long. $20

Private collection, Ohio

This hafted scraper is very thin and well-made; from Runnes County, Texas. $100-125

Grady McCrea collection, Miles, Texas

Dagger, double-barbed, a very rare Mississippian period artifact, made of Dover flint, the classic material. It is either from Kentucky or Tennessee, and is shown in Stone Age in North America, *Vol. 1, p. 235. Ex-colls. Young and Smail.Museum quality*

John M. Maurer collection, Ft. Campbell, Kentucky; photograph by Dan Privett

Spade made of Dover flint, 11-1/2 in. long, from Benton County, Tennessee. This Mississippian period artifact is ex-coll. Mark Clark. This is a high-grade large artifact in top condition. $650

John M. Maurer collection, Ft. Campbell, Kentucky; photograph by Mike Maurer

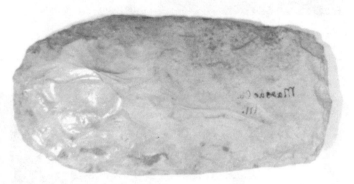

Spade or hoe, flint, well-polished edge. It is 8-1/2 in. long and from Massac County, Illinois. $125

Pat & Dave Summers, Native American Artifacts, Victor, New York

Spade, prehistoric, 7-1/2 in. long. It is from Crittenden County, Arkansas and is made of chert. The artifact has heavy use-polish. $350

Larry Lantz, First Mesa, South Bend, Indiana

Hoe or spade, from Pike County, Indiana. It is made of Mill Creek chert, a whitish-gray high-grade material. Size is 5-1/4 x 11-9/16 in. and the lower, wide end has polish. This is pictured in Who's Who in Indian Relics No. 3. $900

Collection of David G. & Barbara J. Shirley

Notched hoe from St. Louis County, Illinois. Material is a white-gray chert with sections of the original brown exterior. Size, 5-1/2 x 6 in. This Mississippian piece is pictured in Who's Who in Indian Relics No. 1. $1,100

Collection of David G. & Barbara J. Shirley

Frame of Wisconsin artifacts, including points, blades, scrapers, and drills.
                    Collection, $400-500

Robert D. Lund collection, Watertown, Wisconsin

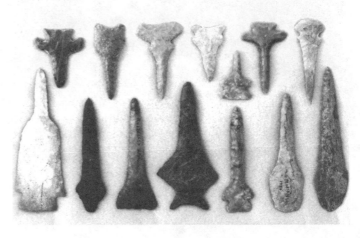

Frame of Wisconsin points and blades, mainly from the Archaic period. The white Dovetail at center is of interest.   *Collection, $600-800*

Robert D. Lund collection, Watertown, Wisconsin

Points and blades, various periods and locations.

Top row, left to right:

Lost Lake, Kentucky.	$35
Plainview (Late Paleo/Early Archaic), Texas.	$140
Thebes blade, Early Archaic, Kentucky.	$120
Pine Tree auriculate, Archaic, Kentucky.	$25
Side-notch drill, Kentucky.	$30
Decatur or fractured-base drill, Kentucky.	$85
Dovetail or St. Charles, exhausted, Kentucky.	$75

Bottom row, left to right:

Etley, 4-3/4 in., Missouri, drill-top.	$75
Adena (Early Woodland), New York.	$50
T-drill, Arkansas (or expanded-base).	$85
Susquehanna, New York state.	$145
Corner-notch, Tennessee.	$95
Sedalia, Illinois.	$70
Beaver-tail Adena, 4-3/4 in., Kentucky.	$140

Pocotopaug Trading Post, South Windsor, Connecticut

Rare early ovoid knife, Paleo period, from Perry County, Illinois. It is made of white Illinois flint and measures 2-7/8 x 6-7/16 in. This piece bears G.I.R.S. authentication number C88-15.   *$1,300*

Collection of David G. & Barbara J. Shirley

Scottsbluff point or blade, Late Paleo/Early Archaic period, from Adams County, Colorado. This artifact is made of gem material, translucent white and orange agate. This fine piece is 3-1/2 in. long. $525

Steven D. Kitch collection, Pueblo, Colorado

Harahey knife, made of Alibates flint. It is from Pratt County, Kansas, and is 5 in. long. This is an excellent example of a four-way bevel. $195

Steven D. Kitch collection, Pueblo, Colorado

Hopewell (Middle Woodland) blades, all left to right:

Jefferson County, New York.	$125
Knox County, Indiana, Coshocton flint.	$150
Near Elizabethtown, Kentucky, 4-1/8 in.	$200
Normanskill flint, New Haven, Connecticut.	$375
Allegany County, New York, 4-5/8 in.	$175

Pocotopaug Trading Post, South Windsor, Connecticut

Collection of points and blades from Mississippi, Louisiana, Texas and Arkansas. Many different types and materials are represented. Each, $25-175

Wilfred A. Dick collection, Magnolia, Mississippi

Late Woodland blade, from Fairfield County, Ohio. Material is blue-gray Upper Mercer and length is 3-3/8 in. This piece has restoration in two places, at the lower blade edge and basal corner. $30

Private collection, Ohio

Paiute Indians, on the Kaibab Plateau, near the Grand Canyon of the Colorado, in northern Arizona. Photo by John K. Hillers, Powell Expedition, 1871-1875. The Indians here are playing the game of "Ni-aung-pi-kai," or "Kill the Bone."

Photo courtesy Utah State Historical Society, Collection of Smithsonian Institution

CHAPTER III

ARTIFACTS OF ORGANIC MATERIALS

Artifacts made from mammal and shellfish parts were common in prehistoric times. Relatively few of the objects survived to the present. Such organic materials, like wood artifacts, have largely disappeared due to the combined actions of time, moisture, and bacteria.

Antler, from deer and elk, was a much-used raw material for tools and weapons. Flaking rods of antler helped make the incredible numbers of chipped objects, and deer tines were often used for projectile points. Antler, due to the hardness and availability, was used in much of North America, including all of the Continental U.S.

Horn, usually from the so-called buffalo (the American bison), was made into ladles, spoons, and ceremonial objects. In the northern reaches of the Rockies, horn also came from mountain goats and bighorn sheep. Horn strips were sometimes used to reinforce bows, and the material was made into knife handles, charms, and decorations.

Ivory had been widely used in the Alaskan region (see later chapter) and northern Canada. Ivory artifacts form a scarce class, especially for prehistoric items in the adjoining United States. Among animals that provided ivory were the walrus and narwhal, a mammal with a single twisted tusk which may have inspired the unicorn legend.

To a limited degree ivory also came from the twin tusks of long-dead mastodon and mammoths, preserved in permafrost. Smaller objects made from the teeth of other sea creatures are sometimes referred to as ivory.

ANTLER, HORN, AND IVORY ARTIFACTS

Horn spoon, Plains Indian, unusual carved handle, cow horn, and 10 in. long. Probably 19th century.   G-$250

Buffalo horns from old headdress, Taos Pueblo, ca. 1800s.   D-$125

Elk horn point, from southern Oregon, 3-1/4 in. long, thinly notched at base. Narrow, may be an arrowpoint.   C-$50

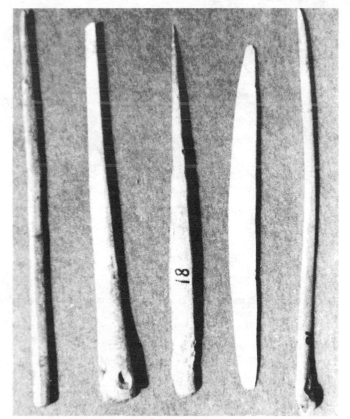

Horn spoon, 8-1/16 in. long, with sinew sewn beaded handle in colors white, green, yellow, and blue. Material is cow horn, and piece is ca. 1910. $400

Photo courtesy of Crazy Crow Trading Post, Denison, Texas

Six deer-antler tools, from Archaic site in Kentucky near Ohio River. Excavated from rock shelter, longest piece is just over 4 in. It is believed these are flint-chipping tools; all six sections in good condition.   *All $25*

Private collection

Five long bone awls, from Texas sites, and late prehistoric era. These were excavated from a Panhandle Pueblo site along with 2-notch and 3-notch Harrell points. Awls are 6 in. to 7 in. in length.   C-$40-100

Photo courtesy of Wayne Parker, Texas

Northwest Coast of Canada totem carved horn ladle, 10 in. long, Haida. It is made of black mountain goat horn, constructed in two pieces and attached with three copper rivets. Handle is totem carved; Northwest Coast of Canada to Alaska, ca. 1860-1880.$850

Frank Bergevin, Port Of Call, Alexandria Bay, New York

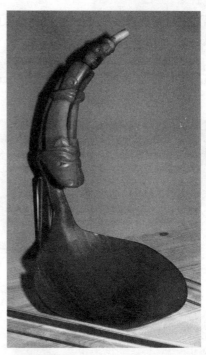

Tlingit horn spoon, 4 x 9 in., a beautiful carving in a material that took great skill to process and work. Ca. 1890.

Historic Interiors, Sorrento, British Columbia, Canada

Bear claw necklace, with longest claw 5 in. long. Inside of claws is painted with vermilion; the necklace was made from the now-extinct prairie grizzly. Piece is Northern Plains and ca. 1870.   *Museum quality*

Nedra Matteucci's Fenn Galleries, Santa Fe, New Mexico

Walrus tusk cribbage board, 11 in. long. The tusk has images of swimming seals and polar bears. Alaska, ca. 1880. $335

Frank Bergevin, Port Of Call, Alexandria Bay, New York

Horn spoon, large 11 in. length, with curved handle done in quill-work. Probably recent, but good piece.   C-$135

Spoon or ladle, Plains Indian, of bison horn, 12 in. long, no damage, some painted designs on handle portion.   D-$140

Deer-antler arrowpoint, Kentucky rock shelter, 2-1/4 in. long; base hollowed out for arrow shaft.   C-$10

Horn spoon or ladle, wide-bowled, 7 in. long and 4 in. wide at shallow bowl. Northwest Coast, probably historic and late 1800s.   C-$275

Horn ladle, Nez Perce, deer horn dipper, 8-1/4 in. long, of bent and shaped horn. No decoration, but good lines.   C-$265

Elkhorn scraper, 13 in. long with right-angle curve; has a snub-nose scraper of quartz still in position. Held by rawhide bindings and pitch. Horn polished by much use; condition good.   D-$350

Ivory bar, incised, western Canada, 3-1/2 in. long and about 1/4 in. thick. Both sides have a series of zigzag lines in parallel rows of three. Possibly a gaming token or marker; actual use unknown. Golden brown with slight age cracks.   C-$225

Horn spoon, Sioux, hand-carved.   D-$65

Freshwater pearls, evidently necklace beads, probably Hopewellian, approximately seventy drilled pearls, none in good condition.   C-$130

Elk teeth, set of seven, drilled at bases for suspension.   C-$50

Antler Atl-atl hook, 6-3/4 in. long and averages 1 in. in diameter, rare piece, removed from North Carolina rock shelter. Material in medium-good condition. Notched at end to receive lance base.   C-$275

Ivory pendant, northern California, 2-3/4 in. long; may have been made from walrus ivory, but uncertain. Drill hole at one end. Oval shape.   C-$160

Horn spoon, Plains Indian; 11 in. overall length; has beaded handle. Pre-1900.   G-$255

Antler pick, 13 in. long, from prehistoric period, probably 4,000 years old. Tip shows polish from long use, but rest of material is chalk-like. May once have had wood handle.   C-$90

Elk horn blade, adz with wooden handle. Piece is 12 in. long, good condition.   G-$250

Elk horn hide scraper, ivoryized from much use, good condition.   G-$265

BONE ARTIFACTS

Bone items were made from the skeletal material of many animals, from raccoons to whales. They were less common in the American Southwest, but other regions had a wide variety of such artifacts. These ranged from turkey wing-bone flutes to deer-bone awls to elk-horn hoes. Flint and obsidian blades shaped the bone.

Long polished-bone hairpin, 5-7/8 in. long, light incised lines along shank sides.   C-$80

Portion of bone flute or whistle, said to have been recovered from Kentucky.   C-$125

Bone spatula or hide-working tool, tapers to sharp rounded blade at end, shows heavy polish in lower regions. Old label states it is from Henderson, Kentucky.   C-$45

Private collection

Bone hoe, made from bison shoulder blade, with original handle.   D-$275

Bone awl, from New York, 4-5/8 in. long, made of splintered deer bone. From late prehistoric site.   C-$40

Bone whistle, Tennessee, 3-1/8 in. long. Has incised lines in spiral design around sides.   D-$90

Bone comb, probably Iroquois, with rounded comb teeth that resemble outstretched fingers of the hand. Piece is 4-1/2 in. high; two effigies on top, resembling facing animals, species unknown.   C-$400

Bone hide scraper, Mesa Verde area of Colorado, 7-1/2 in. long, and made ca. 1900. Perhaps bison bone, with working edges smoothed by use; has quartzite blade.   C-$160

Necklace elements, from Wyoming dry cave, consisting of eight bone beads, each about 1 in. (25mm) long, and three bear canine teeth, averaging about 2-1/2 in. long. Canines drilled at rear; fangs and beads in good condition. Age unknown.   C-$225

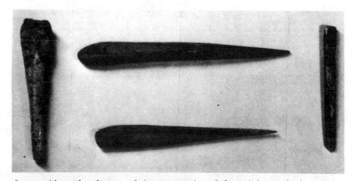

Long wide turkey bone awl, in two sections left to right, each about 3 in. long and polished from much use.

Center: two fine bone awls or needles, all from West Virginia rock shelter, longest about 5 in. The small holes are modern-drilled by an earlier collector who secured pieces together with cord.   C-$65

Private collection

Strand of assorted beads, made of bone and shell, with largest bead 3/4 in. in diameter. These are probably prehistoric.   C-$40-50

Photo courtesy of Robert C. Calvert, London, Ontario, Canada

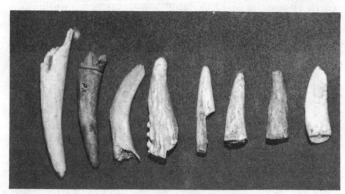

Deer antler tines showing prehistoric working and cuts for snapping off. One is from Pennsylvania and others from Mississippi.   Each, $5

Wilfred A. Dick collection, Magnolia, Mississippi

Collection: A fine assemblage of shell artifacts in central frames, with flint points. Surrounding artifacts include stone celts, axes, flint blades, gorgets, discoidals, plummets, and a spatulate form. All pieces are from Tennessee.   C-Not listed

Photo courtesy of Joseph D. Love, Chattanooga, Tennessee

Bear canine tooth, from Shiawassee County, Michigan. Such objects were often used for decorative artifacts. $65

Collection of David G. & Barbara J. Shirley

Deer antler projectile tips or points, all from Mississippi.   Each, $30

Wilfred A. Dick collection, Magnolia, Mississippi

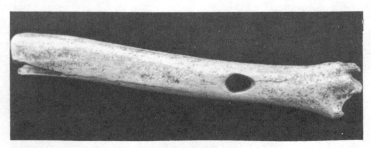

Unusual artifact, a bone arrow-shaft straightener. It was found in Haskell County, Oklahoma, by the owner. $145

James Bruner collection, Oklahoma

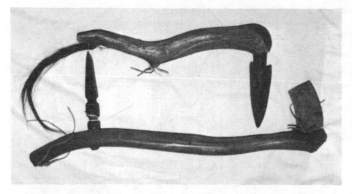

Elkhorn clubs, Arapaho.

Top: horn with metal point, horse-hair drop, hide wrist-band, and paint in colors of yellow, red, and green. The upper example is ex-coll. Green. These are ca. 1840-60.   *Each, $1,200*

Private collection, photo by John McLaughlin

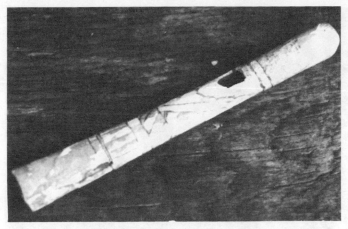

Bone whistle, Archaic period and ca. 2000 BC, from Lewis County, New York. It is geometrically incised. Size, 1/2 x 6 in., scarce artifact. *$195*

Frank Bergevin, Port of Call, Alexandria Bay, New York

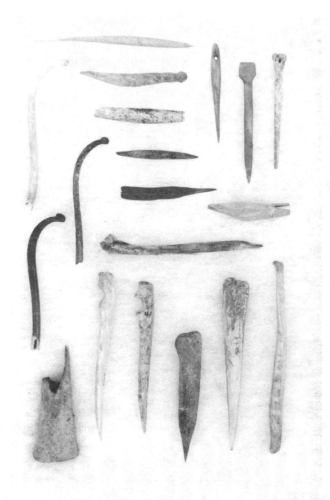

End fragments of carved bone artifacts, both from Kentucky. Study value

Wilfred A. Dick collection, Magnolia, Mississippi

Bone tools and implements, including needles, perforators, fish-pins, awls, hair-pins, etc. These came from the Columbia River area and are ca. 1850-1900.   *$195*

Morris' Art & Artifacts, Anaheim, California; Dawn Gober photograph

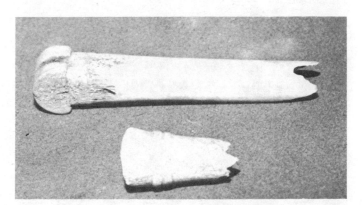

Bone and shell artifacts, prehistoric.

Bear canine teeth, Kentucky.	*$30-35*
Bone awls, Kentucky.	*Each, $10*
Needles, lower right, Maine.	*$8*
Elk teeth, shell crescent, from New York.	*$30*
Center shell gorget, from Connecticut.	*$25*

Pocotopaug Trading Post, South Windsor, Connecticut

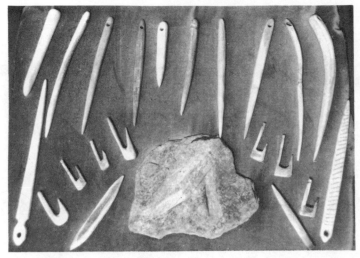

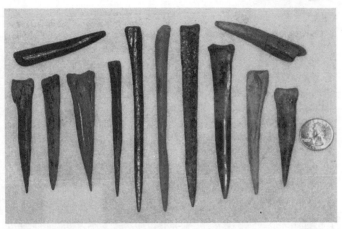

Bone artifacts. These include fish hooks, awls, needles, and hairpins. A well-used sandstone sharpening slab is included. Each, $40-150

Private collection

Bone awls and pins, probably fairly late prehistoric, with quarter giving scale. These were made from deer bones and were found along rivers by the owner in 1997. Kansas. Unlisted

Found by Daniel Fox; photo by Caroline Fox, Manhattan, Kansas

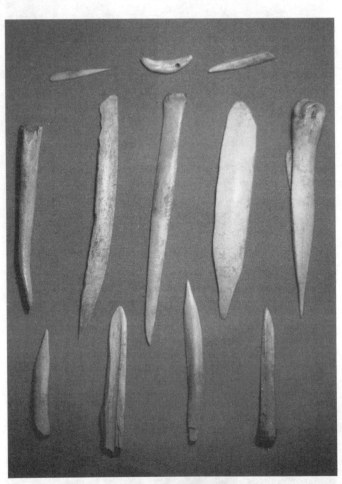

Bone tools, awls, punches and perforators, longest example 6-1/4 in. Often such tools were made of deer bone. These came from the San Jose area of New Mexico. Group, $200

Jack Baker collection, Ozark, Missouri; David Capon photograph

Bone knife, rare artifact, with worn lower region or blade, incised lines on handle (top). It is late prehistoric and measures 7 in. long; material may be bear bone. This was found in a California cave in 1927. $950

Private collection

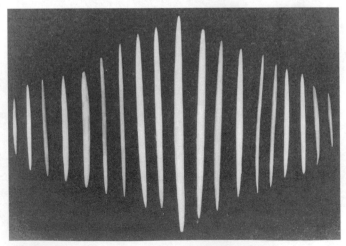

Bone needles, bi-pointed type, Mississippian period, 1-1/2 to 6-3/4 in. long. Color range is from cream and reddish brown to near-black. Georgia. $250

Bruce Butts collection, Winterville, Georgia

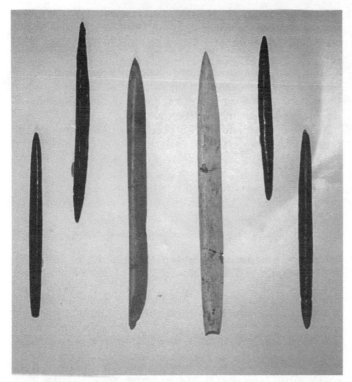

Bone points and pins, various prehistoric time-periods, these 6 to 8 in. long. They are made of deer bone and all were found in Florida. *Each, $20-50*

Scott Young, Port St. Lucie, Florida

Raccoon penis-bone perforator, from Georgia, 3-1/8 in. long. Knobbed at one end, smaller end has been sharpened by abrasion. Piece in outline forms part of an "S" curve. Found on late prehistoric site. C-$15

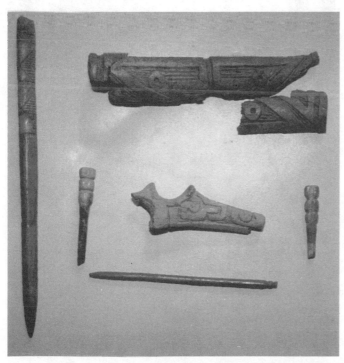

Carved bone artifacts, late prehistoric times, pin on left 6-1/4 in. long. These were found in the Lake Monroe area, Florida. *Each, $25-500*

Scott Young, Port St. Lucie, Florida

Ceremonial ladle, Hupa, 11 in. long, carved from bone; handle decorated with central cutouts and expanded serrations just above bowl. Used for important feast occasions. C-$260

Bone flaking tool, broken and reglued. Piece is 5-1/2 in. long and 1-1/2 in. wide G-$16

Bone whistle, 7 in. long, emits a single-pitch tone. Made from deer or antelope bone. Piece collected in California, early 1900s. D-$125

Elk-bone perforator, 3-7/8 in. long, one tip ground to sharp point. Shows much use; surface very smooth. C-$13

Deer bone awl, from Mimbres, New Mexico. D-$25

Bone fish hook, from Alabama coastal site, 1-1/4 in. long, fine condition. D-$60

Bone awl, polished, from Missouri, 3 in. long and 1/4 in. in diameter. G-$35

Bone hairpin, decorated, 7-1/2 in. long, nearly pointed at tip, expanded at base end. Designs of crossed and dotted lines for about half distance from base to tip. Highly polished overall; has a yellow-brown color. C-$165

Bone awls, excavated or quill flatteners G-$15 each

Bone fish-shaped wand, Tlingit, 15-1/2 in. long, recent and still used in ceremonies. C-$150

Bone harpoon tip, Oregon river valley, 4 in. long, double barbs on each side; socketed base for insertion into long wooden shaft. Base has knobs or protrusions for securing line that was fastened to the tip. D-$165

Split bone awl, Missouri, 3-3/4 in. long. G-$19

Bone needle, polished, from Dickerson Cave, Kentucky, 4 in. long and 1/4 in. in diameter. G-$30

Bone fishkiller club, made of marine animal bone, 19-1/4 in. long. Plain, heavy, 2-7/8 in. in diameter at striking end. Handle end has circular extension like a baseball bat for non-slip hold. Weathered, a bleached pale gray, but good condition. D-$550

Bone needle, polished, from Kentucky, 4-1/2 in. long and 1/2 in. in diameter. G-$40

Bone comb or hair decoration, Woodlands region, historic Indian, probably Iroquois. About 2-1/2 in. wide at base, part of human figure effigy on comb back. Figure would have stood about 5 in. high, but head broken off. Several teeth missing from comb but a fine example. D-$300

Bone fish hook, 1-1/2 in. long, very thin, of deer bone. Highly polished; line end has groove near top. C-$45

Bone scraper, Blackfoot, 12 in. long. Piece has original metal scraper blade. This is 19th century. G-$275

Bone bead, polished, probably part of a necklace, 1 in. long and 1/2 in. wide; well-drilled. Faint circular incised lines on surface, now almost obliterated. C-$12

End-drilled pieces of polished bone, probably necklace segments or miniature pendants. Probably deer bone,

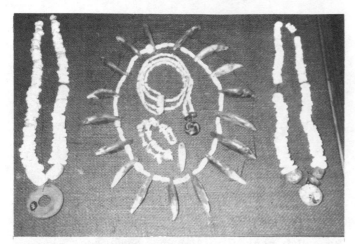

Prehistoric shell beads and necklace of beads and bear teeth.

Left, necklace.	$150-250
Center, bear-tooth necklace.	$350-500
Right, necklace.	$150-250

Philip L. Russo collection, Danbury, Connecticut

from Colorado rock shelter. Bone pieces are nearly matching in size, averaging 2-1/8 in. long. There are fourteen in all.   D-$150

Bone needle, from Todd County, Arkansas, 5 in. long and 1/4 in. in diameter. Good polish and with a perforated eye.   G-$65

Bone pendant, Louisiana, about 2 in. wide and 3-1/2 in. long, end-drilled with a single hole. Rectangular form, age unknown, incised with series of x-like marks on one side.   C-$95

SHELL ARTIFACTS

Shell, the exoskeletons of a multitude of fresh and

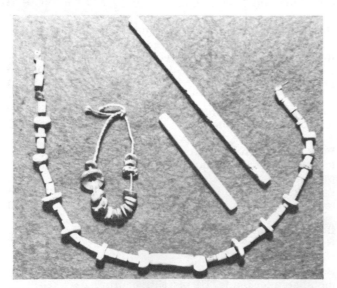

Shell ornaments, from Pennsylvania and New York, ca. 1550-1700s. Long tubular "hair pins," small strand of circular disk "wampum," large strand of shell disk beads and "European" wampum, barrel-shaped.

Hair pipes.	$50-95
Wampum strand this size.	$15-30
Large mixed strand.	$70-125

Gary L. Fogelman collection, Pennsylvania

salt water species, had a long and extensive period of usage for artifacts. Amerinds used shell, with some minor changes, for spoons, containers, and hoes. Other shell portions became pendants and bracelets.

Tiny segments of larger shells became the disc and tubular beads of early and historic times. The well-known "wampum" beads served as a medium of exchange even to the first colonists in New England.

Shell—like some high grades of flint, copper, and other desired materials—is an example of far-flung trade in prehistoric times. Gulf of Mexico conch shell was used by Ohio's Gravel Kame Indians 4,000 years ago. Pacific abalone shell was traded into the Southwest at the close of the BC years. Other bivalve halves were even treated with pitch and saguaro cactus acid by the legendary Hohokam to become the first etchings in the world.

Shell rings and shell pendants, two of each, from Arizona, average 1 in. in diameter.   G-$50 for the four

Shell effigy gorget, Fort Ancient, late prehistoric, illustrating the human face with weeping-eye motif. Specimen is 4-1/8 in. high and 3-1/8 in. wide, with some parts missing at lower shell fringes or "chin" area.   C-$500

Shell dipper or spoon, from a shell-mound site in Kentucky. 5 in. long and 3-1/4 in. wide. Mussel-shell. One long side has been notched in early times.   C-$85

Shell gorget, marine, Mississippi culture, found in Georgia, 5 in. high; inscribed with "eagle warrior" motif, lines not all clear. Depiction is faded and shell is not in good condition.   C-$475

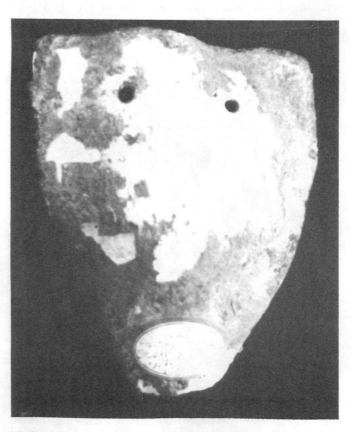

Mask, made of marine shell, from Smyth County, Virginia. Mississippian in origin, these are rare and in good condition. $400

Rodney M. Peck collection, Harrisburg, North Carolina

Shell pendants, large pendant 6 in. long. Small examples are abalone, from the Channel Islands, California. $145

Morris' Art & Artifacts, Anaheim, California; Dawn Gober photograph

Trade wampum necklace, rare Seneca origin and Dutch-made with five crescents and a shell bird or duck effigy pendant, 25 in. plus 5-1/4 in. drop. From near Lima, New York, these are ca. 1640-1660 and ex-coll. Wray. $2,900

Pat & Dave Summers, Native American Artifacts, Victor, New York

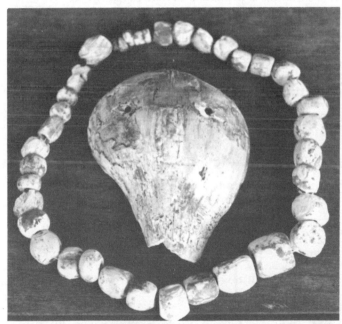

Center, Mississippian shell mask with bas-relief and drilled features, 3 x 4 in. Ca. AD 1200-1600, Arkansas. $900

Necklace, Mississippian period, thirty-nine beads with largest 3/4 in. This shell strand is 18 in. long. $175

Frank Bergevin, Port Of Call, Alexandria Bay, New York

Pendants, abalone shell, both from Contra Costa County, California, and ca. 1000-2500 BP.

Left: "Banjo" form, 3 x 4 in. high. Material is black abalone, rare. $400

Right: "Horned" pendant, 3-3/8 x 3 in. high, red abalone, very rare. $400

Collection of, and photograph by, Michael W. Hough, California

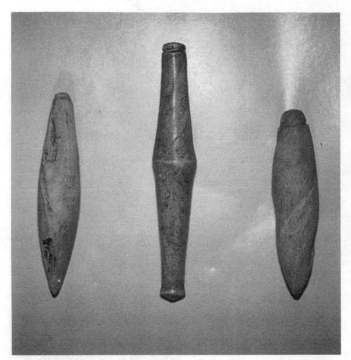

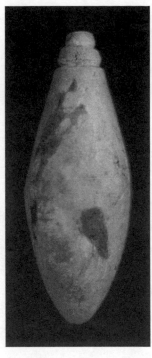

Shell plummet, Mississippian period, double rings at top, 1 x 2-3/4 in. This polished example made of conch shell is rare, and from Seminole County, Florida. $400

Bruce Butts collection, Winterville, Georgia

Plummets, Late Archaic into Early Woodland, these examples made from columella shell. All are from the Charlotte Harbor region, Florida. Left to right:

Plummet, 3-5/8 in., well-shaped.	*$50*
Ornate plummet, 4-3/8 in., ivory color, well-polished.	*$300*
Plummet, 3-1/4 in., typical form.	*$35*

Scott Young, Port St. Lucie, Florida

Shell beads, disc-shaped, about 21 in. long. Necklace of prehistoric graduated-size. Largest discs in center measure 5/8 in. There are approximately 140 beads in the strand. C-$295

Shell bead strand, tube type, length 26 in. Material is from Arkansas. G-$125

Shell necklace with drilled cougar fang pendant, probably Mississippian, late prehistoric. There are seventeen freshwater mussel beads, pendant drilled very much off-center, all in fair condition. Beads have average length of 3/4 in.; pendant is 1-1/8 in. long. C-$125

Conch shell pendant, (#E-18), Seneca, ca. 1680-1700. With two small suspension holes, it is 3-1/2 in. in diameter and from Livingston County, New York. Unlisted

Iron Horse collection, Blasdell, New York

Shell beads, Arkansas, disc and barrel types, and length is 20 in. C-$85

Shell beads and pendant, which is carved in the form of an animal; strand is 17 in. long. G-$75

Shell gorget, engraved, Mississippian period, 4 x 4-3/4 in. Central motif depicts man dancing or flying. Excellent condition, some surface flaking due to age. C-$750

Shell fish hook, made of abalone shell, coastal California. Piece is 1-1/2 in. long, nice curve, good condition, notched for string, excavated find. C-$45

Shell heishi, early Indian string, restrung to be worn. G-$395

Abalone shell pendant, decorated, 4-1/8 in. long and about 2 in. average width. Single drill-hole at one end, scalloped cutouts at other end; from California. C-$175

Strand of shell beads, graduated sizes and well-shaped beads, 40 in. length. G-$250

Shell pendant, one side with heavy polish, drilled with three holes. It is 1-3/4 in. long and 1-1/2 in. wide, from Virginia. G-$20

Strand of shell beads, graduated, from Tennessee, 19 in. long; well-shaped. G-$125

Shell hoe, Virginia, 4 in. long and 2-1/2 in. wide. Made from shell of a freshwater mussel. Single hole in thick central portion for handle. Shell somewhat deteriorated. C-$25

Effigy shell head of alligator; strange piece excavated in Arkansas; it is undrilled and 2 in. long. G-$75

Tube shell beads, Northern California, made by pump-drilling abalone shell. G-$185

Conch shell plummet, from Florida, double grooved at the top. Piece is 4-1/4 in. long, slender, about 1 in. in diameter at center. Lower end tapers to near-point. Discolored with age.   C-$90

Otter hide necklace with large sea shell ornament, possibly a personal amulet.   G-$165

Grooved shell bead, from Tennessee, 3-3/4 in. long, perforated at each end to be worn as a pendant.   G-$30

Marine shell beads, string of approximately fifty, recovered from site in Tennessee. Beads average 3/4 in., or 3/8 in. long and 3/8 in. in diameter. Well-preserved necklace.   C-$185

Shell heishi beads, strand from Arizona, 31 in. long, prehistoric, very well made.   G-$175

Shell ornaments in the shape of birds, from California. Two have holes; the third is undrilled. Average size, 1-1/4 x 1-1/2 in.   G-$75 set

Shell disc, perforated with hole in the center; 2 in. in diameter.   G-$15

Suggested Reading

Miles, Charles. *Indian & Eskimo Artifacts of North America*. New York: Bonanza Books, 1963.

Indian woman and dog, with axe and firewood. Picture taken in state of Washington, date unknown.

Photographer unknown; courtesy Photography Collection, Suzzallo Library, University of Washington

Indian woman weaving a basket. Note completed basket, two partially finished, and supply of spare weaving materials. Picture taken in state of Washington, ca. 1897-1899.

Photographer, Anders B. Wilse; courtesy Photography collection, Suzzallo Library, University of Washington

CHAPTER IV

AXE FORMS

Indian axes are a touchmark of prehistoric occupation on the land. Most were made of some type of hardstone which worked well and provided a durable cutting edge and a pounding surface. The first well-made hardstone axes, as opposed to chipped flint, were made about 6,000 years ago. Then Amerinds discovered how to shape stone by pounding, grinding, and polishing.

Pecking and abrasion was the second of the three great tool-making methods. A stone a bit larger than the axe-to-be was selected. This was struck rapidly and repeatedly with a smaller hammerstone, each blow powdering and removing bits of stone.

Grooves were pecked and ground, except for celts. The axe was then polished, perhaps with sand and leather. Sometimes the entire axe head was so-treated; more often, the lower blade and groove area only were polished.

The groove, of course, was for the handle, and helped secure the axe while in use. This matter of the groove appears to follow a logical sequence, with the oldest axes being full-grooved, or entirely circled with the handle channel.

Later axes were either three-quarter grooved or half-grooved, depending on period and region. The most recent axe form, used until the arrival of Whites, was the celt. This was essentially a long and narrow grooveless axe, and was mounted in a hole or socket of a rather thick-ended handle.

Some areas did not follow this exact progression, and the full-grooved axe was used by some later peoples. Whatever the type, the axe heads are scattered over most of North America. There is an interesting theory that a prime use for axes in prehistoric times wasn't for battle, or even for felling trees, though such woodwork was certainly done. Instead, axes were an aid in obtaining sufficient firewood for heat, light, and food preparation.

The collecting of axes is a major field. Prices can range from several dollars for a battered, low-grade specimen to $1,500 for a fine trophy-grade ceremonial axe.

The rare monolithic (one-stone) axes are late prehistoric copies of the celtiform axe—complete with handle. There's really no top price limit to axes of this type. But the average price for the average axe is probably in the $60 to $125 range.

For the many thousands of collectible axes, a number of guidelines are used to judge axe quality. Material is important, with a compact, close-grained stone most desirable. According to several knowledgeable axe collectors, size and condition are the two key factors, followed by shape or type. Large sizes are preferred to smaller sizes, because these have more "visual impact" and represent more workmanship by the prehistoric creator.

As with all early Amerind works, condition—the presence and amount of damage or absence of same—is vital. (A particular perfect axe might be worth $200 to a collector; half the same axe, nothing.) Some axe types are considered extra-good, because they have additional, often regional, "extras."

Examples might be the Michigan barbed axes, with the end projecting grooved ridges, or the fluted Wisconsin varieties. These have various arrangements of shallow channels, usually at an angle to the actual axe groove. The purpose of such varieties is not known; it may have been only decorative.

Still other axe value determinants are overall workstyle and balance and symmetry along several examination planes. The blade edge or bit ought to be regular and without heavy use-damage. Grooved ridges, if present, should be even and similar. Polish adds to value; the more the better.

Fakes exist in all axe categories, but abound in two. One is the low-cost axe, made of a softer stone (brown and gray sandstone seem to be popular) with the axe made first, then the groove pecked in. Widely sold in the $25 to $100 range, these axes are fine examples of nothing.

A tougher area is the well-made trophy-grade hardstone axe-head, complete with a few just-still-visible peck marks. Consult with advanced collectors before laying out any large sum, and if the piece is at all questionable, pass it by.

FULL-GROOVE AXES

Full-groove axe, Minnesota, 8-1/4 in. long and about 5 in. wide. Unusual in that groove is very near the center of axe, not closer to pounding poll. Little polish, a very utilitarian form, fine condition.   C-$125

Axe, Richland County, Ohio, 7-3/4 in. long and 3-3/4 in. wide. Fine condition.   G-$375

Grooved axe, miniature, Ohio, highly polished, 3 in. long and 2 in. wide; material is a dark green color.   G-$60

Full-grooved axe, Michigan. Blade tapers to about half of extreme width, 4-1/4 in. at grooved ridges. Piece is 6-1/2

Full groove axe, 4 x 6-3/4 in., and very heavy. Semi-polished, with some nicks, this piece is from Michigan.   C-$150

Photo courtesy Bob Brand collection, Pennsburg, Pennsylvania

in. long, made of a white or gray stone. Some original wear on blade edge, but only average. C-$215

Full-groove axe, from Iowa, 5 in. long and 2-5/8 in. wide; a dark brown color. G-$55

Full-groove axe. Arizona, 6 in. long, of a black basaltic rock. Groove is near rounded poll, with long, polished blade and excurvate blade edge. D-$235

Full-groove axe, Missouri, 6-1/4 in. long and about 4 in. wide. Some damage to lower blade region, probably prehistoric breakage, disfigures piece. C-$50

Full groove axe, 4-3/4 x 8-1/4 in. Unpolished, but a good example of a Pennsylvania axe. From the Delaware River area. C-$95

Photo courtesy Bob Brand collection, Pennsburg, Pennsylvania

Full-groove axe, Illinois, 3-1/8 in. long, and well-polished over all surface. Shallow groove. C-$85

Full-groove axe, from Illinois, perhaps ceremonial. Piece is 14-1/2 in. long and 8 in. wide and was a surface find on Archaic site. Well-polished in groove and lower blade regions; peck-marks remain on other surfaces. C-$795

Axe, raised groove, dark gray. Found while excavating for the railroad building in St. Louis, 7-1/4 in. long and 4 in. wide. Some damage to bit. G-$225

Full-groove axe, probably Middle Archaic, with pronounced ridge around groove, upper and lower areas.

Full groove axe, 4 x 7-1/4 in. and very heavy. Somewhat crude, but an unusual type; semi-polished, and with several nicks. C-$400

Photo courtesy Bob Brand collection, Pennsburg, Pennsylvania

Axe is 10-1/4 in. long of dark compact stone; high polish, especially on blade. C-$550

Full-groove axe, small, black 4-3/8 in. high and 2-3/4 in. wide. Groove is shallow but very regular, good overall polish to piece. Blade edge shows mild battering. C-$70

NOTE: A **full-groove axe**, the Midwestern trophy-grade axe, is not represented here. Sometimes these are also **three-fourth groove**. This axe is made of colorful high-grade hardstone, is between 4 in. and 6 in. long, with ridged groove. No dealer had one in stock, and none have been offered at auction recently. The "going rate" for classic specimens is said to be in the $750 to $4,500 range. One knowledgeable collector stated that probably no more than 300 authentic pieces exist.

Full-grooved axe, 4-1/4 in. long. Archaic, excellent condition. Edge has very mild battering, but piece has overall high polish. C-$75

Private collection

Full-groove round-top axe, 3 x 7-1/4 in. This piece is from New Jersey, unpolished, and with slight nick in the top. C-$125

Photo courtesy Bob Brand collection, Pennsburg, Pennsylvania

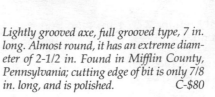

Lightly grooved axe, full grooved type, 7 in. long. Almost round, it has an extreme diameter of 2-1/2 in. Found in Mifflin County, Pennsylvania; cutting edge of bit is only 7/8 in. long, and is polished. C-$80

Photo courtesy Jonas Yoder, Jr., McVeytown, Pennsylvania

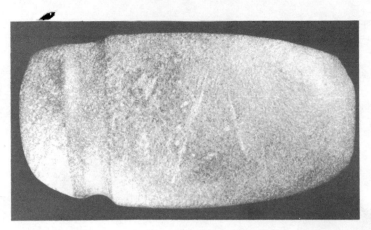

Axe, 4/4 or full grooved, from Pike County, Missouri. Material is a medium-grained granite and size is 8-1/4 in. long; weight is 5-1/4 pounds. $600

Rodney M. Peck collection, Harrisburg, North Carolina

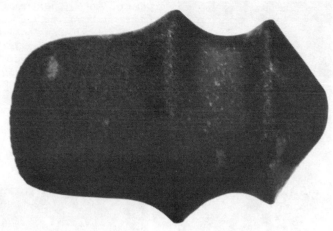

Full-groove axe, Archaic, made of porphyry, black with yellow inclusions. Size is 2 x 3-1/2 x 5-1/4 in. This beautiful example is ex-colls. Scott, Walters and Jardine. $1,200

Collection of David G. & Barbara J. Shirley

Full-groove or 4/4 stone axe, Archaic period, with flattened poll. It is made of gray-green hardstone and is from Horseheads, New York. Size is 1-1/2 x 2-1/2 x 5-1/4 in. $200

Pat & Dave Summers, Native American Artifacts, Victor, New York

Barbed axe, 4-3/8 x 9-7/16 in., 1-3/4 in. thick. This is a fine axe, made of mottled glacial hardstone in green, black and cream. Highly polished, the axe has a few shallow disc or implement strike-marks which do not detract from the high overall artistic merit. A beautiful axe, formerly in the Terry Allen collection, it is from Michigan, county unknown. $1,500

Tom Fouts collection, Kansas

This photo is the reverse of axe

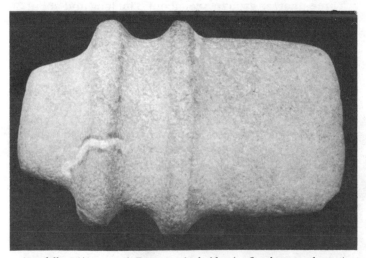

Axe, full or 4/4 grooved, Eastern raised-ridge (or Southern trophy axe), Allegheny County, North Carolina. Made of medium-grained granite, it is 9-3/4 in. long and weighs 8-1/2 pounds. This is a museum quality axe, very rare. $5,000 +

Rodney M. Peck collection, Harrisburg, North Carolina

Full-groove or 4/4 axe, 2-1/4 x 4 in. This fine axe is made of tan quartzite and would date to about the Middle Archaic period, ca. 4000 BC. Louisiana. $350

Richard F. Hughes collection, Louisiana

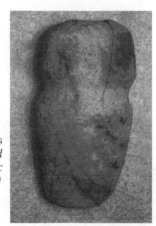

Trophy axe, (#A/977), full-groove, Archaic period, hardstone. The axe is polished, especially in the groove area, and is nicely shaped overall. It measures 3-1/4 x 4-7/8 in. and is from Pennsylvania. $750-1,150

Iron Horse collection, Blasdell, New York

Axe, (#E-2191), full-groove, Archaic period, gray hardstone. At 5 x 7-1/4 in., this axe is one of the better 4/4 grooves to come from the state, being large, well-shaped, and highly polished. The groove area is quite uniform for type, and the blade edge is smoothly excurvate. It was found near Yellow Bud, Ross County, Ohio. $850-1,200

Iron Horse collection, Blasdell, New York

THREE-FOURTH GROOVE AXES

(also called "three-quarter groove")

Three-quarter groove axe, black and white granite, Brown County, Illinois, 7 in. long and 4 in. wide. An exceptional axe.   G-$450

Three-quarter groove axe, from Southwestern cliff dweller site, and with wide, shallow groove near large and rounded poll. Stone head is 6-1/4 in. long, of black material, with very small cutting edge, 1-7/8 in. long, curved. Fine condition.   D-$225

Three-quarter groove axe, very large, Southeastern U.S., possibly ceremonial size. Axe head is 13-1/4 in. long and 7 in. wide below groove. Good condition; not polished.   A-$220

Three-quarter groove axe, Hohokam. Arizona, 9-1/2

Three-fourth groove axe, 4 x 6 in. Piece is very good condition, with a small nick on the back; semi-polished.   C-$300

Photo courtesy Bob Brand collection, Pennsburg, Pennsylvania

in. long, with typical wide and shallow groove. A little over 3 in. wide; stone head tapers to a small, rounded blade edge.   D-$160

Three-quarter groove axe, Western U.S., 5-3/8 in. long. Narrow groove is rather deep; perfect condition. High polish in groove and all of blade area. Edge good.   C-$175

Three-quarter groove axe, 7 in. long and 3-1/2 in. wide, with slight basal flute, from Jersey County, Illinois. Material is dark green and white in color.   G-$300

Three-quarter groove axe, Southwestern U.S., perfect condition. Has made-up (recent) handle for display, but axe head is original and fine.   A-$115

Three-quarter groove axe, 9 in. long and 5-1/2 in. wide, and nearly 4 in. thick. Overall high polish. A-$200

Axe, three-quarter groove, exactly 3 in. long and about 5/8 in. thick. Well-made piece.   C-$100

Three-quarter groove axe, Missouri, 6 in. long and 4-1/2 in. wide.   G-$170

Three-quarter groove axe, about 6 in. long and about 3 in. wide, made of a dark, dense material. High polish in lower blade region.   A-$100

Three-quarter groove axe, hardstone, Missouri, 4 in. long and 3 in. wide.   G-$90

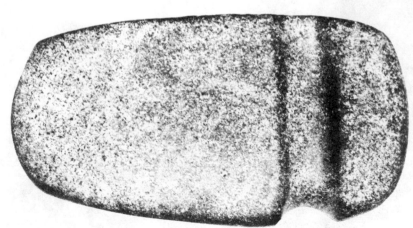

Very fine three-quarter axe, Archaic period, made of brown fine-grained stone. It is 8-1/2 in. long and 4-1/2 in. wide; weight is 7 lbs. This axe has exceptionally fine lines, and was found in Illinois.   C-$350-700

Photo courtesy John P. Grotte, Illinois

Right:

Three-fourth groove axe, 3-1/4 x 6-1/2 in. with the Keokuk groove. From Pike County, Illinois, this is a good piece, semi-polished. It was formerly in the E.W. Payne collection. C-$300

Photo courtesy Bob Brand collection, Pennsburg, Pennsylvania

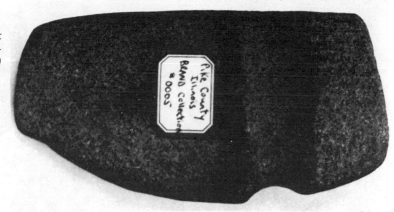

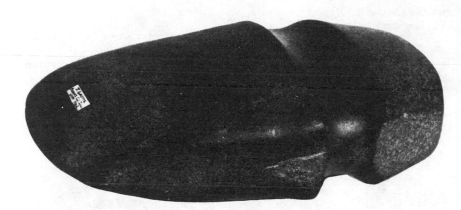

Fine three-quarter grooved axe, of a granite-like fine grained brown stone. Axe is 8-1/2 in. long, and 4-1/2 in. wide and 2-5/8 in. thick. It weighs 6 pounds and was found in Adams County, Illinois; this axe is very finely made. C-$500-800

Photo courtesy John P. Grotte, Illinois

Axe, 3/4 grooved, from Coles County, Illinois. This very fine axe is made from brown porphyry. It is 10-1/4 in. long and weighs 9 lbs. $3,500

Rodney M. Peck collection, Harrisburg, North Carolina

Archaic axe, three-quarter grooved, 7-1/2 in. long; weight is 7 lbs. This example is made of a heavy dark hardstone with medium polish. It was found during construction of Mohawk Dam in Ohio. $300-350

Larry Garvin collection, Ohio

Three-fourth groove axe, 3-1/2 x 8 in., from Pike County, Illinois. Material is a greenish-black; piece is semi polished, fine condition. C-$450

Photo courtesy Bob Brand collection, Pennsburg, Pennsylvania

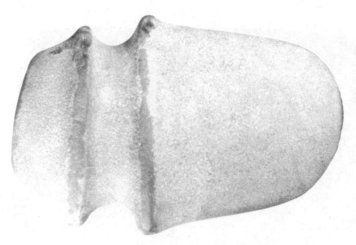

Axe, full or 4/4 grooved, Eastern raised-ridge type, from Sevier County, Tennessee. Material is a fine-grained granite. Size, 8-3/4 in. long, weight 5-3/4 lbs. $700

Rodney M. Peck collection, Harrisburg, North Carolina

Prehistoric 3/4 x 4/4 groove axes.

Back row: left to right: Illinois, 6 x 8-1/2 in.; Georgia, 4 x 9 in; axe 3-1/2 x 9 in.; Missouri, 4 x 8-1/2 in.
Bottom row: center axe from Arizona is 2-1/2 x 9 in. The two small 4/4 groove axes to either side are from the U.S. Northeast.   Each, $75-600

Philip L. Russo collection, Danbury, Connecticut

Axe, 3/4 grooved, Saline County, Missouri. Material is a fine to medium grained granite; axe is 8-3/4 in. long and weight is 7 lbs. $1,300

Rodney M. Peck collection, Harrisburg, North Carolina

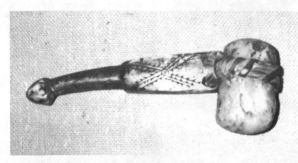

Rare complete club, jade head with carved and decorated ivory handle. The handle is about 10 in. long. This artifact was found in a cave along the Columbia River in Oregon. From an old collection, all parts of the club are original.   Museum quality

Philip L. Russo collection, Danbury, Connecticut

Axe, 3/4 groove, size 2-3/4 x 6-1/2 in. high. It is made of greenish black hardstone which is probably diorite. These are usually called Hohokam axes after the early people that used similar axe designs. This artifact was found near El Rito, New Mexico. $450

Jack Baker collection, Ozark, Missouri; David Capon photograph

Three-quarter groove axes, dark hardstone, from Wisconsin. These are solid, well-made artifacts from the Archaic period. Axes are difficult to find anymore without implement strikes which produce scratches and scars.   The two, $250-375

Robert D. Lund collection, Watertown, Wisconsin

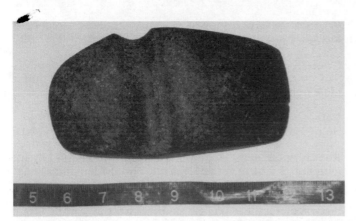

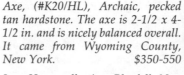

Axe, (#K20/HL), Archaic, pecked tan hardstone. The axe is 2-1/2 x 4-1/2 in. and is nicely balanced overall. It came from Wyoming County, New York. $350-550

Iron Horse collection, Blasdell, New York

Three-quarter groove axe, Late Archaic period, made of dark hardstone. It measures 3-1/2 x 6 in., has a ridged groove and crisp, clean lines. This is an excellent axe with good polish and was located by S. Umscheid along Salt Creek. Leavenworth County, Kansas. $600-1,000

Collection of Daniel Fox; photo by Caroline Fox, Manhattan, Kansas

Axe, (#HL), Archaic period, polished mottled hardstone. This axe measures 3 x 4 in. and has a contracting poll area above the polished groove. It was found in Tioga County, New York. $450-600

Iron Horse collection, Blasdell, New York

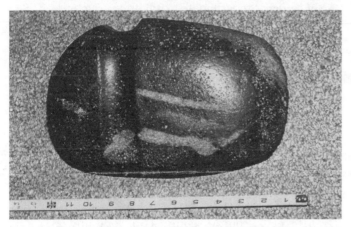

Three-quarter grooved axe, 7 x 11 in. and with weight of 15 1/8 pounds. This is a beautiful, top-of-the-line piece made of dark hardstone with quartz inclusions. Note the classic clean lines and high polish. This superb example of prehistoric artwork (Middle to Late Archaic) was found by W. Jauer in 1937 in LaSalle County, Illinois. $3,500

Rainbow Traders, Godfrey, Illinois

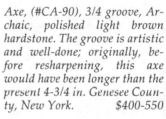

Axe, (#CA-90), 3/4 groove, Archaic, polished light brown hardstone. The groove is artistic and well-done; originally, before resharpening, this axe would have been longer than the present 4-3/4 in. Genesee County, New York. $400-550

Iron Horse collection, Blasdell, New York

Axe, Hohokam, three-quarter groove, 8 in. long and 3 in. wide. Bit is highly polished. G-$260

HALF-GROOVE AXES

Half-groove axe, 4-1/4 in. long and 2-3/4 in. wide, good groove but blade is canted off to one side, giving a lopsided appearance. Made of a close-grained sandstone-like material. C-$40

Half-groove Keokuk-type axe, rectangular outline, 3-3/4 in. long. Made of a dark compact stone; groove and blade area well polished. Crisp, clean lines on this specimen. C-$115

Half-groove axe, from Missouri, 7 in. long and 3-1/4 in. wide, well-shaped and polish over entire surface. Edges, front, and rear undamaged. No damage, fine specimen. C-$400

Half-groove axe, unremarkable, 4 in. long and 2-3/4 in. wide. Lacks polish; poll area is battered, blade average. C-$25

Southwestern axe, usually termed Hohokam by collectors, made of black diorite with weathered finish. New Mexico. $150

Larry Lantz, First Mesa, Indiana

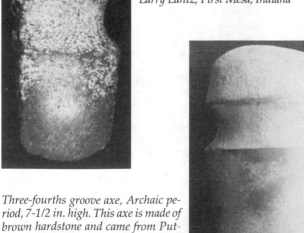

Three-fourths groove axe, Archaic period, 7-1/2 in. high. This axe is made of brown hardstone and came from Putnam County, Georgia. $450

C. H. Baggerley collection, Nicholson, Georgia

Keokuk half-groove axe, classic form, 2-3/4 x 6-1/4 in., 1-5/8 in. thick. It is made of dark brown hardstone, and the type is illustrated in Bruce Filbrandt's 1997 book, Keokuk Axes. This example was found by L. Oakleaf in the 1930s on his father's farm near Mound Valley, Labette County, Kansas. $650

Tom Fouts collection, Kansas

Half-groove Keokuk-type axe, made of a highly polished granite-like stone, black and tan color. Axe is 4-1/4 in. high. From Iowa. Blade edge forms very pleasing excurvate contour. D-$165

CELTS

(ungrooved axes)

Celt, from northern Louisiana, 7-1/4 in. long and 3-1/4 in. wide, well polished. Made of green and black material, no damage, good lines. D-$130

Celt, large, polished. From Shelby County, Illinois. Piece is 7 in. long and 3-1/4 in. wide. G-$225

Stone celt, fine gray, 5 in. long and 2-1/4 in. wide. No damage. G-$55

Celt, rectangular Hopewellian, central Ohio, 6 in. long and 2-3/4 in. wide at blade, both sides flattish. No damage. Made from a yellow and tan stone. Good lines. C-$100

Celt, miniature, 2 in. long and 1 in. wide. G-$25

Granite-like celt, fine speckled, 10 in. long and about 4 in. wide. Polished cutting edge; celt is cylindrical in shape, and even poll area is well polished. C-$135

Caddoan celt, Arkansas, dark gray stone; 5 in. long and 1-3/4 in. wide. G-$40

Hardstone celt, average form, late prehistoric, from Illinois. Piece is 5-1/2 in. long and 2-3/4 in. wide, about 2 in. thick. Several minor plow scars, otherwise good condition. D-$35

Granite celt, squared-base type, 5-7/8 in. long and 2-3/4 in. wide. Good polish in lower blade area; two minor plow marks that disfigure blade side. C-$22

Celt, from Virginia, 5-1/4 in. long and 2-1/4 in. wide. Stone is a light gray color. G-$19

Rectangular celt, Hopewellian, from Illinois, 9-1/4 in. long and 3-3/4 in. wide near bit, and evidencing almost perfect balance. All lines pleasing; entire surface area polished to a uniform medium-high gloss. No damage; piece looks as if it has never been used. Granitic stone approaches coal-black. C-$550

Greenstone celt, dark, outstanding polish, good condition. It is 4-1/4 in. long and 2-1/4 in. wide. G-$80

Celt, miniature, 1-3/8 in. long, from Iowa, found during tilling of garden. Proportionate to full-size specimens. C-$40

Celt, 2-1/4 in. long, slightly flared blade corners, found in Missouri. Black and white hardstone. C-$85

Flare-bit celt, fine polished miniature from Oklahoma, 2-1/2 in. long and 1-1/2 in. wide. G-$45

Celt, dark green, from eastern Texas, polished bit, 5 in. long and 2-1/4 in. wide. G-$45

Slate celt, banded, 6-3/4 in. long, from Illinois, and exactly 3 in. at greatest width. Cylindrical form, black bands on green background. One agricultural equipment mark toward top of rounded poll, not deep. C-$60

Granite celt, from Missouri, 4 in. long and 2-1/4 in. wide, rectangular form. High polish overall, and speckled black and white material. No damage; perfect proportions. C-$75

Celtiform tools, all from Canada, and averaging 5 in. in length. Piece in center may be unfinished; all in fine condition. C-$10-40 each

Photo courtesy Robert C. Calvert, London, Ontario, Canada

Adz blades, all late prehistoric, Adena culture, Midwestern.

Top: Lower portion of larger Adena adz, salvaged in rear section, 3-1/4 in. long, colorful material. C-$20
Left: Black Adena adz, edge shows heavy wear, good form. C-$30
Center: Small brown stone Adena adz, exactly to scale of much larger specimens, 3-1/4 in. long. C-$25
Right: Adena adz blade, almost identical to black specimen at left; edge is sharp. C-$30

Private collection

Three fine Midwestern celts. L to R:

Fine late prehistoric Hopewellian celt, nicely tapered. Polish on lower blade, 5-3/8 in. long.　　　　　　　　　　　　C-$65

Slender tapered celt, probably late prehistoric, made of a brownish quartz. Unusual material and good lines to piece.　　　C-$95

Large Hopewellian celt, nearly round at center, heavily polished over entire surface. Brown material, black inclusions, granite-like stone.　　　　　　　　　　　C-$115

Private collection

Small selection of late prehistoric artifacts, bottom left, longest 3-1/2 in.

Top row, L to R.

Small celt　　　　　　　　　　C-$15

Rectangular Hopewellian celt, perfect form and highly polished overall.　　C-$40

Slate celt, probably Adena, good edge and well-rounded.　　　　　　　　　　C-$20

Celt or chisel, well-polished overall, two small damaged areas appear as light-colored spots.
C-$15

Chisel, well-tapered but no polish. May be fragment from larger specimen.　　C-$10

Private collection

Unusual 3/4 grooved axe, from Franklin County, Ohio, and 6-7/8 in. long and 3-5/8 in. wide. Made of grayish quartzite material. Axe has narrow ridge running from front of groove to lower blade, then up rear portion to flatish area behind groove. Also, blade size is small for axe of this size.　　　　　　　　　　C-$300

Private collection

Fine 3/4 grooved axe, 7-1/2 in. long and 3-1/4 in. wide below notch. Very good condition, some polish, Franklin County, Ohio. Archaic period; axe is made of a compact brownish material.　　C-$325

Private collection

Chipped flint artifacts with polished blade areas. L to R:

Flint celt about 5 in. long, blade region highly polished.　　　　　　　　　　C-$50

Flint celt or chisel, lower blade region nicely polished, good edge.　　　　　C-$20

Flint chisel, highly polished blade area, small working edge.　　　　　　　　C-$35

Private collection

Celtiform tools, hardstone and slate, 4-1/2 in. to 6 in. long. All from Canada, and evidencing varied degrees of workstyle and condition.　　　　　　　C-$5-40 each

Photo courtesy Robert C. Calvert, London, Ontario, Canada

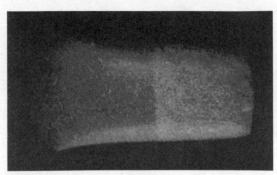

Flared-bit celt, Mississippian period, 6-1/2 in. high. Material is a fine close-grained green and black hardstone and hafting area is denoted by change in polish and color. The celt was found near Piasa Creek, Jersey County, Illinois. $550

Rainbow Traders, Godfrey, Illinois

From left to right:

Celts and gouges, average-good condition, made of slate and hardstone. All from Canada. C-$5-30 each

Large celts, possibly Woodland period, one 10 in. long, the other 8-3/4 in. Blade lengths are 2-1/2 in. both from Canada.

Left (longest): C-$30
Right: C-$30

Photo courtesy Robert C. Calvert, London, Ontario, Canada

Celt or ungrooved axehead, pink rose quartzite, bullseye pattern, 1-3/4 x 3-5/8 in. This material is rare for a celt but was sometimes used for top-of-the-line bannerstones. The celt was found by the owner in June of 1997. Louisiana. $500

Richard F. Hughes collection, Louisiana

Celt, Woodland period, 7 in. long. This is a well-made example in greenish-brown hardstone, from southern Indiana. $165

Blue Coyote Trading Post, Nashville, Indiana; Pat Nolan photograph

Celt, Woodland period, 9 in. long. Probably a Hopewell piece with the rectangular outline, it is made of dark hardstone and was found in southern Indiana. $225

Blue Coyote Trading Post, Nashville, Indiana; Pat Nolan photograph

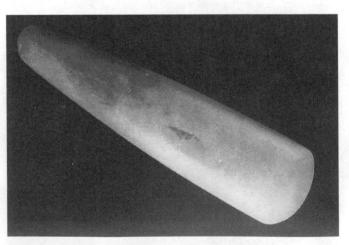

Celt, tapered poll type, 11-3/4 in. long. This Mississippian ungrooved axe is exceptionally large and fine, and is made of greenstone. Bartow County, Georgia. $1,200

C. H. Baggerley collection, Nicholson, Georgia

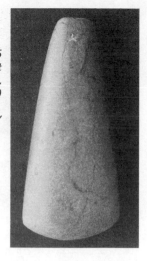

Celt, probably Woodland period, 4-3/5 in. long. This is an above-average celt in greenstone, from Early County, Georgia. $250

C.H. Baggerley collection, Nicholson, Georgia

Pointed-poll celt, Mississippian period, 2 in. long. It is made of black hardstone and was found in Bartow County, Georgia. $100

Bruce Butts collection, Winterville, Georgia

Celt, tapered-poll, probably Mississippian in origin. It measures 5-1/10 in. long and is nicely polished. Made of greenstone, the celt is from Jackson County, Georgia. $450

C.H. Baggerley collection, Nicholson, Georgia

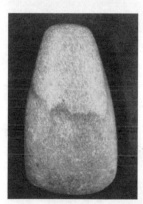

Celt, Woodland or Mississippian period, 4-1/2 in. high. It is made of greenstone and is well-polished. Georgia. $150

Bruce Butts collection, Winterville, Georgia

Celt, Dallas phase, Mississippian period, 7-1/2 in. long. It is made of polished greenstone and is very thin, with a sharp bit. Tishomingo County, Mississippi. *Museum quality*

Bruce Butts collection, Winterville, Georgia

AXE VARIETIES

Celt, lightly-grooved, Indiana, with the tapering characteristics of the celt and very light axe-like full grooving. Piece is about 6 in. long, and groove was pecked in at no great depth. Celt head is lightly polished overall except for groove.　　　　　　　　　　　　　　D-$80

Barbed axe, Porphyry, Michigan, 7 1/4 in. long and 3-3/4 in. wide, very colorful material. Outstanding specimen that has been pictured in archaeological publications.　　　　　　　　　　　　　　　G-$1,000

Flared-bit celt or spatulate form, nearly 6 in. long and 2-1/2 in. wide at blade-edge tips. Well-contoured and made of a dark, compact material.　　　　　D-$135

Stone monolithic axe, black, 15-3/4 in. long, and 6-1/4 in. high at celtiform head height. Copy is one-piece stone of complete celt-axe with handle. Piece has exceptional polish overall. Very rare; probably no more than a few hundred complete specimens exist. Late prehistoric. (Private collection)　　　　　　　　　　C-$4,500

Flare-bit celt, fine condition, polish on blade. Piece is 7-1/2 in. long and 3-1/4 in. wide.　　　G-$115

Fluted axe, from Wisconsin, three-quarter groove, 6-1/2 in. long, with fluting running parallel to groove and lower blade regions. Fluting is very shallow but regular.　C-$450

Notched celt, from Indiana, 3-1/2 in. long, with pecked notches on side edges. Faces polished; interesting specimen and not common.　　　　　　　　　C-$85

Hardstone spud-type celt, from Missouri, 13 in. long and 3-1/4 in. across at blade corners, with extended

Southern long-poll celts, Mississippian period, all nicely tapered. They range in length from 11 to 13 in. and materials are greenstone and light-colored hardstone. All exhibit exceptional workmanship and have a high degree of polish. *Each, $700-1000*

Bruce Butts collection, Winterville, Georgia

Unusual duo-blade celt, from collection in New Jersey. Material is light green, very compact, almost resembling soapstone. Both edges fine condition, overall polish. Piece is 6-1/4 in. long and about 3-1/2 in. wide.   D-$55

Private collection

Axe, 4/4 grooved, Eastern raised-ridge type or Southern trophy type. From Granville County, North Carolina, material is a quartz diorite. It is 10 in. long and weighs 9 lbs. This is a rare, museum-quality axe. $3,000

Rodney M. Peck collection, Harrisburg, North Carolina

blade corners, dark granite. Highly polished all over, especially in blade region. Probably ceremonial; no use marks whatsoever.   C-$1,000

Barbed-ridge axe, from Michigan, extremely fine with groove extensions at both ends, top and bottom. Material is a gray speckled granite, and piece is 8-1/2 in. long, average width for piece. Perfect condition. Axe poll is almost pointed. Fine polish.   D-$795

Spud or flare-bit celt, celtiform, found in eastern Minnesota, about 8 in. long and 3-1/2 in. wide at blade corners. Each face has three shallow grooves for unknown reasons. Uncommon specimen.   D-$500

Fluted axe, from Wisconsin, three-quarter groove type, 6-1/2 in. long, with single central flute on each blade side. From this, other grooves radiate. Rounded poll also has two grooves on sides, which follow contour of the top. Unusual, interesting example of multiple fluting.   D-$995

Flare-bit celt, 11-3/4 in. long, and 4-1/8 in. across at blade edges, blade sides and edge highly polished, body of piece retains some peckmarks.   C-$525

Flare-bit celt, from Missouri, 6-1/2 in. long and 2-1/2 in. wide.   G-$80

Double-groove axe, from northern Missouri, 5-3/4 in. long and about 2-1/2 in. wide. Unusual. Lower groove a bit deeper than upper groove. Green, compact stone.   C-$170

Double-groove axe, Iowa, 6-1/2 in. long and 2-7/8 in.

wide. Black granitic stone. Distinct double groove, and lower blade is in perfect condition. Little polish.   C-$170

Long-poll celt, Lower Mississippi Valley, 6-1/4 in. long and 1-3/8 in. wide. Fine example and undamaged; unusually slender for type.   D-$125

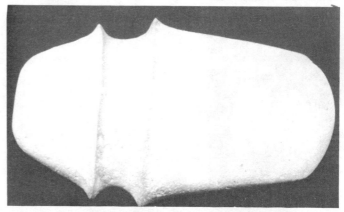

Axe, full or 4/4 grooved, Eastern raised-ridge type from Washington County, Virginia. It is made of a fine-grained granite material; size, 8-1/2 in. long, 4 lbs. in weight. $700

Rodney M. Peck collection, Harrisburg, North Carolina

Hump-backed axe or adz, 6-1/2 in. long and 2 in. wide and thick at central ridge. Blade is at wider end, and piece is in excellent condition; not a common artifact. Material is a green hardstone.   C-$150-250

Photo courtesy Robert C. Calvert. London. Ontario, Canada

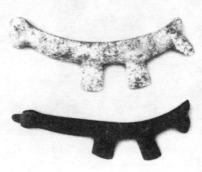

Top: "slave-killer" ceremonial axe, 15 in. long. Item was traded for at the mouth of the Columbia River in 1840 by Joseph Moore, Mate of the ship Salem Queen.
Bottom: "slave-killer" ceremonial axe, 15 in. long. This piece was found about 1833 on the Oregon coast. C-Museum quality; no value listed

S.W. Kernaghan photo; Marguerite Kernaghan collection

Half-groove axe, Iowa, 3-1/2 in. long and 3-1/4 in. wide. Well polished, fine color, perfect condition except for tiny chip from cutting edge, depression polished. C-$120

Hardstone adz, 4-7/8 in. long and 1-7/8 in. wide at curved cutting edge. Flat bottom, very minor damage to rounded end. D-$75

Three-quarter groove axe, from Arizona, 9 in. long and 3-1/4 in. wide at groove area. Good polish in groove and on lower blade. Fine overall form. D-$180

Monolithic axe, 9-1/2 in. high and 20 in. long. Mississippian period, and a ceremonial item. This specimen was found by Colonel Masion east of Tazewell, Tennessee, in the early 1900s.
C-Museum quality; no value listed

S.W. Kernaghan photo; Marguerite Kernaghan collection

Axes and celts, at center a trophy-grade axe, 10 in. long, 3/4 groove with a fine edge. Lower right is a rare pocket axe, 4/4 or full-groove. All are from the Columbia River area. Each, $25-350

Morris' Art & Artifacts, Anaheim, California; Dawn Gober photograph

"Slave-killer" axe, from Oregon coastal region, made of hard slate. The neck of the effigy was broken and has been reglued. Museum quality

Private collection

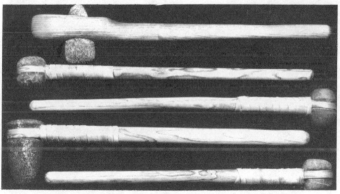

Ancient stone tools with modern museum-demonstration type handles. Shown are three grooved hammerstones and a celt (top) and grooved axehead (bottom). Hafting designs are based on extant specimens found in rock shelters or underwater; hafting done by Deer Creek Enterprises, Ohio. Each, $250-375

Larry Lantz, First Mesa, South Bend, Indiana

Full-groove axe found in Oklahoma County, Oklahoma. This interesting artifact is 11 in. long, made from light brown hardstone. $300

Larry G. Merriam collection, Oklahoma City, Oklahoma

Adena celt, Early Woodland, material a gray-green hardstone. Well polished, this artifact is from Monroe County, Ohio, and is 5-1/8 in. long.   *$145*

Private collection, Ohio

Michigan barbed axe, from Shiawassee County, Michigan. Made of porphyry, it is black and green with tan inclusions. Size is 1-5/8 x 3-3/4 x 6-3/4 in. and it has G.I.R.S. authentication number 0-6.   *$3,000*

Collection of David G. & Barbara J. Shirley

Stone artifacts.

Top: axe or hoe, brownstone, from Mississippi.
                                              $100
Bottom: graystone axe, from Michigan. $100

Wilfred A. Dick collection, Magnolia, Mississippi

Celt made of rock crystal or clear quartz, transparent, 1-9/16 x 4-1/8 in. This rare and fine piece is from Hardin County, Ohio, and probably Woodland period in origin. This example is one of a very few ever found in the Eastern Midwest.　　　　　Museum quality

Larry Garvin collection, Ohio

Celt, Woodland period, from Midland, Michigan. It is made of brownish-tan banded slate with black banding. Size, 5/8 x 2 x 6-3/8 in. Slate is an unusual celt material. A scarce artifact.　　　　　$600

Collection of David G. & Barbara J. Shirley

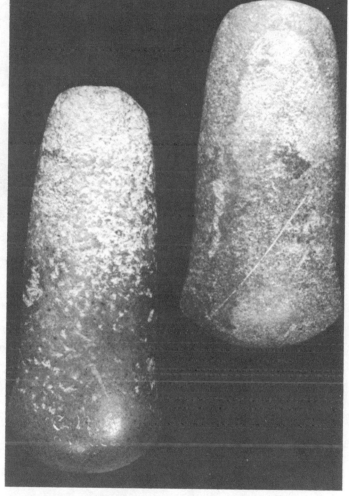

Celts, flared-bit, from Alexander County, Illinois. Material is fine to medium-grained granite

Left: 8-1/2 in. long.　　　　　$400
Right: 7-1/2 in. long.　　　　　$400

Rodney M. Peck collection, Harrisburg, North Carolina

Copper celt, Late Archaic Old Copper culture, from Barron County, Wisconsin. A personal find by the owner, it measures 19/16 x 4 in. It is in very good condition.　　　　　$325

Dennis R. Lindblad collection, Chetek, Wisconsin

Celt collection, many sizes, materials, and styles. These are from the states of Alabama, Arkansas, and Mississippi.   Each, $15-195

Wilfred A. Dick collection, Magnolia, Mississippi

Grooved axes, all Archaic period. Five are full-groove with example at top right three-quarter groove.   The group, $250-350

Robert D. Lund collection, Watertown, Wisconsin

Celts or ungrooved axes from the Woodland period, different sizes, styles and materials. Second artifact from the bottom appears to be an adz or gouge. This is a good small collection.   Collection, $150-225

Robert D. Lund collection, Watertown, Wisconsin

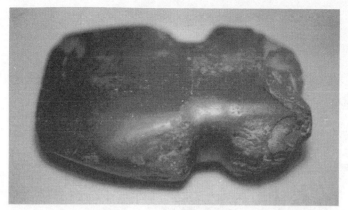

Axe, an unusual triple-notch type, polished side grooves with extra notch atop the poll. The dense, black material is probably diorite, typical of many better grooved axes in the Southwest. Notch location suggests this artifact may have been hafted for use as an adz for secondary woodworking. Size is 3-1/2 x 5-1/2 in. for the artifact, found near Rio Puerco, New Mexico. $225

Jack Baker collection, Ozark, Missouri; David Capon photograph

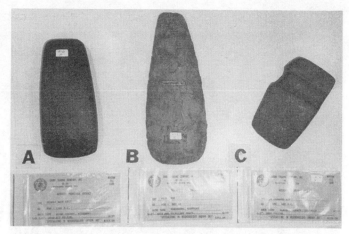

Midwestern edged tools, center example 8 in. long.

A) Square-back celt, dark hardstone, good bit polish. $145

B) Flint spade or hoe, late prehistoric period, Vanceburg area, Kentucky. $245

C) Axe, 3/4 groove, dark hardstone, well-shaped, Hancock County, Illinois. $175

Caddo Trading Company, Murfreesboro, Arkansas

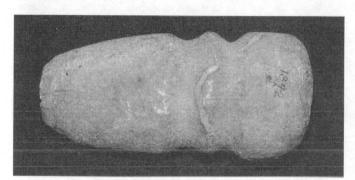

Axe, (#1842/HA-HL), pecked tan hardstone, Archaic, unusual double full-groove form. It measures 3-1/8 x 6-3/4 in. and was found in Allegany County, New York. $350-550

Iron Horse collection, Blasdell, New York

Axe, (#4234/E2188), Archaic period, pecked and polished mottled tan hardstone. It is 2-7/8 x 6 in. long and has an unusual double 3/4 groove. It was found in St. Charles County, Missouri. $500-750

Iron Horse collection, Blasdell, New York

The famous hogan, the earth-covered dwelling of the Navajo Indians. Note the woman grinding material with a mano and stone metate. Also note the Navajo blanket to the right of hogan doorway. Dwellings like these were common into the early 1900s, photo ca. 1930.

Photo courtesy of Utah State Historical Society, Collection of Smithsonian Institution

White House ruins, Canyon de Chelly National Monument, Arizona. The photograph was taken from the valley or canyon floor. Lower buildings extended higher originally, though tree-trunk ladders may have been used to reach the upper level.

Lar Hothem photo

CHAPTER V

STONE COLLECTIBLES

"Stone" here means hardstone, natural rocks commonly used in prehistoric times to make artifacts. This chapter deals with a variety of classes, among them the curious discoidals, food grinders, pulverizers, and the mundane hammerstones. There are effigies, utensils, and many others also.

For each grouping, a slightly different set of measures determine collector interest and help set fair market values. All of these artifacts are relatively simple in design, except for effigy figures.

Portrayals of human and animal figures from early times have always been premium collector items. In this all stone-collectible area, the one aspect to be examined is the "first appearance."

Assuming the article is genuine—and no listing or photograph of a known questionable piece has been put in this book—there are some questions to be considered. Is the artifact pleasing? Why? Does it bother or confuse you? Again why? Is it larger or smaller than usual for the type—and is it too large or too small for your taste? Does it, as is, give a feeling of completeness, of well-accomplished form?

Granted, this is looking at early Indian items as art—but that is what is being done these days. Again, the value range can be jolting. A plain oval pestle, little more than a natural cobble with some wear-marks, can have literally no market value. A long ceremonial-grade pestle, say from the Northwest U.S. region and evidencing supreme care in the making, can easily be in the $1,000 to $3,000 class.

There is still some diversity of opinion as to what discoidals ("discs" to collectors) are. It is agreed that they are found in the Mississippi watershed area and are late prehistoric. Numerous historic-period reports state they were rolled along the ground and were used as targets for arrows and thrown darts in a game called "Chunkey."

However, the workmanship displayed for many fine examples suggests they were more than utilitarian in nature, at least the better specimens. And there is a definite lack of damage which would have resulted from such violent use. A superb specimen sold a few years ago for $1,000, but the average disc price would be worth $100 to $200.

Plummets are still another enigma; few are listed here because they were commonly made of materials other than hardstone. Plummets are shaped like elongated eggs with a hole or groove at the smaller end. Most are meticulously made, well-proportioned, and polished.

For a long time, it was thought they were fishing or net sinkers. New thought is that they were bolas weights and were secured by short thongs in sets of three to five. In use, they were whirled and thrown to bring down waterfowl or small game.

The following information on spatulates was written by Torn Browner of Davenport, Iowa, who has contributed greatly to the prehistoric section of the book. Used with permission.

"Spatulates, commonly known as spuds, probably began around AD 500, having evolved from the Woodland culture's flare-bit celts. Like celts, many spatulates show hafting lines where they were attached to wooden handles. Spatulates continued to evolve until the end of the Mississippian period, about AD 1700.

"It is uncertain where spatulates began; however, the Mississippi River Valley north of St. Louis is an educated guess. This assumption is based on the large numbers of spuds found in the region and the fact that Cahokia seems to be the divisional point between Northern and Southern traditions.

"'The heart area' of the Northern Tradition seems to be Illinois, Missouri, Indiana, and Ohio. Northern Tradition spatulates are made of fine-grained granites and occasionally slate. The earlier types tend to have thicker bodies like celts, oval cross-sections, and rounded bits. As time progressed, the polls became thinner and more rounded. The bits became more elongated and convex. To the north, the polls became shorter; likewise, the further south, the longer the polls tend to be.

"Southern Spatulates tend to have rounded and long polls. The material of choice tends to be green-stone or slates. The bits flatten and become almost square in classic types, with tally marks or grooves being common. The Southern Tradition heartland is southern Illinois, Missouri, Kentucky, Tennessee, Georgia, and Alabama. Cahokia, near St. Louis, Missouri, seems to be the area where the two traditions met."

Unfortunately, because of space limitations, this section can only give a sampling of the rich and varied field of hardstone Indian collectibles.

SPATULATES OR SPUDS

Granite spud, 10 in. long and 1-1/4 in. wide, made of well-polished material, good overall form. This piece was broken and restored.   A-$150

Elongated spud, 13-1/4 in. long and 1-7/8 in. wide, with good material, blackish fine-grained hardstone. Beautiful form, evenly flared bit, high polish; one slight plow-scar along poll side but barely visible. Rare item in size and shape.   C-$1,700

Granite spud, 10 in. long and 2 in. wide at bit. Bit or blade area has softly rounded corners instead of sharp shoulders.   A-$95

Granite spud, 8 in. long and 3 in. wide, well polished and good form. Fine condition.   A-$360

Banded slate spud, 7-1/2 in. long and 1-3/8 in. wide, made of a finely banded green and black material. Good shape and overall polish, no damage.   C-$625

Northern tradition spatulate, 9 in. long and 3 in. wide at flared bit. This specimen is one of the finest of the type. Note the lighter hafting band 3-1/2 in. from the bit tip. Rounded bit and oblong poll show it to be from about AD 900. Material is a gray, polished granite; this piece is from Fulton County, Illinois   C-$1,500

Courtesy Ferrel Anderson, photographer; Thomas Browner collection; Davenport, Iowa

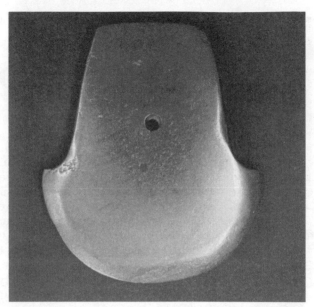

Southern spatulate, Mississippian, 4-1/2 x 5-3/8 in. It is made of highly polished greenstone and was found in northeastern Alabama.   *Museum quality*

Bruce Butts collection, Winterville, Georgia

Late southern-type spatulate or spud form, 5-3/4 x 5-1/8 in. A large specimen of a rare type, it lacks the drilled hole common in many pieces. Exfoliation of the surface and large size identify this as authentic. There are generally no genuine artifacts of this type on the market. Specimen is made of red and tan limonite, and is from Woodruff County, Arkansas.   C-$200-500

Courtesy Ferrel Anderson, photographer; Thomas Browner collection; Davenport, Iowa

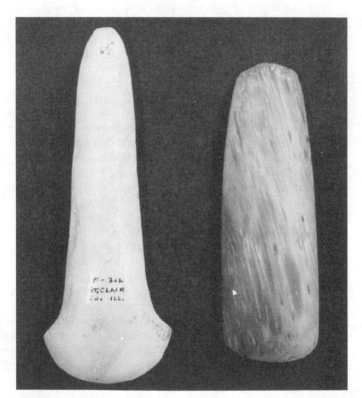

Mississippian period edged artifacts:

Left: spud, 6-3/4 in. long, polished white flint, St. Clair County, Illinois. $1,000
Right: celt, 5-3/4 in., petrified palm wood, Tishomingo County, Mississippi. $500

Bruce Butts collection, Winterville, Georgia

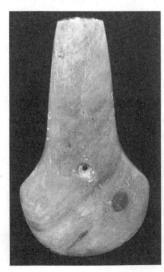

Spud, Mississippian culture, this example 5-1/2 in. wide and 10 in. high. It is nicely made from green banded slate and is in fine condition. Probably southeastern U.S. $1,000

Richard F. Hughes collection, Louisiana

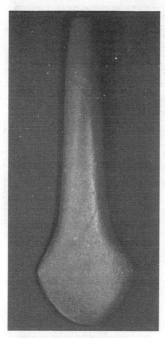

Squared-poll spud, polished hardstone, Mississippian period. This fine artifact is made of black hardstone and measures 12-3/4 in. long. Ex-collections Waters, Johns, B.W. Stevens and DeLime, it is from Trigg County, Kentucky. Museum quality

Bruce Butts collection, Winterville, Georgia

DISCOIDALS

Double-cupped discoidal, 3-1/4 in. wide and 1-3/8 in. high, light tan granitic material and overall high polish. Midwestern piece. C-$185

Discoidal, Tennessee, uncupped and of a black material. It is 2-1/4 in. in diameter and 1-1/4 in. high. G-$120

Double-cup late Woodland discoidal, 2-3/4 in. in diameter. This specimen is notable for its deep cups, perfect symmetry, and polish; even the cups are polished, which is unusual for most discoidals. The piece is from Des Moines County, Iowa, and is made of rhyolite. C-$475

Courtesy Ferrel Anderson, photographer; Thomas Browner collection; Davenport, Iowa

Double-cup Woodland discoidal, 4-1/4 in. in diameter and 2 in. thick. Made of black granite, this is an Ohio piece. The specimen has good size, shape and deep cups. It also lacks color and sharply delineated cup rims; not quite unique enough to command the top discoidal prices of $400-500. Perfect condition. C-$400

Courtesy Ferrel Anderson, photographer; Thomas Brewer collection; Davenport, Iowa

Cahokia type discoidal, 3 in. in diameter. This is a classic Cahokia discoidal with deep cups and prominent rims. This piece is made of gray granite and is from Pike County, Illinois. C-$500

Courtesy Ferrel Anderson, photographer; Thomas Browner collection; Davenport, Iowa

Quartz discoidal, pink and black, 3-1/2 in. in diameter and 1-1/2 in. high, slightly cupped each side. Piece is from Illinois. G-$260

Miniature discoidal, 1-1/4 in. in diameter and 3/8 in. thick, very shallowly cupped, medium-good polish. Rare. C-$80

Quartz discoidal, cups on each side (double or duo-cupped), and has a golden color. Piece is 2-1/4 in. in diameter and 3/4 in. thick. G-$200

Hardstone discoidal, made of a light-colored close-grained stone. Cupped on both sides, perfectly round, smooth finish. A bit over 4 in. in diameter, and 1-3/8 in. thick at outer rim. Hole at center where the bottom of cups meet. C-$595

Hardstone discoidal, pink with deep cups, 2-1/4 in. in diameter and 1-1/4 in. thick. G-$330

Quartz discoidal, duo-cupped, nearly 6 in. in diameter and 2-1/8 in. thick. Polished to a high gloss overall, no damage or imperfection in stone. Piece glitters with quartzite inclusion when strong light strikes it; very pleasing piece. C-$1,550

Discoidal of pottery, only 1-1/2 in. in diameter, and with decorations of incised lines scratched into surface. C-$13

Discoidal from Tennessee, double-dish (duo-cupped) form, perfectly scooped and "dimple" in center of cup on each side. Piece is 3-3/4 in. in diameter, made from fine orange-red stone. C-$550

Double-cupped discoidal, Indiana, 2-7/8 in. in diameter and 1-1/4 in. thick. D-$135

Biscuit-type discoidal, 2-1/8 in. in diameter, made of black and reddish hardstone. Perfect and polished. C-$140

Quartzite double-cupped discoidal, 2-1/2 in. in diameter and of a dark green steatite. Outside rim has a single meandering line incised around it. C-$200

Sandstone discoidal, battered around outside rim, 2-1/4 in. in diameter. C-$30

Stone discoidal, Jersey Bluff type (has somewhat flattened portion around both outside rims) and made of an attractive yellow, green, black, and pink granite. Discoidal was found in Adams County, Illinois, and is 3-3/4 in. in diameter, 2-1/4 in. high. It displays exceptionally fine workmanship. C-$950

Photo courtesy John P. Grotte, Illinois

Discoidal, Jersey Bluff or Cahokia type, found in Humphrey County, Tennessee. It is 2-3/8 in. in diameter and 1-1/4 in. high. From Mississippian times, it is made of a colorful reddish purple and gray quartz. C-$500

Photo courtesy John P. Grotte, Illinois

Tan and brown striped discoidal, Jersey Bluff or Cahokia type. It is 3-1/2 in. in diameter and 2 in. high, and from Mississippian times.   C-$295

Cahokia-type white quartz discoidal, with outer rim nearly joining central cups on both sides. Found in Madison County, Illinois, this would be a Mississippian period artifact. It is 2-5/8 in. in diameter, and 1-1/4 in. high.   C-$625

Photo courtesy John P. Grotte, Illinois

Jersey Bluff type discoidal, 2-5/8 in. in diameter and 1-1/2 in. high. Made of a dark green material, from Adams County, Illinois, and highly polished. Probably from Mississippian period.   C-$260

Photo courtesy John P. Grotte, Illinois

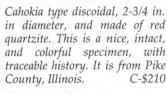

Biscuit-type discoidal, 3-1/4 in. in diameter. Material is a brown and tan claystone. The piece is from Menard County, Illinois, very colorful, and nicely polished.   C-$350

Courtesy Ferrel Anderson, photographer; Thomas Browner collection; Davenport, Iowa

Cahokia type discoidal, 2-3/4 in. in diameter, and made of red quartzite. This is a nice, intact, and colorful specimen, with traceable history. It is from Pike County, Illinois.   C-$210

Courtesy Ferrel Anderson, photographer; Thomas Browner collection; Davenport, Iowa

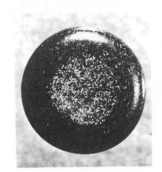

Biscuit-type discoidal, 2-7/8 in. in diameter and made of black diorite. The specimen shows high polish, center pecking, and very shallow cupping; it was found on an early Woodland site on the bluffs near Quincy, Illinois.   C-$425

Courtesy Ferrel Anderson, photographer; Thomas Browner collection; Davenport, Iowa

Discoidals or gamestones, Mississippian period. Top row, left to right:

Sandstone, not well-made, Mississippi. $20
Pottery, cupped both sides, Arkansas. $35
Sandstone, smooth, well-made, Arkansas. $55
Sandstone, rough and thick, Mississippi. $20
Sandstone, smoothed, Arkansas. $35
Center, fine double-cupped disc, nicely shaped and worked, Mississippi. $350
Miniature beside coin, Northwest U.S., Snake River area $80

Wilfred A. Dick collection, Magnolia, Mississippi

Discoidal, perforated with 1/4 in. hole, Mississippian period. It is made of cannel coal and is from Trigg County, Kentucky. $325

Marguerite L. Kernaghan collection; photograph by Marguerite L. and Stewart W. Kernaghan, Bellvue, Colorado

Discoidal, Mississippian period, made of cannel coal. It was found in Trigg County, Kentucky, and is 2-1/2 in. in diameter. $225

Marguerite L. Kernaghan collection; photograph by Marguerite L. and Steward W. Kernaghan, Bellvue, Colorado

Stone artifacts, all from Mississippi.

Top: sandstone discoidal. $25
Center left: polisher(?), mano(?). $25
Center: brownstone discoidal. $85
Center: right, pestle. $10
Bottom: well-shaped mano/pestle. $35

Wilfred A. Dick collection, Magnolia, Mississippi

Salt river type discoidal, 4-1/2 in. in diameter and 2-1/4 in. thick. A large and colorful specimen. Salt River discoidals vary from other types in that the circumference is not oval, but comes to a fine edge like a "V." They are found in the Mississippi River area above St. Louis, Missouri. This piece is made of red quartzite and came from the LaSalle-Peru area of Illinois. C-$750

Courtesy Ferrel Anderson, photographer; Thomas Browner collection; Davenport, Iowa

Double-cup discoidal, sometimes called a "dimple" cup, from the Mississippian era. The disc is 4-3/4 in. in diameter and is a classic piece. Note the well-defined edges and dimple. Large size, polish, and symmetry make this an outstanding artifact. Made of brown granite, this comes from Ohio County, Kentucky. C-$675

Courtesy Ferrel Anderson, photographer; Thomas Browner collection; Davenport, Iowa

Discoidal, Mississippian period, dark gray granite-like hardstone, 1-7/8 in. thick and 3-1/2 in. in diameter. This was found along Pumpkin Creek in Labette County, Kansas. $250

Tom Fouts collection, Kansas

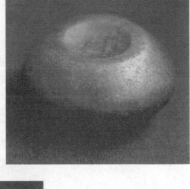

Discoidal, Salt River type, Mississippian period, 3-3/8 in. in diameter. The material is reddish quartzite and it came from St. Genevieve County, Missouri. $800

Bruce Butts collection, Winterville, Georgia

Discoidal, Mississippian, Tennessee type, 5-1/4 in. in diameter. This is an exceptional discoidal, made of honey-colored translucent quartzite. Carroll County, Georgia.
Museum quality

Bruce Butts collection, Winterville, Georgia

Discoidal, Tennessee type, Mississippian period, 5-1/8 in. in diameter. This is one of Georgia's finest of type in white translucent quartzite. It is from Greene County, Georgia. Museum quality

Bruce Butts collection, Winterville, Georgia

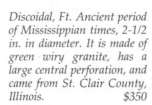

Circle roller discoidal, miniature, Mississippian period, 1-1/2 in. in diameter. It is made of white quartzite and is polished. Georgia. $150

Bruce Butts collection, Winterville, Georgia

Discoidal, Ft. Ancient period of Mississippian times, 2-1/2 in. in diameter. It is made of green wiry granite, has a large central perforation, and came from St. Clair County, Illinois. $350

Bruce Butts collection, Winterville, Georgia

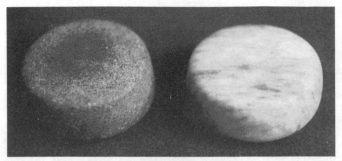

Circle roller discoidals, Mississippian period. These were designed to roll in circles so as to go into different pockets at the end of the rolling alley or Chunkey court.

Left: 3-1/2 in. in diameter, green wiry hardstone, Georgia. $400
Right: 3-1/4 in. across, mottled gray hardstone, Georgia.
Museum quality

Bruce Butts collection, Winterville, Georgia

Discoidals, Mississippian period, various localities, all left to right:

Dark red stone, 2-3/5 in. diameter, double-dished, Butler County, Ohio. $250
Pink with black spots, 2-9/10 in. diameter, double-dished, Pike County, Illinois. $250
Brown hardstone, 2-9/10 in. diameter, Schuyler County, Illinois. $250
Tan biscuit style, 3-1/2 in. diameter, western New York state. $200
Biscuit style, 3-3/4 in. diameter, dark brown, Carroll County, Missouri. $190

Native American Artifacts, Victor, New York

Barrel-type discoidal, 2-3/4 in. in diameter and 2-1/8 in. thick. Average good condition; not much polish. D-$45

MORTARS & PESTLES
(Eastern U.S.)

MANOS & METATES
(Western U.S.)

Boulder mortar, round, from California beach site. It is 9 in. across, and the pounding hole in center is about 4-1/2 in. across. Exterior surface of mortar is fairly smooth. C-$40

Pear-shaped pestle, probably Archaic, 3 in. high, found in Alabama. Made of a dull-colored hardstone. C-$20

Mano or hand-held corn-grinding stone from Missouri, 2 in. high and 3 in. wide. G-$13

Bell-type pestle, 6-1/2 in. high and 3-5/8 in. wide at basal diameter. Top expands slightly while central section is about 2 in. in diameter. Piece is made of a yellow-tan material and there is high polish on the central shaft. C-$150

Stone pestle, Oregon, 8 in. high. Cylindrical form, and tapering from top to base. Base has an extended band 2

Mortars or seed-grinding containers, stone, from the Northeastern U.S. Fine examples such as these are not common. Each, $50-250

Philip L. Russo collection, Danbury, Connecticut

in. high; top has similar but smaller band. Central portion of cylinder forms a handgrip. C-$155

Roller-type pestle, Vermont, 11-1/2 in. long and about 2 in. diameter. Some polish around circumference, and polished at both ends, rounded in same areas. C-$90

Stone mortar, from North Carolina, oblong and about 10 in. long. Top depression for holding seeds averages 3/4 in. in depth. Center shows extensive wear. C-$30

Pole-shaped mano, New Mexico, 9-1/2 in. long. Chip on one end, otherwise fine condition. G-$40

Mortar and pestle, round, latter over 14 in. in diameter and 7-3/4 in. high. Pestle about 10 in. high. (May not have been an original set, but looks like they belong together.) Central California origin. C-$140

Mortar and pestle, mortar height 14 in. and diameter 16 in.; the pestle is 16 in. long and 4 in. in diameter. From the Columbia River area, the artifacts are ex-museum and ca. AD 1600-1800. $425

Morris' Art & Artifacts, Anaheim, California; Dawn Gober photograph

Pestles or seed-grinders, many different materials; all left to right:

Top: ex-Parks collection.	$30
Well-shaped bell type, Ohio.	$50
Small bell type, Ohio.	$25
Bell type with groove, Michigan.	$95
Bell type, Kentucky.	$25
Center: brownstone, Mississippi.	$10
Brownstone, Alabama.	$20
Brownstone, Mississippi.	$20
Hematite, iron ore, Mississippi.	$50
Hematite, from Mississippi.	$50
Bottom: roller type, Ohio.	$50

Wilfred A. Dick collection, Magnolia, Mississippi

Metate or grinding slab for the mano; seed-grinder is 19 in. long, large for the type. Made from a loose-grained stone, upper working surface ground down from long use. Northwestern Nevada.   C-$80

Stone metate, flat, from Texas near Mexican border, about 7 in. long. Grinding stone has three protrusions on bottom in triangular pattern, like short legs.   C-$75

Mano or hand-stone for grinding grain or seeds, oblong, 7 in. in length. Underside flat; may have been used with both hands. Probably prehistoric Hohokam, Arizona, and made from a slate-gray porous volcanic rock. C-$25

Paint mortar, bird-faced, Oregon, perhaps depicting a hawk. Piece is 7 in. high, 4 in. in diameter, and in battered but good condition. Made from a rough-grained river boulder. Effigy has indented eyes, projecting beak.   C-$500

Stone pestle, decorative and cylindrical, probably Yurok, and 16-1/2 in. long. Piece is 3-1/4 in. in diameter at base. Extended ring near bottom and near top. Fine and highly polished stone.   C-$675

WOODWORKING TOOLS

Stone gouge, grooved, New York, 8-1/4 in. long and 2-1/8 in. wide at rounded cutting bit. Groove on underside runs from bit to poll end. (Such length is unusual, as many are only partially grooved.) Light tan stone, high polish.   D-$325

Hardstone chisel, black, 4-3/8 in. long, and 1 in. wide, tapered to straight blade at one end, rounded at other. No damage, some heavy use-marks on bit or blade edge.   C-$90

Mano (hand stone) and metate (grinding platform) set, with metate measuring 12 in. wide and 25 in. long. It is 4 in. thick and weighs 83 lbs. The two were found near San Jose, New Mexico.   Set, $150

Jack Baker collection, Ozark, Missouri; David Capon photograph

Mano (hand stone) and metate (grinding platform) set, with metate 12 x 18 in. and 2 in. thick, 33 pounds weight. The metate is made of tan hardstone and came from near El Rito, New Mexico.   Set, $100

Jack Baker collection, Ozark, Missouri; David Capon photograph

Three-quarter groove adz, from Georgia near Florida line; 9 in. long. Well-finished overall, some use-marks; this is not a particularly common type of artifact.   C-$225

Hardstone gouge, New Jersey, 6-1/8 in. long, deeply scooped concave groove on underside running half the length of piece. It is 1-1/2 in. wide at the cutting edge. D-$90

Hump-backed adz, from Indiana, 6-3/4 in. long, with protruding ridge on topside, evidently to aid hafting. Believed to be a woodworking tool. Made of a gray-black material, and piece is about 2 in. wide. Nice polish, no damage. C-$495

OTHER STONE ARTIFACTS

Sandstone shaft smoother, from South Dakota, 4 in. long. The flat stone has a straight groove along the top, about 1/2 in. across and 3/8 in. deep. C-$35

Stone adz handle, from southwestern Washington, 11-3/4 in. long with a down-curved handle grip. Unusual, but without the once-attached adz head. Well-made piece; well worn. C-$225

Hardstone bowl, rare piece from northern Alabama, 9-5/16 in. in diameter, nearly 3 in. high. Polished inside and out. Pink, close-grained stone, but not Catlinite. Probably a ceremonial item; possibly Mississippian period in origin. C-$695

"Donut stone," California, 3-1/2 in. in diameter, and with central hole 1 in. across. Made of a compact hardstone, no damage, highly polished piece. May have been a clubhead. C-$175

Food pulverizer, historic Sioux, stone head 4 in. high, flat bottom, used for tenderizing meat, crushing seeds and making pemmican. An all-purpose tool, with plain wrap-around leather covered handle 14 in. long. D-$150

Stone bowl, from Oregon, 2-1/4 in. high, about 5 in. in diameter, of smooth brown stone. Edges chipped in a number of places. A-$75

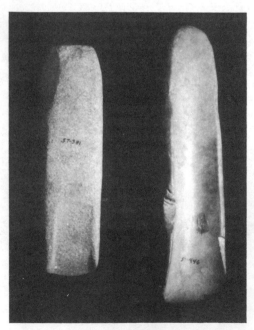

Gouges, hardstone, both from the New England area. Left example is concave for several inches while the right example is concave nearly full-length.
Each, $195

Rodney M. Peck collection, Harrisburg, North Carolina

Adena (Early Woodland period) adz-blade, black tool-grade hematite, from Belmont County, Ohio. It is 1-3/4 in. long and very highly polished overall. Nice piece. $35

Private collection, Ohio

Sandstone spool, very late prehistoric (Mississippian), and from Ohio. Piece is 3-1/8 in. long, and has incised wavy lines on central part of cylinder, which is concave. It is thought that sandstone spools were used with pigment to ceremonially decorate the body. C-$950

Rock crystal pebble pendant or bead, smoothed almost flat on one side, left naturally rounded on the other. Hole had been drilled in one end, but had broken through. Very small hole 1/16 in. had been drilled in opposite end. Period unknown; picked up on Midwestern site that has produced Archaic and Woodland artifacts. C-$45

Sandstone awl-sharpener, 3 in. long, with several thin grooves on upper surface. Believed to be "needle tracks." C-$15

Ceremonial club, from British Columbia, Canada. Piece is 16 in. long, and with human head at base of handle. Blade has a blunt cutting edge; weight is just over 4 pounds, and made of a compact dark gray stone. C-$1,100

Hardstone pendant, 2-3/4 in. long and 1-3/8 in. wide, made of a fine-grained salt and pepper colored hardstone. Surface hole drilled in smaller end, from both sides. Surface is highly polished. Perfect condition, from Illinois. C-$625

Plain stone club, of the "fish-killer" type, miniature form, only 7-1/2 in. long and 7/8 in. in diameter. Quite unusual; has small hole drilled in handle end. C-$450

Steatite or soapstone bowl, 12 x 16 in. and about 5 in. deep. Exterior walls about 1-1/2 in. thick. Recovered from central California, and in undamaged condition except for extreme wear on upper edges. A rare item. C-$825

Cupstone, about 12 in. long and 4 in. wide, with two depressions in top about the size of a silver dollar. Common on Archaic sites in Midwest, purpose uncertain. C-$12

Plummet, from Archaic site, 2-3/4 in. long and 1 in. in diameter. Made of pink sandstone, top grooved. Perfect. C-$30

Plummet, granite, 1-1/2 in. long and 5/8 in. in diameter. Very shallow groove about in middle. C-$35

Drilled stone tube, 3-7/8 in. long, flat on bottom, highly polished surface. Piece has a central hole and is about 1/2 in. in diameter. Stone mottled green and white, one small scratch across top. C-$185

Faceted or beveled-face adz, Archaic period, from Muskingum County, Ohio. Material is a blue-gray hardstone, possibly diorite. Size is 1-3/4 x 4-5/8 in. $145

Private collection, Ohio

Notched celt, probably Woodland period, with material a fine-grained gray hardstone. This piece is from Mercer County, Pennsylvania and is 4-7/8 in. long. Notched celts are scarce wherever found. $70

Private collection, Ohio

Stone turtle effigy paint bowl, contemporary, made of gray hardstone. From Minnesota, the bowl is 3-1/8 in. long. $250

Michael F. Slasinski, Saginaw, Michigan

Stone book effigy, found in Saginaw, Michigan, in 1930. Made of close-grained gray hardstone, it dates from the 1700s. Size, 7/8 x 1-9/16 x 2-5/8 in. $150

Michael F. Slasinski, Saginaw, Michigan

Hardstone tools, all from Wisconsin. Types include cupstones or miniature mortars and pestles or mauls.   *The group, $150-275*

Robert D. Lund collection, Watertown, Wisconsin

Sandstone scooped bowl, Massachusetts, 9 in. in diameter and about 3 in. high. Rounded base, and vessel is rather roughly made, time period unknown; much damage to rim area.   C-$100

Hammerstone, ungrooved, 3-1/2 in. high, well-polished overall. Both ends evidence some battering. This was a tool used to make other tools.   C-$5

Fully grooved hardstone maul or club head, 4-1/2 in. high and over 2 in. thick. Groove about 1/4 in. deep; this could be considered a heavy-duty hammer-stone. D-$50

Three-quarter groove hammerstone, from Pennsylvania, 1-3/4 in. high and 1-1/4 in. wide. Well-polished, perfect condition. Groove area has very smooth finish.   C-$40

Kneeling figure, sandstone, undoubtedly Mississippian, from Georgia. An old excavated find, it depicts a clothed woman; figure is 15-1/2 in. high, and weight is over 15 pounds. Well-detailed, especially face (private collection).   Museum quality

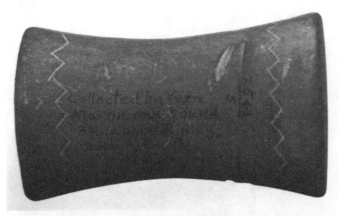

Spool made of tan sandstone, from Brown County, Ohio. It is 1-1/8 x 2-1/8 x 37/16 in. and is well-shaped, with incised zigzags. It was assigned G.I.R.S. authentication number C89-33.   *$1,250*

Collection of David G. & Barbara J. Shirley

Pelican-stone charm, effigy figure, California. It somewhat resembles the neck, head, and beak of that bird. Piece is 4-7/8 in. high with extended base.   C-$600

Hardstone drilled object, purpose unknown, 2-1/2 in. high and 1-1/2 in. wide at flattish base. Smaller, rounded top was drilled from both ends and shows much wear. Unpolished.   C-$95

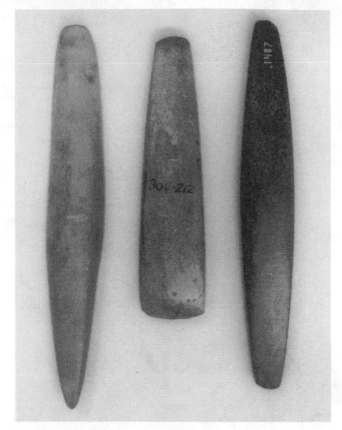

Mississippian ground and polished stone tools, left to right:

Pick, 5 in. long, greenstone, Tennessee.	*$100*
Double-bit chisel, 3-3/4 in., greenstone, Tennessee.	*$60*
Double-bit chisel, 5-1/4 in., green slate, Pennsylvania.	*$60*

Bruce Butts collection, Winterville, Georgia

Knobbed gouge, Archaic period, 1-3/4 x 7-5/8 in. long. This scooped-face gouge is an unusual type found in the Northeast. Made of green hardstone, it came from near Delaware Water Gap, Pennsylvania.   *$900*

Scott Young, Port St. Lucie, Florida

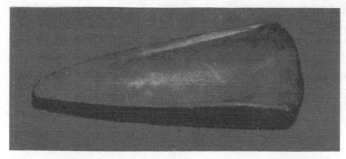

Gouge, (#AK-41), Archaic, green slate, fully grooved from blade edge to poll tip. The gouge measures 1-3/8 x 4 in. and was found near Savannah, Wayne County, New York. $350-550

Iron Horse collection, Blasdell, New York

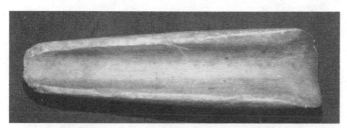

Gouge, (#K-10/HL), light brown slate, fully grooved for length, highly polished. This excellent example measures 2 x 7-3/16 in. long and is Late Archaic in time, ca. 4000-2500 BC. Allegany County, New York. $550-800

Iron Horse collection, Blasdell, New York

Gouge, (#J-5/HL), Late Archaic ca. 4000-2500 BC, gray-green slate. This very fine gouge is crisply shaped, highly polished, and measures 1-7/8 x 8-1/2 in. long. It came from along the Genesee River, Allegany County, New York. $700-1,100

Iron Horse collection, Blasdell, New York

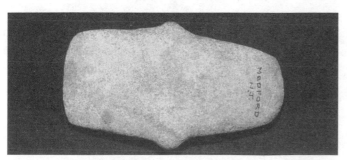

Knobbed adz, (#AK-6N3), Archaic period, made of tan pecked and smoothed hardstone. This adz has the midlength side projections (aids in hafting the head to a wooden handle) that provided the name, and the cutting edge is left in the photograph. The example is 2-7/8 x 5 in. long. Medford area, New Jersey. $500-750

Iron Horse collection, Blasdell, New York

Faceted adz, (#J-10/HL), Lamoka phase of the Early Archaic in the Northeast, polished green slate. This fine example, with the typical three facets or flat surfaces on the rounded face, measures 2-1/2 x 6-7/8 in. long. The adz (a secondary wood-working tool) came from Wyoming County, New York. $550-800

Iron Horse collection, Blasdell, New York

Squared/rectangular pestle (a scarce type compared with the usual rounded "roller" type pestles) from the Wills Creek area, Coshocton County, Ohio. It is made of yellow and tan hardstone and measures 2-1/4 x 1-5/8 x 8-3/4 in. Surfaces are highly polished. $45

Private collection, Ohio

Rounded gamestones, both Texas.

Left: hematite, Harrison County. $50
Right: Ogallala chart, Gregg County. $20

Willie Fields collection, Hallsville, Texas

Effigy bowl (?), gray stone, well-made, top scooped, bird head at one end. The artifact has tally marks on the sides and is nicely polished. It is from Mississippi. $500

Wilfred A. Dick collection, Magnolia, Mississippi

Incised stone, purpose unknown, from Cache County, Utah. While the time-period is unknown, Pinto points were found on the same site, suggesting Desert Late Archaic after 3,000 BC. It measures 1-1/2 x 2 in.   *Museum quality*

Randall Olsen collection, Cache County, Utah

Stone artifacts, left to right:

Anvil, brownstone, Louisiana.	$25
Smoothed and polished anvil or polisher, well-made, Mississippi.	$25
Anvil, brownstone, Louisiana.	$25

Wilfred A. Dick collection, Magnolia, Mississippi

Stone bowl, reddish interior, well-shaped and finished, from Arizona. $165

Wilfred A. Dick collection, Magnolia, Mississippi

Incised stones, probably Late Archaic and Desert culture, with polish and shallow lines. Size range is from 1 to 1-1/2 in., and all are from Cache County, Utah. These may be broken Atl-atl stones, but this is far from certain. Very interesting examples.   *Museum quality*

Randall Olsen collection, Cache County, Utah

Handled pestle made of volcanic rock, probably Western U.S. $85

Private collection

Notched flint hoe, with lower edge polished from use. This artifact is from northern Alabama. $350

Private collection

Spade blade, flint, from northern Alabama. The wide lower working edge is polished from use. $450

Private collection

L to R: drilled pebble, unknown use. Good drilling, but rest of stone rough, medium polish only. C-$10

Donut stone, California, 3-1/3 in. across, very fine central hole. High polish overall. May have been a club head. C-$165

Unusual slate cutting tool, or for chopping tasks; has characteristics both of notched celts and 3/4 grooved axes. Good edge, probably Archaic period. Midwest. C-$30

Private collection

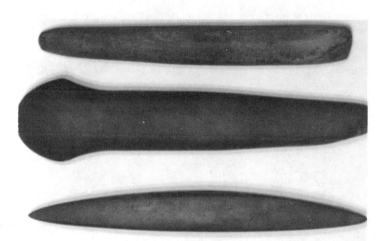

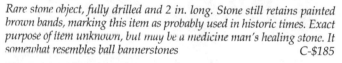

Large and fine artifacts, various periods.

Top: Mississippian chisel, 8-1/4 in., Tennessee. $500
Middle: Well-polished slate spud, Mississippian period, Spencer County, Indiana, 9-5/8 in. $1,500
Bottom: very fine Late Woodland ceremonial pick, blue and black slate, 1-1/8 x 9 in., from western New York state. $800

Pat & Dave Summers, Native American Artifacts, Victor, New York

From left to right:

Rare stone object, fully drilled and 2 in. long. Stone still retains painted brown bands, marking this item as probably used in historic times. Exact purpose of item unknown, but may be a medicine man's healing stone. It somewhat resembles ball bannerstones C-$185

Photo courtesy Robert C. Calvert, London, Ontario, Canada

Unknown stone object, probably prehistoric, found near London, Ontario. Piece is 4-1/2 in. long and has a hole 1/2 in. deep at one end, with incised marks along end sides. Unfinished pipe? Effigy form? C-$70

Photo courtesy Robert C. Calvert, London, Ontario, Canada

Unusual stone object, purpose unknown, 4 in. long. Item may be a preform, but appears to be a complete artifact. Made of a compact green stone, and found near Komoka, Ontario. This has been identified as a monolithic adz handle. C-$350

Photo courtesy Robert C. Calvert, London, Ontario, Canada

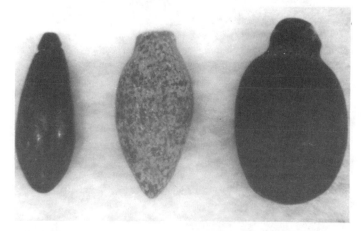

Plummets or plumb-bobs, Late Archaic and Early Woodland, left to right:

Hematite plummet, Schuyler County, Illinois, 2-5/8 in. $285
Granite plummet, South Windsor, Connecticut, 2-3/4 in. $160
Fairly rough plummet, 3 in., from Massachusetts. $45

Pocotopaug Trading Post, South Windsor, Connecticut

Hematite cone, 1-5/8 in. in diameter and 3/4 in. high. It is from Adams County, Illinois, of a colorful red hematite. This piece is flat-based. C-$275

Photo courtesy John P. Grotte, Illinois

Hematite cone, measuring 1-7/16 in. in diameter and 7/8 in. high. It has a small concave dimple on the flat bottom center. Piece is from the river bottoms of Adams County, Illinois, and probably dates from Woodland times. The surface of this cone is partially exfoliated or in the process of flaking.   C-$325

Photo courtesy John P. Grotte, Illinois

Plummet of hardstone, drilled and grooved at one end. It is 3 in. long, and 1-1/2 in. in diameter. Object almost resembles an effigy form, perhaps of a manatee, but resemblance is probably accidental. Found in Fairfield County, Ohio.   C-$65

Photo courtesy Bob Champion, Ohio

Grouping of plummets, all three quite different L to R:

Polished hardstone plummet, 2-3/8 in. long, glossy surface.   C-$60
Small egg-shaped hematite plummet, very shallowly grooved near top.   C-$40
Fine-grained sandstone plummet, grooved near top for attachment.   C-$30

Private collection

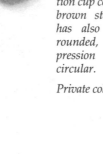

Left: concretion cup container, may have been for paint, about 2 in. in diameter, center worn smooth.   C-$25

Right: notched pebble net-sinker, though exact use of these artifacts is not known. Frequently found near streams in the Midwest.   C-$10

Bottom: small concretion cup container, dark brown stone. Outside has also been nicely rounded, central depression is absolutely circular.   C-$25

Private collection

Collection of grooved mauls with a biscuit-type discoidal at top center. These are from various prehistoric periods and materials are different kinds of stone. All were surface finds in Pratt County, Kansas.   Each, $100-200

Collection of Eugene and Marcille Wing

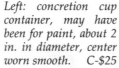

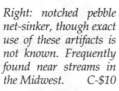

Left: tear-drop plummet, 4-3/8 in. long and 1-1/8 in. wide. Made of pink and black mottled granite, this item is from the Los Angeles area of California.   C-$500

Middle: tear-drop plummet, 4-7/8 in. long, made of a black and red mottled granite. It is from the Sacramento area of California.   C-$600

Right: drilled plummet, 4-3/8 in. long and 1 in. in extreme diameter. Made of a yellow and brown granite, this too is from the Sacramento, California area.   C-$500

Courtesy Ferrel Anderson, photographer; Thomas Browner collection; Davenport, Iowa

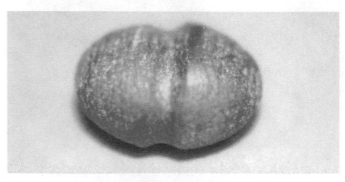

Club-head, full or 4/4 groove, head 1-1/2 in. wide and 1-7/8 in. high. Material is a brownish-yellow hardstone for this well-made example, found in the El Rito Mountains of New Mexico. $85

Jack Baker collection, Ozark, Missouri; David Capon photograph

Maul, 3/4 groove, size 3-3/4 x 6 in. high. This is a well-made example in brown hardstone, which was found near Sandia Park, New Mexico. $200

Jack Baker collection, Ozark, Missouri; David Capon photograph

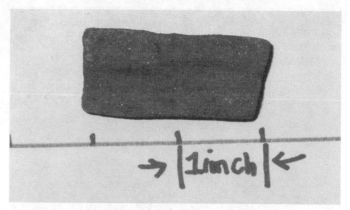

Shaft abrader, also called arrow straightener, sandstone, size 1 x 2 in. Made by Late Plains culture people, this was picked by the owner in 1996. Riley County, Kansas. $75

Found by Daniel Fox; photo by Caroline Fox, Manhattan, Kansas

Collection of Woodland and Mississippian artifacts, all surface finds on one site over a 30 year period, ca. 1935-1965

Clockwise from lower left: Sandstone abrader or shaft-shaper; grooved maul; Keokuk (1/2 groove) axe; discoidal; flint spade. Center, top: Greenish-brown hardstone pipe. Center, bottom: Catlinite pipe. All are from Labette County, Kansas. Unlisted

Fouts-Lyerla collections, Kansas

Necklace of steatite or soapstone beads, very nicely shaped and polished, probably late prehistoric. There are thirty-nine beads present and the string is 54 in. long. These rare beads came from California. Museum quality

Private collection

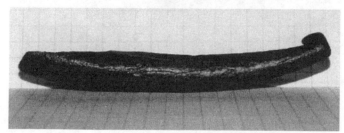

Atl-atl shaft portion with launching hook, an extremely rare artifact. This item probably predates bow use in the region where found. (Scale, five squares are one inch.) It was picked up along the Big Blue River, Potowatomi County, Kansas. Unlisted

Private collection

Donut stones, prehistoric, thought to be stones used with sticks for club-heads. Size-range here is 2 to 6 in. in diameter and materials are sandstone, steatite and serpentine. California. Each, average $250

Private collection

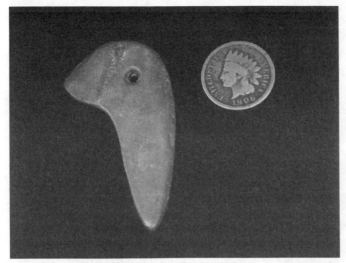

Pendant, effigy in red jasper, in bird head or bear claw form. It measures 1-1/8 x 2-1/8 in. and was a personal find of the owner in April of 1997. Louisiana. Unlisted

Richard F. Hughes collection, Louisiana

Three unusual prehistoric artifacts, all from Illinois, Middle to Late Archaic and Early Woodland periods.

Left: slate full-groove axe, 3 in. high, from near Indiana state line. $125
Middle: rare knobbed hardstone celt, 3-3/4 in. high, Macoupin County. $450
Right: hematite plummet, Godar style, drilled top, Pike County. $100

Rainbow Traders, Godfrey, Illinois

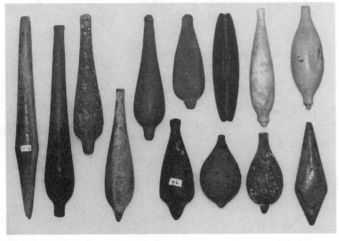

Charmstones, the West Coast equivalent in some cases to the eastern U.S. plummet, ca. 500-2,000 BP. This is a fine collection, and lengths here range from 3-3/16 to 8-7/8 in. Materials are various hardstones, and different shapes, sizes, and colors are represented. These examples came from the San Francisco Bay area and the San Joaquin Valley region of California. $125-400

Collection of, and photograph by, Michael W. Hough, California

Ulu knife with comb, (#349), brown slate, 3-1/2 in. deep and 7-1/8 in. wide. This scarce early knife form was ground into shape and has use-polish on the comb or backing portion. St. Lawrence County, New York. $550-850

Iron Horse collection, Blasdell, New York

Ground slate points and knives, (#6), ca. 4000-2500 BC, black and gray slate. These range in length from 2 to 5 in. and came from miscellaneous counties in New York.   *Each, $25-400*

Iron Horse collection, Blasdell, New York

Ulu knife with comb, (#D11559/OD-2), red slate, 2-5/16 in. deep and 5-3/4 in. wide. Ground into shape, this scarce blade form has a smoothly contoured blade edge. The ulu was found in the St. Lawrence River, Jefferson County, New York.   *$650-950*

Iron Horse collection, Blasdell, New York

Spruce Tree House, Mesa Verde National Park, Colorado. This is one of the better-preserved Anasazi cliff-dwellings or cliff-villages, being protected from much of the weather by the rock overhang.

Lar Hothem photo

Square Tower House, Mesa Verde National Park, Colorado. The existing four levels of the tower make it one of the highest in the Southwest. Other towers at other ruins may have competed, but they have largely crumbled with time.

Lar Hothem photo

CHAPTER VI

BANNERSTONES AND RELATED OBJECTS

The introduction to this chapter was written by Thomas E. Browner, officer of the Central States Archaeological Societies, Inc. and a man thoroughly knowledgeable in the field. Used with permission.

"Bannerstones are a loose category of Archaic artifacts. In outline, bannerstones or banners are symmetrical, usually winged artifacts possessing a drilled center hole or notches. Large numbers of blending forms in a great variety of stones lead to difficulties in classifications as well as value.

"Beginning in the Southeast portion of the United States, bannerstones, over a period of centuries, migrated North and Westward. Evolving with territorial expansion into more eccentric forms and utilizing finer grades of stone, some of the banners are top collectors' pieces today.

"As Atl-atl weights, bannerstones were simple tubular forms. Later, the advanced types were too large and thin to take the pressures of hard everyday use. Theories of social status emblems and tribal or religious significance have been placed on the later types.

"As in any commerce, a tangible object must be matched with an intangible concept (called value) for it to change ownership. Artifacts like bannerstones are one-of-a-kind. Each is different, and therefore values as absolutes do not exist. An artifact is only worth what an individual collector is willing to pay for it. Such a value must be viewed as an extension of the collector's personality, thus reflecting personal taste, interest, and income.

"One collector alone can set the price for a particular class of artifacts by purchasing all that are presented at a higher than normal market value. However, this is unusual as market value is normally determined by the demand of larger groups of collectors, all bidding for a limited number of genuine artifacts.

"In 1912, Warren K. Moorehead stated, 'the farther away from the source of supply, the more valuable the material—shell, copper, hematite.' Of course, he was referring to the economic importance to the Indians. It is interesting to note that the finished artifact today is worth the most in its region of origin. Local artifacts, being the most prized by local collectors, command premium prices.

"Besides demand and location of origin, artifacts generally follow a broad range based, in order of importance, on these factors:

1. Rarity of type
2. Perfection
3. Workmanship
4. Material

5. Size
6. Color
7. Pedigree

"These are self-explanatory, with the possible exception of pedigree. Pedigree means a traceable history, beginning with a list of previous owners and ending with photographs in various publications and books. It is a line of ancestry.

"Unfortunately, fakes and fakers do exist. A pedigree does not guarantee genuineness, but it does increase the collector's chances. Many of the fraudulent specimens being produced today are so realistic that they almost defy detection.

"Therefore, only purchase what you know about, and then only from reputable dealers and collectors. Never buy if you have any doubts about a piece. Ask to take the artifact on approval for a reasonable time. This will allow you the opportunity to trace the history and secure other opinions.

"There are no experts, only collectors like yourself with more knowledge and experience. Anyone can be fooled. Unfortunately, one of the byproducts of this situation is that the unknown, the slightly out-of-type and the unusual are characteristically branded as frauds. The final forms are much treasured and therefore do not tend to change hands as often.

"In choosing a bannerstone, a collector must check the planes, drillings, patination, manufacturing techniques, etc. Many old pieces were scrubbed to bring out the ancient color. The Indians salvaged many specimens. Thus a double crescent banner could end up as a butterfly type. Therefore, even genuine specimens may not be without recent fault or ancient change or profile.

"Are the planes normal for the type? Is the patination even, including edges and salvaged sides? Are the drillings tapered? Has the surface defoliated? Are there any so-called 'worm marks'? Once authenticity has been established, merit as to value must be made on the basis of type, perfection, size, color, and so forth.

"Unusual range highs and lows may be caused by some of the following factors. Obvious bleaching, scrubbing, or the use of oil, shellac, or other caustic agents may lower the value of an artifact by as much as 50 percent. On the other hand, a good pedigree could increase the asking price by 20 percent. Buying an artifact in its home locality might cost an extra 30 percent.

"The finest artifacts of a type could demand a price two or three times the going range high. Prices are generally higher at shows than in homes. However, travel expenses and the reluctance of collectors to sell cherished pieces often makes the dealer's price the only price available.

"Unlike some other collectibles, there are a very limited number of genuine, intact Indian artifacts. Many of these have gone into the vaults of museums and schools and civic organizations and are not readily available for study. In many cases the pride of ownership, more than the object's true value, is a prime objective of the collector.

"Finally, common artifacts remain common.

"The increase in the number of collectors has driven the prices of better grade specimens higher each year. Therefore, buy for the long range appreciation of your investment by selecting the best of what is offered to you. Rare specimens will only become more valuable with time." (T.E.B.)

BANNERSTONES

Slate banner, from Michigan, butterfly type, not drilled in center, but nicely grooved either side, perfect. Wings are 4-1/4 in. wide from tip to tip.   C-$750

Geniculate bannerstone, Illinois, 3-1/4 in. long and 2 in. high, banded slate, some minute original damage in hole region; very colorful blue-black material.   C-$550

Pick banner, 3-7/8 in. long, worked so that bands converge near center, adding to attractiveness. Some battering to slate near one end of central drill hole, unimportant to overall appearance. Somewhat crescentic form.   A-$300

Double crescent banner, 5 in. wide and 3-1/8 in. high, some damage to three of the four arms or wings. Central portions, including hole, are fine. Retains good polish; ideal for restoration.   C-$750

Geniculate banner of banded slate, size about 3 x 3 in., pristine condition and a scarce Archaic form. All corners well-rounded, oblong hole, and extension comes to a rounded tip.   A-$470

Winged banner, of banded slate, remaining portions measuring 5 x 3 in. Lower wing edges broken in prehistoric times, and piece was salvaged by grinding down broken areas to balance the appearance. Salvaged regions not quite as well done as original edges.   A-$300

Winged banner, 3-1/8 in. wide and 1-5/8 in. high, banded slate, of a type sometimes called "butterfly." Finished on exterior; cane-drilled hole not quite completed.   C-$325

Pick banner, curved and 4-1/4 in. long and 1 in. wide, with the slate a banded black, and gray background.   D-$300

Chlorite pick banner, hardstone, 2-3/8 in. long and 1-1/4 in. wide at center. Completely drilled and color an amber-yellow (hard to describe). Very minor surface scratches here and there, original, with polish extending into the scratches, which are really only faint lines.   C-$950

Tubular banner, Kentucky, 2-3/4 in. long, rounded top and sides, flat bottom, drilled for entire length. Material a dark gray unbanded slate.   A-$185

End-view of a fine hourglass-type bannerstone. Made of a colorful rose quartz, piece was reed-drilled approximately halfway through center. Length is 2-3/8 in. and width is 1-1/8 in.; artifact was found in Adams County, Illinois.   C-$750

Photo courtesy John P. Grotte, Illinois

Winged banner, Wisconsin, 3-3/4 in. wide and 2-1/8 in. long, hardstone and made from a material resembling granite. Undrilled, but highly polished specimen.   C-$400

Fluted ball banner, Ohio, 1-7/8 in. long and 1-1/8 in. wide. Very colorful green slate with red and black bands. Some very slight original damage around one end of drill-hole.   C-$160

Notched-ovate banner, rare, Midwestern Archaic, 5-3/8 in. long and 3-1/4 in. wide, banded slate. Some restoration to two of the curved tips. Notched in center of convex edges.   C-$1,100

Winged bannerstone, 4-1/8 in. between tips. About 1 in. of one wing has been carefully restored. Reddish slate with black bands, colorful.   C-$575

Pick banner, a hardstone similar to diorite, smooth-grained, good polish. Piece is 4-7/8 in. long and slightly pointed on one end, slightly flattened on other. No damage; unusual.   C-$450

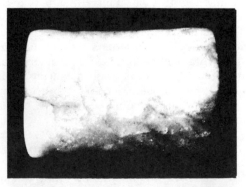

Hourglass bannerstone, from Fulton County, Illinois. It is 2-15/16 in. long and 1-3/4 in. wide, made of a fine grade of quartz. Drilling is slightly broken out at one end, color is not evenly distributed, nor vivid. Yet it is a good, acceptable artifact; if everything were perfect, it could be worth closer to $1,000.   C-$750

Courtesy Ferrel Anderson, photographer; Thomas Browner collection; Davenport, Iowa

Crescent banner, hardstone, 3-3/4 x 2-1/2 in. and illustrated in Indian and Eskimo Artifacts of North America. Material is a brown, fine-grained granite.   C-$775

Courtesy Ferrel Anderson, photographer; Thomas Browner collection; Davenport, Iowa

Unfinished butterfly bannerstone, from Chenango County, New York. It is 6 in. wide and 2-3/4 in. long. Not completed because the drilling missed and bypassed. Shape only fair, and a wing chip breaks the outline. Made of a green and black banded site.   C-$400-650

Courtesy Ferrel Anderson, photographer; Thomas Browner collection; Davenport, Iowa

Double-bitted axe bannerstone, from Pope County, Indiana. It is 5-1/2 in. wide and 3-3/4 in. long, and made from green and black banded slate. Exceptional shape; note the even color and the centered eye (in banding). Both size and color help make this specimen one of the finest of the type.   C-$1,250-2,000

Courtesy Ferrel Anderson, photographer; Thomas Browner collection; Davenport, Iowa

Butterfly bannerstone, brown and black banded slate, 4-1/2 in. wide and 2 in. long. Two minor edge nicks do no major harm to this banner. Note also the light "worm trail" from left to right on specimen, moving down at about 45-degree angle. Such markings are within the natural material.   C-$650-900

Courtesy Ferrel Anderson, photographer; Thomas Browner collection; Davenport, Iowa

Butterfly bannerstone, 5 in. wide and 1-7/8 in. long from Miami County, Ohio. Material is a green and black banded slate. An earlier collector scrubbed the piece with steel wool to bring out the colors, but destroyed the surface patina. This should never be done.   C-(without scrubbing) $400-500

C-(after scrubbing) $135-185

Courtesy Ferrel Anderson, photographer; Thomas Browner collection; Davenport, Iowa

Ball bannerstone, 1-5/8 x 1-1/2 in. from Bureau County, Illinois, piece is made of green and black banded slate. Note high degree of polish on this well-banded banner.   C-$425

Courtesy Ferrel Anderson, photographer; Thomas Browner collection; Davenport, Iowa

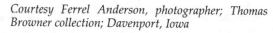

Salvaged double-crescent bannerstone, 4-3/8 in. long and 1-1/2 in. wide. Piece is from Kent County, Illinois. Current appearance of this banded-slate artifact is that of a butterfly or double-bitted axe banner form; crescentic extensions were ground off in prehistoric times.   C $500-700

Courtesy Ferrel Anderson, photographer; Thomas Browner collection; Davenport, Iowa

Quartz butterfly bannerstone, 3 in. wide and 1-5/8 in. long. It is from Cedar County, Missouri, made of white quartz with reddish tinges. Perfect in every detail, it lacks only color and more size to command the highest prices. Edges are nicely rounded and wings are proportionate to the size of the barrel.   C-$1,250-2,000

Courtesy Ferrel Anderson, photographer; Thomas Browner collection; Davenport, Iowa

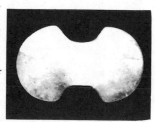

Undrilled fetish knobbed lunate bannerstone, made of brick-colored hematite. It is 2-7/8 in. wide and 1-5/8 in. long. This specimen is rather crude in form, but does represent a one-of-a-kind object. It is from Hudson County, Tennessee.   C-$350

Courtesy Ferrel Anderson, photographer; Thomas Browner collection; Davenport, Iowa

Wisconsin winged bannerstone, from Clark County, Missouri. It measures 3-3/4 x 2 in. and is made of a black and white porphyry. This specimen was expertly restored in one corner; in 1956 it was purchased for $300. The exceptional color and workmanship make this artifact a rare collector's item.   C-$1,250-2,000

Courtesy Ferrel Anderson, photographer; Thomas Browner collection; Davenport, Iowa

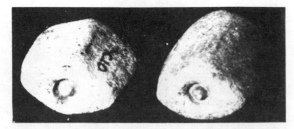

Unfinished bannerstones, each measuring 2 x 2 in. These clearly show the drilling (hollow cane type), with central "islands" protruding about 1/4 in. Both are Archaic and found in northeast Mississippi. The C10 piece is made of quartz material. C-$90 each

Photo courtesy Jim Northcutt, Jr., Corinth, Mississippi

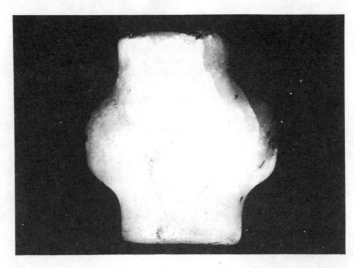

Salvaged double-crescent bannerstone, 3-7/8 in. wide and 3-1/8 in. long. Material is a green and black banded slate. One prong was broken in ancient times, and the other three ground down to create a symmetrical piece. C-$850-1,400

Courtesy Ferrel Anderson, photographer; Thomas Browner collection; Davenport, Iowa

Biface bottle bannerstone, 2-1/2 x 2 in. It is a fine white quartz with small black inclusions. Though small, it is well-documented since the beginning of the 1900s; most collectors will pay more for a traceable artifact. From southern Indiana. C-$1,450-2,100

Courtesy Ferrel Anderson, photographer; Thomas Browner collection; Davenport, Iowa

Rectangular barreled bannerstone, 4-1/8 x 2-3/4 in. The symmetry and raised barrel are the major features of this artifact. Material is a pink and black granite. It is from Preble County, Ohio. Most bannerstones offered for sale can be considered in the more common classes. C-$1,200-1,600

Courtesy Ferrel Anderson, photographer; Thomas Browner collection; Davenport, Iowa

Hourglass bannerstone, from Adams County, Illinois and made of green quartzite. It is 2 in. long and 1-15/16 in. wide, and might be considered a common specimen. Browner: "Size is small and shape only fair; with most of its history lost, it is reduced to an orphaned piece of common art." C-$750-1,100

Courtesy Ferrel Anderson, photographer; Thomas Browner collection; Davenport, Iowa

Tube type bannerstone, 1-1/4 in. wide and 2-1/2 in. long, made of a green stone material. Hole measures 1/2 in. at both ends; tube has a flat bottom. Archaic, it was found near the Hatchie River in Alcom County, Mississippi. C-$525

Photo courtesy Jim Northcutt, Jr., Corinth, Mississippi

Triangular dual bannerstone, from Hancock County, Illinois. It is 4-1/4 in. long and 2-7/8 in. wide, made of mottled granite. This is both a rare piece and somewhat controversial, in that only a portion of its history has been traceable. C-$1,750-2,250

Courtesy Ferrel Anderson, photographer; Thomas Browner collection; Davenport, Iowa

Pebble bannerstone, from Boone County, Missouri. It is 2-1/2 in. wide and 1-1/2 in. long, made of a tan sandstone. Bannerstones began like this, a simple perforated pebble around 4000 BC. This specimen was only shaped slightly by flattening the circumference. Many banners are believed to have been Atl-atl weights. C-$125

Courtesy Ferrel Anderson, photographer; Thomas Browner collection; Davenport, Iowa

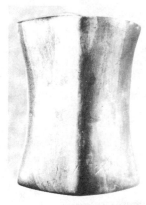

Hourglass bannerstone, 3 in. long and 2-1/4 in. wide, from Randolph County, Illinois. Has the classic shape. At some early time, a person scratched the initial "W" on it; this fault would be penalized to some degree by different collectors. Made of reddish-brown slate; material could be better for the artifact type. C-$850-1,300

Courtesy Ferrel Anderson, photographer; Thomas Browner collection; Davenport, Iowa

Single-face bottle bannerstone, from Lincoln County, Missouri, 3 in. long. Note the flared lips forming mini-rectangles at both ends. Topside is gracefully rounded, bottomside is flat. The material is red quartzite. C-$1,450-1,750

Courtesy Ferrel Anderson, photographer; Thomas Browner collection; Davenport, Iowa

Bannerstone, tubular with reverse groove, from Hopkinsville, Kentucky. Made of green and black banded slate, size is 1 x 1-13/16 x 3-1/4 in. $600

Collection of David G. & Barbara J. Shirley, Michigan

Undrilled Wisconsin winged bannerstone, 2-1/2 x 1-3/4 in. From Illinois, it is made of mottled granite. The specimen is a bit thick and lacks good polish. C-$135

Courtesy Ferrel Anderson, photographer; Thomas Browner collection; Davenport, Iowa

Drilled center banded slate bannerstone, Archaic times, and 4-1/2 in. in length. Found near Pembroke, Ontario, Canada. C-$400

Photo courtesy Howard Popkie, Arnprior, Canada

Knobbed lunate bannerstone, from Delaware County, Ohio. It is 5-7/8 in. long and 2 in. wide. Piece is made of green and black banded slate.   C-$1,050-1,450

Courtesy Ferrel Anderson, photographer; Thomas Browner collection; Davenport, Iowa

Pick-type bannerstone, light green to medium green mottled chlorite, Archaic period. From Fairfield County, Ohio, it is ex-colls. Dr. Copeland and Dr. Meuser. With good design, finish and coloring, this is a small but top piece. Size, 1-5/16 x 2-15/16 in. $2,500-3,200

Private collection, Ohio

Winged bannerstone, 4-1/2 in. long; from near Pond Mills, near London, Ontario. While not shown in photo, piece is fully drilled. C-$300-350

Photo courtesy Robert C. Calvert, London, Ontario, Canada

Pick bannerstone, Archaic period, material a dark green chlorite with small black specks. Size is 1-1/2 x 4-1/16 in. It is from Marion County, Ohio, and ex-coll. Dr. G.F. Meuser. This is a very collectible and well-made specimen. $2,500-3,300

Private collection, Ohio

Winged bannerstone, from Branch County, Michigan, in light brown banded slate with darker brown bands. It is 7/8 x 2 x 5-3/32 in., and bears G.I.R.S. authentication number C89-32. $2,400

Collection of David G. & Barbara J. Shirley

Pick-type bannerstone, from Ohio, made of green banded slate. It is 4-3/4 in. long and ex-coll. McNight. The fine specimen has had the slate worked so that the concentric bands accent the central drill-hole.
                                                                    Museum quality

Bill & Margie Koup collection, Albuquerque, New Mexico; Bill Koup photograph

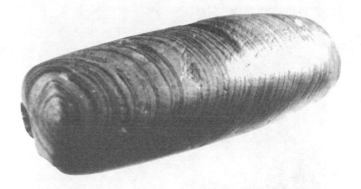

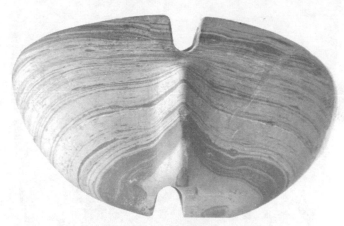

Tube-type bannerstone, made of tan banded slate, 3-5/8 in. long. It was found near Ft. Ancient in Warren County, Ohio, and is from the Archaic period. This is a solid old piece with good patination. $275

Larry Garvin collection, Ohio

Winged bannerstone, Cass County, Michigan. It is made of fractured banded slate, greenish-gray with dark banding. Size is 1-1/4 x 3-3/16 x 4-3/4 in. The banner is pictured in Prehistoric Artifacts. $1,300

Collection of David G. & Barbara J. Shirley

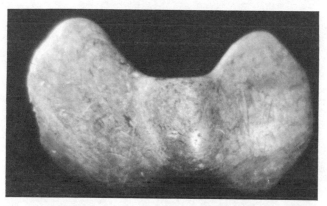

Winged bannerstone, green and black hardstone, from Bedford County, Pennsylvania. It is 1 x 2-3/4 x 4-1/4 in. and ex-coll. Foote. $395

Pat & Dave Summers, Native American Artifacts, Victor, New York

Panel bannerstone, gray banded slate with black banding. It measures 5/8 x 2-1/16 x 2-7/16 in. Panels are scarce banner types. This artifact was pictured in Central States Archaeological Journal, 1988, Vol. 35 No. 3. It is from the Midwest. $1,100

Collection of David G. & Barbara J. Shirley

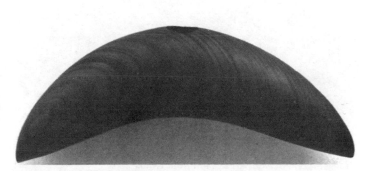

Winged bannerstone Type A, from Midland County, Michigan. Made of gray banded slate with darker bands, it is 2-1/2 x 4-5/16 in. This is one of the top five of the type. It has G.I.R.S. authentication number 221. $2,500

Collection of David G. & Barbara J. Shirley

Curved pick bannerstone, Midwestern, gray banded slate with dark banding. It measures 1-1/4 x 6-15/16 in. This is a fine old piece, ex-colls. Dr. Bunch, Payne, McClain and Smith. It has G.I.R.S. authentication number C88-14. $2,100

Collection of David G. & Barbara J. Shirley

Shuttle-type bannerstone, very thin for size, 2-1/2 in. wide. It is unusual for the area where found, Pickaway County, Ohio, near Circleville. Circleville itself was named for a prehistoric Hopewellian earth-work. Ex-colls. E. Good and Dr. G. Meuser (number 3211 over 5).   Museum quality

Bill & Margie Koup collection, Albuquerque, New Mexico; Bill Koup photograph

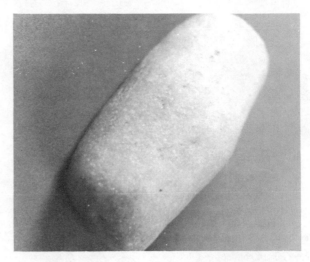

Humped center bar amulet, Early Woodland period, made of cream-colored quartzite. This interesting piece was found near Volney, Michigan and is 13/16 x 2-11/16 in. long. The end-drilling was started but not completed, possibly due to the extreme hardness of the material. $300-450

Private collection, Ohio

Expanded-center Adena gorget, Early Woodland period, material a translucent tan-cream quartzite. It is 1-7/8 x 4-5/8 in., from Knox County, Ohio, and ex-coll. R. Leatherman. It is undrilled but appears finished, a rare gorget type in this material. $450-500

Private collection, Ohio

Humped-center bar amulet, Early Woodland period, material a translucent tan-cream quartzite. From Logan County, Ohio, hole-drilling was started at each end but not completed. The base of this 13/16 x 4-1/8 in. specimen is scooped or concave. $450-650

Private collection, Ohio

Loafstones, Archaic period, both from Ohio.

Left: cream-colored quartzite, Crawford County, ex-coll. A.T. Wehrle, 1-1/2 x 2-1/8 in.
Right: tan-cream banded quartzite, 1-5/8 x 2-5/16 in., from Ross County.   Each, $175-275

Private collection, Ohio

Boatstone, Woodland period, scooped on reverse (shown). It is drilled with two 3/8 in. holes. This polished piece is from Calloway County, Kentucky. $525

Marguerite L. Kernaghan collection; photograph by Marguerite L. and Stewart W. Kernaghan, Bellvue, Colorado

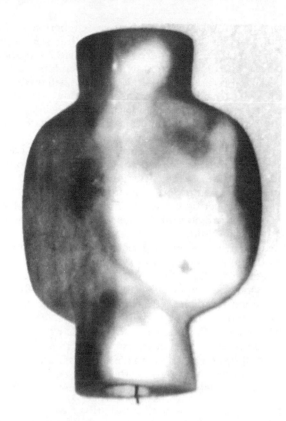

Bannerstone, highly developed bottle shape, ferruginous quartzite. It is 2-1/4 x 3-3/4 in. and is from Kentucky. $1,200

Marguerite L. Kernaghan collection; photograph by Marguerite L. and Stewart W. Kernaghan, Bellvue, Colorado

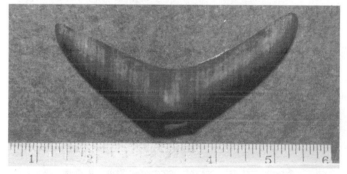

Bannerstone, (#HL/TAL), Archaic period, green banded slate. It is 1 in. thick and 4 in. wide, tally-marked, and gracefully formed. Allegany County, New York. $550-900

Iron Horse collection, Blasdell, New York

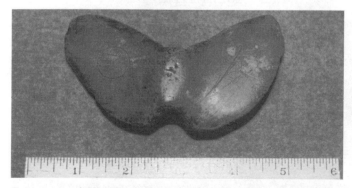

Bannerstone, (#H141/B19), Notched Crescent Class C form, 4-1/4 in. across. Archaic, it is made of green banded slate and came from the Canandaigua Lake region of Ontario County, New York. $800-1,400

Iron Horse collection, Blasdell, New York

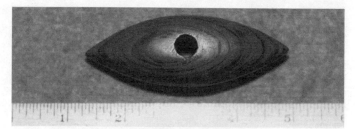

Bannerstone, (#HL-W), Archaic, Pick type, 1-1/4 x 3-3/4 in. It is made of banded green slate with the drill-hole positioned within the banding. Wyoming County, New York. $400-700

Iron Horse collection, Blasdell, New York

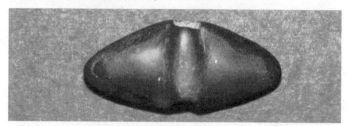

Bannerstone, (#MG), Winged form, Archaic, 3-3/4 in. wide. The material is red and purple shale and the banner was picked up along the Hudson River, Green County, New York. $500-750

Iron Horse collection, Blasdell, New York

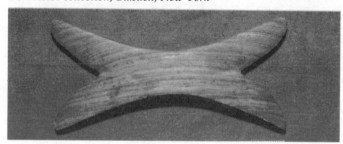

Bannerstone, (#AK-1), Double Crescent form. This is a very rare Archaic banner type in pristine condition, 6-1/4 in. wide. It was found south of Henderson Harbor, Jefferson County, New York. Museum quality

Iron Horse collection, Blasdell, New York

Bannerstone, (#AK-96), Double-Notched Butterfly Class C form, Archaic period, green banded slate. This graceful piece is 4-1/4 in. wide and from New York state. $1,200-1,800

Iron Horse collection, Blasdell, New York

Duo-tipped slate pick, from Canada, 5-1/4 in. long and 7/8 in. wide. Material is a dark gray slate, not banded. Piece is well-shaped but undrilled. C-$275

Panel banner of very attractive, thinly-banded slate, 3-1/2 in. long. Edges have regular tally notches. As is common for the form, one end of the banner is slightly larger than the other. Central hole runs lengthwise; good condition. A-$300

Hardstone banner, Midwestern origin, 2-3/8 in. wide and 1-7/8 in. long, made of chlorite (?), well-drilled, no damage. Small but perfect; highly polished buff-colored surface. C-$875

Quartz bannerstone, 1-7/8 in. wide and 2-3/4 in. long. Made of a well-polished translucent quartzite having black inclusions. Perfect condition, but undrilled; drill-hole was just started, never completed. C-$325

Crescentic pick banner, 3-1/2 in. long, with central hole 1/2 in. in diameter. Very symmetrical, nicely polished, made of dark, close-banded slate. From an old collection. A-$170

Lunate banner, about 5 in. across at the tips, which lack the typical notches or grooves. One arm is slightly shorter than the other and projects at a different angle than does its twin. No restoration and unusual in an unbroken or damaged condition. A-$245

ATL-ATL WEIGHTS

There is considerable evidence that at least some bannerstones served as Atl-atl weights. It is easy to imagine some of the heavier and more compact forms employed in this manner, more difficult in the case of the large, thinwinged types.

Banners, already described, can be quickly (and incompletely) summarized. They are artifacts with a single large round or ovate central hole, and with symmetrical protrusions on both sides of that hole. Only a form like the atypical geniculate family alters this "rule"; even then, set on edge, the symmetry is regained.

Atl-atl weights generally lack a large central hole and tend to be flat or concave on the bottom. As a broad class, they are long, narrow, and may have squared or rounded sides and top. Many forms have grooves or drill-holes for attachment.

It is believed weights were both functional and ornamental. Functional, because the weight would have given some added impetus to the lance-throw. They also would have served as a counter-balance when the flint or obsidian-tipped lance was in place.

They are ornamental, because many varieties are extremely well made, small works of fine proportions and high polish and static grace. Some were effigy forms, adding perhaps luck and magic to the hunter's foray.

Atl-atl weights were used over the entire Continental U.S., and into Canada and Mexico. It is believed the weights were used from early Archaic times until around AD 500,

giving the Atl-atl/lance weapons system perhaps 8,000 and more years of dominance. Early weights were somewhat plain and crude, little more than flattened rocks that could easily be glued or fastened to the wooden lance-thrower.

What is, and what is not, a weight will no doubt be as hotly debated in the future as it is today. New thought is that any prehistoric Amerind artifact that is long, thick, flat-bottomed—and served no other obvious function—may well have been a weight.

Because many of the weights are highly collectible, and these may include some slate and hardstone gorget and boatstone forms, the fakers have been at work. Some of the fraudulent specimens go back to the early years of the century and are now beginning to look old.

There are so many classes of weights that it is difficult to give guidelines on what to watch out for. Drill-holes for weights should be conical, from the tapered flint drills, and not of uniform diameter. Note that drilling, good drilling, adds much to the value of a piece.

One of the more difficult fakes to deal with is the authentic-improved piece, an old artifact that has been recently drilled to increase the value. In most cases, this will be obvious; after all, a semiskilled person is working on an object that is thousands of years old. The marks of steel tools are not the same as those made by prehistoric implements.

Generally, the patina, the microscopically thin surface layer, is disturbed. If in doubt, do not collect the piece.

Atl-atl weight, stone, Klamath River area of Oregon, 3 in. long and 1-5/8 in. high, speckled white stone. Flat bottom, piece nicely grooved front, the back, and across the center. Surface well-polished. D-$275

Boatstone, Arkansas, 3-3/4 in. long and 1-1/4 in. wide. Bottom side, flat on edges and deeply hollowed out or scooped. Good work style, high polish overall, perfect condition. D-$325

Stone Atl-atl weight, excavated from a cave shelter in Arkansas. Found in the same occupational zone as Gary points, and from the Archaic period. Weight is 2-1/2 in. long. C-$75

Photo courtesy Wayne Parker, Texas

Pick-type bannerstone, from Logan County, Ohio, one of the state's better examples. Material is gray and green banded slate with dark gray banding, and size is 1-1/16 x 1 x 5 in. Pictured in Who's Who in Indian Relics No. 1 (p. 118), it has G.I.R.S. authentication number 203. $1,800

Collection of David G. & Barbara J. Shirley

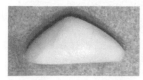

Stone Atl-atl weight, excavated from a cave shelter in Arkansas. Found in the same occupational zone as Gary points, and from the Archaic period. Weight is 2-1/2 in. long. C-$75

Photo courtesy Wayne Parker, Texas

Atl-atl weights, shaped shell, set of nine, from northern Kentucky. Each has a basic triangular shape, corners rounded; each is drilled with central hole about 5/8 in. in diameter. Placed together and approximating original positions, set is about 4 in. long and 1 1/4 in. wide. Segments evidence polish, and each is carefully made. C-$285

Atl-atl, hardstone weight, state of Washington, 3-3/8 in. long. Bottom is flat, top has two longitudinal grooves and is highly polished. Made of a compact tan stone. C-$240

Sandstone weight, from Scioto River Valley, Ohio. It is 3-1/2 in. long and 1-5/8 in. wide, about 3/8 in. thick. Perfect, and an early specimen. Otherwise, an unremarkable piece. C-$35

Banded-slate boatstone, drilled and scooped, Indiana, 3-7/8 in. long and 1-5/8 in. wide. Flattish base has been scooped to a depth of nearly 1/2 in. Some battering on the ends, but shallow and polished all over. C-$225-275

Bar amulet, dark-colored slate, from Michigan, 4 1/2 in. long and 1-5/8 in. wide. D-$285

Atl-atl weight, bar-type grooved, 4 in. long and 7/8 in. wide, and made of a blackish slate. Bottom flat, top rounded, with two thin grooves about 3/8 in. from each end. Unusual and well-finished piece. C-$295

Layer-slate weight, from New York, 2-3/4 in. long and 1 in. wide, with rounded top. Rough finish. C-$70

Grooved weight, 3-1/8 in. long and 7/8 in. wide; light-colored slate. Bottomside flat, top rounded, wide groove across the center. Semi-polished, good condition. D-$135

NOTE: There are other forms that are almost certainly weights, although currently called by other names. These are covered in other chapters consistent with nomenclature. Such artifacts include some late Archaic Glacial Kame gorgets and some Woodland (Adena) bi-holed forms, which are often undrilled.

Suggested Reading

Knoblock, Byron W. *Bannerstones of the North American Indian.* La Grange: Privately published, 1939.

The quarterly journals published by many archeological societies are excellent sources for additional information. See the last chapter.

Bannerstones, Archaic period, top row left to right:

Hematite, drilled, Mississippi. $150
Saddle type, drilled, Mississippi. $325
Winged, brownstone, drilled, Mississippi. $90

Second row left to right:

Broken half, polished, Mississippi. $20
Hematite, polished, undrilled. $50
Broken polished section. $20
Bottom from Mississippi, polished. $20

Wilfred A. Dick collection, Magnolia, Mississippi

Rock art, Indian Petroglyph State Park near Albuquerque, New Mexico. These two figures, pecked into the dark basalt rock, represent birds.

Lar Hothem photo

Petroglyphs, unknown prehistoric period, animals and circle motifs. Such early rock art is fast disappearing due to careless visitors, vandals, and weathering. Southern Illinois.

Dennis R. Arbeiter, Godfrey, Illinois

CHAPTER VII

BANDED SLATE ORNAMENTS AND OBJECTS

In a vast region ranging from the Mississippi watershed area, east to the Atlantic Coast, and from north of the Great Lakes, south nearly to the Gulf, slate was a favorite material in prehistoric times. Much of this slate was of glacial origin, and the slate was traded far into non-glaciated areas. The slate was compact and colorful, and it worked well.

The beauty of banded slate certainly attracted prehistoric crafts-people, just as the finished artifacts attract collectors today. Very simple methods were used to turn out some very well-designed and executed objects. The peck and abrasion method was employed, basically the same used for making hardstone tools.

When the final form was approached, the piece was ground against loose-grained stone; some very delicate work could be done in this fashion. Lastly, the surface was polished and any drilling put in.

For slate artifacts, determinants of present-day value include size of the artifact and the condition. The greater the damage, the greater the loss of value. Collectors seek symmetrical slate, and the pattern, regularity, and boldness of the bands count for much.

Especially admired are pieces where the slate has been worked so the bands are either in harmony with the artifact's lines, or emphasize a key part of the artifact. An example is a panel banner with the slate bands all at the same angle on the top surface. Another is when bands converge to emphasize the eye region of a birdstone.

Slate surfaces should be highly polished and have no serious scratches, either from prehistoric use or today's agriculture equipment. (A surprising amount of breakage and damage occurs when unknowing people acquire fine artifacts and treat them as mere stones.) In the general slate categories of pendants and gorgets, drilling is important. Pendants generally have one hole, and gorgets two or more. Both tend to be long and flat, with varied widths.

All holes should be artistically placed, at the same space from sides for pendants and the same from sides and ends for most gorgets. While some collectors admire very thin slate pieces for the workmanship involved, others seek thick slate for the weight and contoured three-dimensional artistry.

Fakes exist. In the more valued classes, like birdstones, several knowledgeable people have stated there are probably more fraudulent than genuine pieces. There are lucky occurrences. One man bought a box of junk at a farm sale for the bag of nails he saw at the top. After getting it home, he discovered something else on the bottom. His cost was a dollar. His prize was a hardstone, perfect-condition birdstone, worth in excess of $1,000.

Another man bought two birdstones from a pawnshop owner, because they looked good and were priced at only $300 each. With the average "bird" selling in the $1,500 range, they were a bargain providing they were authentic. They were not authentic, and hence, not a bargain.

For the average slate pendant, gorget, birdstone, or effigy, the prices listed here are about market, but many examples can be obtained for far less. A good slate artifact collection can be put together, made up of under $100 pieces, but it is still buyer beware. Know your seller or get a written guarantee that the piece can be returned for a refund if it proves to be questionable.

SLATE PENDANTS

One-holed slate pieces, if they are in fact completed by drilling, are termed pendants. It is believed they were worn around the neck like a large medallion. As prehistoric decorative items, great care seems to have been used in making many of them, though their relative thinness—1/8 in. to 3/8 in.—makes them rather fragile.

Anchor-type slate pendant, 5 in. long and 1-1/2 in. wide at expanded lower base. One anchor prong is a bit smaller than the other.   A-$150

Biconcave pendant, from Missouri, exactly 4 in. long and 1-7/8 in. wide at ends, made in gorget form, but centrally drilled with single hole instead of usual two holes. Material is a green slate with green bands.   C-$210

Rectangular banded slate pendant, 5 in. long and 2 in. wide. Single large hole drilled from both sides, about 1-3/4 in. from one end. Very nice black bands against a reddish slate.   C-$325

Anchor-shaped pendant, 4-1/4 in. long and 1-1/2 in.

wide, with minor damage.   G-$170

Trapezoidal slate pendant, 5 in. long and 2 in. wide at base and 1-1/4 in. wide at top, with single suspension hole. Perfect condition, good polish, very symmetrical.   A-$285

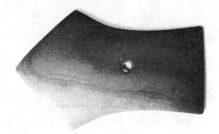

Very unusual Hopewellian shield-shaped pendant, of fine banded slate, piece is 1/8 in. short of 5 in. Topside is slightly convex; underside is very slightly concave. Very symmetrical and an outstanding type specimen.   C-$2,500

Private collection

L to R:

Pointed-end pendant, perhaps salvaged from large artifact in early times, 2-1/8 in. long. C-$25

Large and good anchor-type pendant, made of a high grade yellowish slate. Perfect condition, from Ohio, about 5 in. long. C-$225

Fine rectangular pendant, made of a smooth-grained hardstone; may have been salvaged from larger gorget in early times. C-$50

Private collection

Keyhole pendant, Adena culture, from Christian County, Kentucky. It is gray banded slate with darker bands and measures 2-7/16 x 4-9/16 in. It is pictured in Prehistoric Men of Kentucky, *1910, p. 202. It has G.I.R.S. authentication number C88-12.* $2,500

Collection of David G. & Barbara J. Shirley

Bell-shaped pendant, Woodland period, Ashland County, Ohio. Material is gray banded slate with dark banding and size is 3/16 x 2-5/8 x 4-3/16 in. This very well-made piece has G.I.R.S. authentication number C88-9. $1,000

Collection of David G. & Barbara J. Shirley

Trapezoidal pendant, tallied top, Ohio, tan hardstone. Size, 1/8 x 1-1/2 x 3 in. G.I.R.S. authentication number C89-28. On left. $600

Trapezoidal pendant, on right, with Adena (one side) drilling, from DeKalb County, Indiana. Made of dark gray and yellowish-white hardstone, it is 1/16 x 2-1/16 x 5-1/32 in. Ex-coll. Dougherty, it bears G.I.R.S. authentication number C88-23. $2,000

Collection of David G. & Barbara J. Shirley

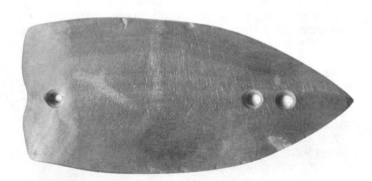

Sandal-sole gorget, Glacial Kame culture (Late Archaic), from Van Buren County, Michigan. Made of banded slate, the material is light red to gray-brown. Size, 3/16 x 2-1/8 x 4-1/2 in. The artifact has prehistoric salvage or repair at the wide end. $500

Collection of David G. & Barbara J. Shirley

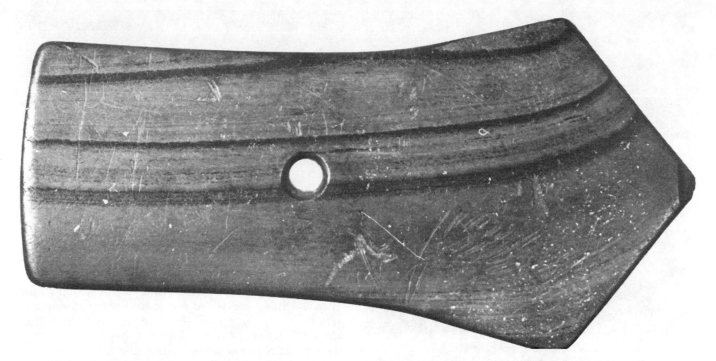

Pentagonal or shield-shape pendant, Late Woodland period, a very superior specimen. Made of banded glacial slate, it is 4-7/8 in. high. It was found along the Old Portage Trail in Summit County, Ohio.
Museum quality

Bill & Margie Koup collection, Albuquerque, New Mexico; Bill Koup photograph

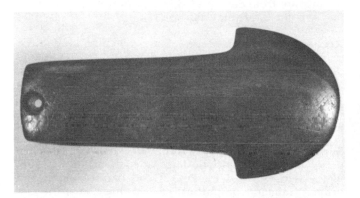

Anchor-type pendant, Early/Middle Woodland, from Franklin County, Ohio. Made of brown, black, and tan banded slate, it measures 2-1/8 x 4-1/2 in. Ex-coll. Max Shipley. $1,000

Collection of David G. & Barbara J. Shirley

Shovel pendant, (#116), tallied lower edges, green banded slate. This Hopewell (Middle Woodland) artifact has unusual double suspension holes and is 1-1/2 in. wide by 4-7/8 in. long. Erie County, New York. $550-800

Iron Horse collection, Blasdell, New York

Anchor Pendant. Hardstone, greenish gray, 5-5/16 x 2 x 3/8 in. G.I.R.S. Allen County, Ohio. $2,500

Pendant, (#HL/1985), Archaic or Woodland, 1-5/16 x 4-3/8 in. Made of green slate, this pendant is from Allegany County, New York. $300-400

Iron Horse collection, Blasdell, New York

Pendant, (#1647/HL), Notched Shovel form, Hopewell people, green banded slate. Typical of this type, the suspension hole is positioned far down on the artifact instead of near the top end. This example measures 2 x 4-7/8 in. and is from Allegany County, New York. $400-600

Iron Horse collection, Blasdell, New York

Pendant, (#308), Woodland timeframe, green banded slate with cream-white inclusions. The large piece is 2-1/4 in. wide and 6-1/2 in. long, and has an unusual angled base. Onondaga County, New York. $600-900

Iron Horse collection, Blasdell, New York

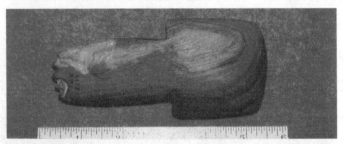

Shovel-shaped pendant, (#E-333), Late Hopewell of Middle Woodland times, with fringed top. This undrilled example is made of green banded slate and measures 2-1/4 x 5-1/8 in. long. It is from Seneca County, New York. $300-400

Iron Horse collection, Blasdell, New York

Pendant, (#HL), Woodland period, green banded slate. This well-made artifact is 1-7/8 in. wide and 4-5/16 in. high. It was found in Allegany County, New York. $350-500

Iron Horse collection, Blasdell, New York

Adena bell-shaped pendant, about 4 in. long, large central hole in upper portion, with tally marks (regular incised lines) at pendant top. A-$175

Slate pendant, 3-1/2 in. long and 1-1/2 in. wide at base. Nicely balanced pendant; partly restored. A-$40

Slate shovel-shaped pendant, 4-1/2 in. long and 1-3/4 in. wide; very good lines to this piece. A-$100

Pendant, (#1826), Woodland period, gray-green slate. This pendant, with polished surface and centered drill-hole is 1-3/4 x 4-1/4 in. It came from Allegany County, New York. $300-500

Iron Horse collection, Blasdell, New York

SLATE GORGETS

These artifacts typically have two holes, but variations have three or more. As with pendants, hardstone examples exist, but they are rare and high-priced. Most gorgets are long and thin. They are believed to have been ornaments, although how they were used is a matter of individual belief. Some gorgets that average about 1-1/2 in. in width, are thick and drilled, may have been Atl-atl weights. The gorget class pulls together some rather dissimilar types.

Two-hole expanded center gorget, 5-1/2 in. long, very well drilled, Midwestern Woodland period. D-$255

Hardstone two-hole gorget, from Illinois, 4-1/8 in. long and just under 2 in. wide and only 5/16 in. thick; very well drilled. Highly polished, holes symmetrical and equidistant from ends and sides. Granite-like stone with black, white, and yellowish colors. C-$900

Reel-shaped gorget, Hopewellian, 4-1/2 in. long and 3 in. wide, angular and very well balanced. Made of attractive banded slate. Surface has a high polish; in perfect condition and from an old collection. A-$400

Rectangular gorget, two-hole, 1-1/4 x 3-1/4 in., clay-colored slate. One plow-mark across face, not deep. C-$80

Sandal-sole gorget, a rare form, Glacial or Gravel Kame period of Late Archaic. Bottom wider than the 2 in. top; piece is just over 6 in. long. Good banded slate, and drilled in diagnostic pattern of 3 in-line holes, the last about 1/2 in. from top. A-$500

Expanded-center gorget, large slate, 6-1/4 in. long and 1-3/4 in. wide in center, very good overall form. A-$425

Concavo-convex slate gorget, 4-1/4 in. long and 2-1/4 in. wide at ends. Drilled with two well-placed holes. A-$350

Humped slate gorget, 4-1/4 in. long and 1-3/4 in. wide, drilled with two holes. Piece has good lines. A-$200

Adena expanded-center gorget, about 4 in. long, holes equidistant from ends, drilled in Adena style from bottom side only. In perfect condition. A-$135

Elliptical gorget, 5 in. long and about 3 in. wide at center. Woodland era; two holes equidistant from rounded ends. C-$700

Slate gorget, very large, 7-1/4 in. long and 2-3/4 in. wide at lower "instep" region. A rare 3-hole sandal-sole type. Symmetrical and well-finished. A-$370

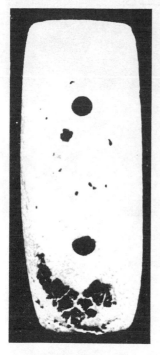 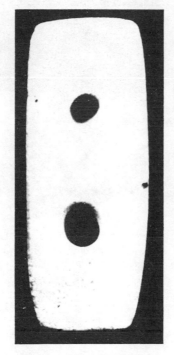

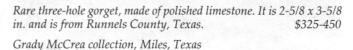

Rare three-hole gorget, made of polished limestone. It is 2-5/8 x 3-5/8 in. and is from Runnels County, Texas. $325-450

Grady McCrea collection, Miles, Texas

Unusual bar gorget, 2-9/16 in. long and 1 in. wide. It is a humped-back type, made of galena and is covered with a thick white pulina. Both obverse and reverse are shown. It evidences conical drilling and may be from the Adena culture, Woodland period. Found in Adams County, Illinois. C-$125-150

Photo courtesy John P. Grotte, Illinois

Stone gorget, 3-1/4 in. long 2 in. wide and 1/2 in. thick; it is made from a red stone material. It was found in Tennes-see. C-$150-200

Photo courtesy Jim Northcutt, Jr., Corinth, Mississippi

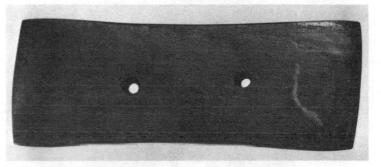

Rectangular two-hole gorget, from Hancock County, Ohio. It is made of banded slate in greenish-gray with darker banding. Size, 1/4 x 2-1/4 x 6 in. It bears G.I.R.S. authentication number C89-24. $1,000

Collection of David G. & Barbara J. Shirley

Slate gorget, 3-1/2 in. long and 2-1/8 in. wide at center. Very well drilled with two holes; slate highly polished, and in good form. Item came from near Brant-ford, Ontario. C-$175-250

Photo courtesy Robert C. Calvert, Lon-don, Ontario, Canada

Slate object, drilled, 5-1/4 in. long and 1-1/2 in. wide, 1/4 in. thick. Piece is damaged at top end. C-$25-30

Photo courtesy Robert C. Calvert, London, Ontario, Canada

Spineback gorget, Glacial Kame culture, from Allen County, Ohio. It is gray banded slate with darker bands and size is 7/8 x 1-3/8 x 4-3/8 in. Pictured in the Meuser collection (p. 74) it bears G.I.R.S. authen-tication number 221. $1,250

Collection of David G. & Barbara J. Shirley

Spineback gorget, Glacial Kame culture, gray and tan banded slate. A rare gorget form, it is 1 x 1-3/4 x 4-1/16 in. It has been assigned G.I.R.S. authentication number 219. $650

Collection of David G. & Barbara J. Shirley

Gorget, six-holed, 2-1/4 x 3-3/8 in. It is made from an unusual material, red hardstone with mica inclusions. This atypical piece is from Montgomery County, Ohio. $300

Larry Garvin collection, Ohio

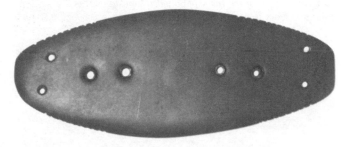

Eight-hole gorget, four in-line and two smaller pairs of extra holes, from Coryell County, Texas. This unusual piece is 2-1/2 x 6-1/2 in. $1,350

L.M. Abbott, Jr. collection, Texas

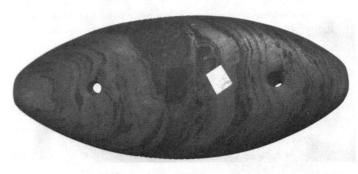

Elliptical gorget, Adena and Early Woodland period, with twelve tally marks on each side. From Allen County, Ohio, it is made of banded slate, gray with black bands. Size is 1/4 x 2-5/8 x 6 in. This fine piece of slate has G.I.R.S. authentication number C89-26. $2,400

Collection of David G. & Barbara J. Shirley

Three-hole pendant or gorget, black well-polished slate, 3 x 3-5/8 in. Found in Ross County, Ohio, the piece may be Glacial Kame culture from the Late Archaic. $275-350

Larry Garvin collection, Ohio

Elliptical gorget, Adena or Early Woodland culture, from Knox County, Ohio. Made of greenish slate with darker bands, it measures 1/4 x 2-8/16 x 6-1/2 in. The large and well-finished artifact is ex-colls. Wehrle, Walters and Jardine. $1,250

Collection of David G. & Barbara J. Shirley

Spineback gorget, Glacial Kame (Late Archaic) culture, Sandusky County, Ohio. Material is banded slate in green, purple, and black. Size is 1-1/2 x 1-3/4 x 4-1/4 in., and the form is highly developed. Ex-colls. Diller, Ritchie and Driskill. $1,500

Collection of David G. & Barbara J. Shirley

Eyed birdstone in green banded slate, fine lines, from Huron County, Ohio. Ex-coll. P. McNight, it is 5 in. long. Museum quality

Bill & Margie Koup collection, Albuquerque, New Mexico; Bill Koup photograph

Slate gorget, 2-3/4 in. long and 2 in. wide, 1/4 in. thick. Found in Brant County, Ontario; made of well-banded slate and is nicely drilled. C-$75-100

Photo courtesy Robert C. Calvert, London, Ontario, Canada

Humped or hump-type gorget, Glacial Kame (Late Archaic) culture, from Hardin County, Ohio. It is 4-1/2 in. long and made from banded slate of the slipped or faulted variety (see change in pattern). Museum quality

Bill & Margie Koup collection, Albuquerque, New Mexico; Bill Koup photograph

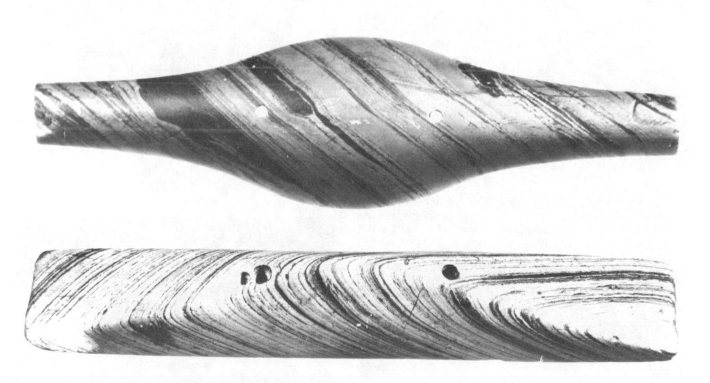

Superb and extremely high quality prehistoric gorgets, each 5-3/4 in. long.

Top: expanded-center Adena gorget, Franklin County, Indiana, green banded slate.
Bottom: keeled gorget, Sandusky County, Ohio. Ex-colls. Diller and Steere.
Both museum quality

Bill & Margie Koup collection, Albuquerque, New Mexico; Bill Koup photograph

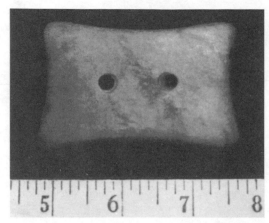

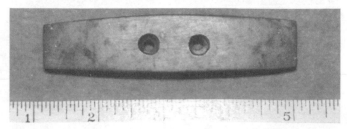

Gorget, Early Woodland (Adena) quadriconcave type, 3 in. wide. The material is streaked green slate probably of glacial origin, and the artifact is from New York. $215

Larry Garvin, Back to Earth, Ohio

Rectangular gorget, (#HL) Woodland period, green slate. The gorget measures 7/8 x 3-7/8 in. and was found near Cuba Lake, Allegany County, New York. $400-650

Iron Horse collection, Blasdell, New York

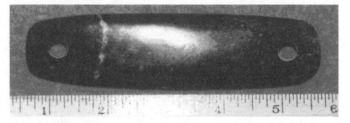

Rectangular gorget, (#HL-1984/A), Woodland, polished black hardstone. This unusual and nicely formed gorget measures 1-1/8 x 5 in. long and was picked up in Allegany County, New York. $600-850

Iron Horse collection, Blasdell, New York

Quadriconcave gorget, (W2-319/156), Adena of Early Woodland times, green banded slate. This example (named for the four incurvate edges), is 1-5/8 x 3-1/4 in. long. It is from the heartland of Adena activity, Ohio. $275-400

Iron Horse collection, Blasdell, New York

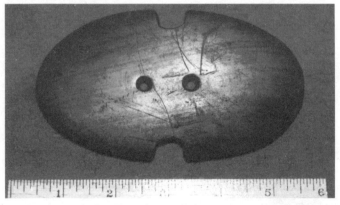

Indented gorget, (#HL-350), probably Early Woodland, banded green slate. Well-made and with good polish, this scarce type example measures 2-3/4 x 5 in. It came from Allegany County, New York. $700-1,100

Iron Horse collection, Blasdell, New York

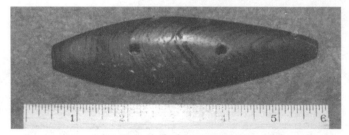

Gorget, (#2HL), two-hole elongated form, Woodland period, banded green slate. This fine gorget with good polish is 1-1/2 in. wide and 5-1/4 in. long. Allegany County, New York. $450-700

Iron Horse collection, Blasdell, New York

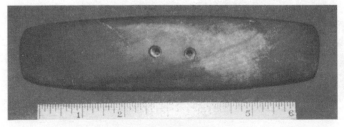

Rectangular gorget, (#HL-1984/B) Woodland period, green banded slate, large size at 1-3/4 x 7 in. This exceptional piece (with the close-together holes that may signify Hopewell origin) came from Allegany County, New York. $700-1,100

Iron Horse collection, Blasdell, New York

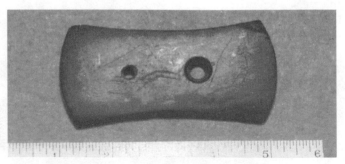

Biconcave gorget, (#G-10), Adena of the Early Woodland period, this piece made of black slate. It is highly unusual and desirable, being engraved with many human figures. The gorget (Atl-atl balance weight) is 1-3/4 x 4 in. long and came from Livingston County, New York. $700-1,000

Iron Horse collection, Blasdell, New York

Slate gorget, cross-shaped, two holes, 3 in. long and 1-3/4 in. wide. Projecting arm ends have a concave outline. Perfect condition. A-$260

Key-hole type gorget, dark banded slate, central hole high up and near top which is irregular to a small degree. Sides and bottom with nicely rounded contours. Average size. A-$175

Adena oval-shaped gorget, 4 in. long and 2-1/4 in. wide; well-drilled from a dark slate. Bands barely visible. D-$225

SLATE BIRDSTONES

Birdstones are from the Late Archaic period and are top-of-the-line for slate collectors. Most "birds" have a head and beak, a flat-bottomed body, and a tail region. Many are drilled with two holes, front and rear on bottom, forming "L"-shaped holes. Obviously, they were attached to something, but no one has yet proven what that might be.

All that can be said today is that birdstones do resemble a bird setting a nest. Strangely, wings are never depicted in any way. Birdstones are found in a 500-mile range of Lake Erie, and many examples come from New York state and the Canadian provinces. A great many have been found in Ohio, Indiana, Illinois, and Michigan.

Banded slate birdstones, 5-3/4 in. long and 1-1/2 in. wide. Classic Glacial Kame elongated type, forward-slanted head and long beak. A-$1,200

Slate birdstone, 4 in. long and 1-1/2 in. wide, good shape, perfect condition. A-$900

Slate birdstone head, broken from body. Head is 1-1/2 in. long; break area salvaged by grinding and base of neck has a slight groove around it, as if for thong attachment. C-$175

Slate birdstone, 4 in. long and 1-1/2 in. wide, good lines. The piece has been restored. A-$185

Birdstone head, "popeye" type of green and black material. It is 1-1/4 in. long, and was salvaged in prehistoric times. The break is ground so that head sits firmly and erect. C-$250

Elongated banded slate birdstone, classic style, 5-7/8 in. and 1-1/2 in. wide at flared tail. Very graceful design and well-drilled. C-$1,600

Black slate birdstone, not drilled, and found at Point Peely, Ontario, Canada. It is 5-1/4 in. long and appears completely finished except for basal holes. Slight scrapes on one side, some damage to left side of head, minor. Very good lines to birdstone. C-$1,250-1,700

Photo courtesy Robert C. Calvert, London, Ontario, Canada

Slate birdstone, unusual form, and 6-1/4 in. in length. Found near Onondago, Ontario, near the Grand River. Like other birdstones, this is probably from Late Archaic times. The specimen is not drilled. C-$1,300-2,000

Photo courtesy Robert C. Calvert, London, Ontario, Canada

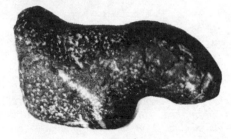

Pre-form birdstone made of a green, mottled hardstone and 3-1/2 in. long and 1-3/4 in. high. Found near Komoka, Ontario, Canada. This piece evidences slight polishing. C-$75-150

Courtesy Robert C. Calvert, London, Ontario, Canada

Birdstone, from near Suult St. Marie, Ontario, Canada. Piece is 3 1/2 in. long and 2 in. high at head and tail. Hardstone material, undrilled, and is probably an unfinished specimen. Good form. C-$600-900

Courtesy Robert C. Calvert, London, Ontario, Canada

Slate birdstone, from near London, Ontario, Canada. Of banded material, piece is 4-3/8 in. long. Birdstone has well-drilled base and is tally-marked on sides of neck, body and tail. Very small damaged area on left side, original. Incised mouths on birdstones are not common. C-$1,400-2,000

Photo courtesy Robert C. Calvert, London, Ontario, Canada

Slate birdstone, from Victoria County, Ontario, Canada. This is a fine popeyed specimen, and measures 4-1/8 in. in length. Piece is drilled on bottom ridges and is in perfect condition. C-$3,200-4,000

Photo courtesy Robert C. Calvert, London, Ontario, Canada

Birdstone, (#6/70), Late Archaic period, red slate. It is 1-7/8 in. high and 5 in. long, with small protruding eyes. This birdstone was found in Burlington County, New Jersey. $2,000-3,000

Iron Horse collection, Blasdell, New York

Birdstone, Late Archaic period and Glacial Kame culture, 1-13/16 x 5-1/4 in. and 3/4 in. thick. This is a nicely formed bird in gray and black banded glacial slate. Boone County, Indiana. $3,000

Richard F. Hughes collection, Louisiana

Birdstone, (#HL-28), Late Archaic period, well-polished dark slate, 1-1/4 in. high and 4-3/8 in. long. It came from Allegany County, New York. $2,500-3,500

Iron Horse collection, Blasdell, New York

Birdstone, (#K-14/HL), Late Archaic elongated subtype, banded slate, 1-5/8 in. high and 5-3/4 in. long. It was found in Allegany County, New York. Unlisted

Iron Horse collection, Blasdell, New York

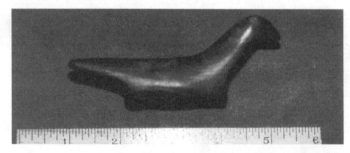

Birdstone, (#HL-352), Late Archaic period, long-necked subtype. This birdstone is 1-1/2 in. high and 4 in. long, and was found in Yates County, New York. $3,000-4,000

Iron Horse collection, Blasdell, New York

Birdstone, (#AK-582), Late Archaic period, with partial neck drilling, banded green slate. It is 1-1/2 in. high and 3-3/4 in. long, and came from Livingston County, New York. $1,500-2,500

Iron Horse collection, Blasdell, New York

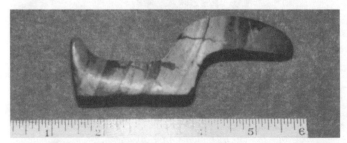

Birdstone, (#1176), Late Archaic period, light brown, beautifully banded slate. A large-headed subtype, it is 1-5/8 in. high and 4-1/4 in. long. New York state. $3,000-4,000

Iron Horse collection, Blasdell, New York

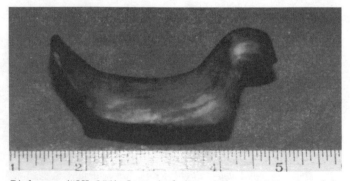

Birdstone, (#HL-351), Late Archaic period, gracefully shaped in banded green slate. It is 1-1/2 in. high and 3-1/4 in. long. Yates County, New York. $2,500-4,000

Iron Horse collection, Blasdell, New York

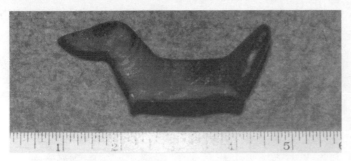

Birdstone, (#HA/DV), Late Archaic period, green banded slate. It is 1-1/2 in. high and 3-5/8 in. long. This type has bottom front and rear ridges for the drill-holes. The birdstone was found near Fillmore, Allegany County, New York. $3,000-4,000

Iron Horse collection, Blasdell, New York

Slate birdstone, 4 in. long and 1-1/4 in. wide; a small-base type.   A-$365

Quartzite birdstone, 4-1/2 in. long and 2-1/4 in. wide. Piece has been restored.   A-$150

Porphyry birdstone, popeye type, 4-1/4 in. long and 2-1/8 in. wide, 2-3/4 in. high. Made of a mottled black and yellow material.   C-$6,000

EFFIGY SLATES

While no one really knows how birdstones were used, neither is it known what effigy slates represent. They most resemble "lizards," or salamanders, but many forms are so highly stylized that not much more can be said. Some forms resemble animals like swimming beavers or otters; others look like a snake that has swallowed a large meal.

Effigies are rarely drilled. They have a flat bottom, a head region, jutting shoulders, and generally taper into a tail region. Some were crudely made while others are superb specimens of the slate-workers' art.

In the opinion of the writer, these are Atl-atl weights from the Middle Archaic time frame. The market value of better specimens is beginning to approach that of average grade birdstones.

Banded slate effigy stone, Midwestern area, 5 in. long. Head squared off, shoulders very high, short neck region. Body and tail tapered very nicely; overall, well-made and polished piece.   A-$650

Slate effigy stone, 4-1/8 in. long, nicely tapered with

Boatstone: flat, uncupped primary form. (Browner): "Boatstones are an Archaic cultural manifestation. Like bannerstones, they seem to have begun in the Southeastern states. From simple uncupped bars used as Atl-atl weights they evolved into intricately shaped and deeply cupped artifacts of unknown use. Boatstones continued into Mississippian times and some of the forms are incised and show rare symmetry and workmanship."

This piece is 3-3/4 in. long and is made from a brown sandstone. It is from Yell County, Arkansas.   C-$250-400

Courtesy Ferrel Anderson, photographer; Thomas Browner collection; Davenport,

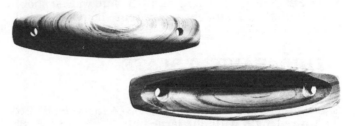

Drilled slate boatstone, top and bottom views. This boatstone is of the rounded type and is a near-perfect example of the type. In size, color, and workmanship it would have few equals. Note the excellent cupping, typical of the type. This piece is 4-1/2 in. long and 1-1/4 in. wide at center. Made of a green and black banded slate, it is from the Grand Rapids, Michigan area.   C-$800-1,100

Courtesy Ferrel Anderson, photographer; Thomas Browner collection; Davenport, Iowa

Ceremonial pick made of slate, and 13-3/4 in. long. It is well polished and in good condition, from Brant County, Ontario. An unusual artifact type.   C-$200-300

Courtesy Robert C. Calvert, London, Ontario, Canada

Paint palette, 10-1/2 in. in diameter, made of slate. Design is a repeated bird motif; this piece was found near Memphis, Tennessee, in 1837 and is late prehistoric, Mississippian era.   C-$2,000

S.E. Kernaghan photo; Marguerite Kernaghan collection

abrupt expansion near head region. Dark-colored and banded slate. C-$675

Slate effigy figure, 5 in. long and 1-1/2 in. wide. Piece has a wide, elongated body, small head, and broad tail. It resembles the profile of a beaver more than a salamander. A-$175

Slate lizard effigy, 4 in. long and 1-1/2 in. wide, very rounded features including head, shoulders, and short tail. Perfect condition, well-polished. A-$325

Slate beaver effigy, 4 in. long and 1-1/2 in. wide. Rather an abstract depiction, rare form, fine condition. A-$360

Slate effigy or lizard, 5 in. long and 1-1/2 in. wide. Piece has squared-off head and tail ends, very narrow and jutting shoulders. No damage. An exceptionally well-made and attractive piece. A-$775

Slate effigy form, 4 in. long and 1-3/4 in. wide at shoulders. Blunt head, straight taper from shoulders to tail. Perfect condition. A-$165

OTHER BANDED SLATE ARTIFACTS

Slate tube, 3-1/4 in. long and 1-3/4 in. wide, drilled for entire length with one large hole. A-$185

Banded slate phallus, depicting male penis glans, 3-5/16 in. high, resting on enlarged flat base. Realistic and colorful material, black bands on reddish background. Unknown time period. Surface find in western Ohio. C-$550

Slate bar amulet, 7-3/4 in. long and 3/4 in. wide, with raised section, ridge-like, in center. Beautiful flowing lines, and high-quality slate. C-$700

Banded slate spud (unusual flared-bit celtiform axe), 10-1/4 in. long and 3-1/8 in. wide at blade tips. Dark green slate with reddish bands. D-$650

Banded slate tube or tubular pipe, 7-1/4 in. long and 3/4 in. wide. Good lines; piece has been restored. A-$250

Slate bar-weight, 3-3/4 in. long and 1 in. wide, notched in center. A-$55

Slate pestle, 6 in. high and 4 in. in basal diameter, bell-type. A-$70

Slate pestle, 19-1/2 in. in length and 2-1/2 in. in diameter, long roller type. A-$200

Plummet, Late Archaic to Early Woodland period, 3-1/4 in. long. This is a beautiful example, grooved at the top for attachment to a cord. Louisiana. $400

Richard F. Hughes collection, Louisiana

Plummet, Late Archaic to Early Woodland, 3-3/4 in. long. This large and fine specimen is made of near-black hardstone and is nicely polished. Louisiana. $450

Richard F. Hughes collection, Louisiana

Boatstone, (#HL-4), Woodland period, green banded slate. It measures 1 x 4-7/8 in. and is shown with the flat bottom facing up. Seneca County, New York. $450-700

Iron Horse collection, Blasdell, New York

Slate axe, 8-1/2 in. high and 4-3/4 in. wide. A-$160

Slate pendant, 3-1/4 in. long and 1-3/4 in. wide, thin and rectangular, one hole at end. Piece interesting because one face is cross-hatched with incised lines. C-$180

Slate lizard effigy, 4-7/8 in. long, bulbous-body type, rounded "tail," tally-marks around shoulder ridge. Perfect condition, very nice banding. C-$1,000

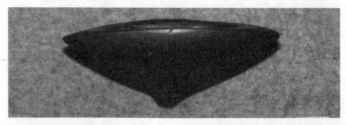

Boatstone, (HL-967), Woodland, green slate. This is a well-polished specimen with the knobbed top pointed down, excurvate base up. Measuring 1 x 4 in., it came from near Hornby Lake in Steuben County, New York. $800-1400

Iron Horse collection, Blasdell, New York

Plummet, (#E-449), Late Archaic to Early Woodland, 1-1/2 x 5-1/4 in. high. The large plummet is made of pecked and smoothed hardstone, and has a thin attachment groove at the top. Erie County, New York. $450-750

Iron Horse collection, Blasdell, New York

Boatstone, Early Woodland period, this example in mottled hardstone. Size 1-1/4 x 4-1/4 in. for this well-shaped and polished artifact which is fully scooped on the bottom. This was found by John Bond in the year 1916. Collinsville area, Illinois. $650-800

Collection of, and photograph by, Steve Granger, Hallsville, Texas

Boatstone, (#HL-2), Woodland period, made of polished dark hard-stone. It is measures 1-1/8 x 3-3/8 in. and came from near Belfast, Allegany County, New York. $900-1,500

Iron Horse collection, Blasdell, New York

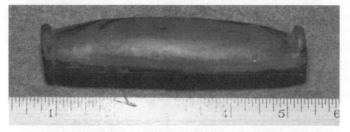

Bar Amulet, (#K-9), Early Woodland period, banded slate. This well-made example with ridged ends is 3/4 x 4-1/2 in. long. It came from Wyoming County, New York. $800-1,200

Iron Horse collection, Blasdell, New York

Boatstone, (#75/22), Woodland period, unusual material, red slate. This superb example has a fully scooped base, is drilled with the typical two holes, and measures 7/8 x 7 in. long. $1,000-1,500

Iron Horse collection, Blasdell, New York

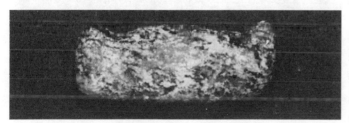

Bar Amulet, (#A-5), Early Woodland period, in very desirable hard-stone colored black and cream. It is 1 x 3 in. and was found in Chautauqua County, New York. $1,000-1,500

Iron Horse collection, Blasdell, New York

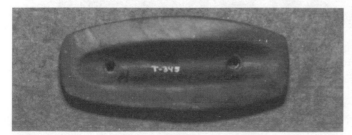

Boatstone, (#T-345), Woodland period, banded slate. Seen from the bottom, it is fully scooped and has two drill-holes for attachment to the Atl-atl or lance-throwing stick. Size, 1-1/2 x 3-3/4 in. This well-made example is from Guernsey County, Ohio. $700-1,000

Iron Horse collection, Blasdell, New York

Spineback gorget, 4-3/8 in. long, with single protruding knob between two drill-holes. Fine banding in specimen and highly polished surface. C-$975

Animal-head effigy, 1-7/8 in. long, unknown species, picked up on Illinois Archaic site. C-$180

Suggested Reading

Townsend, Earl C. Jr. *Birdstones of the North American Indian.* Indianapolis: Privately published, 1959.

Boatstone; deep cup type (Browner): "This example represents the end of boatstone evolution. This specimen is notable in both its deep cup and its extremely thin walls. Minor chips at one edge detract a bit, but do not harm overall value. Boatstones are usually made of banded slate. However, quartz, granite, sandstone, limestone, and steatite were also used."

This piece is 2-3/4 in. long and 1-7/8 in. wide. Made of brown sandstone, it is from Independence County, Arkansas. C-$600-850

Courtesy Ferrel Anderson, photographer; Thomas Browner collection; Davenport, Iowa

Bar amulet, Early Woodland, from Indiana. It is made of light gray banded slate with darker bands, and is 3/4 x 1-5/32 x 3-13/16 in. The reverse ends are string-worn between the holes. Ex-coll. Parks, and G.I.R.S. authentication number C88-6. $950

Collection of David G. & Barbara J. Shirley

Fine slate tube, 3-5/8 in. long, of green slate with bold black bands. Perfect condition; completely drilled and straight, from small to larger end. Old markings, "Forest, Hardin County." An Ohio piece, probably Archaic period. C-$275

Private collection

Bar amulet, Early Woodland, Butler County, Ohio. Made of rare hardstone, light green with brown spots, it measures 15/16 x 13/16 x 3-5/8 in. Ex-colls. Dr. Meuser and D. Driskill. It was assigned G.I.R.S. authentication number C89-30. $900

Collection of David G. & Barbara J. Shirley

Bar amulet, Early Woodland and Red Ochre, Noble County, Indiana. It is gray banded slate with darker bands and measures 7/8 x 9/16 x 3-7/8 in. It is assigned G.I.R.S. authentication number C88-4. $800

Collection of David G. & Barbara J. Shirley

Shell ornaments, Pennsylvania and New York, ca. 1700s. Values depend on decoration, finesse, and condition, with purple items being worth more than white due to rarity.

Top: talon or claw effigies, lizard effigy.   Each, $25-35
Middle: turtles and "ducks," in center.   Each, $100-300

Gary L. Fogelman collection, Pennsylvania

Bar amulet, Red Ochre Early Woodland, from Tiffin (Seneca County), Ohio. Made of gray banded slate with darker banding, it is 7/8 x 1-1/4 x 3-1/4 in. It bears G.I.R.S. authentication number C88-26. $600

Collection of David G. & Barbara J. Shirley

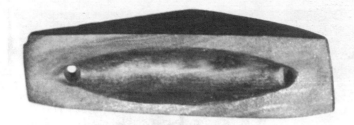

Boatstone, scooped and drilled, rare angular type, from Howard County, Indiana. Made of gray banded slate with darker bands, it was found by Arthur Hunt in 1934, and is ex-colls. Stubbe, Schmatz, Doming and Mear. $1,200

Collection of David G. & Barbara J. Shirley

Bar amulet, Early Woodland, undrilled and made of black and white hardstone. From Portage County, Ohio, it is 1-1/8 x 15/16 x 2-3/4 in. It is pictured in the Dr. Meuser book (p. 40) and Ohio Slate Types (p. 69). The artifact bears G.I.R.S. authentication number C89-31. $1,750

Collection of David G. & Barbara J. Shirley

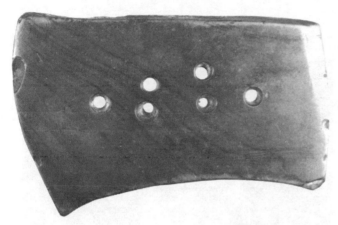

Drilled slate artifact, possibly a reworked gorget or pendant. It is probably from Ohio, 2-1/2 x 4 in., and is made of highly polished banded slate. $150-175

Larry Garvin collection, Ohio

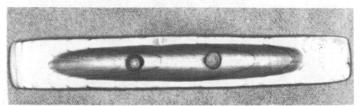

Boatstone, Woodland period, very finely drilled and scooped (bottom view). Made of gray banded slate with darker bands, size is 15/16 x 1 x 6-25/32 in. This piece has G.I.R.S. authentication number 216. This is an exceptionally long and well-made boatstone. $3,000

Collection of David G. & Barbara J. Shirley

Slate blade, highly polished and well-shaped, from Maine. Material is gray slate with wide dark gray bands. This particular piece has been pictured in several early publications.   Museum quality

Collection of David G. & Barbara J. Shirley

Stone and slate artifacts, various regions.

Far left: gorget, New York, slate. $125
Top left: gorget, St. Joseph County, Michigan, banded slate, elliptical type, 5-1/2 in. $140
Top right: gorget, Adena, sandstone, Kentucky. $95

Center, left to right:

Gorget, granite, Kingston, Massachusetts. $75
Pendant, hematite, grooved, Ohio. $35
Pendant, human effigy, salvaged, from Waterbury, Connecticut, rare. $375

Bottom left to right:

Gorget, Adena boat-shaped (Hopewell type but with Adena cone-shaped drilling, from bottom), Ohio. $55
Pendant, Indiana, ex-coll. Parks. $90

Pocotopaug Trading Post, South Windsor, Connecticut

Bar amulet, Early Woodland period, from St. Joseph County, Michigan. Made of gray slate with light and dark banding, it is 7/8 x 7/8 x 5-1/4 in. It carries G.I.R.S. authentication number C89-29. $1,700

Collection of David G. & Barbara J. Shirley

Bar amulet, Early Woodland, from Huron County, Ohio. Made of gray banded slate with darker bands, it is 11/16 x 3/4 x 7-3/8 in. One of the finest bar amulets to come from the state, it is pictured in Who's Who in Indian Relics No. 2 (p. 175). Ex-coll. Jack Walters, and with G.I.R.S. authentication number C88-3. $3,400

Collection of David G. & Barbara J. Shirley

Plummets or plumb-bobs, Late Archaic and Woodland, top row left to right:

Sandstone, grooved, Mississippi.	$100
Greenstone, drilled, Louisiana.	$50
Brownstone, grooved, Mississippi.	$125
Hematite, drilled, Louisiana.	$50
Hematite, drilled, Louisiana.	$30
2nd, left to right: Sandstone, Mississippi.	$25
Polished sandstone, Mississippi.	$15
Sandstone, cupped ends, Mississippi.	$15
Grooved brownstone, Louisiana.	$20
Grooved and polished, Louisiana.	$35
Bottom, stemmed, Mississippi;	Each $35

Wilfred A. Dick collection, Magnolia, Mississippi

Drilled stone artifacts. Top row, left to right:

Greenstone gorget, Mississippi.	$125
Gray stone, tally-marked, Mississippi.	$175
Reddish-brown gorget, Mississippi.	$150
Middle, left to right: Boatstone.	$35
Humped, lined drill-holes, Mississippi.	$125
Gray boatstone, two holes.	$125
Bottom: clay pendant, Mississippi.	$125

Wilfred A. Dick collection, Magnolia, Mississippi

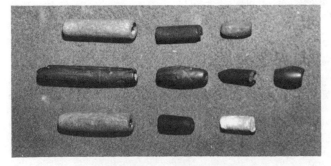

Redstone beads, elongated types, all drilled and polished. These came from the Poverty Point area of Louisiana.   Each, $15-95

Wilfred A. Dick collection, Magnolia, Mississippi

Pentagonal or shield-shaped pendant, Late Hopewell, from Brown County, Ohio. Material is gray banded slate with darker banding, and size is 2-31/64 x 4-7/16 in. It carries G.I.R.S. authentication number C88-13. This piece is nicely balanced. $875

Collection of David G. & Barbara J. Shirley

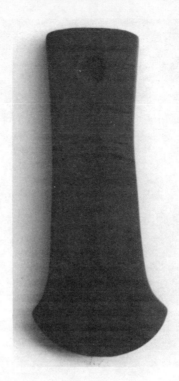

Anchor pendant, Woodland period, from Hardin County, Ohio. Material is gray banded slate with darker banding and size is 5/16 x 1-3/4 x 4-1/4 in. Ex-coll. Driskill #D-133. G.I.R.S. Authentication number C88-8. This is a very attractive artifact. $900

Collection of David G. & Barbara J. Shirley

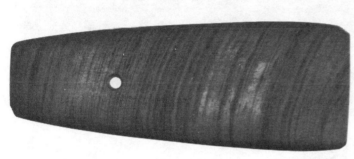

Trapezoidal pendant, Williams County, Ohio. Material is greenish-gray banded slate with darker banding. It is very thin and 2-1/32 x 5-9/32 in. This artistic piece has G.I.R.S. authentication number C88-10. $1,100+

Collection of David G. & Barbara J. Shirley

Unusual view of Cliff Palace Ruins, Mesa Verde National Park, Colorado. Seen at top right, it is obvious how difficult it is to reach the site and how easy it was to defend.

Lar Hothem photo (Upper right in photo)

CHAPTER VIII

ARTIFACTS OF COPPER AND HEMATITE

Copper and hematite, both found in natural deposits, were much-used to make artifacts in prehistoric North America. They were, however, quite dissimilar and were worked in entirely different ways.

Copper was mined—dug from near the land surface—for thousands of years in the Lake Superior region, and copper artifacts are still being found today. Copper was formed by hammering the malleable material into new and useful shapes. This process—treating the metal almost like a plastic stone—was the third great tool-making method used in prehistoric North America.

Despite extensive copper use, and beginning with the Old Copper Culture (5000 BC) in Northcentral U.S., Amerinds above the Mexican-U.S. border did not smelt copper; it was cold-worked. There is some evidence that Woodland and later-period groups heated the metal, but only so it could be pounded into thinner sheets and more varied forms. The small late-prehistoric cast bells (lost-wax process) of the Southwest have not been proven to have been made in the region.

The use of copper for tools, weapons, ornaments, and ceremonial items spans more than 7,000 years, and the material was widely traded in early times. Among the groups which made important use of copper were the Middle Archaic peoples centered in what is today Wisconsin, the Glacial Kame peoples of 1500 BC, the Hopewell groups of 200 BC-AD 500, Southeastern Amerinds of Mississippian times, and Northwest Coastal groups well into historic times. Other Amerinds valued copper and made artifacts from it.

Much copper was made into routine tools, but much was also reserved for specialty items and artistic creations. These range from beads to headdress ornaments, and from finger rings and bracelets to panpipe whistle sets.

Collectors look for size in a copper piece, good condition, and an even color. Weight, an indication of solid copper, is a factor. Appearance is important. Rare artifacts, like a matched pair of earspools in good condition, would be especially desirable, as would any copper with artistic forms or human figures.

There are some fraudulent prehistoric copper pieces around, but the early copper is difficult to fake convincingly. The forms—awls, points, celts—are easy enough to pound into shape. But two factors limit reproductions. One is corrosion or chemical erosion of the artifact itself. The other is a colorful patina.

Depending on whether the artifact was under water or beneath the earth, various mineral salts leach away copper parts, giving a characteristic pitted surface. A colorful patina appears on the surface. It is often a shade of dark green or brown. It is not easy to put the two together in a way that matches the appearance of an authentic specimen.

COPPER ARTIFACTS

Socketed copper blade, overall length, 5 in., hafted by a wide base that has been pounded around to form an almost closed socket. Lightly patinated and good condition. C-$225

Flat-stemmed copper blade, 5-1/2 in. long, with stem the same thickness as blade, 3/16 in. All parts in good condition. C-$300

Copper rattail-hafted blade, blade-back straight, blade edge excurvate. Piece is 4 in. long, beautiful green patina. Said to have been found in shallow waters of a lake. Some corrosion on thin parts of blade but metal not weakened. C-$170

Socketed copper blade, 6 in. long and about 2 in. wide at mid-length. Center of black portion of socket base also has a small hole for a handle peg. Light patina, good condition. C-$240

Copper celt, flared bit, fine shape. Piece is 3-3/4 in. long and 3 in. wide, with much patina. G-$180

Copper chisel, Wisconsin, and 5-1/4 in. long and 1-3/8 in. wide, 3/8 in. thick. Base shows some hammerstone battering. Very unusual, good condition. D-$175

Copper beads from Midwestern late prehistoric site. Nine beads of similar small size, 1/4 in. diameter. Un-

usual. C-$120

Copper Adena bracelet, Woodland period, contains about 300 degrees of arc, tapered tips. About 3/8 in. thick at center. Scarce artifact from an admired culture. C-$450

Curved copper semi-lunar knife, Wisconsin. It is 4-1/2 in. long, has two upright tangs formerly secured to wooden handle, now gone. Blade averages 1/4 in. thick. C-$260

Copper rattail point, unusual in that it is also tanged and with shallow notches at sides of point. Piece 3 in. long.

Copper celt from Alpena, Michigan. It is red-brown with green patination and measures 1-3/16 x 3-5/16 in. This is a very good piece of prehistoric copper. $300

Collection of David G. & Barbara J. Shirley

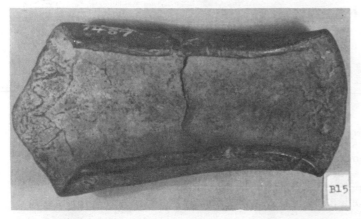

Copper spud or adz from Wisconsin in Old Copper Culture, open-ended design. Note the stress fracture in the metal from use. $900

Courtesy E. Neiburger/Andent, Inc.

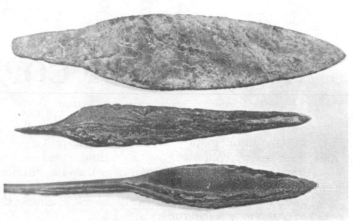

Three types of copper spear points or blades, Old Copper Culture, from Wisconsin. Top: flat blade. Middle: short-tail. Bottom: rat-tail. Each, $350-600

Courtesy E. Neiburger/Andent, Inc.

Opposite view of the copper spud or adz with stress fracture in the metal. The longitudinal ridge put in for strength runs the length of the piece. $900

Courtesy E. Neiburger/Andent, Inc.

Curved copper knife (semi-lunate), surface-found in Wisconsin. It is Old Copper Culture, with hafting tang for handle. $450-700

Courtesy E. Neiburger/Andent, Inc.

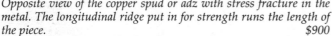

Copper knife with solid haft, from Wisconsin, Old Copper Culture. It is just over 5 in. long. $450-600

Courtesy E. Neiburger/Andent, Inc.

Copper celt, 6 in. long, from northeastern Wisconsin. It is Old Copper Culture and ca. 3000 BC. This artifact has a fine taper to the form. $500-700

Courtesy E. Neiburger/Andent, Inc.

Copper rat-tail type spear head, Old Copper Culture, eastcentral Wisconsin. The unusually long haft area is actually longer than the blade itself. $500-700

Courtesy E. Neiburger/Andent, Inc.

Copper spud or adz blade, from northcentral Wisconsin. Note the closed corner (see arrow) design of manufacture which provided greater strength. $800-900

Courtesy E. Neiburger/Andent, Inc.

Copper spud adz blade, from northern Wisconsin. The bent-side section of the artifact once had a wooden handle. $400-600

Courtesy E. Neiburger/Andent, Inc.

Various copper artifacts.

Top: spear or projectile point. $95
2nd row: copper pendants, some more detailed and elaborate. Each, $30-125
3rd row: points and tubular beads, beads from Southeastern U.S. Each, $15-40

Wilfred A. Dick collection, Magnolia, Mississippi

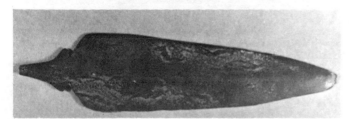

Copper spear point or blade from central Wisconsin, Old Copper Culture of the Late Archaic period. The hefting is very unusual, being a combination of notching and stemming. $600-850

Courtesy E. Neiburger/Andent, Inc.

The reverse of copper spear point or blade from central Wisconsin showing unusual tang. $600-850

Courtesy E. Neiburger/Andent, Inc.

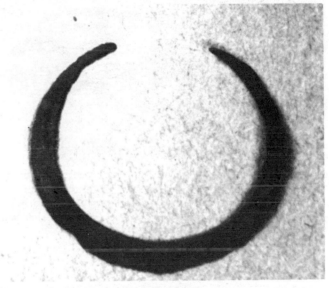

Copper open ring, possibly personal facial ornament, a personal find by the owner in Barron County, Wisconsin. It is delicate and fine, 1-1/2 in. in diameter. $135

Dennis R. Lindblad collection, Chetek, Wisconsin

Copper celt, form Alpena, Michigan. It is reddish with green patination and measures 1-1/2 x 6-7/8 in. This is a fine early artifact. $500

Collection of David G. & Barbara J. Shirley

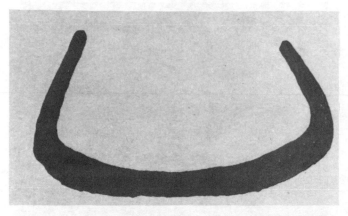

Copper crescent knife, probably from Middle to Late Archaic period, 1-3/4 x 3 in. wide. A personal find by the owner, it is from Barron County, Wisconsin. $150-200

Dennis R. Lindblad collection, Chetek, Wisconsin

Rare artifacts made of clear crystal quartz.

Left: cone, Woodland period, 1-1/8 x 2-3/16 in., Ross County, Ohio. $325-500
Right: hammerstone, unknown period, Wyandot County, Ohio, 1-1/2 x 2-1/8 in. $150-250

Private collection, Ohio

Catlinite pendant, found by Patricia McCrea. It has two holes drilled, one through the side and one through the top; 2-1/4 in. long. It is from Runnels County, Texas. Museum quality

Grady McCrea collection, Miles, Texas

Copper crescent handled knife. Old Copper culture of the Late Archaic period, from Barron County, Wisconsin. A personal find of the owner, it is 4-1/2 in. wide and 5-1/2 in. high. This design, with the one-piece closed handle, is quite rare. Very good condition. $600-850

Dennis R. Lindblad collection, Chetek, Wisconsin

Reverse of above pendant

Copper socketed spearpoint or pike, very heavy, very fine condition. It is 9/16 in. wide at the base and 4 in. long, with a median ridge on one side. This was a personal find by the owner in Barron County, Wisconsin. $325

Dennis R. Lindblad collection, Chetek, Wisconsin

Copper harpoon, rolled shaft, with a very distinct barb and delicate tip. Old Copper culture, this item is 4 in. long. It was a personal find by the owner in Barron County, Wisconsin. $375

Dennis R. Lindblad collection, Chetek, Wisconsin

Socketed copper spearpoint or blade, with characteristic median ridge and very symmetrical shape; good condition. This 4-3/4 in. specimen was a personal find by the owner in Barron County, Wisconsin. $240

Dennis R. Lindblad collection, Chetek, Wisconsin

Double-pointed (?) copper awl, perforator or pike, unusual configuration, quite pointed on both ends. It is 5 in. long, and a personal find by the owner in Barron County, Wisconsin. $250-350

Dennis R. Lindblad collection, Chetek, Wisconsin

Copper knife blade with handle, Old Copper culture. This fine piece is 4-3/4 in. long, a personal find by the owner in Barron County, Wisconsin. $215

Dennis R. Lindblad collection, Chetek, Wisconsin

Copper spearpoint, rolled-shaft type, 3-1/2 in. long. The blade edge is very sharp all around to the stem beginning. Very good condition. It was a personal find by the owner in Barron County, Wisconsin. $250

Dennis R. Lindblad collection, Chetek, Wisconsin

Copper awl or perforator, very precisely made and with little sign of wear. It is 4-3/8 in. long and a personal find by the owner in Barron County, Wisconsin. $160

Dennis R. Lindblad collection, Chetek, Wisconsin

Double-notched/stemmed copper blade or point, very rare type and thought to be much earlier than the socketed blades with median ridges on both faces. It is 7/8 x 2-3/4 in. and a personal find by the owner in Barron County, Wisconsin. $225

Dennis R. Lindblad collection, Chetek, Wisconsin

Copper rat-tail point, very good condition, and a personal find by the owner. It is 2-3/4 in. long. Such artifacts may also have been knife blades. $150

Dennis R. Lindblad collection, Chetek, Wisconsin

Copper knife with one-piece handle, Old Copper culture, it is in very good condition and 4-3/4 in. long, a personal find by the owner in Barron County, Wisconsin. $215

Dennis R. Lindblad collection, Chetek, Wisconsin

Socketed copper point, a personal find by the owner in Barron County, Wisconsin. It is 3-1/8 in. long. $175

Dennis R. Lindblad collection, Chetek, Wisconsin

Tangs both slightly bent. Nice patina overall. C-$135

Conical copper point, 2-1/2 in. long; patinated. D-$60

Copper chisel, northern Michigan, 1 in. wide at center, 4-7/8 in. long. Medium corrosion, convex blade edge, flat poll, good lines. D-$320

Duo-tipped copper awl, Michigan, 8-1/8 in. long and 3/8 in. in diameter in center. Has medium corrosion, overall good condition. C-$400

Copper celt, Minnesota, 7 in. long and 2-3/4 in. wide at bit, 1-1/2 in. wide at squared poll top. Nice patina and good lines. C-$450

Copper fish-hook, Wisconsin, 1-1/2 in. long. Made of a thin roll of beaten copper, twisted and pounded into shape. C-$40

Copper needle, Minnesota, 3-1/8 in. long, bent and badly corroded. C-$15

Copper celt, New York state, 3-3/4 in. long and 1/2 in. thick. Green patina, very regular lines. C-$210

Copper celt, 4-3/8 in. long and 2-1/8 in. wide. Found in 1969 in Wisconsin. C-$365

Copper celt, late prehistoric period, 1-1/4 x 3 in. and 1/4 inch thick. The flared blade corners hint that this might be from the Woodland period, especially the Hopewell people. It was found in the Boot Heel area of Missouri. *$350*

Jack Baker collection, Ozark, Missouri; David Capon photograph

Copper fish-hook, 1-1/4 in. long made from rolled and pounded copper strip. Good condition. C-$30

Tapered-stem blade, 3-1/2 in. long, lightly corroded. It is not known whether this form was knife or spear as blade edges are similar and excurvate. D-$100

Copper needle, historic period, from Apache site near Cajote, New Mexico, and ca. 1850. D-$30

Chief's copper, contemporary Northwest Coast, made and signed by Lelooska. A-$700

HEMATITE ARTIFACTS

Hematite, an iron ore, is colored steel gray to black and from dull to brilliant red. It has a double distinction, for it was used for both artifacts and paint in prehistoric times. Many cultures, including the Red Ochre peoples, valued powdered hematite or ochre in rituals. Occasionally paint cups are found with ochre traces still in them.

This hard material, from examination of unfinished pieces, was made into artifacts by the familiar peck and abrasion method. Hematite was widely used for both tools and strange artifacts that seem to have had no utility, like the Woodland-era cones that resemble tiny mounds.

Hematite was preferred for certain artifacts, like the plummets and some small adz-blades, and almost any artifact made of hard-stone is likely to have a counterpart, somewhere, in hematite. Some of the artifacts become exfoliated. That is, the surface peels and flakes away, becoming uneven.

Collectors look for good shape and pleasing lines. Size is of some importance, but hematite artifacts tend to be rather small due to weight. A high polish is admired, plus few or no rough areas remaining from the original nodule of ore.

At present, fakes are not a serious problem, partly because hematite is a difficult material to work due to its hardness. Apparently, artifacts made today would not be a paying proposition.

Hematite cone, 3/4 in. high and 1-1/2 in. in diameter A-$60

Red hematite celt, 1-5/8 in. long and 1-5/8 in. wide, with polish on bit. G-$55

Hematite plummet, 3-1/8 in. long, drilled at small end, classic tear-drop shape. Polished overall, black color. D-$160

Hematite celt, Missouri, 3-1/2 in. long. G-$35

Hematite plummet, 2-7/8 in. long, one end rounded and grooved, other end pointed. Slender and well-polished. C-$140

Hematite cone, 1-1/4 in. high and 1-1/4 in. in basal diameter. A-$33

Hematite pendant, 3-1/4 in. long and 1-1/2 in. wide at bottom. Well-made, with single large drill-hole at top center, rust-red color, highly polished. C-$260

Hematite plummet, 2 in. high and 1 in. diameter. A-$42

Hematite gorget, 3-1/2 in. long, rectangular form, two drill holes; has highly polished surface, no damage.C-$410

Hematite discoidal, 1-1/2 in. high and 2-1/2 in. in diameter. Very good color in this extremely well-made piece. G-$360

Hematite plummet, extra-large size. It is 3-1/4 in. high and 1 in. in diameter. A-$155

Hematite birdstone, 2-1/4 in. long and 1-1/2 in. high. A-$795

Hematite plummet, 1-3/4 in. high and 3/4 in. diameter. A-$55

Hematite celt, 3-3/4 in. long and 1-3/4 in. wide. A-$70

ARTIFACTS MADE FROM OTHER NATURAL MATERIALS

Cannel coal gorget, 6-1/2 in. long and 2-1/4 in. wide. Three-hole sandal-sole type, fine condition. A-$550

Sheet-mica cut-out, ca. AD 500, Hopewellian and Midwestern, 1-3/8 in. long. Piece depicts the canine tooth of a bear. Base has a small drill-hole. Material probably imported from the Carolinas via early trade. A scarce piece, because mica layer flakes easily. C-$150

Cannel coal disc, 2-1/4 in. in diameter, 1/8 in. in thickness, probably late prehistoric. Use unknown. C-$10

Mica strips, thin, curved, each with minute holes at one end. Seven pieces, each measuring 1-1/8 in. long and resembling eagle or hawk claws. Rare decorative ornaments. From southern Ohio. C-$12 each

Cannel coal pendant, 2-1/4 in. long and about 1 in. wide, drilled at smaller end. D-$45

Meteoritic iron chisel, collected in state of Washington, and remaining section 3-1/4 in. long. Lower blade in good condition but back portion of piece broken in early times. Rare piece. C-$275

Jadeite blade, probably for woodworking adz, from West Coast of Canada, 4-3/8 in. long. Has typical concave adz blade and good condition. Rare material and probably very early. C-$695

Galena (lead ore) pendant, 2-1/4 in. long 3/4 in. wide, and pale white color. Undrilled, so may also have been intended as a small gorget. C-$40

The Papago potter: Edward S. Curtis, photographer.

Photo courtesy National Photography Collection, Neg. #C-30076, Public Archives of Canada

CHAPTER IX

CERAMICS—Pottery

(Considerable writing and material was contributed to this chapter by John W. Barry, P.O. Box 583, Davis, CA, 95617, who is especially knowledgeable in the contemporary Pueblo pottery field. He contributed the entire pre-listings sections, selections from his Indian Rock Arts catalog, and suggestions for further reading. Used with permission.)

INTRODUCTION

Reflections of Native American art through the ceramic media equal and often surpass artistic expression through weavings, jewelry, and canvas. Traditional ceramics usually are executed with natural materials and methods employed for several centuries.

Recognizing that there are contemporary styles using contemporary materials and methods to create ceramic Indian art, the skiff, creativity, and inspiration of the artist are inherent in every piece of Pueblo pottery. These people have an apparent need, coupled with a natural artistry, to express beauty.

It is a natural sequence of events that there is an increasing awareness of this art form as we take shelter from the complexities of our society, examining values and searching for natural aesthetics.

There are several excellent books on American Indian Pottery. For those interested, a list of references is included at the end of this article. The purpose of this chapter is to provide an overview of this art form.

Within the scope of our discussion, ceramics is defined as items crafted from clay by Native Americans. This includes numerous types, styles, colors, designs, and shapes to include beakers, vases, bowls, bottles, scoops, mugs, plates, pitchers, animal and human figurines, jars, and ladles and effigy vessels.

Pottery collectors differ in what they collect, as do collectors of any other art form. Some collections represent either prehistoric, historic, or contemporary pottery. Some single out one pueblo, others may collect a certain style from one or several areas, while still others may collect only miniatures, non-traditional pottery, or pottery produced by a single potter. The choice is great.

I suggest that you consider concentrating on a particular theme if you plan to become a serious collector; otherwise, choose a few pieces which compliment your decor. The objective is to pursue this art form in a manner which provides you the most enjoyment.

HISTORIC DEVELOPMENT AND CLASSIFICATION

Archaeologists and anthropologists (Martin, et. al. 1947) estimate that pottery made its debut in North America 2,500 years ago. Fine ceramics were made by the Hohokam people of the Southwest in 200 BC, and by the Mogollon culture around the opening of the Christian era (Tanner 1968). Later Indian immigrants may have brought pottery types to North America, as suggested by similarities to some Asian types.

But pottery had already been established in the New World. Pottery is of immense importance to the archaeologist in classifying, dating, correlating cultures, and providing valuable clues to their rise and fall.

Pottery is a sensitive indicator of changes within a culture. It shows the influences and mixing of other cultures, and when found *in situ* with burials or ceremonial chambers it provides the archaeologist opportunities to understand the user's lifestyle. A two-name system is used by archaeologists to describe distinctive pottery classes, such as Mesa Verde Black-on-White.

Prehistoric pottery. Classifying prehistoric pottery, particularly those pieces found east of the Mississippi River, is best accomplished by geographic area because there was simultaneous development in various geographical areas. For those interested in more of an in-depth study of the pottery produced by various cultures, books such as Martin, Quimbly, and Colliers' book, *Indians Before Columbus*, should be reviewed.

Historic pottery. Historic pottery, chronologically, is pottery produced after the arrival of Coronado to the area of New Mexico in 1540. Some define historic pottery as that produced after 1600 AD, while others use 1700 AD.

Pueblo V: 1700 to Present. Pottery was produced by many of the pueblos during the early part of the period, at the pueblos of Acoma, Cochiti, Walpi, Sichomovi, Hano, Skungopovi, Shipaulovi, Mishongonovi, Isleta, Jemez, Laguna, Nambe', Picuris, Sandia, San Ildefonso, San Juan, Santa Ana, Santo Domingo, Zia, Taos, Pojoaque, Tesuque, and Zuni.

Pottery from this period reflects the most advanced of all pottery produced in North America. There were great varieties of types, styles, decoration, colors, and designs. This and the contemporary expressions which are an extension of the Historic Period provide the most commonly collected and desirable pottery for the collector.

By 1900 AD pottery seemed destined to extinction. Except for ceremonial and very limited utilitarian use, native pottery was not in general use or needed by the Indian. The reason was the ready availability of cooking and eating ware from the Anglo Culture.

The 20th century has seen a dramatic revival of pottery and the emergence of new types and styles. Thanks to the efforts and encouragement of the traders, museums, and numerous interested individuals, pottery continues and even flourishes in parts of the Southwest. Pottery is now being made for market by all the inhabited pueblos of the Southwest.

Traditional pottery is now being made by the Cherokee and Catawba. Other pottery forms and styles are appearing on the market from tribes throughout the United States. For the most part, however, they are non-traditional in design or manufacture.

CONTEMPORARY POTTERY

Visiting a potter at home is a rewarding experience. Most potters are more than willing to visit and explain the process of making pottery. They usually have pots in various stages of production and, depending upon your timing, you may see a group of pots being removed from their primitive-type firing pit. The potter will show you the clay, polishing stone, and pots awaiting delivery to customers.

It is advisable to make an appointment before your visit. Winter is the best time to visit and make your purchases. At that time you will not be competing with other tourists and various public shows and markets, which require a large inventory. Potters also will keep their better pieces for these shows. Some reservations require that you check in with the reservation officials or Pueblo governor's office before visiting potters within their boundaries.

Most Indian pottery produced today is made by Southwestern pueblos and rancheria people of Arizona. The Southwest pueblos, which produce significant amounts of pottery, include the pueblos of Santa Clara, San Ildefonso, Zia, Cochiti, Jemez, Zuni, Acoma, and the Hopi (First Mesa). There is somewhat limited production at San Juan, Tesuque, Santo Domingo, San Lorenzo (Picuris), Taos, Laguna, Pojoaque, Isleta, Sandia, San Felipe, Santa Ana, and Nambe.

The rancherias, including Maricopa, Yuma, Pima, and Papago, have either ceased making pottery or produce relatively small amounts. Generally the latter has not shared the popularity of Pueblo wares. The Navajo make a traditional working ware primarily for their own use; however, some Navajo pottery is sold to the public. Through Federal programs designed to provide employment to the Utes and Sioux, non-traditional kiln-fired ceramics with Indian motifs are produced in limited quantities for the tourist market. With the popularity of Indian pottery more of the nontraditional types will undoubtedly appear on the market.

POTTERS—A PROFILE

There are many excellent ceramic artists today producing a great variety of pottery. Their excellence equals and may even surpass the accomplishments of well-known Indian potters. They are producing traditional styles and patterns. Others are creating contemporary ceramics which express an unlimited imagination of style, media and shape, such as the carved pots made by Joseph Lonewolf.

Young potters such as Laura Gachupin of Jemez Pueblo and Thelma Talachy of Pojoaque Pueblo are making outstanding examples of contemporary pottery with a balance of traditional designs and contemporary styles. Virginia Ebelacker at Santa Clara Pueblo specializes in traditional black storage jars. Her award-winning pieces are sought-after by museums and collectors.

Seferina Ortiz of Cochiti uses traditional methods to produce storytellers, figurines, and pots with lizards. Like the other potters, she learned from her mother and finds a ready collector market for her pots. Minnie Vigil of Santa Clara is a prolific potter who produces an outstanding variety of styles and colors. These potters have two traits in common: they are outstanding artists and are willing to share their enthusiasm of the art with you.

METHOD OF PRODUCTION

There were five basic methods used by North American Indians to make pottery. None employed a potters wheel or anything resembling a wheel.

1. Coil Method. Rolls of clay are built upon a clay base in a spiral manner. The sides of the pot are developed by successive coils and the sides are smoothed by a piece of gourd, shell, or smooth stone. The Hopi and Rio Grande pueblos use this method today.

2. Coil Method with Paddle and Anvil. This method is similar to the coil method except that coils are rarely applied spirally. A paddle and anvil are used to thin and compress the seams. The rancheria and prehistoric people of the Middle and Lower Gila River district of Arizona used this technique.

3. Paddle and Anvil Method. No coils are used, but the paddle and anvil were used as described above. Some Northern Plains Indians used this method.

4. Modeling Method. Eskimos probably used this method which consisted simply of modeling clay into the desired form by hand.

5. Molded in Basket Method. In this method a layer of clay was molded to the interior of the basket. During the firing process the basket is lost, producing a pot with indentations of the basket on the exterior. This is probably one of the first methods used to produce pottery in the Southwest.

There are two types of firing processes, commonly referred to as oxidation and reduction. In the oxidation process the fire, having access to air, burns hot and clean. In the reduction process the fire is cooler and fueled with animal manure to produce carbon.

Red ware and lighter colored pots are produced by the oxidation method while the popular black pots from Santa Clara and San Ildefonso are fired by the reduction process. Firing usually lasts for about three hours and may reach temperatures up to 1500 degrees F.

A skillful potter can produce a small simple pot in about two hours, exclusive of drying and firing, which may take at least another fifteen hours. Large pots require several weeks to complete, depending upon the amount of decoration and polishing.

Present-day Pueblo pottery is made essentially in the same manner as prehistoric pottery. Women usually are the potters, although assistance is often provided by son and husband in decorating the pottery. In recent years several men have become known as outstanding ceramic artists, such as Tony Da, Carlos Dunlop, and Joseph Lonewolf.

Maria Martinez's husband Julian was probably the first modern day male potter. He decorated many of Maria's pots. Pottery making is usually learned from mother or grandmother.

The type and source of clay, which dictates the color and use of the final product, varies widely among the pueblos. Clay collected from the Rio Grande pueblo area usually turn red or orange when fired, while those west and north turn white to gray. Proper selection and preparation of the clay are essential to making a quality pot.

The pulverized clay is mixed with water and cured for several days. The clay must be uniformly moist. A base is formed free hand and coils of clay are used to build the side. Vessel walls are thinned usually by a gourd rind and the outer sides are polished with a smoothed river pebble. After the pot is allowed to dry it is decorated with vegetal or mineral paints. The process, although simply presented, requires skill, patience, and experience.

SELECTING A PIECE OF POTTERY

Your initial reaction to a piece of pottery should guide your ultimate selection. If the piece is aesthetically pleasing initially, in all probability it will remain so if it satisfies other secondary characteristics. Disregard price if possible, particularly if you are looking for collector pieces. A collector piece is defined as one made by a famous potter, is usually unique, and probably demands a high price.

First look for cracks. Cracks do occur during the firing and cooling process. Some are readily detectable while others are very inconspicuous. Be sure to examine the pottery interior. Prehistoric pottery usually has chips and cracks. Although these affect the price, they are not particularly objectionable because of the rarity of prehistoric pottery.

It is best to avoid any pot which has a crack or chip because it will always be of lesser value. Experienced collectors have their own method of testing for solid pottery. One common test is to tap the rim of the pot with your fingernail, as you would to evaluate a crystal wine glass. There should be a resonant sound and not a thud. Many pieces of pottery such as miniatures and figurines are not suitable to this test. Symmetry or overall evenness is important, and the pot should sit tall, not lopsided.

Polished pottery such as Santa Clara Pueblo black ware should be smooth and even-textured. Polishing of the bowl's exterior sides and bottom represents additional effort of the potter, usually not encountered in most pottery. The design should be symmetrical, lines relatively even and designs balanced. Condition dictates prices of contemporary, historic and prehistoric pottery. Note that when handling a pot, always place one hand on the bottom.

Generally each Pueblo or pottery-producing reservation has a style and technique which is culturally acceptable. What might be acceptable or even necessary to one may be entirely unacceptable to another.

An example would be black firemarks on Taos pottery which reflects higher firing temperatures necessary for utilitarian purposes. These would be unacceptable to fine Santa Clara red ware. Round bottom Navajo pots also serve a purpose for open-fire cooking while decorative San Ildefonso pots with a round bottom would be unacceptable as a decorator or collector's item.

One cannot generalize about color. Many potters experiment with various color, media, and combination. If you are a traditionalist, look for color, particularly in polychrome pieces, which represent the traditional style. Most pots are painted before firing which fixes the color. If the paint rubs off, reconsider your purchase.

Inexpensive pots from a few pueblos are painted after firing. These represent a style and it is your decision whether or not they have a place in your collection. These are not to be confused with some of the outstanding oil and acrylic painted pots from Zia made by Madinas which have appeared in recent years and are in demand by collectors.

Look for small pits on the surface. Some pots from Acoma and other pueblos have impurities and tempering materials essential to strengthening and bonding. Occasionally pitting may develop after firing. Ibis is no reflection upon the skiff of the potter; depending upon the severity, it may affect the pot's appeal and value.

Some of the traditional type pots from the pueblos of Zia, Taos, Picuris, Acoma, and Santo Domingo are utilitarian while most pots from other pueblos are strictly decorative. Your dealer or the potter will discuss this with you.

Properly seasoned pots from Taos and Picuris are excellent for oven use. Although some Indians may use their native pottery for special purposes, cost usually dictates that the pot be displayed as a piece of art. There is a wide choice and the informed buyer will make fewer mistakes in selection. If you are inexperienced, buy from a knowledgeable dealer or a recognized potter.

THE FUTURE

The future of all Indian arts and crafts is dependent upon the attitude, motivations and changing culture of the Indians. Pottery is no exception, although there are several full-time potters making a living as ceramic artists. They are motivated by economic benefits as well as by a need for recognition of their accomplishments. As long as there is an appreciation of pottery it will continue to be produced.

Quality pottery by recognized potters will continue to appreciate in value. Historic and prehistoric pottery will become part of institutional collections and this will result in less pottery being available to private collectors. Styles will continue to change with the imagination of the artists. This creativity is essential to the future vitality of this art.

(J.W.B)

Broken section of pottery vessel, found near Calabogie, Ontario, Canada. A Canadian archaeologist has identified the section as "Black-necked" type, typical of the late Huron-Petun people of southern Ontario, Age: AD 1450-AD 1550.   C-$14

Photo courtesy Howard Popkie, Arnprior, Ontario, Canada

EASTERN AND MISSISSIPPI WATER-SHED PREHISTORIC POTTERY

Pottery bowl, from Arkansas, 7 in. high and 7-1/4 in. in diameter. No restoration or cracks; piece has cross-hatched rim design. G-$300

Ceramic bowl, Mississippi culture, 8 in. wide and 3-1/2 in. high; rim has coiled baked clay resembling 3-strand rope twist. One major break has been skillfully restored. Except for rim decoration, a plain but well-made piece. D-$250

Iroquois vessel, round-bodied, 5 in. high and 5-1/2 in. wide at mid-body. Reinforced upper rim decorated with incised lines. Gray-white in color; pot is in good condition. C-$425

Ceramic bowl, Mississippi culture and from Louisiana, 8-1/2 in. diameter and 3-1/2 in. high, painted lines decorate the straight sides. One section of the bowl bottom has been restored. C-$200

Effigy bowl, Caddoan, 3 in. high and 8 in. wide. Piece has three raised head-like nodes on an outstanding polished and engraved friendship bowl. Lines filled with red pigment. G-$1,000

Ceramic vessel, Mississippi culture, Tennessee, 9 in. diameter and 4 in. high, circular and with knobs on the rim; has a reinforced rim. No decorations. C-$325

Grayware bowl, from Arkansas, 5 in. high and 7 in. in diameter. Fine condition. G-$90

Ceramic vessel, flare-top, Louisiana, 13 in. high and 8-1/2 in. in diameter. It has cord-marked decoration on the surface, and is a brown-gray color. Round body and rim. No restorations. D-$425

Ceramic effigy vessel, from southeastern U.S., 8-1/2 in. high. Human figure depicts kneeling man; some red paint remains on exterior. Vessel damaged and restored in base area, also in several sections of the rim. Figure is fine. D-$575

Caddo seed jar, late prehistoric, from Craighead County, Arkansas. This well-formed pot is 5 x 7 in. Unlisted

Private collection

Pottery bottle, Southern Cult, rare, 8-1/2 in. high and 7 in. in diameter. Four human hands go around the bottle, in raised relief. No restoration, but some very minor rim and body damage. G-$950

Ceramic "teapot," Quapaw, 8 in. high and 9-1/4 in. diameter. Painted red, white, and brown; in fine condition. G-$1,600

Pottery bowl, from Woodland site in Pennsylvania, 6 in. high and 6 in. in diameter, thick shell-tempered piece. No decoration and no handles. Very early vessel, probably BC period. C-$270

Frog effigy vessel, fine ceramic, 4 in. high and 7 in. long. Superb work style, finely detailed, and with a rattle head; no restoration. G-$850

Ceramic vessel, Caddoan, from Arkansas, late prehistoric times. It stands 9 in. high and rounded base is 9-1/2 in. in diameter. Deeply incised with swirling-circle pattern. Well-done, no damage, and no restoration. C-$975

Turkey effigy rattle bowl, 10 in. in diameter and 6 1/2 in. high. From Mississippian mound-builder period. G-$650

Water bottle, Caddoan, 9-1/4 in. high and 6-1/2 in. wide. No designs, but piece has a fine slick black finish and fine balance, only very minor repair. G-$425

Miniature bottles, Caddoan, group of six, averaging 2 in. in height. Some fine engraved examples, and sold as a group only. G-$350

Vessel, Iroquois, square-bodied, New York, 7 in. high and 5-1/2 in. wide at top. Top rim is decorated with incised ladder-like markings, while body has parallel fines. Gray-black color and no restoration. D-$525

Water bottle, Mississippi culture, from Missouri, with some minor restoration. Piece is 7 in. high and 7 in. diameter, with a pedestal base. G-$160

Water bottle, from Arkansas, 7 in. high and 6 in. in diameter. Good shape. G-$155

Perforated disc base water bottle, found in Arkansas, 8 in. high and 6-5/8 in. in diameter. Perfectly balanced with some restoration to rim and base. G-$260

Bird effigy vessel, from Florida, 5 in. long, ca. AD 500. Well-executed and originally hand painted features, now gone. An unusual piece and in fine condition. C-$775

Caddoan vessel with incised exterior, from Oklahoma. This large pot is 8 x 9 in. and very thin. Unlisted

Private collection

Pottery balls, found with sixteen others on the bank of the Tennessee River near Savannah, Tennessee. Each shows evidence of having been in a fire. Use uncertain; may have been heated and used as we use charcoal, or dropped in a vessel for heating and cooking. Each is about the size of a golf ball. Mississippian culture.   C-$4 each

Photo courtesy Jim Northcutt, Jr., Corinth, Mississippi

Compound bowl, gray ware, Mississippi Valley. It is 4 in. high.   Unlisted

Private collection

Two pottery shards, found near Pickwick Dam, Tennessee. They are rare for the area because of the thumbnail impression in darker piece and forefinger and thumbnail impression on the other. These are probably Mississippian in origin. The larger shard is 5 in. long.   C-$4

Photo courtesy Jim Northcutt, Jr., Corinth, Mississippi

Shell-tempered pot, from Hardin County, Tennessee, and probably from the Mississippian culture. Pot is 5 in. high and 5-3/4 in. across at top opening; circumference is 22 in.   Unlisted

Private collection

Mound Place incised bottle, Mississippi period, in gray ware. This beautiful piece is 9-1/2 in. high and the decorating is very well-done.   Unlisted

Private collection

Medallion pot, gray ware, from Mississippi County, Arkansas. This well-shaped ceramic is 5-1/4 in. high. Unlisted

Private collection

Gray ware frog effigy bowl, from Arkansas, 3 in. high and 5 in. diameter. Unlisted

Private collection

Southeastern U.S. pottery, both from Arkansas and both Caddoan.

Left: vase form, 4 in. in diameter and 4 in. high.
Right: jar or vase, 4-1/2 in. in diameter, 4 in. high.   Unlisted

Private collection

Piecrust bowl, tallied rim, Mississippian period. This gray ware pot is 3-1/8 in. high and 6-1/2 in. in diameter.   Unlisted

Private collection

Duck effigy bowl, gray ware, from Arkansas. This interesting vessel is 7 in. high at the head and 6 in. in diameter.   Unlisted

Private collection

Cat-serpent effigy bowl, gray ware, from Arkansas. It is 7 in. in diameter and 6-3/4 in. high. A fine Mississippian-era ceramic, it is in top condition.   Unlisted

Private collection

Medallion pot, gray ware, from Mississippi County, Arkansas. This well-shaped ceramic is 5-1/4 in. high.   *Unlisted*

Private collection

Ceramic vessel, 4-1/2 in. high and 8 in. diameter, plain ware. Gray color, and found in Canada. Vessel is ca. AD 700-1100.   *Unlisted*

Photo courtesy Howard Popkie, Arnprior, Canada

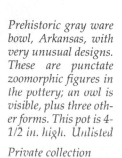

Prehistoric gray ware bowl, Arkansas, with very unusual designs. These are punctate zoomorphic figures in the pottery; an owl is visible, plus three other forms. This pot is 4-1/2 in. high. Unlisted

Private collection

Hooded humpback effigy jar, 5-1/4 in. high, gray ware, and a well-executed ceramic. It is from the Mississippi Watershed region.   *Unlisted*

Private collection

Mississippian bowl, piecrust or tallied rim, gray ware, from Arkansas. It is 2-3/4 in. high and 6-3/4 in. in diameter. Unlisted

Private collection

Humped human effigy figure pot, from Arkansas, 7-1/2 in. high. This female figure is done in tan and gray, and is in top condition.   Unlisted

Private collection

Narrow-top bottle, prehistoric, Mississippi Valley, plain ware or gray ware. It is 6-3/4 in. high.   Unlisted

Private collection

Southeastern U.S. prehistoric pottery.

Left: Hodges engraved, Caddoan, 5-3/4 in. in diameter, 3-1/2 in. high.
Right: Woodland, brushed exterior and pie-crust rim, 5 in. in diameter, 3-3/4 in. high.   Unlisted

Private collection

Grouping of pottery trowels, used for shaping and smoothing pottery vessels. Made of tan or gray baked clay, the highest is 3-1/2 in. All from Arkansas.   Unlisted

Private collection

Prehistoric vase-bottle, Caddo, swirl design of red on white, from Arkansas.   Unlisted

Private collection

Strap-handled pots, various decorations on the exteriors, all from Arkansas. *Unlisted*

Private collection

Various pottery types, decorated examples on right and left, all from Arkansas. *Unlisted*

Private collection

Pottery types, tall bottle at center, all from Arkansas. *Unlisted*

Private collection

Water bottle, prehistoric Southeastern U.S., incised concentric circles, from Arkansas. It is 8 in. high and a well-formed piece. *Unlisted*

Private collection

Effigy bowl, prehistoric Southeastern pottery, "Wounded Hawk" form. It is 7-1/2 in. in diameter and 8-3/4 in. from crest to tail. This fine piece is from Arkansas. *Unlisted*

Private collection

Prehistoric Southeastern pottery, Crocket Curvalinear, from Arkansas. It is 6-1/2 in. in diameter and a pleasingly formed pot. *Unlisted*

Private collection

Southeastern U.S. prehistoric pottery.

Left: Campbell Compound jar over jar, 5-1/4 in. diameter, 4-3/4 in. high.
Right: Northeastern U.S. prehistoric pottery. Seneca (Iroquois) jar, sawtooth rim, 4-1/2 in. diameter, 4-1/4 in. high. *Unlisted*

Private collection

Duck or snake effigy bowl, from Cross County, Arkansas. A scarce vessel, it is 12-3/4 in. long.   Unlisted

Private collection

Tripodal water bottle with bulbous feet, Mississippi County, Arkansas. This is a fairly scarce type.   Unlisted

Private collection

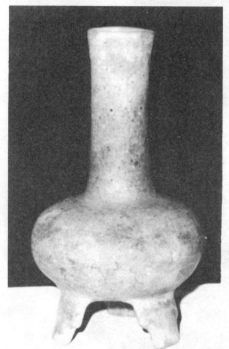

Tripodal water bottle, extra-fine, with slab type stepped feet. It is from eastern Arkansas.   Unlisted

Private collection

Stirrup bottle, Mississippi County, Arkansas. This work has excellent shape and finish.   Unlisted

Private collection

Tripodal water bottle with bulbous feet and disc or platform type base. This is a unique piece because of the basal style; from Mississippi County, Arkansas.   Unlisted

Private collection

Rounded bottle pot, shouldered, gray ware or plain ware. It is 7-1/2 in. high.   Unlisted.

Private collection

Carinated bowl or bottle, gray ware, prehistoric. It is 5 in. high and 6-1/2 in. in diameter. *Unlisted*

Private collection

Mississippian period ceramic jar, ca. AD 1000-1500, Barton/Parkin style. It is from Arkansas, 5 in. in diameter and 6 in. high. *Unlisted*

Private collection

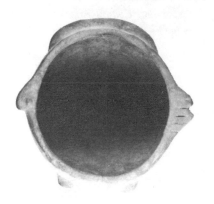

Fish effigy bowl, prehistoric, gray ware, from Arkansas. This fine bowl is 5-1/2 in. from nose to tail. *Unlisted*

Private collection

Group of miniature pottery bowls, prehistoric, Mississippi Valley. These are made of tan or gray pottery. The duck effigy bowl, front, is 3-1/2 in. in diameter. *Unlisted*

Private collection

Late prehistoric Southeastern U.S. bowl, Caddoan, from Arkansas. It is Friendship Engraved, 7-3/4 in. in diameter. *Unlisted*

Private collection

Group of miniature bowls, prehistoric, from Arkansas. These are gray or tan in color; the front bowl is 2-5/8 in. high. *Unlisted*

Private collection

Prehistoric pottery vessels, various shapes, all from Arkansas. Unlisted

Private collection

Seed jar, prehistoric (late), from Clark County, Arkansas. It is 6 in. in diameter and 6-3/4 in. high. Unlisted

Private collection

Bowl in the effigy of a sleeping goose, very scarce, from Pemiscot County, Missouri. Length from head to tail is 10-1/2 in. and the bowl diameter is 9 in. It is in fine condition. Unlisted

Private collection

Large flared-rim bowl, very good condition, from Arkansas. Unlisted

Private collection

Prehistoric Southeastern pottery, Military Road vase, 10 in. high. This nicely flared pot is from Arkansas. Unlisted

Private collection

Pottery bowls, 7 to 12 in. in diameter, two with reddish paint. All from Arkansas.   *Unlisted*

Private collection

Southern U.S. pottery, mainly from Arkansas, miniature examples in front row. The sun-disc effigy in front, 2nd from right, is from Louisiana.
                                                                Unlisted

Private collection

Prehistoric pottery.

Left: Caddo engraved vase, very light and thin, 6 x 6 in., from Oklahoma.   *Unlisted*
Right: Caddo engraved bowl, extremely light and thin, 5 x 6 in., from Oklahoma.   *Unlisted*

Private collection

Outstanding effigy pottery. Deer bowl (Arkansas); frog bowl (Arkansas); human figure (Mexico); human figure (Arkansas); duck bowl (Arkansas); large duck bowl (Arkansas); dog (Mexico); Sun effigy (Louisiana); miniature bird bowl (Arkansas); center bird bowl (Louisiana).   Unlisted

Private collection

Prehistoric Southeastern pottery, both from Arkansas.

Left: Foster Trailed incised, 5 in. in diameter, restored.
Right: Foster Trailed incised, 5-3/4 in. in diameter.   Unlisted

Private collection

Late prehistoric pottery, both pieces from Arkansas.

Left: hunch-back human effigy, 3-3/4 in. high, Cross County.
Right: miniature water bottle, 3-1/2 in. high, Bell plain design.   Unlisted

Private collection

Compound vessels, Mississippian era.

Left: rare; one side is buff, the other dark gray, 8 in. wide, from Pemiscot County, Missouri.
Center: disc base, Mississippi County, Arkansas, 7-3/8 in. wide.
Right: Mississippi County, Arkansas, 6-1/2 in. wide and 3 in. high.   Unlisted

WESTERN PREHISTORIC CERAMIC VESSELS

Vessel, Anasazo/Pueblo III, 12-1/2 in. in diameter, exterior and interior decorated with geometric squares and alternating bands of white and red. Small portion of bowl rim has been expertly restored. Quite impressive piece.   C-$895

Geometric design bowl, Mimbres, 10 in. in diameter and 5 in. high, with usual kill-hole. Restored.   G-$650

Anasazi handled mug, Colorado, stands 4-1/2 in. high, with geometric motif painted on sides. In perfect condition.   C-$400

Seed pot, or storage vessel, from Colorado. Painted with varied motifs and Pueblo I or II period. It is 12-1/2 in. high and 18-1/2 in. in diameter. Unusual item, and in fine condition, no restoration.   C-$1,050

Ceramic bowl, Mimbres, 11-3/4 in. in diameter, with checkerboard design in black and white on interior. Has small kill-hole in bottom, otherwise perfect condition.   D-$725

Corrugated jar, Coal Mine Mesa, 14-1/2 in. high and 11 in. diameter. Some rim damage.   G-$400

Handled ceramic pitcher, Anasazi, but looks almost modern. Piece is 10-1/2 in. high, with expanded base. Bottom has circular streaks, top has lightning pattern. Some restoration to handle, but not major.   D-$650

Vessel, Mimbres, 3 in. high and 9 in. in diameter. Red on white concentric rim bands with inner concentric bands. Star in center and kill-hole.   G-$850

Corrugated ceramic jar, Anasazi, 9 in. in height, some original damage to base but could be restored.   C-$325

Ceramic jar, Salado, 7-1/2 in. in diameter and 5 in. high. Geometric designs, excellent condition, and ca. AD 1200–AD 1450.   G-$750

Black on white pitcher, Chaco Canyon, 4-1/2 in. high and 4 in. in diameter.   G-$400

Ceramic bowl, Zuni, prehistoric, with stylized horned toad (?) motif painted around interior. Piece is circular, 13-1/4 in. in diameter, and has some damage to rim area. C-$725

Ceramic bowl, Anasazi, about 4 in. high and 13 in. in diameter. Semicircular designs painted inside, except for bottom. Rim is damaged in several places.   D-$475

Pottery bowl, Jeddito, 3 in. high and 8 in. in diameter. Geometric painting inside and out, in mint condition. This piece is ca. AD 1400.   G-$500

Large ceramic spoon or scoop, Southwestern Indian, probably Hohokam, 9-1/4 in. long, and shallow. Decorative interior lines of yellow and brown. Handle cracked in places.   C-$265

Casa Grande effigy bowl, 4-1/2 in. high and 7-1/2 in. in diameter. Has bird-like head and four legs which were broken off and smoothed.   G-$550

Black on white bowl, 5 in. high and 6 in. in diameter. The piece has a stylized human effigy figure on the bottom and interior. Large chip missing from the rim.   G-$625

Pottery vessel, Hohokam, 11-1/2 in. in diameter, undecorated, good condition; top opening 7 in. in diameter. Base is fire-darkened and heat-cracked.   C-$300

Four Mile Ruin bowl, 4 in. high and 9 in. in diameter. Polychrome, with geometric design. Painted inside and out; this is a restored piece.   G-$850

Black on white pitcher, 3-1/2 in. high and 4-1/2 in. at base. Geometric designs, Tularosa type, good condition.   G-$350

Ceramic, Salado, 5 in. high and 7 in. in diameter. Geometric designs, and ca. AD 1200-1450.   G-$550

Bowl, Mimbres, 6 in. in diameter. Has a well-executed rabbit design, only usual minor deterioration, ca. AD 1250.   G-$1,250

Bowl, Casa Grande, unusual square shape, mint condition. Piece is 2-1/2 in. high and 4-1/4 in. diameter. Note: It had a miniature axe, polished stone pendant, miniature bowl, and a shell ring all inside bowl when it was found. All included.   G-$625

Food bowl, Zuni, 4 in. high and 12 in. in diameter. Painted geometric designs inside and out, and one small area of restoration on the bottom.   G-$1,300

Effigy ceramic, Casa Grande culture, from New Mexico, 6 in. high and 5 in. wide. Human male, superb detail, excellent condition.   G-$850

Black-on-white bowl, 3-1/2 in. high and 6 in. in diameter. This type is called a "seed pot" by collectors. It has a small crack on the rim but is in excellent condition. Anasazi culture, from San Juan County, Colorado, near Mesa Verde, ca. AD 1100-1300.   C-$500

Photo courtesy Claude Britt, Jr., Many Farms, Arizona

Mesa Verde ladle or dipper, 10 in. long and with bowl 4-1/2 in. diameter. Anasazi culture, from Mancos, San Juan County, Colorado. The handle is restored; otherwise in fine condition. This piece would be worth $300-400, if not restored and perfect, ca. AD 1150.   C-$295

Photo courtesy Claude Britt, Jr., Many Farms, Arizona

Pottery, prehistoric, Salt River red ware from Arizona, 6 in. in diameter. It is ca. AD 800-1000. $200

Pocotopaug Trading Post, South Windsor, Connecticut

Gila bowl, AD 1100-1300, from Arizona. Size is about 5 in. in diameter; it is red on the exterior and has a black on buff interior. Interesting design, and overall in mint condition. $500

Alvin Lee Moreland, Corpus Christi, Texas

Mesa Verde mug, 5 x 4-1/2 in. and decorated with black mineral paint on a white background. Anasazi culture, from Yellow Jacket, Colorado, and ca. AD 1100-1300.   C-$475

Photo courtesy Claude Britt, Jr., Many Farms, Arizona

Anasazi canteen, from Colorado, 6 in. wide at widest. Ca. AD 1100-1300, it has a fine design. There is a pressure crack and a minor rim chip. $650

Alvin Lee Moreland, Corpus Christi, Texas

Pottery, prehistoric, Salt River red ware from Arizona, 6 in. in diameter. It is ca. AD 800-1000. $200

Pocotopaug Trading Post, South Windsor, Connecticut

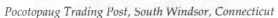

Tularosa olla, black on white, very symmetrical and about 13 in. in diameter. It has pitting on one side and some wear to paint; otherwise, very good condition for this early and rare vessel form. $895

Alvin Lee Moreland collection, Corpus Christi, Texas

Southwestern prehistoric pot, zoomorphic decoration, brown and cream. Size is 3-3/4 in. high and 6-3/4 in. in diameter. This piece is very well-made and in top condition. $500-700

Private collection

Prehistoric olla, Salado red ware, Anasazi. It is 6-1/2 in. in diameter and 6 in. high. Ex-museum, it is ca. AD 1200-1400. $425

Morris' Art & Artifacts, Anaheim, California; Dawn Gober photograph

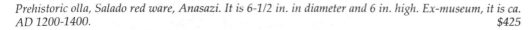

Prehistoric Southwestern pottery, black on white, Anasazi. From Arizona, it is 9 in. diameter and ca. AD 1000-1200. $250-300

Pocotopaug Trading Post, South Windsor, Connecticut

Southwestern prehistoric pot, Anasazi, black on white interior with red exterior. It is from Arizona and 7 in. in diameter, ca. AD 1000-1250. $500-575

Pocotopaug Trading Post, South Windsor, Connecticut

Southwestern prehistoric pot, 2-1/2 in. high and 5-3/8 in. in diameter. It is black and cream on red, a well-made ceramic from Arizona. Unlisted

Private collection

Southwestern pottery vessel, corrugated utility gray ware. It was formed by pinching together the side-coils as they were layered up. Size 3-3/4 in. in diameter and 3-1/4 in. high. AD 1000-1400. $250

Private collection

Southwestern prehistoric pottery, Mogollon, from the Gila River area of southeastern Arizona. Ca. AD 1000-1250, it is 7 in. in diameter. $200-250

Pocotopaug Trading Post, South Windsor, Connecticut

Southwestern prehistoric pottery, Anasazi, black and white interior, red exterior, 6-1/4 in. in diameter. It is ca. AD 1000-1200. $175-225

Pocotopaug Trading Post, South Windsor, Connecticut

Prehistoric bowl, Mimbres, black on red, from the Mogollon Rim. It is 4 x 7 in., ex-museum and ca. AD 1100-1300. $600

Morris' Art & Artifacts, Anaheim, California; Dawn Gober photograph

Gila bowl, from Arizona, 7 in. in diameter. The exterior is red and the interior is a black on buff design, a geometric pinwheel. This pottery piece is cracked and glued in two places. $550

Alvin Lee Moreland, Corpus Christi, Texas

Bowl, Mimbres, 3-1/2 in. high and 9 in. in diameter. Design is concentric rim bands with inner-spaced geometrics; with kill-hole. C-$950

Ceramic bowl, Anasazi/Pueblo-III, 14 in. in diameter, interior painted with swirls and zigzag lines, exterior similar. No damage, no restoration. G-$950

Black on white pitcher, Chaco Canyon type, 5-1/2 in. high and 4 in. in basal diameter. Geometric design and good condition. G-$375

Diegueno olla or storage vessel, Southwestern California, 13 in. high and 8 in. wide, mouth 4 in. wide. Restoration to rim and part of bottom. C-$400

Black on white mug, Anasazi, 5-1/2 in. high and 6 in.

Pottery vessels, late prehistoric period ca. AD 800-1200.

G) Appliqué jar, 11 in. high, Bowie County, Texas. Unlisted
H) Incised jar, 11 in. high, minor repair, Miller County, Arkansas. Unlisted

Caddo Trading Company, Murfreesboro, Arkansas

in diameter. Has a rope-twist pottery handle, in excellent condition. Piece is ca. AD 950. G-$425

Brownware, Mogollon, polished 9 in. high and 9 in. in diameter. Piece has heavy restoration and is ca. AD 400-600. G-$325

Ceramic bowl, black on orange, Bedehochi type, 3 in. high and 6-1/2 in. in diameter. Zone geometric design. G-$525

HISTORIC CERAMICS

Pottery vessel, Hopi, 4-7/8 in. high and 5-1/2 in. in diameter. Unsigned, ca. 1920, mint condition. G-$500

Ceramic pot, Zia, 4-1/2 in. high, 6 in. in diameter, with brown slip. Red and black painted bird designs; cracked and repaired, but with good appearance. Zia Pueblo, ca. 1940. Marked S.P. Medina. G-$400

Ceramic vessel, Acoma, 4-1/2 in. in diameter, stylized animal depicted, nice finish and good design. C-$295

Vase, Hopi, Sikyatki revival style, ca. 1935. G-$315

Polychrome plate, San Ildefonso, 2 in. high and 10 in. in diameter, ca. 1920. G-$450

Pottery vessel, black and orange decorations on white with white interior. It is 6-1/2 in. high and 9-1/2 in. in diameter. This piece was made at Acoma pueblo in the 1950s. $700

Courtesy The Curio Shop, Anderson, California

San Ildefonso jar, 3-1/2 in. high and 4-1/2 in. in diameter. This pueblo is the home of the famous potter Maria Martinez. Although Ildefonso pottery is quite heavy, not thin like the Zia and Acoma, prices of well-finished pieces are rather high. C-$850

Photo courtesy Harvey and Rose King, Muskogee, Oklahoma

Acoma pueblo pot, black and orange-red on tan, ca. 1890. In beautiful condition, this fine work is 11-1/2 x 11-1/2 in. $6,500-7,000

Dennis R. Phillips/Fine American Indian Art, Chicago, Illinois

Pottery, Acoma pueblo, 12 in. diameter and 12-1/2 in. high, orange-red and black on white. This fine piece is ca. 1890. $6,500-7,000

Dennis R. Phillips/Fine American Indian Art, Chicago, Illinois

Pottery vessel, abstract bird decoration in red and black against white. This fine pot is 6 in. high and 8-1/2 in. in diameter. It is from Acoma pueblo and was worked in the 1950s. $700

Courtesy The Curio Shop, Anderson, California

Pottery, high bowl, Acoma pueblo, 8 in. in height. It is red and black on cream with a red interior. Ca. 1890-1910. $400-500

Pocotopaug Trading Post, South Windsor, Connecticut

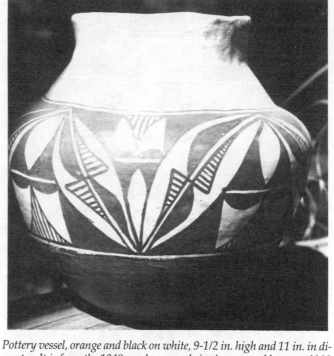

Pottery vessel, orange and black on white, 9-1/2 in. high and 11 in. in diameter. It is from the 1940s and was made in Acoma pueblo. $900

Courtesy The Curio Shop, Anderson, California

Acoma pueblo pottery bowl, black, yellow-buff, and orange-red against cream, ca. 1910. It is 8 in. high and 11 in. in diameter. $875

Private collection

Acoma pueblo pottery bowl, white and black, from the 1940s. It is 8 in. high and 10 in. in diameter. $525

Private collection

Pottery vessel, yellow and black designs with yellow interior, Acoma pueblo. It is 9 in. high and 9-1/2 in. in diameter. This well-made pot is from the 1950s. $1,100

Courtesy The Curio Shop, Anderson, California

Acoma pueblo pot, red and black designs on creamy white, 11-1/4 in. high and 12-1/2 in. in diameter. This very fine piece is ca. 1900. $7,500

Dennis R. Phillips/Fine American Indian Art, Chicago, Illinois

Pottery vessel, insect motif in black, yellow, and orange, 6 in. high and 7-1/2 in. in diameter. It is from Acoma pueblo and was made in the 1930s. $850

Courtesy The Curio Shop, Anderson, California

Pottery vessel, black design on white with orange interior, 8 in. high and 9 in. in diameter. This is from Acoma pueblo and was made in the 1940s. This is a very artistic pot. $1,600

Courtesy The Curio Shop, Anderson, California

Pottery olla, Acoma, ca. 1920, size 9-1/2 in. diameter and 7-1/2 in. high. Very symmetrical and the thin wall has a good ring tone. Colors are orange with black and white designs. White slip shows some crazing, otherwise in excellent condition. Ex-coll. Fruchtel. $650

Sherman Holbert collection, Fort Mille Lacs, Onamia, Minnesota

Historic pueblo pot, Acoma, 7 in. high, black and orange-red on cream, ca. 1920s. $395

Pocotopaug Trading Post, South Windsor, Connecticut

Pottery vessel, Acoma pueblo, New Mexico, black and orange on white, with orange interior. This fine piece is 7 in. high and 8-1/2 in. in diameter; it was made in the 1950s. $950

Courtesy The Curio Shop, Anderson, California

Zia pueblo bowl, animal motif, from the 1920s. It is 9 in. high and 10-1/2 in. in diameter. Designs are black against a light tan ground; this is a fine early pot. $1,650

Private collection

Pottery vessel, 7 in. high and 4-1/2 in. in diameter. It has a five-color design and is from Acoma pueblo. It was made in the 1950s and has a pleasing color combination. $950

Courtesy The Curio Shop, Anderson, California

Pottery vessel, black deer with red heartlines against white, orange interior. This fine pot is from Acoma pueblo and 11-1/2 in. high and 9 in. in diameter. It was made in the 1940s. $950

Courtesy The Curio Shop, Anderson, California

Zia pueblo pottery polychrome bowl, 9-1/2 in. high and 11 in. in diameter. It is ca. 1910 and a fine early pot in top condition. $1,200

Private collection

Pottery vessel, very well decorated in black and orange, from Zuni pueblo. It is 9-3/4 in. high and 11 in. in diameter. This fine work was made in the 1930s. $2,100

Courtesy The Curio Shop, Anderson, California

Zuni owl pottery, 12 in. high, brown and orange on white. $750

Private collection, New Mexico

Pottery bowl, Santa Clara pueblo, 4-1/2 x 7-3/4 in. Ca. 1920s, this is a fine period piece, cream on red and highly polished. Condition is excellent, with only a very small interior rim chip. $225

Sherman Holbert collection, Fort Mille Lacs, Onamia, Minnesota

Hopi bowl, unsigned, black and orange-red on tan-cream, 3 x 8 in. From the 1920s, it is in excellent condition. $350

Courtesy John Isaac, Albuquerque, New Mexico

Laguna pueblo pottery vase, orange-red and black against cream, from the 1960s. It is 8 in. high and 8 in. in diameter. $400

Private collection

Bowl or pot, Cochiti pueblo, black on cream white. It is a top-level work, approximately 11 x 14 in. in diameter, and ca. 1880 $8,500

Dennis R. Phillips/Fine American Indian Art, Chicago, Illinois

Santo Domingo pueblo pot, black on tan-cream, ca. 1890. This top condition piece is 8-1/2 in. in diameter and 9-1/4 in. high. $2,500

Dennis R. Phillips/Fine American Indian Art, Chicago, Illinois

Pottery vessel, Isleta pueblo, New Mexico, 2-3/4 in. high and 5-1/2 in. in diameter. It has orange and black designs on white and is of museum quality; a rare historic bowl from the 1880-90s. $1,350

Courtesy The Curio Shop, Anderson, California

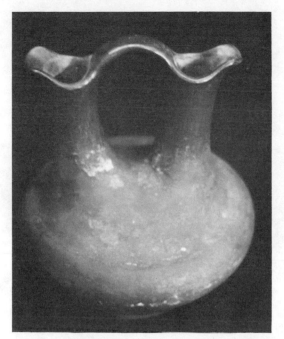

Red ware wedding vase, very early San Ildefonso piece, 1870-1880s. It measures 10 x 14 in. and is in excellent condition. $1,400

Larry Lantz, First Mesa, South Send, Indiana

Storage jar, large size, Zia pueblo, 17 in. high and 20 in. in diameter. This four-color polychrome pottery piece is ca. 1910 and quite rare and beautiful. $45,000

Courtesy Adobe Gallery, Albuquerque, New Mexico

Pueblo bowl, orange-brown and black on cream, 9 in. high and 13 in. in diameter. This fine piece is ca. 1925. $1,100

Courtesy John Isaac, Albuquerque, New Mexico

Picuris pottery vase, 9 in. in diameter and 9-1/2 in. high. It is tan-orange and from the early 1900s. $500

Private collection

Olla, Laguna pueblo, four-color polychrome pot in pleasing design. It is 12 x 12 in. and ca. 1900. $9,500

Courtesy Adobe Gallery, Albuquerque, New Mexico

Historic pueblo pot or vase, orange-red and black on cream, 11 in. high, ca.1920s. $300

Pocotopaug Trading Post, South Windsor, Connecticut

Polychrome pot in black and red-orange against white, Acoma. It is 5 x 5-1/2 in., in perfect condition and made by Virginia Lowden ca. 1970. $550

Marguerite L. Kernaghan collection; photograph by Marguerite L. and Stewart W. Kernaghan, Bellvue, Colorado

Ceremonial plate, San Ildefonso pueblo, 9 in. in diameter. The design is red and black on tan, with the piece ca. 1890. There is some damage and restoration. $950

Courtesy John Isaac, Albuquerque, New Mexico

Storyteller with ten children, Jemez pueblo. It is signed P.M.C., Jemez Pue., and is 5 x 6-1/4 x 7-1/2 in. ca. 1975. $550

Marguerite L. Kernaghan collection; photograph by Marguerite L. and Stewart W. Kernaghan, Bellvue, Colorado

Prehistoric Southwestern pottery bowl, 7 in. in diameter, Snowflake black on white. Small rim chips and crack, no restoration, ca. AD 950-1200. Museum quality

Traditions, Victor, New York

Pot, polished black ware, by Helen Shupa, Santa Clara pueblo. This fine piece, ca. 1985, is 6-1/2 x 5-1/2 in. high. $2,500

Dennis R. Phillips/Fine American Indian-Art, Chicago, Illinois

Prehistoric Southwestern storage jar, large at 18 in. in diameter. Minimal restoration, fine piece. Decoration is black on white in a snowflake design, and the olla is ca. AD 950-1200. *Museum quality*

Traditions, Victor, New York

Casas Grandes prehistoric pot, 7 in. high and 7-1/2 in. in diameter. Decorated with black and red on white, this piece is ca. AD 1200. *Museum quality*

Private collection

Prehistoric Southwestern pottery bowls, Mimbres pictorials, 12 in. and 8 in. in diameter respectively. Minimal restoration to each. These are ca. AD 950-1100. *Museum quality*

Traditions, Victor, New York

Prehistoric Southwestern bowl, St. John's polychrome, 12 in. in diameter, black design on red interior and white-line exterior. Rim kills, no restoration, ca. AD 1175-1300. *Museum quality*

Traditions, Victor, New York

Prehistoric Southwestern mug, Mesa Verde black on white, 5-1/4 in. wide. Stabilized cracks on one side, no restoration. Decidedly modern-looking, this pottery piece is ca. AD 1200-1300. *Museum quality*

Traditions, Victor, New York

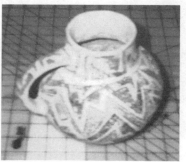

Anasazi pitcher, ca. AD 1100-1500, 6 x 6 in. Ex-collection Morrow, this Southwestern ceramic is repaired and restored. *Unlisted*

Blue Coyote Trading Post, Nashville, Indiana; Pat Nolan photograph

Ceramic jar, Harleton Appliqued, Middle Caddo times. It measures 5 x 6 in. and has no damage or restoration. This beautiful pottery piece came from Titus County, Texas.   Unlisted

Collection of, and photograph by, Steve Granger, Hallsville, Texas

Ceramic Bailey water bottle, 3-7/8 x 4-5/8 in., Late Caddo period. The interesting design represents an owl's face and there is no damage or restoration. Titus County, Texas.   Unlisted

Collection of, and photograph by, Steve Granger, Hallsville, Texas

Ceramic water bottle, in classic Hodges form, Late Caddo period. This is 7-1/2 x 9-1/2 in. The large example is carefully decorated and nicely shaped with high polish, a superb prehistoric piece. Without damage or restoration this is an exceptional pot from Titus County, Texas.   Unlisted

Collection of, and photograph by, Steve Granger, Hallsville, Texas

Mesa Verde olla or storage jar, 14 x 14 in., black pigment on white. This prehistoric pottery vessel is a large and fine example of early work.   Museum quality

David Cook Fine American Art, Denver, Colorado; Jamie Kahn photograph

Ceramic Hodges water bottle, Late Caddo period, 4-3/4 x 5 in. This is a valuable pottery piece due to fine condition, no restoration, design work, and overall quality. Titus County, Texas. Unlisted

Collection of, and photograph by, Steve Granger, Hallsville, Texas

Prehistoric Southwestern pottery effigy jar, 6 in. high and 8 in. across. It is Tulerosa black on white and ca. AD 1200-1300.   Museum quality

Traditions, Victor, New York

Ceramic Rippley hanging pot, Late Caddo period, 3-3/4 x 4 in. This has an unusual breast effigy, well-done designs, and there is no damage or restoration. Camp County, Texas. Unlisted

Collection of, and photograph by, Steve Granger, Hallsville, Texas

Human effigy pot, prehistoric, 6-1/2 in. high and 7 in. deep. This is a nicely made ceramic work from the American Southwest. Museum quality

Scott Young, Port St. Lucie, Florida

Ceramic hanging pot, Johns Engraved, Middle Caddo period. It is 4-5/8 x 5-1/2 in. and is a top example due to rarity of type and no damage or restoration. Titus County, Texas. Unlisted

Collection of, and photograph by, Steve Granger, Hallsville, Texas

Southwestern pitchers, prehistoric and ca. AD 800-1200.

E) Chaco, black on white designs, 8 in. high, Arizona. Unlisted
F) Smaller Chaco pitcher, excellent condition. Unlisted

Caddo Trading Company, Murfreesboro, Arkansas

Ceramic Wilder water bottle, Middle Caddo period, 4-1/2 x 6-1/2 in. It is well-shaped and with good design. With no damage or restoration, this is a quality pot from Cass County, Texas. Unlisted

Collection of, and photograph by, Steve Granger, Hallsville, Texas

Southeastern prehistoric pottery, all from Arkansas:

A) Quapaw Incised bowl, AD 1000-1400, deep and solid, Lee County. Unlisted
B) Friendship bottle, Caddo, 8 in. high, AD 800-1200, Pike County. Unlisted
C) Loop-handle bowl, 6 in. high, AD 800-1200, Cross County. Unlisted

Caddo Trading Company, Murfreesboro, Arkansas

Southwestern prehistoric pottery, ca. AD 800-1200.

D) Four Mile olla, 7 in. high, solid and well-painted, Arizona. Unlisted
E) Anasazi pitcher, 7 in. high, black on white, Arizona. Unlisted

Caddo Trading Company, Murfreesboro, Arkansas

Southwestern prehistoric pottery, AD 800-1000:

E) Corrugated olla, 8 in. high, Anasazi, Arizona. Unlisted
F) Doghead pitcher, 7 in. high, solid, New Mexico. Unlisted

Caddo Trading Company, Murfreesboro, Arkansas

Pot, miniature Acoma, with loop handle. Piece is 2-1/2 in. high and 3-1/2 in. wide. Has good paint and age. G-$350

Fetish bowl, Zuni, depicting frog and water bugs. It is 4 in. high and 9 in. across, in good condition, ca. 1930. G-$165

Bowl, Santa Clara, with incised serpent design. Piece is 5-1/2 in. high and 6-1/2 in. in diameter, ca. 1940, and signed Helen. G-$750

Wedding vase, Santa Clara, 8-1/2 in. high and 7 in. diameter. Good condition, ca. 1920. G-$400

Ceramic, San Ildefonso, 11-1/2 in. high and 12 in. in diameter. Black on black water jar. It has minor rim chips and is ca. 1910. G-$425

Head pot, Acoma, 9 in. high and 12 in. across. It has geometric designs, is in excellent condition and is very thin-walled, ca. 1920. G-$550

Pot, small basket-type miniature Acoma, 2-1/2 in. high and 4 in. in diameter, ca. 1930. G-$700

Ceramic bowl, Hopi, reddish slip, 4 in. high and 8-1/2 in. in diameter. Excellent condition, with red and black painted design, ca. 1930. G-$135

Bowl, historic San Ildefonso, 5 in. high and 11 in. across. Polychrome bowl painted inside and out, geometric design. There is chip damage around lower exterior. G-$750

Jar, Hopi, 4-1/2 in. high and 6 in. in diameter. Not signed, but well done, ca. 1920s. G-$265

Pitcher, Mojave, 5 in. high. Diamond painted design and ca. 1940. G-$150

Rain god, Tesque, 7 in. high, with figure sitting with hands over eyes and bowl in lap, ca. 1920. G-$175

CONTEMPORARY AND/OR SIGNED SOUTHWESTERN POTTERY

Pottery vessel, Santo Domingo, bird effigy, 2 in. high and 4 in. long. Small and well-made. G-$135

Pot, miniature Acoma with lightning designs. A-$55

Bowl, Acoma whiteware with brown flowers painted design, 3 in. high and 4-1/2 in. wide. Piece has large coiled handles. G-$140

Pottery effigy figure, Tesque. A-$50

Pottery vessel, Santa Clara, 3-1/2 in. high and 7-1/2 in. in diameter. Red and white, in mint condition. G-$165

Pottery vessel, Acoma, 8 in. high and 9 in. in diameter, very thin and extremely fine shape. G-$800

Pot, Santo Domingo, 10 in. high and 11 in. across. With geometric checkerboard design and in excellent condition. G-$825

Pot, Hopi contemporary, 5 in. high and 6-1/2 in. in diameter, with stylized bird design. Signed, Emily Komalestewa. G-$395

Pot, Santo Domingo, made by Santana Melchor. A-$115

Pot, miniature Acoma, made by B. Cerno. A-$75

Pot, Santa Clara, made by Jo Ann. A-$110

Zuni polychrome pot, 9-1/2 in. high and 11 in. in diameter. These are no longer being made; ca. 1960. C-$1,500

William Sosa photo; Marguerite Kernaghan collection

San Juan carved polychrome bowl, 3-1/2 in. high and 5 in. in diameter, ca. 1972. C-$500-600

Photo courtesy Harvey and Rose King, Muskogee, Oklahoma

Zia jar, 7 in. in height and diameter. (HK: "Zia pottery has long been recognized as among the best pottery of the Southwest. This is due to precision firing, which produces a 'ring' when tapped, like our fine cut glass. Good Zia pottery will hold water, the only Pueblo pottery that will. The roadrunner, New Mexico's State Bird, is the typical decoration of the Zia. Their pottery is still being used in the kitchen of the Zia household.") Ca. 1973. C-$600-800

Photo courtesy Harvey and Rose King, Muskogee, Oklahoma

Zia pueblo pot with bird motif, 10-1/4 in. both in height and diameter. This fine old ceramic artwork is ca. 1915. $6,500

Dennis R. Phillips, Chicago, Illinois

San Juan carved polychrome bowl, 3-1/2 in. high and 5 in. in diameter, ca. 1972. C-$500-600

Photo courtesy Harvey and Rose King, Muskogee, Oklahoma

Zuni pueblo pottery olla or water jar, 14 in. in diameter. The jar is painted with heart-line deer, a pictographic invocation to the heart or spirit of the deer. Also pictured are birds and traditional geometric figures, ca. 1890s. $7,500

Canfield Gallery, Santa Fe

Acoma or Laguna pueblo pot, in four-color polychrome, 11-1/2 in. high and 12 in. in diameter. This pottery jar has unusual decoration and is ca. 1890. $12,500

Dennis R. Phillips, Chicago, Illinois

San Ildefonso pueblo olla, Maria polychrome, slight fire-clouding but bowl intact. It measures 9 in. high and 12 in. in diameter. Year, 1904. $15,000

Traditions, Victor, New York

Santo Domingo pueblo olla, 11 in. high. This pleasingly decorated high bowl has a hairline crack but no restoration, ca. 1900. $2,500

Traditions, Victor, New York

Acoma pueblo olla, four-color decorations, pot 12 in. high and 13 in. in diameter. This fine piece has no restoration and is ca. 1880. $10,000

Traditions, Victor, New York

San Ildefonso pueblo olla, 9 in. high. This pottery piece has a simple yet bold design in black and red, and there is no restoration, ca. 1920. $2,995

Traditions, Victor, New York

Zia pueblo storage jar, large size at 16-1/2 in. high and 20 in. in diameter. Beautifully decorated with red and black designs, the bird is exceptional. There is a small rim chip but no restoration, ca. 1920. $13,500

Traditions, Victor, New York

Fetish bowl, Zuni pueblo, 1930s. This unusual ceramic piece is 2 in. high and 7 in. in diameter. $350

Blue Coyote Trading Post, Nashville, Indiana; Paul McCreary photograph

Early Hopi(?) bowl, ca. AD 1600s, 4 in. high and 7 in. in diameter. This Southwestern pot has been reglued but has not been restored. $450

Blue Coyote Trading Post, Nashville, Indiana; Paul McCreary photograph

Polychrome pottery vessel, southwestern Pueblo and possibly Zia, 10 in. high. It has red geometric designs on a pale red ground. Early 1900s. $275

Larry Garvin, Back to Earth, Ohio

Pottery bowl, 6 in. wide and 5 in. high, with painted geometric designs. This piece is ca. 1950 and came from Isleta pueblo. $175

Jack Baker collection, Ozurk, Missouri; David Capon photograph

Acoma pueblo olla, 12 x 12 in., beautifully painted in four colors. This outstanding example is ca. 1890. $11,500

David Cook Fine American Art, Denver, Colorado; Jamie Kahn photograph

Hopi canteen, animal figure on side, ca. 1920. $1,400

Crown & Eagle Antiques, New Hope, Pennsylvania

Zuni pueblo olla, 10 in. high and 12 in. in diameter. This pottery vessel has an exceptional design, with birds and heartline deer. There is no restoration done on this piece, ca. 1890. $6,995

Traditions, Victor, New York

Acoma pueblo pot, black and orange-red on tan, ca. 1890. In beautiful condition, this fine work is 11-1/2 x 11-1/2 in.
$6,500-7,000

Dennis R. Phillips/Fine American Indian Art, Chicago, Illinois

Ceramic pitcher, very unusual for Pueblo pottery, San Ildefonso pueblo. It is 10 in. high and 10-1/2 in. in diameter, and is ca. 1910. $650

Private collection

Acoma pueblo pot, 6-1/2 in. high and 9 in. diameter, nicely decorated in black on white, ca. 1930. $650

Tom Noeding, Taos, New Mexico

Zuni pueblo pottery bowl with deer and medallion designs, a fine old piece in excellent shape, ca. 1890. $7,500

Crown & Eagle Antiques, New Hope, Pennsylvania

Maria pot, unsigned but with photographic and paper documentation, 7-1/4 in. in diameter. It is gray on black, ex-collection Britt, and highly polished.   Museum quality

Charles F. and Susan Wood, Ohio

Pueblo ceramic bowls, twisted handles, early 1900s:

Left: 5-1/2 in. diameter, polychrome, Acoma pueblo. $90
Right: 4 in. diameter, polychrome, Isleta pueblo. $65

Frank Bergevin, Port Of Call, Alexandria Bay, New York

Ceramic plate, perfect condition and with feather design, by Maria and Popovi Da. G-$3,500

Pot, Hopi contemporary, 8 in. high and 8-1/2 in. in diameter. Designed with fine-lined center band with geometric neck. Signed, Ruby Shroulate. G-$400

Bowl, Hopi, 3 in. high and 7 in. in diameter, very nice. Signed, Viola Howato. G-$395

Ceramic, Santa Clara, 4 in. high and 5-1/2 in. in diameter. Small black on black piece, with painted knife design. Signed, Minnie. G-$365

Pot, Hopi, 6 in. high and 7 in. in diameter. Shows fine geometric design. Signed, Rondina Huma. G-$450

Bowl, Hopi, 3 in. high and 7-3/4 in. in diameter. Signed, Viola Howato, First Mesa, 1968. G-$995

Seed jar, Santa Clara, 5 in. high and 6 in. across. Design is an incised bear paw. Signed, Minnie. G-$400

Pot, San Ildefonso, made by Blue Corn. A-$75

Pot, miniature Santa Clara, made by Little Snow. A-$75

Cylinder-shape jar, Hopi, 9 in. high and 5-1/2 in. in diameter. Beautiful firing marks and design. Signed, by Sadi Adams, Flower-woman. G-$430

Ceramic miniature, 2 in. high and 4 in. in diameter. Black on black design. Signed, Blue Corn. G-$565

Acoma pot, 8-1/2 in. high and 9 in. in diameter. Fine line work, with geometric wide band. Signed, R.S. G-$400

Ceramic bowl, 6 in. high and 8 in. in diameter. Good design and black on black. By Maria and Santana. G-$2,500

Pot, miniature Acoma, by B. Cerno. A-$65

Pot, Acoma, 7 in. high and 8-1/2 in. across. Zone fine-line design. Signed, Ruby Shroulate. G-$400

Pot, San Ildefonso, made by Florence Naranjo. A-$95

Ceramic bowl, San Ildefonso, 5 in. high and 8 in. diameter. Piece is black on black, feather design. By Blue Corn. G-$2,000

Pot, San Ildefonso, made by Linda. A-$270

Pot, Acoma, 7-1/2 in. high and 9 in. across. Band of fine-line work around center, geometric design on neck. Signed R. Shroulate. G-$375

The following information is a special section on the pottery and artwork of the various Southwestern pueblos. Those that currently produce contemporary (post-1950) ceramic wares are represented. The writer—for this new edition—wishes to thank John W. Barry for special permission to use this material. Examples have been selected at random.

Mr. Barry operates Indian Rock Arts (P.O. Box 583, Davis, California 95617-0583) and is especially knowledgeable in the field of contemporary Pueblo and other Southwest Indian ceramics. His primary business is contemporary Pueblo pottery and he authored the important book, *American Indian Pottery*, which is listed following this section.

CONTEMPORARY PUEBLO POTTERY

Jar-bowl, Acoma Pueblo, black on cream with deer design, by Lucy M. Lewis, 5-3/4 in. diameter, 1977. G-$1,300

Wedding vase, Acoma Pueblo, polychrome with stylized bird, by Marie Z. Chino, 8-1/2 in. high, ca. 1970. G-$1,300

Olla, Acoma Pueblo, brown and tan on cream, by Juanita Keene, 10 in. diameter, 1979. G-$650

Jar, Acoma Pueblo, polychrome with stylized birds, by Ethel Shields, 9 in. high, ca. 1960. G-$600

Tesque miniature wedding vase, 4 in. high and 4-1/2 in. in diameter. Tesque pottery is not fired, but sun-dried and painted with gaudy showcard paints. Many were made as tourist curios, ca. 1975. C-$75

Photo courtesy Harvey and Rose King, Muskogee, Oklahoma

Maria pot, San Ildefonso pueblo, made by Maria Martinez (Marie/Santana), 7 in. high and 9 in. in diameter. This black-on-black piece has the famous knife or feather design. $9,500

Dennis R. Phillips, Chicago, Illinois

Jemez bowl, 7-1/2 in. high and 8-1/2 in. diameter. Some of the pottery was sun-baked for the tourist trade, ca. 1970. C-$150-225

Photo courtesy Harvey and Rose King, Muskogee, Oklahoma

Hopi pot, polychrome decoration, by Rondina Huma. This fine ceramic piece measures 4 in. high and 6 in. in diameter. $1,500

Dennis R. Phillips, Chicago, Illinois

Cherokee jar, 5-3/4 in. high and 5-1/2 in. in diameter. C-$500

Photo courtesy Harvey and Rose King, Muskogee, Oklahoma

Hopi pottery, sculpted bowl with corn ear, 4 in. high and 6-3/4 in. in diameter. This contemporary bowl was made by Fris Nampeyo. $1,500

Dennis R. Phillips, Chicago, Illinois

Hopi pot, interesting and well-done designs, 5 in. high and 6-1/2 in. in diameter. The potter is Fannie Nampeyo who did the work, ca. 1975. $1,800

Dennis R. Phillips, Chicago, Illinois

Hopi pot, contemporary, 3-3/4 in. high and 4 in. in diameter. It is signed by Adelle Nampeyo. $190

Blue Coyote Trading Post, Nashville, Indiana; Paul McCreary photograph

Jemez pueblo painted pottery vessel, 6 in. high. Made by Juanita Fragua, it has black, red and white paint against a cream ground; the round body has a squared top opening. $125

Charles F. and Susan Wood, Ohio

Hopi pots, Arizona, all by White Swan, all left to right:

Seed pot, 4-1/2 in. diameter.	$135
Vase, 5-1/2 in. diameter.	$275
Small vase, 3-1/2 in. diameter.	$150

Blue Coyote Trading Post, Nashville, Indiana; Paul McCreary photograph

Isleta pueblo contemporary carved pictorial vessel with painted eagle on a cream ground. The combination of techniques is quite artistic. This piece is 5-1/2 in. high and was made by Robin Teller. $500

Charles F. and Susan Wood, Ohio

Hopi pottery bowl, black designs on light red ground, 3-1/2 in. high and 8 in. in diameter. Year, 1917. $200

Tom Noeding, Taos, New Mexico

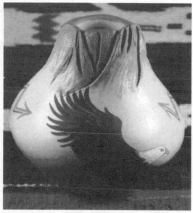

Hopi seed pot, human figure design, 3-3/8 in. high. This pottery piece was made by Lawrence Namoki, 'Kwahu,' and was collected in 1993. $550

Charles F. and Susan Wood, Ohio

Commercial or mold-made pottery vessel, two-spout wedding vase. It is 4-3/4 in. high and has been nicely painted by a pueblo artisan. It is marked "Jojola." $20

Charles F. and Susan Wood, Ohio

Contemporary pottery, "Mesa Verde" style vessel with wooden ladder, 8-3/4 in. in diameter and 7-3/8 in. high. This beautifully sculpted and finished piece was made by Wilfred Garcia and obtained in 1993. $525

Charles F. and Susan Wood, Ohio

Jar, Acoma Pueblo, fine-line design, black on white, 3-1/2 in. high, ca. 1950. G-$125

Miniature, Acoma Pueblo, hand molded, turtle, polychrome turtle shell on white, ca. 1977. G-$20

Corrugated seed jar, Acoma Pueblo, white, by Stella Shutiva, 10 in. diameter, 1979. G-$1,200

Canteen, Acoma Pueblo, polychrome, with Mimbres lizard design, by Emma Lewis, 5 in. in diameter, ca. 1975. G-$600

Storyteller, Cochiti Pueblo, polychrome, by Dorothy Trujillo, 7 in. high, 1979. G-$395

Owl, Cochiti Pueblo, by Seferina Ortiz, 3 in. high, 1979. G-$95

Storyteller, Cochiti Pueblo, polychrome, signed "Felipa," 4 in. high. G-$250

Bowl, Hopi, brown-black on buff, by James Huma, 4 in. diameter, ca. 1970. G-$250

Jar, Hopi, four-color on cream, by Frogwoman (Joy Navasie), 8 in. high, ca. 1978. G-$1,500

Jar-bowl, Hopi, red and black on tan, by Dextra Nampeyo, 5-1/2 in. diameter, 1978. G-$1,700

Jar, Hopi, black and red on orange-tan, by Verla Dewakuku, 7-3/4 in. diameter, ca. 1970. G-$700

Jar-bowl, Hopi, black on tan, 2-5/8 in. high, ca. 1977. G-$65

Seed jar, Hopi, black on cream, 1-3/4 in. high, ca. 1977. G-$75

Jar, Hopi, black on red, 5-1/2 in. diameter, ca. 1965. G-$200

Bell, Isleta Pueblo, polychrome, by Stella Teller, 4 in. diameter, ca. 1975. G-$60

Bowl, Jemez Pueblo "Kiva," tan color, by Juanita Fraqua, 6-1/2 in. diameter, 1978. G-$375

Owl, Jemez Pueblo, polychrome, by Maxine Toya, 3 in. high, 1978. G-$250

Wedding vase, Jemez Pueblo, maize design, by Laura Gachupin, 10-1/2 in. high, 1979. G-$950

Miniature jar, Jemez Pueblo, black on red, 2 in. high, 1979. G-$40

Bowl, Jemez Pueblo, poster paints, 2 in. high, ca. 1970. G-$35

Jar, Jemez Pueblo, polychrome, by Bertha Gachupin, 4 in. diameter, 1978. G-$150

Vase, Nambe/Pojoaque Pueblo, polychrome, by Virginia Gutierrez, 7-1/2 in. high, 1980. G-$185

Bowl, Pecos Revival Pueblo, by Jemez potter, modern with swastika interior design, 5 in. diameter, 1979. G-$500

Textured vase, Pojoaque Pueblo, polychrome, by Joe and Thelma Talachy, 1-1/2 in. high, 1979. G-$95

Bowl, San Ildefonso Pueblo, plain black polish, by Maria Poveka, 5 in. diameter, 1979. G-$1,300

Jar, San Ildefonso Pueblo, by Carlos Dunlap, 4-1/2 in. high, 1979. G-$300

Bowl, San Ildefonso Pueblo, polychrome, by Blue Corn, 5-3/8 in. diameter, some spalling, 1974. G-$950

Vase, San Ildefonso Pueblo, feather design, by Albert and Josephine Vigil, 5 in. high, 1977. G-$550

Bowl, San Juan Pueblo, by Rosita de Herrera, 6 in. diameter, 1976. G-$395

Bowl, Santa Clara Pueblo, incised bird figure, by Art and Martha Cody (Haungooah), 2 in. high, 1975. G-$950

Lidded jar, Santa Clara Pueblo, polished black-ware with bear paw imprint, by Anita Suazok, 7 in. high. G-$950

Plate, Santa Clara Pueblo, Eagle Dancer design, by Goldenrod, 2 5/8 in., diameter, 1980. G-$450

Jar, Santa Clara Pueblo, black-ware with melon design, by Anita Suazo, 3 in. high, 1979. G-$400

Carved vase, Santa Clara Pueblo, black-ware, by Mary Singer, 12-1/2 in. high, 1979. G-$1,200

Pitcher, Santo Domingo Pueblo, double-lipped, by Santana Melchor, 11 in. diameter, ca. 1960. G-$1,100

Jar, Santo Domingo Pueblo, polychrome, with stylized bird, by Robert Tenorio, 9 in. high, 1979. G-$950

Bowl with handle, Santo Domingo Pueblo, polychrome, by Robert Tenorio, 4 in. high, 1977. G-$350

Mud-head figurine, Taos Pueblo, by Alma L. Concha, 5 1/2 in. high, ca. 1975. G-$200

"Rain god" figurine, Tesque Pueblo, tourist item, 6 in. high, ca. 1970. G-$150

Wedding vase, Ysleta-Tigua Pueblo polychrome, by Lucy F. Rodela, 12 in. high, 1979. G-$150

Olla, Zia Pueblo, polychrome with pattern triple-replicated, by Sofia Medina, 12 in. high, ca. 1969. G-$900

Olla, Zia Pueblo, polychrome, stylized red bird decorations in black, by Helen Gachupin, 8-1/2 in. diameter, 1979. G-$350

Jar, Zia Pueblo, polychrome, by Eusebia Shije, 5 in. diameter, ca. 1969. G-$300

Bowl, Zia Pueblo, acrylic painted dancing figure, by J.D. Medina, 10-1/2 in. diameter, 1979. G-$2,800

Jar, Zuni Pueblo, polychrome, by Jennie Laate, 4-1/8 in. high, 1979. G-$400

Olla, Zuni Pueblo, animal designs, polychrome, 9-1/2 in. high ca. 1960. G-$950

Pottery basket with twisted handles, 4-1/2 x 5 in., and fine collector piece. Ca. 1965, black on black matte. By Lucaria Tofoya, Santa Clara Pueblo. Signed.   G-$350

Carved pottery bowl, 5-1/4 in. high and 5-1/4 in. in diameter. Red on tan in carved area, good collector piece. By Helen Tapia, Santa Clara Pueblo. Signed.   G-$300

Pottery dish, 5 in. in diameter, black on black and with feather design. By Ramona Tapia, Santa Clara Pueblo.   G-$300

Pottery dish, 1-3/4 in. high and 6-1/4 in. in diameter. Piece has design on rim and inside of clouds, raindrops, kiva steps and mountains. By Minnie Vigil, Santa Clara Pueblo. Signed.   G-$280

Miniature storage jar, 2-1/4 in. high and 2-3/4 in. in diameter, red, tan, and black with feather design. By Minnie Vigil, Santa Clara Pueblo.   G-$300

Pottery bowl, 4 in. high and 4-1/2 in. in diameter. Piece is red, white and black, with traditional flower design. By Santa Melchor, Santo Domingo Pueblo. Signed. G-$500

Pottery bowl, 3-1/4 in. high and 4-1/4 in. in diameter, black, red, and pale red. Piece has flower and bird design. By Robert Tenerio, Santo Domingo Pueblo. Signed. G-$400

Wedding vase, 7 in. high and 4-3/4 in. in diameter. Piece has traditional Zia bird design. Sofia Medina, Zia Pueblo. Signed.   G-$400

Pottery bowl, 4-1/2 in. in diameter, with bird design. Red, brown on white colors. By Dominguita H. Pino, Zia Pueblo. Signed.   G-$300

Pottery bowl, 5-1/4 in. in diameter. Outstanding traditional piece, red, brown, and white. By Eusebia Shije, Zia Pueblo. Signed.   G-$300

Suggested Reading

"Arizona Highways." (Special Edition) *Southwestern Pottery Today*. Phoenix: Arizona Highway Department, May 1974.

Barry, John W. *American Indian Pottery*. Florence: Books Americana, 1984.

Bunzel, Ruth J. *The Pueblo Potter, A Study of Creative Imagination in Primitive Art*. New York: Dover Publications, 1972 edition.

Dillingham, Rick. *Fourteen Families in Pueblo Pottery*. Albuquerque: University of New Mexico Press, 1994.

Harlow, Francis H. *Modern Pueblo Pottery*. Flagstaff: Northland Press, 1977.

Hayes, Allan and John Blom. *Southwestern Pottery*. Flagstaff: Northland Publishing Company, 1996.

Hyde, Hazel. *Maria Making Pottery*. Santa Fe: The Sunstone Press, 1973.

Lambert, Margaret F. *Pueblo Indian Pottery*. Santa Fe: Museum of New Mexico Press, Popular Series Pamphlet No. 5, 1966.

Martin, Paul S., George I. Quimby and Donald Collier. *Indians Before Columbus*. Chicago and London: The University of Chicago Press, 1947.

Tanner, Clara Lee. *Prehistoric Southwestern Craft Arts*. Tucson: University of Arizona Press, 1976.

Toulouse, Betty. *Pueblo Pottery of the New Mexico Indians*. Santa Fe: Museum of New Mexico Press, 1977.

Water-serpent (Avanyu) pot, 13 in. high and 11 in. diameter. Santa Clara Pueblo, by Belen Tapia.   C-$3,000

Photo courtesy William Scoble. The Ansel Adams Gallery, Yosemite National Park, California

Large San Ildefonso pot, 9-1/2 in. high and 7-1/2 in. diameter, black on black feather design. Pot was made and signed by Maria and Popovi Da, and received by present owner as a gift from Popovi Da in 1962.   C-$8,000

Small San Ildefonso pot, (near Santa Fe, New Mexico), 2-1/2 x 3-1/2 in. Black on black design, made and signed by Maria and Santana, ca. 1958.   C-$450

Marguerite Kernaghan collection; William A. Sosa, photo

Pottery vessel, orange and black designs on white, 9-1/2 in. high and 10-1/2 in. in diameter. It is from Acoma pueblo and was made in the 1960s. $925

Courtesy The Curio Shop, Anderson, California

Pottery vessel, black designs on white with orange interior, Acoma pueblo. It is 7-1/2 in. high and 7 in. in diameter, and from the 1970s. $600

Courtesy The Curio Shop, Anderson, California

Pottery vessel, orange and black on white, orange interior. It is 7-1/2 in. high and 9 in. in diameter, and from Acoma pueblo. It dates to the 1960s. $1,000

Courtesy The Curio Shop, Anderson, California

Pottery vessel, black designs on white with orange interior, Acoma pueblo. It is 7-1/2 in. high and 7 in. in diameter, and from the 1970s. $600

Courtesy The Curio Shop, Anderson, California

Seed jar, Acoma pueblo, black-on-white. It is by Dorothy Torivio, 1 x 2-1/2 in. This delightful miniature is ca. 1991. $250

Courtesy Adobe Gallery, Albuquerque, New Mexico

Seed bowl, Acoma, signed R. Concho, Acoma, New Mexico. It is ca. 1979 with the Mimbres gila monster designs. Size is 3 x 5 in.; perfect condition. $700

Marguerite L. Kernaghan collection; photograph by Marguerite L. and Stewart W. Kernaghan, Bellvue, Colorado

Polychrome singer with five children and one dog, Acoma, signed Frances Torivio, Acoma, New Mexico. It is 4 x 7 in. and ca. 1975. $525

Marguerite L. Kernaghan collection; photograph by Marguerite L. and Stewart W. Kernaghan, Bellvue, Colorado

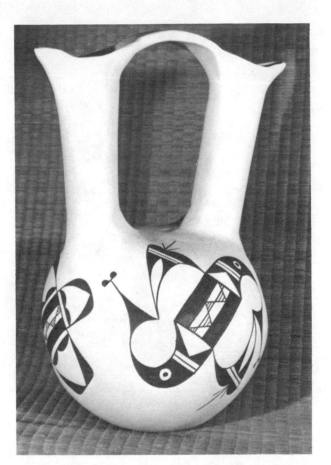

Pottery double-necked vase or pitcher, brown-black and orange designs on white. It is 14 in. high and 8 in. wide and was made in the 1970s. It is from Acoma pueblo. $1,200

Courtesy The Curio Shop, Anderson, California

Olla, polychrome, Acoma pueblo, with heartline deer design. It is by Lucy Lewis, 5-1/4 x 6-1/4 in., ca. 1968. $2,200

Courtesy Adobe Gallery, Albuquerque, New Mexico

Bowl, black-on-black with feather design, 3 x 5 in. This superb pot was purchased in Colorado in 1979 for $250, according to receipts of the previous owner. It was made by Adam and Santana, (Martinez), San Ildefonso pueblo. $650-900

Hothem collection, Ohio

Storyteller with five children, polychrome, signed D. Trujillo, Cochiti, New Mexico. Size is 5 x 7-1/2 in., ca. 1975. $550

Marguerite L. Kernaghan collection; photograph by Marguerite L. and Stewart W. Kernaghan, Bellvue, Colorado

Bowl, black-on-black, by Maria Martinez and Popovi Da. This is a fine example by famous potters, being 3-1/4 x 7 in., ca. 1960. $3,500

Dennis R. Phillips/Fine American Indian Art, Chicago, Illinois

Storyteller figurine, Santa Clara from Cochiti pueblo. It is by Louis and Virginia Naranjo, 6-1/4 in. high and ca. 1992. $995

Courtesy Adobe Gallery, Albuquerque, New Mexico

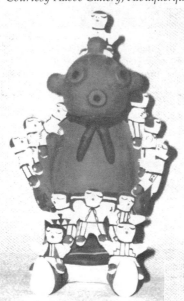

Mudhead storyteller with 13 children, Hopi, signed Norma Sakenima, Hopi, Hoteville, Arizona. It is 6-1/2 x 12 x 17 in. and ca. 1980. $900

Marguerite L. Kernaghan collection; photograph by Marguerite L. and Stewart W. Kernaghan, Bellvue, Colorado

Maria Poveka (Martinez) polished black ware bowl, San Ildefonso pueblo, ca. 1950. A superb plain bowl, it is 3 x 9-1/2 in. $3,000

Dennis R. Phillips/Fine American Indian Art, Chicago, Illinois

Drummer figure, Cochiti, made by Seferina Ortiz. The drum was made by her husband Guadalupe Ortiz, a famous drum maker. This figure received Second Place at the 1983 Santa Fe Indian Market. This 5 x 10-1/2 in. work has several turquoise sets, ca. 1980. Museum quality

Marguerite L. Kernaghan collection; photograph by Marguerite L. and Stewart W. Kernaghan, Bellvue, Colorado

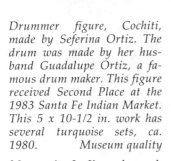

Black-on-black bowl, by Marie Martinez/Santana, and ca. 1950. This beautiful piece is 6 in. in diameter. $1,200

Dennis R. Phillips/Fine American Indian Art, Chicago, Illinois

Black-on-black bowl made by Margaret Tafoya, ca. 1960. The beautiful ceramic work is in mint condition, and 9 in. in diameter. $3,000

Courtesy John Isaac, Albuquerque, New Mexico

Maria jar, Maria and Popovi Da, San Ildefonso pueblo, black-on-black. It is 7-1/2 in. high and 9-1/4 in. in diameter, ca. 1970. A top-grade piece. $7,500

Courtesy Adobe Gallery, Albuquerque, New Mexico

Maria pot, by Maria and Popovi Da, San Ildefonso pueblo, black on-black plate. It has gun-metal finish, is 2 in. deep and 11-1/4 in. in diameter, ca. 1960s. A superb piece. $9,500

Courtesy Adobe Gallery, Albuquerque, New Mexico

Contemporary Pueblo pottery, all left to right:

Acoma black and red on white.	$75
Jemez bowl, 6 in. diameter.	$150
Jemez small bowl.	$65
Acoma pottery owl.	$175

Pocotopaug Trading Post, South Windsor, Connecticut

Black-on-black vase, round base and squared top, 13 in. high. By Flora Naranjo, the vase is ca. 1975; condition is mint. $950

Courtesy John Isaac, Albuquerque, New Mexico

Seed jar, Hopi, polychrome, 3-1/2 x 4-1/2 in. It is by Dextra Quotsquiva Nampeyo, and ca. 1992. $1,400

Courtesy Adobe Gallery, Albuquerque, New Mexico

Pottery vase, Santa Clara pueblo, signed M. Tafoya. It has the bearpaw design and is 9 x 11 in. $900-1,000

Larry Lantz, First Mesa, South Bend, Indiana

Polychrome shaped vessel; it has only the firing hole in the bottom and no other opening. It is carved and decorated with seed beads, turquoise and coral, and is a very beautiful piece. Size is 3-1/2 x 10-1/2 in.   Museum quality

Marguerite L. Kernaghan collection; photograph by Marguerite L. and Stewart W. Kernaghan, Bellvue, Colorado

Recent stoneware effigy lidded container, gray-black designs on speckled tan. By Robert Tenorio, it is 8 in. in diameter. $150

Courtesy John Isaac, Albuquerque, New Mexico

Polychrome pot, Jemez pueblo, signed R. Sandia, Jemez. This fine bowl is ca. 1984 and 4-1/2 x 10-3/4 in. $650

Marguerite L. Kernaghan collection; photograph by Marguerite L. and Stewart W. Kernaghan, Bellvue, Colorado

Polychrome bowl, Hopi, signed Melda Nampeyo, ca. 1985. This pottery piece is well-painted and a good collectible pot. $550

Marguerite L. Kernaghan collection; photograph by Marguerite L. and Stewart W. Kernaghan, Bellvue, Colorado

Carved egg-shaped pot, Hopi, ca. 1988. The maker is C.R. Claw Nampeyo; perfect condition and 4 x 5-3/4 in. It has the Kokopelli design. $875

Marguerite L. Kernaghan collection; photograph by Marguerite L. and Stewart W. Kernaghan, Bellvue, Colorado

Jar, polychrome, Hopi, by Elva Nampeyo. It is 11 in. high and 16 in. in diameter, ca. 1980s. $5,000

Courtesy Adobe Gallery, Albuquerque, New Mexico

Jar, fluted, contemporary example from Laguna pueblo. It is 13 x 13 in., by Andrew Padilla, ca. 1992. $895

Courtesy Adobe Gallery, Albuquerque, New Mexico

Santa Clara pueblo canteen by Margaret Tafoya, red ware with bearpaw imprint, ca. 1960. This is a top-grade pottery piece. $3,000

Dennis R. Phillips/Fine American Indian Art, Chicago, Illinois

Carved pottery jar, Santa Clara pueblo, black, with Avanyu (water serpent) design, by Teresita Naranjo. It is 4 x 6-1/2 in., ca. 1991. $2,500

Courtesy Adobe Gallery, Albuquerque, New Mexico

Maria bowl, San Ildefonso pueblo, done by Maria Poveka. This lovely black bowl is 3 in. high and 9-3/4 in. in diameter, ca. 1960. $3,500

Dennis R. Phillips, Chicago, Illinois

Seed jar, miniature, Santa Clara pueblo buff on red. It is by Delores Curran, 1-3/4 x 1-3/4 in., ca. 1980. $695

Courtesy Adobe Gallery, Albuquerque, New Mexico

Santa Clara pueblo pot, polished red ware, by Margaret Tafoya. It is 4 in. high and 7 in. in diameter, and is ca. 1980. $3,500

Dennis R. Phillips, Chicago, Illinois

Acoma pot, black design on creamy white, 5-1/4 in. high. This fine piece was made by Darla Davis and is a contemporary item. $125

Blue Coyote Trading Post, Nashville, Indiana; Paul McCreary photograph

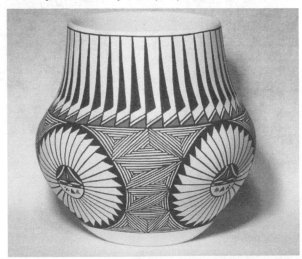

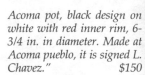

Pottery bowl, Acoma pueblo, 7 x 7-1/2 in. wide. Nicely fired and with very precise designs, this New Mexico piece is just a few years old. Museum quality

Collection of Eugene and Marcille Wing

Acoma pot, black design on white with red inner rim, 6-3/4 in. in diameter. Made at Acoma pueblo, it is signed L. Chavez." $150

Blue Coyote Trading Post, Nashville, Indiana; Paul McCreary photograph

Acoma pueblo pot, contemporary, 6 in. high and 7 in. in diameter. The exterior designs are in red and black and the inner rim is red. The ceramic piece is signed by L. Garcia. $250

Blue Coyote Trading Post, Nashville, Indiana; Paul McCreary photograph

Acoma pueblo pottery turtle, black design on white, 3-1/4 in. long. Nicely handpainted, done by Eva Concho. $45

Charles F. and Susan Wood, Ohio

Acoma pueblo pottery Christmas ornament, green design on red. This hand-painted piece is 2-3/4 in. in diameter and was made by J. Garcia. $30

Charles F. and Susan Wood, Ohio

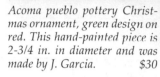

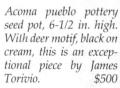

Acoma pueblo pot with parrot design, 3-7/8 in. high. It was made by B. Victorino and is nicely painted. 1993. $100

Charles F. and Susan Wood, Ohio

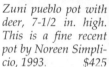

Acoma pueblo miniature seed pot with complex design of white on black, 2 in. in diameter. With small opening at the top, this was made by Dorothy Torivio. $200

Charles F. and Susan Wood, Ohio

Zuni pueblo pot with deer, 7-1/2 in. high. This is a fine recent pot by Noreen Simplicio, 1993. $425

Charles F. and Susan Wood, Ohio

Acoma pueblo pottery seed pot, 6-1/2 in. high. With deer motif, black on cream, this is an exceptional piece by James Torivio. $500

Charles F. and Susan Wood, Ohio

Commercial pottery bowl with mold-marks removed, seed pot form, with exceptional hand-applied paintwork by Brenda Charlie, Acoma pueblo. It is 5 in. in diameter and the designs are black on white. $140

Charles F. and Susan Wood, Ohio

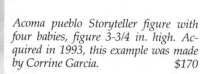

Acoma pueblo Storyteller figure with four babies, figure 3-3/4 in. high. Acquired in 1993, this example was made by Corrine Garcia. $170

Charles F. and Susan Wood, Ohio

Acoma pueblo seed pot, 8-1/2 in. in diameter and 7 in. high, with feather design around top. Obtained in 1993, this was made by Wilfred Garcia. $400

Charles F. and Susan Wood, Ohio

Santa Clara pueblo black Bear Paw pot, 8-1/2 in. high. This polished example was acquired in 1993 and was made by Sharon Naranjo Garcia. $775

Charles F. and Susan Wood, Ohio

Acoma pueblo Storyteller figure, pottery by Peggy Garcia. This example is 4-1/2 in. high. $170

Charles F. and Susan Wood, Ohio

Santa Clara pueblo miniature bowl, 2 in. in diameter, with Avanyu or Water Serpent design. This fine black pot was made by Jennifer Naranjo. $95

Charles F. and Susan Wood, Ohio

Santa Clara pueblo miniature pot with Water Serpent design, beautifully made, carved and polished. It is 2-1/4 in. in diameter and was made by Kevin Naranjo and Marian Rose, ca. 1993. $625

Charles F. and Susan Wood, Ohio

San Ildefonso pueblo carved red ware pot with Water Serpent design. Just 1-7/8 in. in diameter, the bowl has the Serpent's eye of round turquoise. The miniature bowl was made by Lyle Gonzales and the design was by John Gonzales, father of Lyle. 1993. $110

Charles F. and Susan Wood, Ohio

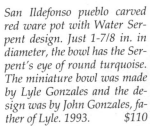

San Juan pueblo incised vase, red ware with mica slip paint on irregular (lower) surface which produces some glitter. This carved vessel, 5-1/2 in. in diameter, was made by Dominguita Naranjo. $350

Charles F. and Susan Wood, Ohio

Acoma pueblo miniature seed pot, rabbit design in black on white. This piece is 2-1/4 in. in diameter and was done by Rachel Concho. $90

Charles F. and Susan Wood, Ohio

San Ildefonso pueblo pottery bowl, red rim and red design on cream, 4-3/4 in. in diameter. This striking piece was made by Albert Vigil. $175

Charles F. and Susan Wood, Ohio

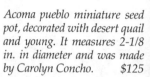

Acoma pueblo miniature seed pot, decorated with desert quail and young. It measures 2-1/8 in. in diameter and was made by Carolyn Concho. $125

Charles F. and Susan Wood, Ohio

Acoma pueblo canteen or water jug, 7 in. in diameter. The design is red and black against cream for this pottery piece made by Loretta Joe. $225

Charles F. and Susan Wood, Ohio

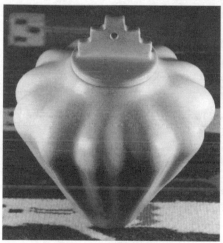

Laguna pueblo melon bowl, cream-colored, 7 in. in diameter and 9-1/2 in. high. This outstanding pottery piece was made by Andrew Padilla. $875

Charles F. and Susan Wood, Ohio

Acoma pueblo miniature plate, 2-1/8 in. in diameter. Decorated with flute-player and cornstalk, it was made by D. Reano. $30

Charles F. and Susan Wood, Ohio

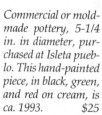

Commercial or mold-made pottery, 5-1/4 in. in diameter, purchased at Isleta pueblo. This hand-painted piece, in black, green, and red on cream, is ca. 1993. $25

Charles F. and Susan Wood, Ohio

An 1891 photo taken by Gravill of Deadwood, with original caption: "Home of Mrs. American Horse. Visiting women at Mrs. A's home in hostile camp." Note the proliferation of White-made goods throughout the encampment. Interestingly, one of the more valued things in nearly treeless regions were the long poles for the tepees.

Photo courtesy of South Dakota State Historical Society

CHAPTER X

HISTORIC TRADE-ERA COLLECTIBLES

The field of trade-era objects has two aspects. One is that the objects were made, for the most part, by Europeans for trade with the Indians. And, although whites used some of these items (axes, kettles, and the like) themselves, the artifacts have been identified with Amerinds ever since.

In short—and for the only such chapter in this book—these are Indian collectibles not actually made by Indians.

Before, during, and after the great fur trade of the 1700s and early 1800s, axes and other edged tools were popular. After the utilitarian objects were obtained, apparently the decorative items were sought. Trade silver and glass beads were much in demand, partially because they were well-made and attractive, but also because they were made of materials unknown to the Native Americans.

BASIC TRADE AXE FORMS

Most trade axes were of wrought (hand-forged) iron, made in the American Colonies, Canada, and Europe. The iron head had a round or oval hafting "eye," a long, often back-slung blade and an inlaid steel cutting edge. Inferior specimens sometimes lacked this last feature, being traded to unsuspecting recipients, making the axe both brittle and nearly useless. Trade axes were used throughout the 1700s and most of the 1800s, until factory-made examples became widely available.

Similar axe and tomahawk heads are being made today for the frontier aficionados and can be mistaken for old and valuable pieces. A certain amount of pitting and scabbing should be on genuine specimens, and the lap-weld around the eye and flowing into the flat blade is usually visible. Value is much less if the steel cutting edge is missing.

Condition is important: a small, intact specimen is more to be desired than a larger piece with much serious rusting and large chips missing from the blade. To paraphrase a knowledgeable Midwestern collector, one should look for a good piece in good condition, at a good price.

A legible and traceable marker's stamp, town or state of origin, or a date will add to specimen value. All three make a very desirable, and rarely obtainable, combination. (Information in this paragraph, by the way, also pertains to the pipe-tomahawks.) Many axeheads have been surface finds, and will show the signs of having been weathered for many years.

TRADE-ERA AXE HEADS

Trade-iron axe head, northern Illinois trading-post site, 6-3/4 in. long. Round hafting eye; some corrosion, but average, ca. 1830.   G-$200

Metal trade axe, 5-1/2 in. long and 2 in. wide; nice shape. It has a hole in the back portion, and was possibly used as a pipe.   G-$200

Belt axe, found on an historic Indian site in Iowa, 4-1/4 in. high. Small, squared, with oblong haft receptacle or eye. Cutting edge good, condition good. Probably late 1800s.   C-$160

Metal trade axe, 7-3/4 in. long and 3-1/2 in. wide, good size, ca. 1700.   G-$240

Trade iron axe head, 8 in. long and blade 5-3/8 in. wide at cutting bit. No haft or handle. Nicely hand-forged, light age pitting, and a solid piece.   D-$255

Axe head, from northern Ohio; 6-1/4 in. high. Badly corroded blade. Undamaged, but heavy rust has eaten out portions of the lower blade and portions of the eye-strap.   C-$90

(The following five listings, of metal axe and pipe-heads only, are courtesy of Bob Coddington, Illinois. Note that these are 1970 figures. In the writer's opinion, values would now be five or six times as high).

Tomahawk head of iron, with surface rust, recovered by means of a metal detector on site of old Ottawa or Huron village along bank of Thames River in Ontario, Canada. This was not far from the site of "The Battle of the Thames" (1813) where the American General Harrison de-

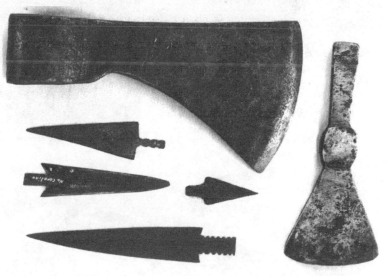

Trade iron and steel artifacts. Top center: trade axe, 6-1/4 in., from New York. $180

Axe with extended poll, Connecticut. $190

Trade points, lower left examples, bottom 4-1/2 in.   *Each, $10-45*

Pocotopaug Trading Post, South Windsor, Connecticut

Historic trade axe, about 8 in. long. Iron is somewhat battered and corroded around the upper haft portion, the eye.   D-$125

Photo-Lar Hothem

Iron axe head, 8-1/4 in. long and 4-3/8 in. wide. Heavy blade is typical of belt axes of this type. The eye is rounded, showing evidence of flattening. The entire head is uniformly pitted and shows a fine brown patina. No doubt it was highly prized as tool and weapon. Touchmark has not yet been identified; piece is ca. late 1700s/early 1800s.   C-$350-475

Photo courtesy Sheridan P. Barnard, Franklin, Massachusetts

Three trade-era iron axes, with middle specimen about 6 in. long. Top and middle pieces have damaged blade edge; bottom piece, marked "ARIT" is heavily worn.

Axes: Left	D-$185
Middle	D-$185
Right	D-$60

Iron pipe tomahawk with 27 in. ash stem. A horse design is stamped on both sides of the blade. A human skull bone is tied to the stem-handle. Ca. 1870.   Museum quality

Nedra Matteucci's Fenn Galleries, Santa Fe, New Mexico

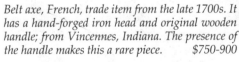

Belt axe, French, trade item from the late 1700s. It has a hand-forged iron head and original wooden handle; from Vincennes, Indiana. The presence of the handle makes this a rare piece. $750-900

Larry Lantz, First Mesa, South Bend, Indiana

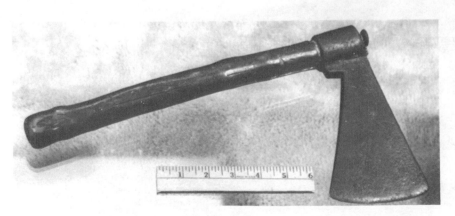

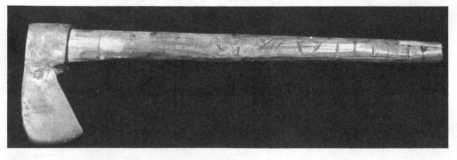

Trade iron axe head with very old handle, both in fine condition. $350-500

Collection of David G. & Barbara J. Shirley

224 →

Trade axes, each with an original wooden handle. These are from Northeastern U.S., and are very scarce items. Each, $400-700

Philip L. Russo collection, Danbury, Connecticut

Trade axes, each with an original wooden handle, all from Northeastern U.S. Note the very different handle styles for each; all are probably hardwood. Each, $400-795

Philip L. Russo collection, Danbury, Connecticut

feated the Shawnee Chief, Tecumseh, and General Proctor of the British Army, in the War of 1812. Tecumseh lost his life. This piece was part of a cache of trade tomahawk heads in an old iron pot with a mixture of mud and beads. Item must have been in new condition when cached; it appears to have never been used, although it is rusted. Has the steel insert on leading edge of blade. This piece is the "modern" type squaw hatchet. (1970) C-$95

Iron pipe-tomahawk head. British-type bowl of either American or English manufacture. (1970)C-$225

Belt hatchet head, found on Chippewa National Forest site, Old Leech Lake Indian Reservation, while digging a well. Steel insert in leading edge of blade. This type of squaw axe was popular as trade commodity and was widely distributed by the Hudson Bay and X.Y. companies. Ca. 1780. (1970) C-$200

Spontoon-type tomahawk head, obtained from Six Nations (Iroquois) Reserve at Brantford, Ontario. Piece is of

the squaw hatchet variety, of Trois Rivieves, or Chautiere, Quebec (Canada) manufacture. Heavily rusted, and a very early French type, ca. 1750. (1970) C-$280

Squaw hatchet head, of early trade variety. Recovered by Peter Cloud, a Chippewa Indian, on Squaw Point of Leech Lake, Minnesota, while plowing garden on site of Chief Flatmouth's old Pillager Chippewa village. From its condition, this piece was evidently discarded as being worn out, and of no further use, ca. 1780 (1970) C-$75

HAFTED TRADE-ERA HEADS (complete)
(Information courtesy Bob Coddington, Illinois)

So-called squaw hatchet with very unusual haft, elaborately decorated with carvings of diamonds, stars, etc. Top of handle has thirteen carved five-point stars encased in "Vs" at each end. Ring in end of haft. This piece could possibly have belonged to a frontiersman (White) during the American Revolution, or a friendly Indian ally of the original Thirteen Colonies. (1970) C-$350

Iron squaw hatchet, haft decorated with brass braid tassel, probably from tunic facings, or epaulet of British or French uniform tunic; ca. 1760-1780. (1970) C-$375

Squaw hatchet of iron, haft decorated with trade tacks and five large white bead sets, typical trade items; ca. 1780.   (1970) C-$265

PIPE-TOMAHAWKS

Better specimens of the pipe-axe/tomahawk (best not to use the terms "pipe-hawk" or "hawk" around serious collectors) are considered a high-art form. Ranging from plain to fancy to presentation-grade—these with the original handle—they grace a limited number of collections.

Still, the writer is aware of several instances where good pipe-tomahawks were purchased at farm auctions for nominal sums, at two to ten percent of actual value. In the world of Amerind collectibles, such things happen.

It may not be possible to totally fake a complete pipe tomahawk (considered by collectors to be pipes, not weapons) head and handle. Beyond the factors of metal working and the head, there is the problem of properly shaping and aging the wood handle-stem. More likely, and to beware of, is an oldish handle hafted to a good but mediocre head.

Usually the fit is not close, the wood is not a seasoned hardwood, and the whole is not a unit. The two sections just do not belong together. If the haft is supposed to be original, or at least of comparable age, both head and handle should evidence a believable amount of wear.

And conversely, an ornate handle will usually not accompany a very plain pipe-tomahawk head. Also, don't be too impressed with the assertion that the piece belonged to famous "Chief So-and-So," for this usually cannot be documented.

Pipe-tomahawk; head is 7-1/4 in. high, blade has 17-7/8 inch cutting edge. Original or at least very old handle, 15-3/4 in. long. Fine condition; ca. 1780. C-$1,400

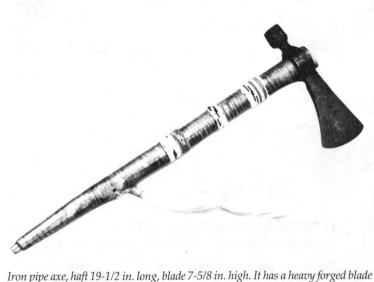

Iron pipe axe, haft 19-1/2 in. long, blade 7-5/8 in. high. It has a heavy forged blade of flaring design, while pipe bowl is crudely made and shows some repair. The maple haft appears to have been a later addition and shows multi-beaded cuffs and a horse hair suspension. The piece is typical of the Midwest-Great Lakes region; it is ca. early to mid 1800s. Note beaded strips on handle. C-$1,900-3,000

Photo courtesy Sheridan P. Barnard, Franklin, Massachusetts

Spontoon-type pipe tomahawk head, no haft; 9-1/2 in. long and 3-1/2 in. wide. Spontoon-types have a spear-like blade instead of a curved blade.   G-$500

Rare spontoon-head pipe-tomahawk, no haft; 10-3/4 in. long, and seems to be all iron. Reported to have come from historic Indian site in Kansas.   C-$550

Trade tomahawk with hammer poll; 10 in. long and 3 in. wide. Found in New York; ca. mid-18th century.   G-$195

Brass pipe tomahawk, good and original head, with a later (but still old) undrilled handle. Stem-handle is file-burned and beaded.   D-$850

Pipe tomahawk, head only; in good, sound condition.   D-$500

Brass pipe tomahawk, of later Reservation period. Original stem, but value reduced when an uninformed person sanded the wood.   D-$550

Pipe-tomahawk, presentation-grade. French or British and probably late 1700s. Piece is from western Pennsylvania, and head is 6-1/2 in. high. Length, with handle, 17 in.; handle may be maple wood. Good condition, and blade has pewter inserts in shape of half moon and stars.   C-$1900

Brass pipe-tomahawk with original handle. A genuine piece of fine style and quality.   G-$1,100

Iron tomahawk, cast blade with heart cut-out. Handle is lead inlayed with bands and crosses; ca. 1880-1890.   D-$500

Pipe-tomahawk, authentic early wooden handle, brass head with only minor battering damage at pipe poll. Attractive.   D-$995

Good brass pipe-tomahawk, guaranteed genuine and in excellent condition. Nice patina on brass, file-burned handle, partially beaded.   G-$900

Pipe tomahawk with old handle; iron head in good condition, has the steel insert. Plain but solid piece.   D-$800

Pipe tomahawk; length of haft is 19-1/2 in. and head is 5-1/2 in. Brass pipe tomahawk with original wood haft. Heavily worn. Leading edge formerly held dovetailed steel bit. Floral motif on bowl and blade; ca. 1790.   G-$825

(The following listings in trade-iron section are courtesy Bob Coddington, Illinois. Values are 1970, and in the writer's opinion, are currently less than one-third fair market prices.)

Typical early trade iron pipe-tomahawk, with curl at base of haft. Very plain; ca. 1790.   (1970) C-$375

Iron pipe-tomahawk, massive British Broad-Arrow marked with superb inlays of pewter or silver on haft. Type presented to chiefs by British government for loyalty and friendship.   (1970) C-$600

Iron pipe-tomahawk with unusual flaring pipe bowl. Slim narrow blade, with pewter-inlayed haft; ca. 1780-1800.   (1970) C-$600

Left:

Iron spike axe, with haft 18 in. long, and blade 7-1/2 in. high. The axe head has a long, straight spike of square cross-section, eye is wedge-shaped; flared blade shows definite notches on the edge. Haft is ovoid in cross-section, decorated with brass tacks; suspensions of hairpipe and beads appear to be a later addition to the axe. Style attributed to Western Great Lakes East to New England. Piece is mid-1700s to early 1800s.   C-$1,900-3,000

Photo courtesy Sheridan P. Barnard, Franklin, Massachusetts

Far Right:

Steel pipe axe, haft 20-1/2 in. long and blade 7-3/4 in. high, 2-3/8 in. wide. The undecorated, drilled and cylindrical wooden handle has a flared steel blade of fine manufacture. The blade is attached with a flanged, engraved pipe bowl of cylindrical shape. Handle is a later addition to the head. This is a Plains region pipe, ca. late 1800s.   C-$2,000-3,000

Photo courtesy Sheridan P. Barnard, Franklin, Massachusetts

Cheek-cah-kose (Little Crane) presentation grade pipe tomahawk. Little Crane was a Chief of the Potowatomi, with a village at the headwaters of the Tippecanoe River in northern Indiana. Three views: Left and right sides of head; and full view. Head is of engraved pewter, with a brass screw-out bowl. The blade is hallmarked (DV) over a coronet. Presentation pieces of this quality are rare. Ca. 1767.   C-$5,000

Photo courtesy Bob Coddington, Illinois

Plains Indian artifacts, with pipe bag shown elsewhere. Top: pipe-tomahawk with a large steel head that is pierced with a diamond cutout. The haft is decorated with brass tacks and file-branding with a suspension consisting of brass wire, brass beads, talons, teeth and an 1847 one-cent coin. Length, 26 in.; ca. 1860s-1870s.   *Museum quality*

Dave Hrachovy, Cedar Glen, California

Great Lakes weaponry. Top: ball-headed club, polished hardwood, ca. 1760. $4,500

Bottom: pipe-tomahawk, original handle, hand-forged head with steel blade, oak handle with silver inlays and carved horn mouthpiece. Rare piece, ca. 1780. $3,000

Private collection; photo by John McLaughlin

Pipe-tomahawk with original handle, ca. 1860-1870, and a style often favored by Plains Indians. It has the handle decorated with beads and tacks. Head, 10-1/2 in. high; handle, 25 in. long. $1,800-2,500

Philip L. Russo collection, Danbury, Connecticut

Pewter pipe-axe elaborately engraved with bleeding heart, leaves and scrimshaw on one side of blade. Large turtle, bow and what appears to be initials "L.H." and profuse engraving. Bowl is deeply and elaborately engraved. Handle is inlayed with pewter bands.   (1970) C-$650

Iron pipe-axe, small short handle with "wi ix" burned in haft. Example of the early French type, strap tomahawk, very old, and heavily rusted, ca. 1695-1710. (1970) C-$335

Trade-type pipe-tomahawk of wrought iron, severely plain, scroll type mouthpiece, probably of British manufacture. Strap type with steel insert on leading edge of blade; ca. 1770-1800.   (1970) C-$325

Excellent French-type pewter pipe-tomahawk of presentation quality with Trois Rivieves, Quebec (Canada) markings; pewter inlays. Type presented to Canadian chiefs for loyalty; ca. 1750.   (1970) C-$600

Pewter pipe-axe; very fine presentation with half-moon and star cut-out, acorn-shape pipe bowl. A wolf is engraved with leaves and star on one side of the blade. Handle has nice pewter inlays. From a Canadian collection; inscription dated 1797.   (1970) C-$650

Brass pick-type spontoon tomahawk, "J.H." over sword. The pick is four-sided. Piece has a beautiful handle inlayed with silver and bone, overall an exquisite work of art; ca. 1760.   (1970) C-$550

TRADE SILVER ORNAMENTS

Even before a man named Paul Revere invented a rolling press to flatten silver bars to a predetermined thinness, trade silver artifacts were very popular items. In addition to the flat pendants and brooches, crosses, and gorgets of myriad forms, there were solid-cast and hollow-cast effigies.

Such forms ranged from turtles to beavers to the esoteric and much-admired "kissing otters," touching noses and swimming, seen from above. Hudson Bay Company contributed countless fine specimens, most of which went into the Northern reaches of the United States, the top fur producing regions.

Trade silver copies are being made today from a metal called nickel silver, a combination of copper, nickel, and zinc. It is cheaper and more durable than pure silver. Such copies are very good and they sell for a fraction of genuine trade silver.

Unfortunately, most are not marked as reproduc-

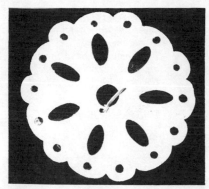

Trade silver brooch, 2 in. in diameter, and with elliptical and circular cutouts, scalloped rim, and touchmarked "DE." Sheet silver, and perfect condition. C-Above $250

Photo courtesy Bob Coddington, Illinois

From left to right:

Trade silver beaver pendant, solid-cast silver, 1-1/4 in. long. C-Above $250
Trade silver turtle pendant, 3/4 in. long, and solid-cast silver. C-Above $200
Trade silver turtle image, 3/4 in. long and hollow-cast silver. Touchmarked on back. C-Above $200

Photo courtesy Bob Coddington, Illinois

From left to right:

Trade silver cross pendant, 1-1/4 in. high, drilled for suspension. Piece has incised lines on face. C-$250

Trade silver cross, 7/8 in. in length. Piece has inscribed lines on face, with touchmark "DS" This was purchased with the original string of trade beads, not shown; price was for the entire necklace. C-$350

Small trade silver cross pendant, 1 in. high, and with circular loop for cord. C-$250

Photo courtesy Bob Coddington, Illinois

Trade silver crown/hat-band, Iroquois, 5/8 in. high and 24 in. around. This superb piece is Northern United States/Ontario, Canada, and ca. 1790. $895

Pat & Dave Summers, Native American Artifacts, Victor, New York

From left to right:

Trade silver masonic emblem, 1-1/4 in. high. Pin that hold brooch is visible in center. C-$150

Trade silver brooch, circular form and with cross-shaped cutouts; piece is 3/4 in. in diameter, of sheet silver. C-$125

Hatchet-shaped trade silver brooch, 1-1/4 in. high. C-$125

Photo courtesy Bob Coddington, Illinois

From left to right:

Trade silver beaver pendant, solid-cast silver, 1-1/2 in. long. Touchmarked on rounded back. C-$250

Trade silver beaver, 1-3/8 in. long, hollow-cast silver. Touchmarked "B" on back. C-$260

Trade silver beaver pendant, solid-cast silver, 1-1/4 in. long. C-$240

Photo courtesy Bob Coddington, Illinois

Trade silver artifacts, early historic period.

Top: cross, 4-3/4 in. high, engraved with beaver gnawing down a tree. $650
Bottom: brooch, 1-7/8 in., with touchmark "CA." $300

Both items came from Monroe County, Illinois, and are very scarce.

Pocotopaug Trading Post, South Windsor, Connecticut

Trade silver brooch, showing silver tongue used for fastening to clothing. The "DS" touchmark may be David Stroughton, who worked in Canada in the early 1800s. Size, about 1-1/2 in. high. $85

Private collection

Trade silver ornaments.

Left: nose ring, 1760-1820.	$125
Top right: small English/Cayuga cross, ca. 1760.	$185
Bottom left: large "Council Fire" brooch, ca. 1760-1820.	$250
Bottom right: superb brooch, ca. 1760-1820.	$300

Pat & Dave Summers, Native American Artifacts, Victor, New York

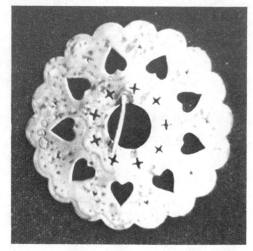

Trade silver brooch, Onondaga, British-made, with heart and cross designs. This exquisite piece is 3 in. across, ca. 1790, and has the maker's touchmarks. $250

Pat & Dave Summers, Native American Artifacts, Victor, New York

tions. Amerind trade silver may have a blackish tarnish and may be somewhat corroded. It should show some signs of one and a half to two centuries of age.

Double-bar cross, 4-1/2 in. high; trade silver of typical thin sheet metal. The top has a small silver ring for suspension; piece was probably worn as a pendant. Good condition. C-$350

Trade silver pendant, 1-7/8 in. wide and 2-1/4 in. high; single suspension hole at top. Piece has star cutouts and floral designs. Touch-marked by maker. Probably Canadian; from the Great Lakes area. C-$275

Trade silver brooch, with both suspension hole and backpin; about 2 in. high. Piece is somewhat corroded and has a council fire cut-out design; said to be an excavated find in Upper Michigan. C-$160

Trade silver finger ring, 13/16 inch in exterior diameter. Plain, but not common; fair condition. C-$110

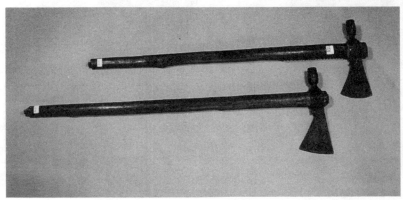

Pipe-tomahawks, White-made, iron heads and wooden handle/stems. Note the small extended mouthpieces at the ends of handles. Late 19th century. Top: $3,500; bottom: $4,500

Crown & Eagle Antiques, New Hope, Pennsylvania

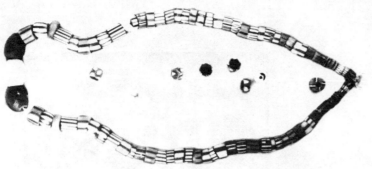

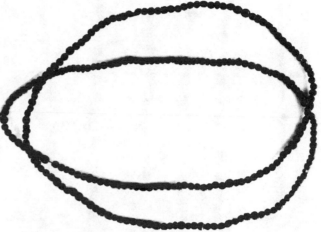

Large strand of Western U.S. trade beads, large blue beads to either side of central large white bead; said to have been screened from an historic Indian site.   C-$125

Private collection

French trade beads, with 248 beads in the two strands. Beads average 1/8 in. diameter, and came from a Brant County site in Ontario. Such beads were used before 1650. Beads are red, blue, white and amber.   C-$130-175

Photo courtesy Robert C. Calvert, London, Ontario, Canada

Small trade silver brooch, 2-1/8 in. high, with rounded triangular shape; has pin on back for attachment. It has masonic symbol cut-out decorations; touchmarked by maker.   C-$145

Large circular trade silver brooch, 3-1/8 in. in diameter; scalloped edge. Has pin at cut-out center; extremely good workmanship and condition, no corrosion. Touchmark of 1728 Canadian silversmith.   C-$600

Trade silver headband, 6 in. in diameter; sheet silver, with heart and diamonds cut-outs. Perfect condition; slight pitting only, touch-marked.   C-$1,200

Trade silver cross, 3-1/4 in. long. Holed for suspension and with decorative tool impressions. Thick-cast, touchmarked.   C-$325

Trade silver buttons, high-domed and backed. Very decorative and well-made.   Each, C-$30

Trade silver cross, 4-3/4 in. high; double-bar type. Piece is touch-marked.   C-$425

Trade silver beaver, 5-1/2 in. long and solid-cast silver. Fine condition, professionally tested (not German silver) and weight is one pound. Touchmarked.   C-$1,200

Trade silver beaver pendant, 2-3/4 in. long; solid-cast, touchmarked. Canadian or U.S. Colonies; ca. 1780.   C-$500

Trade silver beavers, each 1-3/4 in. long; hollow-cast. Set of three, each is touchmarked and perfect condition.   C-$725

Trade silver cross, 5-1/2 in. high; double-bar type, sheet silver. Excellent condition and touchmarked.   C-$550

Trade silver armbands, pair, 4-1/4 in. in diameter; sheet silver. Edges scrolled, otherwise plain. Fair condition.   C-$525

GLASS TRADE BEADS

The early trade-glass beads were usually medium to large in size. These are different from the countless tiny "seed" beads that were worked into designs on bark or fabric or leather. The "major" trade beads were worn in strands of a dozen to many hundreds.

Such glass beads were largely made in Europe, especially the old glass-manufacturing towns of Italy. And the crafts people made there were some wonderful products. Solid-colored, faceted, round, oblong, multi-colored—all found their way to North America. There was also heavy traffic into Africa, and many beads sold today as "American Indian" have actually come from Africa.

Glass beads are being reproduced, of course, so it is best to first check the seller's credentials. Good beads may show extensive wear around the hole-ends. Some may be chipped, with such edges not sharp. Single beads to the advanced collector may be worth from a few cents to $25 or $30 and more depending on rarity.

Fine strand of old trade beads, found on site near the Red River in Texas. Strand is 20 in. long, graduated from small size to larger, and with heavy patina They are at least late 1600s, and may have been traded by the Spanish. G-$175

Cranberry red glass beads; 24-inch-long strand. G-$85

Strand of mille fiore trade beads.   A-$45

Blue glass beads, 26-inch strand; with smaller striped beads interspersed.   G-$90

Trade beads, 34-inch-long strand. White milk glass in tube shape, with six shell spacers; from Oklahoma. G-$90

Cobalt blue globular beads; 28-inch-long strand. G-$120

Glass trade beads; strand is 20 in. long. Colors are pale red, yellow, blue and black.   G-$55

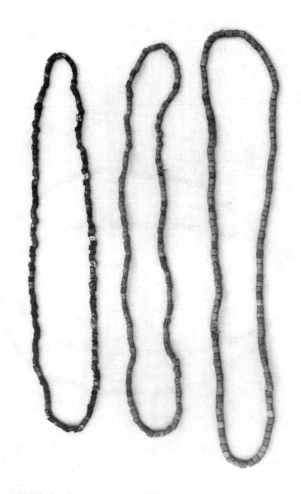

Beads and trade beads, all found in California. Group $95

Lee Hallman collection, Telford, Pennsylvania

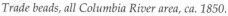

Trade beads, all Columbia River area, ca. 1850.

Left: Russian cobalt blue, faceted, heavy patina, 24 in. long. $175
Center: Russian light blue faceted, highly prized, The Dalles area, 26 in. long. $160
Right: Russian light blue faceted, The Dalles, highly prized, strand 28 in. long. $175

Morris' Art & Artifacts, Anaheim, California; Dawn Gober photograph

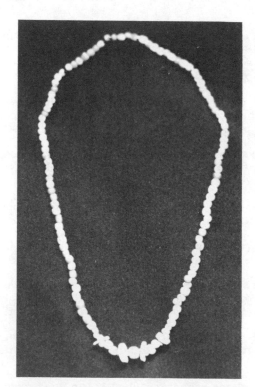

Glass trade bead necklace, early Seneca Iroquois beads plus four shell disc beads, strand 32 in. long. From near West Bloomfield, New York, these are ca. 1610-1630 and ex-coll. Wray. $500

Pat & Dave Summers, Native American Artifacts, Victor, New York

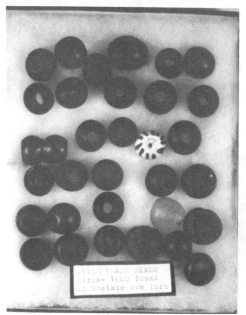

Dutch trade beads from New York state, ca. 1640. These are scarce early beads. Each, $25

Lee Hallman collection, Telford, Pennsylvania

Trade beads, exceptional frame, 130 round drawn-glass Seneca beads in various colors. These were found in the 1930s on a pre-1687 site near Victor, New York. Ex-coil. Wray, of Rush, New York. $400

Pat & Dave Summers, Native American Artifacts, Victor, New York

Russian Blue glass trade bead necklace, 27 in. long, ca. 1850. It is from Alaska and ex-coll. Wray. These attractive beads are in several shades of blue. $220

Pat & Dave Summers, Native American Artifacts, Victor, New York

Yellow fancies beads, wound polychrome glass, thirty-two beads in the necklace. Smallest: 5mm; largest:10mm; longest:15mm. These are from the 1700s. $75

Wendy Wolfsen collection, Michigan

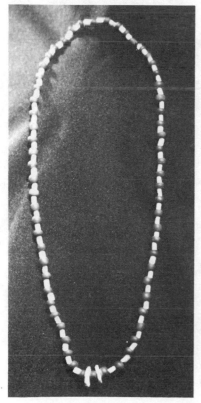

Shell wampum necklace, sixty white shell beads and sixty-three red glass trade beads plus two shell discs. This rare Seneca adornment is from near Victor, New York, ca. 1675-1687, and ex-coll. Wray. $360

Pat & Dave Summers, Native American Artifacts, Victor, New York

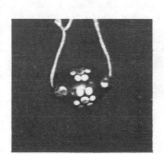

Ambassador pressed glass polychrome bead, 34mm long, from the 1800s. This is a beautiful and relatively scarce bead. $35

Wendy Wolfsen collection, Michigan

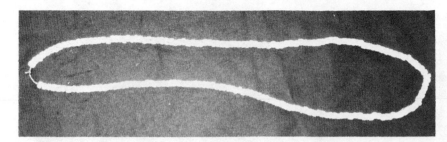

Gooseberry drawn glass beads, translucent with solid white stripes. This string has twenty-six beads, each 3mm in size. From the late 1700s. $50

Wendy Wolfsen collection, Michigan

Wound glass polychrome glass beads with blue striped designs. The beads, from the 1700s, are 12mm; the necklace has fifty-seven beads. $70

Wendy Wolfsen collection, Michigan

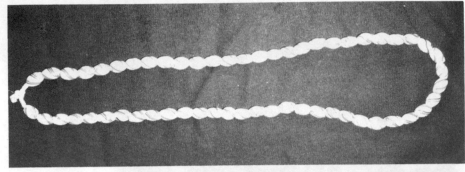

Wound glass polychrome beads with red, blue and brown floral designs. Beads are 12mm. The necklace, from the early 1700s, has fifty-one beads. $70

Wendy Wolfsen collection, Michigan

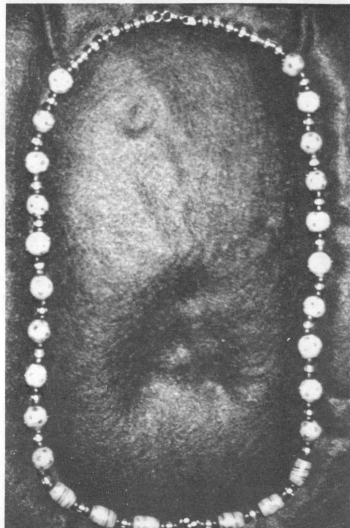

Silver gorget, crescent form, edge decorations, 7 in. across. Touchmarks identify the maker as Frances Crump, 1767, London, England. This rare, historic artifact came from Talladega County, Alabama. Museum quality

Bruce Butts collection, Winterville, Georgia

Necklace, Venetian glass beads, large yellow fancies 12mm diameter, small red beads 4mm. These beads are from the AD 1700-1800 period. $100

Wendy Wolfsen collection, Michigan

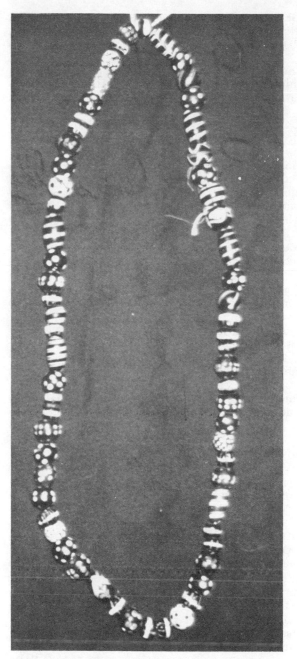

Silver and brass ornaments and jewelry, brooches and pendants, ca. 1750-1840. These items are from western New York.   Each, $150-800

Iron Horse collection, Blasdell, New York

String of glass beads, both wound and pressed, sixty-four beads including: Fancy polychrome beads, eye beads, horn beads, pink pineapple bead, oval fancies, feather bead, etc. Size range is from 6 to 24mm, and they are from the 1700s. $135

Wendy Wolfsen collection, Michigan

Trade beads, type Tia Commashuck meaning Chief of the Beads, not Indian Chief. These were traded by the Lewis and Clark expedition; they are ca. 1800-1850.

Smaller, 20 in. strand. $95
Larger, 28 in. strand. $140

Morris' Art & Artifacts, Anaheim, California; Dawn Gober photograph

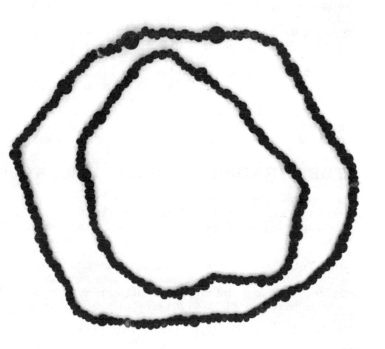

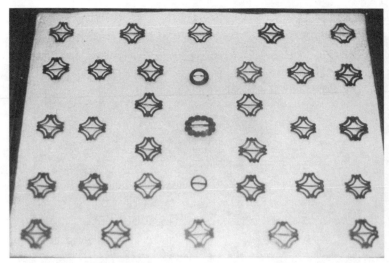

Silver brooches, each with tongue for securing to hair, clothing or blankets. All are of thin silver, from western New York. Each, $100-200

Iron Horse collection, Blasdell, New York

Hudson Bay white beads, 26 in. long with Cornaline d'Aleppo red beads. G-$125

White milkglass trade beads; extremely long strand of 90 in. Tube shaped with average bead length of 1 in. (25 mm). G-$190

Red "whiteheart" beads, with one section of blue beads; strand is 27 in. long. G-$110

Round trade beads, pale red. Strand length is 24 in.; ca. late 1800s. G-$115

Tile beads, 28-inch strand; various colors. G-$110

Pale blue and white trade beads; strand is 20 in. Beads have a heavy patina and are from site on the Tennessee River. G-$150

Faceted Russian blue beads; strand is 33 in. long. G-$145

Small red glass beads, from northwest Oklahoma; strand of 22 in. long. G-$115

Trade beads; 24-inch-long strand of green glass beads, with 13 amber glass beads. G-$125

Deep cobalt-blue beads; strand of 24 in. long. They are round and all the same size; a beautiful strand. G-$135

Fine old trade bead necklace, 22 in. long, with two large dentilium shells, large blue chevron beads and red "whiteheart" beads. G-$155

OTHER TRADE-ERA COLLECTIBLES

Winchester Indian rifle, tack-decorated, with history attached via tag. Condition only fair; throat of stock rawhide-wrapped, may be split. Decorated with brass trade tacks. A-$700

Indian Police rifle, caliber 45/70; a Remington-Keene repeating rifle. Difficult to obtain today and a problem with fakes, due to premium prices. Guaranteed authentic and collected on a Dakota Reservation. G-$1,800

Old musket, average condition for metal, wood stock not good. Last decorated with brass tacks in Plains Indian style. D-$800

Indian musket, old Barnett trade piece. Stock has minor repair that does not affect value; overall fair-good condition. D-$2,600

Cut-down trade musket; old and with brass tack decorations. From a Montana collection. D-$500

Northwest trade gun, by Barnett. The earliest of the Barnett's marked 1805 and in original flintlock. Possibly saw service at the start of the Northwest Company or the American Fur Company, etc. Absolutely genuine; circle fox visible on stock. G-$3,600

Metal arrowpoint, 4-1/2 in. long. A good old piece, and Cree type from South Dakota. G-$45

Iron arrow point, Tesuque Pueblo; 18th or 19th century. D-$50

Brass arrowhead, from historic Indian site in New Jersey. Probably salvaged from white-made brass kettle or utensil. Piece is 1-1/2 in. long and triangular-shaped with small stem. C-$30

Taos Pueblo arrow, 24 in. long; wooden shaft with blood-line and metal point. Sinew wrapped, good condition. G-$110

Old converted musket, with old brass tacks showing Indian use; authentic. G-$600

Rare 1866 Winchester carbine, with all wood carved in various Northwest Coast designs. A-$2,700

Barnett trade musket in original percussion, late trade period. Once covered with brass tacks on wooden portions, many now removed. D-$2,800

Spear or lance point, fine hand-forged early piece. Excellent condition. D-$175

Old brass trade pail, as traded or issued to the Indians. These were once common on reservations, but now are scarce. D-$195

Gun barrel hide scraper, made from the barrel of a trade musket; hide-wrapped. D-$175

Strike-a-light, hand-forged; an excavated find. D-$60

Sioux steel-tipped arrowhead. G-$30

Three metal lance heads, average length is 5-1/2 in.; different sizes and types. Sold as group of three. G-$225

Trade-iron lance head, from Iowa; 9 in. long, with a maximum thickness about 3/8 in. Head is triangular and in good condition. Iron is slightly pitted. C-$265

Copper trade token, from New Mexican trading post ruins. D-$15

Russell Green River trade knife, 9-1/2 in. long. Has an antler handle and old leather sheath. G-$250

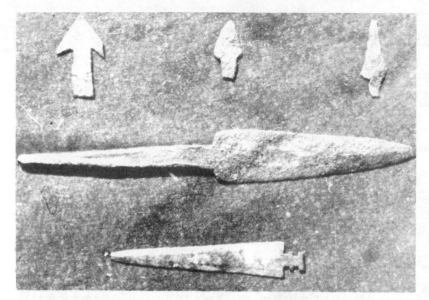

Metal trade-era projectile points and large blade. Top three are Indian-made from barrel hoops. The long blade or spear was Indian-made from a file. Bottom point was a Comanchero trade item, with four basal notches. All from the historic period, 100 to 300 years old. Artifacts are from 1 in. to 7-1/2 in. in length. C-$20-175

Photo courtesy Wayne Parker, Texas

Glass trade beads, chevron type, white and light green color. These are ex-collection Foley. The beads are from the 1800s. $100

T.R.H. collection, Indiana

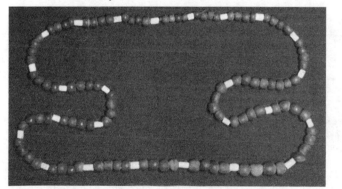

Glass trade beads.

Top: ruby red translucent Hudson's Bay beads, 36 in., Canada, 1800s. $95
Lower center: rare Seneca beads, 26 in., ca. 1850. $235

Native American Artifacts, Victor, New York

Trade beads, red glass (104) and white shell wampum (twenty-five), Seneca, ca. 1670-1687, ex-collections Schoff and Wray. $300

Native American Artifacts, Victor, New York

Skinning knife in old case; trade-steel and possibly made from an old file. Plains Indians, but sheath plain and deteriorated. D-$180

Drilled Germanic coin pendant, found in central Ohio. Site has produced gunflints and brass points that were Indian made from salvaged metal. Reverse of coin reads, "12 Einen Reichs Thaler, A. 1771." Hole made with hot needle awl, as there is minute silver-melt on both sides of small hole. C-$55

Hand-forged strike-a-light, good old excavated item. (Such pieces were the steel in flint and steel kits for fire-making). G-$85

Historic Midwestern gunflint, 3/4 inch long; native-chipped from Ohio flint, probably late 1700s. Found on Muskingum River site that has produced objects from that era. Uncommon. G-$12

Steel strike-a-light; good condition. D-$55

Trade iron hoe, 5-3/4 in. high and 5-7/8 in. wide, with circular hafting hole partially forming hoe top. Some corrosion along rounded sides, but cutting edge very good. C-$145

Iron fish-spear head, from Columbia River region; head is 7 in. long and 4-1/2 in. wide. Perhaps used during annual salmon run. Each tine has a single barb. Apparently a trade piece. C-$160

George Washington peace medal; the facing bust that has considerable mention in the peace medal book. Silver plated and guaranteed genuine. G-$1,400

Rectangular soapstone bullet mold, 3-1/2 in. long and 2-1/8 in. wide. Picked up near a South Dakota historic Indian site, with two cavities for round bullets. Both halves are present. Probably early 1800s. C-$140

Spark-striker, "knuckle-buster," 3-3/4 in. long. Type is made from an old steel file, with ends upturned in an artistic fashion. Fine condition. C-$90

Suggested Reading

Kuck, Robert. *Tomahawks Illustrated*. New Knoxville: Brookside Enterprises, Ohio, 45871.

Peterson, Harold. *American Indian Tomahawks*. Heye Foundation: Museum of the American Indian, 1971.

Prucha, Francis P. *Indian Peace Medals in American History*. University of Nebraska Press.

The Museum of the Fur Trade Quarterly, Rt. 2/Box 18, Chadron, Nebraska 69337; Charles E. Hanson Jr., editor/director.

Trade era spearpoint or knife, metal, from the 1700s. $150

Lee Hallman collection, Telford, Pennsylvania

Peace medal, British, 1757, rare. $1,000

Private collection, New Mexico

Trade-era iron, two axe heads, knife or spear with socketed handle and a harpoon head. Each, $150-300

Philip L. Russo collection, Danbury, Connecticut

Iron arrowhead found in the Custer battlefield area. $35

Lee Hallman collection, Telford, Pennsylvania

Barrel-strap iron points for arrowheads, from the 1870s. Each, $30

Lee Hallman collection, Telford, Pennsylvania

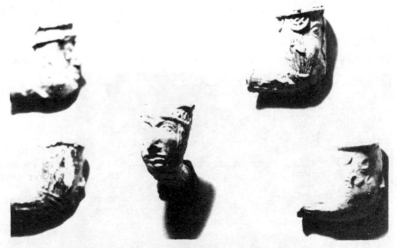

Trade-era clay pipes, human face or effigy variety. Such pipe bowls were made in molds, pressed into shape. The clay is kaolin, a white, yellow or gray material found in deposits in New England area and some Southeastern states. C-$12 each

Private collection

Two steel-blade knives, with beaded sheath fitting blade to right. Left: a single-edge blade fashioned from a discarded saw blade; blade riveted to a section of antler forming a handle. Piece is Northern Plains Flathead, Montana, ca. mid to late 1800s. Right: typical "butcher" type trade knife, with steel blade marked "Bozum," a wooden split handle and riveted brass hardware. The piece is Montana Sioux, and ca. mid to late 1800s. C-$1,200 each

Photo courtesy Sheridan P. Barnard, Franklin, Massachusetts

Trade-era clay pipes, some plain and some with effigy faces. Condition is average-good, for most pipes were mold-made from a high-quality clay called kaolin. Ca. 1800.   C-$12 each

Lar Hothem photo

George Washington peace medal, 2-1/2 in. in diameter. Item is made of pewter and dated 1789. This medal was not made by the U.S. government but by a fur trade company. This medal was much-coveted by the Indians.   Museum quality

Nedra Matteucci's Fenn Galleries, Santa Fe, New Mexico

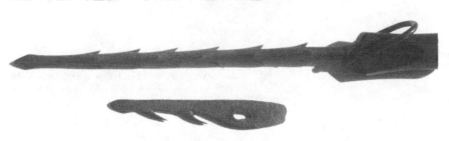

Trade-era artifacts, historic period.

Top: iron harpoon from Alaska, probably Russian Bottom: iron harpoon point, Alaska, once fitted to a wooden shaft. These are unusual artifacts.   Museum quality

Private collection

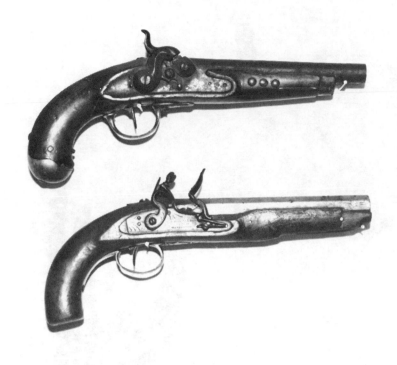

Indian pistols. Top: unmarked German or Austrian percussion that is tacked and shows much use. Ca. 1840s-1850s.

Bottom: "P Powell & Co./St. Louis" marked flintlock with 56 caliber brass barrel marked "London." Forearm is painted and gun has been well-used. This very rare pistol was probably a kit gun made of component parts for the early Missouri River trade. Ca. 1840s-1850s.   Both museum quality

Dave Hrachovy, Cedar Glen, California

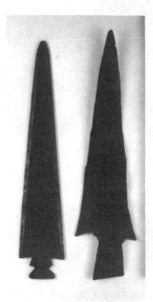

Indian-manufactured barrel-strap metal points.   Each, $35-45

Lee Hallman collection, Telford, Pennsylvania

Trade-era clay pipes, plain variety, and common over Eastern U.S. historic sites.   D-$12 each

Private collection

Plains lance, made of wood, brass, tacks and steel. The shaft is made from calvary flagpole and the tip is a Sheffield blade. It is 6 feet long and 19th century. $2,000

Private collection, photo by John McLaughlin

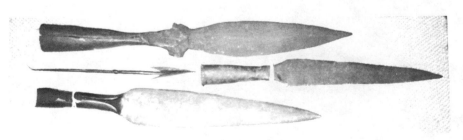

Trade-era iron spears or blades, socketed handles, three different blade configurations. Note also the barbed harpoon head. All are from the Northeastern U.S.   Each, $125-500

Philip L. Russo collection, Danbury, Connecticut

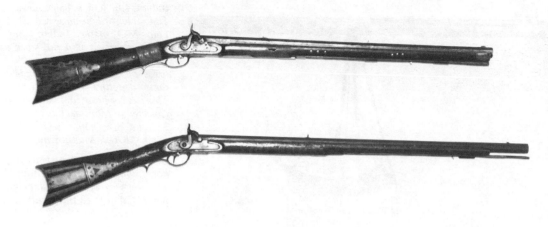

Indian guns, fur trade era. Top: "Warranted" marked on the lock of this fifty caliber full-stock Plains rifle which has a hide repair on the cracked wrist and was tacked by the Indian. Obtained in 1950 from the Goff Creek Lodge on the North Fork of the Shoshone River by Yellowstone Park in Wyoming. It was originally collected by John Goff, a well-known hunter at the turn of the century who was Teddy Roosevelt's guide on his bear and mountain lion hunts. Ca. 1830s-1840s.

Bottom: "J. Fordney/Lancaster Pennsylvania" marked Indian gun of fifty caliber. It is a full-stock percussion Plains rifle with brass tacks on the cheek rest. It is a contract gun made in 1837 for the American Fur Company. Ca. 1830s-1840s.   Both museum quality

Dave Hrachovy, Cedar Glen, California

Indian guns, top: Folsom shown elsewhere. Bottom: "Conestoga Rifle Works/Lancaster, Pennsylvania" marked Indian gun of fifty-five caliber. It is a full-stock percussion Plains rifle with a hide repair at the wrist and saddle wear showing Indian use. These guns were made by Leman for the Western trade. Ca. 1860s-1870s. $3,000-4,000

Dave Hrachovy, Cedar Glen, California

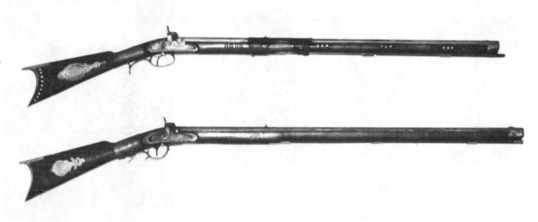

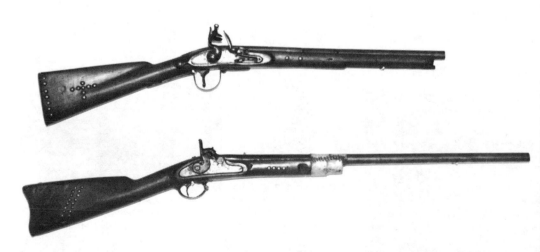

Indian "carbines." Top: "Parker Field & Son/1860" marked Indian trade gun of sixty caliber, shortened barrel with cutdown stock into carbine size for horseback. Original flint with tacked stock and brass serpent sideplate. These guns were used by the Hudson Bay Company for the Indian trade, ca. 1860s. Bottom: Springfield percussion rifle marked "1864" and cut down into carbine size with shortened barrel and forearm. The gun is tacked and has much saddle wear; a hide wrap served as a barrel band. This piece was obtained from a North Dakota museum which had acquired it from an Indian family on the Standing Rock reservation. Ca. 1860s.
                Both museum quality

Dave Hrachovy, Cedar Glen, California

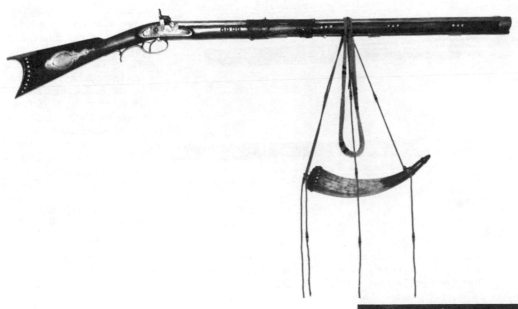

Indian gun and powder horn. Top: "Henry Folsom & Co./St. Louis MO" marked Indian gun of 56 caliber. It is a full-stock percussion Plains rifle with brass tacks and a buffalo hide wrap denoting Indian usage. This is a very rare St. Louis gun collected in Montana by Arnold Marcus Chernoff. It is ca. 1860s-1870s. Museum quality

Bottom: Plains Indian powder horn with beaded cord strap. The horn is brass-tacked and painted, and is 13 in. long. Ca. 1860s-1870s. $2,500-3,000

Dave Hrachovy, Cedar Glen, California

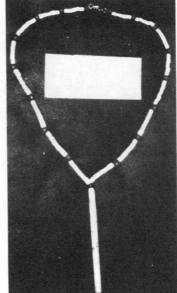

Wampum (white shell) and dark red glass beads from New York state. The small wampum beads are 7mm long, the glass beads are 8mm, the long shell bead 130mm. All are ca. 1660. $475

Wendy Wolfsen collection, Michigan

Trade iron items.

Left: axe-head, 6 in. long, New York state, ca. 1860. $130
Center: 17th century French iron oar steering guide, 4-3/4 x 8-1/2 in., Irondequoit Bay, New York. $115
Right: iron axe, Cayuga, three touch-marks, 4 x 6 in. From Cayuga Lake, New York, ca. 1680. $65

Pat & Dave Summers, Native American Artifacts, Victor, New York

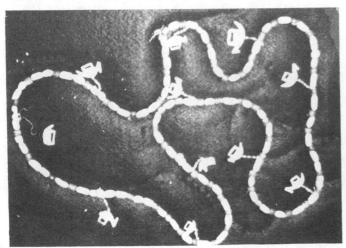

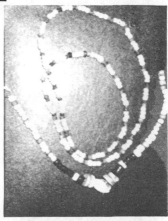

Necklace, drawn and wound glass trade beads with copper animals in sheet-metal cut-outs. Large beads 15mm, seed beads 3mm, small beads 8mm, copper animals 31mm. This fine and rare necklace is early AD 1700s. $1,000

Wendy Wolfsen collection, Michigan

Glass and shell beads: Large glass (wound) white, 5mm, small glass white 4mm, small pre-white hearts 4mm, large pre-white hearts 10mm, large shell bead 20mm, small shell beads 4mm. All are from California and ca. 1790-1810. $95

Wendy Wolfsen collection, Michigan

Necklace, wound glass beads mainly in pale greens, bead diameter 6mm. These early beads, ca. 1700-1740, are from Hamilton County, Tennessee. $65

Wendy Wolfsen collection, Michigan

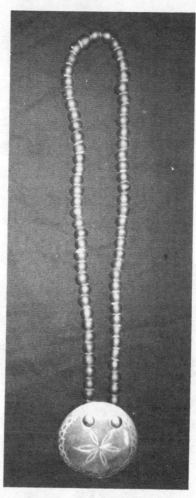

Translucent olive-colored glass beads with silver pendant. Beads, 9mm, pendant, 71mm. This necklace is late 1700s to early 1800s, and in beautiful condition. $395

Wendy Wolfsen collection, Michigan

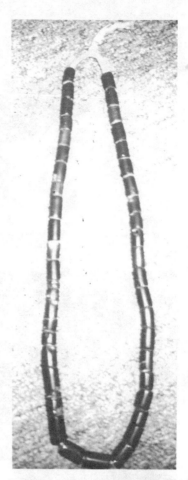

Necklace, tubular drawn glass beads of the yellow heart design, bead length 14mm. This fine necklace is from the AD 1600s, with rich, reddish-amber colored beads. $150

Wendy Wolfsen collection, Michigan

Necklace, blue Russian faceted glass beads, drawn, graduated string. Beads: Smallest 4mm, largest 10mm, longest 23mm. These are ca. 1720s to 1800s. $200

Wendy Wolfsen collection, Michigan

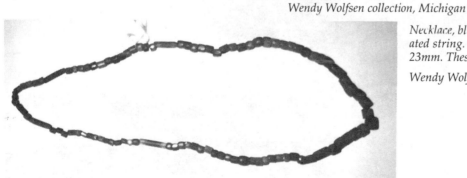

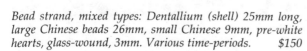

Bead strand, mixed types: Dentallium (shell) 25mm long, large Chinese beads 26mm, small Chinese 9mm, pre-white hearts, glass-wound, 3mm. Various time-periods. $150

Wendy Wolfsen collection, Michigan

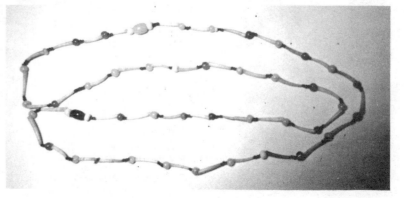

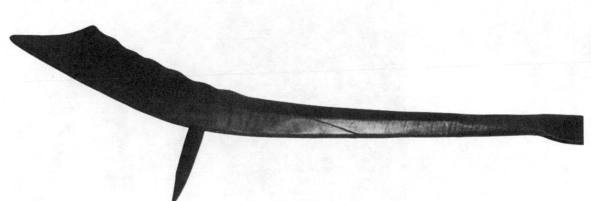

Gunstock club, polished hardwood with steel knife-like blade, ca. 1840. $1,300

Private collection, photo by John McLaughlin

Tomahawk, curved-spike top and flared blade, wooden handle coated with red ochre, ca. 1780. $3,000

Antiques & Art, Piedmont, South Dakota

Northern Plains Hudson's Bay dag with Indian-made copper handle. This piece is 2-1/2 in. wide and 12-1/2 in. long. The blade is marked "Jukes Coulson & Co.," and it is ca. 1865. $9,500

Forrest Fenn, Santa Fe, New Mexico

Brule Sioux dag constructed from a large rasp, 14-1/2 in. long, the handle made from half a bear̄s mandible. There are many modern-made bear-jaw dags, but this example dates to ca. 1865. $15,000

Forrest Fenn, Santa Fe, New Mexico

White-manufactured mold-made clay pipes, Midwestern, late 1800s. Such inexpensive ceramic pipes, with long reed stems, were used by both Whites and Indians. Each, $6-10

Larry Garvin, Back to Earth, Ohio

Bayonet dag, Hudson's Bay, with Indian-made mountain sheep horn handle, 12 in. long. This rare, early example is probably from a Great Lakes tribe and ca. 1820. $12,000

Forrest Fenn, Santa Fe, New Mexico

Trade-era pottery pipe, 1-1/2 in. high, post-Contact period. This decorative mold-made pipe is 1-1/2 in. high and came from the Sandia Park area of New Mexico. $25

Jack Baker collection, Ozark, Missouri; David Capon photograph

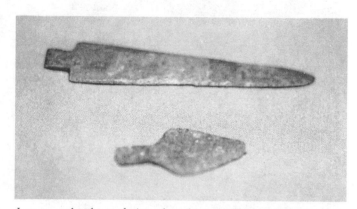

Iron arrowheads, trade iron from historic times, longest example 3-3/4 in. Both were found in the El Rito Mountain region, New Mexico. Short, $25 Long, $125

Jack Baker collection, Ozark, Missouri; David Capon photograph

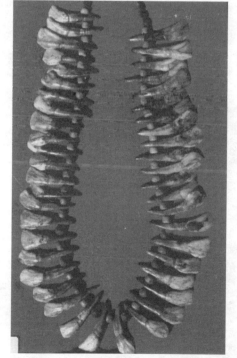

Necklace, trade beads in brass and glass with bovine teeth. This piece is 1920s, 20 in. long, and was once used in a Wild West show. $175

Blue Coyote Trading Post, Nashville, Indiana; Pat Nolan photograph

Historic-era copper trade kettle, from northeastern Mississippi. Early copper and brass kettles are scarce items. $250

Wilfred A. Dick Collection, Magnolia, Mississippi

Indian woman, in state of Washington, seated before rough-plank dwelling, squatting on rough mat. Note small-mesh fishnet in background and fiber strands in hand, perhaps for basketry work. Ca. 1900-1905.

Photographer, Norman Edson; courtesy Photography collection, Suzzallo Library, University of Washington

CHAPTER XI

BASKETS

(The writer wishes to thank Dick Weatherford, Washington State, for the introduction to this chapter on basketry and for the books in the Suggested Reading section of it. Used with permission.)

Like most of the great Aboriginal Art in existence today, the baskets of the Indians of North America were intended primarily for everyday use. The decorations applied and woven in the curious shapes, whimsical lids, and hanging feathers and beads may look useless, but they all attest to the Indians' talent for making what is useful also pleasing to the eye and touch.

Baskets in collections today are, for the most part, only the very latest representations of the craft. Baskets, trays, woven mats and clothing, reed and stick toys, and jewelry existed in prehistoric times all over the world, as surely did the more durable arrowheads, spear points, pipes, pottery, and other ceremonial rock and wood art.

But because textiles are more susceptible to disintegration with age and use, the vast majority of baskets, trays, and mats by which we judge the art as practiced by the Indians of North America have been made in the past 200 years, and most of those since 1880.

Collectors of baskets may judge the commercial value of an item by different standards. For some, age alone determines value. That is, any basket in any condition more than, say, 150 years old, is automatically rare and expensive. Others are more interested in the aesthetic properties: shape, coloring, and patina, the use of the fiber—how tightly the basket is coiled or woven—how carefully the shape and size of the coils and other elements are matched, and how well the decorative fiber matches the structure fiber.

Still others collect only baskets whose condition is near to new as possible. And, finally, there are those who collect for size only, or for decorative motifs, or for tribal area and type. All of these are reasons for collecting baskets, but not all of them determine commercial or market value per se.

For example, age alone is not a sufficient reason for a basket being valuable, especially if the basket, although quite old, is crudely made or heavily damaged or aesthetically unpleasant. Size also does not determine value, since a very large basket may bring a smaller price than a very small, finely woven and decorated piece.

Value is itself a relative term, and monetary value is only one factor to be considered in making up a collection. Sentimental association is as real to the collector as cash value, but sentimental value more often than not cannot be expressed to others and usually cannot be marketed.

For the serious collector, then, who wishes to gather some baskets, regardless of their sentimental value or particular age, for the purposes of show, personal enjoyment, and, possibly, investment, there are some things to consider before buying.

The first rule of collecting anything is that the condition of each piece must be excellent. Baskets—like books, stained-glass windows, arrowheads, beaded vests, Navajo rugs, and other collectibles—must be in fine condition in order to bring and retain high prices. Baskets with broken edges, repairs, re-dying or painting over, missing parts, holes, etc., are simply not as valuable as perfect pieces, and they never will be, even if they are restored.

Having slightly damaged baskets in a collection does not necessarily diminish the value of the collection, but it doesn't help much either. Of course, some baskets are so rare as to put the lie to the absoluteness of the condition rule, but the exceptions are very few indeed.

Next to condition, the aesthetic qualities of a basket determine value. The qualities are difficult to explain in this short space, and they won't mean much to the collector who has not seen and studied a number of baskets. But aesthetic qualities include the fineness of the weaving and/or coiling, the regularity of the design, and the degree to which it enhances the shape of the basket itself—as opposed to detracting from its shape by being too large or small or complex or simple to be comfortably accommodated on the piece.

One of the most pleasing qualities of North American Indian basketry is its sensory appeal. Good baskets feel and look and even smell natural; they are well-shaped and well-made. The genius of them is that they incorporate art in the utilitarian object, that they make what is useful also pleasing to touch and see. That quality is difficult to assess and describe. It is easier to appreciate with the senses, and that is one reason why many examples of baskets are pictured in this book.

Collectors who read this will note that I have not touched on such considerations as materials and tribal groups as determinants of market value. I agree that what a basket is made of and who made it have something to do with the value of it. But these values are more relative to the collector's own tastes, and they are first subject to the standards of condition and aesthetic quality mentioned above.

Certainly, a finely made Tlingit or Washoe basket brings more on the market than a small, plain, rather crude Pomo basket. But beginning collectors will not be able to make successful determinations of value without some more study. I suggest it is not wise to study, or even to buy, simply for tribal area or material.

One must see many types of baskets themselves, as well as pictures of them, in order to get a clear idea of their shapes, designs, and materials. Most larger state, city, and university museums have some baskets to see and compare. And the collector will want to frequent the auctions, antique shows and shops, Indian gallery showrooms, and the like before making any selections.

I strongly suggest that the collector also read about baskets, how they are and were made, materials and methods of construction, designs, shapes, age, etc. The collector who relies purely upon rumor and the seller's word is very likely to be unhappy about some purchases.

It is always best to know, to be able to judge independently and with some authority, the baskets one is likely to pay a good deal of money for. See Suggested Reading for a few selected major reference works for the collector. These will, in addition to this book, provide necessary information.

(D.W.)

The basket listings in this section have been set up in alphabetical order according to tribe. This has been done so that baskets by known Indian groups can be easily located.

While not all basket-making Indian groups are represented, these are some of the baskets likely to be encountered. Historic and recent baskets are included, plus many contemporary examples. A wide selection has purposefully been included here.

Apache shallow-bowl basket; 14 in. in diameter, with designs in stars and crosses. Condition is fair. D-$1,400

Apache shallow-bowl basket, 18 in. in diameter, and in excellent condition. Designs of dogs, men, and horses; two major breaks on rim, which do not detract from value. C-$1,600

Apache burden basket, 11-1/2 in. high. Typical construction with hard leather or rawhide bottom, plain, average condition, and showing much wear; c. 1920s. D-$750

Apache burden basket, 6-1/2 in. across and 5 in. high; contemporary. Geometric pattern, with tin cones hanging from buckskin straps. G-$155

Apache burden basket, 8 in. across and 6 in. high; contemporary. Geometric pattern; tin cones on buckskin straps. G-$255

Apache burden basket, 12 in. across and 10-1/2 in. high; contemporary. Negative pattern with tin cone danglers; excellent condition. G-$550

Apache grain barrel basket, 11 in. high and 10 in. in diameter. Geometric designs with eight human figures. Rim of basket shows some wear and repair, but generally in nice condition; ca. before 1900. G-$750

Apache grain or seed container basket, 17 in. high. Has geometric designs in black, on tan background. Extra-fine overall condition; ca. early 1900s. C-$1,800

Apache plaque basket, 16 in. in diameter and 5 in. high. Geometric design with nice stitch; good condition. G-$1,200

Apache plaque basket, 22 in. in diameter and 6 in. high. Design: Twenty dog and men figures. One bad spot 3 in. from rim, and condition fair. G-$2,100

Apache miniature basket, 5-1/2 in. across and 1 in. high. Good condition, with radiating-star design. G-$400

Apache storage basket, 14-1/2 in. in diameter. Black chain-link and human figure decorative motif on side. C-$850

Apache basketry tray, 10-1/2 in. in diameter, and very old; ca. late 1800s or 90s. C-$350

Apache wedding basket, 13 in. in diameter and very old. D-$100

Apache water-bottle basket (or "tus"), 17 in. high. Has coating of pitch to make it waterproof. Collected about 1935. Good condition and not common. C-$1,200

Apache water-bottle basket, 13-1/2 in. high. One of two horsehair handles remaining. Pitch missing in small sections. Piece is not well preserved. Old. C-$325

Apache water-bottle basket, 5 in. across and 9 in. high; pine-patch covering. Contemporary. Has leather carrying straps. G-$160

Mescalero Apache lidded basket, 7 in. wide and 5 in. high. Good condition; ca. 1900. G-$360

Western Apache basket, 12 in. across and 2 in. high, with a moderate stitch. Whirlwind design in bottom and geometric design on exterior. G-$425

Athabascan birchbark basket, and Washo basket, both one auction lot. Athabascan is 2-3/4 x 4 in.; Washo is 1-1/2 x 3-1/2 in. A-$130

Bannock/Shoshone berry basket, 8 x 8-1/2 in. A-$110

Bannock basket, 8-1/2 x 13 in. A-$95

Bannock/Paiute gathering basket. A-$70

Bella-Bella basket-covered jar. A-$50

Bella-Coola cedar-bark basket, state of Washington; 12-1/4 in. high. Decorated with intertwined cedar root strips, and of some age. C-$135

Contemporary baskets.

Left: Passamaquoddy lidded basket, 6-3/4 in. in diameter. Wood splint and sweetgrass. C-$35
Right: Penobscot lidded basket, 3-1/2 in. in diameter. D-$25

Photo courtesy American Indian World, Ltd., Denver, Colorado

Burden basket, White River Apache, Arizona. Used as a utility basket by Indian women, carried on the back and supported by a strap from the person's forehead. Excellent condition; 18 in. wide and 10 in. high; ca. 1940. Museum quality

Photo courtesy W.J. Crawford, The Americana Galleries, Phoenix, Arizona

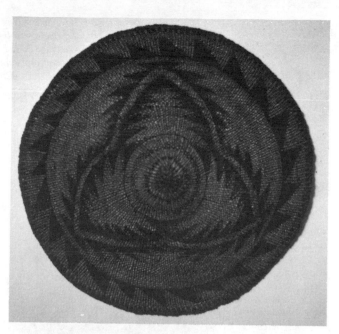

Modoc twined tray, the design woven with dyed porcupine quill. It is 18 in. in diameter and ca. 1880. $1,200-1,500

Terry Schafer collection, Marietta, Ohio

Papago basket, chocolate brown on tan ground. This piece is in very good condition, with a top diameter of 7-1/4 in. and height of 4-3/4 in. $65-85

Private collection

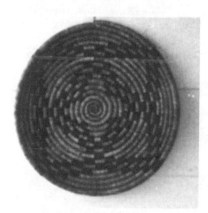

Papago basket, chocolate brown on tan ground. This piece is in very good condition, with a top diameter of 7-1/4 in. and height of 4-3/4 in. $65-85

Private collection

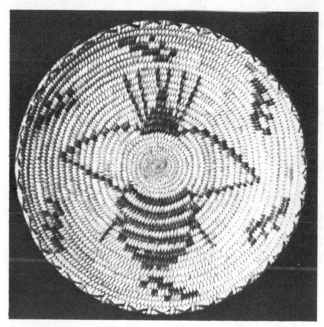

Papago coiled figural tray, woven with yucca and sumac root (red), very finely woven. It is 6-1/2 in. in diameter and ca. 1930. $600-800

Terry Schafer collection, Marietta, Ohio

Basketry jar, coiled, decorated with humans and saguaro cactus forms. This exquisite Pima work is 9-1/2 x 8-1/2 in. It is ca. 1920. $690

Pat & Dave Summers, Native American Artifacts, Victor, New York

Yurok basket, 9-1/2 in. in diameter and 7 in. high. Design is diamonds and rectangles. Piece is in good condition and probably early 1900s.   C-$425

Photo courtesy R. M. Weatherford, Washington

Maidu basketry plate, 14 in. diameter, from Northern California. Coiled, ca. 1900.   C-$2,500

Courtesy LaPerriere collection, California

Wood-splint basket, recent, about 12 in. high and 15 in. in diameter. This could either be a Great Lakes area piece, but is more likely Cherokee-made, ca. 1950. Note characteristic way each handle end is worked back through the wood, which is typical of Cherokee work. Collected in Ohio; bottom is square and top opening is round. Perfect condition.   C-$165

Private collection

Hupa basket, Northern California, 10 in. diameter, ca. 1910.   C-$700

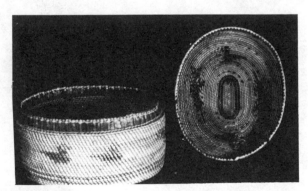

Makah lidded basket, Northwest Coast, 2-1/2 in. high, fair condition, ca. 1930.   C-$155

John Barry photo

Hupa-Yurok basketry hat, from Northern California, 7-1/2 in. top diameter. Twined, early 1900s.
          C-$170-200

Courtesy LaPerriere collection, California

Makah lidded basket, Northwest Coast, ca. 1940.   C-$180

John Barry photo

Hupa basketry hat, 4 in. high, ca. 1910.   C-$500

Bob LaPerriere photo

Hupa basket, 4 in. high, ca. 1910. C-$400

Bob LaPerriere photo

Western Apache basket, 10 in. diameter, from Arizona, ca. 1930. Coiled at five coils per inch, fourteen stitches per inch. C-$500

Courtesy LaPerriere collection, California

Apache basket, 21 in. high, ca. 1910. C-$5,500

Photo courtesy John Barry

Havasupai plaque, Arizona, 11-1/4 in. diameter. Materials are willow and devil's claw, fifteen coils per inch, thirteen stitches per inch. Coiled, representation of two women, men, and dogs. By Karen Martinez, 1974. C-$500

Courtesy LaPerriere collection, California

Lidded basket, Yurok-Hupa-Karok group. Northern California, 6-3/4 in. top diameter. Twined, ca. 1910. C-$750

Courtesy LaPerriere collection, California

Lummi basketry bottle, from Bellingham, Washington, fine condition, ca. 1930. C-$400

John Barry photo

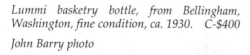

Lummi basketry bottle, from Bellingham, Washington. Item 11-1/2 in. high ca. 1930. C-$350

Photo LaPerriere

Klamath basket, Southern Oregon, 6 in. top diameter. Twined, soft and flexible, early 1900s. C-$300

Courtesy LaPerriere collection, California

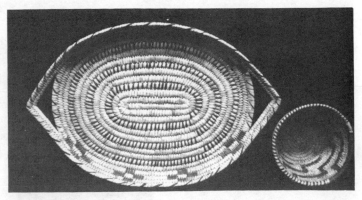

Klamath basket, Southern Oregon, 5 in. top diameter. Twined, with yellow porcupine quill decorations, early 1900s. C-$200

Courtesy LaPerriere collection, California

Papago basketry.

Center: large serving tray basket, 12 x 18 in., late 1800s to early 1900s period. $265

Right: bowl basket, 6 x 6 in., early 1900s. $145

Larry Lantz, First Mesa, South Bend, Indiana

Papago basket, 10 in. diameter at top. Southern Arizona. Coiled, six stitches per inch, contemporary. C-$200

Courtesy LaPerriere collection, California

Papago basketry bowl, different and larger view of basket shown elsewhere, 6 x 6 in. $185

Larry Lantz, First Mesa, South Bend, Indiana

Papago basket, 6-3/4 in. top diameter, southern Arizona. Coiled, eight stitches per inch, zoomorphic designs, 1930s or earlier. C-$200

Courtesy LaPerriere collection, California

Papago basket, 6-1/2 in. top diameter, coiled at four coils per inch, eight stitches per inch, southern Arizona, mid-1900s. C-$150

Courtesy LaPerriere collection, California

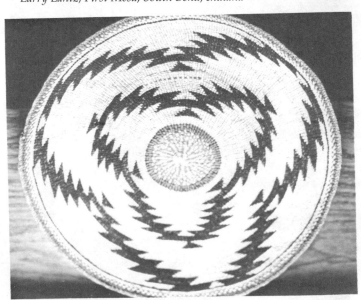

Shasta twined tray, woven with beargrass and maidenhair fern stems. Ca. 1900, it is 16 in. in diameter and 2 in. high. A very attractive weaving. $900-1,200

Terry Schafer collection, Marietta, Ohio

Maidu feast basket, 8 x 14 in., brown diamonds on tan. In fine condition, this ca. 1895 work is a rare historic piece. $4,000

Courtesy John Isaac, Albuquerque, New Mexico

Olla basket, Apache, nicely executed diamond and triangle designs. This rare item is ca. 1880. $6,500

Crown & Eagle Antiques, Inc., New Hope, Pennsylvania

Wicker bowl, Hopi Third Mesa, 9 in. in diameter, ca. 1930s. $85-115

Pocotopaug Trading Post, South Windsor, Connecticut

Pima basket, dark brown against a light brown ground, 9 in. in diameter. It is from the 1930s. $350

Private collection

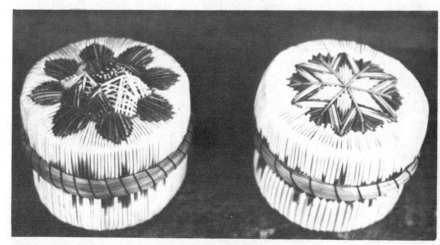

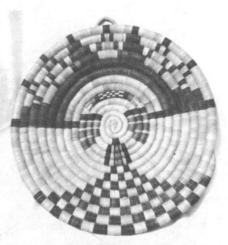

Penobscot quilled birch-bark round covered boxes, the designs done in natural and dyed porcupine quills (red, yellow, green, and blue). They are sweetgrass-wound by thread on cover edge. Southeast Seaboard of Canada, ca. 1940s, 3 in. in diameter. Each, $90

Frank Bergevin, Port of Call, Alexandria Bay, New York

Hopi wedding basket, 10-1/2 in. in diameter, from the 1970s. It has black and red designs against yellow-tan. $150

Private collection

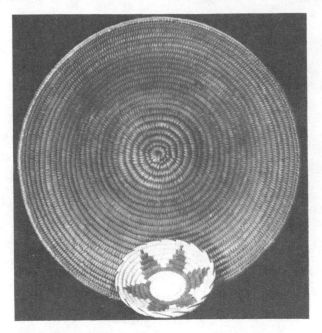

Southwestern Indian basketry.

Large center basket: Navajo-style wedding basket actually made by the Jicarilla Apache, 8 x 16 in. with faded old polychrome design. From the 1800s. $650-750
Small center basket: Papago, 5 in. in diameter, star design bowl from the 1940s. $125

Larry Lantz, First Mesa, South Bend, Indiana

Basket, Chiricahua Apache, from the early 1900s. It is 5-3/4 x 15-1/2 in. in diameter and is a coiled basket in dark red, orange and black decoration on an undyed background. Collected in the Southwest, this large and attractive basket is in a fine state of repair. $600

Sherman Holbert collection, Fort Mille Lacs, Onamia, Minnesota

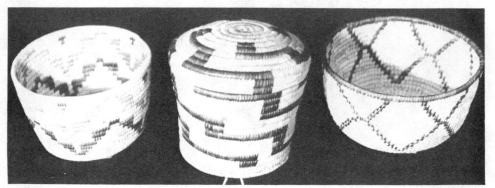

Papago baskets, various sizes and designs, from the 1930s to the 1940s.   Each, $135-250

Larry Lantz, First Mesa, South Bend, Indiana

Wicker plaque, Hopi Third Mesa, whirlwind design, 12 in. in diameter. It is ca. 1930s. $175-200

Pocotopaug Trading Post, South Windsor, Connecticut

Papago basket, 12 in. long, with black human figures against a yellow-tan background. This is a well-made basket in mint condition. $500

Private collection, New Mexico

Papago basket, 13-1/2 in. diameter, 1950s. $600

Courtesy Tom Noeding

Papago burden-basket, diamond-step design, ex-museum. It is 10 x 10 in. and a very well-made basket. Ca. 1880-1900. $475

Morris' Art & Artifacts, Anaheim, California; Dawn Gober photograph

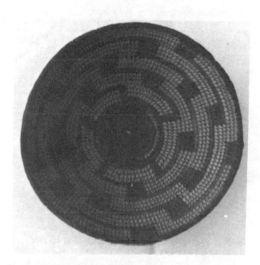

Busket, Pima, 7 in. in diameter, attractive design, ca. 1890-1910. $150-200

Private collection

Basket, vase or jar form, Pima, 8 in. high. This well-made example is ca. 1890-1910. $150-175

Pocotopaug Trading Post, South Windsor, Connecticut

Wedding tray, Navajo, pre-1930, size 3-1/2 in. high and 12-1/4 in. in diameter. Possibly made by the Paiute, this coiled basket is in natural rust and brown. A fine example of a traditional ceremonial item. Ex-coll. Fruchtel. $275

Sherman Holbert collection, Fort Mille Lacs, Onamia, Minnesota

Basketry bowl, Hopi Second Mesa, bundle-coiled, 8 in. in diameter. It is from the 1940s. $110

Pocotopaug Trading Post, South Windsor, Connecticut

Papago basket, medium wear on interior and exterior, yellow and caramel designs on tan background. Has top diameter of 5-5/8 in. and height of 2-5/8 in. $45-65

Private collection

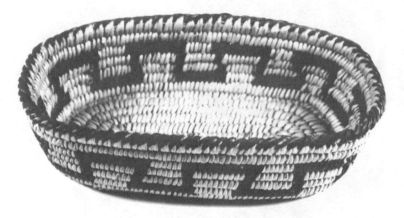

Basket, Papago, chocolate-brown designs on tan, 7 in. in diameter. It is ca. 1900-1920. $125-165

Pocotopaug Trading Post, South Windsor, Connecticut

Papago basket, brown designs on light tan ground. Oblong, size is 3 x 5-3/8 x 1-3/8 in. high. Condition is excellent. $55-75

Private collection

Pima basket, medium brown design on light brown or tan ground, perfect condition. Size, 3-1/2 x 9-1/2 in. $900-1,300

Marguerite L. Kernaghan collection; photograph by Marguerite L. and Stewart W. Kernaghan, Bellvue, Colorado

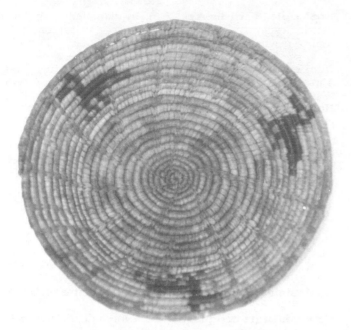

Figural basket, Papago, bird motif, 9 in. in diameter. It is ca. 1900-1910. $150-175

Pocolopaug Truding Post, South Windsor, Connecticut

Wedding tray, Navajo, basketry in several subtle colors, 14 in. in diameter. This fine example is ca. 1910-1920. $300-350

Pocotopaug Trading Post, South Windsor, Connecticut

Wicker plaque, Hopi Third Mesa, 12 in. in diameter, black and tan-yellow central design and inner rim of green and red. Ca. 1940s. $200-250

Pocotopaug Trading Post, South Windsor, Connecticut

Birch bark storage baskets, size from 3 x 5 x 3 in. to 6 x 10 x 5 in. These are made from birch bark, spruce root, and cherry bark, and all are from the eastern and western Sub-Arctic and Alaska. Ca. 1860-1920. Each, $45-400

Historic Interiors, Sorrento, British Columbia, Canada

Southwestern basketry.

Left: Hopi Second Mesa, bundle-coil, 6 in. in diameter, 1910-1920. $125-150
Right: Papago, 5 in. in diameter, ca. 1940-1950. $65-95

Pocotopaug Trading Post, South Windsor, Connecticut

Quilled birch bark baskets, 2 x 3 in. to 3 x 10 in. Materials are birch bark and porcupine quills; the baskets are from central Ontario and northern Michigan. Ca. 1900-contemporary. Each, $60-400

Historic Interiors, Sorrento, British Columbia, Canada

Chehalis basket, 4-1/2 x 9-1/2 in.   A-$45

Chehalis basket, 4-1/4 x 6-1/4 in. Has woven designs of geometrics and crosses; in mint condition.   A-$250

Chemehuevi basket, 11-1/2 in. across and 2 in. high, with a design of two geometric concentric bands. Piece has a moderate stitch; good condition.   G-$750

Chippewa birchbark basket, 4-1/2 in. high and 9-5/8 in. in diameter. Designs done in sweetgrass and quill.   A-$70

Coushatta swampcane basket, collected in Louisiana in the 1950s. Size, 4-3/8 in. in diameter.   C-$75

Coushatta basket tray, 6 in. in diameter; two unusual handles. Made of coiled pine needles, small floral designs, slight damage to bottom.   D-$65

Cowlitz lidded basket, 3 x 4-1/4 in.   A-$145

Cowlitz basket, 10-3/4 x 14-1/4 in.   A-$430

Fraser River basketry trays; two sold as one lot. A-$75

Fraser River basket, 7-1/4 x 9 x 7 in.   A-$145

Hat creek basket-covered wine bottle, 10 in. high. It has lightning design in redbud weave. Good condition. G-$230

Hat Creek basket, 3-1/2 x 6-1/4 in.   A-$325

Havasupai basketry bowl, 7 in. across and 4 in. high. It has red aniline dye swastika pattern; good condition.   G-$725

Havasupai basket, coiled fiber, 11-3/4 in. in diameter. Design is a series of small, connected triangles. C-$400

Havasupai basketry plaque, or plate, 12 in. in diameter. It has orange and black geometric "crepe paper" design.   G-$525

Hoopa basketry hat, 3-3/4 in. high and 7-1/4 in. across; made of close-twined weave. Fine condition. (Hupa).   C-$460

Hopi coiled-bowl basket, 9-1/4 in. in diameter; faded floral designs. Basket in overall good condition. C-$235

Hopi coiled-bowl basket, 7 in. in diameter, with geometric designs on sides. Average to good condition; bottom somewhat deteriorated.   D-$175

Hopi coiled-bowl basket, Second Mesa, 4 in. high and 4 in. in diameter.   A-$45

Hopi wicker-bowl basket, 9 in. in diameter; excellent condition. Geometric designs on side.   C-$255

Hopi corn-sifter basket, recent, with sturdy hoop around top. Wicker form is 15 in. in diameter; decorated with spiral designs radiating out from center.   C-$190

Hopi miniature plaque, Second Mesa, 4 in. across. Contemporary and has a polychrome star design.   G-$100

Hopi miniature bowl, 1-1/2 in. across and 1-1/2 in. high. Second Mesa contemporary, with geometric design.   G-$110

Hopi miniature coil plaque, 3-1/4 in. in diameter. D-$40

Hopi miniature coil plaque, 2-1/2 in. in diameter. D-$30

Hopi coiled plaque, 14-1/2 in. across. Old. Second Mesa; ca. 1930.   D-$330

Hopi coiled tray, 14-1/2 in. in diameter. Third Mesa.   A-$110

Hopi basketry tray, 1 in. in diameter; Second Mesa. Has mythical figure as central design.   C-$270

Hopi wickerwork tray, 17-1/4 in. in diameter; very regular designs in black.   C-$365

Hupa cooking basket, 3-1/8 x 5-1/4 in.   A-$90

Hupa covered basket, 8 in. in diameter, with geometric designs in tan and cream colors. Some damage to one portion of bottom, but not major.   D-$175

Hupa basketry hat, 6-5/8 in. in diameter.   A-$155

Hupa basketry hat, 7 in. in diameter and 4 in. high. Made using half-stitch; piece has two geometric and concentric bands.   G-$300

Hupa basketry mush bowl, 3-1/2 in. high and 6 in. in diameter. Tan and light brown colors, nice design, perfect condition; ca. 1900.   G-$275

Karok basketry cradleboard, sit-down style. Piece is finely woven basketry, with sun shade in yellow quillwork.   G-$500

Karok basketry mush bowl, 5-1/2 in. across and 3-1/2 in. high. Reverse pattern; good condition.   G-$180

Karok oval-shape basket with inverted bottom; 10 in. long and 7 in. wide, 5 in. high. Half-twist polychrome design; good condition.   G-$265

Klamath basket, 3-1/2 x 6-1/2 in.   A-$40

Klamath trinket basket, 3 in. high, 4 in. in diameter. Simple design in brown colors; excellent condition.   G-$145

Klamath gambling tray, 14 in. in diameter. Good condition; ca. 1900.   G-$595

Klikitat basket, 4 x 4-1/2 in.   A-$155

Klikitat gathering basket, with undulating and raised rim top. Basket is 11-1/4 in. high; medium-good condition.   C-$265

Klikitat miniature basket.   A-$50

Klikitat baskets, both miniature, sold as one lot. A-$110

Klikitat basketry trunk with lid, 14-1/2 in. across, 15 in. high and 26-1/2 in. long. It has a polychrome geometric design and is in nice condition.   G-$1,100

Kuskokwim River basket, with yarn trim. Piece is 5-1/2 x 6-1/2 in.   A-$55

Lilooet basket, 12-1/2 x 16 in. and 14 in. high. A-$245

Lilooet basket, 8-1/4 x 10-1/4 in. and 12-1/2 in. high.   A-$60

Maidu basketry bowl, 6 in. across and 3 in. high. In traditional Maidu pattern, average weave, good condition. Piece is ca. 1910.   G-$410

Maidu miniature basket, 1-1/4 in. high, 1-3/4 in. in diameter. Very tight and regular weave; perfect condition.   C-$240

Maidu basketry tray, 8-1/2 in. in diameter.   A-$100

Makah lidded basket, 4 in. across and 2 in. high. Geometric banded design in polychrome.   G-$125

Makah basket, 7 in. in diameter, with zig-zag designs on side. Slight fraying at one portion of rim. Tight weave.   D-$135

Makah basketry covered bottle, 12 in. high. Good condition.   G-$275

Makah basketry covered bottle, 12-1/2 in. high, weaving with figure design.   A-$145

Makah basketry covered bottle, one-half pint whiskey; 6-1/2 in. high.   G-$190

Makah/Nootka basketry-covered bottle, 12-1/4 in. high.   A-$165

Salish baskets, various sizes, made of cedar splints, spruce roots, and cherry bark. These are from British Columbia and ca. 1860-1920.   *Each, $300-800*

Historic Interiors, Sorrento, British Columbia, Canada

Makah jewel basket.   A-$40

Makah/Nootka miniature baskets, two, sold as one lot.   A-$35

Makah basketed net float and small basketry covered bottle; sold as one lot.   A-$110

Makah twisted-twine basket, 5 in. in diameter. C-$85

Mandan basket, circular and 8 in. high. Wood splint, rare item and quite old.   C-$500

Mission basket, 18-1/2 in. in diameter and 10 in. high. Very large, minor rim damage; ca. 1900.   G-$1000

Mission basket, from California, 20 in. across and 12 in. high. Has a six-point negative star in bottom.   G-$280

Mission basket, 6 in. in diameter and 2 in. high. Bowl-shape; geometric design with star pattern on bottom. Average weave and condition.   G-$235

Mission plaque, 15 in. across, 2-1/2 in. high. Made of variegated juncus grass; average weave.   G-$360

Mission basketry tray, 12 in. across and 2-1/2 in. high. Made by the California Mission Indians. Mint condition.   G-$850

Miwok basket, 12 in. high and 7 in. in diameter. Good condition; ca. 1900.   G-$700

Modoc hat, 6 x 11-1/2 in.   A-$195

Modoc hat, 7 in. in diameter.   A-$135

Modoc basketry cap, 6-1/4 in. in average diameter and about 5 in. high. Diamond decorations.   C-$290

Mohawk sweetgrass gift baskets, two; sold as one lot.   A-$45

Navajo wedding basket, 15 in. in diameter. Tight weave; ca. 1860.   D-$210

Navajo wedding basket, 13-1/4 in. in diameter. A-$245

Nootka basket, 9 in. high and 15 in. in diameter. Tan with black and brown designs depicting early seafaring scenes. Lidded; perfect condition.   C-$1,800

Nootka basket, old, 2-5/8 x 4-1/8 in.   A-$120

Nootka whaler's hat, 10-1/2 x 10-1/2 in.   A-$495

Ojibwa wicker basket made of peeled willow and collected in Minnesota. About 8 in. high. Not recent, but not of great age.   C-$105

Splint collecting basket, Indian group unknown, New England area. Piece is 8 x 9 x 5 in. high. Wood well-woven, good condition.   C-$155

Maine Indian birch-bark container, 9-1/4 in. wide and 14 in. long. Possibly a blueberry collecting basket. Average wear. Old and not common.   C-$145

Penobscot white ash basket, 13 in. long and 7 in. wide. Ribbed and handled; recent.   C-$115

Passamaquoddy "curlicue" basket, 5 in. high. Round and made of ultra-thin strips of brown ash. This type of "whatnot" basket often had a cover; if so, it is now missing.   C-$35

Passamaquoddy basket, Maine, stands 18-3/4 in. high. Splint-woven of brown ash. Carved wood handles on opposite sides of top. Style is the familiar commercial fish-scale basket. Tightly woven and contemporary. C-$155

Paiute coiled-bowl basket, 4-3/4 in. in diameter; beaded exterior. A few beads missing, but an exceptional work.   C-$400

Paiute lidded basket, 5 in. high and 6-1/2 in. across. Has polychrome geometric design.   G-$375

Paiute basketry covered bottle, 10 in. high. Good condition; ca. 1900.   G-$230

Southern Paiute basketry hat.   A-$130

Paiute hat, 8-1/2 in. across and 5-1/2 in. high. It has two geometric concentric bands.   G-$230

Paiute seed jar, 8 in. high and 5-1/2 in. in diameter with in-and-out weave for design; a single concentric band.   G-$170

Paiute basketry water jar, 7-1/2 in. high and 5-1/2 in. across. Has pine pitch on outside and horse-hair handles. Nice condition.   G-$200

Panamint basket, 10-1/2 in. across and 5 in. high. Design is two geometric concentric bands with rim ticking; there are fifteen stitches and five coils to the inch.   G-$1,100

Panamint basket, 10-1/2 in. across, 4 in. high. Has reversing diamond pattern, with unusual start on bottom. Fair condition, with some rim damage.   G-$695

Papago basket, 13 in. in diameter, 4-1/2 in. high. Faint geometric designs on sides.   C-$240

Papago lidded basket, 5 in. in diameter and 3-1/2 in. high. Made of bleached yucca and devil's claw, it has large butterflies on side and coyote tracks on lid.   G-$240

Papago miniature basket, 1 in. high, 1-1/2 in. in diameter. Brown with white simple designs.   C-$125

Papago oval basketry tray, 12 in. wide and 15 in. long and 3-1/2 in. deep. Loose weave typical of Papago, and with brown design. Good condition.   G-$180

Papago plaque, 15 in. in diameter, 3-1/2 in. high; old. Design is concentric squares from center.   G-$340

Papago waste paper basket, contemporary, 10 in. in diameter and 12 in. high. Design of dogs and men. G-$260

Pima basketry bowl, 16 in. in diameter and 5 in. high. Has salt and pepper design, and is in fair condition. G-$635

Pima coiled-bowl basket, 6-1/2 in. high, with geometric designs. In poor condition; has extensive damage. C-$70

Pima shallow-bowl basket, 17-1/2 in. in diameter, with star design. Extra-good condition.   D-$450

Pima fretwork basket, 16 in. in diameter. In nice condition and old; early 1900s or before.   G-$440

Pima grain barrel, 12-1/2 in. high and 11 in. in diameter. Has large open mouth and geometric design. Good condition.   G-$850

Pima lidded horsehair miniature basket, 1 in. in diameter and 1 in. high. Has a geometric design element. G-$85

Pima coiled plaque, 11 in. in diameter, with "maze" design on bottom. Average good condition.   C-$385

Pima miniature basketry plaque, 2-3/8 in. in diameter. Very uniformly woven, with geometric design. Good condition.   C-$100

Pitt River basket, 8 in. across and 7-1/2 in. high. Has geometric design interspersed with snow flakes. G-$465

Pitt River basket, 10 in. in diameter. In good condition; ca. 1900.   G-$240

Pomo basket, 6 in. in diameter.   D-$175

Pomo basket, 9-1/4 in. in diameter; beaded, coil manufacture. Two sizes of shell beads used to set off basic stepped-pyramid design.   C-$410

Pomo beaded boat-shaped basket, 4-1/2 in. long and 3-1/2 in. wide and 1-1/2 in. high. Has green beaded background, with red beads for geometric pattern. Fully beaded.   G-$750

Pomo feathered basket, from California, about 12 in. in diameter. Decorated with blue, green and white feathers. Condition is good.   A-$295

Salish (Coastal) miniature baskets, two; sold as one lot.   A-$95

Salish (Coastal) basket, 5 x 7-1/2 in.   A-$30

Satsop basket, twined, 7-1/2 x 12 in.   A-$220

Seminole coiled basket, 4 in. high and 6-1/2 in. in diameter, with coils of sweetgrass. Basket is plain and has flat cover; undecorated. Collected in the 1950s. C-$110

Shasta miniature basket.   A-$70

Shasta basket, 3-1/4 x 5-1/2 in.   A-$135

Shasta basket, 3 in. high and 6-1/2 in. in diameter. Geometric designs; exceptionally good condition.   C-$180

Shoshone burden basket, 10 x 12-1/2 in.   A-$135

Shoshone basket, 5 in high. Plain utility container; good condition.   C-$120

Siletz burden basket, 9 x 18 in.   A-$75

Skokomish berry basket, 6-3/4 x 8-1/2 in.   A-$190

Skokomish basket, 5 x 7 in.   A-$65

Thompson River lidded basket, British Columbia, Canada; 4 x 4 in.   A-$155

Thompson River basketry trunk, with lid. Dimensions are 15 in. across, 27 in. long and 15 in. high. Piece has imbricated diamond and cross designs. Fair condition. G-$1,600

Tlingit basket, 6 in. in diameter and 4-1/2 in. high. Geometric design, medium stitch, excellent condition. G-$895

Tlingit basket with butterfly designs, 4 x 6-3/4 in. A-$145

Tlingit basketry tray, 5-3/4 in. in diameter and 1-3/4 in. high. A-$75

Tlingit basket, 5 in. in diameter and 6 in. high. Good condition; ca. 1880. G-$750

Tlingit lidded basket, 4-1/2 x 6-1/2 in. A-$760

Tlingit basket, 5-1/2 in. high and 6 in. across. Design of two concentric geometric bands; slight damage to piece. G-$500

Tlingit basket, measuring 2-1/2 x 3-1/8 in. A-$50

Tsimshian lidded basket, 4-3/4 x 7 in. A-$60

Tulare basket, California, 9 in. high and 16-1/2 in. in top diameter. Small base and flaring top. Lightning decorations on exterior sides. Fair condition. C-$1,400

Tulare basket, 21 in. in diameter and 11 in. high; very large. Pattern is two bands of polychrome rattlesnake designs. Condition excellent. G-$3,000

Tulare basket, 7-1/2 in. in diameter and 3-1/2 in. high. Piece has serrated step pattern, polychrome and squaw stitch. Condition good. G-$325

Tulare basket with rattlesnake designs. A-$165

Washo basket, 2-3/4 x 6-1/4 in. and 4-7/8 in. high. Oval shape. A-$210

Washo basket, 7-1/4 in. in diameter, with banded exterior design. Has close weave, and is in good condition. C-$240

Washo basket, 7 in. in diameter and 4 in. high, with geometric design. G-$175

Washo basket, 10-1/2 in. in diameter and 5-1/2 in. high. Single-rod construction; design is a serrated concentric band. G-$315

Yavapai olla, a fine example of the storage basket. A-$235

Yokuts burden basket. A-$155

Yurok basketry mortar skirt or grain-catching hopper. A-$210

Yurok miniature tobacco basket, 2-1/2 x 2-3/4 in. A-$85

CANADIAN INDIAN BASKETS

It should be noted that some of the baskets already listed are also Canadian in origin. The names sometimes represent a basket-making region rather than a specific Indian group. Among such baskets are Frazer River and Thompson River in British Columbia, Western Canada.

Plaited wood-strip basket, 14 in. in diameter and 8-1/2 in. high. From Vancouver Island; work is good and serviceable. Probably a gathering basket for roots or shore seafoods. No decoration, fair condition. C-$120

Ash-splint basket, 16-1/2 in. high and 1-1/2 in. wide at rounded shoulders; alternating dark and light brown colors. Collected in Southeastern Canada. Basket design is from square at the bottom to round opening at top, with nice merge; ca. 1900. C-$170

Small nondescript basket, from Central Canada, 3-7/8 in. in diameter; wood splint. Original colors of separate plaits were red and black, now faded. No cover. Good condition. C-$55

Historic-period basket, from Canada ,just above the Montana border. Piece is 7-1/2 in. in diameter and from an old collection. Material is a kind of reed, species unidentified. No decorative work. Basket is in good condition. C-$200

Pima basket, 3 in. deep and 13 in. in diameter. In top condition and with a careful design, the basket is ca. 1910. $1,000

Dennis R. Phillips, Chicago, Illinois

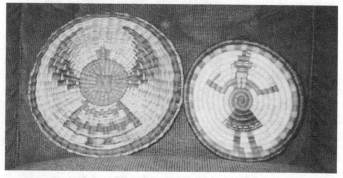

Two Hopi baskets, ca. 1930-1950, both from northern Arizona, good comparison photograph.

Left: 13-1/2 in. diameter, figural, wicker, rabbit-brush, yucca and sumac. $250
Right: 11 in. diameter, figural, coiled basketry, yucca. $250
Rainbow Traders, Godfrey, Illinois

Apache figural tray, large and in fine condition with excellent designs. It is ca. 1900 and 15 in. in diameter. Made of willow and devil's claw, this is an attractive, well-made basket. Southwestern Arizona. $2,400

Rainbow Traders, Godfrey, Illinois

Basket, White Mountain Apache, figures done in negative design. This large basket measures 14-1/2 in. in diameter and is 17-1/4 in. high. It was woven of willow and devil's claw and is ca. 1890. Because it is large, figural and with negative design, topped by superb condition, this is a very collectible piece. Southwestern Arizona. $20,000

Rainbow Traders, Godfrey, Illinois

Apache basketry olla, 20 in. in diameter and 21-1/2 in. high. Materials are willow root, yucca, and devil's claw. Human or animal figures are typical of Apache basketry, this ca. 1900. $22,500

David Cook Fine American Art, Denver, Colorado; Jamie Kahn photograph

MISCELLANEOUS BASKETS

Northwest Coast basketry hat, 13-1/2 in. in lower diameter, flat crown, and 9 in. high. For rain protection, this basketry hat has a very tight weave. Unusual. C-$775

Miniature sweetgrass basket, Eastern Woodlands, 3 in. in diameter, with cover. D-$45

Miniature sweetgrass basket, Eastern Woodlands, 2 in. in diameter, with cover. D-$40

Northern California basketry mortar skirt, 9-1/2 in. high. It is 14 in. across the open top and 4 in. across the open bottom. Whole is shaped like a funnel, and the shield kept the pounded meal from flying from the mortar and being lost or mixed with grit. Historic; with diamond and lightning design. C-$950

Basketry head ring, about 4-1/2 in. in diameter, open center, about 1 in. thick. Used between top of head and carrying pot for steady transport of water vessel, etc. From Southwestern U.S., and old. C-$135

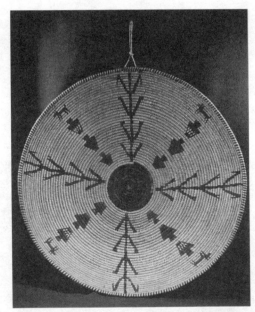

Apache coiled basket, with designs of four corn stalks with ears of corn, twelve Apache ollas, and four quadrupeds. In mint condition, the basket is 3-1/2 x 16-1/2 in. In fineness of weave and being both figurative and pictorial, it is a spectacular and rare basket. Ca. 1900. $5,000-7,000

Terry Schafer, American Indian Art & Antiques, Marietta, Ohio

Maidu basketry gambling tray, 16 in. in diameter, nicely patterned, ca. 1900. $1,585

Indian Territory, Tucson, Arizona

Basketry hats, both finely woven and ca. 1920.

Left: Karok. $645
Right: Yurok. $565

Indian Territory, Tucson, Arizona

Basket group, periods ca. 1880-1940. This is a good representative collection of baskets, described clockwise from upper left corner.

Large Pima basket with best-of-show ribbon. $750

Oblong Mission basket. $150

Large Pima bowl with dog figurals, some rim damage. $400

Old oblong Papago basket, "good luck" whirling log (swastika) symbol. $150

Shallow Papago tray with three horsehair miniatures.   All, $150

Tight Jicarilla Apache square tray. $250

Center left: cone-shaped Maidu basket. $500
Upper center: old corn plant figural, California. $750

Rainbow Traders, Godfrey, Illinois

Mission storage basket, 13 in. high and 20 in. across the top. The yellow basketry material is juncus reed from southern California. The basket was formerly in the Glenbow Museum in Calgary, Canada. Ca. 1890-1900. $3,200

Indian Territory, Tucson, Arizona

Artifact grouping, two baskets, beadwork and pipe.

Center top: Panamint olla (rare) with network design. $2,400

Pewter inlaid pipe with original quilled stem, ca. 1890. $3,500

Lower right: Cahuilla corn plant basket, shown elsewhere, California. $750
Upper left: Iroquois beaded picture with tintype of Victorian lady. $150

Rainbow Traders, Godfrey, Illinois

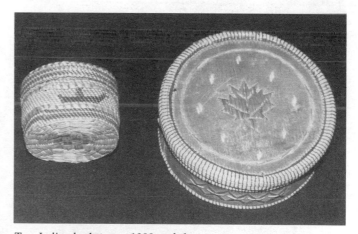

Two Indian baskets, ca. 1900, as below:

Left: Makah, 2-1/2 in. diameter, Washington state and British Columbia, made of sweetgrass. $175
Right: Ojibway, 4-1/2 in. diameter, birchbark and quillwork leaf design on lid, northern Minnesota and southern Canada. $150

Rainbow Traders, Godfrey, Illinois

Pomo feather basket, 7-1/2 in. in diameter and 2 in. high. The designs are worked in feathers colored yellow, purple-black, green, and white. This rare early basket is from northern California. $2,500

Terry Schafer, American Indian Art & Antiques, Marietta, Ohio

Chemehuevi coiled basket, 3 in. high and 16 in. in diameter. Materials are desert willow and devil's claw for this exceptional basket. It came from the Colorado River area near Needles, California, ca. 1900. $3,000

Terry Schafer, American Indian Art & Antiques, Marietta, Ohio

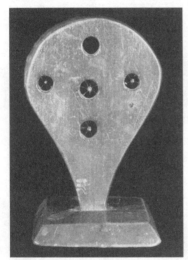

Northern California basketry material splitter and sizer, used to split and size fibers for making fine baskets. The rare artifact is 3 in. high and 1-1/2 in. wide, and is made of wood with metal cutters. Ca. 1880. $1,000

Terry Schafer, American Indian Art & Antiques, Marietta, Ohio

Basket, Pomo, 17 in. in diameter, woven of willow, redbud, and sedge root. This excellent basket is ca. 1880-1910 and has beautiful design planning and execution. Central California. $2,200

Rainbow Traders, Godfrey, Illinois

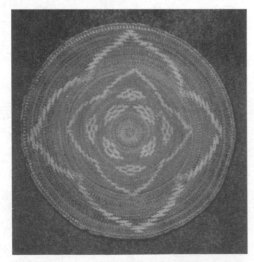

Klamath gambling tray, 17 in. in diameter, made of cattail and beargrass. The large tray came from southern Oregon and is ca. 1890. $2,000

Terry Schafer, American Indian Art & Antiques, Marietta, Ohio

Basketry items: Large Apache tray and three Pomo bowls. All, left to right: $1,500; $2,800; $750 and $2,200

Crown & Eagle Antiques, New Hope, Pennsylvania

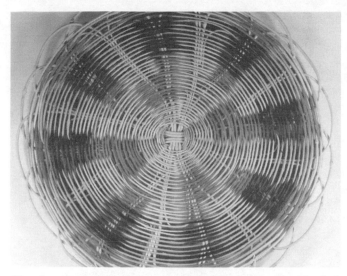

Cherokee mat, web-weave honeysuckle, 11 in. in diameter. The dark brown and red dyes were made from walnut and bloodroot. North Carolina. $30

Charles F. and Susan Wood, Ohio

Hopi coiled basketry plaque, 8-1/2 in. in diameter. With designs in red and dark brown, it was made by Christine Saufkie. $100

Charles F. and Susan Wood, Ohio

Wall basket, maple and walnut splints, 14 in. high. The tag reads: "Certified Indian Enterprise/Indian Arts and Crafts Board/U.S. Department of the Interior." Ca. 1993. $45

Charles F. and Susan Wood, Ohio

Nest of five Penobscot baskets, ash splints and sweetgrass, ca. 1920-1940. Old Town, Maine. Set, $250

Native American Artifacts, Victor, New York

Hopi coiled basketry plaque, 10-3/8 in. in diameter. This well-done example is by Vernita P. $140

Charles F. and Susan Wood, Ohio

Ojibwa or Chippewa lidded birchbark box, floral quill designs. With handle, this box measures 4 x 5 x 8 in. and is ca. 1950. Minnesota. $290

Native American Artifacts, Victor, New York

American Indian basketry, back row left to right:

Alaskan tray, coiled beach grasses, 13 x 15 in., ca. 1950. $375
Zuni wicker basket, natural colors, 18 in. diameter, ca. 1920. $195

Front row, left to right:

Hopi wicker plaque, spider-web design, 10-1/2 in. diameter, ca. 1940. $200
Oval Papago coiled basket, natural and brown, 11 in. long, ca. 1940. $70
Hopi coiled tray, 6-1/2 in. diameter, ca. 1950. $95

Native American Artifacts, Victor, New York

Southwestern prehistoric basket, 8-1/2 in. in diameter and 4-3/4 in. high, gray-brown color. Basket has a medium-tight weave, no remaining decoration. Found during excavation of a dry cave in New Mexico. Reed used, but is now very brittle.   C-$425

Cone-shaped California burden basket, 17 in. high; would have been used with the forehead strap or tumpline. Tribe unknown. A plain piece, showing average and acceptable wear.   C-$1,600

Southwestern Oregon basketry cooking pot, 11 in. high and 13-1/2 in. in diameter. Circular, with extremely tight weave. Stepped pyramid designs, reinforced rim. Used with water, meat and roots; hot rocks were dropped in to boil the water and cook the food. Historic; damage to bottom.   C-$500

Suggested Reading

James, George W. *Indian Basketry*. San Francisco, 1902 (reprinted)

Mason, Otis T. "Aboriginal American Basketry: Studies In A Textile Art Without Machinery." *Annual Report of the U.S. National Museum* (1902): 1904. New York: Doubleday.

Miles, Charles, and Pierre Bovis. *American Indian and Eskimo Basketry: A Key to Identification*. San Francisco, 1969 (reprinted).

Klamath basket, stripe design of dark brown against light yellowish brown, from southern Oregon. It is 5 x 9 x 13 in., ex-museum, and ca. 1920. $425

Morris' Art & Artifacts, Anaheim, California; Dawn Gober photograph

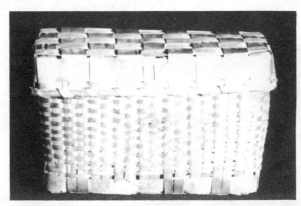

Klamath basket, stripe design of dark brown against light yellowish brown, from southern Oregon. It is 5 x 9 x 13 in., ex-museum, and ca. 1920. $425

Morris' Art & Artifacts, Anaheim, California; Dawn Gober photograph

Iroquois (Mohawk) ash-splint basket, "strawberry" form, covered and edged with sweetgrass. Ca. 1940s, it is 3-1/2 x 5-1/4 in. $110

Frank Bergevin, Port of Call, Alexandria Bay, New York

River cane basket, Cherokee, large size, from the 1940s. $350

Larry Lantz, First Mesa, South Bend, Indiana

Lidded basket, Penobscot, splint and sweetgrass. It is 8 in. in diameter and ca. 1920-1940. $65-85

Pocotopaug Trading Post, South Windsor, Connecticut

Yokuts basket, human figure motif, 7 in. high and 10 in. in diameter. Design is dark brown on tan and this is a fine work, possibly from the 1920s. $1,200

Private collection

Splint basket, Mohawk, 7-1/2 in. in diameter. This well-made work is ca. 1880-1900. $90

Pocotopaug Trading Post, South Windsor, Connecticut

Tsimshian baskets, Northwest Coast, all made of spruce root and bear-grass.

Left: 7 in. high, ca. 1920s. $125-175
Center: grizzly bear in false embroidery, 10-1/2 in. high, ca. 1880-1900. $400-500
Right: 7-1/2 in. high, ca. 1920s. $150-200

Pocotopaug Trading Post, South Windsor, Connecticut

Basketry water bottle, Paiute, still showing traces of pine pitch coating. Ex-museum, it is 10 in. in diameter and 13 in. high, ca. 1880. $350

Morris' Art & Artifacts, Anaheim, California; Dawn Gober photograph

Handkerchief basket, Penobscot, 9 in. square, unusual lid or top. Ca. 1920s. $50-60

Pocotopaug Trading Post, South Windsor, Connecticut

Basketry vase, Penobscot, splint and sweetgrass, 8 in. high. In fine condition, it is ca. 1920-1940. $90

Pocotopaug Trading Post, South Windsor, Connecticut

Twined hat, high-crowned, Yurok. In perfect condition, it is 7 x 10-1/4 in. and ca. 1920. $800-1,300

Marguerite L. Kernaghan collection; photograph by Marguerite L. and Stewart W. Kernaghan, Bellvue, Colorado

Twined hat, Hupa, perfect condition. The design is maroon, black, and cream against a cream background. It is 3-1/4 x 6 in. and ca. 1900. $500-750

Marguerite L. Kernaghan collection; photograph by Marguerite L. and Stewart W. Kernaghan, Bellvue, Colorado

Twined hat, Karok, perfect condition. Design is black and brown against a cream ground. Size is 3-1/2 x 6-1/2 in.; ca. 1900. $500-750

Marguerite L. Kernaghan collection; photograph by Marguerite L. and Stewart W. Kernaghan, Bellvue, Colorado

Shasta basket, step design, from northern California. Ex-museum, it is 5 in. in diameter and 4 in. high, ca. 1920. $200

Morris' Art & Artifacts, Anaheim, California; Dawn Gober photograph

Beehive basket, Northeastern Woodlands, splint and sweetgrass. It is 8-1/2 in. in diameter and ca. 1920s. $125-150

Pocotopaug Trading Post, South Windsor, Connecticut

Sewing basket, Penobscot, 7-1/2 in. in diameter. It is a well-made example, ca. 1920s. $75-100

Pocotopaug Trading Post, South Windsor, Connecticut

Lidded box, basketry, Makah, 5 in. in diameter. This delicate work is ca. 1890-1900. $125-160

Pocotopaug Trading Post, South Windsor, Connecticut

Birch-bark basket, Micmac-Abenaki, maker Jim Rouix. Ca. 1980. Size of this pleasing piece is 5 x 5-3/4 in. $140

Marguerite L. Kernaghan collection; photograph by Marguerite L. and Stewart W. Kernaghan, Bellvue, Colorado

Lidded basketry box, Nootka, 4-1/4 in. in diameter. This is a well-made Northwestern Coast artwork, ca. 1920s. $150-200

Pocotopaug Trading Post, South Windsor, Connecticut

Strawberry basket, Iroquois, so-named because of basket shape and design. It is 5-1/2 in. in diameter, decorated with curlicues. Ca. 1910-1930. $75-100

Pocotopaug Trading Post, South Windsor, Connecticut

Indian basket, split white oak, late 1800s, Chickasaw, from Mississippi. $125

Wilfred A. Dick collection, Magnolia, Mississippi

Close-up and different view of the Cherokee basket shown elsewhere. It has the government authorization tag from a North Carolina reservation and the weaver's name. Exceptional basket with documentation. $395

Larry Lantz, First Mesa, South Bend, Indiana

Picnic basket or carrying basket, Salish, 7 x 10 x 14 in. It has an imbricated butterfly design in black on yellow-tan. Ca. 1910-1925. $250-300

Pocotopaug Trading Post, South Windsor, Connecticut

Splint basket, Pequot, lidded, 14 in. diameter and 12 in. high. Nicely stamped, it is ca. 1860-1880. $275-325

Pocotopaug Trading Post, South Windsor, Connecticut

Splint basket, Pequot, potato-stamped, 8 in. square. This excellent piece is ca. 1880s. $150-200

Pocotopaug Trading Post, South Windsor, Connecticut

Maidu basket, 7 in. width, six coils per inch, thirteen stitches per inch, Northern California. Coiled, dark material redbud, ca. 1890. C-$1,000

Courtesy LaPerriere collection, California

Basket, Tlingit, designs in cedar bark and bear grass. This pleasing piece is 6 in. high, ca. 1920s. $300-400

Pocotopaug Trading Post, South Windsor, Connecticut

Hupa-Yurok basketry hat, from Northern California, 7-1/2 in. top diameter. Twined, early 1900s. C-$170-200

Courtesy LaPerriere collection, California

Pit River basket, Northern California, 4 in. high, ca. 1910. C-$375

Bob LaPerriere photo

Apache basket, 10 in. diameter, ca. 1910. C-$550

John Barry photo

Makah lidded basket, Northwest Coast, 4-5/8 in. high, ca. 1940. C-$200

John Barry photo

Makah lidded basket, fair condition, 2-1/4 in. high, ca. 1940. C-$75

John Barry photo

Maidu basket, coiled bowl, 4 in. high, ca. 1910. C-$900

Bob LaPerriere photo

Maidu baskets, both 3-1/2 in. diameters, Northern California. Miniatures, coiled, dark material redbud, early 1900s. Top specimen with stain.

Left: C-$200
Right: C-$300

Courtesy LaPerriere collection, California

Tsimshian basketed bottle.

Southern Alaska, 3 in. bottle height plug 2-1/2 in. wooden totem. Twined, inkwell, carved stopper with paint. Ca. 1910.　　C-$800

Courtesy LaPerriere collection, California

Washo basket, 6 in. wide diameter, 4 in. high. Northern California. Coiled plain black fern design (Mt. Brake). Seven coils per inch, fifteen stitches per inch, ca. 1890.　　C-$800

Courtesy LaPerriere collection, California

Nootka-Makah basketry bottle, from Vancouver, British Columbia. Twined, 11-1/2 in. high, early 1900s. C-$500

Courtesy LaPerriere collection, California

Washo single-rod coil basket, Northern California, 6 in. top diameter. Coiled at six coils per inch, ten stitches per inch, uncertain age.　　C-$300

Klikitat basket, age uncertain, from Washington state. Top diameter 5-1/4 in., 3 in., high. Coiled, six stitches per inch.　　C-$150

Courtesy LaPerriere collection, California

Modoc bowl basket, 8-1/4 in. diameter. Northern California, ca. 1910.　　C-$400

Bob LaPerriere photo

Yurok basket, by Geneva M. Maltz, Northern California, 2 in. high, ca. 1974.　　C-$150

John Barry photo

Tulare (Yokut) basket, 4-1/4 in. top diameter. Northern California. Coiled, in snake pattern, thirteen stitches per inch.   C-$300

Courtesy LaPerriere collection, California

Tlingit basket, 6 in. high, Southern Alaska. Twined, early 1900. This specimen with tear damage.

Torn condition.   C-$300

In perfect condition.   C-$400

Courtesy LaPerriere collection, California

Eastern mono cooking basket, Northern California, 14 in. top diameter. Coiled twelve stitches per inch., seven coils per inch. Black zig-zag design, ca. 1900.   C-$2,000

Courtesy LaPerriere collection, California ▼

Hopi basketry plaque, 11 in. diameter. Northeastern Arizona. Coiled, pre-1940; from Second Mesa, this is the old type, thick, with more subtle colors.   C-$300

Courtesy LaPerriere collection, California

Left: Pit River burden basket, small size, 7 in. high. Twined. Shasta area of Northern California, uncertain age.   C-$350

Courtesy LaPerriere collection, California

Right: basket, probably Shastan Group, Northern California, 17 in. in height and top diameter. Large burden basket, somewhat crude, some rim repairs, possibly early 1900s. C-$2,500

Courtesy LaPerriere collection, California

Pomo basket, age uncertain, Northern California, 2 in. top diameter. Coiled, ten coils per inch, twenty-three stitches per inch With war-canoe design.   C-$500

Courtesy LaPerriere collection, California

Navajo wedding basket, usually not made by Navajos, Northeastern Arizona, 9 in. diameter. Coiled, and contemporary.   C-$150

Courtesy LaPerriere collection, California

Eskimo basket, 13 in. high, Alaska, ca. 1960. C-$400

Courtesy LaPerriere collection, California

Shoshone basket, southeastern California. From East of Sierras, probably Inyo County. Coiled, lightning design, fourteen stitches per inch. Stabilized, pre-1900. C-$1,800

Courtesy LaPerriere collection, California

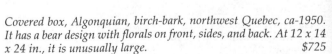

Far Left: Hat Creek basket, Shasta area of northern California, 6-1/2 in. wide. Twined, about early 1900s. C-$350

Courtesy LaPerriere collection, California

Left: Salish basket, British Columbia or Washington state, 8 in. top diameter. Imbricated design, coiled, four coils per inch. Ca. 1910. C-$250

Courtesy LaPerriere collection, California

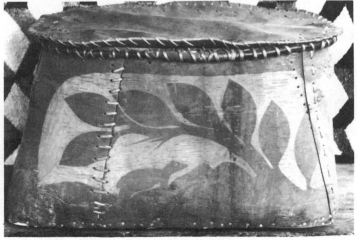

Covered box, Algonquian, birch-bark, northwest Quebec, ca-1950. It has a bear design with florals on front, sides, and back. At 12 x 14 x 24 in., it is unusually large. $725

Frank Bergevin, Port of Call, Alexandria Bay, New York

Iroquois (Mohawk) ash-splint basket, potato-stamped, early 1900s. It is natural ash with strips of painted green ash, stamps in faint red. Size, 11 x 17 x 17 in. $375

Frank Bergevin, Port of Call, Alexandria Bay, New York

Iroquois (Mohawk) ash-splint basket, potato-stamp designs in green and red on one strip. Size is 4 x 13 x 15 1/2 in. $225

Frank Bergevin, Port of Call, Alexandria Bay, New York

Twined hat, Yurok, perfect condition. It is 3-1/2 x 6-1/4 in. and ca. 1900. $500-700

Marguerite L. Kernaghan collection; photograph by Marguerite L. and Stewart W. Kernaghan, Bellvue, Colorado

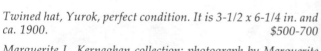

Twined hat, Yurok, perfect condition. It is 3-1/2 x 7-1/2 in. and ca. 1920. $400-650

Marguerite L. Kernaghan collection; photo by Marguerite L. and Stewart W. Kernaghan, Bellvue, Colorado

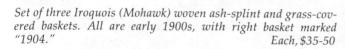

Set of three Iroquois (Mohawk) woven ash-splint and grass-covered baskets. All are early 1900s, with right basket marked "1904." Each, $35-50

Frank Bergevin, Port of Call, Alexandria Bay, New York

Indian woman with child in suspension-type wooden cradle. She is rocking the cradle with cord and foot. Note reed or fibre matting, basket, and woven tapestry in background. Picture taken at Neah Bay, Washington, ca. 1890.

Photographer, Samuel Gay Morse; courtesy Photography Collection, Suzzallo Library, University of Washington

CHAPTER XII

BEADWORK AND QUILLWORK

American Indians are widely recognized to have done the world's finest decorative work with beads and quills. Quills were used in the Eastern Woodland regions, the Rocky Mountains, and parts of Canada. The Plains Indians and many other groups favored beads. Quills and beads were sometimes used on the same item.

Porcupine quills were processed and dyed before use; the beads were ready-made trade goods. While generalizations regarding Amerind objects are somewhat difficult, there are basic design differences. In the Eastern Third of the country, bead or quillwork designs were often floral patterns, rounded designs. Western areas had more geometric patterns, angular designs.

The Indian appreciation for things of beauty meant that even everyday objects were sometimes decorated. Ceremonial items, like the fine pipe bags, were often heavily beaded in pleasing color combinations. In this chapter are some collecting areas in which bead or quillwork is especially important.

Value factors include the kind of item decorated, with a complete work (a bandolier bag, for example) more admired than a part of an original piece (a pipe bag panel, for example). The complexity of the design counts considerably, involving both the design and the quantity of beads. A typical beadwork design employs many thousands of small beads.

Fully beaded items, such as fetishes, are generally higher priced than a partially beaded object of the same size and type. The percentage of beads missing or quills lost or damaged is of great importance in arriving at a value.

The condition of the leather or trade cloth to which beads or quills are secured is to be regarded; a supple, quality leather is much better than poorly tanned and cracked leather. Indian-tanned leather is generally desired over commercial leather.

PIPE BAGS—FULLY OR PARTIALLY BEADED

Sioux pipe bag, old and of fine quality; large size and good condition.   G-$850

Cheyenne pipe bag, 22-1/2 in. long, with very nice beaded exterior over soft leather. Fringed and beaded tassels add another 7 in. to length. Good condition.   D-$1,100

Sioux pipe bag, 7 in. wide and 35 in. long, including fringe. Quillwork is 50 percent missing, but beadwork is excellent and in geometric design with various colors of beads on white background.   G-$1,150

Cheyenne pipe bag, partially beaded, fully fringed. A-$360

Cree pipe bag, beaded panel at bottom is 6 x 6 in. Done on fine Indian-tanned leather. No quillwork, usual for this type. One side shows floral design and other side shows teacup and flowers beaded on white background. Old, and in nearly perfect condition.   G-$850

Sioux (?) pipe bag, quillwork and beadwork missing a considerable percentage of units.   D-$575

Sioux pipe bag, 12 in. long with fringe extra. The beaded panel at bottom is 4 x 7 in. and in excellent condition. Probably pre-1890.   G-$500

Sioux pipe bags, private collection, per each. C-$900-1,700

Sioux pipe bag with full drop that is nicely quilled.   D-$1,100

Cheyenne pipe bag, well beaded and quilled; good condition.   D-$800

Sioux pipe bag, rebuilt. Old beadwork panels with new buckskin top, quillwork and fringe. Good designs and colors.   G-$700

Lady's pipe bag, Chippewa (Ojibwa), with appliqué stitching on both sides. This fine piece is from the 1880s. $750

Larry Lantz, First Mesa, South Bend, Indiana

Arapaho pipe bag, standard size, with fringed bottom. Lower sections very well beaded in red, white, black, and buff colors. Excellent condition, and ca. 1890. D-$1,495

Photo courtesy Crazy Crow Trading Post, Denison, Texas

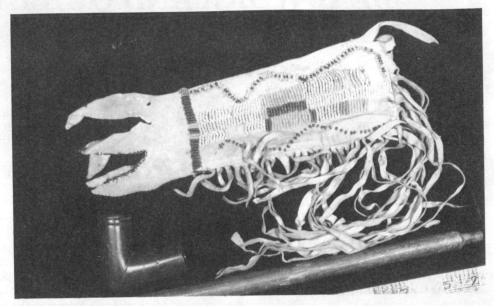

Sioux miniature pipe bag with Catlinite "L"-shaped pipe and original cylindrical stem 13 in. long. The complete set is from Mandan, North Dakota, and ca. 1870s.

Pipe and stem	$775
Pipe bag	$400

Larry Lantz, First Mesa, South Bend, Indiana

Sioux beaded pipe bag, 36 in. long, good design, well-beaded, and ca. 1870-80. D-$1,500

Photo courtesy Winona Trading Post, Santa Fe- Pierre & Sylvia Bovis

Plains Indian (probably Sioux or Northern Cheyenne) pipe or tobacco bag, geometric beadwork designs in five colors against a white ground. This is a beautiful fringed bag, ca. 1890-1900. $750

Tom Fouts collection, Kansas

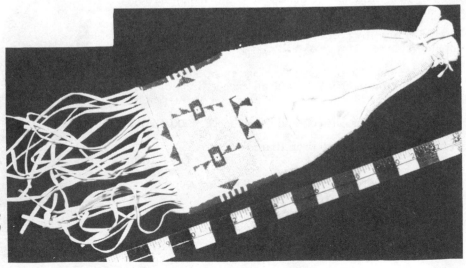

Pipe bag, Sioux, from South Dakota. It is sinew-sewn and brain-tanned, ca. 1880-1890, with rectangular panel beaded in red, white, and two shades of blue. This is a fine bag. $1,000

Larry Lantz, First Mesa, South Bend, Indiana

Beaded and quilled pipe bag, Sioux, 25 in. long. It is brain-tanned, ca. 1880-1890s, in excellent condition. Beadwork is geometric against a green ground. $2,000

Larry Lantz, First Mesa, South Bend, Indiana

Early Cheyenne pipebag, painted and fringed hide, 17 in. long. Embroidered front and back with beadwork in a bar design symbolizing the warrior's accomplishments in battle. This rare bag is ca. 1870s. $14,000

Canfield Gallery, Santa Fe

Pipebag, Northern Cheyenne, ca. 1870-1880. This fine example measures 7 in. wide and 24 in. long. Materials are buffalo hide, trade beads, quillwork, horsehair, and tin cones. Plains area. $2,500

J. Steve and Anita Shearer, Torrance, California

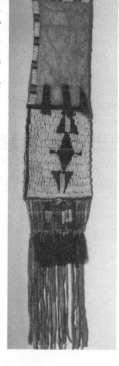

Pictorial pipebag, Sioux, of soft fringed hide with Venetian glass bead panels on each side, and geometric figures and blue horses outlined in red. On one side reads "$50" and on the other side is "$60" and a series of letters. These are indecipherable but may be a Lakota word or name. Between the beadwork panel and hide fringe there is a panel of spiral columns of bohemian glass beads. Ca. 1900. $6,000

Canfield Gallery, Santa Fe

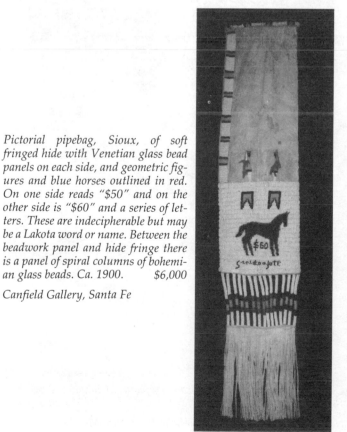

Pipe bag, Flathead Indian, 26 in. long with fringe. This fine bag is made of tanned hide and has a geometric design. Ca. 1890-1900. $2,750

Historic Interiors, Sorrento, British Columbia, Canada

Sioux pipe bag, beaded, and with unusual parfleche bottom. A-$495

Plains Indian pipe bag, fringed and quilled; good condition. D-$950

Cheyenne pipe bag, old and of very large size for a Cheyenne. Typical designs with fringed, quilled, drop. Piece has slight damage. G-$1,100

Cree pipe bag, 7 in. wide and 28 in. long including fringe. No quillwork, as is common on this style bag, but has a beaded panel of stylized flower on both sides. Varicolored beads on white background. Almost perfect condition. G-$1,050

QUILLWORK

(Additional quillwork listings are in the Clothing chapter)

Plains Indian hair roach, nicely quilled, with horsehair. D-$295

Quilled coat, hide with floral quilled designs on front and back. Beautiful early piece with about 20 percent of quillwork gone but in excellent condition. Colors are bright. G-$1,650

Cheyenne armbands, beaded and quilled. A-$145

Sioux quilled armbands, trimmed with ermine fur. Quilled danglers; pair 12 in. in circumference. Good condition; ca. 1900. G-$175

Hair ties, pair, nicely quilled. D-$125

Hair ties, quilled pair, with brightly colored fluffs and tin-cone danglers. G-$70

Sioux quilled cuffs with American flag designs, good quality and condition. Pre-1900 items. G-$500

Quilled birch bark box, 5 in. on a side and 2-1/4 in. high. Flower designs done in dyed and natural quills (dyed, red, and green); dried grass edging, with sides done in natural quills. Collected at Wisconsin Dells, Wisconsin. This is a Chippewa box, from the early 1900s. C$375

Photo courtesy Bill Post collection

Dance wand, 14 in. long. Plains Indian with wooden handle and quilled head; recent. C-$65

Quilled cradle, Arapaho. Top fully quilled in natural and purple quills. Quilled strips down side to cloth base; replaced boards but was done correctly. A beautiful example; ca. 1870. G-$3,300

Hair drop, very old, with trade beads and quillwork. D-$220

Quilled pouch, 7 in. circular size. Front fully quilled, with quills dyed red, green and orange. Collected in 1930s from Big Sorrell Horse, a Blackfoot Indian in Montana. Piece is excellent, early and rare. G-$1,100

Quilled basket, Eastern Woodlands, 3-1/8 in. in diameter, with fitted, original cover. Interior is birch bark, the whole covered with dyed porcupine quills; brown background. Probably early 1900s. Good condition. C-$175

Quilled breastplate with American flag motif, 21 in. long. Piece is ca. 1885. *Museum quality*

Nedra Matteucci's Fenn Galleries, Santa Fe, New Mexico

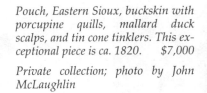

Knife sheath, quilled on black buckskin, Central Great Lakes region. This rare piece is ca. 1800. $3,000

Private collection; photo by John McLaughlin

Pouch, Eastern Sioux, buckskin with porcupine quills, mallard duck scalps, and tin cone tinklers. This exceptional piece is ca. 1820. $7,000

Private collection; photo by John McLaughlin

Quilled horse mane hair piece, 14 in. long. The quills and hair are dyed red; tin cone jangles hang on the quilled leather. Ca. 1870. Museum quality

Nedra Matteucci's Fenn Galleries, Santa Fe, New Mexico

Quilled moccasins, Great Lakes and early, ca. 1790. These adult-size moccasins are quilled and ribboned on brown hide. $4,500

Private collection; photo by John McLaughlin

Quilled birchbark lidded box, with alphabet sampler letters. This charming piece is 3-1/2 x 4-1/4 in. in diameter, from Canada ca. 1930. Ex-coll. Casterline. $150

Pat & Dave Summers, Native American Artifacts, Victor, New York

Plaque, Chippewa, Great Lakes area, quilled florals on birchbark with grass border. It is 7 in. in diameter and ca. 1940s. $65-85

Pocotopaug Trading Post, South Windsor, Connecticut

Quilled birchbark lidded box, Woodlands region. It has a colorful floral design in blue-green, pinkish-red, and yellow; size is 4 x 9-1/4 in. in diameter. Ex-coll. Casterline. $550

Pat & Dave Summers, Native American Artifacts, Victor, New York

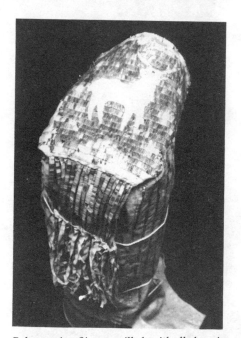

Baby carrier, Sioux, quilled, with elk done in quillwork. Materials are quills, cloth, and hide. This fine work is ca. 1880. $4,000

Private collection, photo by John McLaughlin

Northern U.S. quilled hatband, 1 in. wide and 24 in. long, leather with porcupine quills in orange, white, blue, and berry. With average wear but in good condition, this band is probably from the early 1900s. $300

T.R.H. collection, Indiana

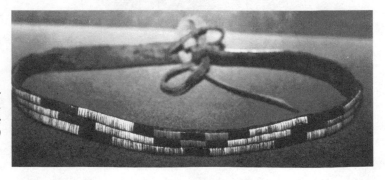

Quilled hair ornaments, center example 3-1/2 in. long, porcupine quills on leather backing. The smaller ornaments have blue and red quills against white, while the larger has yellow, gold, and red quills against white. Possibly Great Lakes region, early 1900s. $150

T.R.H. collection, Indiana

Sioux quilled sheath and old knife, with red and white quills bordered with black quills with yellow accents. The sheath is in mint condition and is ca. 1910. $745

Indian Territory, Tucson, Arizona

Sioux woman's beaded and quilled work or smoking bag, with antelope head. This design is the same both front and back, and the bag is 11-1/2 in. long. Ca. 1870. $5,500

Forrest Fenn, Santa Fe, New Mexico

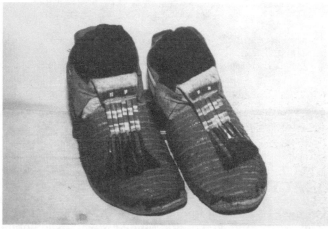

Sioux man's moccasins, quills and beads, with quillwork in red, white, and blue and with quilled tassels. These rare moccasins are in outstanding condition. Ca. 1880. $4,500

Traditions, Victor, New York

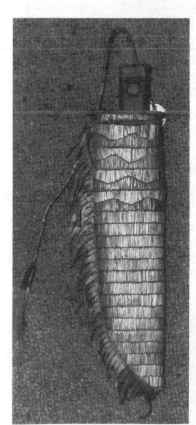

Upper Missouri quilled knife sheath and knife, Yankton Sioux, sheath 9-1/2 in. long. This is beautiful early quillwork, ca. 1865. $18,000

Forrest Fenn, Santa Fe, New Mexico

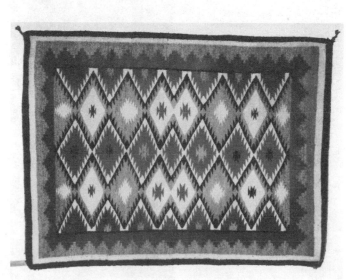

Navajo rug, 39-1/2 x 51-1/2 in., black, white, gray, and red. Ca. 1940. $395

Native American Artifacts, Victor, New York

Navajo rug, 36 x 57-1/2 in., one small stain otherwise excellent condition, ca. 1950. $325

Native American Artifacts, Victor, New York

BEADED AWL CASES

Awl case, 8 in. long fine. Fully beaded example, Cheyenne, with white, green, and blue beadwork. Old horsehair dangles with tin cones; ca. 1900.   G-$350

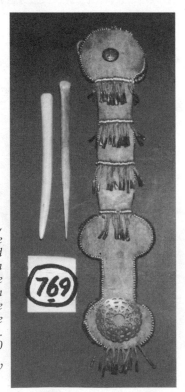

Awl case or knife sheath, Apache, 19-1/2 in. long. There are tin cones and beads around the edges, a U.S. Cavalry button at the top, and a Woodland type German Silver brooch which decorates the bottom. Two bone awls are shown with this piece which came from Arizona. Ca. 1865. $3,000

Forrest Fenn, Santa Fe, New Mexico

Awl case, Sioux, fully beaded, with beaded drops; extra-fine condition and old.   D-$180

Awl case, Apache, 14 in. long. Beaded in geometric designs with tiny seed beads. Larger beads and tin-cone dangles; good condition.   D-$395

Awl case, 12 in. long, with circular design done in blue, yellow, and red beads. Sound condition; pre-1900 item.   G-$170

Awl case, nicely beaded Plains Indian piece.   A-$95

Awl case, with bone awl; 9 in. long plus fringe. Wooden top, and fully beaded.   G-$260

BEADED CARRIERS—VARIOUS TYPES

Beaded bag, probably Nez Perce, 9 in. wide and 12-1/2 in. long; all frontal beading intact. Simple star-like designs, two small and one large. Leather is dry but could be treated.   C-$475

Beaded bag, 8 x 9 in., a beautiful item. Bag has a blue background with roses and leaves design, with many early cut-glass beads. Excellent condition.   G-$260

Beaded pouch, Sioux; similar to a strike-a-light bag.   G-$160

Beaded bag, Plains Indian, 6 x 8-1/4 in. Well-beaded on one side; good condition.   D-$425

Beaded bag, Woodland Indian style; 6 x 6 in. Beadwork is done on black velvet as was usual; floral design with all beadwork intact. Top rim of bag shows some wear. G-$250

Bandolier bag, Chippewa, a large bag with typical floral designs on velvet. Good condition.   G-$1,200

Paint bag, a rare Sioux item; 12-1/2 in. long. Nearly full beaded and with beaded fringes. A pouch-type container, it still has interior traces of ochre or powdered hematite. Beads are red, yellow, and green.   C-$950

Bandolier bag, Menominee, 38 in. long and 11 in. wide. Fully beaded and in very good condition; ca. 1880.   G-$1,200

Horseshoe-shaped pouch, classic Sioux, fully beaded and fringed. Piece is ca. 1885.   C-$1,000

Leather bag, Woodlands Indian, 6-1/4 in. high. Beaded front in typical floral pattern. Possibly Ottawa in origin. The pouch is fully fringed on all sides except top, which is closed by a beaded flap.   C-$625

Wall bag, Sioux (?), 12 in. long. Fully beaded and with tin cone jangles. Nice condition; ca. 1910.   G-$255

Belt pouch, with beaded eagle design.   A-$110

Pitt River bag, 10 x 10 in.; triangular design. It has the highest quality loomed bead work and is of the type done only by Indians on the Pitt River, Oregon. Specimen has an amber background, with blue and white geometric designs and beaded handle; ca. 1930.   G-$450

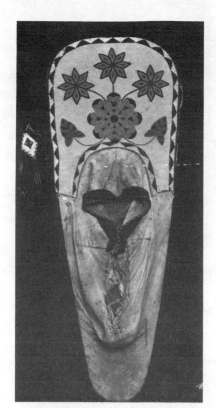

Baby-carrier, Nez Perce, wood frame with hide, cloth and beadwork. This is an ultrafine example, ca. 1890. $6,500

Private collection, photo by John McLaughlin

Small beaded bag, Eastern Woodlands/Great Lakes area, fringed sides. The floral motif is done in red, white, blue, green, and black. $325-400

Collection of David G. & Barbara J. Shirley

Baby-carrier, Ottawa, painted wood, cloth and beadwork. This exceptional piece is ca. 1880. $2,500

Private collection; photo by John McLaughlin

Beadwork.

Top left: Iroquois bag, floral motif both sides, ca. 1890. $195
Top right: Chippewa loom-beaded bag, 5 x 6-1/2 in., butterfly and floral pattern. $415
Bottom left: Plateau bag, 7 x 11 in., 1890s, stylized eagle. $300
Bottom right: Iroquois beaded bag, 6-1/2 x 7-1/2 in., floral motif both sides, 1880s, fine work. $475

Larry Lantz, First Mesa, South Bend, Indiana

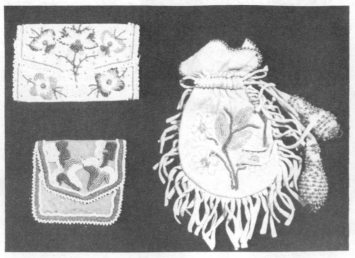

Bandolier bag, Chippewa, ca. 1880-1910. It is 16-1/2 x 36 in., and has exceptionally colorful beadwork. This piece has been restored and stabilized to preserve a rare piece of primitive art. $1,950

Sherman Holbert collection, Fort Mille Lacs, Onamia, Minnesota

Beaded containers.

Top left: Iroquois (Oneida) needle case, 3 x 4-1/2 in., late 1800s, bird and floral motif. $300
Bottom left: Northwest Coast (Tlingit) charm bag, 3 x 3 in., seed beads on green trade cloth, ca. 1875. $400
Right: Chippewa circular bag, late 1800s, brain-tanned, beaded both sides, beaded pompom draw-pulls. $340

Larry Lantz, First Mesa, South Bend, Indiana

Beaded bags.

Left: tobacco bag, Chippewa, seed beads in abstract design, 6 x 7-1/2 in., from Hayward, Wisconsin. It is late 1800s. $215
Right: shown elsewhere in book. $265

Larry Lantz, First Mesa, South Bend, Indiana

Beaded bags.

Left: wall-pocket bag, Winnebago, black velveteen front, sugar sacking on back, 7 x 22-1/2 in. Seed beads are in abstract floral design, ca. 1880s. $1,000
Right: Plateau bag, Yakima, 10 x 11 in. It is contour-beaded in red, blue, and lime green, ca. 1880s. $995

Larry Lantz, First Mesa, South Bend, Indiana

Drawstring bag, Chippewa, floral beading in reds, white, green, and blue. It is 4 in. high and ca. 1880-1890. $265

Pocotopaug Trading Post, South Windsor, Connecticut

Bandolier bag, Potowatomi style, ca. 1860-1870. It is 17 x 41 in. and a truly great example of mid-1800 Indian bead art. Appliqué floral beadwork accents and separates the nearly flawless choke cherry pattern loom work of the tabs and strap. This is a giant bag compared with most loomed bandoliers. $3,450

Sherman Holbert collection, Fort Mille Lacs, Onamia, Minnesota

Baby carrier, Ute, done in wood and hide, decorated with paint and beading. It is ca. 1880. $3,500

Private collection, photo by John McLaughlin

Woman's bag, Chippewa, late 1800s. Made of brain-tanned hide, it is 6 x 6 in. and has a beaded looped handle with seed beads in fishnet pattern on both sides. A fine piece. $725

Larry Lantz, First Mesa, South Bend, Indiana

Pocket, Iroquois, Great Lakes area beadwork ca. 1885-1895, 4 x 4-1/2 in. The fine beading is done on black and red cloth. $135

Pocotopaug Trading Post, South Windsor, Connecticut

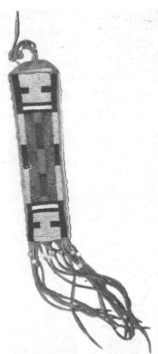

Sheath, Crow, hide with beadwork. This may be a whet-
stone case, ca. 1890. $800

*Private collection, photo by
John McLaughlin*

Bag or purse, Micmac, drawstring top, Great Lakes region. This is
a very fine example of a scarce item with colorful beading. It is 7-
1/2 x 11 in., ca. 1840-1860. $625

Pocotopaug Trading Post, South Windsor, Connecticut

Wallet, Seneca, Great Lakes area beading, item 2-1/2 x 4 in.
Beads are in seven different colors, item ca. 1860-1870. $110

Pocotopaug Trading Post, South Windsor, Connecticut

Pocket or bag, Iroquois, colorful floral design with red cloth edging and white beads in looped fringes. Ca. 1880-1890, it is 5 in.
wide. $110

Pocotopaug Trading Post, South Windsor, Connecticut

Bag or pocket, Iroquois, very colorful and attractive beading
on black with red fringes, 5 x 6 in., ca. 1850-1860. $350

Pocotopaug Trading Post, South Windsor, Connecticut

Women's dress, Shoshone, pony-beads with buckskin. This superb piece is from the mid-1880s. **$25,000.** *Courtesy Canfield Gallery, Santa Fe, New Mexico.*

Warshirt, Blackfoot, beaded and fringed. This excellent hide artwork is ca. 1875 and in top condition. **$50,000.** *Courtesy Canfield Gallery, Santa Fe, New Mexico.*

Red River Metis style coat and bag, coat size 44 and bag 7 x 10 in. Materials are brain-tanned moose leather, deer hair, beaver fur, pewter buttons covered with quillwork, and loom-woven quillwork on both coat and bag. **Coat: $4,500; Bag: $1,500**. *Artwork by Brent Boyd, Ontario, Canada.*

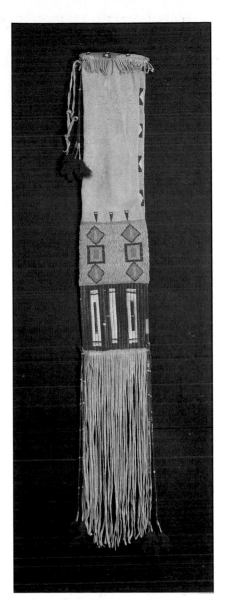

Warshirt, Northern Plains Indian, with colorful and intricate quillwork. This very rare piece is mid-1800s. **$75,000**. *Courtesy Canfield Gallery, Santa Fe, New Mexico.*

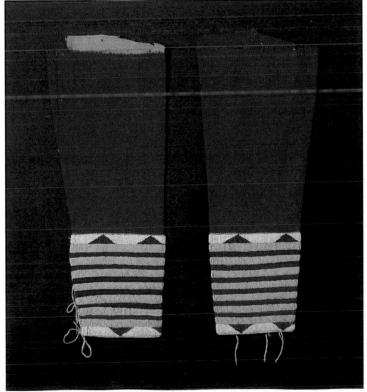

Pipe bag, Arapaho, 36 in. long. Nicely fringed and in bright and pleasing colors, this piece is from the late 1800s. **$6,000**. *Courtesy Canfield Gallery, Santa Fe, New Mexico.*

Women's leggings, Crow, beaded trade-cloth, from the late 1800s. The beading is in top condition. **$3,000**. *Courtesy Canfield Gallery, Santa Fe, New Mexico.*

Beaded decorative sash, fringed, 1/2 in. wide and 45 in. long. Over a dozen different colored beads were used, and nearly 4,000 are in the sash. Good condition. **$75**. *Private collection.*

Medicine bundle case, Crow/Nez Perce, from the mid-1800s. It has fine geometric designs and exceptional fringing. **$7,500**. *Courtesy Canfield Gallery, Santa Fe, New Mexico.*

Martingale or horse collar, Crow, many bold colors, from the 1800s. This is a scarce and fine item. **$15,000**. *Courtesy Canfield Gallery, Santa Fe, New Mexico.*

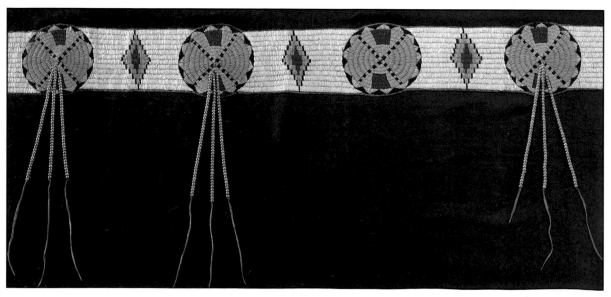

Cheyenne beaded blanket strip, ca. 1870s. **Unlisted.** *Courtesy Morning Star Gallery, Santa Fe, New Mexico.*

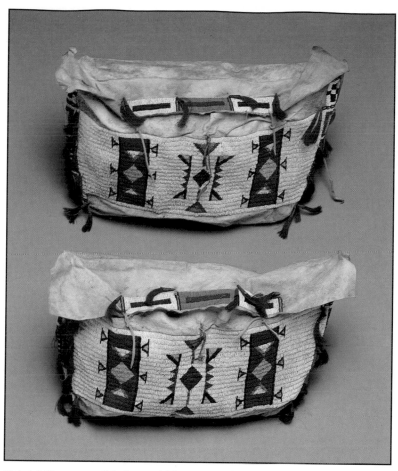

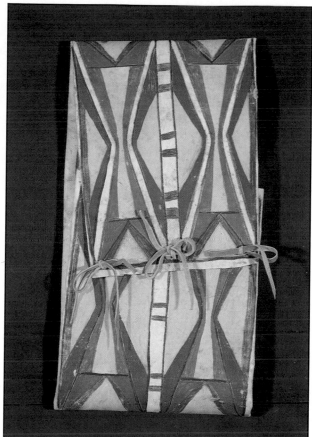

Pair of Sioux possible bags, 19th century. **Unlisted**. *Courtesy Morning Star Gallery, Santa Fe, New Mexico.*

Parfleche, Plateau, from the late 1800s. Done in half a dozen colors, this fine piece measures 14 x 28 in. **$5,000**. *Courtesy Canfield Gallery Santa Fe, New Mexico.*

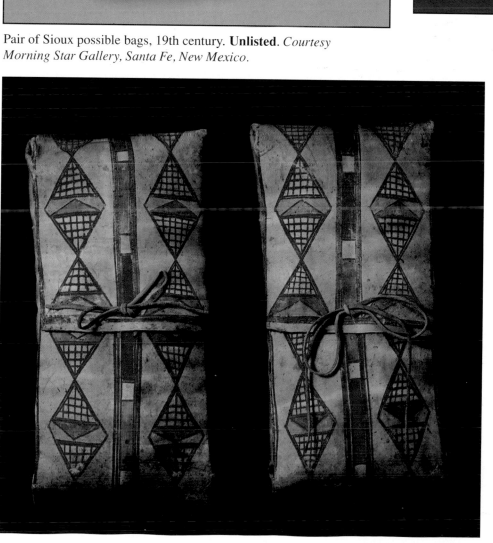

Parfleche, Plateau, each approximately 14 x 28 in. This pair is closely matched and from the late 1800s. **$6,000**. *Courtesy Canfield Gallery, Santa Fe, New Mexico.*

Pipe bag, Sioux, with finely done pictorial motif. This beautiful piece is 29 in. long and from the late 1800s. **$10,000**. *Courtesy Canfield Gallery, Santa Fe, New Mexico.*

Rifle cases (Top to Bottom): Cheyenne, 1870s; Sioux, 1870s; Crow, 1870s. **Unlisted**. *Courtesy Morning Star Gallery, Santa Fe, New Mexico.*

Old Navajo dolls, ca. 1940. Sizes, 6-3/4 x 7-1/4 in. and 10 in. tall. These evidence signs that they were played with frequently. They are trimmed with beads, metal belt, etc. **Small: $250-350; Large: $400-600**. *Courtesy Marquerite and Stewart Kernaghan collection, Bellvue, Colorado.*

Great Lakes region beaded pin-cushion, 5-1/2 in. corner to corner, type sold in Niagara Falls area, early 1900s-1940s. **$60**. *Private collection.*

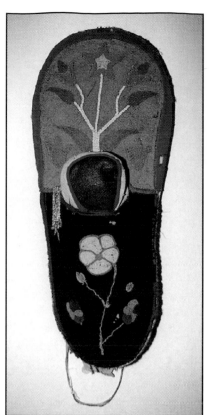

Doll cradle, Nez Perce, ca. 1880-1890. Size is 9 in. wide and 22 in. long. Wooden cradle backing, trade cloth, and trade beads materials. From the Bruce Johnson collection, Marin County, California. **$1,500**. *J. Steve and Anita Shearer, Torrance, California.*

Southern Cheyenne beaded dolls, male and female, large doll 15 in. high. The woman wears a dress and the man a painted coat, while both have beaded leggings. These are exceptional figures with exceptional work. Ca. 1865. **Pair: $22,000.** *Forrest Fenn, Santa Fe, New Mexico.*

Hopi Kachina, 11-3/4 in. high, wood with leather, fur, and feathers. It is from Arizona. **Unlisted.** *Collection of Eugene and Marcille Wing.*

Neo-Revival Navajo textile, contemporary, 30-1/2 x 49-1/2 in. A very graphic banded style blanket, it contains natural indigo green and rich shades of indigo blue. There are also multiple shades of natural cochineal red. **$6,800**. *The Child's Blanket, Highland, California.*

Navajo Germantown yarn blanket, 51-1/4 x 83 in., done in black, green, yellow, and white against red. Ca. 1890. **$14,500**. *David Cook Fine American Art, Denver, Colorado; Jamie Kahn photograph.*

Neo-Revival Navajo pictorial textile, contemporary, 38-1/2 x 44-3/4 in. All natural dyes include indigo and cochineal. This magnificent pictorial is the only rendering of an Anglo-European religious figure known to exist containing indigo and cochineal natural dyes. **$4,500**. *The Child's Blanket, Highland, California.*

3rd Phase Chief's weaving, approximately 4 x 6 ft., stripes and diamonds. This beautiful old blanket is in very good condition for its age, having been made ca. 1890. **Unlisted.** *Dennis R. Phillips, Chicago, Illinois.*

Teec Nos Pos weaving, approximately 4-1/2 x 7 ft., lovely and highly detailed. It is ca. 1910. **Unlisted.** *Dennis R. Phillips, Chicago, Illinois.*

Neo-Revival Navajo pictorial textile, contemporary, 33-3/4 x 51-1/2 in. The trains and houses pictorial contains all natural dyes with alternating bands of natural indigo blue and green, cochineal red and purple, osage orange and cutch brown. **$4,200**. *The Child's Blanket, Highland, California.*

Tlingit feast ladle and basket. **Unlisted**. *Courtesy Morning Star Gallery, Santa Fe, New Mexico.*

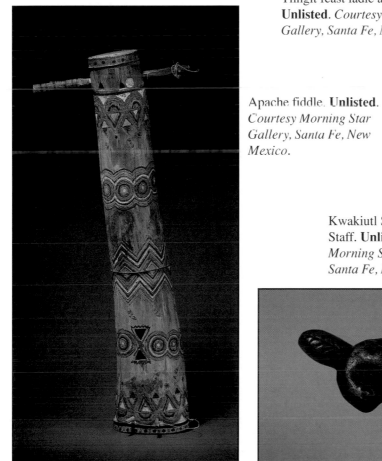

Apache fiddle. **Unlisted**. *Courtesy Morning Star Gallery, Santa Fe, New Mexico.*

Kwakiutl Speaker's Staff. **Unlisted**. *Courtesy Morning Star Gallery Santa Fe, New Mexico.*

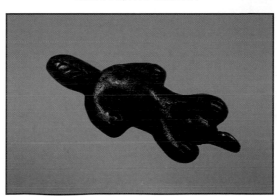

Solid-cast silver beaver, trade-era, touchmarked "TR," 2-3/4 in. long. From Canada, ca. late 1700s. **$450**. *Private collection.*

Iroquois False Faces, standard sizes plus one miniature, carved wood, paint, and horsehair. These have varying dates, ca. 1870-1940. **Each: $850-5,000**. *Traditions, Victor, New York.*

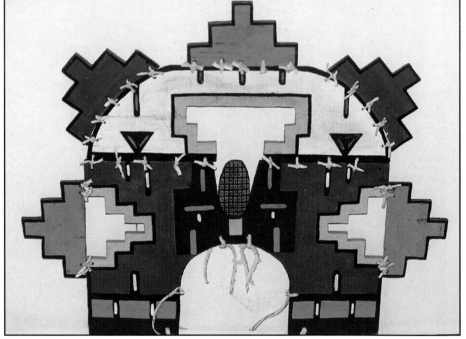

Hopi tableta, 23 in. high, made of cottonwood, deerskin, and commercial pigment. Ca. 1940s. **$650**. *Robert F. Manchester, Schenectady, New York.*

Northwest Coast cedar hawk mask, 13-1/2 in. high, abalone eyes, ca. 1930. **$600**. *Native American Artifacts, Victor, New York.*

Group of Apache baskets. **Unlisted**. *Courtesy Morning Star Gallery, Santa Fe, New Mexico.*

Footed basket, Papago, 4 x 7-1/2 in. top diameter. **$60**. *Private collection.*

Papago basket, Southwest, 3-3/4 x 6-1/2 in. top diameter. **$90**. *Private collection.*

Papago basket, Southwest, 2-1/4 x 7-1/8 in. top diameter. **$75**. *Private collection.*

"One of the most pleasing qualities of North American Indian basketry is its sensory appeal. Good baskets feel and look and even smell natural; they are well-shaped and well-made. The genius of them is that they incorporate art in the utilitarian object, that they make what is useful also pleasing to touch and see."

- Dick Weatherford, Washington State

Papago basket, Southwest, worn, 4-1/8 x 10 in. top diameter. **$75**. *Private collection.*

Hopi basketry plaque, Southwest, 9-1/2 in. in diameter, very fine condition. **$60**. *Private collection.*

Tlingit basket group. **Unlisted**. *Courtesy Morning Star Gallery, Santa Fe, New Mexico.*

Group of Pueblo pottery.
Unlisted. *Courtesy Morning Star Gallery, Santa Fe, New Mexico.*

Ocoma Olla. **Unlisted**. *Courtesy Morning Star Callery, Santa Fe, New Mexico.*

Zuni Olla. **Unlisted**.
*Courtesy Morning
Star Gallery, Santa Fe,
New Mexico.*

Ceremonial pottery
bowl, Zuni, diameter
12 in. This beautiful
ceramic in top condi-
tion is from the late
1800s. **$12,000**. *Cour-
tesy Canfield Gallery,
Santa Fe, New
Mexico.*

Santa Clara pueblo pottery, three fine examples by accomplished potters, described largest to smallest sizes. Incised bowl by Margaret Tafoya; fluted bowl by Helen Shupla; miniature by Nancy Youngblood. **Unlisted**. *Dennis R. Phillips, Chicago, Illinois.*

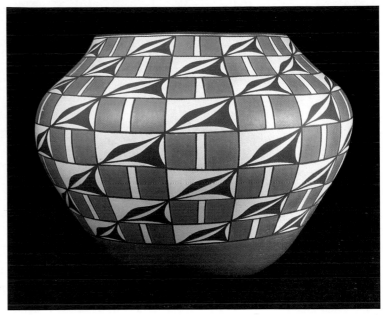

Dominquito S. Tomasita, 5-1/2 x 7-1/2 in. diameter, ca. 1960s-1970?. **$350**. *Indian Rock Arts, Davis, California.*

Laguna, 12-1/2 in., ca. 1989. **$900**. *Indian Rock Arts, Davis, California.*

Acoma, 12 in. diameter, ca. 1950s. **$900**. *Indian Rock Arts, Davis, California.*

Laguna, 3 x 3-1/4 in. diameter, ca. 1920, jar. **$250**. *Indian Rock Arts, Davis, California.*

Acoma, 12 in. diameter, ca. 1940s-1970?. **$1,100**. *Indian Rock Arts, Davis, California.*

Acoma, 10 in. diameter, ca. 1984, Barbara & Joe Cerno. **$1,800**. *Indian Rock Arts, Davis, California.*

Zuni, 10-1/2 in. diameter, ca. 1989, by A. Peynetsa. **$575**. *Indian Rock, Arts, Davis, California.*

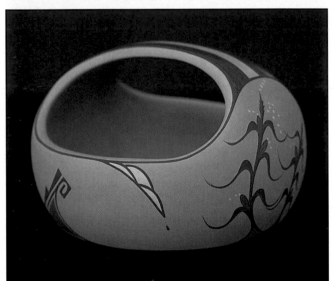

Jemez, Laura Gachupin, ca. 1985. **$795**. *Indian Rock Arts, Davis, California.*

Jemez, Bertha Gachupin, seed jar, 6 in. diameter, ca. 1987. **$395**. *Indian Rock Arts, Davis, California.*

Santa Clara, Lois Gutierrez, ca. 1982. **$1,450**. *Indian Rock Arts, Davis, California.*

Cochiti Storyteller figurine, 8-1/2 in. high. Made by Denise Martinez, contemporary. **$250**. *Tom Noeding, Taos, New Mexico.*

Cochiti pueblo Storyteller figure, pottery piece 10-1/2 in. high. It was done by Pablo Quintana and acquired in 1993. **$400.** *Charles F. and Susan Wood, Ohio.*

Commercial or mold-made pottery form, piggy bank, accented with red and black paint, 6-3/8 in. long. It is marked "Feliz, N. Mex." **$25.** *Charles F. and Susan Wood, Ohio.*

Jemez pueblo Nativity scene figures, three of eight pieces; the tallest is 6 in. Pottery figures are very well-made and painted; done by Linda Fragria and obtained in 1993. **Set of eight: $1,100**. *Charles F. and Susan Wood, Ohio*.

Hopi Kachina, black figure elaborately costumed, ca. 1940. **$3,000**.
Crown & Eagle Antiques, New Hope, Pennsylvania.

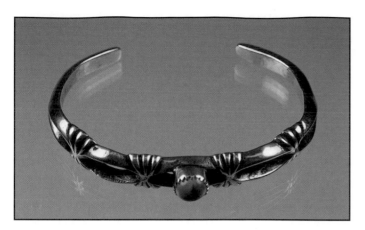

Sandcast silver bracelet, recent, marked "N. TSO." **$140**. *Private collection.*

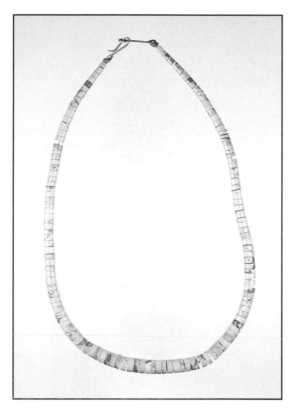

Turquoise necklace, graduated beads, old, 16 in. strand. **$175**. *Private collection.*

Pendant, 3-3/8 in., signed "Effie C. Zuni." **$100**. *Private collection.*

Navajo and Zuni bracelets. Silver and turquoise. **Unlisted.** *Courtesy Morning Star Gallery, Santa Fe, New Mexico.*

14K gold yei pendant on red coral heishi and matching bracelet. Pieces are inlaid with red and pink coral, lapis, and Chinese turquoise; designed by Ray Tracey. **Necklace $7,500.** **Bracelet $7,500.** *Courtesy Ray Tracey, Galleries, Santa Fe, New Mexico.*

14K gold yei pendant on collar. Pendant is inlaid with sugilite, opals, and embellished with diamonds. Diamonds also set in collar; designed by Ray Tracey. **$10,000**. *Courtesy Ray Tracey Galleries, Santa Fe, New Mexico.*

14K gold heartline bear necklace inlaid with lapis, Chinese turquoise, red coral, and diamonds; designed by Ray Tracey. **$18,000**. *Courtesy Ray Tracey Galleries, Santa Fe, New Mexico.*

14K gold yei pendant on seed pearls, bracelet and earrings inlaid with sugilite, opals, and diamonds; designed by Ray Tracey. **Pendant on pearls: $6,000; Bracelet: $7,000; Earrings: $1,200**. *Courtesy Ray Tracey Galleries, Santa Fe, New Mexico.*

14K gold pendant, bracelet, and earrings inlaid with sugilite, pink coral, opals, and diamonds; designed by Ray Tracey. **Pendant: $7,000; Bracelet: $8,000; Earrings: $2,500**. *Courtesy Ray Tracey Galleries, Santa Fe, New Mexico.*

Sterling silver yei earrings inlaid with lapis and opal; designed by Ray Tracey. **$450**. *Courtesy Ray Tracey Galleries, Santa Fe, New Mexico.*

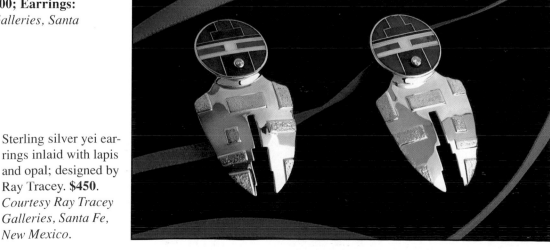

Modern Cherokee pipe, light pink pipestone and sourwood handle, pipe 12-1/2 in. long. North Carolina, 1994. **$60**. *Charles F. and Susan Wood, Ohio.*

Necklace with Thunderbird pendant. Owner's father acquired from an Indian in 1938 by trading string of a dozen large trout. Backing made from an old single-sided record and the bone and turquoise side extensions are glued on with piñon sap. From near Jemez pueblo. **Unlisted**. *Jack Baker collection, Ozark, Missouri; David Capon photograph.*

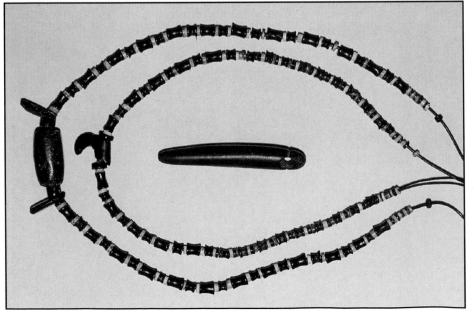

Necklaces of hourglass beads, 1000-2500 BP, bead length 3/16-1/2 in. Beads made of ground and polished black steatite. Quite scarce; ex-collection Johnson. **Each: $300**. Center: stone pendant, 1000-2500 BP, 3-1/4 in. long. Drilled and grooved at the top, it is made of polished dark hardstone. **$100**. Necklaces and pendant are from Contra Costa County, California. *Collection of, and photograph by, Michael W. Hough, California.*

Three stone discoidals. Right: Perforated-center disc, 3-1/8 in. in diameter, possibly from Ohio. **$400**. Center: Large disc, 4-3/8 in. in diameter, from Illinois. **$800**. Left: Very unusual flint disc, 2-1/4 in. in diameter from Tennessee. **$650**. *Photo courtesy Summers Redick, Worthington, Ohio.*

Near-ceremonial class stone pestle, probably Northwest Coast region, prehistoric, of a highly polished dense black material. Piece is 6-3/4 in. long and 3-1/2 in. across at base (larger) end. **$1,100**. *Photo courtesy Summers Redick, Worthington, Ohio.*

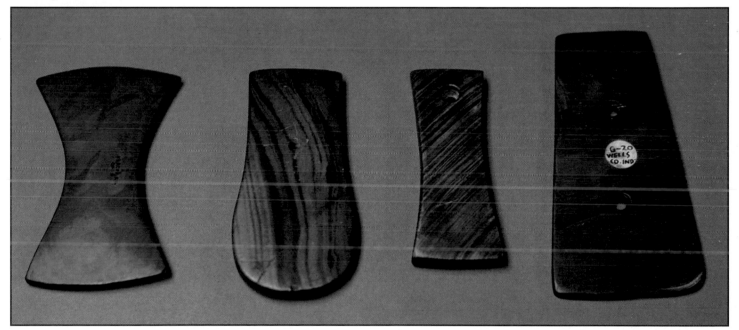

Four slate pieces, prehistoric, of different kinds of banded slate. Left to Right: A biconcave gorget, undrilled, 5 in. long, **$400**; a keyhole-type pendant 5 in. long, very symmetrical, **$600**; a bell-shaped pendant 4-1/2 in. long of very good work style, **$450**; a rectangular two-hole gorget from 6 in. long, with one large and one small end. **$675**. *Photo courtesy Summers Redick, Worthington, Ohio.*

Polished flint spade, 10 in. long and 4-1/4 in. wide. In position photographed, top side is excurvate, bottom side flattish. Piece shows good use-polish. **$450**. *Photo courtesy Summers Redick, Worthington, Ohio.*

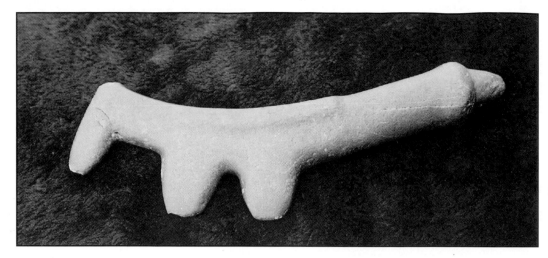

"Slave-killer" axe, 14 in. long, ca. AD 800-1200. This example in animal effigy form has a slate appearance but is made of hardstone. It is pictured in *Indian & Eskimo Artifacts of North America*. This rare object came from the California - Oregon state line area. **$8,500**. *Rainbow Traders, Godfrey, Illinois.*

Celt, (#FJ-10), Iroquoian, ca. 1650-1750. The flared-bit polished celt is made of highly unusual material, Catlinite, and measures 1-1/4 x 5-1/8 in. It came from near Seneca Falls, Seneca County, New York. **$650-1,000**. *Iron Horse collection, Blasdell, New York.*

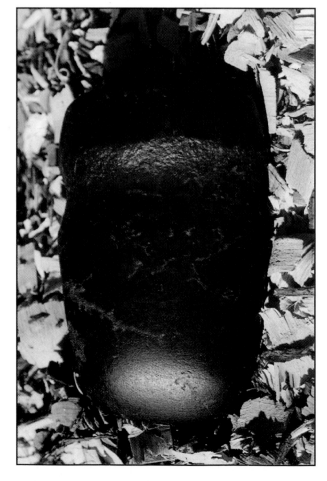

Trophy axe, (#7G), full groove with raised groove ridges. This fine Archaic axe is made of pecked and polished gray hardstone and measures 3-1/4 x 5-1/2 in. high. It is from Pennsylvania. **$650-1,000**. *Iron Horse collection, Blasdell, New York.*

Full-grooved, or 4/4, axe made of near-black hematite or natural iron ore, it has no damage and has good overall polish. This example was found in Cass County, Texas. **$225-300**. *Collection of, and photograph by, Steve Granger, Hallsville, Texas.*

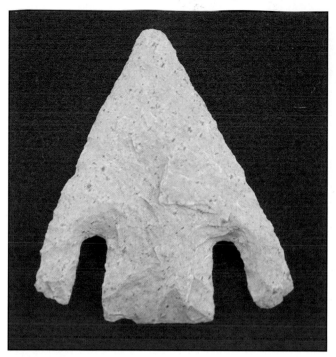

Calf Creek blade, about 2-1/4 in. long, found by owner in Sequoyah County, Oklahoma. These are Early Archaic, ca. 7000 BC. **$195**. *Courtesy James Bruner collection, Oklahoma.*

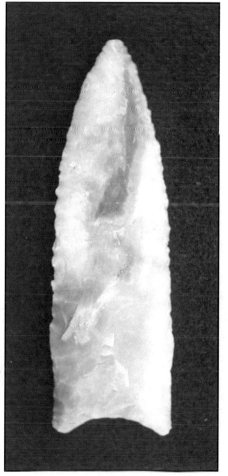

Meserve, Dalton-related and Late Paleo/Early Archaic period, found in Haskell County, Oklahoma, by owner. This piece is 3 in. long. **$300**. *Courtesy James Bruner collection, Oklahoma.*

Dalton, 3-1/2 in. long, Late Paleo/Early Archaic, found in Haskell County, Oklahoma, by owner. Undamaged daltons are not common. **$200**. *Courtesy James Bruner collection, Oklahoma.*

Corner-tang knife, Late Archaic period, found in Muskogee County by owner. These are fairly scarce blades. Length, 3 in. **$350**. *Courtesy James Bruner collection, Oklahoma.*

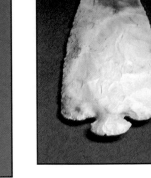

Dovetail blade, over 4 in. long of translucent Flintridge material, white and rust-red. Very slight damage to tip, but fine form and superb chipping. **$400**. *Photo courtesy Mike Miller, Lancaster, Ohio.*

Fine flint blades of exceptional size and workstyle. Left to Right: 4-1/2 in. long beveled-edge type, **$450**; 6 in. long turkeytail, **$650**; base-notched blade 4-3/8 in. long, **$400**.

Plainview, Late Paleo/Early Archaic, found by the owner in Haskell County, Oklahoma. Length, 3 in. **$300**. *James Bruner collection, Oklahoma.*

Two flint celts or adzes, one 8-1/4 in. long, the other 9-1/4 in. long. Of cream-brown flint, both are highly polished. **Each: $425**. *Photo courtesy Summers Redick, Worthington, Ohio.*

Plainview, 2-3/4 in. long, fine point or blade found in Haskell County, Oklahoma, by owner. **$300**. *James Bruner collection, Oklahoma.*

Selection of Guilford-Type Points, averaging 2-3/4 in. long. Of various types of chert and flint, all are from the North Carolina region. **Each: $20**. *Photo courtesy Summers Redick, Worthington, Ohio.*

Typical point and blade types found by owner in eastern. Oklahoma. **Unlisted**. *James Bruner collection, Oklahoma.*

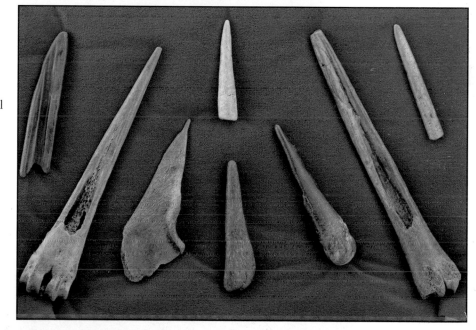

Bone awls, all found in Haskell County, Oklahoma, by the owner. **Frame: $200**. *James Bruner collection, Oklahoma.*

Fine frame of typical points and blades found in east-central Oklahoma by the owner. **Unlisted**. *James Bruner collection, Oklahoma.*

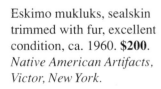

Eskimo (Inuit) doll, 12 in. high. Material for the costume is sealskin and rabbit fur, while the face is ivory. In top condition. Alaska, ca. 1920-1930. **$250**. *J. Steve and Anita Shearer, Torrance, California.*

Eskimo mukluks, sealskin trimmed with fur, excellent condition, ca. 1960. **$200**. *Native American Artifacts, Victor, New York.*

Pocket or bag, Iroquois, Great Lakes area, cross motif against red cloth, 3 x 4 in. It is ca. 1860-1870. $85

Pocotopaug Trading Post, South Windsor, Connecticut

Bag, Iroquois, Great Lakes area beadwork, colorful floral designs. It is ca.1875-1885 and 6 x 7 in. $200-250

Pocotopaug Trading Post, South Windsor, Connecticut

Bandolier bag, Great Lakes region, floral designs in beadwork over cloth. Ca. 1880.   Museum quality

Morning Star Gallery, Santa Fe, New Mexico

Bag or pocket, Osage, heavily beaded, 6-3/4 x 8 in. It is from Kansas and ca. 1860-1880. $185

Pocotopaug Trading Post, South Windsor, Connecticut

Sioux knife and sheath, 11 in. tall, fully beaded on side, and ca. 1880.   D-$1,400

Photo courtesy Winona Trading Post, Santa Fe-Pierre & Sylvia Bovis

Kiowa strike-a-lite bag, a flint-and-steel container. Piece is 8 in. high, nicely beaded, and with cone "tinklers" top and bottom. With suspension thong, ca. 1880.   D-$900

Photo courtesy Winona Trading Post, Santa Fe-Pierre & Sylvia Bovis

Cheyenne beaded pouch, beaded both sides on buffalo, 3 x 4 in. Half a dozen different colors were used for the wheel-like design. Ca. 1880. $800

Private collection

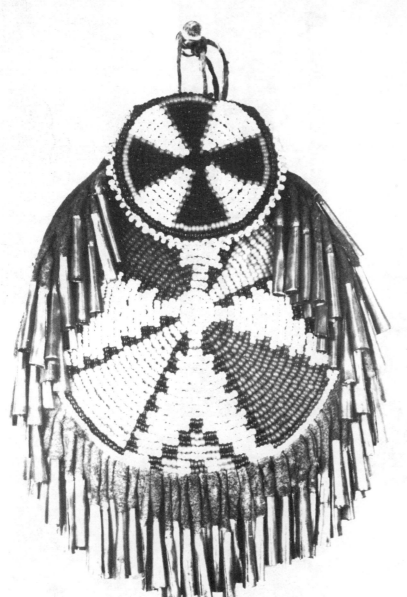

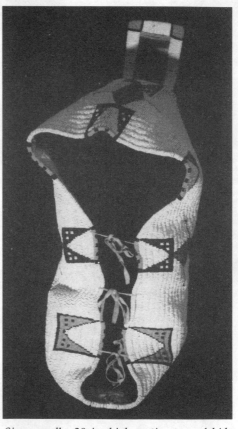

Sioux cradle, 20 in. high, native tanned hide with glass beads. In very fine condition and nicely designed. Ca. 1890. $11,500

David Cook Fine American Art, Denver, Colorado; Jamie Kahn photograph

Apache beaded bag, 7-1/2 in. long. Piece has tin cone jangles, and is ca. 1880.   *Museum quality*

Nedra Matteucci's Fenn Galleries, Santa Fe, New Mexico

Cheyenne or Sioux knife sheath, 12 in. long, elk hide over liner. Multi-colored beads and quillwork fringed danglers make this an ornate object from the 1870s. $6,800

Private collection

Apache beaded pouch, 3-1/2 x 4-1/2 in. plus tassels with brass beads. The beadwork in red, white, and blue seed beads has an American flag representation. In excellent condition, this piece is year 1912. $450

T.R.H. collection, Indiana

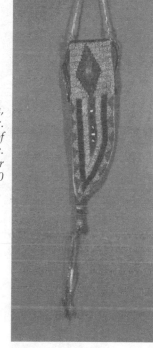

Cheyenne or Arapaho knife sheath, 11 in. long, beaded hide over liner. The rare case has a record in beads of coups and kills on the sheath reverse. This is documented from the year 1868. $10,000

Private collection

Cheyenne or Sioux knife sheath, 8 in. long, beaded both sides. Sinew-sewn, the sheath has small faceted glass beads that sparkle. In top condition, it is ca. 1870-1880s. $6,000

Private collection

Central Plains knife sheath, 9-1/2 in. long, hide over buffalo liner. This beautiful case with geometric designs in six colors is ex-collection Fenn and ca. 1880. $6,000

Private collection

Blackfoot carrier or cradle, Blackfoot from Alberta, 16 x 40 in. with fringe, wool, canvas, and glass beads. The beadwork is very attractive and the carrier is in fine condition. Ca. 1890. $5,500

Historic Interiors, Sorrento, British Columbia, Canada

Crow wooden cradleboard, three cutout hearts at top, cloth wrap with beaded floral design. This fine piece measures 9 x 20 in. and is ca. 1905. Montana. $1,250

Native American Artifacts, Victor, New York

Sioux quilled doctor's bag or purse, with quilled drops and hawk bells. It is 14 in. long and colors are red, yellow, and purple. South Dakota, ca. 1890. $8,500

Forrest Fenn, Santa Fe, New Mexico

Iroquois beaded pouch, side two, with bird on an arrow and two American flags. Early 19th century. $3,500

Crown & Eagle Antiques, New Hope, Pennsylvania

Cree possible bag, lined, black velvet with twelve bead colors. Size is 17 x 19 in. on the attractive floral-decorated piece, ca. 1880-1890. $740

Native American Artifacts, Victor, New York

Iroquois beaded pouch, side one, a unique pictorial presentation of Indian life. Shown is a man with bow and arrow, a tepee, and woman using a stump mortar. Early 19th century. $3,500

Crown & Eagle Antiques, New Hope, Pennsylvania

Oneida Grand River bag, black velvet and beads in many colors, ca. 1820-1890. This fine bag came from the Tonawanda Reservation, western New York. $250-350

Iron Horse collection, Blasdell, New York

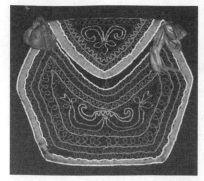

Seneca Grand River bag, black velvet, red ribbon, and beads. It is ca. 1820-1860 and from western New York. $300-400

Iron Horse collection, Blasdell, New York

Micmac Grand River bag, red cloth, green ribbon, and beads in floral patterns. Ca. 1820-1890, the bag is from the Tonawanda Reservation, western New York. $275-350

Iron Horse collection, Blasdell, New York

Kiowa shot bag, 2-1/2 x 4 in., buffalo hide, sinew, beadwork, and brass button. The reverse is also beaded, in horse-track pattern. Ca. 1880-1900. $400

Frank Bergevin, Port of Call, Alexandria Bay, New York

Iroquois beaded pockets, ca. 1860-1880, left to right:

Pocket, 6 x 6 in., felt, satin, canvas, beadwork, New York state. $190

Pocket, 4 x 5 in., felt, satin, canvas, beadwork, New York state. $110

Frank Bergevin, Port of Call, Alexandria Bay, New York

Beaded bag, 11 x 12 in. Blue background with Nez Perce woman beaded as design. Well-done piece and scarce pictorial bag. Excellent condition.　　G-$400

Beaded tobacco bag, average condition.　　D-$425

Beaded bag, 6-1/2 in. long, Woodland floral patterns. Beaded front and back on black trade-cloth velvet. Good condition; collected in the Great Lakes area.　　C-$400

Beaded bag, Iroquois, 6-1/2 x 7-1/2 in.. Beaded both sides on velveteen with red cloth binding. Good specimen; ca. 1920.　　G-$260

Strike-a-light bag, Sioux, 3-1/2 x 6 in.; flint and steel. Beaded one side, with carrying strap; good condition.　　C-$365

Beaded bag, Apache, buckskin with typical bead fringe and geometric designs.　　G-$240

Plateau bag, 11 in. high and 9 in. wide. Fully beaded using glass beads; floral design.　　G-$330

Carry-all bag, Woodlands Indian, 11 in. high and 11-1/2 in. wide. Rounded bottom and lower edge of closing flap. Beadwork design on black velvet. Had carrying strap, now missing. Very good condition; very few beads gone.　　C-$525

Beaded bag, 5-1/2 x 6 in. Caddo, fully beaded including flap and handle. Buckskin with cloth lining. Piece has an unusual looped bead fringe; ca. 1890.　　G-$265

Beaded belt pouch, Plateau area.　　A-$100

Strike-a-light bag, beaded in Plains Indian style.　　D-$235

Beaded bag, 9 x 10 in.; zipper top with handles. Beads used to make bag are 40-50 years old. Gray background with stylized floral designs; excellent condition.　　G-$280

Medicine bag, Plains Indian, worn around the neck. Rare item; ca. 1880.　　D-$295

Tobacco bag, bead designs of standing Indian, and American flag. Slight damage.　　G-$375

Beaded container, Apache, 8 in. wide and 5 in. high. Black on buff designs.　　C-$190

BEADED BOTTLES

Beaded bottle, 28 in. tall. Done by the Paiute Indians after they ceased doing basket work. Extra-large specimen. White background with variety of geometric designs. Perfect condition.　　G-$850

Beaded bottle, very small, 2-1/4 in. high and 3/4 in. wide. With top, specimen is done on yellow beaded background with black and green geometric designs. Perfect.　　G-$135

Beaded bottle, 18 in. high. It has a zig-zag pattern done in red, white, blue and black beads; very attractive.　　G-$515

Beaded bottle, 5 in. high. Beaded on small perfume bottle. Fully beaded, including bottom, with early crystal beads. Beads have red and blue geometric designs.　　G-$165

Nez Perce beaded bottle, fully beaded in green, blue, white, and red seed beads over leather covering bottle and stopper. It is 5-1/2 in. high and ca. 1880s. $165

Frank Bergevin, Port of Call, Alexandria Bay, New York

Plains Indian fetish, 6-1/2 in. long; lizard form, but more nearly resembles a horned toad. Beaded design on top, beaded strip around edges, limbs and tail.   C-$565

Beaded turtle umbilical fetish, for twins; two turtles are fastened together. Sioux Indian and extremely rare.   G-$925

Lizard fetish, 6 in. long and 2 in. wide. A Sioux piece, it has blue beads on greasy-yellow background and two horsehair dangles on each end. One seam coming apart but easily repaired. Excellent condition; ca. 1890. G-$415

Turtle fetish, 4 x 2-1/2 in. Multi-colored beadwork on commercial leather; done on reservation in the 1920s. A few beads missing, but in excellent condition.   G-$165

Turtle umbilical fetish, a Sioux beaded piece. Old and in good condition.   G-$400

MISCELLANEOUS BEADED AND QUILLED PIECES

Chippewa beaded panel, floral designs done on velvet. Possibly a pillow cover originally. Old and fine condition.   G-$285

Crow beaded panel, 12 x 12 in. Red trade cloth. Floral motif; considerable moth damage and some beads missing.   G-$140

Beaded necklace, probably Ottawa. Piece is 18 in. long and 3/4 in. wide at sides and back, 2 in. wide at lower portion. Small beads in red, green, and yellow. Very well done and unusual.   C-$400

Beaded cigarette case, Chippewa; contemporary. D-$30

Sioux cuffs, 5 x 10 in., with 4 in. of fringe on edges. Fully beaded; light blue background with red, blue, and yellow geometric designs. Excellent condition; ca. 1930s. G-$285

Beaded blanket strip, Northern Cheyenne; flag designs.   A-$795

Crow belt, 39 in. long and 2-3/4 in. wide. Standard Crow stitch and colors in lavender, blue, yellow, and red.

It is on harness leather and has brass tacks. Some beadwork is loose and some missing, but in generally good condition. Pre-1890.   G-$275

Athabascan beaded hair ties.   A-$18

Beaded watch fob, Plains Indian; ca. 1920   D-$40

Beaded belt, Sioux, 28 in. long and 2 in. wide. Fully beaded and in fine condition.   G-$400

Beaded sash, Woodland loom-beaded specimen.   D-$160

Contour beadwork, four fine and old pieces; sold as one lot.   A-$110

Choker, 14 in. long and 3/4 in. wide; fully beaded. Made by Blackfoot Indians sometime prior to 1930 when it was collected. An original scalp may be hanging from this choker, making it a very rare piece.   G-$385

Arm bands, full beadwork over rawhide on these Sioux items.   D-$165

Beaded cuffs, pair, Yakima.   A-$110

Beaded strip, Cheyenne, 25 in. long and 1-3/4 in. wide. Sinew-sewn beadwork in excellent condition; ca. 1900.   G-$295

Beaded head band, Sioux, 20 in. long, with beads sewn on buckskin. Ends have ties.   G-$75

Beaded bag front, rest of bag gone; 5 x 5-1/2 in. Beadwork is excellent and complete. Done in old cutglass beads, depicting bird motif. A good basis for a new pipe bag.   G-$60

Beaded dress yoke, Apache.   A-$35

Beaded arm bands, pair, Ponca. Fully beaded on trade cloth; ca. 1890.   D-$200

Bugle bead vest, very old.   A-$600

Baby bonnet, Sioux; fully beaded and nice condition.   G-$650

Beaded belt, 33 in. long and 2-3/4 in. wide. Fully beaded with overlaid stitch, not loomed. White background, geometric designs in red, yellow, blue, and green beads, backed with cloth. Not too old, but in excellent condition.   G-$295

Ceremonial spoon, early 1900s, 16 in. long. The wooden handle is decorated with trade cloth and glass beads. Northern Plains. $300

Blue Coyote Trading Post, Nashville, Indiana; Paul McCreary photograph

Apache beaded belt set, native-tanned hide with glass beads, copper and brass. Ca. AD 1910-1915, this women's set includes 7 in. knife sheath, 8 in. awl case and 3 x 3 in. pouch. Arizona. Set, $900

Blue Coyote Trading Post, Nashville, Indiana; Paul McCreary photograph

Beaded purse, glass beads on oilskin in half a dozen colors, 6-1/2 x 10 in. Ojibway, this is an attractive "railroad bag" beaded both sides, ca. 1940s. Eastern Canada. $450

Blue Coyote Trading Post, Nashville, Indiana; Paul McCreary photograph

Storage bag, Arapaho, ca. 1880-1890. It is 10 in. high and 11 in. wide, and is made of elk hide with decorations in seed beads. The moon and star are Ghost Dance symbols on this unusual bag from a Montana collection. $3,000

J. Steve and Anita Shearer, Torrance, California

Tobacco bag, Northern Cheyenne, ca. 1860-1870. The bag measures 6 in. wide and 21 in. long. This rare piece is made of deer or antelope hide and has blue and white pony beads and tin cones on the leather fringes. It was collected at Taos pueblo, New Mexico. $3,000

J. Steve and Anita Shearer, Torrance, California

Plains whetstone case, 2-1/2 in. wide and 6-1/2 in. high, ca. 1860-1880. Nicely beaded in colors against a white ground, materials are buffalo hide and trade beads. This piece is Northern Sioux or Arapaho. $750

J. Steve and Anita Shearer, Torrance, California

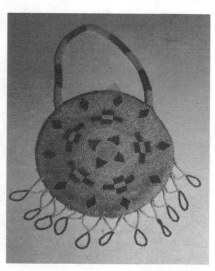

Round bag, Yakima, ca. 1900. This example is 9 in. in diameter and has a cloth interior, with exterior covered with seed beads. It is from a collection in Oregon. $500

Steve and Anita Shearer, Torrance, California

Saddle bag, one of a pair, Crow Indian. It is ca. 1890-1910 and each is 6 in. wide and 7 in. high. Material is cowboy boot top leather, muslin cloth, and trade beads, and the horse is done against a ground of blue beads. Crow Agency, Montana.   Pair, $3,000

J. Steve and Anita Shearer, Torrance, California

Crow purse and mirror bag, Montana, respectively 4 x 7 in. and 6 x 23 in. (with fringe). An old purse and mirror with hide and glass beads, these are ca. 1900-1920. Set, $1,500

Historic Interiors, Sorrento, British Columbia, Canada

Ration ticket pouch or holder, Apache, ca. 1880-1890. It measures 4 in. wide and is 8 in. high; it was made of deer hide decorated with trade beads and tin cones. This unusual and scarce item was obtained at an antiques show at Glendale, California. $500

J. Steve and Anita Shearer, Torrance, California

Crow quirt, 14 in. long plus whip, wooden handle with wristband of trade cloth, brass bell, and glass beads. Ornate piece is ca. 1880. $6,500

David Cook Fine American Art, Denver, Colorado; Jamie Kahn photograph

Historic Interiors, Sorrento, British Columbia, Canada

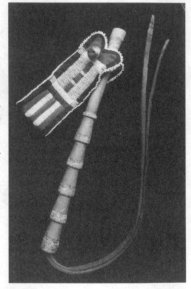

Tlingit wall pocket, hide and glass beads with double-headed bird, 9 x 13 in. The pocket is ca. 1890. $425

Historic Interiors, Sorrento, British Columbia, Canada

Great Lakes region beaded sash, loom-beaded with yarn and glass beads, 33 in. long. This example has geometric designs in six colors and yarn fringes. It is ca. 1900. $900-1,200

Terry Schafer, American Indian Art & Antiques, Marietta, Ohio

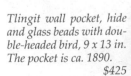

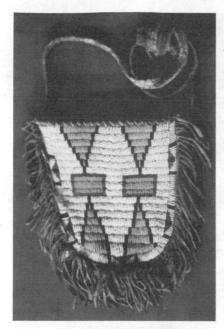

Cheyenne shot pouch, 6 x 7 in., buffalo leather and glass beads in black, yellow, red, and blue against white. This pouch is ca. 1870s. $6,500

Private collection

Yakima cradleboard top, beautiful beadwork with red and yellow roses and butterfly, all against a white ground. The strong colors give a three-dimensional look to the beadwork, ca. 1920-1940. $975

Indian Territory, Tucson, Arizona

Northern Plains Indian coin pouch, 2-1/2 x 3-1/4 in., envelope type. This piece has seed beads in five colors and is beaded front and back. With certificate of authenticity, the coin pouch is year 1910. $200

T.R.H. collection, Indiana

Plains Indian umbilical amulet, 2-1/2 x 5 in., hand-sewn leather with red, white, light and dark blue seed beads. An American flag is depicted within the diamond-shaped border. Early 1900s. $450

T.R.H. collection, Indiana

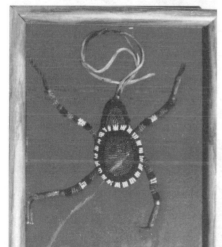

Beaded amulet, early 1900s, 3 x 3 in. It is made of native-tanned hide with glass beads. This is a Northern Plains item, from Montana. $300

Blue Coyote Trading Post, Nashville, Indiana; Pat Nolan photograph

Quilled birchbark heart-shaped box, 5-1/2 in. across, birchbark, quills, sweetgrass, and thread. It is ca. 1900 and from Ontario, Canada. $65

Frank Bergevin, Port of Call, Alexandria Bay, New York

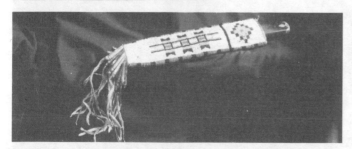

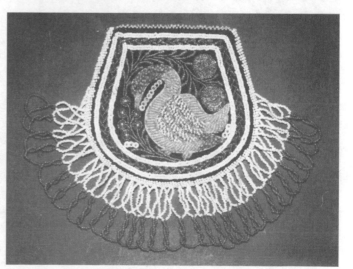

Beaded knife sheath, Sioux, early 1900s, 12 in. long. It is made of native tanned hide and is decorated with glass beads. $450

Blue Coyote Trading Post, Nashville, Indiana; Paul McCreary photograph

Iroquois pictorial pouch with waterbird centerpiece and florals, beautiful condition, ca. 1890s. $2,850

Crown & Eagle Antiques, New Hope, Pennsylvania

Loom-beaded belt, Northern Plateau area. A-$65

Beaded strip or belt, 46 in. long and 3 in. wide. Sinew sewn on buckskin in yellow, blue and red. G-$425

Wrist cuffs, beaded pair, Plains Indian. D-$145

Frame of seed beads, 8 x 12 in. Multi-colored seed beads in floral motif, on trade cloth. D-$75

Beaded pillow, Chippewa, 6-1/2 in. square. Has floral beadwork designs with beaded edging in seven colors. Quite unusual. D-$135

Beaded armbands, Flathead Indian. A-$38

Beaded headband, Sioux, beads on buckskin; ca. 1900. D-$80

Armbands, Blackfoot, 10-/2 in. long and 1 in. wide quilled dangles. Collected in Montana in 1932, but much older. Pair. G-$185

Beaded headband, loom-beaded Cree; ca. 1885 D-$85

Pin cushion, Chippewa, 8 in. long. Piece has floral design in very small (18/0) beads, red, dark green, blue, pink, and yellow. G-$130

Headband, Sioux, beaded with string hair-drops. D-$150

Beaded belt, Indian group unknown, 30 in. long and 3 in. wide. Loomed work; white background with seven deer woven into the design. G-$325

Suggested Reading

Whiteford, Andrew H. *North American Indian Arts.* New York: Golden Press, 1970.

Duncan, Kate C. *Northern Athapaskan Art: A Beadwork Tradition.* Seattle: University of Washington Press, 1989.

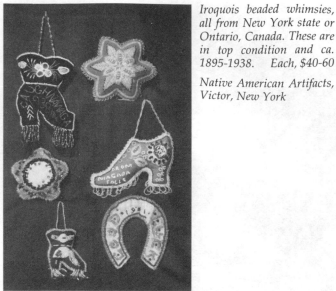

Iroquois beaded whimsies, all from New York state or Ontario, Canada. These are in top condition and ca. 1895-1938.   Each, $40-60

Native American Artifacts, Victor, New York

Mohawk beaded watch holder, used at night to hold a watch upright so that the sleepy owner could see the time at a glance. Leaf design, 5-1/4 x 9 in., ca. 1890. $175

Native American Artifacts, Victor, New York

Woman's purse, Sioux, fully beaded, 4 x 8in., ca. 1880. $1,000

Freya's Collectibles, Banff, Alberta, Canada

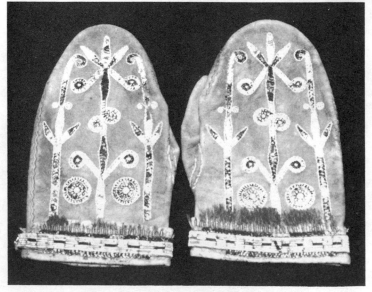

Quilled hide mittens, Eastern Great Lakes, Huron (?), with porcupine quills, tin cones, and dyed animal hair. Ca. 1750. $5,000

Private collection, photo by John McLaughlin

Beaded bag, 2-1/2 x 4 in., the beading done in brown, green, and white on one side and brown, blue, black, and white on the opposite side. The leather is Indian-tanned. $200-250

Collection of David G. & Barbara J. Shirley

Quilled birchbark boxes, Mohawk, contemporary, container with beaver design 7 in. long. These are well-made and nicely decorated. Each, $75-175

Pocotopaug Trading Post, South Windsor, Connecticut

Cap, beaded brimless Iroquois in classic form, blue velvet and colored glass beads. It is 3 x 7-1/4 in. in diameter, Six Nations, Canada, and ca. 1870. $600

Pat & Dave Summers, Native American Artifacts, Victor, New York

Loom-beaded sash, Winnebago, very early 1900s. It is beaded in green and yellow against white and is very heavy. This fine piece is 90 in. long. $850

Larry Lantz, First Mesa, South Bend, Indiana

Beaded sash, Winnebago, early 1900s. It is 1-1/4 x 68 in., with blue beading on a white ground. $225

Larry Lantz, First Mesa, South Bend, Indiana

Knife sheath, Chippewa, ca. 1890-1910. It is 4 x 18-1/2 in., with attractive appliqué beadwork, floral design, in red, brown, blue, crystal, orange, and two shades of green on a white beaded background. There are twenty-five metal cone suspensions. This is an exhibition, dance or ceremonial item as the sheath does not have a knife opening. $675

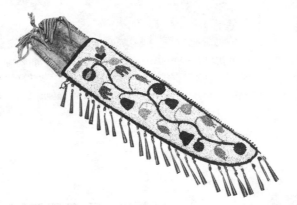

Sherman Holbert collection, Fort Mille Lacs, Onamia, Minnesota

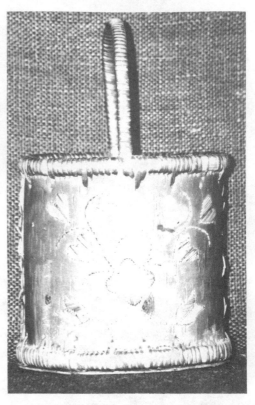

Quilled birch-bark basket, basswood handle, quilled floral and hearts design. Good condition, the box is 6 x 7 x 7 in., Chippewa, and ca. 1900. $200-250

Marguerite L. Kernaghan collection; photograph by Marguerite L. and Stewart W. Kernaghan, Bellvue, Colorado

Apron (dance costume), Chippewa, Leech Lake Reservation, Minnesota. Ca. 1920s, it is 18 x 20 in. and black velveteen beaded in a floral pattern of red, white, blue, green, and yellow seed beads. Edging is yarn with pink piping. $175

Sherman Holbert collection, Fort Mille Lacs, Onamia, Minnesota

Knife case, Chippewa, hide, wood, cloth, and floral beadwork. It is 14 in. long and ca. 1900. $1,200

Private collection, photo by John McLaughlin

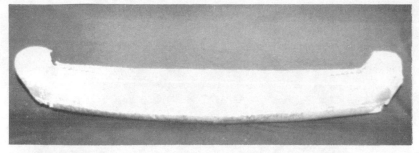

Model canoe, birchbark, with porcupine quill designs. It is a large 42 in. long, ca. 1910, and ex-coll. Casterline. $650

Pat & Dave Summers, Native American Artifacts, Victor, New York

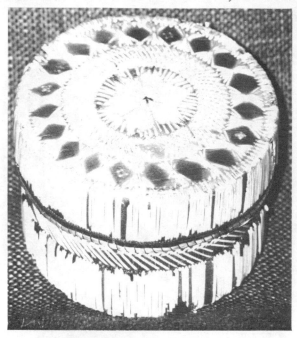

Quilled birchbark box, Chippewa, many quills missing. This 3-3/4 x 5-3/4 in. box is ca. 1900.
$150-225

Marguerite L. Kernaghan collection; photograph by Marguerite L. and Stewart W. Kernaghan, Bellvue, Colorado

Fine Sioux beaded saddle blanket, leather, 25 in. wide and 46 in. long. Excellent designs, well-balanced piece, ca. 1880.   D-$2,000

Photo courtesy Winona Trading Post, Santa Fe-Pierre & Sylvia Bovis

Winnebago beaded bandolier bag, 36 in. long and 18 in. wide, beaded floral motifs. Note the superb condition of this excellent example of Indian art, ca. 1880.   D-$1,600

Photo courtesy Winona Trading Post, Santa Fe-Pierre & Sylvia Bovis

Beaded purse, 5 in. long, not counting strap. Tourist item, Southwestern states and possibly Apache work. Ca. 1950.   C-$55

Private collection

Small Delaware beaded purse, 6 in. in diameter, with nicely balanced floral design on front. About 100 years old, it is ca. 1870-80. D-$325

Photo courtesy Winona Trading Post, Santa Fe-Pierre & Sylvia Bovis

Baby-carrier, Cheyenne, done on hide with cloth, beads, and bells. This fine piece is ca. 1880. $3,000-4,000

Private collection; photo by John McLaughlin

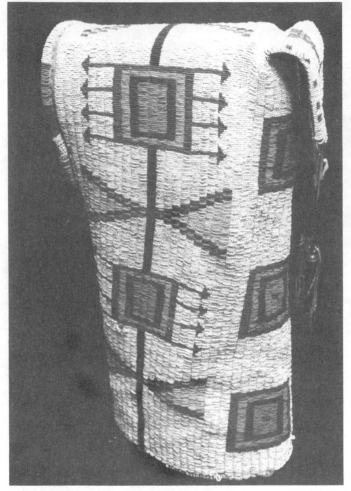

Baby-carrier, fully-beaded, in hide, metal, cloth, beads, and bells. This Sioux artwork is ca. 1875. $4,000

Private collection; photo by John McLaughlin

Beaded purse with ribbon handle, fine floral beading on both sides, Iroquois. This excellent work is 7 in. square, from Quebec, Canada, and ca. 1880. $525

Pat & Dave Summers, Native American Artifacts, Victor, New York

Beaded purse, Woodlands, with ribbon handle and lovely floral beading on both sides. This piece is 5 in. square and ca. 1875. $150

Pat & Dave Summers, Native American Artifacts, Victor, New York

Plateuu bug, beaded, Nez Perce, 10 x 12 in., floral pattern, from the 1890s. Fine condition. $475

Larry Lantz, First Mesa, South Bend, Indiana

Pocket, Iroquois, Great Lakes area beadwork ca. 1885-1895, beading done on black and red cloth. It is 3-1/2 x 4 in. $100

Pocotopaug Trading Post, South Windsor, Connecticut

Beaded bags.

Left: woman's possible bag, Sioux, beaded border and twisted beaded handle, 4-1/2 x 6 in., 1890s. $285
Right: woman's bag, Oglala Sioux, brain-tanned, beaded both sides, 8 x 8 in. $300

Larry Lantz, First Mesa, South Bend, Indiana

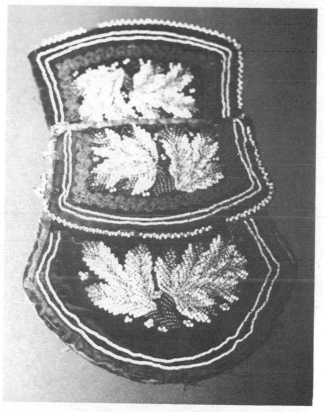

Beaded purse, early Tuscarora, with floral design on both sides. This 7-1/2 in. square purse is from the Tuscarora reservation and ca. 1865. $300

Pat & Dave Summers, Native American Artifacts, Victor, New York

Knife case, Seminole, alligator hide, buckskin, and beads. This unusual and fine piece is ca. 1860. Museum quality

Private collection, photo by John McLaughlin

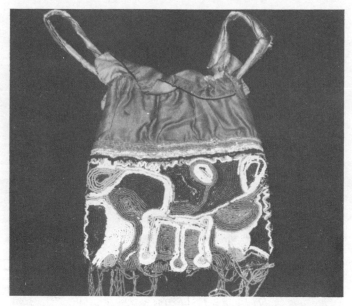

Lady's bag, Seminole, silk, cloth, and beadwork, ca. 1850. Museum quality

Private collection, photo by John McLaughlin

Plains items.

Right: baby carrier, Cheyenne, with umbilical fetish. It is wood, cloth, hide, beads, tacks and paint, ca. 1870. $5,000 Lower left: fetish, Nez Perce, beaded fringes. Unlisted

Private collection, photo by John McLaughlin

Bag, Iroquois, very attractive beading in many colors against black with red edging. Ca. 1875-1885. $225-300

Pocotopaug Trading Post, South Windsor, Connecticut

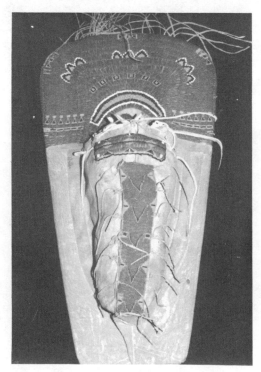

Baby carrier, Ute, wood and hide, decorated with paint and beading. This excellent work is ca. 1880. $3,500

Private collection, photo by John McLaughlin

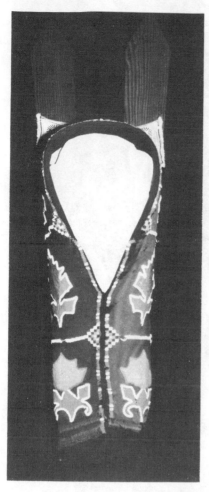

Baby carrier, Kiowa, consisting of wood, tacks, hide, cloth, and beadwork. This high-quality piece is ca. 1890. $10,000

Private collection, photo by John McLaughlin

Bandolier bag, Ojibwa, very fine beadwork throughout, 26 x 48 in. It is ca. 1890. $5,500

Freya's Collectibles, Banff, Alberta, Canada

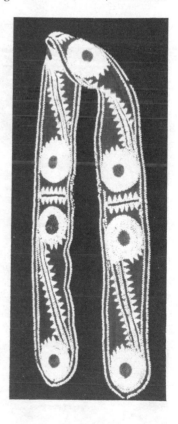

Bandolier bag, British Columbia, Canada, bag size 6 x 9 in. Done with bird, geometric, and floral designs against red, it is ca. 1930s. $225-300

Pocotopaug Trading Post, South Windsor, Connecticut

Sash, Choctaw, red stroud, black braid, and interesting beadwork design. Ca. 1850. $1,200

Private collection, photo by John McLaughlin

Bandolier bags, finely decorated and in superb condition, both ca. 1870. Each, $3,000

Private collection; photo by John McLaughlin

Sash, Seminole, wool cloth, red yarn, ribbon, and beads, ca. 1850. $3,000

Private collection, photo by John McLaughlin

Beaded octopus bag, Tlingit, contemporary, 22 in. long. $1,200

Freya's Collectibles, Banff, Alberta, Canada

Winnebago beaded sashes.

Top: 38 in. long with ties, red, green, yellow, and black on white, early 1900s. $160
Bottom: 36 in. long, red, green, and brown against white, 1890s. $210

Larry Lantz, First Mesa, South Bend, Indiana

Cuffs, fully beaded, Winnebago. The beads are loomed and mounted on leather, well-worn but beads in place. Size each is 3-1/4 x 10 1/2 in., and period is ca. 1910-1920. $700-1,000 pair

Marguerite L. Kernaghan collection; photograph by Marguerite L. and Stewart W. Kernaghan, Bellvue, Colorado

Garrison cap, men's size, beaded in many colors. This outstanding Iroquois work is in pristine condition and is 11-1/2 in. long. It is ca. 1850-1870 and from Ontario, Canada. $700

Pat & Dave Summers, Native American Artifacts, Victor, New York

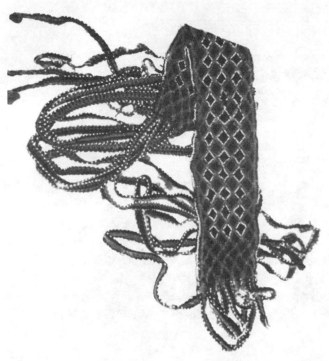

Sash, Creek or Cherokee, yarn with beads in diamond design. Ca.
1850. $2,000

Private collection, photo by John McLaughlin

Cloth panel with tassels, beaded floral design, Woodlands
region. This pristine and well-done piece is 14 x 21-1/2 in.
and ca. 1890. Highest quality. $1,250

*Pat & Dave Summers, Native American Artifacts, Victor,
New York*

Glengary hat, Iroquois, multi-colored beads on black with red
ribbon trim and ties. This is a fine early piece. Unusual. $450

Michael F. Slasinski, Saginaw, Michigan

Whimsies, Iroquois, Great Lakes area beadwork.

Left: pillow dated 1924, 6 x 6 in. $75
Right: shoe form with delicate beading. $55

*Pocotopaug Trading Post, South Windsor,
Connecticut*

Puye Cliff Dwellings, Santa Clara Indian Reservation, New Mexico. This is a series of cave-like rooms excavated into the canyon wall. Additional ruins are on the mesa top, while the cave-rooms extend for nearly a mile. Puye was settled in the early to mid AD 1500s.

Lar Hothem photo

Interior of Far View Ruins, Mesa Verde National Park, Colorado. The very large structure was made of above and below-ground rooms, carefully walled with fitted stone blocks.

Lar Hothem photo

CHAPTER XIII

PIPES

Pipe forms began in the Archaic time-frame, and various types were made throughout North America. Generally pipes were made from a select material, a hardstone, that was both compact and colorful.

The form, in principle, is simple: A pipe has an enclosed area that contains the smoking material—tobacco, as we know it, was not used widely until historic times—and a smaller, intersecting hole through which the smoke was drawn. Pipes range from large to small and effigy to plain, with workstyle from passable to superb.

Pipes are classified according to shape: tube, elbow, elongated, platform, and so forth. Some are mere bowls, while others are complete with stems and incised decorations. Earlier pipes tend to be simple; later forms are more elaborate. Many specimens took a great deal of time and skill to make and are avidly sought by collectors today.

For this discussion, pipes can be divided into two large collecting fields. As with many other Amerind collectibles, these are before (prehistoric) and after White-contact times (historic period). Prehistoric pipes tend to be the most varied in form, the most geographically divergent.

Historic Plains Indian style pipes are much more similar for the times. There is a certain sameness of size, design, and material, with Minnesota red pipestone (also called Catlinite) the common stone. Such pipes were also popular in the Great Lakes area and other regions.

Value considerations for prehistoric pipes include material from which the pipe is made, with harder substances ranked higher than loose-grained stone. Polish is important, as are size and workstyle. All drilling should be complete and well done. Some tube-type pipes combine the two in a single elongated hole.

Effigy pipes usually command higher prices than ordinary pipes, and depictions of the human figure are especially valued. The rare Hopewellian effigy pipes—often mini-sculptures of birds or animals—can be worth in excess of $2,000.

Historic times had many White-made pipes. They ranged from the rare Russian lead stem-and-bowl pipe of the far Northwest to numerous baked-clay and porcelain pipes of White mold-manufacture. The pipe-tomahawks of Eastern regions (covered elsewhere) are yet another example. The big collector item, however, is the Indian-made Plains-style pipe.

The typical Plains Indian Catlinite smoking instrument had a high, rounded bowl and a stem-receptacle of similar proportions. In profile, the two form either an "L" or an inverted "T" shape. Some pipe forms were two-piece, with the stem connecting the receptacle. And the stem, in turn, was either of wood or Catlinite.

Better pipes were stored and transported in the beaded and/or quilled pipe-bags, and were used on special occasions. The current value range for Plains-style pipes is $500-3,000, and more for extra-fine specimens. Most pipe heads are about the same size, so this is not usually a big value factor.

Overall workmanship is important, plus surface polish and completed and accurate drilling. Twisted-wood or paneled-wood stems are more desired than plain wooden stems, and Catlinite stems are sought-after. Pipes that can definitely be associated with an actual (and famous) Indian leader are in the minority, and should be thoroughly documented.

It is pointed out that contemporary Catlinite pipes are being made by American Indians at the Pipestone National Monument in Minnesota. These are modern reproductions that much resemble Plains style historic specimens; they sell in a range of $50-200, and, with wood stem, are from 12 in. to 30 in. in length.

PREHISTORIC STONE PIPES

Sandstone tube pipe, 4-1/2 in. long and 1-1/4 in. in diameter. A well-made piece, fully drilled the length. A-$110

Caddo long-stem pipe, 9 in. long. Piece is from Arkansas and has minor stem breaks, but repaired; no bowl damage. Nice item. G-$350

Hardstone tube pipe, 10-1/4 in. long and 1-1/4 in. in diameter near center. Made of black compact stone, highly polished on surface. Larger end evidences some battering, but nothing major. D-$795

Bowl-type pipe, 1-1/2 in. long and 1-1/2 in. high, and made of Ohio pipestone. A-$75

Round bowl-type pipe, made of compact light sandstone. Large hole 1/2 in. in diameter with smaller hole for stem. Pipe, with rounded bottom, is 1-3/4 in. high. C-$120

Diegueno Indian soapstone tube pipe, 5 in. long and 1 in. across at smoking end. Drilled entire length, small to larger hole, no damage. C-$475

Cylindrical banded-slate pipe bowl, flat bottomed; 2-1/8 in. high, exterior highly polished, good banding. D-$185

Wine-glass type pipe, Washington state, 4-1/2 in. long and 7/8 in. wide at end. Polished stone resembling steatite, well carved, perfect condition. D-$525

Sandstone effigy pipe, 4 in. high and 3-1/4 in. wide. A cranelike bird is depicted, with beak touching ground, and bowl on back. Restored. A-$370

Clay pipe, 4 in. long and 2-1/2 in. high, from Brant County, Ontario, Canada. This is a sturdy and well-made piece, late prehistoric or early historic. C-$50-80

Photo courtesy Robert Calvert, London, Ontario, Canada

Stone effigy pipe, platform type, 3 in. high and 1-1/4 in. wide. Probably Woodland; pipe bowl top made in image of a turtle in its shell, a common Midwestern Hopewellian motif. From Canada, Lake Huron region. (Condition uncertain.)   C-$400-650

Clay pipe, 3-1/8 in. long and 1-3/4 in. high, and 1-1/2 in. diagonally across pipe bowl. This is a Canadian piece and may be Neutral or Attawandoron in origin.   C-$135

Stone elbow pipe, excavated from a Texas Panhandle Pueblo site near Spearman. It is made from a material that is very fine-grained; a charred smoking substance is still inside the bowl. Bowl top has incised markings; pipe is 2 in. length, and probably dates AD 900-1300.   C-$175

Photo courtesy Wayne Parker, Texas

Stone pipe, prehistoric, unusual squared and elongated form. Larger end has pipe bowl, with connecting hole for stem in center of bottom side. Smaller end has two drill-holes connecting in "L" configuration. Smaller end is additionally grooved, and there are several deep grooves on topside-which would have been pipe front when in use. Unusual, and tallynotched. Piece is 2-1/2 in. long.   C-$275-375

Photo courtesy Robert C. Calvert, London, Ontario, Canada

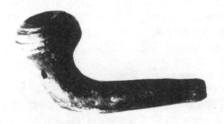

Clay pipe, 3-1/2 in. long and 2-1/4 in. high and found near Hyde Park, London, Ontario, Canada. A well-shaped and sturdy late-prehistoric or early historic pipe.   C-$200

Photo courtesy Robert Calvert, London, Ontario, Canada

Effigy clay pipe, 5 in. long and 3-1/4 in. high at top of effigy head. Effigy types of artifacts tend to be more valued than plain types; this is a Canadian piece.   C-$275

Photo courtesy Robert C. Calvert, London, Ontario, Canada

Pipe (bean type), a well-shaped pipe made of steatite, nicely polished. It is from Stokes County, North Carolina. $900

Rodney M. Peck collection, Harrisburg, North Carolina

Stone pipe, made of banded slate, and an unfinished item. Pipe is 2-1/4 in. long and is drilled at both bowl and stem ends. Bowl top has a curious set of lines around bowl, which could have been centering guide for drilling, or just decoration, or a symbol representing the four directions.   C-$100-175

Photo courtesy Robert C. Calvert, London, Ontario, Canada

Bent-tube pipe, found in Lancaster County, Pennsylvania. $165

Lee Hallman collection, Telford, Pennsylvania

Tubular pipe, probably Adena and Early Woodland, material a tan colored quartzite. Size, 1-1/4 x 2-5/8 in.; from Hardin County, Ohio, this pipe has fine lines and a high polish. Unusual material for the type, and a plus for the piece. $750-1,000

Private collection, Ohio

Hopewell (Middle Woodland) platform type pipe, 1-1/2 in. high and 2-5/8 in. long. Material is a dark close-grained stone, possibly steatite. It is from the Scioto River area, Pike County, Ohio.   Museum quality

Larry Garvin collection, Ohio

Prehistoric pipes.

Left: pottery elbow-type pipe, from Arkansas. $175
Center: pottery bird-head effigy pipe, Louisiana (shown elsewhere). $175
Right: small polished stone pipe. $125

Wilfred A. Dick collection, Magnolia, Mississippi

Prehistoric pipes.

Left: bird-head pottery pipe, from Louisiana, different view. $175
Bottom left: Caddo pottery pipe, Arkansas. $200
Right: stone tubular pipe, the earliest type, Mississippi. $200

Wilfred A. Dick collection, Magnolia, Mississippi

Prehistoric pipes, various regions.

Top left: alate form (winged), steatite, 8-1/2 in., from North Carolina. $2,500
Tube pipe, steatite, 5 in., California. $700
Tube pipe, Ohio pipestone, 4 in. $350
Elbow pipe, steatite, 2-1/2 in. long, Virginia. $300

Pocotopaug Trading Post, South Windsor, Connecticut

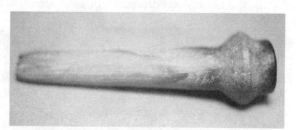

Pottery pipe, late prehistoric or early historic period, 4 in. long. This is a Pueblo type with enlarged end for the smoking substance. It was found near Alcalde, New Mexico. $295

Jack Baker collection, Ozark, Missouri; David Capon photograph

343

Effigy pipe, 4 in. high, made of sandstone. This example was found in southern Indiana. $250

Blue Coyote Trading Post, Nashville, Indiana; Pat Nolan photograph

Canoe pipe, Mississippian period, 3 in. high and 5-1/2 in. long. Made of pottery, this is one of the finest of type known to exist, being rare in this condition and with excellent detail. Rome area, Georgia. Museum quality

Bruce Butts collection, Winterville, Georgia

Green soapstone or steatite pipe, from Virginia. Piece is 5-3/8 in. long and has a bowl at one end of a flat base. Some damage to expanded rim of bowl, now expertly restored. C-$550

Platform-type pipe, steatite, 4 in. long and 1-1/2 in. high. Nicely polished. A-$220

Raised-bowl pipe, with flat stem extending for 3-3/4 in.; height is 1-1/2 in. Stem is just over 1 in. wide, with raised ridge along top center. A-$600

Effigy platform pipe, pipestone, 3 in. long and 1-3/4 in. high, depicting a bird. Piece is done in Hopewellian fashion. Head is restored. A-$375

Steatite elbow-type pipe, 2-1/2 in. long and 1-1/2 in. high; very well polished. A-$155

Sandstone effigy pipe, 3 in. high and 2 in. long, depicting a human figure with arms around the bowl. Piece is broken, but not seriously. A-$290

Steatite pipe, large bowl 4-1/4 in. high and with smaller stem about 2-3/4 in. long. Highly polished. D-$525

Tubular pipe, pipestone, 7 in. long and 1-1/4 in. wide, with fully drilled, tapering hole. A very well-made piece, though broken and restored. A-$800

Granite effigy pipe, 3-1/2 in. high, 1-1/2 in. wide. Bird figure with bowl on the back. A-$320

Sandstone pipe, 2 in. high. Made to represent a sitting frog or toad. Pipe has large smoking hole in middle of the back. Good condition, and a well-made piece. Intensive wear around top of bowl. C-$260

Hopewellian platform-type pipe, 4-3/4 in. long, sandstone. Very nicely carved and proportioned. Piece is unfinished, having never been drilled for bowl or stem. C-$300

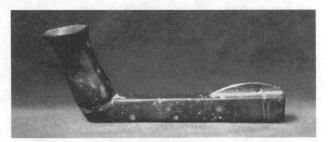

Creek Indian pipe, historic period, 2-1/2 in. high and 5 in. long. It is gracefully carved from black steatite and came from Talladega County, Alabama. Museum quality

Bruce Butts collection, Winterville, Georgia

Steatite pipe, tubular form, 1-1/4 in. in diameter and 3-1/2 in. long. Ends lightly scarred, all minor, surface highly polished. D-$140

Sandstone pipe, 2-1/4 in. high; barrel type. Late prehistoric, Midwest. Some damage to top of bowl. C-$125

Slate pipe, 4-1/4 in. long and 1-1/8 in. in diameter; tubular form. Good banded material, high polish, drilled completely through, no damage. C-$325

Stone pipe, 3-1/2 in. long and 1-7/8 in. high; elbow type. Squared edges, rather heavy in appearance, well-polished surface. One chip from mouthpiece area, but minor. C-$300

Pipe, Northwest Coast "wineglass" tubular variety; 2-7/8 in. long and 7/8 in. in diameter at larger end, hole drilled the length. Smaller "bottom" mouthpiece end had hole drilled in corner, possibly for securing thong. D-$475

Steatite bird-effigy pipe, with sitting bird facing pipe bowl; 4-1/4 in. long. Small scratches on surface, none deep. Unusual; unknown time period, but prehistoric. Effigy well carved. C-$1,350

Sandstone pipe, elbow-type, 2-3/4 in. long and 1-1/4 in. high. Plain, but well-made. From Oklahoma, and prehistoric. Surface still rough. D-$100

Pipestone pipe, 4-1/8 in. long; platform type. Concave platform base, plain bowl. Perfect condition, highly polished. C-$1,600

"L"-shaped pipe of greenish pipestone, 2-1/8 in. long. Bowl has two incised lines around top near rim. C-$215

Platform-type pipe of limestone, 3-1/2 in. long and 1-3/4 in. high. A-$175

Disc-bowl pipe, Illinois, 1-3/4 in. high and 2-1/2 in. long. Made of gray-white material; has a short rounded stem. C-$425

Effigy pipe of sandstone, 5 in. long and 3 in. high; possibly representing a sitting bird with squat body and raised head. A-$800

Iroquois pipe, pipestone, 5 in. long and 2 in. high. Bowl and stem form right angle; top of bowl has a widened, flat rim. The piece has been restored. A-$175

Elbow-type pipe, North Carolina, expanded bowl set at right angles to squared base. Material a yellowish compact stone. Piece is 3 in. long. C-$550

Large platform-type pipe, 4-7/8 in. long and 3-1/4 in. high. Made of a polished dark brown stone, no damage. Well-polished; bowl fully drilled and stem partially drilled. C-$900

Granite elbow-type pipe, 4 in. long and 2-1/2 in. high. A-$165

Iroquois pipe, 4-1/2 in. long and 2 in. high; long-stem type. Round bowl, tubular stem, made of pipestone. This piece has restoration. A-$175

Tubular pipe, state of Washington, 5-1/8 in. long, of a type called "wineglass." Made of a compact black stone. One end flares abruptly, other end tapers to rounded and expanded mouthpiece. Slight damage to rim of smoking bowl, but minor. C-$650

Elbow-type stone pipe, 3-1/2 in. long and 1-3/4 in. high. Made of a fine-grain yellowish siltstone. Well-made and with good polish. C-$475

Quartzite barrel-type pipe, 2 in. high and 1-3/4 in. in diameter, with hole for stem in center which connects with smoking compartment. A-$195

INDIAN-MADE HISTORIC PIPES

Red pipestone pipe, 19-1/2 in. long; made in the form of a pipe-tomahawk. Plains Indian and probably late 1800s. C-$525

T-shape Catlinite pipe; bowl 3-1/4 in. high and overall length 22-1/2 in. Round stem with carved and painted design. G-$650

Catlinite pipe head, Plains Indian, with redstone head 4-1/4 in. high and 6 in. long. Well-carved and nicely polished. Probably late 1800s. C-$425

Catlinite pipe, old, with stem of pipestone also. A-$310

Red pipestone pipe, head 7 in. long and with 18-1/2 in. wood stem. D-$675

Catlinite pipe and stem, early period, both showing great age and use. G-$525

Catlinite T-shaped effigy pipe, squared stem and bowl, with horsehead prow beautifully carved. Early 1900s. $2,500

Crown & Eagle Antiques, New Hope, Pennsylvania

Pipe, T-shaped, Catlinite with pewter banding, Great Plains region. A large pipe, it measures 4-1/2 x 8-1/2 in. and has a crest between the bowl and handle end. Ca. 1880-1900. $400

Frank Bergevin, Port Of Call, Alexandria Bay, New York

Pipe, Catlinite, 9 in. long and 4 in. high. A classic specimen of the Plains Indian style. Carved and polished; Northern Plains region, and mid-1800s. G-$550

Pipe, with original pipe bag; Sioux, and pre-1900. A-$1,000

Tube pipe, historic Chumash Indian, of green steatite. A-$165

Pipe bowl, 4 in. long and 3-1/2 in. high. Ornately sculpted Catlinite pipe bowl in unusually elaborate design. Surface worn to a fine patina. Northern Plains and mid-1800s. G-$675

Eskimo pipe, with Siberian influence. Carved from wood, with inlayed pewter decorations. A-$875

Pipe bowl, 10 in. long and 4 in. high. Catlinite pipe bag, with pierced-design "fin" between end and bowl. Cheyenne, and ca. 1900. G-$540

Catlinite pipe and stem, with early spiral-carved stem. Top quality piece and in very nice condition. G-$650

Sioux Catlinite pipe, with head 3 in. high and 8 in. long, with carved snake. The twisted wood stem is 15 in. in length. Piece is ca. 1920. G-$525

Sioux Catlinite pipe, 3 in. high and 7 in. long. Wooden stem is 17 in. long. Carved squirrel facing the bowl. This piece is ca. 1920. G-$475

Blackfoot pipe, Reservation-collected in the early 1900s. Bowl is black and carved in Blackfoot design; wooden stem, with old collection. Excellent condition. G-$700

L-shaped Catlinite pipe; head is 1-1/4 in. high and short wooden stem is 6 in. long. Old label reads, "Kiowa, from Missouri River." G-$350

Catlinite Sioux pipe, finest workmanship and condition. Pipe bowl and lower portions are inlayed with lead or pewter. C-$1,100

Sioux Catlinite pipe, bowl 6 in. long and 3 in. high in the form of an eagle claw with cone. Wooden stem is 17 in. long; ca. 1920. G-$550

Sioux Catlinite pipe with quilled stem. Collected prior to 1900 and formerly in a major collection, Oklahoma. An early and fine piece. G-$950

Sioux Catlinite pipe, bowl 4 in. high and 8 in. long, with solid Catlinite stem 17 in. long; ca. 1880.   G-$650

Hupa soapstone tube pipe, California, ca. 1890. D-$150

Catlinite pipe, Western Plains Indian; bowl is 3 in. high and 5 in. overall, with wood stem an additional 17-3/4 in. Bowl is cracked at base, but line is barely visible. D-$675

Suggested Reading

Bierer, Bert W. *Indian Artifacts in the Southeast. A Sketchbook*. Columbia, South Carolina: privately published, 1977.

Hart, Gordon. *Hart's Prehistoric Pipe Rack*. Indiana: privately published, 1978.

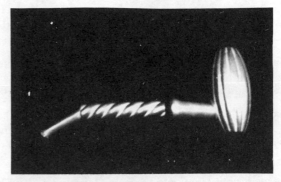

Red Catlinite "squaw pipe" with an intricately carved stem and bowl, each a separate piece. Pipe is about 7 in. long, including the spiral-carved stem.   D-$575

Photo courtesy Crazy Crow Trading Post, Denison, Texas

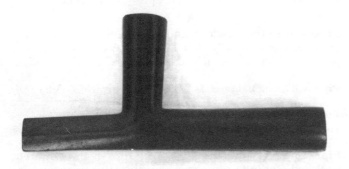

Catlinite pipe bowl, Hunkpapa Sioux, 4-1/2 x 8-1/2 in. This ex-museum piece has clan markings on the stem and is ca. 1880. $550

Morris' Art & Artifacts, Anaheim, California; Dawn Gober photograph

Great Lakes region pipes, Catlinite and pewter, ca. 1800.

Top right: human head and animal head. $3,500
Bottom left: human head and animal, fenestrated lower platform. $5,000

Private collection; photo by John McLaughlin

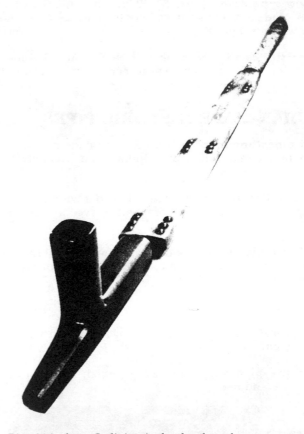

Pipe, 31 in. long. Catlinite pipe bowl and wood stem ornamented with brass tacks and wrapped with plaited quilling. Northern Plains area, and pre-1900.   *Museum quality*

Photo courtesy Kenneth R. Canfield, Plains Indian Art, Kansas City, Missouri

French trade pipe, historic, from Ontario, Canada. Piece is 2 in. high and 2 in. long, quite well made and in fine condition. C-$125

Photo courtesy Robert C. Calvert, London, Ontario, Canada

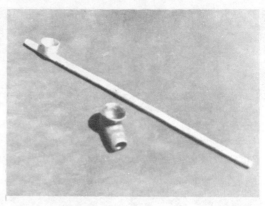

Caddo pipes, Mississippian period.

Top: extra-long example at 9 in., with bowl thimble-size; from southwest Arkansas. This is a very fragile piece. $300-500
Bottom: short-stem pipe, dark color, southwest Arkansas. $150-250

Private collection

Historic-era pipe, Plains style with long base and high bowl at one end, black steatite with pewter inlays. This is a large pipe, 3-3/16 x 7-5/16 in., from Sandusky County, Ohio, where it may have been traded in. This is a very well-made example with solid inlays and high material polish. $1,000-1,500

Private collection, Ohio

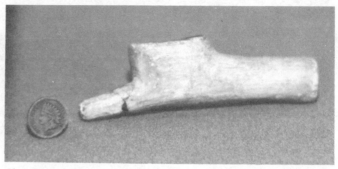

Clay pipe, prehistoric and in repaired condition. This pre-Iroquois smoking instrument is 4-1/2 in. long. $250

Pat & Dave Summers, Native American Artifacts, Victor, New York

Bear effigy pipe, gray steatite, from southern Tennessee. Museum quality

Private collection

Pottery pipes, Mississippian era.

Left three: Mississippi County, Arkansas, fine conditions.   Each, $85-150
Right: pipe from Desha County, Arkansas. $125+

Private collection

Catlinite pipe, Ottawa, ca. 1840-60. This "L"-shaped pipe has two engraved bands at the ends of the stem and bowl and three projections at lower front. It is from northern Michigan (shown elsewhere). $400

Larry Lantz, First Mesa, South Bend, Indiana

Platform pipe, Hamilton Culture (AD 600-700), from Hamilton County, Tennessee. It is made from dark gray steatite, with a quartz vein. Size, 2 x 10-3/4 in. This is a museum-quality piece. $10,000-12,000

Rodney M. Peck collection, Harrisburg, North Carolina

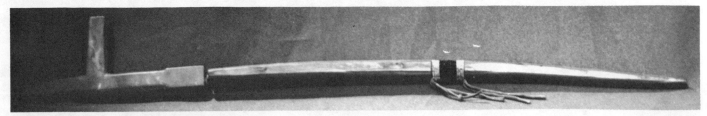

Catlinite (Minnesota red pipestone) pipe with beaded wooden stem, Northern Sioux. The bowl is 4-1/2 x 8 in. and the stem is 20-1/2 in. long. It is ca. 1900 and the stem portion is ex-coll. Casterline. $1,100

Pat & Dave Summers, Native American Artifacts, Victor, New York

Contemporary curly maple effigy pipe, highly polished, from Traverse City, Michigan. Made in the 1950s, the pipe is 16-1/4 in. long. $200

Michael F. Slasinski, Saginaw, Michigan

Catlinite pipe-tomahawk pipe, incised with floral and geometric designs. This excellent Sioux piece is 7-1/2 in. high and 13-1/4 in. long. Ca. 1890-1900. $1,000

Pat & Dave Summers, Native American Artifacts, Victor, New York

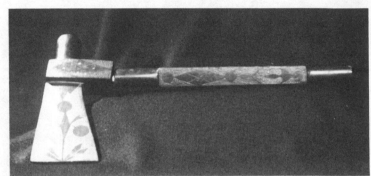

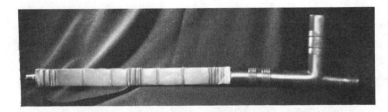

Catlinite pipe bowl and stem, Plains Indian, an exquisite piece. It is 25 in. long and from the late 1800s. $2,400

Pat & Dave Summers, Native American Artifacts, Victor, New York

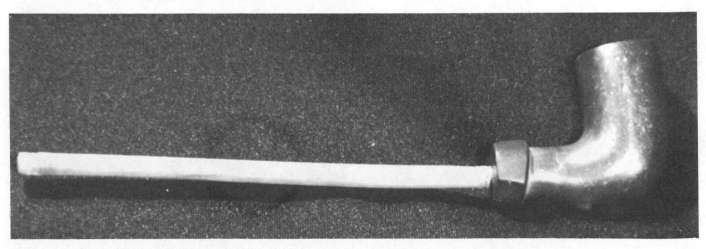

Catlinite pipe bowl with contemporary reed stem, bowl 1-7/8 x 2-1/8 in. This graceful knobbed and faceted pipe is ca. 1860-1870. $325

Pat & Dave Summers, Native American Artifacts, Victor, New York

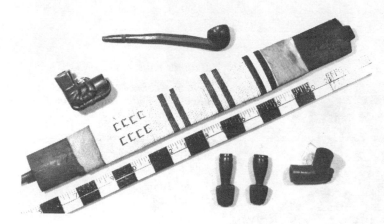

Catlinite pipes, various origins. These are Sioux, Chippewa, Fox, and Ottawa, and all are from ca. 1850-1890s. Note the original Sioux beaded ash stem with horse-track designs.

Pipes.   Each, $150-550
Stem alone. $500

Larry Lantz, First Mesa, South Bend, Indiana

Catlinite pipe, Sioux, classic form from Dane County, Wisconsin. This fine, large pipe is late 1800s. $750

Larry Lantz, First Mesa, South Bend, Indiana

Catlinite pipes.

Top left: Sioux "L"-shaped, 2-1/2 x 4 in., 1860s. It has three engraved lines on the bottom. From St. Paul, Minnesota. $450
Sioux "T"-shaped bowl with original Catlinite stem, 17 in. overall. From South Dakota, scarce. $900-1,300

Larry Lantz, First Mesa, South Bend, Indiana

Catlinite pipes.

Top left: Ottawa "L"-shaped, 2 x 2-1/2 in., 1840-1860. Note engraved rings on stem and bowl; from Michigan. $400
Top right: Sioux "L"-shaped, with lead or pewter inlaid lines on bowl, 1850-1860, North Dakota. $350
Bottom: shown elsewhere in book, Chippewa Voyager-type pipe, 6-1/2 in. long, solid Catlinite, with seven engraved lines on bowl. $450

Larry Lantz, First Mesa, South Bend, Indiana

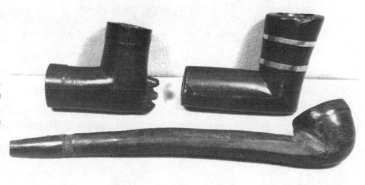

Catlinite pipes.

Left: Sioux "L"-shaped, 2-1/2 x 4 in., 1860s, with three engraved lines. It is from St. Paul, Minnesota. (shown elsewhere). $450
Right: Chippewa "T"-shaped, 1-3/4 x 3-1/4 in., from Cass Lake, Minnesota. Ca. 1840-60. $395

Larry Lantz, First Mesa, South Bend, Indiana

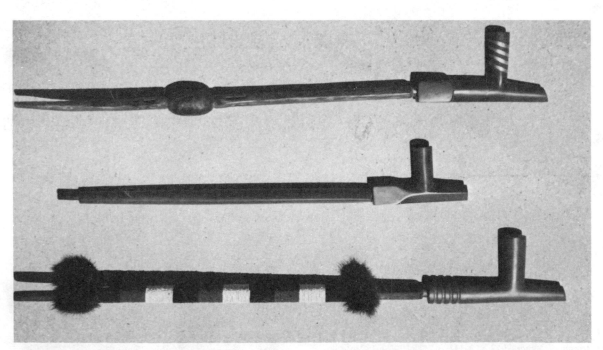

Plains Indian (Sioux) Catlinite Pipes with wooden handles, both plain and decorated with fur and beads. Lengths, 22-1/2 to 30 in. long. They are in perfect condition. Each, $600-1,450

Marguerite L. Kernaghan collection; photograph by Marguerite L. and Stewart W. Kernaghan, Bellvue, Colorado

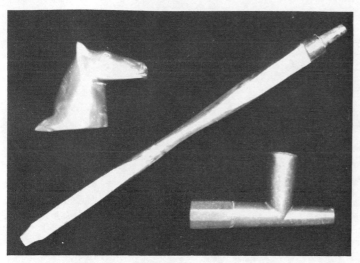

Catlinite artifacts.

Top left: Sioux, horsehead, 2-3/4 x 3-1/2 in., 1890s, probably an un-finished pipe. It is from North Dakota. $250
Center and right: 12 in. original ash stem, carved so that flat surfaces occur on all four sides; also, "T"-shaped pipe, 1-1/2 x 4-1/2 in.

Pipe and stem $950

Larry Lantz, First Mesa, South Bend, Indiana

Cup-type pipe bowl, mottled reddish granite, from northern Alabama. Hollow reed stems were often used with bowls like this. $200

Private collection

Plains Indians in Montana, date unknown. Note the fine baby carrier woman carries between tepees, and dramatic feather headdress worn by standing man.

Photographer, Roland Reed; courtesy Photography collection, Suzzallo Library, University of Washington

CHAPTER XIV

CLOTHING, MOCCASINS, AND LEATHERWORK

As with all natural and rendered materials to be worked, historic and recent Amerinds excelled in clothing and footwear.

The leather was well-tanned and supple. Any decorations—beads, quills, paint—were put on with innate taste and practiced skill.

The sums being paid for such items, as evidenced by this chapter, are one indication of the esteem in which such work is now held. Faked pieces have thus far not been much of a problem, due to the complexity of matching both materials and artistic designs. Stone, in some cases, is easier to market than leather.

Articles most in demand appear to be complete and decorated dresses, skirts, vests, and leggings, hopefully with documentation, but usually without. If old and good, these are museum-quality items. Designs should be pleasing, the leather whole, and almost all beads and quills in place. Paint should still be somewhat bold, and the designs still visible. Leather fringes should be mostly intact and the item itself of some size.

For moccasins, Eastern examples tend to be soft-soled and floral-decorated. Moccasins can show some wear, but should not be holed on the bottoms or ripped badly. Sides and top should be in good condition, with most bead and quill designs intact.

Generally, the more beads or quills, the greater the value, whether the piece is historic or recent. And note that items collected before about 1950 tend to be premium-priced.

WOMEN'S CLOTHING

Small girl's dress, 15 in. wide and 20 in. long, Plains Indian design. Base is blue cloth with leather fringe and cowrie shell design; excellent condition and dresses this small are unusual. Pre-1900.   G-$550

Buckskin dress, medium-size, Plains Indian, fawn color and fringed. Some bead decorations.   D-$950

Woman's dress, made of bright purple satin. Hundreds of metal dangles hanging from dress. Excellent condition; Plateau piece. Ca. 1940s.   G-$400

Woman's dress, for tall person, shoulder sections well beaded. Made of doeskin. Superb condition, probably late 1880s; beading excellent, all fringes present. Typical Plains Indian beadwork designs in red, white, and blue. D-$3,200

Woman's dress, single unit, dark brown and 41 in. long. Beadwork strips, in good condition.   D-$975

Woman's dress, small size and Nez Perce. On green cloth, yoke is nicely beaded with blue, black, and red beads. Many cowrie shell decorations. Excellent condition, probably from the 1920s.   G-$875

Woman's dress, Navajo, skirt and blouse, red and blue designs in weave; combined length of pair 53 in. Worn but good condition.   D-$800

Leather vest, woman's size, geometric beadwork designs, some damage to back but beadwork in good condition.   C-$500

Woman's vest, light-colored thin leather, beads, and quillwork, old but in good condition.   A-$400

Woman's leggings, 7 x 12 in., fully beaded with yellow, red, green, and purple beads. Very decorative set; Plateau origin and ca. 1930s.   G-$450

Woman's leggings, Plains Indian, good beadwork, in good condition.   D-$650

Woman-size Apache leather dress, ca. 1900. Nicely tasseled overall; yoke at top has beaded fringe and fine designs on shoulders. D-$8,000

Photo courtesy Winona Trading Post, Santa Fe-Pierre & Sylvia Bovis

Dress, Sioux, Elk Dreamers Society, early 20th century. It is 52-1/2 in. across and 55 in. long including fringes. A fine and well-made dress. $3,500

Crown & Eagle Antiques, Inc., New Hope, Pennsylvania

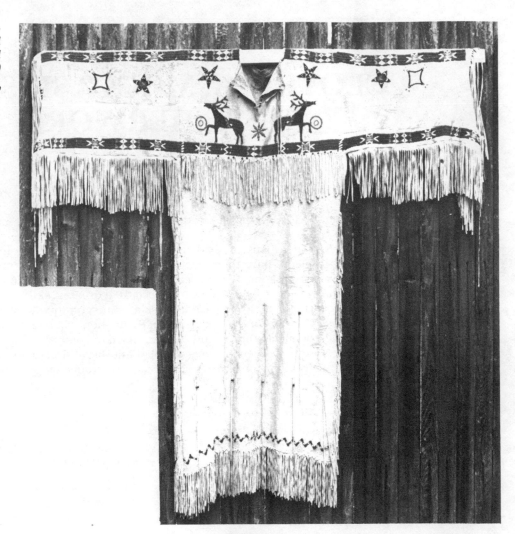

Sioux woman's dress, large size in green trade cloth, with decoration of elk teeth and carved bone. Ca. 1890-1900. $7,500

Antiques & Art, Piedmont, South Dakota

Wedding headdress, Umatilla, pony beads, hide, dentallium shells, and Chinese coins, ca. 1880. Generally sell for $1,000-4,000. $1,500

Private collection; photo by John McLaughlin

Blackfoot woman's beaded yoke, with old Venetian glass tube beads in rows of white, green, and red. Chinese coins hang from yoke. Ca. 1880. $1,950

Indian Territory, Tucson, Arizona

Woodland vest, excellent example of heavy late 1800s type wool vest. Beadwork in many colors, near-mint condition. It is 21-1/4 x 25-1/2 in., ca. 1900. $750

Sherman Holbert collection, Fort Mille Lacs, Onamia, Minnesota

Plains Ojibwa woman's leggings, 6 x 18 in., wool and glass beads. Floral design attractive in six colors against the red cloth. Ca. 1890. $1,250

Historic Interiors, Sorrento, British Columbia, Canada

Woman's leggings, Sioux, beautiful designs and colors. Sinew-sewn on buckskin. In excellent condition. Tag included suggests they belonged to wife of famous Lower Brule Sioux chief. G-$1,350

MEN'S CLOTHING

Man's outfit, quilled, and Blackfoot. Set includes war shirt, pair of gauntlets, rifle case, and knife sheath. Quills are red, yellow, green, purple, and natural, woven on hide. Outstanding and like-new condition. Ca. 1910-20. G-$6,200

Woodlands jacket, 26 in. long, of leather; piece has beadwork included in the cuffs and front, and design on back. Fringes along underside of sleeves. Probably ca. 1930s. A-$625

"War shirt," probably Sioux, beaded front and back. Poor to fair condition overall. Badly stored for a number of years, sections of beadwork are lost. About 75 percent of beadwork remains. Back design better than front. C-$650

Boy's jacket, Crow, floral beadwork and outlined. Lined, made of buckskin with very fine beadwork. Good condition and ca. 1880. G-$925

Leather vest sleeveless, 18-1/4 in. from top to bottom. Beaded in floral designs at bottom and middle of front flaps. Collected in northeastern Pennsylvania and is ca. 1920s. D-$850

Man's vest done on commercial leather and lined in old cloth. Arrows and circles beaded front and back, in orange, yellow, and bright blue colors. Medium-size. Ca. 1920-1930s. G-$425

Leggings, beaded on old blanket material. Beaded panels at bottom. It is 7 x 12 in. Shows ribbon work on edges, slight moth damage. Beadwork nearly perfect. Crow Indian, and ca. 1885. G-$1,400

Man's leggings and vest, matched outfit, Plains Indian style. Both well beaded; ca. late 1880s. D-$1,750

Leggings, 24 in. long and 7 in. wide, with short fringes on outer sides. Cheyenne. A-$400

Leggings, Ponca or Oto Indian. Black trade cloth with tan cloth trim on bottom. All trim outlined in light blue beads with many white stars beaded on cloth. Beautiful yellow fringe on edge. Ca. 1910. G-$900

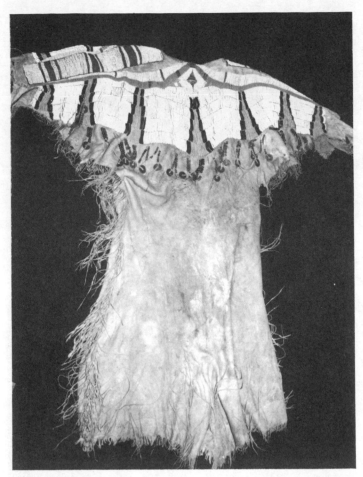

Woman's dress, Nez Perce, hide with pony beads, trade beads, and Chinese coins. Finely beaded shoulder panels. Very fine piece, ca. 1860. $9,000

Private collection; photo by John McLaughlin

Vest, Sioux, men's size 38/40, ca. 1880-1890. Sinew-sewn and beaded on Indian leather, lined with cloth. American flag designs, front and back; bead colors are white background with blue, green, metallic gold, and red white-hearts. Purchased by original collector in South Dakota, 1920, it is ex-coll. Luongo. A superb period piece. $4,500

Sherman Holbert collection, Fort Mille Lacs, Onamia, Minnesota

Ceremonial shirt, Nez Perce, hide and beaded strips with ermine drops. Superb piece is ca. 1900. $15,000

Private collection; photo by John McLaughlin

Men's beaded vest, Flathead, five colors against a white ground. In superb condition ca. 1890. $975

Freya's Collectibles, Banff, Alberta, Canada

Vest, Santee Sioux, men's size 36/38. Front made of buffalo hide, beaded designs of birds and flowers. Beads in red, three shades of blue, amber, yellow, white, black, green, mauve, and orange. Tapestry style cloth for back. Both sinew and thread used for sewing, all hand stitched, ca. 1870-1890. $1,475

Sherman Holbert collection, Fort Mille Lacs, Onamia, Minnesota

Vest, Chippewa, men's size 34. Black velvet lined with cotton; nine buttons are abalone with metal back. Beuling depicts flowers, leaves and vines in colors of old rose, gold, blue, pink, crystal, green, and several shades of yellow. Very good condition, ca. 1890-1910. $1,500

Sherman Holbert collection, Fort Mille Lacs, Onamia, Minnesota

Pictorial vest, Sioux, figures on white beading, top condition. This rare vest is ca. 1890. $7,500

Crown & Eagle Antiques, Inc., New Hope, Pennsylvania

Vest, Chippewa, ca. 1890-1910. Men's size 34, black velvet lined with cotton. Nine buttons are abalone with metal back. Beading depicts flowers, leaves and vines, in colors of old rose, gold, blue, pink, crystal, green, and several shades of yellow. Very good condition, an artistic vest.   1,500

Sherman Holbert collection, Fort Mille Lacs, Onamia, Minnesota

Man-size Sioux leggings, ca. 1880, with fine beadwork designs.   D-$1,500

Photo courtesy Winona Trading Post, Santa Fe-Pierre & Sylvia Bovis

Man's vest, quillwork, Eastern Sioux. Rare example, in top condition. Has a red flower design with white foliage against a red-gold quilled ground, ca. 1880. $9,500

Canfield Gallery, Santa Fe

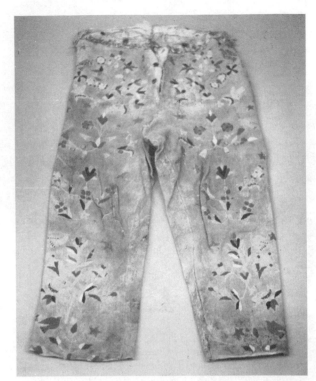

Santee Sioux beaded pants, buckskin with designs in tiny cut-glass beads. Unusual floral work done ca. 1860-1880. $3,500

Antiques & Art, Piedmont, South Dakota

Plains Indian shirt, Dakotas, fringed hide with bands of porcupine quill embroidery across arms and front. Very rare Plains Indian piece, ca. late 1800s. $24,000

Canfield Gallery, Santa Fe

Beaded jacket, Flathead, ca. 1910. Chief's or adult male jacket, has winter weasel (ermine) tails, shell buttons, and beadwork down back. Old museum tag dates 1910. $2,500

Rainbow Traders, Godfrey, Illinois

Plains Indian man's shirt, beaded and fringed hide with ermine, scalp-locks, and trade beads. Plains Indian clothing in this high quality and of this age, extremely hard to find. Ca. 1900. $36,000

Canfield Gallery, Santa Fe

Flathead warshirt, native-tanned hide with green pigment, ermine skin, trade cloth, and glass beads. Ca. 1890. $68,000

David Cook Fine American Art, Denver, Colorado; Jamie Kahn photograph

Nez Perce leggings, buckskin, brain-tanned and fringed. Designs are painted, not beaded. Ca. 1900. $1,450

Indian Territory, Tucson, Arizona

Blackfoot beaded vest, man's size, floral bead designs on black velvet and trade cloth. Came from Cutbank, Montana, ca. 1890. $1,500

Terry Schafer, American Indian Art & Antiques, Marietta, Ohio

GAUNTLETS

Moose hide gauntlets, Nez Perce Indian, 7 in. long. Decorated with cut-glass beads and with beaded floral design panels on backs. Large, excellent condition and ca. 1930s.   G-$450

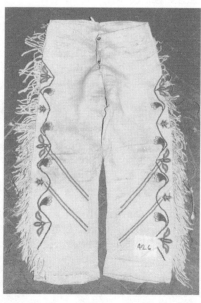

Crow trousers, beaded buckskin, with buckskin and horse-tail fringe. Belonged to Bear In The Clouds, a Crow warrior. Ex-collection Joseph Henry Sharp, who made multiple oil portraits of Bear In The Clouds. $15,000

Forrest Fenn, Santa Fe, New Mexico

Gauntlets or gloves, Plateau, pair, 16 in. long. Made from Indian-tanned leather, floral beading on cuff fronts only. Bead colors are green, ruby, white, blue, yellow, metallic gray, and metallic blue. Beading in perfect condition, ca. 1920-1930. $350

Sherman Holbert collection, Fort Mille Lacs, Onamia, Minnesota

Crow beaded gloves or gauntlets, very attractive beadwork on backs and cuffs. One of better pairs in existence, ca. 1890. $4,000

Antiques & Art, Piedmont, South Dakota

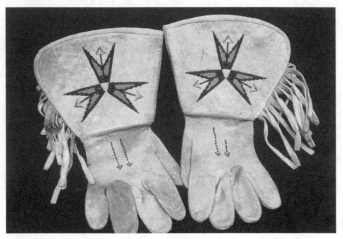

Beaded gauntlets, Western Canada, 12 in. long. Made of native-tanned hide; gloves decorated with glass beads in five colors. 1940s. $350

Blue Coyote Trading Post, Nashville, Indiana; Paul McCreary photograph

Nez Perce man's gauntlets, nicely beaded with fringed cuffs; beads are very small. Ca. 1910. $975

Indian Territory, Tucson, Arizona

Gauntlets, pair, woman's size. Partially beaded on cuffs. Indian-tanned leather, cloth-lined. G-$225

Gauntlets, pair, man-size, 17 in. overall length with 6 in. fringe. Blackfoot, early. Stylized floral designs beaded on cuffs; fingers deteriorated; pair should be set behind glass for preservation. G-$325

Gauntlets, pair, Indian-tanned leather. Simple horseshoe designs beaded on cuff. Medium-size, in excellent condition G-$250

Gauntlets, large and beautiful pair from Northern Plains region. Lined with fur; trade cloth, ca. 1870. D-$350

RELATED INDIAN APPAREL

Man's belt, thick black commercial leather. Plains Indian, 35 in. long, with geometric designs in beadwork. Collected in Montana and in excellent condition. Possibly ca. 1900. C-$450

Two Sioux arm bands, both different, sold as one lot. A-$75

Wolf skin medicine cap, was in University collection. Hair mostly present, some deterioration from age. An original Blackfoot item, very rare, ca. 1800. G-$400

Hair roach, done with porcupine guard hairs and red-dyed horsehair. Piece has a yarn and leather base; old and symmetrical. G-$350

Man's belt, 42 in. long and 2-1/2 in. wide. Beadwork on one side, geometric designs, fair condition, Blackfoot. D-$350

Nez Perce dance apron. A-$50

Rectangular cape, red and blue cloth, 36 in. long and 19 in. wide. Has two loom-beaded strips 1-1/4 in. wide and 10 in. long. Hawk bells attached, small mirrors and brass cone jingles. Unusual item. G-$265

Sioux cuffs, fair condition and workstyle. D-$300

Dew claw medicine piece, made from the hide of a deer leg. Museum quality, decorated with mirrors and brass tacks. Sioux, and very early. G-$675

Man's hair drop, beaded, Plains Indian style. D-$325

Woman's beaded collar, worn around neck and across shoulders. Shell beads cover outside; decorated with glass beads in several designs. Fringed. D-$335

Woodlands apron, design on velvet backing; tree and flowering plants done in beadwork. C-$550

Headband, beaded Plains Indian type, 1-1/8 in. wide and in good condition. D-$240

Penobscot fur hat, ca. 1900. D-$55

Infant's cap, northern Plains region, possibly antelope hide; completely covered on outside with tiny seed beads. It is 4-1/2 in. in diameter, in good condition; an unusual item. D-$700

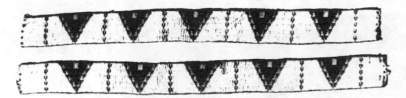

Sioux man's beaded legging strips, 29 in. long and 3 in. wide. All excellent condition, ca. 1880. D-$1,000

Photo courtesy Winona Trading Post, Santa Fe-Pierre & Sylvia Bovis

Smoking cap, probably Seneca or Onondaga, New York state. It is 4-1/4 x 11-3/4 in. Beaded in pattern of green vine with fruits or flowers in many colors. Saw-tooth beaded border in blue trimmed with white. Ex-coll. Fruchtel. Ca. 1870 or before. $525

Sherman Holbert collection, Fort Mille Lacs, Onamia, Minnesota

Dance apron, Ponca-Oto, intricate seed bead design on black velveteen. Size, 15 x 16 in.; this is rare Prairie beadwork, ca. 1885. $525

Larry Lantz, First Mesa, South Bend, Indiana

Sash, Winnebago, 5-1/2 x 96 in. Finger-woven of colorful commercial yarns in light and dark blues and red. Near-perfect example of old multi-strand braid weaving. Ca. 1950. $165

Sherman Holbert collection, Fort Mille Lacs, Onamia, Minnesota

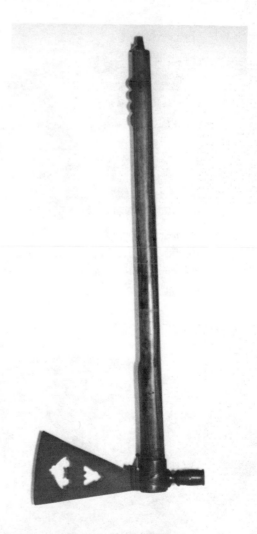

Pipe-tomahawk, Plains Indian. Large steel head with blade pierced, bat and fly design cut-outs. Plain wood haft has four raised projections near mouthpiece. High-grade, collected by Arnold Marcus Chernoff. It is ca. 1860s-1870s. Museum quality

Dave Hrachovy, Cedar Glen, California

Turban, Osage, bear-belly fur edged with trade beads and lined with fabric. Embellished with silver decoration. It is 4 in. high and late 1800s. Museum quality

James Reid, LTD, Santa Fe, New Mexico

Huron(?) cap, multi-colored beadwork over black cloth, very small beads with minimal bead loss. It is 7 in. in diameter, ca. 1850. $1,995

Traditions, Victor, New York

Dress tie and collar, fully beaded, 6 x 15 in. Made of canvas and beads, Blackfoot, and ca. 1890-1910. $350

Historic Interiors, Sorrento, British Columbia, Canada

Shirt, Ute, Intermontane, made of hide, stroud, German silver buckles, silk ribbons, and paint. Quite attractive, rare. 19th century. $4,000

Private collection; photo by John McLaughlin

Gros Ventre arm-bands, 4 x 10 in., from Montana. Pair made of canvas, beads, and silk ribbon with leather fringes. Ca. 1890. $900

Historic Interiors, Sorrento, British Columbia, Canada

Glengarry cap, Iroquois, Great Lakes beadwork in floral motif, many bead colors. Ca. 1870-1880. $425

Pocotopaug Trading Post, South Windsor, Connecticut

Cheyenne young girl's dress, fully beaded with small beads, done by Sylvia Spotted Wolf and her granddaughter, Kim (Cheyenne). Beaded on both sides, recent artwork. $4,985

Indian Territory, Tucson, Arizona

Sioux boy's vest, 20 x 26 in., hide and glass beads. Beadwork is very well-done, ca. 1890. $5,250

Historic Interiors, Sorrento, British Columbia, Canada

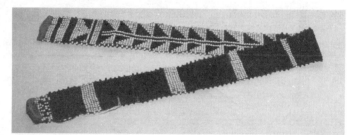

Belt, beaded, 24 in. long. Collected during California Gold Rush, probably Mono Indian. Scarce artwork, ca. 1850. $2,500

Traditions, Victor, New York

Glengarry hat, wool and glass beads, 3 x 4 x 9 in. Beadwork in many colors, Six Nations Iroquois, ca. 1860. $850

Historic Interiors, Sorrento, British Columbia, Canada

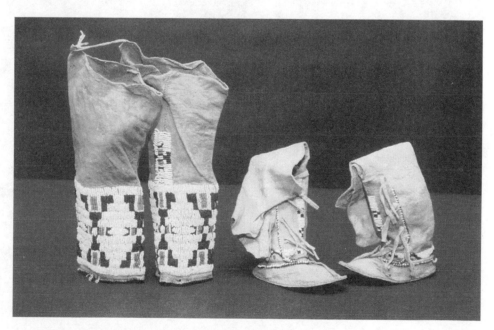

Ceremonial moccasins, Blackfoot, fully beaded in blue, yellow, and red against a white background. Ca. 1880. $2,000

Freya's Collectibles, Banff, Alberta, Canada

MOCCASINS—Adult Size

Cree moccasins, 8 in. long, with quillwork on hide. Simple floral design and in excellent condition; ca. 1900. G-$295

Sioux moccasins, quilled and beaded, man's size. D-$475

Plains Indian beaded moccasins, beaded tops, rawhide bottoms. Very old and in good condition. A-$450

Sioux "ceremonial moccasins," entirely beaded in geometric designs including soles. Adult sizes, good condition, almost all beadwork intact. C-$850

Sioux moccasins, fully beaded, good early designs. Sinew-sewn on buckskin with rawhide soles. C-$425

Cheyenne moccasins, very nicely beaded. D-$450

Taos Pueblo moccasins, beadwork on toes, originally painted in yellow ochre. D-$400

Arapaho moccasins, fully beaded, 10-1/2 in. long. Extremely fine condition with beaded cuffs; have "trail dusters" and red cloth bindings, sinew-sewn, and beaded. Ca. 1910. G-$550

Quilled moccasins, fine early designs, very old. A-$500

Deerskin moccasins, Woodlands Indian, upper parts covered with fine beadwork. Overall reddish leather, and ca. late 1880s. D-$500

Blackfoot moccasins, man-size, partially beaded in blue, lavender, and amber, classic style for this group. Collected on Blackfoot reservation in 1930s. G-$550

Sioux beaded moccasins, good design. A-$295

Sioux moccasins, man-size, light blue background with green and yellow designs. Excellent condition, and ca. 1910. G-$500

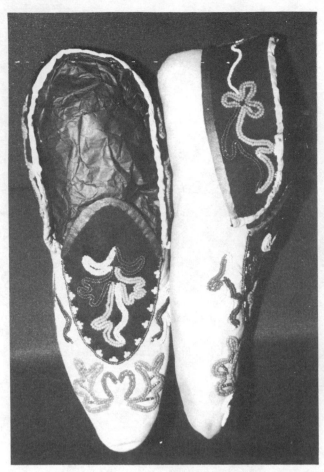

Men's moccasins, Tlingit, very nicely beaded in multiple colors, ca. 1880. $1,200

Freya's Collectibles, Banff, Alberta, Canada

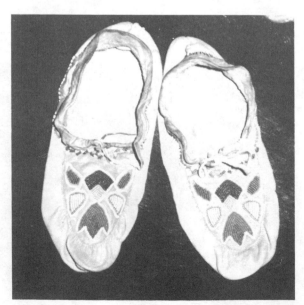

Beaded moccasins, light brown brain-tanned leather, Chippewa. Pair from Michigan, year 1870. $450

Michael F. Slasinski, Saginaw, Michigan

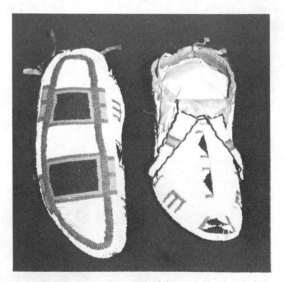

Ceremonial moccasins, Blackfoot, fully beaded in blue, yellow, and red against a while background. Ca. 1880. $2,000

Freya's Collectibles, Banff, Alberta, Canada

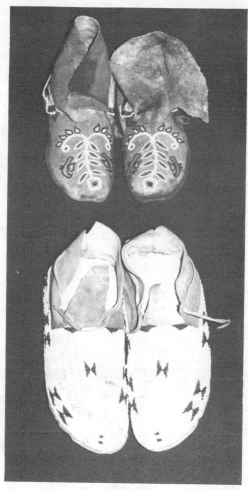

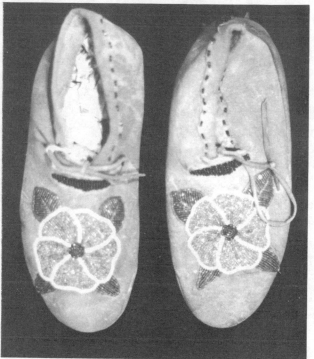

Moccasins, Athabascan, 11 in. long, early 1900s. Seed-beaded in floral designs on smoked moosehide. $375

Larry Lantz, First Mesa, South Bend, Indiana

Plains Indian moccasins, pairs.

Top: Blackfoot men's moccasins, 1865. $650
Bottom: Arapaho men's moccasins, 1880. $850

Freya's Collectibles, Banff, Alberta, Canada

Early Metis men's moccasins with soft soles, delicate beadwork design, year 1865. $600

Freya's Collectibles, Banff, Alberta, Canada

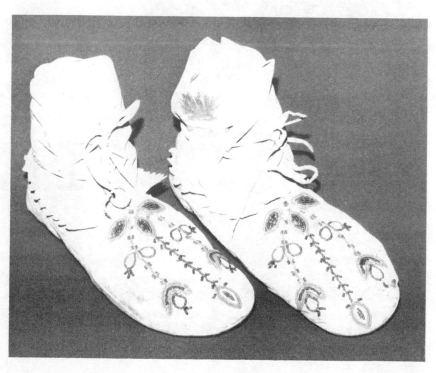

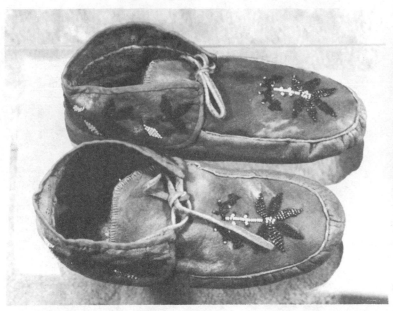

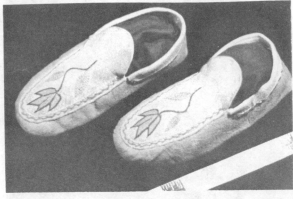

Moccasins, Cree, 9-1/2 in. long. Decoration is thread embroidered in florals, early 20th century. $200

Larry Lantz, First Mesa, South Bend, Indiana

Fine pair of Eastern Woodlands/Great Lakes area moccasins, with beaded tops and ankle-flaps. Condition is very good for age. $395-425

Collection of David G. & Barbara J. Shirley

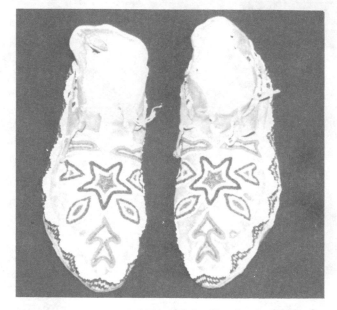

Moccasins, Ute, men's, hide with beading in six colors. Ca. 1870. $1,500

Private collection; photo by John McLaughlin

Moccasins, Mille Lacs Reservation, Chippewa, 10 in. long. Pair made of Indian smoke-tanned leather. Beadwork translucent green and gold, and solid red and brown. Contemporary. $145

Sherman Holbert collection, Fort Mille Lacs, Onamia, Minnesota

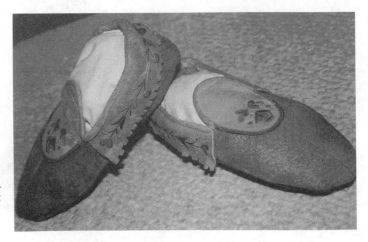

Cree moccasins, very fine embroidery work on buckskin, formerly in a museum. They are 10 in. long, ca. 1940-1950. $365

Indian Territory, Tucson, Arizona

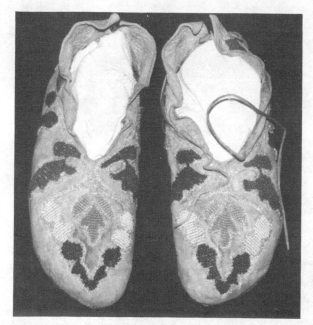

Moccasins, Osage, adult size, leather with beadwork in floral design and seven colors. Ca. 1920. $,500

Private collection; photo by John McLaughlin

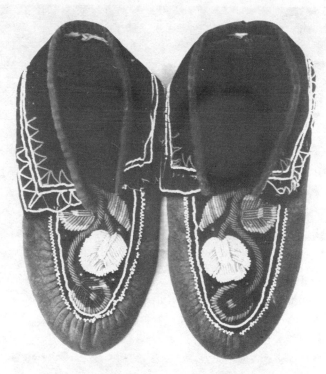

Moccasins, Iroquois, floral beading done in six basic colors against black, including two shades each of white, yellow, blue, and reddish. Very nice pair, ca. 1860-1870. $550

Pocotopaug Trading Post, South Windsor, Connecticut

Moccasins, various groups and periods.

Top left: Canadian Chippewa, 11-1/2 in. long, moosehide, ca. 1920s-1930s. $225

Top right: Shoshone, Indian-tanned leather, seven colors of beads in cascade pattern, ca. 1940-1950. $245

Bottom left: Hudson Bay Eskimo, child's size in sealskin and rabbit, fine condition, attractive, ca. 1950. $95

Bottom center: Dogrib-Canada, brain-tanned moosehide, floral beading, ca. 1930s. $95

Bottom right: Cree Indian, Indian-tanned moosehide, beading in two sizes and many colors, 11 in. long, ca. 1920-1940. $225

Sherman Holbert collection, Fort Mille Lacs, Onamia, Minnesota

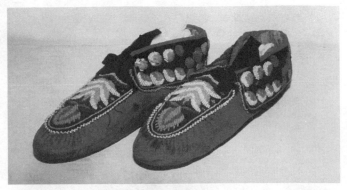

Iroquois moccasins, 9 in. long, floral work done in very small beads with minimal bead loss. These are ca. 1870. $1,500

Traditions, Victor, New York

Moccasins, Sioux, beaded on soles and uppers, 10 in. long. Moccasins made as gifts or for dress occasions often were elaborately decorated with solidly beaded soles. Ca. late 1800s. $6,500

Canfield Gallery, Santa Fe

Kiowa woman's moccasins, high-top, buckskin with beaded trim and fringe. Covered with yellow ochre, probably ca. 1940-1960. $2,875

Indian Territory, Tucson, Arizona

Sioux beaded moccasins, ceremonial type with both beaded soles and uppers. Note the decorative triple tongue-end tassels. Ca. 1880-1890. $4,500

Antiques & Art, Piedmont, South Dakota

Sioux moccasins, beaded buckskin, beads in white, green, black, and red. Well-made pair, ca. 1890. $1,000

Antiques & Art, Piedmont, South Dakota

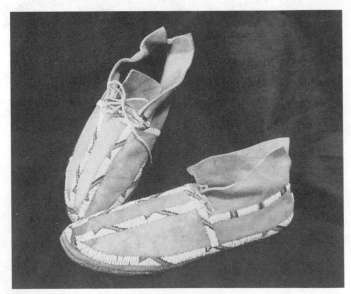

Cheyenne moccasins, 10 in. long. Made of native-tanned leather with glass beads; sewn with sinew, late 1800s. $600

Blue Coyote Trading Post, Nashville, Indiana; Paul McCreary photograph

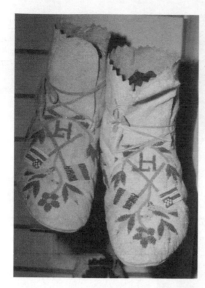

Moccasins, Eastern or Santee Sioux. Moccasins 9 in. long and 9 in. high, decorated with florals and flags. Soles and uppers are deer hide and initials 'HT' on the vamps, ca. 1890-1900. $1,000

J. Steve and Anita Shearer, Torrance, California

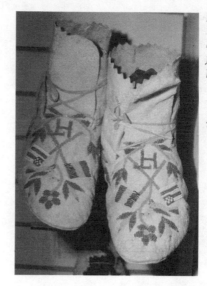

Moccasins, Eastern or Santee Sioux. Moccasins 9 in. long and 9 in. high, decorated with florals and flags. Soles and uppers are deer hide and initials "HT" on the vamps, ca. 1890-1900. $1,000

J. Steve and Anita Shearer, Torrance, California

Nez Perce woman's boots, hide and glass beads, 12 in. high. Nicely beaded in floral designs and ca. 1890. $2,750

Historic Interiors, Sorrento, British Columbia, Canada

Sioux or Assiniboin moccasins, man's size 7, hide, cloth, and glass beads. Ca. 1895-1910. $1,250

Historic Interiors, Sorrento, British Columbia, Canada

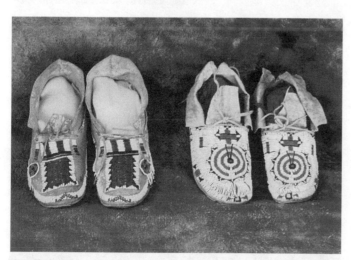

Southern Cheyenne moccasins from Oklahoma, very well made of hide, attractive beadwork. Both in man's size 8, and ca. 1890.

Left: $1,450
Right: $1,800

Historic Interiors, Sorrento, British Columbia, Canada

Sioux moccasins, man's size 8-1/2, hide, cloth and beads with strips of porcupine quills across uppers. Quillwork blue-green and yellow against red. Ca. 1875-1885. $4,500

Historic Interiors, Sorrento, British Columbia, Canada

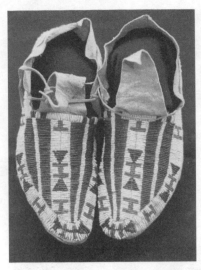

Cheyenne moccasins, native-tanned hide, sinew and glass beads. Colors are red, blue, and green against white. Ca. 1890. $2,750

David Cook Fine American Art, Denver, Colorado; Jamie Kahn photograph

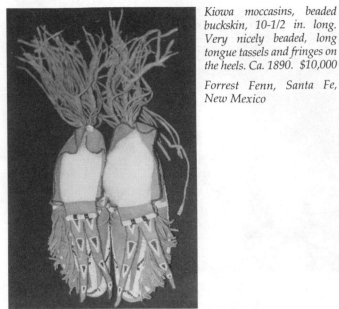

Kiowa moccasins, beaded buckskin, 10-1/2 in. long. Very nicely beaded, long tongue tassels and fringes on the heels. Ca. 1890. $10,000

Forrest Fenn, Santa Fe, New Mexico

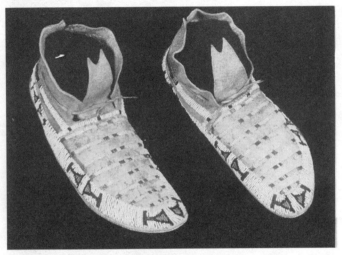

Plains Indian beaded and quilled moccasins, beaded sides and quilled uppers, done on brain-tanned leather. Ca. 1880. $2,500-3,500

Terry Schafer, American Indian Art & Antiques, Marietta, Ohio

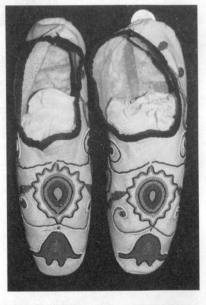

Upper Missouri beaded woman's buckskin moccasins, may be Arikara, made from buffalo parfleche. No later than 1850s. $3,500

Forrest Fenn, Santa Fe, New Mexico

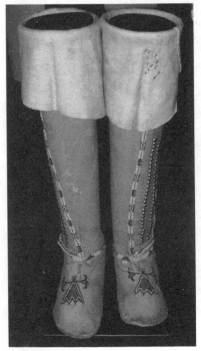

Kiowa woman's hightop moccasins, 19 in. high, beaded, with German silver buttons up the sides. In beautiful condition, ca. 1890. $15,000

Forrest Fenn, Santa Fe, New Mexico

Cheyenne moccasins, beautifully beaded with small beads. In mint condition, sinew sewn with buffalo hide soles. Size is 10 in. long. Ca. 1880. $3,250

Indian Territory, Tucson, Arizona

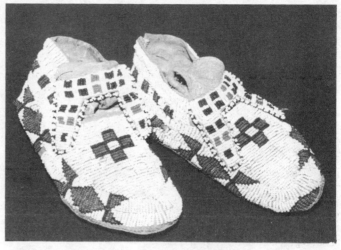

MOCCASINS-Child's Size

Baby moccasins, 5 in. overall length and 2 in. wide. Toes partially beaded; Indian-tanned leather.   C-$135

Plains Indian baby moccasins, single specimen, 4-1/4 in. long. Top area beaded, bottom worn through; very nice beadwork design and that section in good condition.   C-$35-55

Blackfoot baby moccasins, beaded pair.   A-$115

Sioux man's moccasins, parfleche soles, hide uppers with highly intact beadwork in good designs. Ca. 1900. $1,750

Traditions, Victor, New York

Sioux man's moccasins, leather and beadwork, intricate designs on a green ground. In fine condition, ca. 1920. $1,500

Traditions, Victor, New York

Assiniboin boys' moccasins with beaded tongues. Beads red, blue, and green against a white background. Year 1890. $600

Freya's Collectibles, Banff, Alberta, Canada

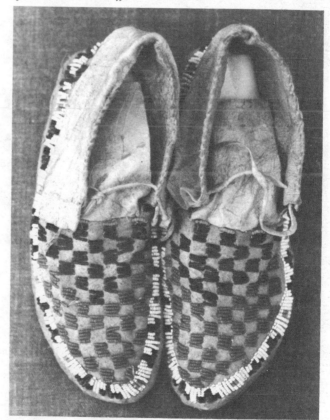

Moccasins, Chippewa. Made of native-tanned moosehide, felt cloth, and beads in floral patterns. Western Ontario, Canada, early 20th century. $285

Frank Bergevin, Port Of Call, Alexandria Bay, New York

Moccasins, Cheyenne, beadwork done in checkerboard pattern of red and green with red, white, black, and green around edges. Ca. 1870s. $575

Pocotopaug Trading Post, South Windsor, Connecticut

Woodlands moccasins.

Left: Iroquois, beaded, 9-1/2 in., ca. 1900. $350
Center: very nice Cree beaded leather, Manitoba, Canada, ca. 1920. $325
Right: colorful beaded leather, Quebec, Canada, 8 in. long, ca. 1890. $375

Pat & Dave Summers, Native American Artifacts, Victor, New York

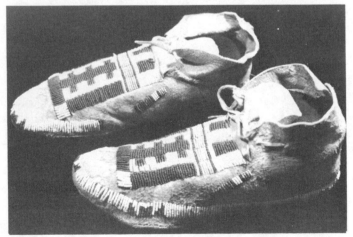

Moccasins, man's, Southern Arapaho, 10 in. long, lazy stitch sewing with seed beads, late 1800s. An exceptional pair. $1,100

Larry Lantz, First Mesa, South Send, Indiana

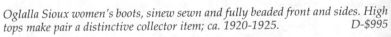

Oglalla Sioux women's boots, sinew sewn and fully beaded front and sides. High tops make pair a distinctive collector item; ca. 1920-1925.   D-$995

Photo courtesy Crazy Crow Trading Post, Denison, Texas

Moccasins, high-top, Sioux, 9-1/2 in. long. Beaded panels are in several colors against white; late 1800s. $695

Larry Lantz, First Mesa, South Bend, Indiana

Sioux (Mixed Blood) child's quilled moccasins, 6-1/2 in. long. Have attractive quilled designs and are ca. 1870. $4,500

Forrest Fenn, Santa Fe, New Mexico

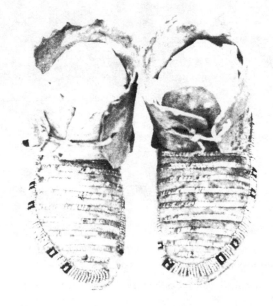

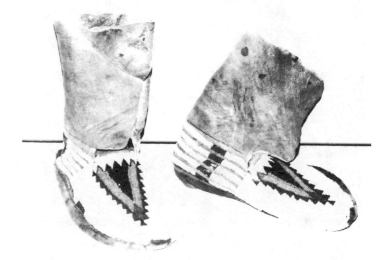

Child's moccasins, 6-1/2 in. long. Orange quillwork bands and an outline strip of pale blue beadwork. Northern Plains area, ca. 1880. G-$550

Photo courtesy Kenneth R. Canfield, Plains Indian Art, Kansas City, Missouri

Pair of Nez Perce beaded man's moccasins, ca. 1880, excellent condition and with fine beadwork overall. D-$1,100

Photo courtesy Winona Trading Post, Santa Fe-Pierre & Sylvia Bovis

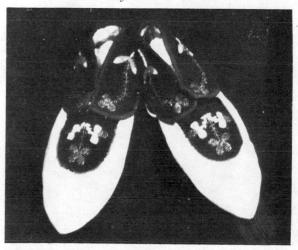

Huron moccasins, 9-1/2 in. long. Smoked buckskin with black cloth flaps and toe panels, beaded floral designs. Like-new condition, and ca. 1890. D-$500

Photo courtesy Crazy Crow Trading Post, Denison, Texas

RELATED INDIAN FOOTGEAR

Apache boots, pair, 27-1/2 in. long. Beaded crosses on toes with small beaded band on tops.   G-$475

Plains Indian beaded moccasins, three, left foot only, in man, woman, and child sizes. Possibly, for reasons unknown, three pairs were divided and marketed. Fine beadwork, excellent condition. All evidence similar handwork; may have been made by same person. Early 1900s.   C-$475

Cheyenne moccasins, pair, beaded.   A-$145

Southern Cheyenne or Kiowa boots, 15 in. high. Decorated with seed beads in strips, on yellow ochred hide. Excellent condition and ca. 1870-80.   G-$1,450

Cree beaded moccasins, pair.   A-$75

Tlingit moccasin tops, pair.   A-$65

Moccasins, Eskimo or sub-Arctic, sealskin with rabbit trim, near-original condition, ca. 1940s. $200-250

Pocotopaug Trading Post, South Windsor, Connecticut

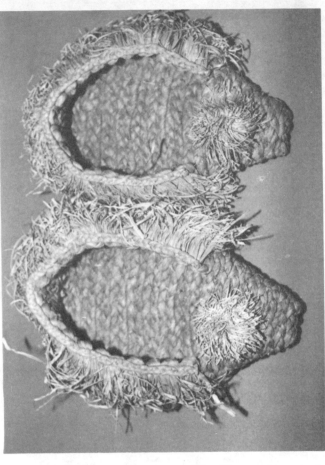

Corn-husk moccasins, yellow-tan in color. They are Iroquois, from New York state, year 1952. $175

Michael F. Slasinski, Saginaw, Michigan

Sandal, from near Pruitt, New Mexico. Such perishable items from prehistoric times are rare, Basketmaker II period. $100-150

Marguerite L. Kernaghan collection; photograph by Marguerite L. and Stewart W. Kernaghan, Bellvue, Colorado

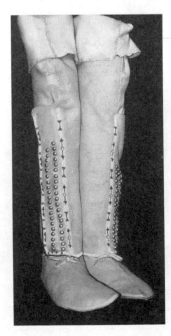

Girl's boots, Kiowa/Comanche. Flaps decorated with beadwork and brass tacks, and condition is exceptional for leatherwork a century old, ca. 1900. $4,000

Canfield Gallery, Santa Fe

Moccasins, contemporary make, left example 9 in. long, left to right:

Cheyenne style, fully beaded	*$350*
Cheyenne style, partial beading	*$150*
Cree, fleece-lined	*$150*

Blue Coyote Trading Post, Nashville, Indiana; Paul McCreary photograph

Dew claw necklace as used by the Sioux and many other tribes. All carved dew claws with trade beads, and pre-1900.   G-$450

Chippewa shoulder bag, 12 x 15 in. with 2-1/2 in. wide carrying strap. Floral designs done in red, green, and white beads. Has beaded tassels.   G-$1,500

Awl case, leather with beadwork, some beads missing; 9 in. long.   D-$150

Miniature pipe bag, probably late 1800s. Deerskin, beaded designs on side, nicely fringed and 10-1/2 in. long.   D-$300

Parfleche knife sheath with painted designs and tacks. Sioux, and old.   G-$275

Dew claw bag, made from the leg skin of an elk. Old piece, very good condition.   G-$475

LEATHERWORK COLLECTIBLES

Plains Indian saddle bags, matched pair, made of rawhide and fringed.   C-$2,500

Parfleche envelope, small, 5 x 9 in. Standard design and excellent condition. Marked "Pendleton, Oregon" and dated 1930.   G-$185

Leather carrying bag, Plains Indian and early. D-$575

Pipe bag, Southern Plains, 27 in. long, nicely glass-beaded, leather fringes, late 1880s.   D-$825

Carrying pouch, Apache, of shaped hide, 7 in. long.   D-$200

Plains Indian lariat or lasso, with eye or slip-loop at one end, knotted at other. Still coiled, rawhide hard. Estimated length 23 ft. Slight mouse-nibble damage, barely noticeable. Averages 1 in. in diameter. Private collector values at $15 per foot. Braided.   C-$460

Painted parfleche envelopes, matching pair, 12 in. high and 26 in. long. Very nice designs painted; in excellent condition. Pairs are hard to obtain. Good art pieces, very collectible.   G-$950

Carrying bag, partially decorated front and back in geometric beadwork, late 1800s. Bag is 3 x 13 x 15 in., worn but good condition. Leather.   D-$350

Strike-a-light bag, 5 x 3-1/2 in. wide, northern Plains region. Leather with beadwork designs on one side. C-$325

Hair roach of deerhide and porcupine quills, very well preserved. Attractive piece, ca. early 1900s.   D-$200

Parfleche box, 6 x 9 x 14 in. All painted designs, early reservation period, nice condition.   G-$425

Leather dance bell straps, set, Plains Indian. Attach to outer sides of legs. Early 1900s, good bells.   D-$160

Parfleche envelope, 8 x 7 in., with flexible leather wrap that closed front. Faint painted design. Plains Indian.   A-$225

Saddlebags, 10 in. wide and unfolded length 62 in. Set classic Apache, rawhide cutouts over red tradecloth. Set is ca. 1890.   G-$1,800

Photo courtesy Kenneth R. Canfield, Plains Indian Art, Kansas City, Missouri

Bow and quiver case with bow, Cheyenne, beaded and quilted. Top-grade piece, ca. 1875. $6,500

Crown & Eagle Antiques, Inc., New Hope, Pennsylvania

Ermine (winter weasel) ceremonial bundle, Blackfoot. Has red and dark blue ribbons and brass tack eyes. Length, 14-1/2 in.; late 1800s. Museum quality

Michael F. Slasinski, Saginaw, Michigan

Quirt, Northern Plains Indian, made from chair leg with brass tacks as decoration. Lash is twisted commercial leather; wrist wrap is tacked saddle leather. Length is 16 in. (handle) and it is ca. 1860s-1870s.
    Museum quality

Dave Hrachovy, Cedar Glen, California

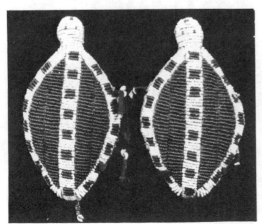

Amulets, turtle effigy, Sioux. Matching pair has green, red, blue, and white beading. Ca. 1800s.
    Museum quality

Morning Star Gallery, Santa Fe, New Mexico

Sioux arrow, point, shaft and fletching complete, 1870s. $125

Lee Hallman collection, Telford, Pennsylvania

Cheyenne/Pawnee arrow, just over 2 ft. long, ca. 1860s-1870s. $150

Lee Hallman collection, Telford, Pennsylvania

Gros Ventre Sioux arrow, metal tip, ca. 1860s-1870s. $150

Lee Hallman collection, Telford, Pennsylvania

Southwestern U.S. arrow, painted in fletching area, ca. 1880s. $125

Lee Hallman collection, Telford, Pennsylvania

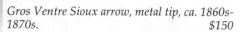

Warclub, stone head with decorations and wrapped wooden handle. An excellent example of a Plains Indian weapon from the 1800s. $400-600

Private collection

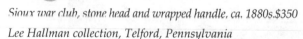

Sioux war club, stone head and wrapped handle, ca. 1880s. $350

Lee Hallman collection, Telford, Pennsylvania

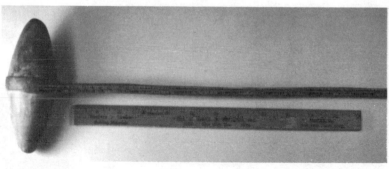

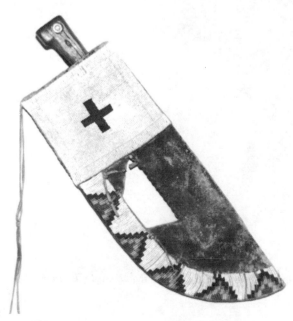

Beaded knife case, Blackfoot. Has Indian-tanned leather with belt cutout; blade made from an old file with a wood handle. Length is 14-1/2 in. for this 1870s-1880s piece. $4,000-5,000

Dave Hrachovy, Cedar Glen, California

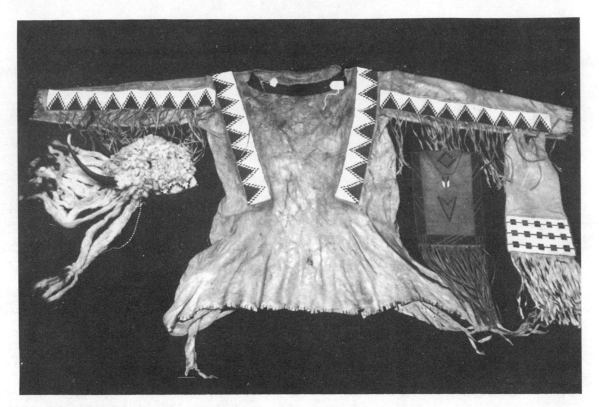

Blackfoot material.

Left: horned headdress, trade cloth, ermine, buffalo horns, and beads, ca. 1890. $3,000
Center: ceremonial shirt, hide, beads, trade cloth, and ochre paint, ca. 1880. $7,500
Right: mirror bag (rectangular), hide and beads, ca. 1890. $1,200
Far right: pipe bag, hide and beaded both sides, ca. 1880. $2,000

Private collection; photo by John Mc-Laughlin

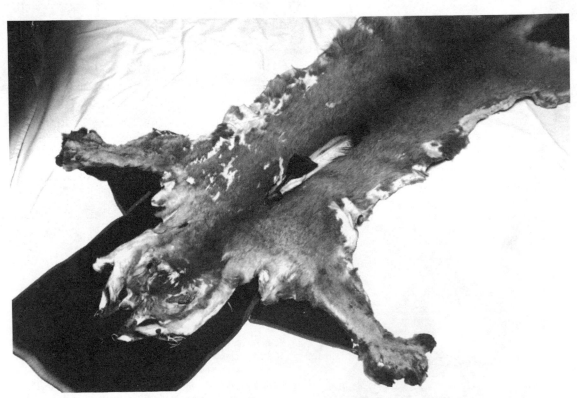

Saddle blanket, Crow, made of mountain lion pelt, cloth, and feathers. This unusual and rare item is ca. 1870. $5,000

Private collection; photo by John McLaughlin

BACK

Coat, Santee Sioux, men's size 40/42. Made from buffalo calf hide; decorated with blue, red, white, and yellow beads depicting flowers, vines, leaves, stars, and horses. Rawhide ties instead of buttons and fringed sleeves and shoulders. A fine old Plains item. Ca. 1880. $4,950

Sherman Holbert collection, Fort Mille Lacs, Onamia, Minnesota

Small Eastern Woodlands/Great Lakes fringed bag with drawstring top and quillwork on side. Quills are dyed red, orange, and white. $325-400

Collection of David G. & Barbara J. Shirley

Shield-cover, Cheyenne, painted hide with feather, ca. 1860. $3,000

Private collection, photo by John McLaughlin

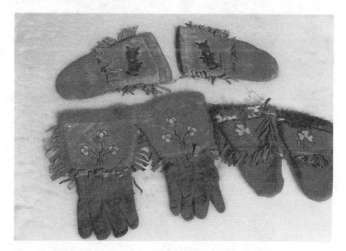

Cree mittens and gauntlets, mid-1900s, adult sizes. Materials are moosehide, rabbit fur, and beads in floral patterns. Omushkegowuk (Swampy Cree) from the village of Kashechewan, James Bay, Ontario, Canada.

Mittens $125-160;
Gauntlets $225

Frank Bergevin, Port of Call, Alexandria Bay, New York

Child's fringed jacket, extensive beadwork, Crow Indian. Very high quality, ca. 1870. $6,500

Freya's Collectibles, Banff, Alberta, Canada

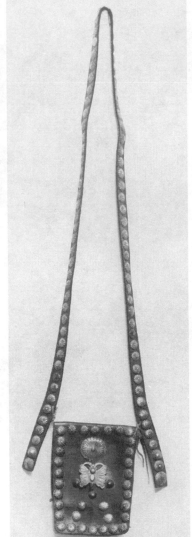

Leatherwork, center examples 15 in. long, all left to right:

Iroquois woman's boots, felt cloth, deerhide, and beads, St. Regis Mohawk Reservation, New York, mid-1900s. $175
Cree gauntlets with embroidery, adult male size, moosehide, rabbit fur, and embroidery thread. Northern Quebec, Canada, mid-1900s. $200
Cree boots, red felt, moosehide, wolf fur, and beads. Northern Quebec, Canada, mid-1900s. $185

Frank Bergevin, Port of Call, Alexandria Bay, New York

Cheyenne dispatch case or sewing kit, 6 x 9 in., made of recycled leather; perhaps a saddle bag. Container is ca. 1870-1880. $600

Private collection

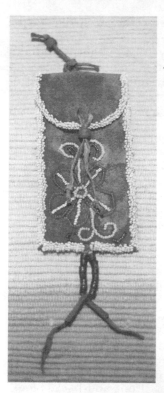

Seneca woman's utility bag, 3-1/2 x 6-1/2 in., made of elk hide. Floral pattern beadwork in four colors, from the 1890s. $375

T.R.H. collection, Indiana

Buffalo rawhide shield, Jemez pueblo, 22 in. in diameter. Holding and carrying thongs passed through the close sets of small black holes. Ca. 1850. $25,000

Forrest Fenn, Santa Fe, New Mexico

Great Lakes area beaded bag, 4-1/2 x 8 in., soft leather hand sewn with cotton thread. Beadwork in red, white, and black octagon-shaped beads. From Michigan, early 1900s. $450

T.R.H. collection, Indiana

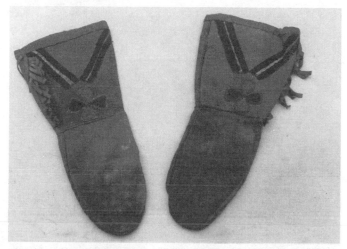

Northern Cree mittens, adult size 14 in. long, beaded clover-leaf pattern, applied trade ribbon, short fringe, all on native-tanned moosehide. Northern Quebec, Canada, ca. 1910. $150

Frank Bergevin, Port of Call, Alexandria Bay, New York

Ration ticket carrier, Reservation period, 3-1/4 x 4 in. Materials are leather and seed beads in red, green, light blue, and royal blue, with red heart beads, brass beads, and bells. Late 1800s. $450

T.R.H. collection, Indiana

Plains Stryklite pouches, ca. 1880-1900. $1,000-3,000

Crown & Eagle Antiques, Inc., New Hope, Pennsylvania

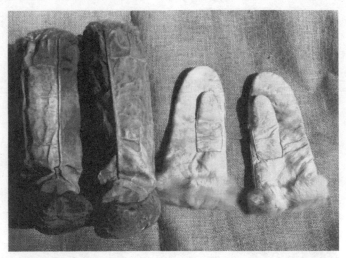

Northern leatherwork, left to right:

Inuit (Eskimo) mukluks, adult size 15 in. high, sealskin. Northern Quebec, Canada. Ca. 1930s. $250
Cree mittens, sealskin, adult size 10 in. long, northern Quebec, Canada, 1940s. $85

Frank Bergevin, Port Of Call, Alexandria Bay, New York

Cree snowshoe boots, adult sizes. Made of moosehide, canvas, and beads; Omushkegowuk (Swampy Cree) from village of Kashechewan, Ontario, Canada, mid-1900s.

Left: $90
Right: $150

Frank Bergevin, Port Of Call, Alexandria Bay, New York

Flint and steel or strike-a-light bag, possibly Apache, with small hawk bells. Size, 3-1/2 x 6-1/2 in. and likely late 1800s. C-$425

The listings that follow have been selected because they are highly unusual or significantly different to warrant presentation. All were selected from Kenneth R. Canfield's Plains Indian Art Catalogues Nos. 1 and 2.

Following is an excerpt from Catalogue No. 1, written by Mr. Canfield. It allows a fleeting glimpse of artistic inspiration in the Plains Indian past. Used with permission.

"The American Great Plains is an awesome sweep of land and sky bounded by mountains and long sinuous rivers. The Northern Plains were dominated by the tribes of the Teton (or western) Sioux, who called themselves collectively the Dakota, and to a lesser degree by the Blackfeet, Crow, Gros Ventre, Assiniboin, and Plains Cree. In the south were Kiowa and Comanche. Cheyenne, Arapaho, and Pawnee

ranged along the western margins of the grasslands. On the east lived Osage, Iowa, Oto, Mesquakie, and Mandan.

"They differed widely by tribe—linguistically and ethnically—but they had much in common socially and culturally. The Northern Cheyenne and Sioux lived in such proximity that their artistic production overlaps.

"The plains tribes shared a way of life imposed upon them by the vast, harsh world in which they lived, a landscape of dazzling color and light, of violent contrast and great distance. Theirs was an environment of blinding white snow, of depths of blue sky, of the carmine red of lifeblood, of the endless green seas of grass on ochre plains.

"Death was always at hand, but they lived serenely, at one with the universe. It seems hardly surprising that a sense of vivid intensity, wonder and magic should communicate itself to the view through the still living art of the Plains Indians."

Note: Values listed are ca. 1975. Current values would be two to six times as high.

PLAINS INDIAN ART

(Courtesy Kenneth R. Canfield)

Whetstone case, 5 in. long. Hide container ornamented with blue and white beadwork front and back. Sioux, from South Dakota, and pre-1890. G-$35

Man's warshirt, 38 in. long. Painted buckskin with beaded strips on shoulders and sleeves; beaded rosettes front and back. Ten winter-pelt weasel skins attached. Beaded geometric designs in orange, black, and pale blue on white background. Collected in Canada; Blackfeet (Piegan), from Alberta, ca. 1910. G-$2,600

Carved wooden flute, 21-1/2 in. long. Cedar, incised in spiral pattern. Lead soundplate surmounted by wooden sound block carved in shape of horse and stained with red ochre. Paper tag affixed to sound block. Eastern Sioux, from Northern Plains area. Mid-1880s. G-$495

Quillwork pipe bag, 28 in. long with fringes. Deerskin tobacco bag embroidered with red and yellow dyed porcupine quills, front and back. Quilled suspensions with tin cone and feather attachments. Old tag attached reads "Quilled pipe bag 1875." Northern Plains, and mid-1870s. G-$1,560

Woman's boots, 25 in. long. Hard-soled, soft yellow dyed deerskin with fringing at tops. Narrow beadwork lines in white, red, and blue encircle tops and ankles and frame the front flaps. Flaps studded with double rows or German silver buttons. Kiowa, Southern Plains area, ca.1875. G-$780

Ration ticket pouch, 4 in. long. Beaded bag with triangular figures of brown, yellow, and light blue on lavender field; flap and thong drawstring. Carry-strap of woven pale blue beadwork. Southern Plains regions, and pre-1900. G-$155

Tepee liner, entire canvas 85 x 142 in. Area of ornamentation 55 x 92 in. Heavy canvas, ornamented in traditional linear pattern; predominately orange bands of beadwork interspersed with red yam tufts. Cornhusk-wrapped suspensions attached to fourteen beaded medallions along top. Each suspension terminates in loop and deer-hoofs. Collected by Reese Kincaid, from Nightwalker family. Cheyenne, from Oklahoma, and ca. 1900. G-$3,500

Sioux "possible" bags, beaded pair. Soft sinew-sewn hide pouches, each 13 x 22 in., decorated with large panels of multicolor geometric beadwork. Name comes from Lakota word meaning a container for any possible thing. Ca. 1875. Pair, $16,000

Canfield Gallery, Santa Fe

Crow quirt, wood handle with pictograph design. Wrapped with beaded buckskin. Ca. 1890. $4,000

Antiques & Art, Piedmont, South Dakota

Sioux tepee or possible bag, buckskin with tin cones, large central beaded panel. Horsehair tufts add decoration. Ca. 1910. $2,500

Antiques & Art, Piedmont, South Dakota

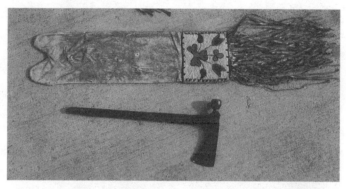

Blackfoot pipe bag, top, fringed top with beaded floral panel, ca. 1890. $1,850

Pipe-tomahawk, bottom, with metal-inlaid handle. Unlisted

Antiques & Art, Piedmont, South Dakota

Close-up of Crow quirt with pictograph design on wood handle. Figures may represent an elk and a bear. Ca. 1890. $4,000

Antiques & Art, Piedmont, South Dakota

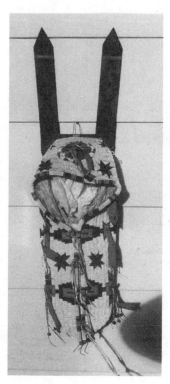

Cheyenne cradle, beautifully beaded buckskin, with tacked wooden slats. Ca. 1930-1940. $6,500

Antiques & Art, Piedmont, South Dakota

Cheyenne/Arapaho beaded saddle bags, with pictograph designs on fringed buckskin. Outside horses are blue; inside horses are red, both on green ground. Ca. 1910. $10,000

Antiques & Art, Piedmont, South Dakota

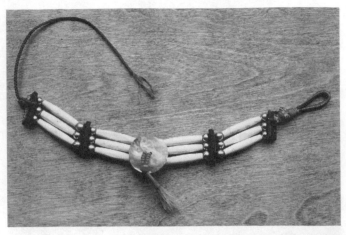

Plains Indian male's choker, made with leather, bone, and silver trade beads. Center is river mussel shell with red glass trade beads, tin cone, and horsehair drop. Leather spacers, bone sections, and silver trade beads strung on sinew. Tie finely braided human hair, ca. 1920-1940. $550

Tom Fouts collection, Kansas

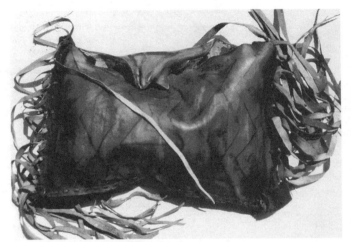

Parfleche, Northern Plains and Blackfoot, 10 x 13 in., made of rawhide with painted geometric designs. Ca. early 1900s. $375

Blue Coyote Trading Post, Nashville, Indiana; Pat Nolan photograph

Man's Northern Plains bone breast-plate, 9 in. wide and 11 in. high. Made of hairpipe bone and leather dividers and trade bells. Came from the Little Soldier or Louis Sitting Bull collection, from Jamestown, North Dakota, ca. 1870-1890. $5,000

J. Steve and Anita Shearer, Torrance, California

Plains Indian (probably Crow or Kiowa) knife and beaded sheath; blade made by trader or blacksmith. Handle is wood wrapped with sinew, Indian made. Sheath of Indian-tanned leather, finely beaded, and edged with a strip of old trade blanket. Set is ca. 1880. $2,000

Tom Fouts collection, Kansas

Woman's dentilia shell breast-plate necklace, 6 in. wide and 21 in. long. Material is dentilia shells and leather divides topped with strip of red ribbon. Came from the Little Soldier or Louis Sitting Bull collection, Jamestown, North Dakota. Ca. 1880-1890. $5,000

J. Steve and Anita Shearer, Torrance, California

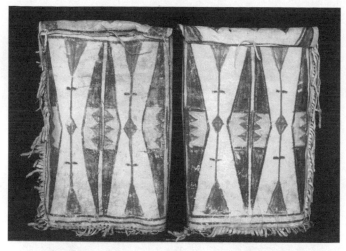

Arapaho parfleche pair, unusual elliptical design, 13 x 20-1/2 in., 4 in. deep. Made of hide with trade pigments in red, yellow, and blue. Ca. 1890. $9,500

David Cook Fine American Art, Denver, Colorado; Jamie Kahn photograph

Ghost Dance dress, Kiowa, 57 in. long. Top made from army flag and bottom from army tenting material. Ca. 1890. $35,000

Forrest Fenn, Santa Fe, New Mexico

Central Plains knife case, hide over recycled parfleche, 11 in. long. Sheath beaded both sides with red, dark blue, and yellow beads against a light blue ground. Quite attractive with beaded fringes, ca. 1870-1880. $7,500

Private collection

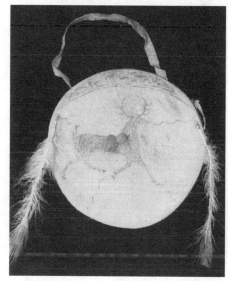

Kiowa Elk Dreamer shield, painted figures on buckskin, shield 9 in. in diameter. Collected from White Eagle, 101 Ranch performer. When guns and bullets became widely used, shields gradually became smaller, but remained as necessary as large ones. Last quarter of 1800s. $20,000

Forrest Fenn, Santa Fe, New Mexico

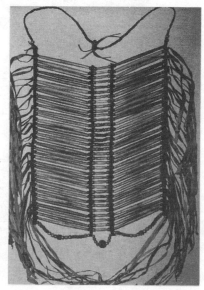

Plains Indian hair pipe breastplate, 9-1/2 x 15 in., bone hair pipes with cobalt blue and red heart beads. Obtained from a Canadian Native American; prior history is unknown. Ca. 1890-1910. $1,800

T.R.H. collection, Indiana

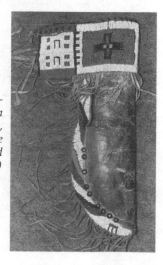

Central Plains knife case, hide over recycled parfleche, 11 in. long. Sheath beaded both sides with red, dark blue, and yellow beads against a light blue ground. Quite attractive with beaded fringes, ca. 1870-1880. $7,500

Private collection

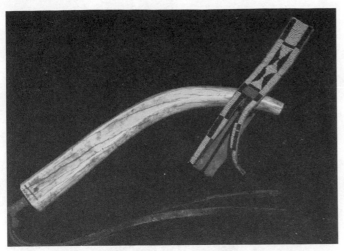

Northern Cheyenne elk-antler quirt, with yellow, green, and white-center red beads. Measures 30 in. long including the leather whip; antler scraped, flattened and incised. Ca. 1865. $8,500

Forrest Fenn, Santa Fe, New Mexico

Sioux Indian boy's outfit, child size fringed shirt with leggings. Material is buffalo hide and beadwork. In excellent condition, ca. 1900. $4,750

Traditions, Victor, New York

Santee Sioux vest and leggings, outfit sized for 5- or 6-year-old boy. Material is buckskin with fine floral beadwork. Ca. 1900. $2,475

Indian Territory, Tucson, Arizona

Crupper for horse, 22 x 42 in., wool, canvas and glass beads. Highly decorative work, Blackfoot, from Montana, and ca. 1890. $2,950

Historic Interiors, Sorrento, British Columbia, Canada

Sioux boy's beaded vest, beadwork on hide, fine edging and designs. In excellent condition, ca. 1885. $3,250

Traditions, Victor, New York

Cornhusk belt, 37 in. long and 6 in. wide. "Cornhusk" actually woven hemp fibers on leather, with geometric designs imbricated in yarn. Three brass buckles; lined with calico. Nez Perce, Plateau area, and pre-1900.   G-$625

Quilled breastplate, 10 in. wide and 16 in. long. Ornate with hide strips wrapped in predominately bright red quillwork in geometric pattern. Ribbon, feather, and tin-cone attachments. Sioux, Northern Plains region, and ca. 1890s.   G-$1,750

Pipe, 29 in. long. Catlinite pipe bowl with wooden stem, wound with braided quilling and feathers. Provenance: Lawson Collection, Philbrook Art Center, Tulsa. Collected by Roberta Lawson, acquired by museum in 1946. Deaccessioned in trade, 1976. Sioux, Northern Plains area, mid-1880s.   G-$885

Pipe tamper, 11 in. long. Carved of ash; end shaped like human foot, wrapped in braided red and white quillwork. Northern Plains region, and ca. 1910.   G-$140

Baby leggings, 6 in. wide and 9 in. high. Diminutive pair, buckskin, outlined with band of geometric beaded figures on blue field. Edges trimmed with faceted metallic beads. Old tag reads "Paul Good Bear, Cheyenne." Cheyenne, Plains region, and ca. 1900.   G-$145

Pair of child's dolls, large doll 13 in. high, smaller doll 11-1/2 in. high. Made of buckskin, trade cloth, animal hair, and yarn. Decorated with beading and blue and red paint. Smaller doll painted with an eagle front and back on its buckskin shirt. Large doll has crescent moon front and back, with cross and falling star pattern under shirt flaps. Painted images similar to those on Ghost Dance costumes of the period. Northern Plains area, and ca. 1895.   G-$440 pair

Toy canoe, 42 in. long and 10 in. wide. Detailed replica of full-size craft. Birchbark sealed with pitch, cedar planking, pine thwarts, tied with cedar root, and fastened with wood pegs. (Compare no. 33 in Norman Feder's catalogue of the Jarvis collection of Eastern Plains Indian art in the Brooklyn Museum.) Ojibwa, and pre-1900. G-$325

Bag, 46 in. long. Otter skin medicine bag of the Mide society, used to hold sacred objects for curing rites. Beaded panels of ribbon-edged velvet. Otter retains claws, skull and teeth, and has one coat-button eye. Red-dyed feathers inserted into nose. Brass thimble attached to one claw. Great Lakes area. Ca. 1870.   G-$825

Ghost Dance vest, 21 in. long. Man's, beaded in pictographic style with blue, green, greasy yellow, and transparent red beads. Front and back are four Ghost Dance-style crows in dark blue faceted beads. On back, three zoomorphic forms with forked tails, perhaps lizards or dragonflies. On front, geometric figures made of stepped triangles, and eight crosses. Sioux, ca. 1890.   G-$1,950

Hairbrush, 12 in. long. Porcupine tail hair brush, with buckskin-wrapped and fringed handle. Beading in transparent red, dark blue and lavender. A strip of quillwrapped rawhide runs brush length. Sioux (?), ca. 1890.   G-$295

Peyote rattle, 15 in. long, not including fringe. Gourd rattle on wooden shaft, stitched with multicolored beadwork. Extensive use of small, faceted beads. Feather tip and cord fringe. Oklahoma, ca. 1930.   G-$210

Dance wand, 18 in. long. Quirt-style dance piece, red painted handle with brass tacks, braided rawhide suspension. Sioux, and ca. 1910.   G-$165

Loop necklace, of mandrel-wound white tradebeads, strung on thongs between rawhide strips. Six red beads, one at center of each strand; top strand broken and re-tied. Cluster of deer-hoof janglers, rough cloth medicine bag stained dark, and tassel of red-dyed horsehair partly wrapped in hide with a wrapping of seed beads all attached. Crow (?),early 1880s,   G-$775

Peyote bag, 5-1/2 in. long. Metallic faceted beads around edge and at center of four-point star. Southern Plains region, ca. 1900.   G-$145

Breastplate, 21 in. in length. Man's, composed of bone hairpins, brass beads, rawhide spacers, and thongs. Provenance: Abourezk collection, Mission, S.D. Sioux, and from the 1890s.   G-$1,000

Tab bag, 12 in. long. Yellow-painted buckskin with beaded patterns of stepped triangles on white background. Pendant is long hide tab with two narrow strips of diagonal black and white beading. Southern Plains area, ca. 1900.   G-$255

Awl case, woman's, 39 in. long with trailers. Large, elaborate. Long beaded trailers. Tin-cone and breath-feather attachments. Southern Plains region, and ca. 1900.   G-$525

Cape or yoke, 37 in. wide. Fringed buckskin edged in cowrie shells and trade beads. (Beaded in geometric patterns as described by Father Peter J. Powell in the Chicago Art Institute catalogue, The Native American Heritage.) Beaded in rose, blue, green, and greasy yellow on deep blue field. Sioux (?), and ca. 1880.   G-$1,450

Bag, 5 in. long. Partly beaded with tiny faceted glass and brass beads. Lined with cotton cloth. Santee (?), and ca. 1895.   G-$140

Suggested Reading

(By the Editors), *The American Heritage Book of Indians.* McGraw Hill Book Company: American Heritage Publishing Co., Inc. 1961.

Koch, Ronald P. *Dress Clothing of the Plains Indians.* University of Oklahoma.

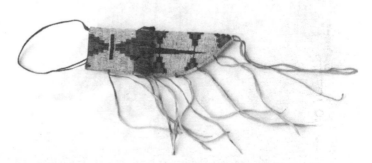

Knife sheath, Southern Cheyenne, fully beaded, fringed, with row of tin cones. Ex-museum, 10 in. long, ca. 1880. $400

Morris' Art & Artifacts, Anaheim, California; Dawn Gober photograph

Skull-crusher, Oglala Sioux, handle wrapped with rawhide and 24 in. long. Ex-museum, it is ca. 1880. $375

Morris' Art & Artifacts, Anaheim, California; Dawn Gober photograph

Buffalo hide shield, 1/4 in. thick and 16-1/2 in. in diameter. Green hand painted on center of shield with red dot in the hand. A Plains Indian piece, some Plains tribes pictured hand on shield, war shirt or pony to denote an enemy killed in combat. Old red cloth sewn around bottom edge, decorated with dentallium shells, old ribbed type, all sinew sewn. Remains of bird sinew sewn on edge, probably the owner's good luck charm or fetish. Ca. 1880.   C-$1,900

Photo courtesy Bill Post collection

Blackfoot parfleche, child's size, with painted geometric designs. In excellent condition, a 19th century piece. $1,100

Private collection, New Mexico

Plains shield, with paper-stuffed heron head tied on. Top half painted in rainbow designs of red, black, green, and yellow. Northern Plains, pre-1880.   **Museum quality**

Nedra Matteucci's Fenn Galleries, Santa Fe, New Mexico

Bear cult shield, 16 in. in diameter. Probably Cheyenne or Assiniboin, Montana. Has arm straps, two bears painted in black with humps, probably grizzly. Has two beaded diamonds and beaded tabs. Made of hide shrunk by heat process to 1/4 in. to 5/16 in. thick. Bear hair trim across top of shield. Ca. 1860-70. $1,950

Photo courtesy Bill Post collection

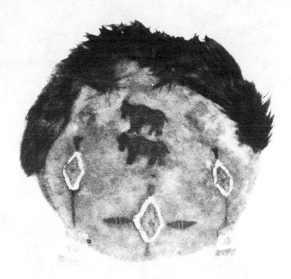

Bandolier bag, Arapaho, made of hide, cloth, and beads. Well beaded, ca. 1870. $800

Private collection, photo by John McLaughlin

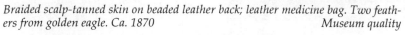

Braided scalp-tanned skin on beaded leather back; leather medicine bag. Two feathers from golden eagle. Ca. 1870   **Museum quality**

Nedra Matteucci's Fenn Galleries, Santa Fe, New Mexico

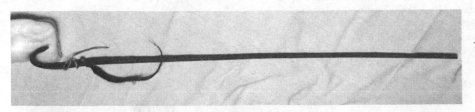

Coup-stick, Plains Indian, 3 ft. long and with finely carved birdhead. Small brass tack eyes, completed with leather and hair. Ca. 1870. $600

Private collection, photo by John McLaughlin

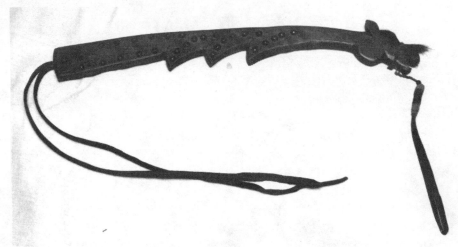

Quirt, Arapaho, done in horse effigy. Wood with brass tacks, leather, horsehair, and beads. Ca. 1900. $2,000

Private collection, photo by John McLaughlin

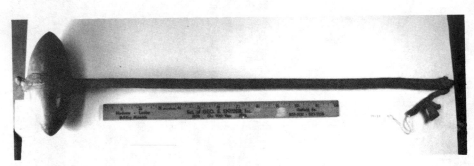

Sioux Ghost Dance war club, with muslin fabric on the handle, ca. 1890. $400

Lee Hallman collection, Telford, Pennsylvania

Arrow, complete with point and guiding feathers, possibly Cheyenne, 1860s. $125

Lee Hallman collection, Telford, Pennsylvania

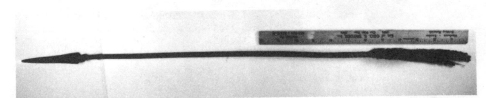

Sioux arrow, point, shaft, and fletching complete, 1870s. $125

Lee Hallman collection, Telford, Pennsylvania

Boy's vest, Sioux, 17 x 20 in., fully beaded and fringed in red. Ca. 1880. $2,000

Freya's Collectibles, Banff, Alberta, Canada

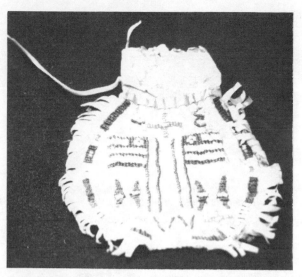

Beaded leather pouch, Plains Indian, beaded both sides. It is 6 x 6-1/2 in. and a colorful item in top condition. From the 1800s. $500

Pat & Dave Summers, Native American Artifacts, Victor, New York

Tobacco bag, Crow, beaded on both sides and nicely fringed. It is 14-1/2 in. long and 1880-1890. $2,250

Larry Lantz, First Mesa, South Bend, Indiana

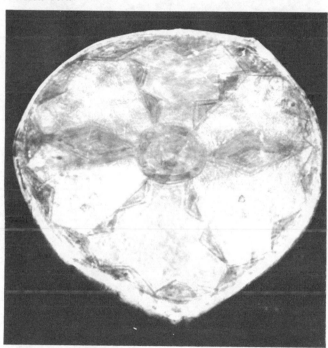

Dance shield, Northern Plains Indian, buffalo hide composition. Has designs in red, yellow, and blue; 16 in. in diameter. Dramatic piece from the 1800s. $1,800

Pat & Dave Summers, Native American Artifacts, Victor, New York

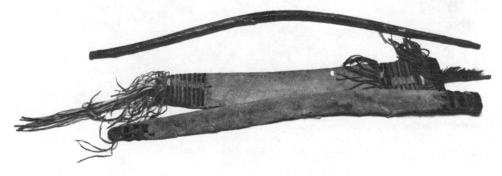

Bow and arrows with bow-case and quiver, Blackfoot. Materials are hide, cloth, beads, wood, feathers, snakeskin, and paint. Rare, ca. 1870. $7,000

Private collection, photo by John McLaughlin

"Pemmican pounder" or tent hammer, stone head with rawhide and wrap-around handle. Sioux, from the Dakotas. $165

Private collection

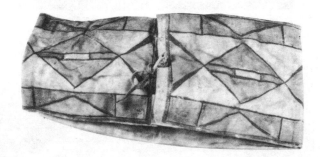

Parfleche container, Sioux, folded size 12 x 26 in. Unused condition, painted in bright blue and orange, with green patterns. Made of heavy rawhide with hair removed, Indian leather ties. Very good condition, age is uncertain. $300

Sherman Holbert collection, Fort Mille Lacs, Onamia, Minnesota

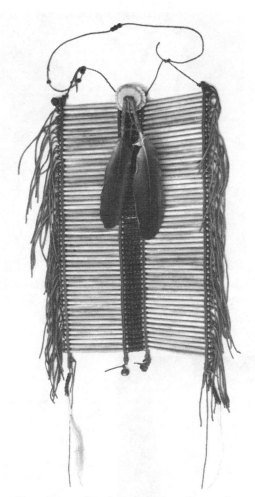

Sioux breast-plate, bone hairpipes, brass, glass beads, antler crown, harness leather, rawhide, sinew-wrapped feathers, hawkbells. 10 x 18 in., from the Pine Ridge Reservation, South Dakota. Contemporary piece. $250

Morris' Art & Artifacts, Anaheim, California; Dawn Gober photograph

Saddle-bag, Plateau. Size, 14 x 100 in. long. Indian-tanned elk hide decorated with old blanket material and some felt. Rare and beautiful piece of Indian costume horse trapping, slight damage and use-marks, probably ca. 1880s. $2,500

Sherman Holbert collection, Fort Mille Lacs, Onamia, Minnesota

Plains Indian drum and drumstick, 9-1/2 in. in diameter. Painted yellow and red, and is ca. 1880s. $600

Private collection

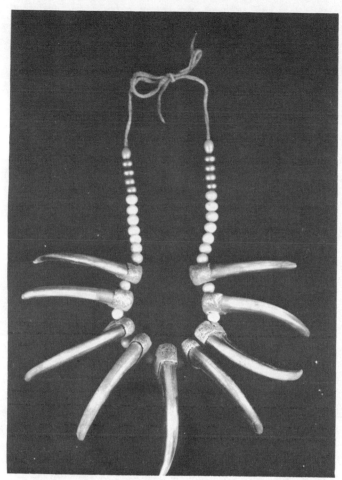

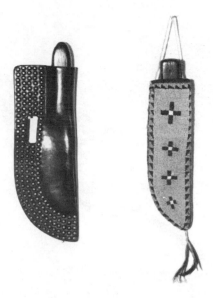

Plains sheath-knives.

Left: saddle leather case with belt cut-out and decorated with brass tacks. Length, 12 in., ca. 1870s. $2,500-3,000
Right: buffalo hide beaded knife case with a tin cone and horsehair drop. Probably Sioux, length 10 in. Ca. 1870s. $2,000-2,500

Dave Hrachovy, Cedar Glen, California

Bear-claw necklace, Northern Plains, with blue beads and brass beads. Ca. 1870.   Museum quality

Morning Star Gallery, Santa Fe, New Mexico

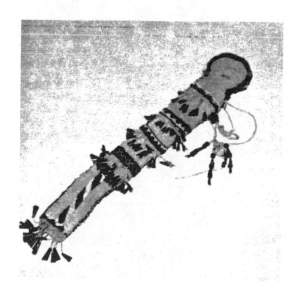

Quirt, Cheyenne, wood carved in "saw-tooth" style. Inside of teeth painted. Lash of commercial leather with fringed tanned hide tie. Wrist strap is tanned hide and beaded in saw-tooth pattern with tin cone drop. Handle length, 18 in. Ca. 1860s-1870s.   Museum quality

Dave Hrachovy, Cedar Glen, California

Awl case, Apache, beaded leather with tin cones, very good condition. This 2 x 15 in. piece is ca. 1880.   Museum quality

James Reid, LTD, Santa Fe, New Mexico

Dag knife, Plateau area, known as beaver-tail, dagger or stabber, with a double-edged blade. Handle made of two pieces of mountain sheep horn, held together with copper rivets. Three brass tacks decorate the handle butt. Quite rare. Length, 9 in. and ca. 1830s-1840s. $6,500-7,500

Dave Hrachovy, Cedar Glen, California

Pipe bag, Cheyenne, beaded, quilted, and fringed antelope hide. Beaded bar design panel and "X" motif quilted panel. Hide fringe decorated with tin cones and horsehair. Length 32 in., ca. 1860s.   Museum quality

Dave Hrachovy, Cedar Glen, California

Plains Indian knives, typical group. Blades were obtained from traders, frontier blacksmiths or home-made from old files, etc. Indian-made handles made of wood, bone or antler with some being wire or hide wrapped. Lengths are 9 to 13 in., ca. the 1800s.   Each, $100-300

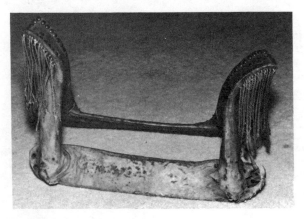

Saddle, Plains Indian, hide-covered, wood decorated with brass tacks. Painted, twisted fringe. The pommel and cantle also painted. Length, 19 in. and ca. 1870s. $3,000-3,500

Dave Hrachovy, Cedar Glen, California

Zippered purse, Plains and possibly Sioux, very nicely beaded, 5 in. long. Ca. 1930s. $150-200

Pocotopaug Trading Post, South Windsor, Connecticut

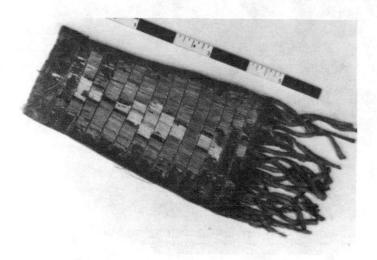

Bow case and quiver with bow and arrows. Plains Indian case two buffalo leather hide compartments hung on wide strap with fringe suspensions. Pony beads decorate mouth of quiver. Bow has quill wrapping on exposed end. Early "user" was collected from Sioux of Sitting Bull's group at Standing Rock Reservation. Arrows, 27 in.; bow, 51 in. long. Set is ca. 1840s-1860s. Museum quality

Dave Hrachovy, Cedar Glen, California

Zippered purse, Plains and possibly Sioux, very nicely beaded, 5 in. long. Ca. 1930s. $150-200

Pocotopaug Trading Post, South Windsor, Connecticut

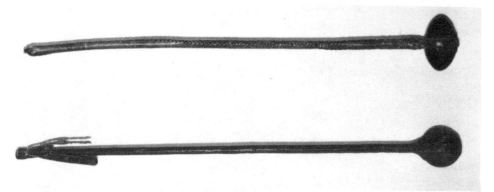

War-clubs, stone-headed with long hide-covered wooden hafts for use on horseback. The round-headed club has a beaded wrist strap of tanned hide. Lengths, 31 and 32 in. respectively. Typical weapons of the mid to late 1800s Plains Indians. Each, $750-1,000

Dave Hrachovy, Cedar Glen, California

Threading snowshoes, Mackenzie River, North West Territories, ca. 1920s.

Photo courtesy National Photography collection, Neg. #C-38174. Public Archives of Canada

CHAPTER XV

WOODEN COLLECTIBLES

The great number of hafted stone woodworking tools from forested and coastal regions of prehistoric North America suggests wooden art and artifacts were once common. Certainly specialized chipped artifacts were also employed to carve wood into useful and pleasing objects. Almost all of such objects have been lost to time, bacteria and the present.

The average person, asked to name early American Indian wood items, might mention some well-known examples. These might be prehistoric bows and arrows, historic Northwest Coast totem poles, Iroquois false-face masks, or a few other memorable examples. With the exception of wood preserved by arid conditions in the Southwest and by permafrost in the far North, very few of such cultural creations survive.

Hundreds of wooden dugout watercraft have been found in the United States and Canada, and recoveries were being made as soon as Europeans arrived. By far the largest number have come from the Eastern U.S., in an area ranging from New England to Florida. Most were sunk in swamps or lakes and became entirely or partially buried in mud and silt. When recovered under scientific conditions, special chemicals are used to preserve the wood.

Following is a very brief listing of early watercraft discoveries, along with some information on each find.

Case	Location	Date Found	Dimensions	Estimated Age
1&2	Ontario, Canada (Lakes?) two dugouts	Unk.	Unk.	2000 years
3	Northwestern Ohio (Lake)	Late 1976	22-1/2 ft. long, 3-1/4 ft. wide	2000-3000 years
4	Southwestern state (River)	1970 (?)	Not large	Unk.
5	Manhattan, New York (Landfill)	1906	Broken half of dugout was 7 ft. long, 3 ft. wide	Unk.
6	Tennessee (River)	1797 (?)	Unk.	Pre-1797
7	Michigan (Lake)	1971	17 ft. long	300 years old; possibly earlier
8	Georgia (River)	Early 1977	24 ft. long	250 years
9	Florida (Lake)	1977/78 (?)	19 ft. long	200 years (sides burned)

Leaving the prehistoric and unknown regions, there are many wood collectibles from historic and recent times. The more desirable items have age, as well as beauty, and are mainly from the 1700s into the early 1900s.

The wood should preferably be a heavy hardwood, with some surface patina due to age. Marks of manufacture, generally from White-supplied iron and steel tools, can be visible but not prominent to the point of distraction. Splitting and splintering should be at the absolute minimum, and wood rot or decay is a serious value depreciation. Some stain is permitted, especially with items like pemmican-pounders, for these are use-signs.

Many wood artifacts were further decorated with quilling (early) or beading (later), brass tacks, or paint. This chapter consists of all-wood collectibles or Indian items that have a major part made of wood.

PREHISTORIC WOOD ITEMS

Wooden rabbit-stick, Southwestern, a slightly flat and curved stick about 23 in. long. Thrown to bring down small game; sticks were retrieved on foot.   C-$250

Oregon Atl-atl, 16-3/4 in. long, recovered from dry cave. Handgrip end thicker, opposite end has antler or ivory hook lance-butt. Shallow groove for the shaft connects the two. Pale evidence of paint remains. Fair condition. Rare.   C-$600

Wood digging stick, Montana, 39 in. long. Lower end heavier and sharpened to point. May have been fire-hardened. Bark peeled from entire length; used for grubbing out roots.   C-$45

Arrowshaft section, 9 in. long, portion somewhere between missing front and back. Flint tools used for shaft smoothing. Marks still show on surface.   C-$40

HISTORIC WOOD ITEMS

Cradleboard, central California, full size. Decorated with sun shade yarn ties.   G-$600

Carved wood club, Papago, potato-masher type, 1800s.   D-$150

Salish-Shaker power stick, Northwest Coast, carved wood with deer toes and cover. Made when Shaker church was influential in the area.   A-$1,500

Spoon, carved wood, Great Lakes region and Huron. Has fine bird effigy handle and is ca. 1870. $350

Private collection, photo by John McLaughlin

Feast bowl, Kwakitul, from Albertsville, British Columbia, Canada. Collected in 1920s, 10 in. high and 19 in. long. Dorsal-fin lid, old green stained colored body, abalone eyes, ivory teeth and side spots. The painted decorations are in red and white. A fine Northwest Coast item. $1,175

Sherman Holbert collection. Fort Mille Lacs, Onamia, Minnesota

Burden-carrier, wood and bark, Iroquois. From the 1800s and ex-coll. Fine piece. Casterline. $425

Pat & Dave Summers, Native American Artifacts, Victor, New York

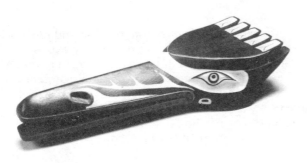

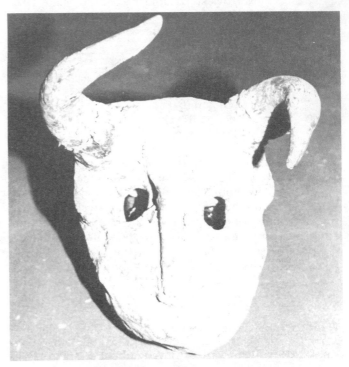

Mask, forehead, Kwakiutl, Northwest Coast. First collected in 1920s. It is 7 in. wide and 21-1/4 in. long. Carefully made, has a remote attachment so wearer can open and close the cormorant effigy bill during dance ceremony. Carved, painted black, red and white. Northwest Coast. $895

Sherman Holbert collection, Fort Mille Lacs, Onamia, Minnesota

Mask, Northwest United States, made of carved wood and horn. This is a nice old piece, unusual. $375

Wilfred A. Dick collection, Magnolia, Mississippi

Toy cedar-wood canoe, Salish, from the late 1800s. It is 18 in. long and nicely painted. Old label reads "Made by Neah Bay Indians, Neah Bay, Washington." $450

Larry Lantz, First Mesa, South Bend, Indiana

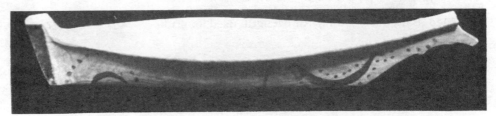

Rare Atl-atl or lance-throwing stick from King Isle, Alaska. Dated by previous owner as being from 1830s. *Museum quality*

Private collection

Another view of wooden lance-thrower from Alaska. Shows finger positioning peg. Atl-atls from North America are very scarce and tend to come from the Southwest or the Far North. *Museum quality*

Private collection

Ball-headed club, one-piece burl wood, mint Seneca Iroquois. Very rare, 26-1/2 in. long. Has fine natural patina overall. From 1800s. $2,250

Pat & Dave Summers, Native American Artifacts, Victor, New York

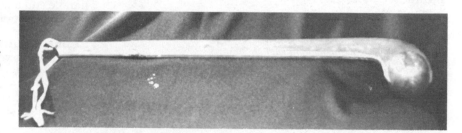

Sugar spoon, Mille Lacs Chippewa, early 1900s. It is 39 in. long. Used with large iron kettles for stirring nearly finished maple sugar. Old and well-used. In very good condition. $125

Sherman Holbert collection, Fort Mille Lacs, Onamia, Minnesota

Club, Sioux, horse-leg effigy form, wood and tacks with file blade. Ca. 1870. $1,000

Private collection, photo by John McLaughlin

Birchbark basket, base larger than top, Northeastern Woodlands, 8 x 11 in. It is a ca. 1940s. $150-200

Pocotopaug Trading Post, South Windsor, Connecticut

Wooden bowls, Great Lakes region.

Left: brown wood, ca. 1860. $1,000-1,500
Right: Winnebago, yellow-blond wood, ca. 1880. $150

Private collection, photo by John McLaughlin

Wood-handled crooked knife, Ree Indian, 8-1/4 in. long, from a site in northern South Dakota. Handle has small knife blade set at lower end. Working edge 1-3/8 in. long. Not common, old. C-$225

Cedar canoe baler, Northwest Coastal group. A-$95

Wooden food container or trencher, late historic, Chippewa, old and unusual. Rectangular, 5 in. deep, 13-1/4 in. long and 7 in. wide. From hardwood, possibly maple. Sides and bottom average 5/8 in. thick; some small age-cracks at ends. Smaller ends have thickened projection for handles. C-$600

Plains cane or dance wand, 19-1/2 in. long, wood; top has tied feathers, base is hide-wrapped. Appears very old. D-$250

Sioux cane or dance stick, a natural wood formation, carved and painted in shape of smiling snake. Colorful, primitive art piece of exceptional note. G-$700

Cherokee stick-ball racket, 27 in. long, wood with rawhide lace. G-$100

Birchbark basket, Northeastern Woodlands, rectangular base and oblong top, 8 x 12 in. It is ca. 1840-1860. $195-225

Pocotopaug Trading Post, South Windsor, Connecticut

Food trencher, Haida (NW Coast), rectangular form, 15 in. long and 9-1/2 in. wide. Ends up-curved, sides down-curved, and piece well-made of spruce (?) wood. Exterior once painted; an old item C-$1750

Spoon, Northwest Coast, Kwakiutl, 14 in. long, curved wood. A-$155

Canoe paddle, possibly middle-1880s, Eastern Woodlands group. All wood, even, flowing lines, well-carved. Upper handle region has some light incising in simple pattern. Fine condition, not common. C-$650

Battan weaving tool, Navajo, ca. 1880. D-$45

Lacrosse stick, probably Canadian Indian, just over 35 in. long. Hitting end has laced rawhide flattish cup, handle end has thong-wrapped section for non-slip use. Excellent condition. C-$250

Beamer or hide-scraping tool, Sioux, 14-1/2 in. long. Two-handed wood handle with metal blade insert. Wood is beautifully grained. G-$225

Cradleboard, central California, full-size. Yarn decorated design on sun shade. Has doeskin straps. G-$450

Ball-headed wood club, Woodland region, Great Lakes area. Carved from single piece of wood, possibly oak burl, and is 22-1/2 in. long. Plain, businesslike piece. C-$1,000

Fertility wooden statue, Eastern Sioux, 14 in. high. Good condition and rare; could be older than ca. 1900. G-$1,950

Cradleboard, Sioux, original wood frame and 24 in. long. Leather over wood, with beadwork designs. C-$800

Ball-headed war club, turn of the century period; head has stone inset. Cross-hatching decoration on handle. Good condition. G-$1,050

Wood stirrups, pair, plain, both with portions of original rawhide fastenings at top. Northern Plains regions, simply carved, nicely matched. C-$300

Fleshing tool, Plains style with metal blade edge; from Taos Pueblo and probably from the 1800s. D-$160

Wooden bowl, made from hardwood log, 7 in. wide and 20-1/2 in. long. Good condition. Undecorated. C-$425

Fleshing tool, Blackfoot, wooden handle with sinew-wrapped metal blade, unusual shape to handle. 15 in. long. G-$200

Wood stirring spoon, California, 14 in. long. Well carved handle. Early historic, from one of the interior desert groups. C-$175

Willow back rest, Sioux, zone-painted with incised tripod legs. G-$950

Fleshing tool, Sioux, wood with metal side blade, ca. 1850. D-$150

Ball-type wooden club, 20 in. long. Ball diameter 4-1/4 in. May be Chippewa, but uncertain. Some incised lines on handle; an old and good piece. D-$875

Wood and leather cradleboard, 21 in. high, a basic wood-slat frame. Whole somewhat deteriorated due to

Birchbark basket, squared base and rounded top, Northeastern Woodlands, 7-1/2 in. in diameter. It is ca. 1940s. $55-70

Pocotopaug Trading Post, South Windsor, Connecticut

lack of past attention. A late 1800s item; some beadwork remains on brittle leather portions.　　C-$525

Four Northwest Coast carvings: Rattle, Adz, Potlatch bowl, and Shaman's spirit bent-box with Ed. All are finely carved.　　C-$1,600 the four

RECENT WOOD ITEMS (1900-1970)

Meat drying rack, Canadian Indian, unusual item. Eight peeled-bark wands secured to three crosspieces; former are 40 in. long; latter about 35 in. and thicker. Collected years ago north of Lake Erie, probably early 1900s. Possibly used to dry or smoke freshwater fish.　　C-$210

Wood totem, Northwest Coast, Raven effigy, old.　D-$175

War club, Northwest Coast.　　A-$155

Paddle-spoon, Tlingit (NW Coast), shaped like miniature dugout canoe paddle, 14-1/2 in. long. (More ornate forms reserved for special occasions. Paddle-spoons used to eat Northwest Coast delicacy called "sopalalli" or "soap-berry," a mixture of berries and cold water frothed with oil from the olachen or candlefish.) Very good condition; relief carving on straight wide lower portion may represent mountain goat.　　C-$525

Wooden bow, 46-1/2 in. long, narrowed and thicker at center. Believed to be from Plateau area, perfect, painted in faint black and red designs. Early 20th century, probably pre-tourist times. Well-done piece.　　C-$365

Paddle-spoon, Northwest Coast, undecorated, 13-3/4 in. long. Fair condition with cracking.　　C-$175

Miniature canoe, Northwest Coast, copy of highprowed sea-going dugouts; it is 3-3/4 in. wide and 19 in. long. Made of thin wood strips and held together with sinew through small holes.　　C-$425

Paiute cradle board, made of wicker and covered with partially beaded hide. Large and well-designed; some wicker missing. Made in 1930s or 40s.　　G-$850

Wooden Iroquois mask, False-Face society, life-size or larger with long horsetail hair. Shell eyes, red feathers and black details. Not older than 1900; may be later.　C-$700

Dance wand, Plains Indian, about 16 in. long. Knob head end has false scalp-lock of long hair, possibly bison beard. Has faded painted lines along shaft. Unusual.　C-$275

Chippewa maple sugar spoon.　　A-$65

Miniature paddles, pair from Northwest Coast, carved, 18 in. long. Have good stylized carving and are ca. 1930.　　G-$250

Iroquois wooden mask, about 12 in. high with exaggerated and twisted features. Ca. 1900.　　C-$725

Lidded birchbark sugar box, Eastern Woodlands Indian, probably used for maple sugar storage. It is 9-1/2 x 11 in. and 7 in. high. Ca. 1930s.　　C-$185

Wooden-frame loom, Plains Indian, late period, probably for sash weaving. About 1-1/2 ft. long and 5 in. wide, with some original thread ties remaining.　　C-$225

Raven rattle, Northwest Coast, 14 in. long and 4-1/2 in. in diameter. Piece is ca. 1930.　　G-$2,000

Chippewa courting flute, 1-1/2 in. in diameter and 15 in. long. Courting object, has double chambers, carved bird head on end, and traces of red and green paint. Decorated with old hide and fringe; ca. 1890. C-$495

Photo courtesy Bill Post collection

Wooden Kwakiutl portrait mask, Northwest Coast carving, 9 in. high. Recent piece; face painted in black and red. Made by Calvin Hunt, ca. 1965. C-$400-550

Photo courtesy R.M. Weatherford, Columbus, Ohio

Birchbark canoe, scraped hearts and floral design, Cree Indian. Made in the 1920s, from Canada. Quite large at 22-1/2 in. long. $275

Michael F. Slasinski, Saginaw, Michigan

Woodland Indian carved trail marker, Ottawa, Michigan, year 1923. Has painted blue highlights, represents a man, a woman, and an owl. Museum quality

Michael F. Slasinski, Saginaw, Michigan

"Buffalo" mask, Cherokee, made in the 1950s. Painted wood, it is from North Carolina. Size is 7 x 12-1/2 in. $185

Michael F. Slasinski, Saginaw, Michigan

Iroquois False Face mask from New York state, year 1920. Face is red-brown, with horsehair. Size, 6 x 11 in. Rare, early artifact. $2,000

Michael F. Slasinski, Saginaw, Michigan

Birchbark canoe, 33-1/4 x 148 in. Rare one-man or hunter's canoe, made by Na-Ah-Qua-Geseg, Mille Lacs Chippewa. Ca. 1959, the only canoe ever offered for sale by maker. Ex-colls. Johnson and Kouba. Museum quality item with historic significance. $2,000

Sherman Holbert collection, Fort Mille Lacs, Onamia, Minnesota

Iroquois Crooked-Face mask, 7 in. wide and 12 in. high, excluding hair. Ca. 1900; painted red and black. The face is wood, the eye areas are metal, and the hair is horsehair. From the New York state Iroquois. $500

Steve and Anita Shearer, Torrance, California

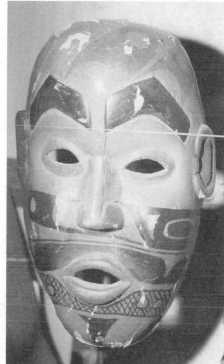

Shaman's mask, Northwest Coast, ca. 1870-1890. It is 6 in. wide and 10 in. high; made of wood and trade paints. Came from a collection in Santa Fe, New Mexico. Rare.
Museum quality

Steve and Anita Shearer, Torrance, California

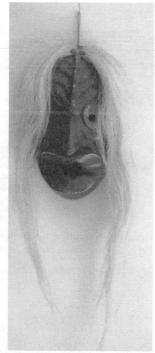

Iroquois False Face mask, 24 in. high with hair, wood, metal, and horsehair. An early piece, ca. 1900. Museum quality

David Cook Fine American Art, Denver, Colorado; Jamie Kahn photograph

Iroquois bird or rabbit snare-net, made with wooden hoop and string loops. It is 19 in. in diameter and ca. 1900. $49

Native American Artifacts, Victor, New York

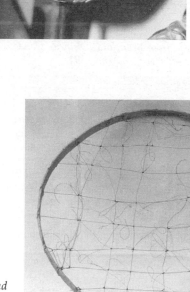

CONTEMPORARY WOOD ITEMS

Navajo cradleboard, 36 in. long.　　　G-$200

Halibut hook, Northwest Coast, carved, done by Tsungani.　　　A-$195

Houseboard, Northwest Coast, signed.　　　A-$165

Apache cradleboard, 36 in. long.　　　G-$275

Carved paddle, Northwest Coast, 15-1/2 in. long. Has painted killer-whale design, signed, John Bennall, Haida.　　　G-$175

Iroquois False Face mask, from Brantford, Ontario, Canada. Face is barn red, hair is white, and eye-plates are copper. Size, 6 x 12 in., 1989.　　　$175

Michael F. Slasinski, Saginaw, Michigan

Iroquois False Face mask, from Brantford, Ontario, Canada. It is oxblood red with copper eyes, size 7 x 11 in., 1991.　　　$175

Michael F. Slasinski, Saginaw, Michigan

Water bucket, 11 x 13 in. high plus handle. Made by Babe Earth, Chippewa, Mille Lacs Reservation, it is ca. 1986. Has reinforced double rim, sealed with spruce pitch; used for carrying water or maple sap.　　　$125

Sherman Holbert collection, Fort Mille Lacs, Onamia, Minnesota

Wooden bowl, prehistoric, with rim. This extremely rare item, 9-1/2 x 14-1/4 in., was found frozen in ice near Shismaref, Alaska.　　　$650

Pat & Dave Summers, Native American Artifacts, Victor, New York

Carved wooden pipe stem, very well done and in top condition.　　　$50

Collection of David G. & Barbara J. Shirley

Great Lakes region baskets.

Left: Mille Lacs Chippewa, 19 x 22 in., birchbark, excellent work. $225
Left center: Mille Lacs Chippewa, rare large basket made by Maggie Kegg, basswood bark. $145
Right center: birchbark, Maggie Kegg, Mille Lacs Chippewa, excellent condition. $225
Right: decorated birchbark basket made by Rose Wind, acquired in 1987. $195

Sherman Holbert collection, Fort Mille Lacs, Onamia, Minnesota

Baby-board, Mohawk, carved wood with painted designs, ca. 1870 .$3,000

Private collection; photo by John McLaughlin

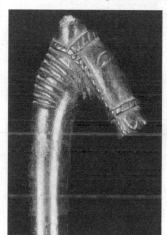

Iroquois Lacrosse sticks, mid-20th century, 3-4 ft. long. Materials are ash and leather and are from the St. Regis Mohawk Reservation, New York. Each, $35-45

Frank Bergevin, Port of Call, Alexandria Bay, New York

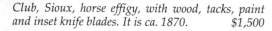

Plains Chief's horsehead walking stick, carved wood, 33 in. long. This unusual item came from North Dakota and is ca. 1880. $5,000

Terry Schafer, American Indian Art & Antiques, Marietta, Ohio

Club, Sioux, horse effigy, with wood, tacks, paint and inset knife blades. It is ca. 1870. $1,500

Private collection, photo by John McLaughlin ▼

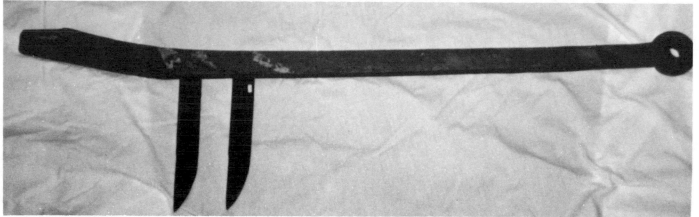

Sioux Indian man performs in the Sun Dance in the Black Hills. Dancer may be blowing on bone whistle or flute.
Photo courtesy South Dakota State Historical Society

CHAPTER XVI

KACHINAS, DOLLS, TOYS, AND MUSICAL ITEMS

Hopi Kachinas are difficult to explain easily, for they are much more than doll-like forms. Kachinas depict Kachina dancers, which in turn represent spirits and forces important to the traditional and modern Hopi lifeway. Even inanimate objects may have such powers.

The Kachina dolls—and there are about 300 different characters that appear regularly and some 200 that appear occasionally—served to instruct Hopi children. Often superbly carved from cottonwood, Kachinas of the late 1880s and early 1900s soon became collector items.

Eventually original supplies were depleted, but demand continued and a new collecting field developed. Today no assemblage of Southwestern Indian works is considered representative without a Kachina or two.

Kachina figures vary in size from a few inches to several feet. Value factors include size and material, with hand-carved wood—some with moveable arms and legs—being a favorite. Modern copies are made by non-Indians in plaster, plastic, and ceramic. For Indian-made Kachinas, the skill of the maker counts for a great deal, and usually the more handwork the higher the value. Beyond the basic figure, Kachinas may be painted, clothed, wear various ornaments, and carry different symbols.

Two important sub-areas for collecting are the old, pre-tourist Kachinas and those made by well-known contemporary Indian artists. The best way to get a good quality Kachina at a reasonable price is to know your source.

KACHINAS

Kachina doll, 9 in. high and ca. 1940s.   G-$210

Hopi "Owl" Kachina, 7 in. high.   G-$175

"Hummingbird" Kachina, 8-1/2 in. high and ca. 1940s.   G-$375

Kachinas, two, old, sold as one lot. Ca. 1920.   A-$180

Hopi "Ogre" Kachina, 7 in. high.   G-$225

Kachina doll, 16 in. high, in form of wolf with bow and arrow, in "Strongbow" form. Made by Fred Kubota; well-painted.   G-$450

Kachina doll, 8 in. high, and ca. 1940s.   G-$225

Sun Kachina, by Tino Youvella, 12-1/2 in. high. $600

The Eastern Cowboys, Scottsdale, Arizona

Warrior kachina or Ewiro Kachina (Hopi name), 22 in. high, 12-1/2 in. width front to back. Unsigned.   G-$1,100

Photo courtesy William Scoble, The Ansel Adams Gallery, Yosemite National Park, California

Kachina made by Willie Tewaquaptewa, 8 in. high, with painted features. In extremely fine condition for age, ca. 1940. $850

Courtesy John Isaac, Albuquerque, New Mexico

Clown Kachina, by Clarence Cleveland, height 10 to 12 in. $425-650

The Eastern Cowboys, Scottsdale, Arizona

White Buffalo Kachina, by Earl Yowytewa, 10 in. high. $395

The Eastern Cowboys, Scottsdale, Arizona

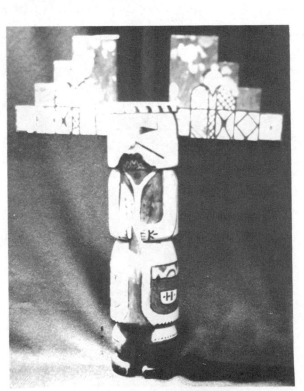

Hopi Kachina, superb Tsitoto Helmet Mask figure of cottonwood, in several well-done colors. It is 19 in. high, from Arizona, and ca. 1940. $900

Pat & Dave Summers, Native American Artifacts, Victor, New York

Owl Kachina, by Preston Ami, 9 in. high. $485

The Eastern Cowboys Scottsdale, Arizona

Eagle Kachina, by Coolidge Roy Jr., 9 in. high. $485

The Eastern Cowboys, Scottsdale, Arizona Owl Kachina, by Preston Ami, 9 in. high. $485

The Eastern Cowboys, Scottsdale, Arizona

Butterfly Maiden Kachina, Hopi Maker Henry Shelton. Done on special order for Marguerite L. Kernaghan, autographed. Size, 6 x 15-1/2 in. Museum quality

Marguerite L. Kernaghan collection; photograph by Marguerite L. and Stewart W. Kernaghan, Bellvue, Colorado

Eagle Kachina, by Ron Duwyenie, 9 in. high. $485

The Eastern Cowboys, Scottsdale, Arizona

Eagle Kachina, by Ron Duwyenie, 9 in. high. $485

The Eastern Cowboys, Scottsdale, Arizona

Kachina, old, Hopi, no action shown. Done in six colors, size is 3 x 11-1/4 in. $550-850

Marguerite L. Kernaghan collection; photograph by Marguerite L. and Stewart W. Kernaghan, Bellvue, Colorado

Chowilawa Kachina, done in seven colors. This figure was made by Jerry Lalapo and is 7-1/2 x 11-1/2 in. $500-800

Marguerite L. Kernaghan collection; photograph by Marguerite L. and Stewart W. Kernaghan, Bellvue, Colorado

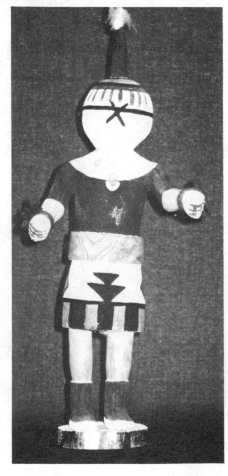

Kachina figure, old, Hopi, with no action shown. Done in seven colors, it is 5-1/2 x 14 in. $550-850

Marguerite L. Kernaghan collection; photograph by Marguerite L. and Stewart W. Kernaghan, Bellvue, Colorado

Mastoff Kachina, Hopi maker Raymond Parkett. This large figure is 8 x 16-1/2 in. $600-1,000

Marguerite L. Kernaghan collection; photograph by Marguerite L. and Stewart W. Kernaghan, Bellvue, Colorado

 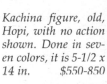

Hopi Buffalo Dancer Kachina. This is a small but powerful carving, in top condition, ca. 1920. $1,800

John C. Hill Antique Indian Art, Scottsdale, Arizona

Hopi Kachinas. On the left is Ho'ote and on the right is a rare Red Buffalo Kachina. Both figures are in very fine condition, ca. 1940s.   Each, $900-1,200

John C. Hill Antique Indian Art, Scottsdale, Arizona

Hopi Buffalo Kachina, by Jimmy K. He was one of the first artists to sign his work (JK), ca. 1940s $1,500

John C. Hill Antique Indian Art, Scottsdale, Arizona

Hopi Butterfly Maiden or Palik Mana, by Jimmy K. One of the most popular forms for Kachinas, ca. 1950s. $2,400

John C. Hill Antique Indian Art, Scottsdale, Arizona

Hopi Kachinas, early dolls. Prices for such early works vary greatly, of the pre-1920 period. $950-2,500

John C. Hill Antique Indian Art, Scottsdale, Arizona

Hopi Kachina, red, cream, yellow, blue and black, 8 in. high. In fine condition, dates to the 1940s. $450

Courtesy John Isaac, Albuquerque, New Mexico

Pang or Mountain Sheep Kachina, Hopi. Appears in bands in an ordinary Kachina dance and has power over rain and spasms. It is 16 in. tall. Kachina is about fifty-five years old and has a later base added about 1940. $1,000-1,700

Marguerite L. Kemaghan collection; photo by Marguerite L. and Stewart W. Kernaghan, Bellvue, Colorado

Konin Supai Kachina, Hopi, appears in a regular Kachina dance. Representation of the Hopi's neighbors to the west, the Havasupai Indians. Maker is Alfred Hitez and size is 6 x 9 in. $450-700

Marguerite L. Kernaghan collection; photo by Marguerite L. and Stewart W. Kemaghan, Bellvue, Colorado

Hopi Kachinas.

Left: giant Kachina, 16 in. high, by Bill Scwiemaenewa. $750
Right: star Kachina, 15 in. high, by Leo Lacapa. $895

Both are made of cottonwood root.

Courtesy John W. Barry, California

Mudhead Clown Kachina carrying a Mudhead
Clown (Koyemsi), Hopi. Appear in mixed or regular dances; sometimes a group appears in a dance of
their own. Comic-characters, enliven serious ceremonies. Only Kachina allowed to do whatever they
want. Made by Robert Kayguoptewa. Size is 5 x
12-3/4 in. $600-950

Marguerite L. Kernaghan collection; photograph
by Marguerite L. and Stewart W. Kernaghan, Bellvue, Colorado

Rattle Kachina
(AYA), Hopi. Name
derived from mask re-
sembling a Hopi rat-
tle. Comes in pairs,
rarely one at a time.
Carries yucca whips
which he uses on a
runner that does not
win a race. Figure
made by Carl Sulu, 7
x 11 in. $500-800

Marguerite L. Ker-
naghan collection;
photo by Marguerite
L. and Stewart W.
Kernaghan, Bellvue,
Colorado

Kachina, Mong or Chief Kachina
(wuwuyomo), Hopi. It is spoken of
as "Old man kachina" because he
is so ancient. Always appears in
groups of four with the Pachavu
Manas whom they lead into the
villages. Appear in Third Mesa extended form of the Powamu, the
Palolokong Ceremony. The maker
is Gilbert Naseyouma; size is 4-1/2
x 14-1/2 in. $600-1,000

Marguerite L. Kernaghan collec-
tion; photograph by Marguerite
L. and Stewart W. Kernaghan,
Bellvue, Colorado

Left-handed Kachina (SUY-ANG-E-IF), Hopi. Carries his bow right
hand. All hunting gear is reversed. Chief Kachina appears as a warrior in the Powamu ceremony. Size is 7-1/2 x 14 in. $600-1,000

Marguerite L. Kernaghan collection; photograph by Marguerite L.
and Stewart W. Kernaghan, Bellvue, Colorado

Chasing Star Kachina, Hopi, done in red, black, yellow, and white. Made by Ernest Chapella, First Mesa. Size is 6-3/4 x 12-1/4 in. $500-850

Marguerite L. Kernaghan collection; photograph by Marguerite L. and Stewart W. Kernaghan, Bellvue, Colorado

Hopi Kachina, 7 in. high, nicely carved in wood. This well-painted example is from Arizona.   Museum quality

Collection of Eugene and Marcille Wing; photograph, Steven A. Wing

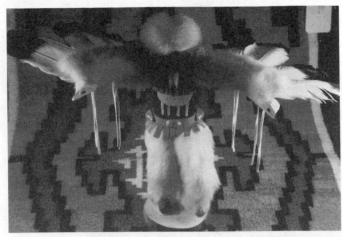

Mask Eagle Kachina, 13 in. high, with detachable mask. This example was made by C. Tom. $200

Charles F. and Susan Wood, Ohio

Mask Eagle Kachina, 12-1/2 in. high, painted body with leather, feathers and fur. It was made by I. Tom. $200

Charles F. and Susan Wood, Ohio

Hopi kachina, Na-ukuita, made of cottonwood. It is 9 in. high and ca. 1965. $100

Native American Artifacts, Victor, New York

Kachina doll, 9-1/2 in. high, ca. 1940s.   G-$250

Hopi "Mouse Warrior" Kachina, 14 in. high and well carved. Signed "N. Seltewa."   G-$425

Kachina doll, 7 in. high and ca. 1940s.   G-$225

"Mana" Kachina doll, 9 in. high and ca. 1940s. G-$250

"Mud-head" Kachinas, set of four on a base.   A-$210

"Mouse Warrior" Kachina, 8 in. high and signed, "S. Jackson."   G-$250

NON-KACHINA DOLLS

"Koshare" doll, with figure holding baby. Piece is 15 in. high and signed, "Regina Naha."   G-$600

Cochiti "Storyteller" doll, with nine babies. Doll is 8 in. high and ca. 1960.   G-$625

Jemez "Storyteller" doll, and six babies. Piece is 7 in. high, and signed, "Toledo."   G-$395

Bear figure with fur, 8-3/4 in. high, made by Renee Pettingrew. $30

Charles F. and Susan Wood, Ohio

INDIAN DOLLS

Indian doll, 13 in. high and from Western U.S., dressed in fringed moccasins, leather skirt. Wood face, nonmoveable arms and legs, good condition. Ca. 1930s   D-$250

Navajo dolls, pair, man 8 in. high and woman 7-1/2 in. high. Modern items done by Navajos and dressed in authentic costumes; all handmade. Contemporary. G-$100

Old Indian doll, 11 in. high, with beaded hair. Face made of old paper or corn husk; figure wrapped in part of an old blanket.   G-$245

Doll moccasins, fully beaded and just over 1 in. long.   Pair C-$95

Old Pacific Plateau beaded doll.   A-$70

White Buffalo Dancer, Hopi; not a Kachina because has no mask. Nicely made and decorated, this 6 x 12 in. figure was made by Murray Harvey, Polacca, Arizona. $500-850

Marguerite L. Kernaghan collection; photograph by Marguerite L. and Stewart W. Kernaghan, Bellvue, Colorado

Navajo doll, probably Indian child's "companion," depicting woman in ceremonial dress. Doll is 10-1/2 in. high and ca. 1910.   C-$300

Sioux pair of man and woman dolls, matched set 11 in. high. The dolls have human hair and are ca. 1900. C-$850

Plains Indian doll, 9 in. high and with wood base. Made for the old tourist trade; hide face with yarn hair and hide dress nicely beaded. Piece has partially beaded cradle on back, with child.   G-$200

Apache gun-dance dolls, averaging 10 in. high. Set of five, hand-carved.   D-$225

Comanche beaded doll with Plains bonnet and ca. 1880-90.   D-$150

Doll moccasins, pair of Sioux family beaded items, old and of good quality.   G-$200

Snohomish basketry dolls, man and woman, both 8 in. high.   A-$180

Child's play or toy cradleboard, late 1800s, and 11 in. high. Leather, partially beaded on wood frame. Good condition and rather scarce item.   C-$375

Miniature cradleboard with doll, 14 in. long and 5-1/2 in. wide. Of old tan buckskin, piece has a fully beaded top section 5 in. wide and 6 in. long.   G-$575

Buckskin dolls, Sioux, pair, both 11 in. high. Female has buckskin face and male has black face made of dried apple. Clothing has beaded decorations; good condition, and ca. 1920.   G-$450

Corn-husk doll, Iroquois, red wooden false face, rabbit fur hair, 5 in. high. From Brantford, Ontario, Canada, and year 1988. $95

Michael F. Slasinski, Saginaw, Michigan

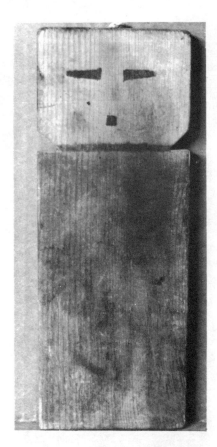

Laguna doll, wooden board, brownish body and tan-yellow face, features in blue-green. In used condition, the doll is 9 in. high. $120

Courtesy John Isaac, Albuquerque

Hano Clown (Koshare), Hopi maker Murray Harvey. Size is 4-3/4 x 12 in. $500-800

Marguerite L. Kernaghan collection; photograph by Marguerite L. and Stewart W. Kernaghan, Bellvue, Colorado

Hand-made doll, Navajo, 16 in. tall and in traditional costume. Beadwork and ceremonial accessories. Early 20th century. $275

Larry Lantz, First Mesa, South Bend, Indiana

Doll, Apache, with cut hide poncho and skirt, high-top moccasins, cloth body and head. With tin cone drops, 14-1/2 in. tall. Ca. 1880.
Museum quality

Morning Star Gallery, Santa Fe, New Mexico

Doll, Cheyenne, beaded and fringed hide dress, with boots and buffalo hair. *Museum quality*

Morning Star Gallery, Santa Fe, New Mexico

Doll, Flathead, hide, beaded dress fringe, red leggings. This superb piece is 16-1/2 in. tall and ca. 1880s.
Museum quality

Morning Star Gallery, Santa Fe, New Mexico

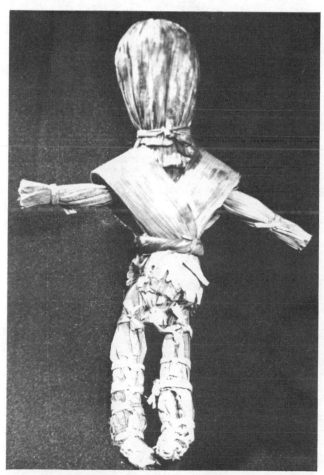

Cornhusk doll, faceless, very old. This Iroquois figure is 11 in. high and an interesting early piece. $125

Pat & Dave Summers, Native American Artifacts, Victor, New York

Left: Doll carrier, Crow, wood, hide, cloth and beads. Well made, ca. 1890. $4,000-6,000

Private collection, photo by John McLaughlin

Doll carrier, Great Lakes region, with cornhusk doll, wood, cloth, yarn, and beads. This interesting item is ca. 1900. $400

Private collection, photo by John McLaughlin

Iroquois cornhusk dolls, 9 in. high, cornhusk bodies and beaded cloth costumes. Ca. 1900.   Pair, $1,200

Traditions, Victor, New York

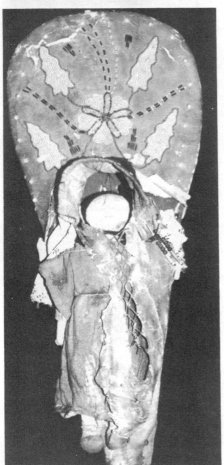

Doll carrier, Plateau, with doll. Made of wood, hide, and cloth, with beadwork. Ca. 1880. $900

Private collection, photo by John McLaughlin

Cheyenne doll, 6 in. high, simply made with wool, sweetgrass and glass beads. It is ca. 1870. $750

Historic Interiors, Sorrento, British Columbia, Canada

Indian doll, from near Eagle, Alaska. It has a cloth body and face with thread-sewn features and finely tanned clothing. Length 15 in. Rare item, collected in the early 1900s. $850

Private collection

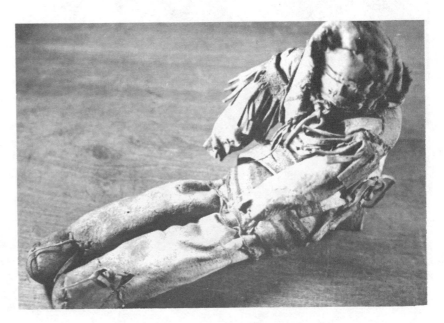

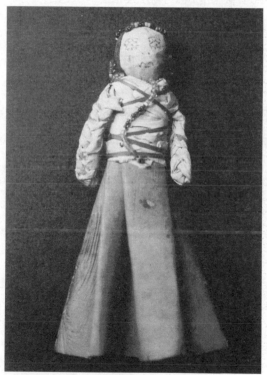

Seminole doll, 5 x 6 in., hand-stitched natural fiber body, cotton dress and trim, seed bead necklace. This is from Florida, ca. 1960. $85

T.R.H. collection, Indiana

Indian doll, about 24 in. in height. Hand made by Kay Bennett, whose Indian name is Kaibah, a full-blooded Navajo Indian. Simulated turquoise nuggets and jocula around doll's neck, and dress and top are velvet. Silver style conchas on belt. Excellent workstyle and condition. Doll made around 1973.   G-$550-650

Courtesy Hugo Poisson, photographer; Edmunds of Yarmouth, Inc.; West Yarmouth, Massachusetts

Great Lakes area birchbark doll, 7 in. high, made of cornhusk and birchbark with handpainted facial features. Doll is early 1900s. $125

T.R.H. collection, Indiana

Iroquois cornhusk dolls, left 5 in. high and right 2-1/2 in. long, bodies cornhusk with wooden false faces. Fine workstyle, ca. 1940s.   Pair, $850

Traditions, Victor, New York

Plains Indian dolls, two riders and three horses, very rare in a set. These are most unusual and turn-of-the-century. Set, $8,500

Crown & Eagle Antiques, New Hope, Pennsylvania

Doll, Canadian Indian made, carved from wood with a thin leather dress. Painted features, and 9 in. high, contemporary. C-$100

Iroquois corn husk doll, 8 in. high and 3-1/2 in. wide. From false face society; good early tourist piece and with some beadwork; well-carved on a wood base. G-$200

Seneca doll, collected in Eastern Canada. Corn husk body with thin cotton dress stained brown. Piece is about 10 in. high. Probably from the 1940s. C-$125

Sioux child's tepee, old, with pictograph drawings and tin cone dangles. Faded, shows considerable age; completely assembled with poles. G-$550

Fraser River miniature cradle, 5-1/2 x 13 in. A-$200

Carved doll in cradle, item 18 in. high and 7-1/2 in. wide. Cradleboard in authentic style; doll has well-carved wood face. Done by LaLooska. G-$575

TOYS AND GAMES

Kiowa toy cradle with slat, 15 in. high. Made up of stained hide and partial beading. C-$850

Beaded buckskin toy tepee, Santee Sioux, an old item and in good condition. G-$650

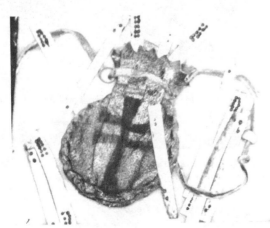

Apache game, hide bag with red decorations, drawstring top. The bone strips have various markings in black and are the playing pieces. A rare set. $1,000-1,650

Marguerite L. Kernaghan collection; photograph by Marguerite L. and Stewart W. Kernaghan, Bellvue, Colorado

Miniature travois, 17 in. long, Plains Indian and old. Two poles and small hide platform; unusual item. C-$200

Miniature Hupa cradle, 3-3/4 x 8-1/2 in. A-$65

Miniature cradle, Paiute style, 14 in. long and 5 in. wide. Has wicker base, covered with hide and partially beaded. Piece is ca. 1930. G-$195

Child's toy travois, Sioux, in very fine condition. G-$225

Hupa cradles, two miniature, sold as one lot. A-$95

MUSICAL ITEMS—DRUMS

Drum, double-headed, painted with buffalo and eagle; a Pueblo piece and ca. 1890. D-$425

Plains-type drum, 14 in. in diameter, made of hide stretched on wood. Painted figure on hide. Old. G-$425

Cree single-head drum, painted head, ca. 1920. D-$225

Drum, California Indian type, 6 in. high and 7 in. diameter. Hide stretched over wood, both ends covered and wood is painted. Good condition. G-$295

Sioux drum, done on square box and 14 in. square. Painted with deer on one side and star on the other; stretched hide covers ends. Good sound and comes with early beater. G-$325

Sioux drum, rawhide covered and laced wood drum, painted designs on ends, with beater. G-$350

Sioux hoop drum, 13 in. in diameter, hide covered single face, and piece has some age. D-$250

Tourist-type drum, 10 in. in diameter, hide stretched over wood frame. Figure painted on hide, trimmed with feathers, and ca. 1940s. G-$225

Indian drum, 11-1/2 in. in diameter, some age. A-$60

Sioux hand-held drum, wood hoop type and hide-covered. Drum is 11 in. in diameter. G-$150

Drum, Pueblo, red horse painted on top, black triangles on sides with yellow and red panels, ca. 1920-1940. Museum quality

Morning Star Gallery, Santa Fe, New Mexico

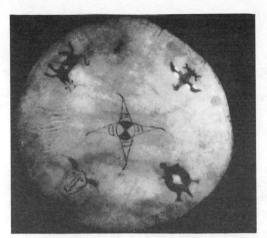

Cree Indian hand drum, 16 in. in diameter. Has very old hand-hewn wooden frame, with painted zoomorphic designs on drumhead. Leather has very small slit; a more modern drum-beater is included.   D-$450

Photo courtesy Crazy Crow Trading Post, Denison, Texas

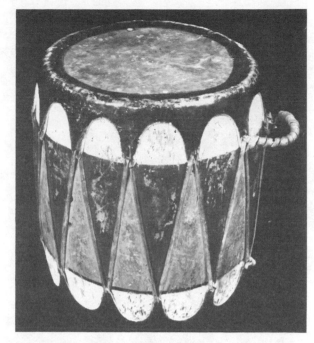

Drum, Pueblo, sides painted in red and green triangles. Ca. 1920-1940.   Museum quality

Morning Star Gallery, Santa Fe, New Mexico

Drum, Pueblo, sides painted in pale plum and green, 7 in. in diameter and 10 in. high. It is ca. 1920-1940.   Museum quality

Morning Star Gallery, Santa Fe, New Mexico

Drum, Sioux, hide and wood with painted background and animal figures. It is 19th century. $4,000

Private collection, photo by John McLaughlin

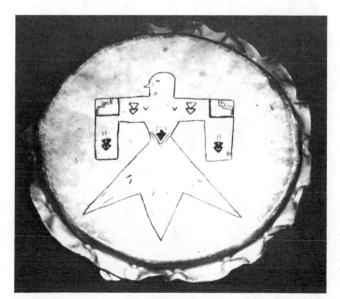

Dance drum, single-head, from the Iroquois on the Cayuga Reservation. With Thunderbird design, diameter is 10-1/4 in.; ca. 1920. $450-700

Marguerite L. Kernaghan collection; photograph by Marguerite L. and Stewart W. Kernaghan, Bellvue, Colorado

Drum, Mide, Great Lakes region, with wood, hide, paint, silk ribbon, and cloth plus sweetgrass. It is 19th century. $1,000

Private collection, photo by John McLaughlin

Drum, Taos Indian, wood and horsehide. This large drum, made for a wedding, is 25 in. in diameter and ca. 1940. $400

Tom Noeding, Taos, New Mexico

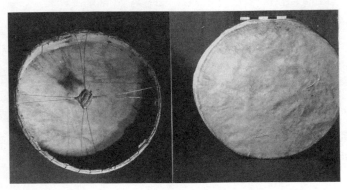

Plains-type drum, 16 in. in diameter and 3 in. thick, with beater. Hide stretched on wooden hoop; no design but pleasing tone. G-$300

RATTLES

Hopi gourd rattle, painted black on white with swastika symbol. D-$150

Peyote gourd rattle, with red, white and blue beadwork; ebony handle has a buckskin figure, recent. D-$225

Medicine rattle, type sold by Northern Cheyenne Indians in Montana. Has a small leather ball on the end with horsehair; handle wrapped in rawhide. Made by Marion King. G-$100

Plains rattle, 10 in. long and 3-1/2 in. wide, done with hide that has been made into the entire rattle. Has a light green painted design; 19th century. G-$250

Medicine rattle, Southwest type, a black leather hoop 4-1/2 in. in diameter, with attached handle. Authentic. G-$300

Comanche rawhide rattle with horsetail decoration. Ca. 1890. D-$225

Elk hoof rattle, part of medicine bundle, extra-fine condition. G-$375

Bird-bone rasp, 9 in. long, from New Mexico. D-$125

Peyote fan, Peyote style with gourd rattle. Seed bead design on wooden handle. Dyed hair on one end and woven leather fringe on the other. G-$400

Plains Indian "bullroarer," a 9-3/4 in. flattened section of wood with hole in smaller end. Item was whirled around the user on a cord, making a humming roar. Painted, but faded. C-$100

Left: Larger ceremonial rattle, companion piece to item on right. It is 5 in. in diameter with overall length 15 in. Pictured on rattle face is the Mide-related supernatural character Misshipeshu, otherwise known as the Underwater Panther, with a supernatural bird. Ca. 1895. C-$400

Photo courtesy Bill Post collection

Right: Small ceremonial rattle, Mide-wiwin Grand Medicine Society, Chippewa (Ojibway), 4 in. in diameter and 14 in. long. From Leech Lake, Minnesota; five small green turtles are on rattle face and edged in red color. All hide including sinew-sewn handle. Ca. 1895. C-$400

Photo courtesy Bill Post collection

Plains drum, rawhide, 16-1/8 in. in diameter. Both sides shown, and drum is ca. 1920s. $200

Native American Artifacts, Victor, New York

Bark rattle, Iroquois, 4-1/2 x 13 in. From New York state, ca. 1900. $200

Pat & Dave Summers, Native American Artifacts, Victor, New York

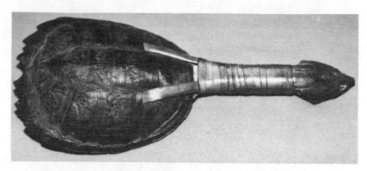

Contemporary snapping turtle rattle, Mohawk, from Ontario, Canada. This interesting piece is 14 in. long. $500

Michael F. Slasinski, Saginaw, Michigan

Turtle rattle, Iroquois, with leather handle winding. This large rattle is 27-1/2 in. long. From New York state, contemporary piece. $475

Pat & Dave Summers, Native American Artifacts, Victor, New York

Wooden bird-effigy rattle, Northwest Coast, Haida. From Canada and in perfect condition. Ca. early 1900s $750-1,100

Marguerite L. Kernaghan collection; photograph by Marguerite L. and Stewart W. Kernaghan, Bellvue, Colorado

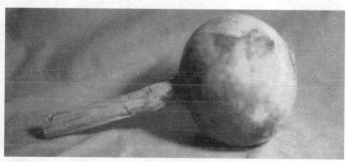

Rattle, consisting of gourd secured to a wooden handle; faint traces of old paint on the gourd. Came from the Navajo Reservation, New Mexico. Historic item. $125

Jack Baker Collection, Ozark, Missouri; David Capon photograph

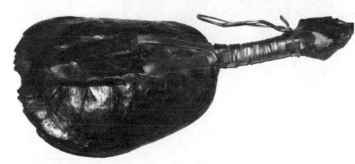

Turtle rattle, Iroquois, 16 in. long. Made of wood with turtle shell, head, and leather, with pebbles. It is 19th century. $1,000

Private collection, photo by John McLaughlin

FLUTES & WHISTLES

Sioux love flute, 21 in. long, well carved and decorated, in good condition. Ca. 1920.   G-$300

Small Sioux flute, sinew wrapped.   G-$295

Bone flute, Plains Indian.   A-$175

Sioux Grass Dance whistle, fine early piece with carved open-mouthed bird head.   G-$425

Mogollon bird-whistle, red pottery, New Mexico. D-$115

Three Nez Perce men, with tepees to side and background. Note the fine necklaces and blankets; photo taken at Colville, Washington, ca.1904. Photographer, Dr. E. H. Latham; courtesy Photography collection, Suzzallo Library, University of Washington

CHAPTER XVII

WEAVINGS: BLANKETS AND RUGS

American Indian weavings are probably the warmest-looking and most useful of Amerind contemporary arts and crafts to live with. You can look at them, walk on them, and sleep under them. Most of the older blankets are quite valuable as collector items, but modern rugs of good quality can be obtained at reasonable prices.

Weaving in North America has ranged from Northwest Coast spruce root mats to Plains robes made of rabbit skin strips. Today, the Navajo weavings are best known. They are certainly one of the Big Four of contemporary Amerind collectibles: Baskets, Blankets and Rugs, Jewelry, and Pottery.

For the record, Pueblo blankets were made for centuries, but the Hopi Indians (here, the men often weave) now do most of the work. The Navajo Indians used natural cotton but then began to raise sheep for the wool.

The wool is chipped, cleaned, and carded before it is spun on a whirling, hand-held wooden spindle. Weft thread may be spun twice, while warp thread, which must be tight and strong, may be spun three times. If the wool is to be dyed, this step takes place next; the dry wool is then rolled into balls, ready for the weaver.

The Navajo woman, the weaver, generally dyes only enough wool for the intended rug. This is for economy, but also so that any one dye color will match in the same rug and not be a different shade. Rugs, and the blankets before them, are woven on an upright loom which the Navajos may have developed and refined themselves. The warp threads (except for some historic Chiefs' blankets, where it is opposite) run up and down on the loom, or the length of the rug when it is completed.

Warp yarn is important, and experts say a wool warp is generally better than a cotton warp. It is more durable, making an all-wool rug, and the two age nicely together.

The weft threads run horizontally on the vertical loom, or the width of the finished rug. These are the design elements, formed by different weft colors. Any pattern will then be formed by the weft yarn. Without getting into a discussion of the actual weaving and tools used, it is enough to say that a good rug takes many hundreds of hours to make and considerable degrees of experience and skill.

There are three colors of wool that might be in any one rug or late blanket, and they are sometimes combined to form different colors in the same rug.

1. **Natural**: Whitish, brown, gray, and reddish black. Blackish wool is often dyed to make a solid black.
2. **Vegetal**: Dyed wool, the dye made from plant stems, roots, bark, etc. There are currently some 135 slightly different vegetal-dye colors. The best of these rugs are said to come from the Klagetoh region.
3. **Commercial**: (synthetic) Called "aniline" dyes, these were widely used in the last quarter of the 1800s and are still popular today.

Here are some of the historic Navajo blanket types, mostly from the 1850-1900 period. These blankets were made for the Navajo's own wearing use and for trade.

The Chiefs' blankets were "exported" to other tribes and were so well-made that only an important person was said to be able to afford them. The best Navajo blankets—especially the complex double-faced blanket with different patterns on both sides using two distinct wefts—could hold water for awhile without seepage.

Shoulder blankets: Ca. 1850 and later, men and women's sizes, simple stripes.

Striped blankets: Wearing blankets common among the Navajos until 1900s.

Banded blankets: "Fancier" striped varieties with additional designs between stripes.

Chief's blankets: Three varieties or "Phases" recognized, ca. 1850-1895:

1st Phase: Stripes of blackish color, red, white, and blue

2nd Phase: Some red stripes divided into blocks; some blocks no longer joined by red. Green sometimes used; designs within blocks.

3rd Phase: Some stripes have large diamond patterns, with the diamonds on the corners, the four sides, plus one in the center, nine in all. Multi-colored. Diamonds later became larger square crosses in some cases. Original 1st Phase stripes now only a small part of background.

Serape/Poncho-style blankets: Early and late periods, ca. 1860s-1880s. Diamond patterns, natural dyes. Some had a slit woven at center to go over the head.

Eye-Dazzler blankets: Ca. 1880-1910. Aniline or commercial dyes used. Blankets had a multitude of designs, especially zigzag lines and smaller, "busy" patterns. Examples had as many as nine different colors.

Other important blankets include pictorial, wedgeweave child's blankets, and the smaller saddle throws. Bayeta blankets were woven, when flannel-like red English blankets were unraveled and the yarn used in Navajo blankets. The period ca. 1850-1870 is considered to be the Classic Period, the golden age of Navajo blankets.

The last major Navajo blanket made a genuine break from the past. It is the transitional blanket, made in many eccentric patterns, some very well done. Ca. 1885-1900, some resembled earlier forms, others reverted to natural and vegetal colors. One significance is that these weavings are the last of the Navajo blankets before the changeover to rugs.

Before the turn of this century, quality, White-made, machine-woven blankets faltered and the White Indian traders decided to try something different.

With the completion of the railroads and the large number of Eastern travelers in Navajo lands, a new demand arose for blankets. But the demand was for blankets used as rugs and tapestries, or floor coverings and wall hangings.

The Indians were encouraged to weave with heavier yarns, and in new sizes with new designs. Except for experiences like the "pound" rugs—when traders bought weavings according to weight, not quality—the enterprises have been highly successful.

Today, there are a dozen or so major Navajo weaving areas, each of which produces distinctive rug styles. The early blankets are commonly classed according to pattern. Today's rugs, except for the Yei rug or blanket and pictorials, were named after the regions where they have been made for many years. But there has been so much departure from traditional and blending of patterns that these identify more rug style than a place style.

Here are some of the better-known contemporary Navajo blanket types:

Burntwater: Central panel in geometric style and a broad geometric border. Vegetal dyes.

Crystal: Simple and elegant patterns, vegetal dyes; these rugs have a certain "modern" look that is quite pleasing.

Ganado: Four-colored rugs; two natural (white, gray) and two aniline (red and enhanced black) colors are used.

Pictorial: Rugs woven with patterns of identifiable objects, people, animals, plants, feathers, etc.

Pine Springs: Designs are similar to Wide Ruins, but more vivid and with contrasting colors; earth tones.

Storm pattern: Symbolic dark geometric forms at the four corners, separated by broad white lightning designs.

Teec Nos Pos: Geometric designs in multi-colored shades, boldly outlined. Aniline dyes.

Two Grey Hills: Basic geometric designs, natural wools used; they are combined, also, to produce buff and gray.

Wide Ruins: Patterns closely follow those of late-Classic wearing blankets; horizontal bands, geometric designs.

Yei weavings: Yei figures copied from sacred sand paintings (part of healing ceremonies). Light in weight compared with other contemporary rugs. These are often hung.

As of 1993, there has been an upsurge in prices for high-quality Navajo rugs. This has been due to a renewed interest in weaving arts, based on a much larger number of collectors competing for a relatively few good rugs. Too, while rug-making has long been considered a craft, many of the pieces have come to be seen as fine art, again with appreciated prices. As cases in point, a $2,000 rug in 1990 might go for $5,000-6,000 today, and a $10,000 rug then might reach above $30,000 today.

OLDER BLANKETS

Navajo saddle blanket, 3 ft. 5 in. x 5 ft. 11 in., diamond patterns in red, natural-wool tufts as fringes. Several small burn holes in this specimen. D-$1,000

Wearing blanket 4 ft. 10 in. x 6 ft. 4 in., diagonal cut fine. Homespun yarns, vegetal dye, good condition. Blanket is ca. 1885 G-$3,500

Serape-style blanket, Navajo, commercial (aniline) dyes, 4 ft. 3 in. x 6 ft. 1 in. Blanket made in four colors, in extra good condition. Ca. 1800s. C-$4,500

Eye-dazzler blanket, size unknown, cotton warp. Large blanket with damage that is repairable. Ca. 1890. G-$1,600

Serape-style blanket, 6 ft. 3 in. x 4 ft. in., striped designs. Condition fair, with normal wear that shows. Late 1800s. C-$2,900

Transitional blanket, 50-1/2 x 63-1/2 in. A-$200

Navajo blanket with red and rust designs, fawn-colored background. Minor moth damage; piece is 3 ft. 1 in. x 5 ft. 7 in. C-$1,150

Transitional blanket, 4 ft. 6 in. x 7 ft. Design is serrated diamond showing heavy wear. Piece is ca. 1890. G-$2,100

Navajo blanket, handspun wool with commercial dyes. Size is 5 ft. x 6 ft. 5 in. Excellent condition because blanket was stored for years. Wedge-weave pattern. C-$3,000

Zuni blanket, man's shawl style, 3 ft. 8 in. x 7 ft. 1 in. Multi-colored vegetal dyes; woven by men only, a rare piece in good condition. Blanket is pre-1920 G-$7,000

Child's blanket of Merino sheep wool, which is like Angora. Rare, and condition excellent. Blanket, red, gray, white, and black, is 30 x 50-1/2 in. Ca. 1875-90. C-$3,000

Photo courtesy Rob Swan Townshende, California

Classic diamond pattern chief's blanket, in colors black, buff, red, and white. In excellent condition, blanket is 49 x 64 in., and is ca. 1880-95.   C-$4,500

Photo courtesy Rob Swan Townshende, California

Classic diamond pattern blanket, in colors, red diamonds in white background and white diamonds in red background, brown borders. Eye-Dazzler patterns, and excellent condition. Blanket is 39-1/2 x 81-1/2 in. It is ca. 1885-90.   C-$5,000

Photo courtesy Rob Swan Townshende, California

Transitional diamond pattern blanket, tight weave, in white, orangeish, and brown. Fair condition, and 47 x 62 in. Ca. 1890-1900.   C-$2,000

Photo courtesy Rob Swan Townshende, California

Diamond pattern blanket, medium-coarse weave, in colors red, white, black, and gray. Excellent condition, and ca. 1895-1910.   C-$1,600

Photo courtesy Rob Swan Townshende, California

Rare Germantown serape-style Chimayo blanket, in excellent condition. Colors are white, red, blue, and yellow. Blanket measures 39 1/2 x 74 1/2 in., and is ca. 1875-90.   C-$3,300

Photo courtesy Rob Swan, Townshende, California

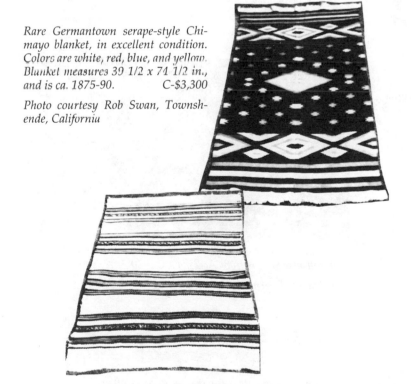

Serape-style woman's blanket, early coarse weave. Black-bordered orange stripes on a cream background. It is 43-1/2 x 64-1/2 in. in very good condition. About Bosque Redondo.   C-$3,300

Photo courtesy Rob Swan Townshende, California

Saddle blanket, Navajo, very old. It measures 25-1/2 x 44-1/4 in. and is black on yellow-tan. $250

Pat & Dave Summers, Native American Artifacts, Victor, New York

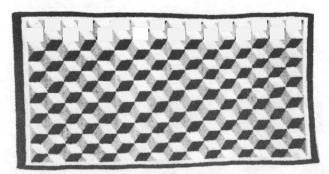

Rug, Navajo, optical illusion pattern., it is 27 x 54 in. and has natural grays and white, the black dye-enhanced to accent the contrast. Unusual and well-done design. Contemporary. $450

Sherman Holbert collection, Fort Mille Lacs, Onamia, Minnesota

Rug, Navajo, 24-1/2 x 30-1/2 in. Pattern is a Teec Nos Pos dazzler in both hand-spun and commercial yarns and in natural color and natural and aniline dyes. The center stars are brilliant red with brown centers, bordered with alternating black, white, gray, and brown, ca. 1980. $390

Sherman Holbert collection, Fort Mille Lacs, Onamia, Minnesota

Ganado rug, red, gray, black, and white wools, with a strong and well executed design. In impeccable condition, this 47 x 69 in. piece is ca. 1970. Museum quality

James Reid, LTD, Santa Fe, New Mexico

Klagetoh rug, 48 x 67-1/2 in., in near-mint condition. This bright and well-made rug is from Arizona, ca. 1930. Museum quality

Collection of Eugene and Marcille Wing

Germantown yarn weaving, Navajo, 28 x 34 in., the style is often called a "Sunday Saddle Blanket" Has a wide red border with black and orange inner borders and zigzags on a green field. Yarn tassels add a decorative finishing touch. Ca. 1890. $4,500

Canfield Gallery, Santa Fe

Ganado weaving, in black, gray and white against a red ground, 59 x 79 in. This colorful and well-done work is ca. 1910. $5,000

Dennis R. Phillips, Chicago, Illinois

Germantown weaving, 43 x 77 in. including fringe. Finely woven, it has nine to ten warps per inch and twenty-four wefts per inch. This beautiful weaving is in fine condition and has an intricate design. Ca. 1890. $15,000-20,000

Terry Schafer, American Indian Art & Antiques, Marietta, Ohio

Navajo blanket, wedge-weave, natural fleece dyed red and yellow. A very fine early blanket, it measures 68 x 88 in. and is ca. 1890. $12,500

David Cook Fine American Art, Denver, Colorado; Jamie Kahn photograph

Navajo wool blanket, done in half a dozen colors, 41 x 54 in. This early weaving is ca. 1880. $2,500

Tom Noeding, Taos, New Mexico

Navajo weaving, 47 x 55 in., frayed on edges, woven in blue, tan, white red and black. Ca. 1910. $695

Native American Artifacts, Victor, New York

Navajo Transitional rug, about 6 x 9 feet, dyed and natural wool yarn. This is a large, well-made rug in excellent condition, ca. 1890-1900. $3,000

Frank Bergevin, Port Of Call, Alexandria Bay, New York

Chimayo blanket measuring 4 ft. 4 in. x 6 ft. 10 in. A-$400

Navajo saddle blanket, 2 ft. 3-1/2 in. x 3 ft. 1 in. Small size, good condition. A-$300

Indian blanket fragment, section cut from old hand-woven blanket. Red background, black designs. Piece is 19 in. long and 13 in. wide, with edges sewn to keep from fraying. All four sides decorated with horsehair. Unusual piece, unknown work. C-$295

Navajo saddle blanket, 3 ft. 7 in. x 4 ft. 8 in., gray and black design. Natural wool, fair condition. D-$750

RECENT AND CONTEMPORARY RUGS

Teec Nos Pos rug, 50 in. x 90 in. Pristine condition, vibrant colors, and a rare piece. Ca. 1920. C-$11,000

Navajo rug, diamond designs in many colors, 3-1/2 ft. x 6 ft., rust-red background with zigzag bands. C-$2,200

Throw rug, Gallup (?), 17 x 39 in. Patterns in black, gray and white, excellent condition. G-$250

Pictorial rug, 48 x 66 in., and all natural wool colors. Weave is medium, and twenty feathers are woven into patterns. Item has a few minor stains and is about 1920s or 30s. G-$1,400

Yei rug, 52 x 72 in. Pattern is five yeis surrounded by Rainbow God. Rug has "lazy lines" and comes with appraisal papers. Piece is about 50 years old. C-$3,500

Navajo rug, 43 x 67 in., in good but worn condition. C-$2,500

Navajo rug, moderated Klagetoh pattern, 5 x 7 ft. Medium weave, contemporary. G-$3,300

Two Grey Hills rug, 30 x 35 in. Standard pattern, colors in tan, brown, black, gray, and white. Rug has a tight weave and intricate pattern. G-$1,600

Navajo Tree of Life tapestry weaving, from Shiprock, New Mexico. This rug type copies sand painting designs. A-$1,300

Navajo rug, Yeibichai dancers and head man. Rug is 4 ft. 8 in. x 6 ft. Very tightly woven and in fine condition. Ca. early 1900. G-$4,750

Two Grey Hills rug, 39 x 47 in. Colors gray, white, brown and black, and in good condition. Ca. 1950. G-$2,000

Early Navajo rug, 33 x 58 in., with fine, tight weave. Good colors and designs; rug has slight stains on one side. G-$800

Wide Ruins rug, tapestry weaving style, 33 x 39 in., all natural wools and vegetal dyes. A-$350

Navajo Sand painting rug, 48 x 51 in., with very fine weave and in excellent condition. Ca. 1950s. G-$3,500

Yei rug, 3 x 5 ft., white background with five Yei figures. Good condition and ca. 1940. C-$2,000

Early Navajo rug, small size, good weave. A-$425

Germantown rug, 24 x 31 in. Red with multi-color Eye-Dazzler pattern. Fringe on bottom intact; excellent condition. Ca. 1900. G-$1,600

Navajo rug, 36 x 60 in. A high quality rug, but dirty and in need of repair. Poor condition. Very old. G-$175

Navajo rug, 3 x 5-1/2 ft., double-diamond pattern with geometric border. Medium-good condition, ca. 1930. G-$800

Small Germantown rug, 22 in. square. Pattern in green and white on red background. Nice condition and ca. 1900. G-$600

Yei rug, 35 x 53 in., multi-colored with brown background. Ca. 1950. G-$1,800

Transitional 2nd phase blanket, 41 x 62 in. Colors are a faded red, white, yellowish, brown, and buff. There is a stain on one side, and condition is fair. Ca. 1880-85. C-$1,300

Photo courtesy Rob Swan Townshende, California

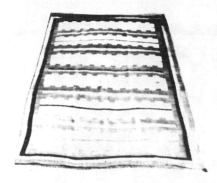

Extremely large terrace/striped chief's blanket, in colors reddish, black, yellow, and white. It measures 60 x 93-1/2 in.; in good condition, with several minor, old repairs. From the transitional period, ca. 1880-1895.   C-$4,400

Photo courtesy Rob Swan Townshende, California

Germantown rug or blanket, black, white, blue, and green designs on red ground. In poor condition, ca. 1890.   C-$2,400

Photo courtesy Jack Barry

Navajo rug, 24 x 46 in., in seven colors. From the Shiprock area, contemporary, and tagged.   D-$325

Photo courtesy of American Indian World, Ltd., Denver, Colorado

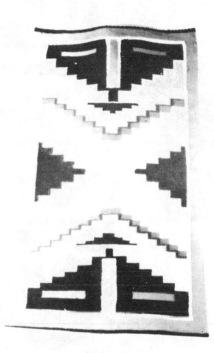

Germantown rug or blanket, blue and green designs outlined in white against red ground. Ca. 1890, good condition.   C-$3,200

Photo courtesy Jack Barry

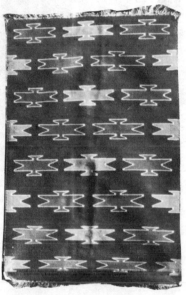

Yei/yebechai rug, about 5 x 8 ft., plus. Tight weave, and very good condition; colors predominately black, white, burnt-orange, and red. Ca. 1920.   C-$2,300

Photo courtesy of Rob Swan Townshende, California

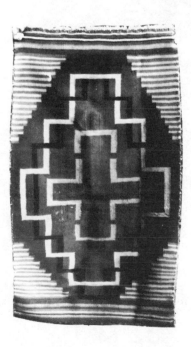

Germantown rug or blanket, green striping, white, black, and blue designs against red ground. In good condition, ca. 1890.   C-$2,900

Photo courtesy Jack Barry

Left: Yei rug, figures in white, buff, and gray against rich brown ground, border in black. Ca. 1973.   C-$800

Photo courtesy Jack Barry

Two gray hills rug, design in two shades of brown plus gray, black, and white, black border, Ca. 1973.   C-$2,100

Photo courtesy Jack Barry

Right: Yei rug, figures in red, yellow, white, and blue-gray against gray ground. Ca. 1973.   C-$900

Photo courtesy Jack Barry

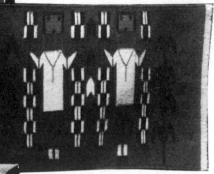

Left: rug, natural and vegetal dyes, ca. 1973.   C-$1,000

Photo courtesy Jack Barry

Right: pictorial rug, natural and vegetal colors, ca. 1973.   C-$1,100

Photo courtesy Jack Barry

Navajo rug, Eye-Dazzler, in colors of brown, gold, white, red, black, and tan. Size is 38 x 72 in. This exquisite rug with very fine weave is ca. 1910. $1,100

Pat & Dave Summers, Native American Artifacts, Victor, New York

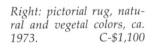

Navajo rug, a fine large weaving in splendid condition. Done in black, white, gray, red, and rust and measures 58 x 84 in. This exceptional rug is ca. 1940. $2,800

Pat & Dave Summers, Native American Artifacts, Victor, New York

Navajo rug, natural white, gray, and dark brown. It has a concentric diamond pattern bordered with a fret design in red, natural white, and dark brown. Size, 66 x 121 in. and ca. 1915. Museum quality

James Reid, LTD, Santa Fe, New Mexico

Navajo rug, natural white, gray, and dark brown. It has a concentric diamond pattern bordered with a fret design in red, natural white, and dark brown. Size, 66 x 121 in. and ca. 1915. Museum quality

James Reid, LTD, Santa Fe, New Mexico

Navajo rug, Eye-Dazzler, red, white, gray, and rust. This fine weaving is 34 x 58 in. and ca. 1925. $650

Pat & Dave Summers, Native American Artifacts, Victor, New York

Navajo rug, done in all-natural colors of white, brown, tan, and camel. This classic weaving is 46 x 76 in. and is ca. 1920. $1,000

Pat & Dave Summers, Native American Artifacts, Victor, New York

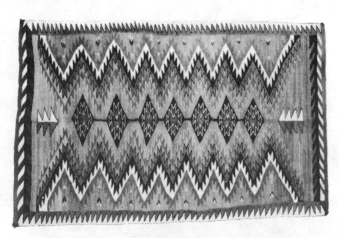

Rug, Navajo, 48 x 74 in. It is pre-World War One and a dazzler with exceptional weave. There are as many as forty color changes across the width of the rug, with each change having an individual outline. Natural gray background with white, red, gold, black, and yellow patterns. $3,000

Sherman Holbert collection, Fort Mile Lacs, Onamia, Minnesota

Navajo rug, lightning pattern, in colors of brown, white, black, and gray. Size is 30 x 57 in., with very fine weave. This well-done rug is ca. 1920. $1,100

Pat & Dave Summers, Native American Artifacts, Victor, New York

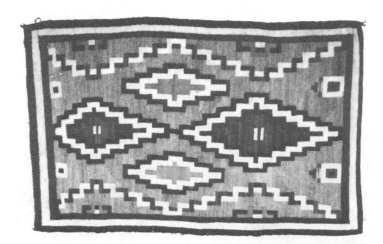

Navajo rug, crystal pattern in colors of gray, red, white, brown, and orange, it is 38 x 59 in., from Crystal, New Mexico, year 1920. $700

Pat & Dave Summers, Native American Artifacts, Victor, New York

Crystal weaving, natural shades of brown with red and yellow ochre in storm pattern. This Navajo work has fine weave and fair condition. It is 34-1/2 x 70 in., and ca. 1915.   Museum quality

James Reid, LTD, Santa Fe, New Mexico

Blanket, Chief's pattern, Germantown third phase, done in white, black, and red. This rare weaving is ca. 1880-1890.   Museum quality

Morning Star Gallery, Santa Fe, New Mexico

Crystal rug, Navajo, 5 ft. 2 in. x 8 ft. 10 in., very good condition. Red and natural shades of white, beige, and dark brown, with a central design and geometric border. With pleasing pattern, it is from the 1930s.   Museum quality

James Reid, LTD, Santa Fe, New Mexico

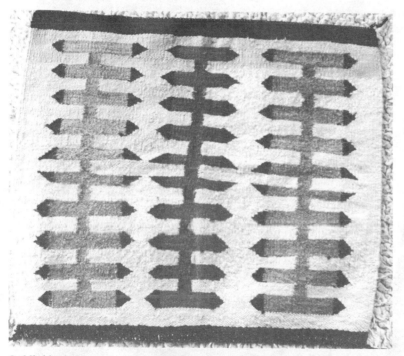

Saddle blanket, Navajo, blacks, grays, rust, and red on tan-cream with black top and bottom borders. It is 28 x 30 in. and ca. 1940s. $275

Pocotopaug Trading Post, South Windsor, Connecticut

Weaving, Germantown Yei, 2 ft. 8 in. x 6 ft. Done in nine colors on a gray background. In mint condition, ca. 1920. $4,200

Courtesy John Isaac, Albuquerque, New Mexico

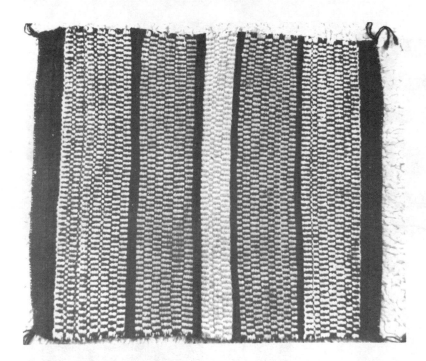

Saddle-blanket, Navajo, twill weave, 27 x 29 in. Done in reds, black, and buff, it is ca. 1930s. $150-200

Pocotopaug Trading Post, South Windsor, Connecticut

Cree rug-runner, all wool, 31 x 87 in., many colors. In excellent condition, this rug is from Canada and ca. 1930s-1940s. $229

Native American Artifacts, Victor, New York

Regional Navajo rug, 43 x 58 in. It is black-bordered with colors of red, black, and two shades of gray against white. Ca. 1920. $600-900

Terry Schafer collection, Marietta, Ohio

Navajo rug, 37-1/2 x 54 in., browns and rust colors on a white field. Ca. 1940. $395

Native American Artifacts, Victor, New York

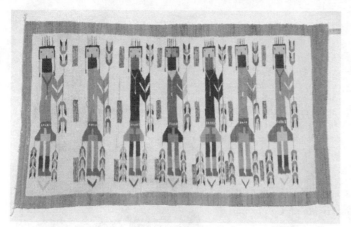

Yei throw-rug, seven figures, many different yarn colors, 28-1/2 x 49 in., ca. 1940. $395

Native American Artifacts, Victor, New York

Navajo rug, Two Grey Hills design, 25 x 35 in., design in several earth shades. $650

Charles F. and Susan Wood, Ohio

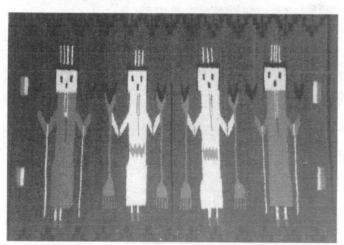

Navajo Yei weaving, 21 1/2 x 30 in., done by Ilene Chico, aged sixty five when the piece was acquired in 1993. $350

Charles F. and Susan Wood, Ohio

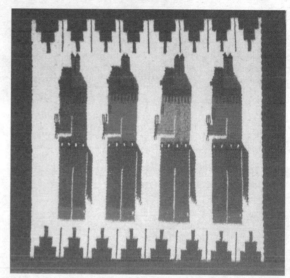

Navajo weaving, Shiprock region, 17-7/8 x 19-1/4 in. This was woven by Ameria Cambridge. $235

Charles F. and Susan Wood, Ohio

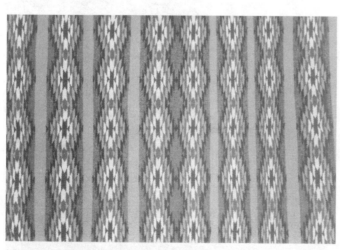

Navajo rug, Wide Ruins design, 23 x 32 in. This weaving is by Edith Brown, Arizona. $525

Charles F. and Susan Wood, Ohio

Yei rug, Navajo from the Ship Rock region, 36 x 48 in., black border and figures in various colors. Ca. 1940. $1,200

Tom Noeding, Taos, New Mexico

Contemporary Southwestern artworks.

Miniature Zia pueblo pot, 2 in. high. $13.50
Small Navajo rug by Sarah Foster, with certificate of authenticity. $85

Blue Coyote Trading Post, Nashville, Indiana; Pat Nolan photograph

Neo-Revival Navajo textile, contemporary, 30-1/2 x 48 in. Child's sized Chief's pattern with navy blue natural indigo dye and a luminous light. Also has medium natural blue indigo with vibrant natural cochineal red/orange stepped geometric diamonds. $2,500

The Child's Blanket, Highland, California

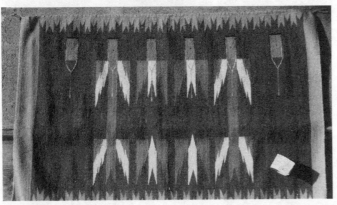

Yei (Bat Wing) weaving, 27 x 33 in., design in white and earth shades. This was made by Louise Begay in 1970. $650

Private collection

Neo-Revival Navajo pictorial textile, 29-3/4 x 48-1/2 in. Babe Ruth rug includes his number three on the jersey. The weaving contains three shades of rich natural indigo blue, a deep cochineal red border, and cochineal dyed orange bats, contemporary. $6,500

The Child's Blanket, Highland, California

Navajo rug, 30 x 60 in., handspun wool. It is gray with a dark brown border and designs in white, red and dark brown. This storm pattern rug is from New Mexico or Arizona and period is 1930-1940. $600

T.R.H. collection, Indiana

Navajo rug, Crystal Trading Post, 49 x 71 in. Bordered in black, white, and red, it is made of natural fleece and aniline dyes. Ca. 1930. $4,000

David Cook Fine American Art, Denver, Colorado; Jamie Kahn photograph

Neo-Revival Navajo pictorial textile, 36 x 50 in. Combination Santa Fe train pictorial and Classic blanket pattern depicts a train robbery and passengers. All natural dyes include various shades of indigo blue and green, cochineal red, osage orange, and cutch browns, contemporary. $7,000

The Child's Blanket, Highland, California

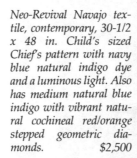

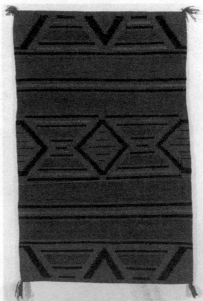

The Child's Blanket, Highland, California

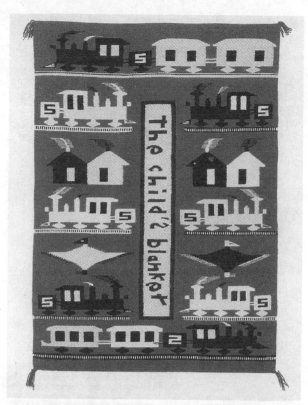

Neo-Revival Navajo pictorial textile, contemporary, 36-1/4 x 51-1/4 in. Pictorial has trains, houses, and birds, and contains deep, navy blue, natural indigo dye, and various shades of cochineal red natural dye. $6,000

The Child's Blanket, Highland, California

Neo-Revival Navajo pictorial textile, 29-3/4 x 49-1/2 in. Often referred to as the "Icon of Navajo Weaving," was recreated from the aniline dyed historic rug located in the collections of the San Diego Museum of Man. Contains rare and beautiful indigo and cochineal natural dyes, contemporary. $8,500

The Child's Blanket, Highland, California

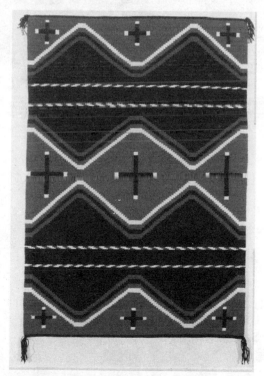

Neo-Revival Navajo Moki textile, 35-1/2 x 51-1/2 in. An elegant Moki textile, it contains thin stripes of rich natural indigo blue dye, brown vegetal cutch, and a stunning cochineal natural red plus Spider Woman crosses of deep navy blue indigo, contemporary. $5,500

The Child's Blanket, Highland, California

Neo-Revival Navajo textile, 31-3/4 x 48 in. Elegant Classic blanket pattern with various shades of indigo blue, green and cochineal red natural dyes, contemporary. $3,500

The Child's Blanket, Highland, California

Neo-Revival Navajo Pictorial textile, 37 x 52-1/2 in. Has fifty-six man figures and all natural dyes. Dyes contain two shades of indigo blue which include a luminous medium blue, a deep cochineal red, and natural white wool, contemporary. $6,500

The Child's Blanket, Highland, California

Neo-Revival Navajo textile, 30 x 48-3/4 in. Classic blanket pattern comprised of stepped diamonds and crosses; contains rare indigo and cochineal natural dyes, contemporary. $3,200

The Child's Blanket, Highland, California

Neo-Revival Navajo textile, 35-1/4 x 51-3/4 in. Represents a serape-style poncho, with the vertical line in the central diamond as the weaver's interpretation of the poncho opening. Weaving has two shades of indigo blue, deep cochineal red, and brilliant indigo green, contemporary. $5,800

The Child's Blanket, Highland, California

Neo-Revival Navajo textile, 30 x 48 in. Very graphic and modernistic-looking, Navajo weaving comprised of various shades of rich natural indigo and cochineal dyes, contemporary. $2,500

The Child's Blanket, Highland, California

Neo-Revival Navajo Chief's textile, 48 x 62 in. Features the 3rd Phase pattern with Spider Woman crosses and rich shades of indigo and cochineal natural dyes, contemporary. $5,000

The Child's Blanket, Highland, California

Pine Springs rug, 34 x 39-1/2 in., natural wools and vegetal dyes. A-$125

Teec Nos Pos rug, 42 x 64 in. Deep red predominates, with black, gray, white, and orange colors. Very good design and in excellent condition. Ca. 1910-1920. G-$1,700

Two Gray Hills rug, 49 x 73 in., colors are gray, white and black. Good condition, and ca. 1910. G-$2,700

Banded rug, 3 ft. 9 in. x 6 ft. 5 in., natural grays and whites, aniline reds, and greens. Pattern may be derived from old wearing blankets. Contemporary. D-$2,300

Navajo rug, 31 x 56 in., vegetal dyed. Pattern is double diamond with outlined design. Nice weave, and contemporary. G-$995

Tapestry rug, Sand painting designs, 53 x 72 in., and multi-colored. Gray background, extremely fine weave, a rare piece. Ca. 1960. G-$14,000

Navajo rug, 5 ft. wide and 7 ft. long, diamond pattern in gray, white, red, and black. Good condition. G-$2,800

Teec Nos Pos rug, 41 x 68 in., diamond pattern. Colors are red, black, and gray, and rug has a good, tight weave. Item is 40 to 50 years old. G-$2,000

Navajo rug, 58 x 83 in., very large and colorful with red, and white swastikas. In good, sound, usable condition. G $1,900

Navajo rug, Klagetoh area, sunrise pattern with bows and arrows. Rug is 45 x 80-1/2 in. A-$1,300

Ganado rug, 32 x 61 in., in good condition. Rug made by Daisy Mano, colors red, white, and gray. Ca. 1920. G-$1,800

Navajo rug, Klagetoh area, measuring 38 x 57 in. A-$300

Navajo rug, small, 20 x 40 in. Natural wool colors in gray, black, and tan. Nice condition. G-$500

Storm pattern rug, 4 x 6 ft. excellent condition. Ca. 1940. G-$2,600

Yei rug, 4-1/2 x 6-1/2 ft., with colors beige, brown, orange, vegetal-red, rust, and blue. There are five central figures surrounded by Rainbow figure. Rug is ca. 1910. G-$2,000

Two Gray Hills rug, measuring 40 x 70 in. A-$1,250

Navajo rug, 2-1/2 x 5 ft. Pattern is double-diamonds with geometric border. G-$500

Pine Springs rug, 30 x 56 in., colors tan, gray, and white. Nice design and perfect condition. Made in 1976 by Florence James. Burntwater Post tag still attached. G-$1,800

Eye-Dazzler rug, 43 x 64 in., natural wool colors and red aniline dye. Handspun wool, and ca. 1920. C-$2,400

Mr. Al R. Packard does business as Packard's Indian Trading Company, of Santa Fe, New Mexico. He is a third generation Indian trader, in Santa Fe since 1929. The writer was referred to Mr. Packard as being one of the most knowledgeable persons in the country on the subject of American Indian weavings, old and new.

Mr. Packard kindly consented to offer six tips on buying a Navajo rug, with two additional observations. These involve aesthetic values of the rugs, and where to buy them. Used with permission.

A PERSON BUYING A NAVAJO RUG SHOULD LOOK FOR THE FOLLOWING:

1) *Symmetry*: Place the rug on a floor without any background design. This way you can tell whether the edges and design are straight or crooked. If there is not an unobstructed area to throw the rug on, then fold the rug in half (warp end to warp end) and see if the width at each end is close to the same. If there is a two inch or more difference on a 6 ft. long rug, then it will look crooked on the floor. Two inches would not matter on a 12 ft. rug, but even an inch would matter on a 4 ft. rug.

2) *Stains*: Although nearly all Navajo rugs have identical designs on both sides, the buyer must be sure to examine both sides. Occasionally there will be a rust, grease, ink, coffee, urine, etc. stain on one side but won't show through. An unethical dealer or weaver would throw the rug down with the un-stained side showing.

3) *Cotton vs. wool warp*: Since the warp in a Navajo rug is completely hidden, the buyer must pull the weft apart to tell whether the warp is cotton or wool. Wool warp is preferred and generally only an expert can tell the difference. However, wool is never quite as white as cotton, and cotton warp really looks (like) and is cotton string.

4) *Weft packing*: For a long lasting rug, be sure that the weft is packed tightly together.

5) *Weft thickness*: The finer the weft threads are spun, the sharper the design will be. Also, the finer the weft, the more expensive the rug.

6) *Design*: The "one of a kind" designs in Navajo rugs offer endless patterns and colors. Peoples tastes differ also, so choose a rug of your own liking.

Do not look for absolute perfection when buying a Navajo rug. Using a primitive loom combined with natural human error cannot result in a perfect product. This is what makes Navajo weaving a true work of art. Buy it for what it is and treat it and enjoy it as you would a painting on your wall.

Buy at a reliable store, preferably an Indian Arts and Crafts Association member. Mexican imitations are saturating the market and although they don't compare with a true Navajo rug, they can fool the uninformed buyer.

(A.R.P)

Bell photo of three Sioux Indians dressed for the Sun Dance, probably in Black Hills. Two of the men are wearing large "sun disc" pendants.
Photo courtesy South Dakota State Historical Society

CHAPTER XVIII

SILVER AND TURQUOISE JEWELRY

Probably no other category of contemporary Amerind art forms has so captured the attention of the general purchasing public as has jewelry. Silver and turquoise necklaces, bracelets, and rings went for surprising sums in the 1970s and 1980s. Few buyers cared, or cared to check, whether the items were either well-made or authentic American Indian-made.

Behind the in-fashion publicity and money came the sharpsters. They proved, if nothing more, that Taiwan has some excellent crafts-people and that modern plastics can be made to resemble the shapes and colors of natural turquoise. More than one disenchanted buyer proudly called in an insurance agent to cover a $1,500 squash-blossom, and found that the acquisition was indeed a good item—at 1/20 the price.

A few years have passed and three major changes have occurred. Many of the offending merchandisers have gone out of business, and consumer-protection agencies have gained some clout. Collectors and buyers have become more street-wise (educated) in the ways and means of purchasing good items.

And the Amerind artisans have themselves come to understand that craft quality in design and manufacture provide both a livelihood and a continuation of buyer/collector demand. It is the general opinion of dealers in contemporary jewelry that very good pieces are still available at reasonable prices; in other words, the investment aspect has not been lost.

Following is information pertaining to a special class of older Indian jewelry known as "Old Pawn." The background story of Old Pawn is fascinating; this, and the description of Old Pawn pieces, along with prices, is courtesy Don C. Tanner's Indian Gallery, 7007-5th Avenue, Scottsdale, Arizona. Reprinted by permission.

OLD PAWN—THE REAL INDIAN JEWELRY

"Old Pawn," when correctly used in conjunction with Indian jewelry, means a piece made by an Indian craftsman, acquired, worn, treasured, and finally pawned by an Indian and sold by the trader when it becomes "dead." The term "old pawn" has a romantic appeal. It represents native ideals, craftsmanship, tradition, and intrinsic worth.

The pawn system today is still used as it was back in the late 1800s. However, the number of traders has diminished markedly due to increased legislative controls and the use of the monetary system. The pawn system began with the Reservation traders and became an integral part of the Reservation economics. Since most business was transacted by barter and exchange, money per se meant very little. Silver coins could be hammered, melted, and cast into jewelry that could be worn, exchanged, or used as collateral for a loan. Guns, saddles, blankets, buckskins, baskets, and robes could be pawned also, but jewelry was most common.

The Southwest Indians used the pawn system regularly, primarily as collateral for a loan to help them get by between sheep shearing seasons, lamb crops, pay checks, etc. In addition they would pawn their jewelry in order to keep it safe when they didn't need it. It also served as the Indian's visible bank account, displaying personal worth. During the summer months there were the ceremonials; to appear at their best, they made every effort to redeem their pawn, even though custom allows the Indian to take out their ornaments without redeeming them, after which they were conscientiously returned.

The Indian's personal jewelry is generally of the best quality. However, some will try to pawn their least valuable jewelry first. The pawn dealers usually have their own set of standards for what they will or will not accept. The pawn dealers then gain a reputation among the Indians by which they know what they can or cannot pawn.

There are some characteristics of "old pawn" Indian jewelry that you can recognize and should be familiar with.

The early jewelry was made out of hammered coins or by casting. In the 1940s, most silversmiths were using sheet silver, which didn't have to be melted or hammered. The older pieces tend to be heavier and larger compared to the newer jewelry. Old jewelry that has been worn should have a patina or light to dark-gray coloration caused by the skin acids, etc. This can be done chemically, so again, you must exercise caution in your selection.

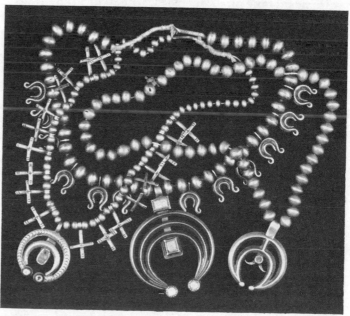

Three Navajo silver Naja necklaces, all ca. 1900. These came out of "Dead Pawn" before World War II. Each, $1,800-4,500

John C. Hill Antique Indian Art, Scottsdale, Arizona

Some bracelets were originally made as plain silver bands, and the stones were set afterwards. Wire bracelets were made by hammering the wire to the desired size. This can be seen by the different thickness and twists of the wire.

Old jewelry was made by designing the bezel to fit the stone. Newer jewelry is the opposite. Some stones were used first as earrings and pendants, then reset in bracelets or rings. Consequently, small holes can sometimes be seen in the reused stones.

The real "old pawn" is becoming a scarce item. However, it is still available in limited quantity through reliable dealers. We see "old pawn" jewelry as an intimate relic of a people and a culture which is slowly and inevitably disappearing into history. This fact alone makes legitimate "old pawn" jewelry valuable in today's market place.

The information that follows—Indian Silversmithing; Navajo, Zuni, and Hopi Silverwork; Santo Domingo Beadwork—has been reprinted with the kind cooperation and permission of Mr. Armand Ortega, owner of the Indian Ruins Trading Post at Sanders, Arizona.

Armand Ortega is a well-known and respected Indian trader, the product of four generations of life among the Indians of the Southwest. His expertise in the field of Native American arts and crafts stems from this life-long experience, during which he learned the intricacies of turquoise, became fluent in the Spanish and Navajo languages, and developed a deep understanding and respect for Indian culture.

INDIAN SILVERSMITHING

Silversmithing is a relatively recent Indian craft which began its development in the late 1850s. The Navajo, the first to engage in silversmithing, used the silver ornaments of the Spanish explorers as a basis for many of their designs. Conchas, originally from the bridles of Spanish horses, influenced the familiar concha belt. The squash blossom is an elongated version of the Spaniards' pomegranate ornament.

The Zunis began their silversmithing in the 1870s with most of the other pueblos learning the art by 1890. Each tribe, influenced differently, developed its own special style. The Zunis worked initially as stone cutters and became well known for their expertise and skill.

Much of the jewelry was originally made by the Indians for their own adornment, and the amount worn signified personal wealth. As the White traders close to the Indians began to see and appreciated the jewelry, they encouraged the craft and supplied turquoise, silver, and finer tools in order to refine the designs and increase quality. The Indians have never mined silver and only mined small quantities of turquoise. White traders today continue to supply them with the materials for their craft.

The first Indian jewelry marketing venture was initiated by the Fred Harvey Company in 1899, selling Indian jewelry on Santa Fe trails and at railroad station shops. Harvey provided silver and turquoise to the area trading posts and paid local silversmiths for finished work. This introduction of Indian jewelry to tourists from across the nation was a contributing factor in the popularity of handmade jewelry, which has grown over the years.

With more silversmiths than ever improving designs and workmanship, it is easy to see how the once crude craft has developed into the art it is today.

NAVAJO SILVERWORK

The work of the Navajos is generally massive and simple in design. The Navajos are expert silversmiths and enhance their silver work with turquoise stones. Along with their silversmithing, the art of sand-casting silver was begun long ago by the Navajo tribe. Recently they have started overlay silver work with the inlay of chips of turquoise and coral in contemporary designs.

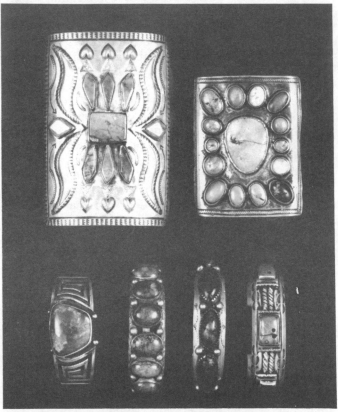

Silver and turquoise jewelry.

Top: Navajo and Hopi Ketohs or bow-guards.
Bottom: early Hopi (left) and early Navajo bracelets, these ca. 1910-1940s.   *Each, $375-950*

John C. Hill Antique Indian Art, Scottsdale, Arizona

Necklace, Navajo, hand-made silver beads with 1946 silver half-dollar pendant. Pendant was worked to present convex surface on head side of coin. Interesting and well-made.   *$125*

Sherman Holbert collection, Fort Mille Lacs, Onamia, Minnesota

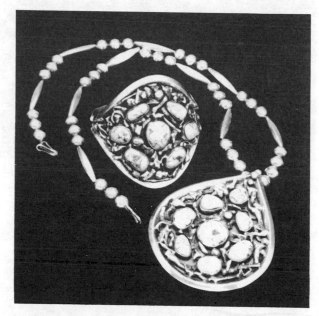

Ear pendants, heavy silver wire bands, silver hollow balls, with blue-green turquoise nugget suspensions. Silver rings are 2-1/4 in. in diameter, set is 3-3/4 in. long. Southwest, ca. early 1900s. $150

Private collection, Ohio

Jewelry, Navajo, silver and turquoise set. Necklace, 3-1/4 in. in diameter, bracelet 2-1/4 in. in diameter. Attractive and matching, seven stones in the bracelet and eight stones with forty-eight hand-made silver beads in the necklace. Ca. 1970. Set, $575

Sherman Holbert collection, Fort Mille Lacs, Onamia, Minnesota

Zuni mosaic inlay ring, man's size. Made from silver contained in one U.S. silver dollar. $175-250

Private collection

Navajo woman's bracelet, silver and turquoise. Stone is untreated, natural turquoise. $500-750

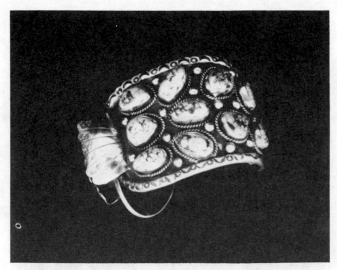

Bracelet, Navajo, silver and turquoise, 3 in. in diameter. Bracelet beautifully made with thirteen attractively mounted turquoise stones; the silver has an intricate pattern. Made by Rose Fransiscus and stamped with her mark. Ca. 1970. $495

Sherman Holbert collection, Fort Mille Lacs, Onamia, Minnesota

Necklace, Navajo, squash blossom, 20 in. long. A very attractive small necklace with eleven well-matched turquoise settings. Hand-made beads, has nice patina. Ca. 1940s. $425

Sherman Holbert collection, Fort Mille Lacs, Onamia, Minnesota

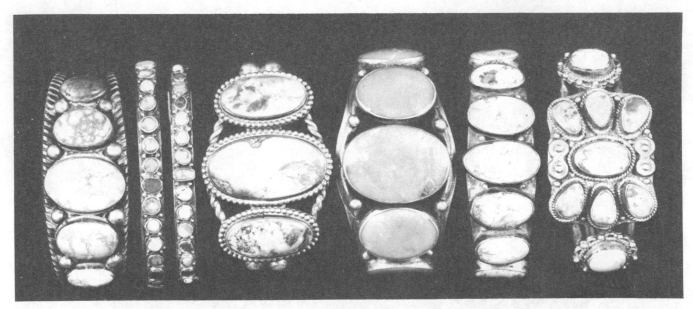

Navajo turquoise and silver bracelets. Workstyle and materials are fine, ca. 1920s-1940s.   Each, $200-800

John C. Hill Antique Indian Art, Scottsdale, Arizona

Concha belt, Navajo First Phase, silver on leather, very well made. It is ca. late 1800s. $10,000

Crown & Eagle Antiques, Inc., New Hope, Pennsylvania

Navajo woman's necklace, silver in floral design with turquoise. $800-1400

Private collection

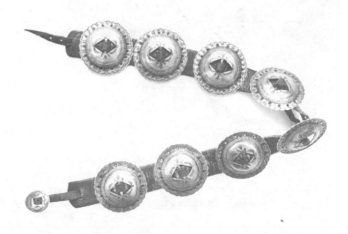

Concha belt, Navajo Second Phase, Transitional, excellent silverwork on leather. It is ca. 1900. $9,500

Crown & Eagle Antiques, Inc., New Hope, Pennsylvania

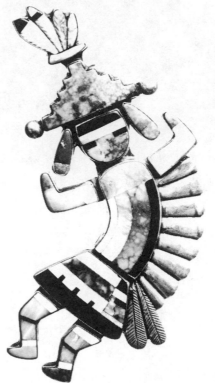

HOPI SILVERWORK

The overlay technique of the Hopi was developed in the 1930s. The Hopi had previously copied many of the Navajo and Zuni styles. With encouragement from the Museum of Northern Arizona, they developed their own overlay technique. Using many of their distinctive pottery designs, Hopi overlay is executed by cutting out a design in silver and attaching it to another layer of oxidized silver, allowing the design to stand out.

Outstanding Zuni inlayed pin, 4-3/8 in. long. Made by master craftsman Lambert Homer Jr. Originally in the Wallace collection, made in 1951. In form of silver Rainbow god, inlayed with Blue Gem turquoise, pink and white shell, red coral, and black jet. On pin back is etched "C.G. Wallace, Zuni," and in print, "Zuni, N.M.," and in black marker, "IOG 100." The inlay fitting is outstanding and condition is excellent.
G-$2,500-3,500

Courtesy Hugo Poisson, photographer; Edmunds of Yarmouth, Inc.; West Yarmouth, Massachusetts

Butterfly pin, Zuni, inlaid with jet, turquoise, mother-of-pearl, and spiney oyster shell. Pin is 4 in. across and ca. 1940s. $900

Crown & Eagle Antiques, Inc., New Hope, Pennsylvania

ZUNI SILVERWORK

The emphasis on the stones rather than the silver characterizes Zuni craftsmanship. The Zunis are expert in cutting and setting stones in clusters, delicate needlepoint and inlays of turquoise, coral, jet, and shell. Setting and cutting stones was well-known to the Zunis long before they began working with silver.

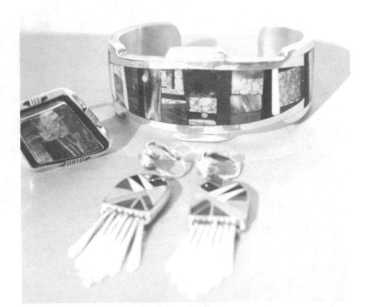

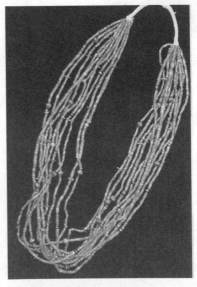

Navajo necklace, ten strands of reddish-orange coral beads interspersed with turquoise and silver beads. Ca. 1890. $4,500

Canfield Gallery, Santa Fe

Contemporary Zuni jewelry, silver set with various precious and semiprecious materials. Includes inlay bracelet and ring, plus earrings.   *Set, $1,100-1,700*

Private collection

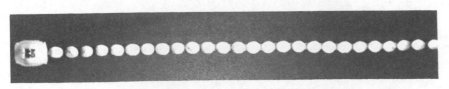

Belt, choice Santo Domingo twenty-six-concha dime sampler belt of silver coins on black leather. Each 3/4 x 1 in. concha is of individual design. Mid-20th century, signed CRZ. Ex-coll. Coriz.$600

Pat & Dave Summers, Native American Artifacts, Victor, New York

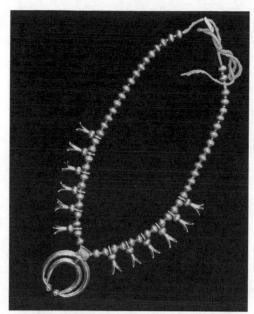

Silver and turquoise "squash-blossom" necklace, Navajo. Old handmade silver jewelry done in artistic style, ca. 1890s. $7,500

Canfield Gallery, Santa Fe

SANTO DOMINGO BEADWORK

Santo Domingo bead work is an ancient art which originally made use of handmade tools and original techniques. Turquoise and coral, as well as assorted shells, are used in their bead making. The material is drilled and the stones are then strung on cord and rolled or ground to the shape and size of bead strands desired.

OLD AND RECENT SILVER AND TURQUOISE JEWELRY

Turquoise necklace, Southwestern Indian, 19-1/2 in. long, consisting of raw stones and finished beads which alternate along the length. Blue turquoise, and very old piece, probably from early historic times. C-$1,000

Turquoise pendant, single, oblong, 1-1/2 in. long, drilled at smaller and thinner end. From a prehistoric Southwestern site, and accompanied by other bone artifacts. C-$150

Navajo chunk necklace, 1900 or before. Jaclas attached, with handmade heishi. All turquoise is natural green. One sing attached. Rare piece; necklace has both age and quality. G-$2,250

Heavy Navajo man's old silver squash blossom necklace, made with U.S. and Canadian dimes. No sets; fastened, necklace is 15 in. long and Naja is 4 in. wide. Has abalone piece tied to top. Sandcast Naja. Pawn piece from Teec Nos Pos Trading Post, Navajo reservation and ca. 1915. C-$1,400

S.W. Kernaghan photo.; Marguerite Kernaghan collection

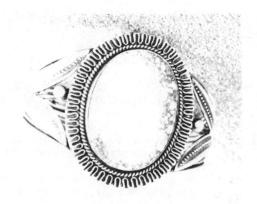

Old Navajo silver and turquoise bracelet. Circumference 6-1/4 in. Stone measures 1-3/4 in. long and 1-1/4 in wide. Fancy silver setting surrounds turquoise, stone along edges gives appearance of being spotted, with dark blue and a lighter blue. At bottom of bracelet back are etched two words, "Joann" and "Becent." Outstanding workstyle and in excellent condition, the piece is ca. 1920s. G-$1,500

Courtesy Hugo Poisson, photographer; Edmunds of Yarmouth, Inc., West Yarmouth, Massachusetts

Pawn belt, Navajo man's with six conchas, each 3 x 3-1/2 in. Buckle and conchas set with turquoise; belt also has seven butterflies and is ca. 1930s. G-$1,900

Silver necklace, Navajo, about 25 in. long, with beads hammered from old silver dimes. Central pendant of silver mounted turquoise. Ca. 1950s. D-$950

Bracelet, Navajo, 2-1/4 in. at widest point. It contains 49 pieces of good turquoise set in silver; beautiful blue stone, excellent condition, old. G-$750

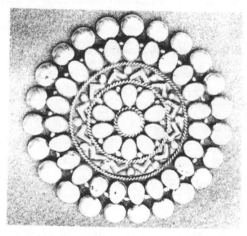

Zuni cluster pin, measuring approximately 3 x 3 in. Stones from the Lone Mountain mine; pin is signed on back in print, "Zuni" and in script, "Lee Mary." There are twenty-three tear-shaped stones on outer rim of the cluster, ten on inner cluster, with one stone set in the center. Workstyle outstanding and pin in excellent condition. Pin made in the late 1950s. G-$1,550

Lee Mary's work has been pictured in the Collector's Edition of Arizona Highways and in several other Indian jewelry books.

Courtesy Hugo Poisson, Photographer; Edmunds of Yarmouth, Inc., West Yarmouth, Massachusetts

Sheet-silver bracelet, 1-1/2 in. wide and set with turquoise nuggets. This is an old piece.   G-$450

Tlingit silver bracelet, by Leo Jacobs of Haines. A-$195

Cockroach, solid silver, 3 in. long and 2 in. wide. Item has eyes of inlayed turquoise, and is quite old and unusual.   G-$225

Silver wrist bowguard, recent Zuni, stamped silver on leather. Large carved central plate, well done.   D-$450

Navajo concha belt; pawn silver, piece has five conchas, five butterflies, and buckle. All inlayed with turquoise and with original leather backing; early period.   G-$1,500

Squash blossom necklace, Navajo, all silver with naja, and blossoms on each side. Necklace has a double row of beads, and is ca. 1950.   G-$650

Assorted Indian silverwork and turquoise:

Concha belt   C-$1,100

Concha belt, (Ca. 1940)   C-$675

Cluster bracelet   C-$1,000

Navajo concha belt, with six hand-stamped silver conchas on leather, with turquoise. Seven hand-stamped butterflies with single stones. Belt has multi-stoned buckle, and piece is ca. 1930.   G-$2,300

Bolo de fastener, Navajo, with pawn ticket attached. Fastener has two turquoise stones and is dated 1970. G-$225

Sunburst cluster bracelet, Zuni, very nice piece and ca. 1940.   G-$995

Navajo concha belt, with eight hand-stamped conchas and buckle.   G-$1,850

CONTEMPORARY JEWELRY

Silver necklace, contemporary Navajo, double beaded. Turquoise inlay of flying birds, crescent naja or pendant, also with chip inlay.   D-$1,075

Navajo pawn belt, woman's size, conchas 1-1/2 in. in diameter. Buckle and conchas inlayed with turquoise; recent work.   G-$850

Concha belt, 32 in. in length, made of nine finely worked, thin silver conchas and a rectangular belt buckle. No stones.   G-$600

Silver concha belt, made by Monroe Ashley, with thirteen conchas each 1-1/2 x 2 in., plus buckle.   C-$700

Silver concha belt, disc-type conchas about 3 in. in diameter, with rectangular silver spacers. All with blue turquoise centers; contemporary Navajo.   D-$1,800

Concha belt, made of nine sandcast silver conchas. Circular pieces, no stones, with belt buckle sandcast and in rectangular shape. Recent or contemporary item. G-$625

Silver bracelet, narrow, turquoise chip inlay, contemporary Navajo.   D-$95

Cast-silver bracelet, 6-1/2 in. in circumference, with a magnificent Blue Gem mine turquoise stone. Stone is 2 in. long Bracelet made in the early 1950s; craft person did outstanding job. Three silver bands support stone and bands have been etched.

Back of the turquoise has silver plate, 3/4 x 1-1/4 in., with intricate design. Bracelet in excellent condition.   G-$2,000-2,600

Courtesy Hugo Poisson, Photographer; Edmunds of Yarmouth, Inc., West Yarmouth, Massachusetts

Silver bracelet, 3/4 in. wide, handmade and contemporary Hopi Indian.   D-$225

Silver bracelet, contemporary Navajo, with turquoise chip inlays.   D-$185

Silver bracelet, rope-twist style, contemporary Navajo.   D-$70

Silver bracelet, wide, man's size, contemporary Navajo. Piece has turquoise chip inlay, traditional designs. D-$275

Finger ring, handmade silver with two blue turquoise stones.   D-$95

Finger ring, 5/8 in. interior diameter, contemporary Navajo and handmade. Set with turquoise chips.   D-$125

Silver earrings, contemporary Navajo, handmade.   D-$60

Silver earrings, contemporary Hopi, simple design in silver overlay.   D-$100

Silver pendant, 1-7/8 in. long, contemporary Hopi handmade, with natural turquoise stone.   D-$170

Silver letter-opener, probably Navajo, and 8-1/2 in. long. Handle is set with one large turquoise stone and one small stone. Very well-done work. Contemporary. D-$100

Keychain piece or small pendant, 2 in. high, of sheet silver and small round greenish turquoise stone. A tourist item, and ca. 1955.   C-$25

Private collection

Silver and turquoise necklace, with one large and three smaller stones. All silver, contemporary styling. D-$1,500

Photo courtesy Howard Shaw, Casa Kakiki, Sunland Park, New Mexico

Silver belt buckle, 2-1/4 x 3-1/8 in., probably Hopi, entirely handmade. D-$295

Silver bolo tie fastener, die-stamped silver, set with turquoise and red coral. Contemporary Navajo. D-$295

Silver Pendant, large size, contemporary Navajo. Traditional inlay designs; chip inlays of turquoise and red coral. D-$425

Silver belt buckle, contemporary Navajo, with design in turquoise chip inlays. D-$300

Navajo cross, solid silver, 3-1/4 in. wide and 5-1/4 in. high. Nice inlayed turquoise center; this is a well-done sandcast piece. G-$200

Silver pin, 3 in. long and sandcast; contemporary Navajo. D-$100

Silver cross-form pendant, 2 in. high, recent Navajo in origin. Piece set with several small turquoise stones. D-$150

Bolo tie fastener, sandcast silver, 2-3/4 in. high, and with elongated natural turquoise stone. Solid silver front, with tool-marked designs. D-$400

Silver brooch, 1-3/4 in. in diameter, set with natural turquoise stones; contemporary Hopi. D-$280

Silver hat band, contemporary Navajo, with a dozen and a half miniature concha plates on leather strip. D-$200

Bolo tie fastener, contemporary Hopi, large, all silver. D-$300

Sandcast silver belt buckle, 3 in. long, contemporary Navajo; double-naja motif, and graceful lines. D-$285

Here are three examples of Indian-owned and operated arts and crafts businesses. All carry a selection of silver and turquoise jewelry.

Hopi Arts & Crafts Guild
P.O. Box 37
Second Mesa, Arizona 86043

Navajo Arts & Crafts Enterprise
P.O. Drawer A
Window Rock, Arizona 86515

Pueblo of Zuni Arts & Crafts
P.O. Box 425
Zuni, New Mexico 87327

The following information on turquoise is courtesy of Mr. Armand Ortega, owner of the Indian Ruins Trading Post, Sanders, Arizona, and reprinted by permission.

TURQUOISE-THE SKY STONE

To the Indians, turquoise has the life-giving power of sky and water and is held in high esteem. This beautiful blue gem that the earth has given is their sign of wealth, as well as a symbol of protection from the forces of evil.

The "sky-stone" has been part of Indian cultures for centuries. The oldest well-documented use of turquoise was the discovery of two turquoise ornaments at southeastern Arizona's Snaketown ruin, estimated to have been made before 300 A.D. Turquoise deposits found in the West have shown evidence of prehistoric mining. It is said that turquoise mining predates any other kind of mining in the United States.

Technically, turquoise is a mineral belonging to the copper group and is found in arid regions of the Southwestern United States and parts of Asia. It is formed by the action of water which deposits it in veins in existing rock. This mother rock creates the markings or matrix which appear in the turquoise as thin black lines, brown or black blotches, iron pyrite or bits of quartz and gives each stone its own natural beauty.

The color of turquoise varies from light blue to deep blue and green. As well as color variations, turquoise has many grades. Of each mine producing turquoise, only a small percentage is of high-grade gem quality. High-grade stones are those with greatest density, hardest consistency, and deepest color, as well as those with the finest matrix pattern or "spiderwebbing" as it is commonly called. Turquoise is sold by carat weight, with high-grade stones costing considerably more per carat because of their quality and scarcity.

As turquoise grades go downward, the hardness decreases accordingly and the color seems to get higher. These medium-to-lower-grades of turquoise are more abundant than the high-grade stone and most often stabilized to increase durability and deepen the color of the stones. Naturally, stabilized turquoise is less expensive than the higher grades but commands a greater price than unstabilized stones of the same grade.

Much confusion exists as to the merits of stabilized turquoise. Many people are under the impression that stabilization alters the true stone, covers faults and makes it less valuable. On the contrary, proper stabilization of turquoise enhances the color and durability of the stone so that it will resist cracking and retain its sky-blue color through the years.

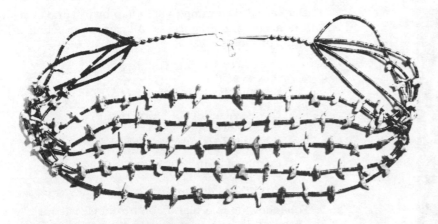

A SHORT STORY OF TURQUOISE

By Edmunds of Yarmouth, Inc.

"Turquoise" comes from the French word meaning Turkish, indicating the origin (Middle East) of the stones. Turquoise is said to bring success in love and money. It is also the birthstone for December. Turquoise has not only found popularity in this country, but goes back to the early civilizations of foreign lands. Queen Zer of the first Egyptian Dynasty owned turquoise jewelry.

Turquoise is found in many locations all over the world. Most of the Southwestern states (Nevada, Arizona, New Mexico, Colorado) produce turquoise ranging in quality from low grade to gem. The mines around Nishapur, in Iran, yield the high quality stones known to us as Persian turquoise. Low to medium grade turquoise is also found in Africa, Australia, China, and Tibet. The Indians of the Southwest were mining turquoise centuries before the White man came to the area. Now the White man mines the stones and the Indians buy from the traders.

Turquoise is cut usually in dome shape. The stones are usually cut so that the finished gem includes some of the matrix in which the turquoise is found. The matrix can be brown, black, yellow, red, or even white in color. Many people judge a stone by how much matrix is in the stone. Some people find the matrix more attractive. One form of matrix which is very popular today is that known as "spiderweb." In this type of turquoise, the matrix is formed in very fine lines which show patterns similar to lifelike spider webs.

Turquoise, especially the lighter blue stone, is a porous stone. Therefore, we recommend removing a turquoise ring before washing dishes, bathing, or washing hands, as the soaps and oils may change the color of the stone. Many Indian rings, especially Zuni inlay pieces, can have their stones loosened by prolonged exposure to water. Zuni rings are almost impossible to size, because the heat used for sizing the ring would harm the stone.

In the past few years turquoise has become very popular. We see the stars wearing it on television, and people from all walks of life wearing it on the street. The jewelry comes in many forms. It can be bought for babies: as silver spoons, diaper pins, bib-pins. It can be bought for grandmothers: as bowls and flatware, as well as the more common earrings, rings, bracelets, and necklaces. The men haven't been forgotten either, as bolas and belt buckles, tie tacs, rings, bracelets, watchbands, money clips, and cigarette cases are being made.

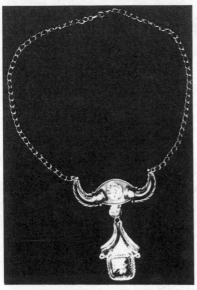

People are suddenly becoming suspicious of stabilized turquoise, when for many years turquoise and most other precious and semi-precious stones have been treated in similar and equally advantageous ways.

Turquoise is a relatively soft mineral and stabilizing does just what it implies—strengthens the stone. This added durability makes the turquoise easier for silversmiths to work with and assures the consumer that daily encounters with water, oils, and moisture will no longer turn the stone a dull green.

Stabilization is scientifically done while turquoise is in rough form using material of a resinous nature which seals the pores of the turquoise while in a vacuum. No foreign or unnatural color is added, since the stabilizing process itself deepens the natural color of the stone.

There is a very old turquoise mine at Cerrillos, southwest of Santa Fe in New Mexico. The material was traded in prehistoric times even into present-day Mexico. Mining there began sometime in the early A.D. centuries.

Other well-known turquoise mines are: Castle Dome, Kingman, Number Eight, Carrico Lake, Fox, Villa Grove, Valley Blue, Battle Mountain, Globe, Lander Blue, Lone Mountain, Morenci, Bisbee, Blue Gem, Poe, and Stormy Ridge.

The following provides additional accurate information about turquoise, including several little-known aspects of this attractive gemstone. This material has been provided by Edmunds of Yarmouth, Inc., of West Yarmouth, Massachusetts and is reprinted by permission.

Zuni inlay necklace and earrings, with total neck-lace length about 21 in. Jewelry set with turquoise, jet, coral and mother-of-pearl. On the back of larger half-moon is scratched the name of the maker, "Margaret Chico." Limited edition of hand silk-screened tiles were made from this outstanding piece in 1975. Workstyle is exceptional and condition is excellent. G-$5,000

Courtesy Hugo Poisson, Photographer; Edmunds of Yarmouth, Inc., West Yarmouth, Massachusetts

Turquoise nugget necklace, 14-1/2 in. long, fastened. Graduated-size natural stone, deep blue. Machine-drilled, hand-shaped and polished.   D-$1,850

Navajo turquoise necklace, two strands of nuggets and strung on gray heishe.   G-$1,100

Navajo turquoise necklace, single strand natural stone strung with white heishe.   G-$950

Like anything else where there is money to be made, people will try to sell anything. There are White men making jewelry that looks like Indian jewelry, and many have even signed the pieces. This is unfortunate, so be sure the person you are dealing with can guarantee that what you have purchased is American Indian made. Beware of plastic sold as turquoise, or inferior turquoise mixed with plastic, or dyed turquoise sold as genuine turquoise. Be sure the person you are dealing with will stand behind the merchandise. Matrix can be faked, as well as the stone itself, by using iodine and also shoe polish.

To prove that so much of the Indian jewelry that is on the market today is not Indian made, that is a fact: The Indians only realize one to two percent of their income from making jewelry; the rest of it comes from sheep herding and harvesting their crops.

TURQUOISE JEWELRY

Heishe turquoise choker necklace, contemporary Santo Domingo Pueblo, and 13 in. long, looped. Made of graduated-size natural turquoise beads.   D-$300

Navajo nugget necklace, with treated turquoise; nuggets strung with white heishe.   G-$950

Turquoise nugget necklace, strung with shell heishe, with coral bead spacers and bear claw capped with silver and turquoise and set as pendant. Contemporary Southwestern.   G-$175

Navajo nugget necklace, turquoise strung with gray heishe; nuggets machine-drilled.   G-$1,200

ABOUT CONTEMPORARY JEWELRY

G.S. Khalsa, of Albuquerque, New Mexico, is an experienced and perceptive dealer in fine contemporary Indian jewelry. Mr. Khalsa consented to offer some tips on buying contemporary silver and turquoise jewelry. Used with permission.

In recent years, American Indian jewelry has become the focal point of American Indian art and crafts. Since its emergence in the eighteen hundreds, Indian jewelry has been sought after and collected.

The great demand for Indian jewelry was at its peak in the early 1970s. The market subsequently became flooded with cheap imports, mass-produced styles and junk turquoise, including plastic imitations.

Because of the growing skepticism as to authenticity, the fever for American Indian pieces subsided as the decade wore on. At present, the market is stabilizing and once again growing in popularity worldwide.

The average buyer or collector who wants to buy quality American Indian jewelry (whether it costs $5 or $5,000) has the responsibility to discriminate between authentic, handmade American Indian jewelry and contemporary Southwestern-style jewelry.

Southwestern-style is usually machine-made, cast jewelry made by non-Indians. For those who are unsure about how to pick authentic, handmade American Indian jewelry, here are some simple guidelines and information.

The three major silversmithing tribes are Navajos, Zunis, and Hopis. Navajo jewelry is easily distinguishable because it features a more elaborate silver work, incorporating a leaf or feather motif. Sometimes Navaho work does not include stones, such as sandcast jewelry.

Navajo woman's necklace, silver and turquoise, naja with in-set small stones. Fine work of art. $1,400-2,000

Private collection

Sandcast jewelry is made by pouring hot molten silver into a mold carved out of volcanic rock.

The Zunis, on the other hand, are expert lapidaries. Stone-on-stone inlay, needlepoint, and cluster work usually predominate their silver work. It should be noted that some Zunis are doing a Navajo style, as, too, Navajos are doing more and more inlay and cluster work. Nevertheless, the work is authentic.

Hopi silver overlay is an altogether different style. The Hopi craftsman uses two layers of silver. The bottom layer is oxidized black. On the top layer, a design is drawn and cut out, then overlaid on the bottom. The final texture to the oxidized layer is achieved by etching lines into the black.

The finished jewelry has a satin-brushed look quite different from Navajo or Zuni style. Stones are rarely incorporated into the design. Although Hopi jewelry is frequently imitated by the Navajos, the imitation may be inferior in quality and lower in price.

The most important aspect to consider in buying American Indian jewelry is choice of retail dealer. Your dealer must be reputable, honest, and willing to guarantee in writing the authenticity of each jewelry piece. Large in-store inventories or memberships in jewelry associations do not necessarily guarantee the dealer's integrity.

A bona-fide dealer has the responsibility to know and share with the customer all pertinent information about his merchandise: Who is the silversmith? Where is the stone from? What quality of stone is it? It is no longer valid to simply name the tribe. Be aware that phrases such as 'Zunistyle' or 'Indian-style' do not guarantee that the piece is authentic or handmade. Well buffed and nicely displayed jewelry is a good indication of how much the dealer respects what is being sold.

When making a purchase, be sure the jewelry is 'clean.' The silver work should be neat, bezels around the stones ought to be seamless, and the soldering carefully done. There should be no sharp edges on the silver work. Insist on natural turquoise stones that are cut and polished, but not treated.

The term 'natural' means genuine. Genuine stones may be real turquoise, but it may be that the stone is of very poor quality and treated to look better. It is considered acceptable that Zuni inlay jewelry and Santo Domingo heishe use stabilized turquoise, which provides the hardness needed for the delicate lapidary work involved. In Navajo silversmithing, insist on natural stones.

Some simple rules of thumb to determine the relative quality of natural turquoise are hardness, intensity of natural color (either blue or green), hardness of the matrix (does it chip out with your fingernail?), and the ratio of turquoise to matrix.

In Zuni channel work, a clean piece will not have filler to gap the distance between poorly cut stones and the silver. The surface of the entire inlay should be very smooth with a brilliant sheen to it. When looking at needlepoint or cluster work, the uniformity of shape and color of the stones determines quality.

To appreciate American Indian jewelry is to become a part of the rich heritage and culture of the American Indians. The 'complex simplicity' of their lifestyle is expressed in their artifacts, sophisticated in design, and workmanship, yet reflecting perfectly the individualism and undying spirit of Native Americans. So many of us long for such simplicity of spirit, and for the intimate communion with Nature from which it is spawned.

The charm and desirability of authentic American Indian jewelry is that it looks and feels like it is made from a perfect mixture of the Southwestern landscape and human spirit, overflowing with the joy of life.

(G.S.K.)

Old Navajo squash-blossom necklace, silver and turquoise. Silver is quite heavy. $1,500-2,200

Private collection

Suggested Reading

Arizona Highways, issue of August, 1974.

Arizona Highways, issue of March, 1975.

Bahti, Mark. *A Consumer's Guide to Southwestern Indian Arts and Crafts*. Albuquerque, New Mexico: Indian Pueblo Cultural Center.

Gillespie, Alva H. *How to Invest in Indian Jewelry*. Albuquerque, New Mexico: Diamond Press.

Rosnek, Carl and Stacey. *Joseph, Skystone and Silver - The Collector's Book of Southwest Indian Jewelry*. New Jersey: Prentice-Hall, Inc., 1976.

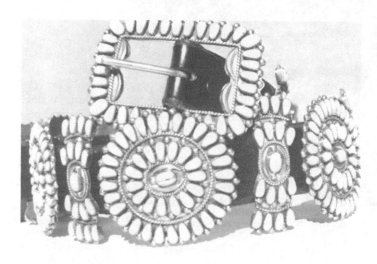

Zuni man's bell, silver and turquoise, matching blue stones. $1,500-2,500

Private collection

Navajo Concha belts. Made of heavy gauge silver and high-grade old turquoise, both on the original leather, ca. 1930s. Each, $2,500-3,500

John C. Hill Antique Indian Art, Scottsdale, Arizona

Newspaper Rock, Indian Creek State Park, Utah. One of the most famous rock art sites in the Southwest, most work was probably done by the Fremont culture, ca. AD 900-1200.

Randall Olsen photograph

Petroglyphs, uncertain prehistoric time, these depicting a series of human stick figures. Rock art in North America has been largely overlooked by the average person; these are rare examples of American Indian natural artwork. Southern Illinois.

Dennis R. Arbeiter, Godfrey, Illinois

CHAPTER XIX

OTHER AMERICAN INDIAN COLLECTIBLES

The material in this chapter is a wonderful assemblage of authentic Amerind items. They are listed in no particular order and without regard to materials, regions or age. The listings either did not fit conveniently into other chapters or the information arrived after individual chapters were closed. Many are one-of-a-kind.

Probably only the Plains-style war club has enough entries for a separate heading. It is practically impossible to locate a particular item for price-comparison, at least on first reading.

This section is probably treated best as a broad survey of Amerind creations for casual reading and general knowledge.

AMERIND COLLECTIBLES

Wool sash, Osage, hand-woven, 54 in. long including fringe. Colors are red, white, and blue, and in nice condition.   D-$115

Powder horn, old Indian, 6-1/2 in. long, with rawhide carrying thong. Wooden end-plug set with large brass tacks which added decoration. Plains Indian, probably mid-1800s.   A-$160

Sioux war club, with rawhide-wrapped handle; fine example.   A-$270

Beaded saddle blanket, high quality with bells, fringed, and in excellent condition. Sioux.   D-$2,500

Chippewa martingale, on cloth with beaded panels. It is 26 x 44 in., with patterns in floral design. Excellent condition.   G-$1,400

Apache rawhide quiver and assorted arrows.   A-$410

Cradleboard, Paiute buckskin covered, moderately beaded. Yarn decorated sun shade.   G-$695

Wool blanket with beaded strip 2 in. wide and 80 in. long. Has four large colorful rosettes.   G-$350

Saddle blanket, possibly Crow Indian. Needs repair.   A-$200

Club with beaded handle, stone head with one chip

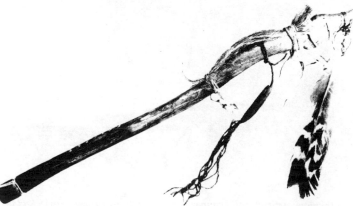

Wooden-horse stick, 24 in. in length. Plains Indian, and ca. 1880.   *G-Museum quality*

Nedra Matteucci's Fenn Galleries, Santa Fe, New Mexico

missing; handle is thin and 12 in. long, fully quilled. Has four cone dangles.   G-$425

Indian Wars weapon, 1873 Springfield carbine, tack decorated stock.   A-$455

Leather awl case, Apache, 12-1/2 in. long. Has rows of small tin bells on yellow leather, with yellow and blue beadwork.   A-$145

Santee Sioux horse bridle, with red and navy trade cloth; canvas-backed, with nice floral designs.   G-$515

Crow bridle with German silver bit; engraved and inlayed German silver with flat headstall. Beaded in typical Crow designs; leather formerly dyed red. Rare piece, excellent condition.   G-$950

Kiowa war club, rawhide wrapped; hide cracking. Ex-museum piece and quite old.   G-$200

Sioux bow with two bone-tipped arrows.   G-$315

Sioux dog travois, sticks and rawhide laced platform. Fine display or museum piece, high quality.   G-$375

Horseman's gauntlets, beaded, Plains Indian and probably Nez Perce, with very small designs in beads on back. Fair condition and ca. 1890.   D-$425

Silver salad fork and spoon, Northwest Coast, both 9-1/2 in. long. Native-incised handles.   G-$425

Sioux war club with rawhide wrapped handle, stone head; an old and good piece.   G-$400

Cradleboard cover, Sioux, beaded, with trade cloth sinew sewn. Geometric design on white back. Colors of beads are red, blue, green, and yellow.   G-$695

Peyote fan, pheasant feathers with finely beaded handle.   G-$100

Buckskin knife and awl case, 8 in. long and 2 in. wide. Small knife and awl included, both with carved handles in shape of bear's head. Tin cone dangles on tassels.G-$350

Painted hide, Northwest Coast, with effigy figure painted on it in brilliant blacks and reds. Very decorative and fine art work.   G-$2,100

Carved halibut hook, Northwest Coast, 10 in. long.   G-$275

Great Lakes region charm bags, various sizes, designs, ages and materials. All ca. 1830-1870. Each, $150-2,000

Private collection; photo by John McLaughlin

Pallette or slate ornament, 3-5/8 in. in diameter, made of thin slate. Late prehistoric, probably originated in or near Tennessee where the type usually found. Information on artifact states it was found near the Old Erie Canal, Defiance County, Ohio. Museum quality

Larry Garvin collection

Figure by Fletcher Healing, 10 in. high, colorful and well-done. $550

Courtesy John Isaac, Albuquerque, New Mexico

Modoc quiver, bear-skin, with ten sinew-wrapped feather drops. Rawhide-sewn and 26 in. long. From northern California, this ex-museum piece is ca. 1880-1900. $425

Morris' Art & Artifacts, Anaheim, California; Dawn Gober photograph

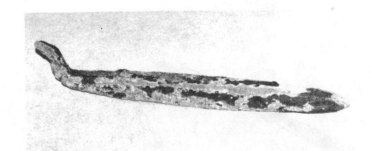

Unknown artifact, solid copper, possibly a non-utilitarian object. Has very squared edges, is 2-1/2 in. long, and in very good condition. Personal find by owner in Barron County, Wisconsin. $100-125

Dennis R. Lindblad collection, Chetek, Wisconsin

Cornhusk artworks, Nez Perce, fiber, yarn and hide.

Upper left: woman's hat, ca. 1920 $400 (general, $300-1,000)
Lower left: Sally-bag, pouch, ca. 1880 $1500 (general, $300-1,500)
Center: bag, ca. 1890 $500 (general, $200-1,000, exceptional up to $2,500)

Upper right: bag, ca. 1910 $400
Lower right: belt-pouch, ca. 1930 $500

Private collection; photo by John McLaughlin

NOTE by the collector regarding cornhusk items: "In general the following are considered when appraising cornhusk bags: Type, condition, beauty, size, fineness of weave, and age. Age is not a major consideration; even modern pieces are highly sought."

Corn-husk bag, Umatilla, 8 x 9-1/2 in., very finely woven; data on old tag reads "Collected near Umatilla Ring, Oregon/1880." Reverse has different pattern. Exceptional item, ca . 1870-1880. $1,000

Larry Lantz, First Mesa, South Bend, Indiana

Copper fishhook, scarce and unusual find by the owner in Barron County, Wisconsin. It is 2-1/2 in. long. $75

Dennis R. Lindblad collection, Chetek, Wisconsin

Rolled copper beads and a clasp, largest bead 1/2 in. diameter. Personal finds by the owner in Barron County, Wisconsin. $75 group

Dennis R. Lindblad collection, Chetek, Wisconsin

"Adoption Papers," unique Seneca Wolf Clan item. Paint on rawhide, signed by Chief Shongo, July 4, 1942. Size 31-1/2 x 38 in., ex-coll. Casterline. $500

Pat & Dave Summers, Native American Artifacts, Victor, New York

Prehistoric artifacts.

Left: Adena gorget, banded slate, LaGrange County, Indiana. $300
Center: salvaged gorget or pendant, note broken-out hole at top center, from Michigan. $200
Right: copper celt, 3-3/4 in. long, Kent County, Michigan. $325

Larry Lantz, First Mesa, South Bend, Indiana

Picture frame, basketry, Thompson River Salish, 6 x 9 in. This unusual piece is ca. 1890-1900. $125

Pocotopaug Trading Post, South Windsor, Connecticut

House wall or foundation material, clay tempered with pine straw or needles, state of Louisiana. Building material of any kind from prehistoric times is unusual.   Study value

Wilfred A. Dick collection, Magnolia, Mississippi

Ghost Dance club, 9-3/4 x 20 in. Has two buffalo horns bound with rawhide and is well-decorated with white, green, blue, and red beads and feather quill. Ca. 1880s. $750

Sherman Holbert collection, Fort Mille Lacs, Onamia, Minnesota

Fossils and small turtle shell that evidence prehistoric human reworking and polishing. Probably picked up as curios and collectibles; all from known prehistoric sites in Mississippi.   Each, $1-$50

Wilfred A. Dick collection, Magnolia, Mississippi

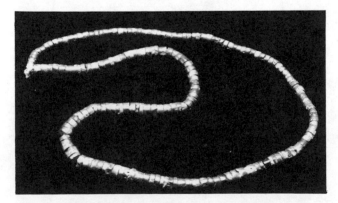

Necklace, unknown origin and time-period, 19-1/2 in. long. Made of pipestone ground into small discs and laced together. Has total of 188 disc-beads. $95

Sherman Holbert collection. Fort Mille Lacs, Onamia, Minnesota

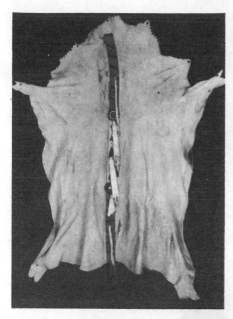

Elk hide with beaded strips, Plateau, beadwork in colors of black, pink, and blue and with ermine drops. Ca. 1890s.

Museum quality

Morning Star Gallery, Santa Fe, New Mexico

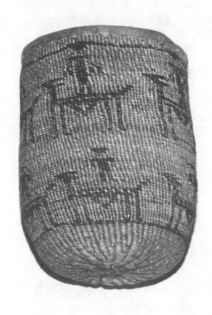

Sally bag, Wasco. These vary greatly in size. This one is typical, about 4 x 10 in. Usually they have figures on them, but some were produced with geometries. Older specimens have condors (they look like butterflies), skeletal human figures, or very intricate geometric designs. Values determined by size, condition, and design. Better examples sell for $3,000-4,000. Size range is 3 x 4 to 6 x 15 in. Example, ca. 1880. $1,500

Private collection, photo by John McLaughlin

Freshwater pearl necklace, rare, from Mississippian period. Consists of eighty small white pearls and came from near Elizabethtown, Tennessee. $1,700

Pat & Dave Summers, Native American Artifacts, Victor, New York

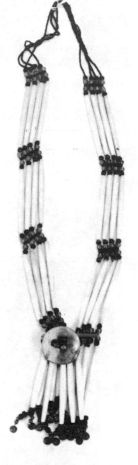

Breastplate, ladies, hairpipe, 28 in. long. Made of thirty-seven hairpipes, ninety-five large black beads, and sixty-nine large gold beads. Has harness leather dividers. Also has thirteen round brass buttons, a bell, a Canadian coin dated 1910, an abalone button, and four strands of black beads at the neck, ca. 1920s-1930s. $850

Sherman Holbert collection, Fort Mille Lacs, Onamia, Minnesota

Bowl game, Chippewa, bowl 11-1/2 in. in diameter. Consists of hand-carved wooden bowl, game pieces, and puzzle bag for same, plus counters. Bowl, ex-colls. Owen and Blessing. Ca. 1940s. $450

Sherman Holbert collection, Fort Mille Lacs, Onamia, Minnesota

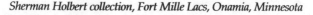

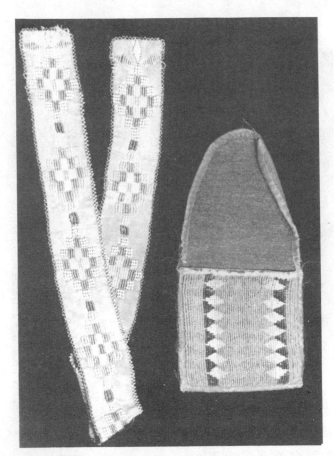

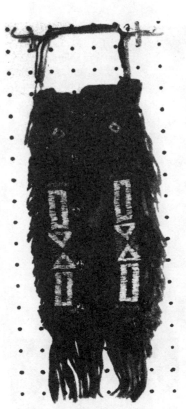

Woodlands beadwork.

Left: Kickapoo belt, 2 x 26 in., seed-beaded in geometrics, 1800s. $475
Right: Sauk charm bag, loom-beaded with cloth backing, 4 x 4 in., ca. 1865. $750

Larry Lantz, First Mesa, South Bend, Indiana

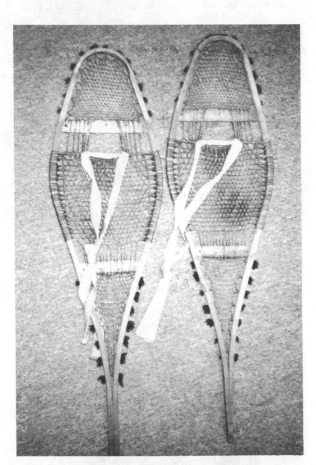

Skookum doll, 6 x 18 in. While many tribes made these as tourist items, they are collector items in their own right. The word "Skookum" in Chinook means powerful or great; older meaning was ghost or spirit. Came from the Northeast but Skookums can be found across the country. $200-275

Marguerite L. Kernaghan collection; photo by Marguerite L. and Stewart W. Kernaghan, Bellvue, Colorado

Indian-made snowshoes, Great Lakes region type, 37-1/2 in. long. $165 pair

Wendy Wolfsen collection, Michigan

Buffalo-horn "skull-cracker," 17-3/4 in. long. Brought to Springfield, Oregon in 1930s by family who came from South Dakota, purchased by them on Pine Ridge Reservation. Sioux item.   C-$500

S.W. Kernaghan photo; Marguerite Kernaghan collection

Baby carrier, Osage, tacks, paint and yarn on wooden board. It is ca. 1900. $1,000

Private collection, photo by John McLaughlin

Moosehair embroidery, Iroquois, very rare, done on black cloth. It is 13-1/2 x 14 in. and ca. 1850. $800

Pat & Dave Summers, Native American Artifacts, Victor, New York

Burden strap or tumpline, Salish, mountain sheep wool and plant fibers. Shoulder strap is 2 x 18 in. with four foot ties at each end. Late 1800s, museum tag reads "Puget Sound." $450

Larry Lantz, First Mesa, South Bend, Indiana

Black slate knives.

Left and right, Oswego, New York.   Each, $35
Center: semi-lunate knife, granite, 4 in. long, from Connecticut. $300

Pocotopaug Trading Post, South Windsor, Connecticut

Assorted adornments or ornaments, consisting of stone beads, drilled obsidian crescent, undrilled obsidian, and jasper pendants. From the Columbia River area, ca. AD 1600-1800. $125

Morris' Art & Artifacts, Anaheim, California; Dawn Gober photo

Fabric sample, extremely rare, made of shredded sagebrush. Made prior to 700 BC, came from a rock shelter in Oregon. Material like this used for sandals, sleeping mats, and the like. $200

Pat & Dave Summers, Native American Artifacts, Victor, New York

Chopper-type hand (?) celt, early, from North Carolina. $75

Private collection

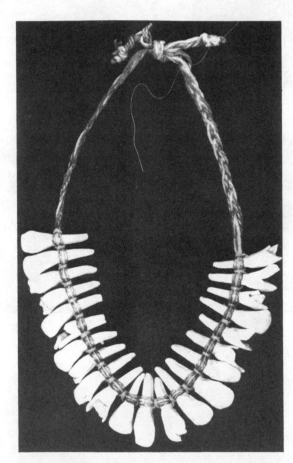

Buffalo tooth necklace, Sioux, collected from Mandan, North Dakota in the late 1800s. Each tooth individually tied with braided trade yarn. $350

Larry Lantz, First Mesa, South Bend, Indiana

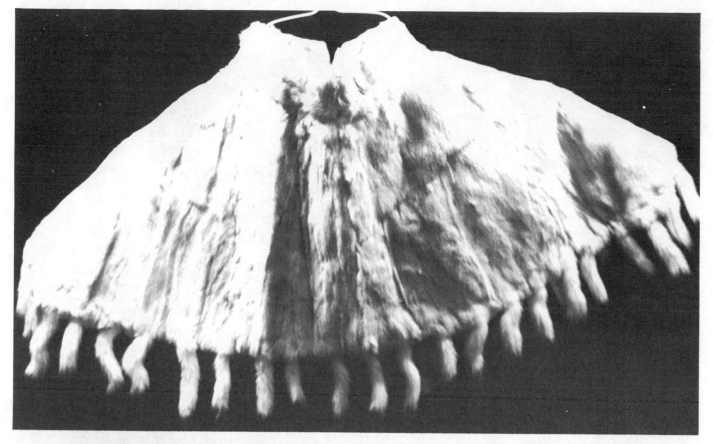

Ceremonial cape, child's size, Winnebago, made from 45 ermine skins. Note the tails; mid to late 1800s, rare item. $700-850

Larry Lantz, First Mesa, South Bend, Indiana

Oil painting by Louis Shipshee, 24 x 30 in., mint condition. $450

Private collection, New Mexico

Restored club, ancient head and new wooden handle. Head found in western Kansas. Club head. $65

New wooden haft. $45

Lee Hallman collection, Telford, Pennsylvania

Alabaster turtle figure by Doug Hyde (Nez Perce, Chippewa and Assiniboin) and 13-1/2 in. tall. Ca. 1985. $6,000

Dennis R. Phillips/Fine American Indian Art, Chicago, Illinois

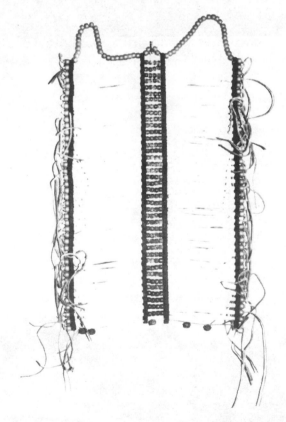

Sioux man's breastplate, of leather thongs, bone tubes, and large beads. It is 20 in. high and 12 in. wide, ca. 1900. $1,950

Photo courtesy Winona Trading Post, Santa Fe–Pierre & Sylvia Bovis

Three Yei Bi Chai masks: Navajo medicine man extremely important during ceremonies. Yei Bi Chai dance held during winter months as major curing ceremony. Yei Bi Chai dancers appear during last two nights of nine day ceremony. Yei represent supernatural beings who have great powers. Yei masks made of buckskin from deer which have been suffocated with sacred meal. Full masks worn by male dancers. Masks are approximately 18 in. long and 14 in. wide; ca. 1920.   C-Each, $1,950

Photos courtesy W.J. Crawford. The Americana Galleries, Phoenix, Arizona

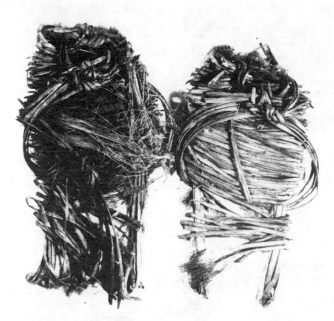

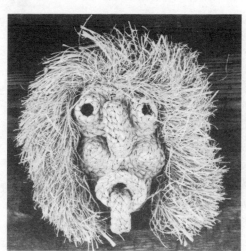

Pair of woven fiber sandals, from cave shelter in New Mexico. Twelve pairs came from site, on privately owned land. Material is yucca plant fibres, and sandals are Anasazi culture.   C-$145-195

Photo courtesy Wayne Parker, Texas

Zuni pueblo bear fetish, malachite, 1-5/8 in. long. Small turquoise slab tied to bear's back with a leather thong. $40

Charles F. and Susan Wood, Ohio

Stereoptic view cards, Comanche and Apache chiefs: Horseback, Heap Wolves, Mow way, and Black Hawk. Early 20th century.   Each, $15

Frank Bergevin, Port of Call, Alexandria Bay, New York

Zuni pueblo fetish, dolphin figure, 3 in. long, done in Picasso marble. Signed with "Scott" and a bent arrow symbol. $40

Charles F. and Susan Wood, Ohio

Algonquian birchbark container with lid, container 8 in. high. With diamond designs, this piece is ca. 1850. $900

Traditions, Victor, New York

Cherokee pottery mug, alphabet on sides, 3-3/4 in. high. Obtained in North Carolina in 1993, it is signed "Bigmeat." $30

Charles F. and Susan Wood, Ohio

Indian gun, 1861 Springfield military piece with stock rawhide-wrapped and tacked. $3,500

Antiques & Art, Piedmont, South Dakota

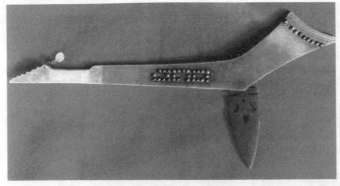

Gunstock club, Eastern Sioux, 28 in. long. Maple handle has dag blade and is decorated with brass tacks and traces of red and yellow paint. $25,000

Forrest Fenn, Santa Fe, New Mexico

Bead necklace, pottery beads, strand 56 in. long. Found near Santa Fe, New Mexico. $150

Jack Baker collection, Ozark, Missouri; David Capon photograph

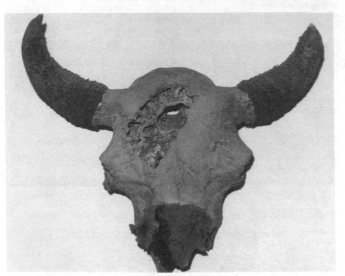

Buffalo skull, Indian-killed, with thick skin and hair still on nose. Skull was cut open to remove brains for tanning. Picked up and owned by Buffalo Bill and was in Buffalo Bill Museum, Cody, Wyoming. $7,500

Forrest Fenn, Santa Fe, New Mexico

Gun case, Cree Indian, 62 in. long. Material is caribou or deer hide, with trade cloth and trade beads. Came from an estate sale in Seattle, Washington, ca. 1870-1890. $2,500

J. Steve and Anita Shearer, Torrance, California

Gun case, Interior Athapaskan in origin. It is 58 in. long and made of caribou hide, trade wool cloth and pony-size trade beads. From the Col. Ben Thompson collection, ca. 1880-1890. $2,500

J. Steve and Anita Shearer, Torrance, California

Pouch, Ojibwa, measures 5-1/2 x 9 in. and beautifully decorated with beadwork. Material is wool trade cloth and trade beads, and the pouch is from the Great Lakes area, ca. 1880. $100

J. Steve and Anita Shearer, Torrance, California

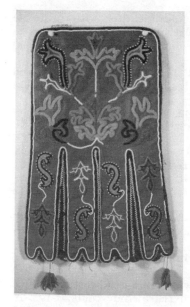

Octopus or fire bag, 10 in. wide and 22 in. long. Made of green trade wool with designs in trade beads with wool tassels. Rare bag, in pristine condition, from the James Flury collection, Seattle, ca. 1880-1900. $5,000

J. Steve and Anita Shearer, Torrance, California

Dance wand, may be Ghost Dance period; 15 in. overall length. Top is comprised of two small horns and handle decorated with beaded horse hair.   G-$400

Tepee bag, probably made from cradle cover. Designs are Sioux, Cheyenne and Crow motifs. Piece is 15 x 23 in. Fully beaded on front and in excellent condition.   G-$975

Haida argillite carving, depicting miniature totem pole. Item is 13 in. high and shows mythical creatures. Ca. 1930 (?).   C-$1,000

Quilled contemporary breastplate, 12 x 20 in. Done in Blackfoot design and excellent work.   G-$775

Bow set, Taos Pueblo, complete with bow case and quiver, painted cedar bow that is sinew strung. Painted war arrows without feathers. Items are ca. 1860-70.   D-$1,200

Cheyenne buffalo hair medicine case, ca. 1900. D-$195

Apache arrow quiver, 15-1/2 in. long, made of soft leather and about 3-1/2 in. wide. Unusual, and good condition.   C-$400

Gueverra long bow with four cane arrows with fancy foreshafts. Set is ca. 1870.   D-$425

Beaded case, 3 x 4 in., with geometric designs in green and white, with blue, yellow, and pink. One beaded fringe missing; Sioux.   A-$95

Fish effigy made of yellow-gray shale, drilled at dorsal fin region, from Virginia. Piece is 2-1/8 in. long, good condition.   C-$85

Sioux bow and quiver case with bow and arrow. Made of moose hide, has beaded edge with fringe and strap. Good condition, ca. 1920.   G-$550

Martingale, Blackfoot, and loom-beaded. Has red, white and blue ribbons, hawk bells and tin cone danglers. Fine condition.   G-$575

Apache saddle bags with intricate cutout designs backed with red trade cloth. Made of rawhide and with long fringe. Such items are seldom encountered.   G-$2,600

Cheyenne baby cradle with fully beaded hood, and with bottom part made of calfskin. Good condition, and ca. 1880.   G-$775

Russell Green River trade knife, old, complete with leather sheath. Rare piece, with a polished antler handle; knife is 9 in. in length.   G-$275

Rifle case, leather, partially beaded, probably an early flintlock or percussion weapon. Case is 4 ft. 1 in. long, and may have been used by a Mountain Man trapper, though certainly Indian-made. Old tag states that piece was collected in Idaho in 1907.   C-$950

War club, stone head, hide-wrapped handle, good condition.   D-$300

Painted parfleche box, Sioux, 11 x 9 x 7 in.   G-$165

Painted pottery tile, 4-1/4 in. wide and 5-1/4 in. high, with painted Kachina face on front.   A-$80

Knife and sheath, Plains Indian, sheath is 9-1/2 in. long, knife blade 5-1/4 in. long, with bone handle. Sheath well beaded and nicely fringed.   Alone, $155

Knife, White-made and used, possibly hide-skinner's tool, blade well-worn.   Alone, $55

Presented as a set, but knife and sheath obviously mismatched.   C-uncertain value

Sioux saddle blanket with 6 in. beaded panels, and with bells and heavy fringe. Excellent condition.   G-$2,600

Parfleche container, Plains Indian, 6-1/4 x 9-1/2 in., painted at one time. Good condition.   D-$215

Indian carrying net, collected in California, over 20 in. long. Woven with wide spaces, each about 2 in. square. Used for transporting unwieldy loads; natural fibers.   C-$200

Bison hide, painted with various designs; very fine work and may show a "count" of years and events. Condition average.   D-$1,400

Bow and arrows, old set, bow 3 ft. 4 in. long, with five arrows. Condition not good; feathers missing from arrows and string from bow; arrows iron-tipped. Set found in old house, had been exposed to elements for many years.   C-$550

Parfleche container, nicely decorated, medium size.   A-$240

Flesher, from Taos Pueblo, 15 in. long. Has wooden handle, inset metal blade, and in fine condition. Ca. 1890. G-$200

Nez Perce corn husk pouch.   A-$95

Plains "egg-head" skull-cracker club, good condition.   D-$300

Sioux saddle blanket, fully beaded on hide, and 36 x 80 in. Has canvas center and yellow fringe; beads on blue background with fine geometric designs and four different colored horses. Perfect condition and ca. 1910. G-$2,600

Knife sheath, Plains Indian, about 12 in. long. Small beadwork designs, geometric pattern, one side, late 1800s.   D-$365

Beaded knife sheath, fringed, some beadwork missing; leather is parfleche, good condition.   D-$345

Horseman's gauntlets, pair, beaded, wide-cuffed. A-$210

Bolo tie fastener, 2 in. high; shell inlayed with jet, turquoise and coral in the form of a quail. Exquisite work by Eliot Quelo, and signed.   G-$1,300

Columbia River basalt carving, 23 in. tall.   A-$335

Woman's hair-pipe breastplate, large and fine, Plains Indian, many beads, all with beautiful patina. Ca. 1880.   C-$2,300

Nez Perce "sally-bag." 7 x 10-3/4 in.   A-$300

Cherokee plaited mat, made of river cane.   A-$25

Quill and deer hair roach, Sioux, good condition, old.   D-$225

Original lance with point, California desert region; lance is 52 in. long, with obsidian point about 3 in. long, still secured with original lashings. Unknown age, but old.   D-$550

Squaw axe, trade iron, 5 in. high. Excellent condition, and blade has flower-like stamping.   A-$75

Wood comb, 9 in. long, with thirteen long wooden teeth. Has early chip-carving and abalone shell inlays. Northwest Coast.   A-$45

Tubular pipe, of a reddish-yellow quality stone, 3-3/8 in. long, just less than 1 in. in middle diameter. Highly polished, in vague effigy of unknown animal. Probably a late B.C. piece, from Archaic and Woodland site in the Midwest.   C-$875

Silver and turquoise concha belt, 34 in. long. Conchas elongated, with much stamp work and well-set with turquoise. Spacers in butterfly shape; ornate buckle, eleven worked silver pieces in all. Good overall tooling. A-$700

Birchbark basket rectangular, 7-1/4 in. long and 3-3/8 in. wide, with floral designs in dyed quills. Historic, Great Lakes area. Probably Canadian Indian.   D-$225

Beaded belt, 30-1/2 in. long, beaded on leather and with tying thongs. Geometric designs done on blue field, with colors red, yellow, and black.   A-$180

Squash blossom necklace, silver and turquoise, large, all beads made from liberty dimes. Naja with seven large stones and ten "blossoms," each with two stones. Well-made piece.   A-$625

Carved bullet 45-70 cartridge, unfired, with lead bullet portion carved to represent human face. Believed to be Indian work; shell casing of brass has heavy patina. From Kansas, estimated to be late-1800s.   C-$65

Trade-silver cross, 2-1/2 in. high, with back touch-marked "Montreal," and front hand-stamped. Suspended on necklace consisting of black beads with silver beads at intervals.   A-$165

Kachina doll, 8-3/4 in. high, painted wood, recent. D-$95

Silver ketoh or wrist bowguard, leather, with turquoise stone in silver attached. Silver plate measures 2-1/2 x 3-1/2 in.   A-$180

Trade-iron arrowhead, 2-1/8 in. long with squared stem serrated on edge for lashings.   C-$35

Shell necklace, 18 in. long, made of thin disc-beads of clamshell. Necklace somewhat resembles puka shell; well-made.   A-$60

Apache bow and two arrows; arrows without points. Bow once painted and is 42 in. long. Documented; pre-1901.   A-$215

Two Pomo arrows, cane shafts with wooden tips; each, 36 in. long, and in very good condition.   G-Each, $75

Rawhide quirt, intricately braided, contemporary. G-$175

Bridle and reins, bridle with some beadwork and lined with trade cloth (on leather); rawhide reins 3-1/2 ft. long.   C-$550

Medicine weasel, pelt stuffed with sweetgrass; piece has beaded eyes and nose.   G-$375

Sioux war club with large stone head and ca. 1900.   D-$165

Cheyenne knife sheath, fully beaded with five colors of beads; 2-3/4 in. wide and 7 in. long. Sinew-sewn rawhide and buckskin, and ca. 1910.   G-$500

Sioux "skull-cracker" war club, wooden handle covered with rawhide, with stone head. Piece is 17 in. long, in good condition, and ca. 1900.   G-$350

Haida silver spoon, fine, old.   A-$365

Umatilla "sally-bag."   A-$85

Sioux cradle cover, fully beaded top triangle with later added Hudson Bay blanket wrap. Good early colors; high quality.   G-$750

Birch-bark container, Canada and Upper Great Lakes area. Made from folded sections of bark; container has reinforced top and is 14 in. long. Worn but good condition.   C-$250

Parfleche knife case, probably Sioux, painted and old; knife goes with case.   D-$475

Frame of Basket-Maker artifacts, projectile point flakers, cordage, yucca strings, rope, and so forth. Shelter finds from New Mexico.   D-$215

Bow-drill outfit, Plains Indian, pump-style with short bow, cord, and wooden drillstick. Probably late 1800s.   C-$325

Rawhide knife sheath, Western Plains, 6-1/2 in. long, made of very heavy leather. Well-done, authentic, old.   D-$200

Hopi painted bow, sinew-strung and with four small game arrows. Items are ca. 1890.   D-$350

Crow Indian beaded knife sheath, 7-3/4 in. long, not in good condition. Many beads are missing; design uncertain.   C-$90

Stone club, Columbia River region, 13-1/2 in. long and about 3 in. wide, with a polished handgrip. Purpose unknown, but may be related to the "slave killer" monolithic axes. May be an unfinished because it is rather thick in proportion to length.   C-$415

Saddle blanket strips, pair, Cheyenne, beaded. A-$460

Hair ties, pair, braided and quilled, good condition. D-$160

Sioux pemmican hammer, rawhide covered handle with granite stone for base; item shows much age and use.   G-$325

Horse martingale, Blackfoot, 12 x 48 in., fringed with 4 in. of basket beads with hawk bells at ends. Collected in the 1930s.   G-$750

Kiowa war club, bound with rawhide; old piece. D-$265

Plains-type war club, 1800s. Stone fully encased in rawhide with rawhide-wrapped handle. Some beaded decoration, but probably added later.   G-$400

Saddle bags, Northern Sioux, buffalo hide with large beaded panels and a heavy fringe; has connecting beaded strips. Scarce and quality item, ca. late-1800s.   G-$2,600

Tsimshian basketry hair receiver.   A-$75

Corn husk bag, 11-1/2 in. long and 13-1/2 in. wide, with geometric designs on one side only. Nicely woven and sturdy, probably ca. 1950.   C-$155

Cheyenne baby carrier, fully quilled hood and partially quilled sides. Full size, ca. 1870.   G-$3,250

Parfleche container, envelope-type, with triangular red and green designs. It is 17 in. long and 12-1/4 in. high, and has wraparound thong fastener.   C-$575

Crow saddle blanket, made of old tepee canvas as base with beaded strip of cloth. Good condition, ca. 1880.   G-$995

Nez Perce corn-husk container, probably for small personal items; unrolled length 17 in. Unusual wool embroidery on sides, and a recent piece.   C-$425

Pomo cane arrows, California, with hardwood foreshaft that is sinew-tied. Ca. 1880.   D- $85 each

Plains Indian bow with three iron-tipped and feather-vaned arrows, all good condition.   C-$410

Sioux umbilical fetish.   A-$160

Napkin ring, unusual, Catlinite, 2 in. in diameter, said to have been traded on an Army post in mid-1800s.

Probably once part of set. Carving on outside depicts Western Army post.   C-$165

Tobacco cutting board, Sioux, in shape of turtle or possibly beaver pelt; has brass tack eyes.   G-$275

Zuni bear-hunting fetish, made of fur, feathers, and beads. A rare item and ca. 1870   D-$165

Plains Indian fan, probably prairie hen feathers (several missing), handle of sinew and some beadwork.   D-$85

Gauntlet gloves, pair, beaded, possibly Crow, with slight damage.   G-$325

Mojave painted bow with one painted arrow; ca. 1870-80.   D-$350

Gila River effigy, 4 in. wide and 8 in. long, good condition with some restoration.   G-$995

Beaded leggings, Warm Springs.   A-$120

Skokomish slate spear, 12 in. long; a ceremonial item and ca. 1860.   D-$145

Salish woven tumpline, Columbia River area, wide leather band and braided rawhide straps. About 20 in. long, fastened.   C-$225

Corn-husk martingale, Nez Perce, 18 in. wide and 31 in. long; rare, and in good condition. Ca. 1900.   G-$1,000

Sioux umbilical lizard, worn but in good condition.   G-$295

Hair ties, pair with beadwork and feather down; small brass dangles or tinklers.   D-$100

Sioux miniature tepee, 14-1/2 in. high, with nine thin lodge poles. Leather covering for structure has remnants of fringe at bottom, so may have been taken from a worn-out shirt or dress. Unusual, fine condition.   C-$425

Mono cradleboard, with woven red and green sash straps and a decorated hood.   G-$575

Horse bridle, trade cloth, with good designs, beadwork in Plains Indian style.   A-$385

Cheyenne beaded sheath and knife, buckskin. Knife is trade steel, edge well-worn, and with antler or bone handle.   D-$350

Shirt, Navajo, with approximately 400 hand-made silver buttons, old.   G-$1,000

Dance sash, 44 in. long and 12-1/2 in. wide, with trade beads the length. Fine condition, old.   G-$500

Rock art at Indian Petroglyph State Park, near Albuquerque, New Mexico. These figures were pecked into the dark basalt lava, probably by the Pueblo peoples, ca. AD 1100-1600. There are many animal and human figures plus unknown designs.

Lar Hothem photo

CHAPTER XX

ESKIMO, ALEUT, AND ALASKAN INDIAN ITEMS

Today two main, but related, groups—with roots stretching far back into prehistory to the Umnak people—inhabit the Alaskan region. They are the Aleuts, who inhabit the Aleutian Islands, and the Eskimos. The word "Eskimo" was a non-complimentary term applied by a Northcentral Amerind group, and it meant something like "Eaters of raw fish."

Eskimos on the coastal areas called themselves "Inuit," while more inland Eskimos were the "Nunamuit." Technicalities aside, all groups were almost totally dependent on fish, birds, and animals.

There are two other Alaskan-area Indian peoples who still make traditional arts and crafts. There are the Athabascan Indians (of inland and coastal areas) and the Tlingit-Haida (southern coastal parts).

Some contemporary painting and sculpting is done, but the emphasis is on items made of ivory, bone, soapstone and woodworking, plus some basketry and clothing. Much work is characterized by combining simplicity and clean, almost stark, but dramatic lines in the best artistic fashions. Some nephrite (jade) is mined northeast of Kotzebue, Alaska, and is made into small objects.

At Little Diomede Island, near the International Date Line and not far from the Russian Siberian coast, a pair of walrus tusks is valued at about $200. However, if the native carvers make the ivory into small art objects, the same ivory can eventually return nearly $2,000.

Not many people, compared with other Amerind items, as yet collect Alaskan-area and Eskimo artifacts and artworks. It would appear to be a very good area to explore. The most valued material is ivory, which usually comes from walrus tusks; sometimes whale teeth are used, and more rarely the single tusk of the narwhal. Included here is some very interesting information about walrus ivory, which will aid in identifying the type used in making certain collectibles.

Special thanks are due Mary Lou Lindahl, General Manager of Alaskan Native Arts & Crafts, Inc., for permission to reprint these facts on ivory, plus other material as noted.

For catalog, write (and enclose a couple of stamps) to: Alaskan Native Arts & Crafts, 425 D. Street, Anchorage, Alaska 99501. The Co-op employs only native craftspeople, and their Trademark is "ANAC."

WALRUS IVORY

Alaskan ivory comes from the walrus that inhabit the Arctic Ocean and Bering Sea areas. Walrus herds generally migrate north in the spring. Around this time, villages along the coast harvest the animal for a variety of uses. Although the walrus provides the main meat supply for many villages the year round, it is a renewable resource, in the same sense that cattle are, and the impact of the Alaskan Native on the walrus herds is far below the herd growth level. The walrus is in no danger of becoming extinct.

The ivory tusk of the walrus protrudes downward from the upper jaw, extending as much as three feet. The tusk has three layers: an inner core of light tan, dark tan, and white; a second layer of soft white and an outer shell that, when properly worked, can be polished to a brilliant sheen.

The ivory is found in three basic forms, identifiable by coloration:

1. New ivory: That which has been recently harvested, the gleaming white color described above.

2. Old ivory: Like that commonly found along beaches, usually tan or brown from exposure to the elements.

3. Fossilized ivory: Often very dark from having been buried in the permafrost for many years.

The Alaskan native peoples, in comparison with better known Amerind groups, have a significantly smaller output of traditional arts and crafts. However, the art forms are so unusual that there is usually little difficulty in assigning an Eskimo, or far northern, origin.

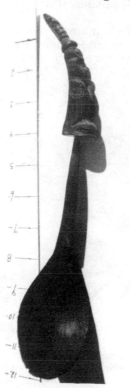

Left: Spoon with detachable ivory carved handle, rare decoration, from Alaska.
The two, $1,000

Private collection

Barbed bird point carved from ivory, 2 in. long, from Alaska. Carefully made with delicate serrations or barbs. $100

Private collection

OLD ESKIMO & ALEUT ITEMS

Bear fetish or toggle, small ivory, Eskimo, 1-3/8 in. long. Ivory is rich amber color; small hole drilled in shoulder region for cord. Perfect condition, and very old.   C-$165

Eskimo bowl oil lamp, steatite (soapstone), oblong, 13 in. long and 9 in. wide, 3-1/4 in. deep. One small end has groove which held twist of moss for a wick. Bottom almost perfectly flat.   C-$300

Rounded fish lure, Eskimo, carved from bone or ivory, and 4 in. long. Curved iron hook set into body; hole drilled at front end, both to represent eyes and to hold fishing line.   C-$195

Eskimo lidded basket, 13 in. in diameter and 9 in. high. Good condition, and ca. 1900.   G-$325

Compound harpoon, portion, carved from bone. Piece is 4-3/8 in. long, has socketed base, drill hole for cord, and cut-out notch in top for harpoon head section. Plain, but very well-made and good lines. Old.   C-$175

Eskimo tobacco container, nicely beaded, and ca. 1900.   G-$275

Eskimo comb, small bone, very old, 2-3/4 in. wide and 1-3/4 in. high. Few teeth are broken, but very well-made.   C-$100

Small ivory effigy, or decorative toggle, Eskimo. Just over 1 in. long, cylindrical, and in the shape of the upper portion of walrus.   C-$195

Eskimo basket, 5 in. high, 10 in. wide and 12-1/2 in. deep.   A-$50

Bone meat hook, Alaska, 14-1/2 in. long with sharply angled ivory inset to form holding barb. Used to catch and strip blubber when butchering large sea mammals. C-$525

Eskimo chipped bear point, made from material resembling chert 3-3/4 in. long. Stemmed, shoulders rounded, edges show extensive wear so may have also been a working blade.   C-$80

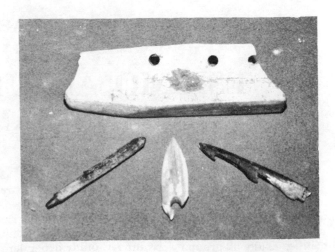

Alaskan artifacts.

Top: section of ivory or bone sled runner, drilled for attachment to sled runner frame. $100
Bottom: harpoon points.   Each, $40

Wilfred A. Dick collection, Magnolia, Mississippi

Eskimo baleen basket, made from the fibrous material in the mouth of some whales, used to screen plankton. It is 4-1/2 in. in diameter and 4-1/8 in. high. Several small ivory animals on lid; all in good condition. G-$575

Carved-ivory snow goggles, from an early group. About 4-1/2 in. wide and 1-1/2 in. high, with drill-holes at ends for fastening cords. Eye-slits are straight lines; very unusual and well-carved item. Prehistoric.   C-$850

Pre-Eskimo whalebone mask, from northern Alaska. Has typical inset eyes with vision slits, protruding and elongated nose, and mouth opening. It is 8-3/4 in. high, and in fair condition. Old.   C-$995

Eskimo walrus ivory hunter's tally.   A-$300

Eskimo or Aleut ivory chisel, with ground-down orca or killer whale tooth set in bone handle. Very rare item.   C-$525

Eskimo wooden point scabbard, a hallowed holster-like device used to protect sharp harpoon tips when stored. Piece is 4 in. long and 1-3/4 in. wide at base; may have been carved from driftwood. Good condition.   C-$100

Walrus-tusk adz-blade, from very early Alaskan coastal site, without handle. Tusk section 8-1/4 in. long. C-$295

Eskimo wooden fire-making set, with curved fire-bow, pointed and worn drill-stick, and fire-base with drilled holes for friction starts. Unusual items, in good condition.   C-$165

Eskimo ulu or woman's knife, with bone handle. A-$45

Eskimo ulu, with walrus design carved on handle.   A-$130

Eskimo ivory hairpin or perforator, 4-1/8 in. long and polished from use. Incised-fine decorations. C-$75

Ivory bow wristguard, attached to inside of lower arm holding bow to protect against bowstring slap. It is 4-1/2 in. long and drilled front and rear for fastening.   C-$275

Sealskin boots, Eskimo, 10 in. long. Made of caribou hide, the pair has snowshoe straps and is beaded with fur tops; from the 1920s. $400

Larry Lantz, First Mesa, South Bend, Indiana

Alaskan artifact, ivory thumb-guard with incised lines, for use with bow and arrows. $95

Private collection

Ivory carving, possibly a miniature totem pole, Tlingit, 8 in. high. Made of walrus tusk, it is ca. 1920-1940. $300-400

Pocotopaug Trading Post, South Windsor, Connecticut

Pre-Eskimo microlith blade, 1-3/8 in. long, evidencing ultra fine chipping, nearly 20 flakes to the inch. Very thin tip; may have served as a barb for harpoon, but actual use unknown. C-$50

Ivory harpoon tip, Alaska, from Dorset site, 3-1/4 in. long. Double barbs on each side, and in good condition. C-$200

Eskimo doll, of carved wood, about 5 in. high. May be from early 1900s; miniature skin parka, probably made of seal gut. C-$190

Eskimo snow shovel, bone blade, about 48 in. in length. Good condition and ca. 1900. G-$365

RECENT ESKIMO & ALEUT ITEMS

Eskimo baleen "wolf-scarer," a long, flat object attached to thong and swung in a circle; makes vibrating, whistling roar. A-$55

Eskimo lidded basket, 4 in. in diameter, 3-3/4 in. high. Coil weave, natural plant fibers. C-$250

Eskimo fossilized ivory bracelet. A-$85

Leather mittens, pair, Eskimo, 14-1/2 in. long with extension for thumb. Coastal Alaska, in fair condition. C-$200

Sealskin boots, pair, Eskimo, thigh-length and man-size, with waterproofed seam stitching. Good condition, and unusual. C-$700

Miniature skin mukluks, footgear, from St. Lawrence Island. A-$45

Eskimo fur doll, from Yukon Delta. A-$60

Aleut basket, Alaskan islands, of braided grass 11 in. in diameter. Has braided carrying strap, and is probably a lightweight collecting basket. C-$525

Walrus ivory carving, depicting a snowy owl. A-$60

Eskimo miniature skin kayak. A-$50

Miniature umiak or woman's boat, actually used by families to hunt and travel, 17 in. long, and gut-covered wooden frame. Four tiny paddles, each about 5 in. long. C-$500

Scrimshaw walrus ivory box. A-$95

Eskimo walrus-tusk etching, soot-impregnated thin incised lines, illustrating wintertime activities. Tusk section just over 13 in. long, decorated both sides. Not signed, and probably ca. 1930s. From Point Hope, Alaska. C-$950

Carved seal, of fossilized ivory, set on base. A-$90

Walrus ivory cribbage board, Eskimo, and ca. 1930. A-$340

Walrus tusk ivory cribbage board, 13-1/2 in. long and lacking game pegs. Fine condition, ivory and golden tan brown. C-$395

Attu lidded basket, miniature style, with fine weave. A-$775

Eskimo lidded basket, 11 in. in diameter and 12 in. high; basket has swirling stairstep design, in good condition. G-$400

Eskimo basket, measuring 5-1/2 x 13 in. A-$60

Eskimo doll, small, with carved-ivory face. A-$65

Soapstone fish, Eskimo carved, done by Tom Mayac. A-$75

Eskimo baleen basket, with ivory seal and bear. A-$300

Eskimo carving of a drummer, done on walrus jawbone. A-$160

Carving, Eskimo, St. Lawrence Island, it is 2-1/4 in. wide and 10-1/4 in. long. Mounted on cross-section of fossil ivory sled-runner and depicts hunter spearing a walrus. A very fine Eskimo art piece. Ca. 1970. $750

Sherman Holbert collection, Fort Mille Lacs, Onamia, Minnesota

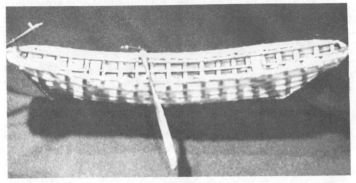

Model whaling or general-purpose boat, sealskin over wood, Eskimo. It is 15-1/2 in. long. $395

Pat & Dave Summers, Native American Artifacts, Victor, New York

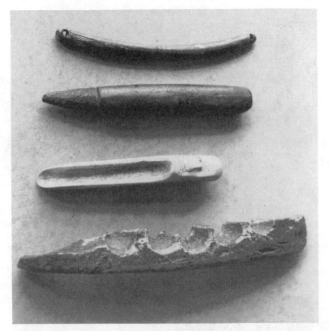

Eskimo (Inuit) bone and fossil ivory artifacts, all top to bottom:

Gorget, bent bone, 5-3/4 in. long. $65

Harpoon segment, 5-7/8 in. long. $70

Bone-marrow scoop, 4-3/4 in. long. $100

Fire hearth for starting fires with bow and stick. $60

Frank Bergevin, Port of Call, Alexandria Bay, New York

Eskimo doll, 14 in. tall, seal-skin outfit and with fossilized ivory face. Ca. 1910. $750

Indian Territory, Tucson, Arizona

Basket, Eskimo, body made of whale baleen, with ivory animal head handle. It is 6 in. high and 7 in. in diameter. Ca. 1940s. $1,500

Crown & Eagle Antiques, Inc., New Hope, Pennsylvania

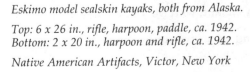

Eskimo model sealskin kayaks, both from Alaska.

Top: 6 x 26 in., rifle, harpoon, paddle, ca. 1942. $279
Bottom: 2 x 20 in., harpoon and rifle, ca. 1942. $139

Native American Artifacts, Victor, New York

Eskimo yo-yo, braided sealskin with a baleen handle.   A-$45

Eskimo lidded basket, polychrome geometric design, 4-1/2 in. in diameter and 4-1/2 in. high.   G-$150

Walrus ivory carved seals, two set on soapstone base; done by Tom Mayac.   A-$45

Eskimo basket, 4-1/2 in. in diameter and 3 in. high. Basket has geometric designs; in good condition. G-$95

The following are recent auction results, all concerning Eskimo items. The material is courtesy Rod Sauvageau, Trade Winds West Auction Gallery, Vancouver, Washington. Used with permission.

Eskimo skin parka.   A-$345

Eskimo basket, large, 13-1/2 x 15-1/2 in.   A-$105

Eskimo whalebone mask, by Alex Frankson of Point Hope, Alaska. Piece has ivory teeth and eyes, with baleen pupils and jade labrets.   A-$185

Eskimo bracelet, ivory on fossilized ivory; a fine carving with gold nugget.   A-$200

Eskimo adz, long-handled and with stone blade and oogruk lashing.   A-$170

Ivory carving, unusual, of Eskimo man hunting walrus with a gun. Polychrome, and ca. 1890.   A-$575

Eskimo caribou hunter's belt, with teeth, beads, and cartridge case suspensions. Belt has 248 sets of caribou front teeth.   A-$2,100

Eskimo bracelet of fossilized ivory, with finely carved relief of polar bears.   A-$205

Eskimo storyboard, with many carved figures attached.   A-$1,250

Eskimo harpoons, two, with ivory harpoon points. One lot.   A-$270

Walrus ivory cribbage board, by Joe Ignatius. A-$390

Eskimo bolas, set of fourteen, used for hunting birds.   A-$55

Eskimo miniature sled, made of caribou jaw, with baleen bottom.   A-$60

Eskimo appliqué skin mat, 38 in. diameter, and an exceptional piece.   A-$1,075

Eskimo tom cod jigging outfit, complete with baleen line, ivory weight and lure.   A-$70

Eskimo whalebone snow shovel.   A-$170

Eskimo carver's box, filled with items relating to carving.   A-$310

Eskimo fish net and line made of hide.   A-$270

Eskimo skin boots, very old.   A-$120

Eskimo kayak paddle, full size.   A-$115

Eskimo cup, made from the jaw of a walrus.   A-$125

Eskimo small-game harpoon, fine piece.   A-$120

Eskimo bow-drills, two.   A-$240

Eskimo doll, fur and wood, from the Kuskokwim River Delta.   A-$45

Eskimo baleen woven box, with ivory lid and bottom.   A-$335

CONTEMPORARY ESKIMO & ALEUT ITEMS

The material that follows is a selection of typical and authentic artifacts and artworks from the Alaskan region. All examples are from the current Alaska Native Arts & Crafts catalog; used by permission. Values are ca. 1980.

Game sled, weight two pounds, with walrus ivory sled on base made of fossilized ivory.   G-$170

Ivory birds, from 1-1/2 in. to 4-1/2 in. in length. Artists include works by Peter Mayac and by Kokuluk. Have wings etched in India ink, colored beaks and feet; can be purchased with or without bases. Smaller birds G-$110
Larger birds G-$165

Whalebone mask, from Point Hope, Alaska, 9 in. high and 6 in. wide. Use of bone shows very few parts of the whale go to waste.   G-$115

(Price range on plain to elaborate masks is $80-135)

Masks, made of caribou skin, with wolf or fox trim; made in community of Anaktuvuk Pass in the Brooks Mountain Range. Size, 9 in. high and 5 in. wide. Masks began as Halloween pranks many years ago, but have since become art objects to the trade.   G-$45-95

"Strong Man" mask, by Willie Marks of Hoonah. Depicts ancient legend in which a youth is strong enough to save his village from sea demons. Item, 9 in. high and 7 in. wide.   G-$135

Ivory pendant, of fossilized ivory, constructed and etched by Lincohi Nayapuk of Shishmaref. Pendant is cross section of fossil ivory. 2-1/2 in. across. Has gold chain.   G-$69

Medium coil grass basket, from Kuskokwim Delta village of Kipnuk, showing use of both dried grass and seal gut. Membrane very thin and strong; it is woven as an overlay to grass. Quality depends on how well the seal gut is tied back into the grass.   G-$142

Miniature harpoon, by Eric Tetpon of Shaktoolik, and 14 in. long. Detachable ivory head is tied to wooden shaft with sinew.   G-$40

Ivory owl by Keith Oozeva, from recently harvested walrus ivory. All three layers of walrus ivory tusk can be seen. Owl's eyes darkened with India ink and wing outlines are etched and counter-sunk.   G-$52

Dyed grass and seal gut basket, 11 in. in diameter and 10 in. high. Basket hand-crafted from marsh grasses collected in summer months; patterns whipped into the basketry by using dyed grass and sometimes dyed seal gut. Made by Mrs. Milton Mandigo of Chefomak.   G-$195

Soapstone carvings on various themes, all hand-carved:

Soapstone bird, 6 in. long, by Levi Tetpon. G-$22

Soapstone kayak, 5 in. long, by Walton Tetpon. G-$42

Soapstone bear, 10 in. high, by Robert Tevuk. G-$230

MUSK OX PRODUCTS

For contemporary fashion-clothing items made from the soft, brown underwool of the musk ox, write:
Musk Ox Producers' Cooperative, 604-H Street, Anchorage, Alaska 99501

Suggested Reading

(By the Editors). *Indians of the Americas.* The National Geographic Society, 1955.

Ivory drum handle, probably Eskimo, from Alaska. $75
Private collection

Alaskan artifacts.

Top: ivory sinew-twister, polished.
Bottom: polished bone or ivory tool.   Each, $70-100

Private collection

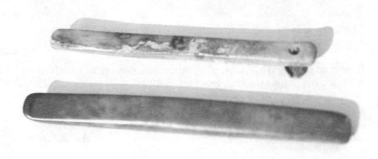

Alaskan artifacts, as follows:

Top row: bone point, slate point or knife, and slate harpoon head.
Center left: ivory fixed barb point.
Bottom row: ivory barbed bird point and ivory spear point.   Each, $30-150

Private collection

Alaskan artifacts.

Top: fishing-net gauge, ivory.
Bottom: fishing-net gauge, made of bone.   Each, $75-125

Private collection

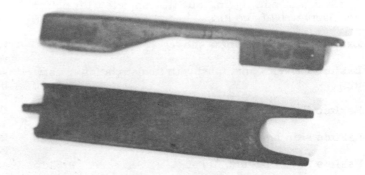

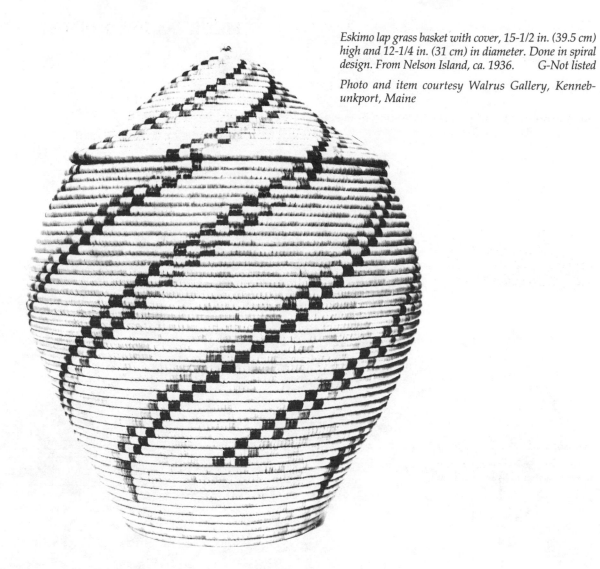

Eskimo lap grass basket with cover, 15-1/2 in. (39.5 cm) high and 12-1/4 in. (31 cm) in diameter. Done in spiral design. From Nelson Island, ca. 1936. G-Not listed

Photo and item courtesy Walrus Gallery, Kennebunkport, Maine

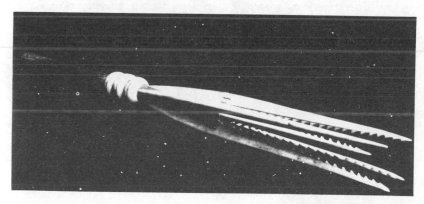

Ivory spear point, Eskimo, 9-3/4 in. (25 cm) long. G-Not listed

Photo and item courtesy Walrus Gallery, Kennebunkport, Maine

Very fine and highly polished Eskimo bone point or blade, 4-1/2 in. in length. Type can be found around Spence Bay in the Arctic. There, frozen ground conditions (permafrost) help to preserve organic materials almost indefinitely. C-$40

Photo courtesy Howard Popkie, Arnprior, Ontario, Canada

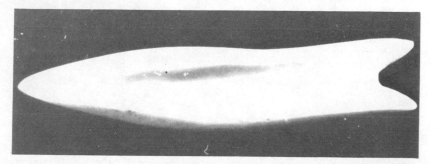

Sioux ration camp in Nebraska. Meat, probably beef or bison meat, dries on racks out of reach of camp dogs. Indians gathered periodically to receive U.S. government food supplies.

Photo courtesy of John A. Anderson collection, Nebraska State Historical Society

CHAPTER XXI

NON-INDIAN ARTWORK

This section highlights works of art produced by non-native or non-Indian artisans whose skill and dedication to accurate renditions will give an idea of the fine work being done today. This helps keep alive some of the old traditions that are, unfortunately, not widely known today.

An example is the work done by Brent Boyd of Ontario, Canada, who specializes in quillwork and embroidery. Mr. Boyd is self-taught and has been studying, reproducing, and restoring artwork for many years. Having learned from examining specimens in private and public museums, he only employs original materials and techniques that will achieve faithful representations. Some of Mr. Boyd's quillwork pieces were used in the motion picture *The Last of the Mohicans*, and he has done restoration for historical societies and private collectors. He also taught a course on quillwork at the St. Regis Mohawk Reserve.

Red River Metis style bag, 7 x 10 in. Brain-tanned deer leather was used, with horsehair, glass beads, and porcupine quills. $1,500

Artwork by Brent Boyd, Ontario, Canada

Sioux/Metis style coat, size 44. It is made of brain-tanned elk, silk ribbon, and quilled buttons. Coat front is also decorated with quillwork. $3,800

Artwork by Brent Boyd, Ontario, Canada

Swampy Cree style bag, 8 x 10 in. With wool fringes, this bag is made of brain-tanned moose leather, glass beads, and porcupine quills. $1,500

Artwork by Brent Boyd, Ontario, Canada

Red River Metis style bag, 7 x 10 in. It is made of leather and is decorated with wool, silk ribbon, tin cones, glass beads, and porcupine quills. $1,500

Artwork by Brent Boyd, Ontario, Canada

Western Great Lakes style bag, 7 x 18 in. Material is brain-tanned deer leather with tin cones, deer hair, and porcupine quills. $1,000

Artwork by Brent Boyd, Ontario, Canada

Red River Metis style knife sheath, size is 12 in. long. The sheath is brain-tanned moose leather and the decoration is porcupine quills. $750

Artwork by Brent Boyd, Ontario, Canada

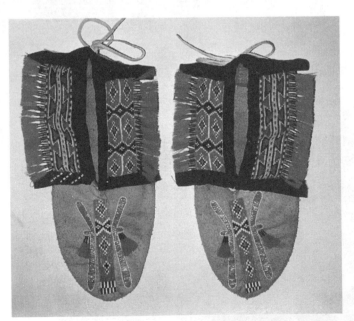

Great Lakes style bag, 10 x 10 in. Material is brain-tanned deerskin with porcupine quills, deer hair, and tin cone dangles. $1,250

Artwork by Brent Boyd, Ontario, Canada

Great Lakes style moccasins, 11 in. long. Made of brain-tanned deer leather, silk ribbon, tin cones, deer hair, and porcupine quills (loom woven), this is a colorful pair. $2,500

Artwork by Brent Boyd, Ontario, Canada

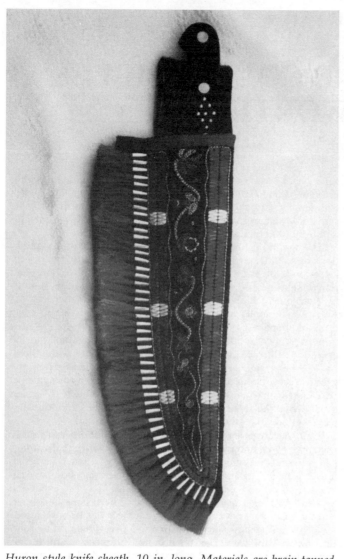

Huron style knife sheath, 10 in. long. Materials are brain-tanned moose leather, moose hair (floral down center of sheath), porcupine quills, brass cones, and deer hair. $1,000

Artwork by Brent Boyd, Ontario, Canada

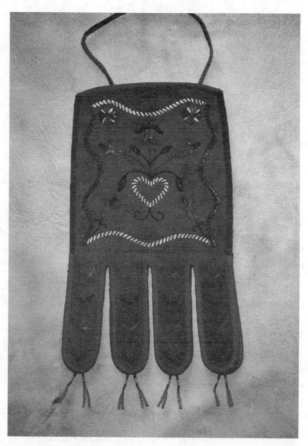

Red River Metis style bag, 8 x 15 in. It is made of brain-tanned moose leather with silk ribbon and porcupine quills. $850

Artwork by Brent Boyd, Ontario, Canada

Huron style moccasins, 10-1/2 in. long. These are made of brain-tanned deer leather, silk ribbon, deer hair, tin cones, and porcupine quills. The ankle flap panels and panels down the moccasin centers are of loom-woven quills. $2,500

Artwork by Brent Boyd, Ontario, Canada

CHAPTER XXII

WHAT ARE AMERIND COLLECTIBLES REALLY WORTH?

Here is a look at the four major sources for prices used in this book. They are each, in their special way, valid interpretations of value.

"A," or auction, depicts an actual, recent, high bid. Because bidders are often present for a pre-viewing, many catalogs do not fully describe the piece sold, or the small details that can make a big difference in bids. Regional and human factors also are important.

An East Coast object may be auctioned on the West Coast at a lower price than in the "home territory," and vice versa. Or, an item may go much higher than usual because of keen competition evidenced by spirited and high bidding. The auction may also cover a large and respected collection, in which case the prices are likely to be higher than usual.

Or, bad weather may keep important out-of-state collectors away, with bids then somewhat lethargic as a result. On the whole, auction prices should "average out" and be a fairly close indication of item values.

"C," or collector prices, would seem to be the most accurate because the owner has had time to study the objects and make comparisons. Contributors were in all cases asked to set a "fair market value," and most did. The collector, in his or her collecting field(s), tends to keep abreast of "going rates." While the collector attempts to purchase and evaluate realistically, other angles can be considered.

People and interests change. In a few cases, collectors got into Amerind objects and then, for whatever reasons, kept the collection but did not continue active collecting. In such cases, the "C" listings were below current market rates and were either dropped from the book or, with the collector's permission, were corrected to reflect current set prices and ranges.

Correspondingly—and the psychology of pricing enters strongly here—several collectors sent photos and descriptions of items that may have been somewhat over-valued, based on the nebulous concept of fair market price. No changes have been made by the writer in this area unless the figure seemed outlandishly high, and then, only with the permission of the collector. It is up to the reader to evaluate the merits of any one piece and relate that to the given figure—quite a learning experience in itself.

Collectors sometimes pay more for an item to complete a type collection. There's another side to prices: collectors tend also to get the bargains, fine pieces at below market averages. In some instances—and all collectors know of them, especially because they always seem to happen to someone else—purchase to value ratio would be a few cents on the dollar. Such windfalls are probably reflected occasionally in this book, being lower priced, but examples are not common.

"D," or dealer, is a good source of study. In most cases dealers are in the field of Amerind collectibles for both love and money. Love, because that is how they choose to spend a great deal of time and effort. Money, because to exist as dealers they must average a certain profit to continue the business.

Dealers, probably more than any other source-category, must be aware of what collectors want and how much they are willing to pay for items, common-grade to select. Many dealers offer a wide range of good pieces. Most concentrate in one of the three major Amerind collecting time-spans: prehistoric, historic, or contemporary.

"G," or gallery, is a special classification. The writer defines a gallery as a business which is concentrated in a limited Amerind collecting field. That area is irrelevant; a gallery usually carries high-quality, authentic pieces. The owner or manager may also be very knowledgeable in his or her own right and tends to deal with advanced collectors.

For the beginner—not referring necessarily to classifications of A, C, D, or G—it would be wise to pay nearly as much attention to the seller as to the desired object itself. To be a good purchase, the item must offer both authenticity and high quality, both of which should also be reflected by the seller.

For example, America is loosening up a bit, getting away from traditional antiques shops, dealers, and second-hand stores in pursuit of collectibles. All of these have been combined in the great buy-sell-trade arenas called flea markets, along with others.

True, tremendous bargains can be obtained when the wise collector spots a good Amerind piece at a giveaway price. Sometimes a tremendous buy turns out to be "hot stuff," stolen goods. Then the collector is left with an item that cannot be displayed or sold, or even admired with an easy mind.

In all categories of Amerind collectibles, but especially those from prehistoric and historic times, there is a chance that damage has occurred. Very minor damage can merely be taken as a sign of authenticity, depending on the type; however, major damage detracts from value. Sometimes, major damage has been concealed by a variety of methods. This may not have been done to deceive, and the seller may not even know that a piece has been restored.

No matter how the item came to be restored and no matter how well the work has been done, the piece is still not as valuable as a complete and original specimen. And it should not be sold as such or paid for as such. Check out the various methods that have been used in any area you are interested in collecting, because restoration can be quite subtle.

Regarding Amerind collectibles as a whole, a friend has some interesting observations: "The goal is to get a superb piece in excellent condition, and at a good price. Steady buying in the $1-10 range indicates that the purchases are just a hobby. In the $10-100 range, it is still a hobby, but has become a more serious one. And in the $100-1,000-and-above range, the buyer is involved with fine art—or had well better be!"

Attribution can be tricky. In buying a historic Amerind item that is said to have been owned by a known historic figure—or a contemporary object made by a "name" craftsperson—be sure all documentation is authentic and in order.

Also be certain that the item being sold is actually from a long-time collection. Many large collections are sold at public auction by specialized auctioneers, and when you buy from them, you can be sure of the source. You are also buying directly from that collection at competitive prices.

Collector demand in a specific area can send prices nearly beyond the financial reach of average collectors. The high prices of good pieces are partly the result of competition, plus some inflation. Also add to this the fast-growing awareness that genuine Amerind items of prehistoric, historic, and recent times are limited in number, while collector demand increases.

Only in the area of recent and contemporary jewelry—silver, turquoise, and other valuable metals and stones—does the material itself make up a significant part of the value. Otherwise, with a few exceptions, the actual material is of limited worth.

What, really, is the value of several pounds of deer hide, the quills from a few porcupines, and the sinew from a bison? And yet, if they are all worked into a Plains Indian dress, the current owner has quite a treasure.

The real worth of the majority of Amerind items has to do with a number of factors. Collectors are intrigued by the fact that Amerinds treated everyday materials in unique ways. These materials were made into items quite different from those known to our prevailing culture.

Beyond the importance of the basic form, decoration of almost any kind, if harmonious with the form, adds to value. In short—and a repetition of what this whole book is about—collecting good Amerind pieces is collecting good art. A Picasso, for instance, is not valued at ten dollars worth of paint and canvas.

As the value of the basic material increases, it contributes to the overall value today. Ivory is generally more valuable than bone, and gem-quality flint more valuable than listless, drab chert. Even in White-made goods, an iron and steel-bladed pipe-tomahawk is more valuable than an all-iron head. The better the material, the higher the price.

For the book, price ranges are helpful because they give an idea of upper and lower price structures. The actual price is even more useful; there is no doubt what the piece sold for or is currently valued at. As to terms used, the words "piece," "specimen," "item," and so on are used interchangeably throughout the book.

People in the field of Amerind collectibles, with only a few collecting area exceptions (old baskets), tend to be vocally aware of the problem of fakes. The writer acknowledges similar feelings, but there is a danger that people who are just beginning collections may feel that every other piece is non-authentic, questionable, etc. Sweeping statements have been made regarding the supposed percentage of fakes in certain collecting areas, and each expert has a different expert opinion.

Several things need to be said. The problem of spurious specimens, bad pieces, is not confined to the field of Amerind collectibles, nor will it be. Artifacts and artworks in the style of earlier periods, and for which a market demand exists, have been around for thousands of years. This is apparent from coins and stamps to furniture, glass, and paintings.

Unless one has many years of in-depth experience, an encyclopedia-like knowledge of all other collecting areas and a computer's capacity and speed of summation, few accurate comparisons can be made. Many collecting fields have the problem of fakes. But, the chances of a person being "taken" decrease in direct proportion to that person's knowledge of what is being collected.

Keeping in mind several key characteristics of Amerind-made collectibles—that they are and were largely created in unique forms and styles, and with a great deal of time spent in their creation—what might be some good collecting areas for the future?

In the prehistoric field, chipped artifacts predominate. Prices tend to be high for large blades and those of exceptional materials. Often overlooked are the mundane tools like scrapers, which may evidence both excellent materials and workstyles.

Some hardstone tools are probably under-priced, but the type varies with the locality. Good axes are now high in price and will certainly go higher. Slate forms, especially the less dramatic specimens, are probably a good bet. Items like effigy slates will one day approach the prices of average birdstones.

In the historic Amerind fields, there are two types of collectibles, those made by Whites and those made by Amerinds. Both have been appreciated greatly in the last decade, with collector focus on items used for war or hunting, in the trade iron field. Strike-a-lights might be good, plus any trade objects entirely or partly made of copper or brass.

Smaller historic Amerind pieces of good beadwork ought to be solid buys, if only because more collectors will be able to afford them in the future. Some plainer containers, basketry, and pottery are still priced at reasonable levels. Often pieces made for the early 1900s tourist trade have excellent quality.

In the contemporary collectibles field, jewelry is still very much in demand. There are so many aspects to this field that only very general guidelines can be given. First, learn as much as possible about good silver, turquoise, and shell. If the contemplated object is a poor-grade piece, it is not a bargain no matter how many times it has been sale-discounted. Also, buy only what appeals to you personally, jewelry you can live with easily and proudly. Last—and even the experts repeat this time and again—buy only from a reputable source. This above all is your guarantee of quality at a fair price.

There are two fields of contemporary collectibles that the writer feels have been somewhat overlooked. One is good baskets by non-famous makers; the other is good weavings by competent makers.

The amount of time—exclusive of gathering and preparing the materials—that goes into a 6-inch diameter basket is amazing. Faye Stouff, Chetimacha Indian basket weaver of Route 2, Jeanerette, Louisiana, advised the writer that at least three days are required to make one of her smaller pine-needle coiled and split-stitch lidded baskets. In the opinion of the writer, the work of this crafts lady—and many similar Indian artisans—will triple in value in the next few years.

Weavings, in terms of time and price, are much the same on a larger scale, with the average non-famous weaver working at something like half the national minimum-wage rate. Reading between the lines of statements made by a number of authorities, here are some things that are happening in the basketry and weaving areas.

The Indian craftspeople have recognized they are spending a great deal of time on work that yields very little monetary return; almost anything else, workwise, pays much better. Contrary to some popular beliefs, most Indians in this country do not make a living with arts and crafts. Probably fewer than five percent are so-involved.

In a number of cases, only a few skilled older people are still at work, and their productions will not be found in the market-place in large quantities. Because of this, it probably wouldn't be a bad idea to concentrate on collecting items made by the smaller Amerind groups. This not only helps support such craftspeople, but their work is often superior to more publicized creations.

Good-quality jewelry, by all signs, is still a good buy, whether from the standpoint of use or investment. In fact, when the U.S. dollar sinks drastically on the international currency market, there are a number of people who place excess funds in quality Indian jewelry.

Pieces purchased are often in the $500-1,000 range, and so do not diminish the supply for the typical collector or casual buyer, or unduly elevate prices. For top-quality pieces, it has always been a seller's market, always in demand.

There was some concern when this book was being put together that auction (A) values would predominate. There is a feeling among some collectors that auction prices tend to be higher than average. "After all," a collecting friend said, "don't forget that the winning bid is one 'raise' above what every other bidder thought the item was worth."

Perhaps so, but auctions still, on average, do not noticeably price items beyond a fair market value. In fact, the writer is aware of non-publicized, single-item sales between advanced collectors, or dealers and collectors, that are well above several type categories listed.

As to what American Indian items are really worth, there is a stock reply that insists any one piece is worth whatever the seller can get for it. This is not really true, because both seller and buyer may have reached a monetary (or trade material) agreement on a value, but that may still be high or low for the type.

It is, the writer suggests, the medium figure (of many such similar-item exchanges) that can give a reasonable idea of fair market value. And the collector goes on from there.

CHAPTER XXIII

HELPFUL AGENCIES

The average person interested in contemporary and traditional American Indian materials might like to know something about two very relevant agencies. One is professional, the other governmental.

The trade organizations is the Indian Arts and Crafts Association, commonly referred to as I.A.C.A. or IACA. The United States government agency is the Indian Arts and Crafts Board of the U.S. Department of the Interior. Both have kindly given permission for use of pertinent facts. IACA is discussed first.

INDIAN ARTS AND CRAFTS ASSOCIATION

The Indian Arts and Crafts Association is a national non-profit association of traders, museums, collectors, individual Indian craftspeople, tribal co-ops, and guilds.

Primary purposes of IACA include the promotion of Indian arts and crafts and the maintenance of high ethical standards. Other activities include national advertising, twice-yearly wholesale markets that attract nation-wide buyers, seminars, publications, legislative support (see, later), consumer information materials, and awards.

Available from IACA, and recommended by the author, are: a set of ten informational brochures on such subjects as buying weavings, jewelry, and pottery (cost five dollars a set); and the current IACA Directory of Members and Buyers Guide (cost ten dollars each). The brochures mainly cover Southwestern items, while the Directory is national.

The IACA is active in introducing and supporting legislation that provides stiff penalties for misrepresentation of Indian arts and crafts. Members are pledged to guarantee honest representation of any and all items they sell. Any member who, after a complete investigation of both sides, is found to be in violation of the IACA Code of Ethics, is ejected from the IACA. The information gathered is turned over to the appropriate authorities if there has been possible violation of federal, state, or local law. All complaints are handled on a confidential basis for the protection of both parties.

Finally, the IACA acts as a clearing house for information that individuals, organizations or firms may request on Indian arts and crafts.

In short, if a business displays the IACA seal of membership, that means the personnel will honestly and correctly represent its merchandise as to nature and origin. The IACA additionally sponsors regular seminars by Indian craftspeople and other recognized experts on both Indian arts and crafts and cultures.

Following, reprinted in full, is the IACA Code of Ethics. All members of the IACA agree to adhere to these principles.

IACA CODE OF ETHICS

1. To honestly represent American Indian arts and crafts as to nature and origin within the realm of their control and to offer return privileges for articles found by the Indian Arts and Crafts Association to have been misrepresented.
2. To abide by all Federal, state, and local, and tribal laws pertaining to Indian arts and crafts, artifacts, and natural resources.
3. To abide by ethical business conduct regarding advertising, appraising, pricing, and guarantees offered.
4. To respect and support ethical business activities of all Indian Arts and Crafts Association members.
5. To encourage consumer confidence in the authenticity of articles identified with the IACA seal.
6. To cooperate with law enforcement agencies and the IACA in the investigation of crimes involving Indian arts and crafts and to promote proper identification of Indian arts and crafts.

Anyone may obtain the Directory of Members simply by a written request, along with ten dollars. Write to: Indian Arts and Crafts Association, 122 La Veta NE, Albuquerque, New Mexico 87108 (505)265-9149

As another example of IACA work, the association has recently drawn up guidelines for ethical appraisal practices. The recommended guidelines section alone has twelve key parts, while eleven containments are suggested for the actual appraisal report.

The purpose of the IACA Appraisal Guidelines is "…to provide a needed service to our clients and to encourage public trust in the objectivity and competence of appraisals performed by IACA members."

Finally, in its role of introducing and supporting legislation, the IACA has been instrumental in amending New Mexico's Indian Arts and Crafts Sales Act, which is considered by many to be one of the few state legal Indian arts and crafts acts with "teeth." It is Chapter 334, 1977 Laws, 1st Session of the 33rd Legislature, State of New Mexico.

According to a past IACA Executive Director (personal communication): "This is now one of the better laws in the U.S. This can and is being used as 'model legislation' in other states which need to up-date and improve existing statutes, and to guide introduction of legislation in other states with no laws."

The act includes a legal definition of terms commonly used (Indian hand-crafted; natural turquoise), required duties of arts and crafts dealers, unlawful acts (mainly, misrepresentation), and possible penalties for such unlawful acts.

Included is possible action by the state attorney general ("…civil penalties not to exceed five thousand dollars per violation…"), as well as a private right of action. This last means the damaged party can sue in district court.

Legislation of the sort just mentioned will, both in the short-term and long-range, help assure the buyer that he or she is getting exactly what the item is supposed to be. Such legislation offers three-way protection, to the authentic Indian-made goods and the Indian craftspeople, the reputable dealers and the buyer.

Another helpful agency is The Indian Arts and Crafts Board of the U.S. Department of the Interior. Established in 1935, the Board promotes the development of Native American arts and crafts—the creative work of Indian, Eskimo and Aleut peoples.

The Indian Arts and Crafts Board concentrated on

stimulating what Indian arts and crafts existed, and engaged in aiding production, marketing and public awareness. Eventually, advisory groups—such as the Navajo Arts and Crafts Guild, and the Alaska Native Arts and Crafts—were soundly established.

A demand for authenticity and quality increased, and training programs were set up. These concentrated on individual craftspeople, with teaching by example. The reason is well-expressed in this extraction from the Board's recent Fact Sheet:

"This is because, in any art of any culture in history, it has always been impossible to separate absolutely the influence of the whole culture from the unique influence of the individual. An artist expresses both background and a special view of it in the work, and an individual whose work is good inspires and stimulates many others in the immediate community and beyond."

The Board actively assists artists and craftspeople to develop cooperative marketing organizations and to advance professional careers. A special emphasis has been placed on helping Native leaders regarding the preservation and evolution of Native culture in the years ahead.

The Board's Advisory Staff has played a major role in helping Native craftspeople and organizations counteract a wave of misrepresentation of imitation Indian-type crafts products that occurred as part of a fashion craze for all things Indian. The Board served as a clearinghouse for information, and successfully gained the cooperation of state and local consumer protection officials, various Federal agencies and newspapers—all to heighten consumer awareness to discriminate between genuine and imitation products.

As a result of these efforts, major distributors began to show a much greater sensitivity to honest representation in their marketing. The staff's continuing effort is to help Native people register trademarks in the U.S. Patent and Trademark Office, so that their work can receive full legal protection when it is marketed.

The Board's Museums, Exhibitions, and Publications Staff administers three Indian art museums. These were founded in the 1930s and 1940s by the U.S. Department of the Interior's Bureau of Indian Affairs, with advisory assistance from the Indian Arts and Crafts Board.

Each of these museums operates in a similar way. There is a permanent exhibition of historic tribal arts of the immediate region, plus a series of changing displays devoted to works by outstanding Native American artists and craftspeople. Sales shops offer the customer some of the finest contemporary artworks to be found.

The museums operate year-round, and there is no admission charge. They are:

MUSEUM OF THE PLAINS INDIAN
P.O. Box 400
Browning, Montana 59417

SOUTHERN PLAINS INDIAN MUSEUM
Highway 62 East
P.O. Box 749
Anadarko, Oklahoma 73005

SIOUX INDIAN MUSEUM
P.O. Box 1504
Rapid City, South Dakota 57701

The sales shops at the museums are operated, respectively, by the Northern Plains Indian Crafts Association, the Oklahoma Indian Arts and Crafts Cooperative and the Tipi Shop, Inc. These highly successful Native American arts businesses are independently operated, provide their own management and handle their own affairs. They buy works directly from the artists and craftspeople. The works are then offered to the public, either at the individual museum or through mail order.

The Indian Arts and Crafts Board's Washington, D.C. office helps the buyer of Indian art in several ways. The Board periodically updates and publishes a Source Directory dealing with American Indian crafts organizations and individual workers. This lists only Native American owned and operated arts businesses throughout the United States.

Copies of the Source Directory can be obtained on request by writing:

General Manager
U.S. Department of the Interior
Indian Arts and Crafts Board
1849 C. Street NW
USDI Room 4004
Washington, D.C. 20240-0001
(202)208-3773

In addition, the Washington office also issues a bibliography listing major books on contemporary Indian arts titles. Single copies of the bibliography will be sent, free, on request. Write the General Manager of the Board at the Washington address.

The writer recommends that the person interested in contemporary Indian arts and crafts obtain both the IACA Directory of Members and the Board's Source Directory. And books listed in the bibliography can be found either in a library (another fine source of Amerind information) or at a bookstore.

The writer also recommends the Indian Craft Shop in Washington, D.C. This retail-only, no mail-order business (operated by Government Services, Inc.) has Indian and Eskimo arts and crafts, these obtained from cooperatives, artists and craftspeople. Hours are 8:30 AM - 4 PM, Monday through Friday. The address is:

Indian Craft Shop
1050 Wisconsin Ave. NW
Washington, D.C. 20007
(202)342-3918

The U.S. Department of the Interior's Bureau of Indian Affairs also deserves mention here. The Bureau, in 1962, established the Institute of American Indian Arts. The purpose, as recommended by the Board, was to provide heritage-centered instruction to Indian youths with artistic talent.

Today, the Institute has achieved an international reputation for creative and innovative education. Now chartered as a junior college, many of the Institute's graduates are in the assertive vanguard of Indian artists and craftspeople.

The Institute has two public exhibits called Student Sales Shows, with a gallery of sales items priced by the students. The exhibits are held in May and December, both in the second week of the month. The Institute of American Indian Arts is located on Cerrillos Road in Santa Fe, New Mexico.

The Institute of American Indian Arts is also responsible for the Traveling Exhibit, called "One With the Earth." The exhibit consists of fine contemporary Indian art, as well as historic pieces from the Institute's Honors collection. The exhibit includes pottery, sculpture, painting, beadwork, weaving, basketry, and other creative works.

In the 1960's, fine Indian works of many kinds began to decorate the offices of the U.S. Department of the Interior. Appreciation spread until even U.S. embassies abroad used Indian art in their decor.

The Traveling Exhibits have toured Europe, the Far East, and South America. And now, full circle, the Exhibits are being shown in Native American communities.

The buyer/collector, it can be seen, has some valuable and powerful agencies which are extremely interested in seeing that American Indian arts and crafts are fairly and accurately represented at all times. Beginner and advanced collectors alike are advised to make use of the available information.

CHAPTER XXIV

DIRECTORY

The Directory is intended as a guide to both selected businesses and further sources of information.

The criteria for inclusion of a shop, dealer, or gallery in this section is that each has, in some important fashion, contributed to putting this book together. Each has been instrumental in providing factual data, photographs, necessary permission for use of material, or all three.

Some of the enterprises are long-established, others are relatively recent. Some keep regular business hours, others are by chance or appointment. As a further help, a brief notation is given regarding the main line of American Indian collectibles for that business. Besides those listed, other items are usually carried as well.

Before making a long trip, it would be best to call ahead and determine hours, current stock, special collectibles you might want to see, and so forth. A few businesses are mainly wholesale dealers to the trade and will be so-noted, You would need to be a dealer to purchase there; however, your favorite shop can handle your order as intermediary.

The Directory to businesses handling American Indian material has been set up on a state basis, alphabetically.

COLLECTORS

Joey Whitlock, 45 Co. Rd. 351, Moulton, AL 35650, (205) 350-2645, Stone and flint artifacts, the Atl-atl

David Hrachovy, P.O. Box 1069, Cedar Glen, CA 92321, (909) 337-9953, Plains Indian weaponry and accoutrements

Marguerite L. Kernaghan, 511 La Escena Drive, Bellvue, CO 80512, (303) 493-4471, All American Indian artifacts

Steven D. Kitch, 631 Wilson Ave., Pueblo, CO 81004, (719) 542-1136, Paleo Points from CO, NE, NM and NY

Philip L. Russo, 59 Lake Ave., Danbury, CT 06810, (203) 792-9885, Indian Artifacts

John & Susan Maurer, 370 Tucson Dr., Fayetteville, NC 28303

Michael Slasinski, 7201 Danny Drive, Saginaw, MI 48609, (517) 781-1152, Woodland Indian tools and implements, masks

Wilfred A. Dick, Rt. 4 Box 14-C, Magnolia, MS 39652, (601) 783-3400, All Indian artifacts

Hothem House, Lar Hothem, P.O. Box 458, Lancaster, OH 43130, (740) 653-9030, Ohio fluted points, prehistoric artifacts; books

James Bruner, Rt. 1 Box 39, Keota, OK 74941, (918) 966-3779, Oklahoma artifacts

Larry G. Merriam, 8716 Old Brompton Road, Oklahoma City, OK 73132,(405) 721-0484, Midwestern and OK flint artifacts, Paleo period

G. Thomas Noakes, 107 Gilshire Dr., Coraopolis, PA 15108, (412) 269-7965, Plateau, Southeast U.S. and Great Lakes regions

Gary L. Fogelman, RD 1 Box 240, Turbotville, PA 17772, (717) 437-3698, Northeastern U.S. artifacts

Lee Hallman, 166 W. Broad St., Telford, PA 18969, (215) 723-9471, Indian artifacts of PA and the Northeast U.S.

Alvin Lee Moreland, 1234 Hayward, Corpus Christi, TX 78411, (512) 855-2321, Prehistoric American and Mexican Indian artifacts

Grady Patrick McCrea, 12637 McCrea Road, Miles, TX 76861, (915) 468-6161, Early Texas artifacts

Willie Fields, Rt. 2 Box 625, Hallsville, TX 75650, (903) 668-3273, Scottsbluff culture

Dennis R. Lindblad, 1628 8th Street, Chetek, WI 54728, (715) 924-4373, Ancient copper artifacts, historic trade goods

Mert Cowley, 611 22-3/4th St., Chetek, WI 54728, (715) 924-4668, Early Wisconsin artifacts

Robert D. Lund, 918 Cleveland St., Watertown, WI 53094, (414) 261-2147, Wisconsin artifacts

Daniel Fox, E-mail, fox2@ksu.edu Kansas flint artifact typology, Florence, Foreacre and Niobria jasper artifacts aged, dated and current value opinions. Researching and referencing local areas for legal hunting grounds. Kansas Indian photo databank.

Steve Granger/Granger Artifacts, 7358 FM 968 West, Hallsville, TX 75650, (903) 668-3452, High-quality flint and pottery

Jack Baker, 1581 E Warren, Ozark, MO 65721, (417) 485-2208, Southwestern U.S. artifacts

Thomas Joseph Waffle, 872 S. Collins Lane, Manhattan, KS 66502, (785) 776-9362, Artifacts of Florence chert, Foreacre chert and Niobrara jasper

Forrest Fenn, P.O. Box 8174, Santa Fe, NM 87501, (505) 982-8520, Western and Midwestern Paleo Indian, Kiowa and Comanche beadwork

Dick Agin, A & B Collection, P.O. Box 1895, Buellton, CA 93427, (805) 688-9329, Artifacts from AZ, NV, WA; Chumash, Santa Barbara and Santa Clara counties, California

Richard F. Hughes, 1309 Summerlin Lane, Bastrop, LA 71220, (318) 281-4818, Southeast prehistoric artifacts

Kenneth Hamilton, 416 S. Walnut, Harrison, AR 72601, (870) 743-2175, Sel-found flint and bone artifacts

Michael W. Hough, 746 N. 17th Street, San Jose, CA 95112, (408) 971-6221, High Plains and West Coast prehistoric artifacts

Bruce Butts, 850 Cherokee Road, Winterville, GA 30683, (706) 742-9578, Artifacts from the Woodland and Mississippian periods

C. H. Baggerley, 4890 New Kings Bridge Road, Nicholson, GA 30565, (706) 546-8432, Archaic flint, Southeastern hardstone, Mississippian pottery

DEALERS

Caddo Trading Company & Gallery, Sam Johnson, Rt. 2, Box 669, Murfreesboro, AR 71958,(501) 542-3652, Moundbuilder art

Indian Ruins Trading Post, P.O. Box 46, Sanders, AZ 86512, (602) 688-2787, Contemporary silver and turquoise

Pierre G. Bovis, P.O. Box 460, Tombstone, AZ 85638, (602) 457-3359, Plains Indian material

Indian Rock Gallery, John W. Barry, P.O. Box 583, Davis, CA 95617, (530) 758-2561, Contemporary Southwestern pottery

Morris' Art & Artifacts, Cliff Morris, P.O. Box 4771, Anaheim, CA 92803, (714) 533-0391, Northwest Coast artworks, historic Plains period

The Curio Shop, Robert Vincent, P.O. Box 1013, Anderson, CA 96007, (916) 365-6458, North and South American Indian culture

Freya's Collectibles, Alan McClelland, 114 Banff Ave. / P.O. Box 1362, Banff, Alberta, Canada TOL OCO, (403) 762-4714, Central and Northern Plains, beadwork

Toh-Atin Trading Company, P.O. Box 2329, Durango, CO 81301, (303) 247-1252 or (303) 247-8277, Wholesale; old and contemporary art

Pocotopaug Trading Post, Alan or John Atkins, P.O. Box 5 77, South Windsor, CT 06074, (203) 644-4476, Prehistoric to historic items, related books

Dennis R. Phillips, 1819 W. Thome Ave., Chicago, IL 60660, (847) 869-6367, Dealer in fine American Indian Art

Edmunds of Yarmouth Inc., P.O. Box 788, West Yarmouth, MA 02673, (617) 775-9303, Contemporary material

Plains Indian Art, 609 Greenway Terrace, Kansas City, MO 64113, (816) 361-1599, Plains Indian items, many types

Casa Kakiki, P.O. Box 111, Sunland Park, NM, 88063(915) 584-0195, Contemporary jewelry

Hyde's, P.O. Box 2304, Santa Fe, NM 87501, (505) 983-2096, Historic, Plains Indian

John Isaac, 2036 S. Plaza NW, Albuquerque, NM 87104, (505) 842-6656, Southwestern textiles, baskets, pottery, kachinas, beadwork

Khalsa Trading Company, 1423 Carlisle NE, Albuquerque, NM 87110, (505) 255-8278, Contemporary jewelry

Morning Star Gallery, Joe Rivera 513 Canyon Rd., Santa Fe, NM 87501, (505) 982, 8187, Pre-1900 art from all North American tribes

Packard's Chaparral Trading Post, 61 Old Santa Fe Trail, Santa Fe, NM 87501, (505) 983-9241, Old and contemporary items

Tom Noeding, P.O. Box 153, Taos, NM 87571, (505) 758-2376, Southwestern Indian artifacts, Navajo rugs, Southwest pottery, beadwork, arrowheads

Native American Artifacts, David and Pat Summers, 45 West Parkway, Victor, NY 14564,(716) 924-5167, Full line of historic and prehistoric artifacts

Port of Call, Frank Bergevin, 65 Church Street, Alexandria Bay, NY 13607, (315) 482-6544, American Indian art and antiquities, world tribal arts

Back To Earth, Larry Garvin, 17 N LaSalle Drive, South Zanesville, OH 43701, (614) 454-0874, Artifacts, fossils, jewelry, books

Crown & Eagle Antiques, Inc., Mrs. Lynn D. Trusdell, Rt. 202, P.O. Box 181, New Hope, PA 18938, (215) 794-7972, Highest quality jewelry, rugs, pottery, stone and beadwork; collections purchased, certified appraisals

Antiques and Art, James O. Aplan, HC 80 / Box 793-24, Piedmont, SD 57769, (605) 347-5016, Plains Indian items, Old West, guns

Crazy Crow Trading Post, 107 North Fannin, Denison, TX 75020, (214) 341-7715, Plains and historic pieces

First Mesa, Larry Lantz, P.O. Box 1256, South Bend, IN 46624, (219) 232-2095, Historical and prehistoric artworks

Don C. Tanner's Indian Gallery, 7007 5th Ave., Scottsdale, AZ 85251, (602) 945-5416, Old pawn jewelry, other varieties

John C. Hull Antique Indian Art, John C. Hill, 6990 E. Main St., Suite 201, Scottsdale, AZ 85251,(602) 946-2910, Rugs, blankets, baskets, old pawn, kachinas, pottery

The Americana Galleries, 3901 East Anne Street, Phoenix, AZ 85016, (602) 268-3477, Ancient and primitive art

The Ansel Adams Gallery, Village Mall/Box 455, Yosemite National Park, CA 95389, (209) 372-4413, Contemporary selections.

Whispering Pines Gallery, 8243 La Mesa Boulevard, La Mesa, CA 92041, (714) 460-3096, Historic and other material

Jay Evetts, Yoder, CO 80864, (303) 478-2248, Navajo blankets, early rugs, historic pottery

Sherman Holbert Collection, Sherman Holbert, Fort Mille Lacs, Star Route, Onamia, MN 56359, (612) 532-3651, Historic American Indian artifacts and artworks

Canfield Gallery, Kenneth Canfield, 414 Canyon Road, Santa Fe, NM 87501, (505) 988-4199, Antique Indian art, Plains artworks, Southwestern pottery

Nedra Matteucci's Fenn Galleries, Alexis Buchanan, 1075 Paseo de Peralta, Santa Fe, New Mexico, 87501, (505) 982-4631, American Indian Art

James Reid, Ltd., Kellie M. Keto, Curator, 114 E. Palace Avenue, Santa Fe, NM 87501, (505) 988-1147, Antique Indian art, Southwest furniture and paintings

Ray Tracey Galleries, Nancy Welker, 135 W. Palace Ave., Santa Fe, NM 87501, (505) 989-3430, Works of Navajo jeweler Ray Tracey, other quality arts

Manitou Gallery, 1718 Capitol Ave., Cheyenne, WY 82001, (307) 635-0019, Original Indian materials

Rainbow Traders, Dennis R. Arbeiter, PO Box 566, Godfrey, IL 62035, (618) 466-0935, Ancient Indian artifacts, historic Indian rugs, beadwork, baskets, pottery

Quillwork by Brent Boyd, Brent Boyd, PO Box 251, Williamsburg, Ontario, Canada K0C 2H0, (613) 535-1139, Quillwork and moosehair embroidery

Blue Coyote Trading Post, Gerry Nolan, PO Box 412, Nashville, IN 47448-0412, (812) 988-6883, Indian art

Shearer Splendor, J. Steve and Anita Shearer, 4455 Torrance Blvd/Suite 493, Torrance, CA 90503-4398, (310) 316-5298, Plains Indian, Plateau, Northwest Coast, Eskimo, California, Southwestern, Great Lakes

Indian Territory, Neil Hicks, 5639 N. Swan Road, Tucson, AZ 85718, (520) 577-7961, Old and new Plains Indian beadwork and artifacts

Traditions, Marty Gingras, 7834 North Road, Victor, NY 14564, (716) 924-7826, Historic and prehistoric Pueblo pottery, Plains beadwork, pre-1900 Iroquois material

Historic Interiors From Thompson Lodge, Alan McClelland, RR#1/S-20/C-1, Sorrento, British Columbia, Canada V0E 2W0, (250) 675-2878, Northern Plains Indian and other beadwork

David Cook Fine American Art, Jamie Kahn, 1637 Wazee, Denver, CO 80202, (303) 623-8181, Historic American Indian art, regional paintings, arts and crafts, furnishings

American Indian Art and Antiques, Terry Schafer, Rt#2 - Box 298, Marietta, OH, 45750, (740) 374-2807, Indian baskets, blankets, rugs, oil paintings, beadwork

Scott Young, PO Box 8452, Port St. Lucie, FL 34985, (561) 878-5634, Southeastern U.S. prehistoric artifacts

Silver Fox Trading Post, Larry Kieser, 5104 King Hill Avenue, St. Joseph, MO 64504, (816) 238-7560, Artifacts from MO, IA and KS

The Child's Blanket, Roger Derda, PO Box 652, Highland, CA 92346, (800) 919-9276, Neo-Revival Navajo textiles with rare indigo and cochineal natural dyes

Iron Horse, Mickey Taylor, 3580 S. Park, Blasdell, NY 14219, (716) 824-2735, Pipes, prehistoric and historic artifacts and artworks

OTHER

Robert C. Calvert, 363 Avondale Rd., London, Ontario, Canada N5W 5B4, (519) 455-4002, Canadian artifacts; hobbyist

Andent, Inc., Ellis J. Neiburger, DDS, 1000 North Ave., Waukegan, IL 60085, (708) 244-0292, Ancient copper artifacts; research

Piedmont Archaeological Society, Rodney M. Peck, 2121 Quail Drive, Harrisburg, NC 28075, (704) 786-6294, The Southeastern U.S.; publications

The Eastern Cowboys, Jay Sadow, 4235 North 86th Place, Scottsdale, AZ 85251, (602) 945-9804, Arts and Crafts of 60 Indian Nations; distributor

Kachina Shop
Denver Museum of Natural History
City Park/2001 Colorado Blvd.
Denver, Colorado 80205 (303)370-6312

BOOKSELLERS

One of the fine pleasures of collecting American Indian items of any kind is learning more about them and the people who made them. Books are an important source of information; following is a source list of booksellers who carry a selection of books on Indian-related subjects.

Collector Books
P.O. Box 3009
Paducah, Kentucky 42001

Hothem House
P.O. Box 458
Lancaster, OH 43130

American Indian Books
9868 Diamond Point Drive
St. Louis, MO 63123

AUCTION HOUSES

Auctions are one very good way to obtain exceptional American Indian items, and here are three that have such sales on a regular basis. Write for information on Indian-item mailing lists.

Garth's Auction, Inc.
2690 Stratford Road
Delaware, OH 43015

Sotheby, Parke Bernet, Inc.
980 Madison Avenue
New York City, 10021

Old Barn Auction
10040 St-Rt. 224 W.
Findlay, OH 45840 (419) 422-8531

AMATEUR ARCHAEOLOGICAL ORGANIZATIONS

The archaeological societies are excellent for learning more about American Indians and their cultures, especially the earlier peoples. The cost of belonging is nominal; while many have regional names, membership is nationwide.

These non-profit organizations concentrate on education, and the dissemination of facts about prehistoric lifeways. Each of the societies puts out a quarterly journal, and these alone are reason enough to become a member.

Most states and regions have such archaeological groups. Six of the major organizations are listed here, from East to West, and some areas between the two. You may write, at no obligation, to the society that interests you. Thus you can easily learn what the society is and does, and how to become a member.

The Central States Archaeological Societies
6118 Scott
Davenport, IA 52806

Eastern States Archaeological Federation
RD #2, Box 166
Dover, Delaware 19901

Genuine Indian Relic Society, Inc.
3416 Lucas-Hunt Road
St. Louis, MO 63121

Ohio Archaeological Society
5210 Coonpath Road
Pleasantville, OH 43148

Oklahoma Anthropological Society
1000 Horn Street
Muskogee, Oklahoma 74401

Oregon Archaeological Society
P.O. Box 13293
Portland, Oregon 97213

COLLECTOR'S WHO'S WHO

A hardcover book series called *Who's Who In Indian Relics* is, in the writer's opinion, invaluable in collecting fields for the prehistoric and historic time-spans. (Early editors were Hubert C. Wachtel, Dayton, Ohio, and more recently, Cameron W. Parks, Garrett, Indiana; recent editor is Ben W. Thompson, Kirkwood, Missouri.)

Each book (with No. 9 published, Nos. 1-8 are collectors' items in themselves) is a North American guide, with biographical data, to hundreds of major collectors. Amerind items range from the early prehistoric to contemporary goods. Many thousands of fine artifacts and artworks are shown.

For further information, write:

Janie Weidner
Who's Who Editor
P.O. Box 88
Sunbury, OH 43074

And for a variety of display frames:

Indian River Display Case Co.
13706 Robins Rd.
Westerville, OH 43081
1 800 444-1280

PUBLICATIONS

There are three publications in the field of American Indian items that the writer highly recommends. These periodicals cover artifacts, handicrafts, and artworks of many kinds. You may write directly to the publications, as listed below, for subscription information.

Editor
The Indian Trader
P.O. Box 1421
Gallup, NM 87305

Editor
American Indian Art Magazine
7314 E. Osborn Dr.
Scottsdale, AZ 85251

Editor
Indian-Artifacts Magazine
RD#1-Box 240
Torbotville, PA 17772

Editor
Prehistoric Antiquities
P.O. Box 53
North Lewisburg, OH 43060

SOME FINAL NOTES...

To remain faithful to materials sent by contributors, and to demonstrate the variety in words, spelling of key terms has not been standardized. In fact, there is often no single "correct" version.

A good example is "heishe" which appears in half a dozen slightly different ways. The guideline has been that such words must resemble one another only to the extent that there is no confusion as to the intended meaning.

If anyone who contributed to the book was not thanked in the Acknowledgment section or listed in the Directory or credited with photographs that were published, you have the writer's apology in advance. Any such oversight will be corrected in subsequent editions.

This book is periodically revised and updated, and there is a need for additional photographs for each edition. If good photographs of quality artifacts and artworks are available, there is a strong possibility that the pictures can be used. For such contributions, please contact the author in care of the publisher.

Since *North American Indian Artifacts* first appeared in 1978, great changes have taken place in the collecting field. An accurate summary of what has happened in the past twenty years would, ideally, require comment from individual experts in each of the collecting categories and in subdivisions of each category. (In fact, this might be a good thing to do for the next edition.) It is now enough to say that very many additional collectors have entered the field, and at all levels of monetary ability and knowledge.

There has developed a great awareness and appreciation of American Indian collectibles, again at all levels and in all areas of the country. It is true that some valuable items can cost hundreds of thousands of dollars, but hundreds of thousands of items cost only a few dollars.

All areas of Amerind collectibles have increased in value, partly due to the influx of new collectors and a growing recognition of the uniqueness and special beauty of the pieces. Those people who studied carefully and bought wisely have seen their acquisitions increase in value many times. Still, an overall guide and a purpose of this book is to consider the investment aspect as secondary to the enjoyment aspect. Ancient or modern, the piece should be something that provides solid satisfaction just in having it around, in seeing and touching and displaying. Such an enlightened attitude honors both the maker and the owner.

At the early end of the collecting spectrum, one can acquire the oldest human-made items in all of North America. In the latest context are those artists and craftspeople who are today working in materials not used in more traditional times, but whose sculptures, jewelry, and paintings add a new dimension to the world of artistic accomplishment. The field, in short, has broadened and grown.

There will be many more changes in the next twenty years of *North American Indian Artifacts*.

Lar Hothem

GLOSSARY

POINT & BLADE TYPES

1/3 Approximate size

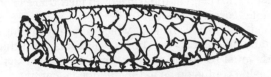

Dovetail (St. Charles) blade

Fluted-base points

Late-Paleo stemmed & shouldered blade

Bifurcated-base point or blade (Archaic)

Leaf shaped Adena cache blade

Folsom (Paleo)

Triangular arrowhead (unnotched)

Clovis-type

Late arrowhead triangular, notched

Woodland Period

Hopewell point or blade (notched)

Northwest Coast gempoint

PROJECTILE POINT PARTS

Adena point or blade (stemmed)

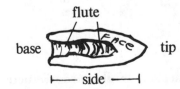

flute

base   Face   tip

side

Triangular blade (no notches or stem)

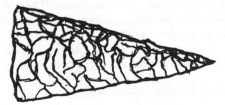

beveled edge

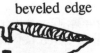

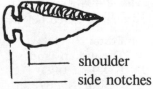

shoulder
side notches

Archaic E-notch beveled blade

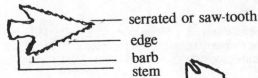

serrated or saw-tooth
edge
barb
stem

Serrate edge point or blade

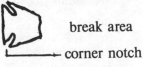

break area

corner notch

COMMON AXE TYPES

Scale: 1/6

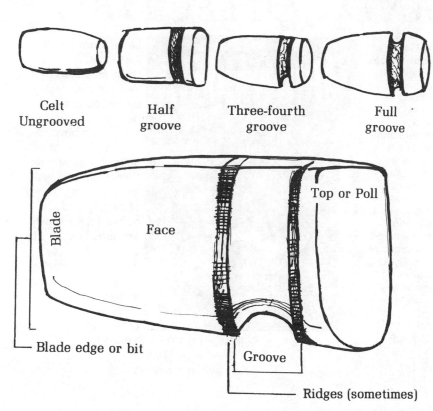

Celt
Ungrooved   Half
groove   Three-fourth
groove   Full
groove

Blade

Face

Top or Poll

Blade edge or bit

Groove

Ridges (sometimes)

GLOSSARY

For Points & Blades

Authentic: Point actually made in prehistoric times.

Bevel: Blade edge that is sharply angled, formed by re-chipping or resharpening edge.

Birdpoint: Small (less than 1 inch) late prehistoric arrowheads, either stemmed or notched at base.

Bifurcate: Point base split into double lobes with indentation similar to notches on sides.

Blank: Otherwise finished point or blade but without base notches or stem put in.

Cache blade: Quantities of points or blades found together in an underground depository or in a mound. Adena cache blades (large, leaf-shaped) are common in the Midwest.

Duo-Notch: Point with double set of notches (rare). A few duo-tipped points also exist.

Fake: Modern-made point passed off as authentic and old.

Flute: Channel-chip taken from both faces of Paleo point, extending towards tip. The shaft end fitted with the grooved portion and allowed deep penetration in target animal.

Fracture-based: Special chipping technique that knocked off long thin slivers of flint from point edges. Usually done on base bottom, occasionally on lower shoulders. May have been a chipping "short-cut."

Gempoint: Smallish points made of very high grade (colorful and/or translucent flints), commonly found in the Pacific Northwest.

Glossy: Flint with high surface sheen, usually denoting quality.

Grinding: Point base of blade with sharp edges ground off and smoothed. Evidently done so binding thongs were not cut.

Haft: A method of fastening to shaft or handle, generally notches or stem. A "hafted shaft scraper" once had a handle.

Notches: Matching indentations in point base area, may be in base, at point corners or sides.

Obsidian: Common in western regions, this natural volcanic glass exists in shades of red, brown, and black.

Patina: Surface coloration or thin deposits from soil chemicals; in short, how point exterior differs from interior flint.

Percussion flaking: Large flakes removed by direct or indirect blows from flaking hammer.

Pot lid marks: Conical depressions in flint that prove the item was once in a fire. Heat caused moisture in tiny hollows to expand and blow out a section of flint.

Pressure flaking: Controlled flaking that used finger pressure to create delicate work, edge retouch, deep notches, etc.

Questionable: Point or blade is probably not "good," i.e., is a fake.

Reproduction: Modern point made without intent to deceive, as exercise in chipping skill.

Serrations: Saw-tooth projections on blade or point edges.

Stem: Hafting method at base where flint extends in a central column.

Tip-base: The top and bottom of point or blade.

Translucent: Chipped material that transmits a certain amount of light; usually means high quality.

Warpoint: Small, late prehistoric general-purpose arrowheads with triangular configuration, without notches or stem.

YOUR GUIDES TO ANTIQUES AND COLLECTIBLES

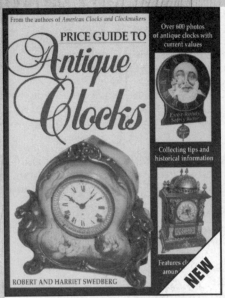

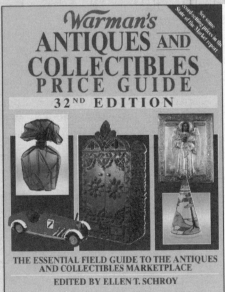
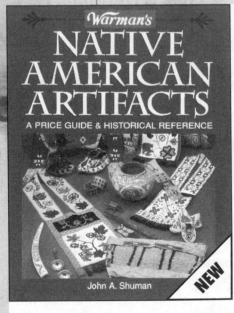

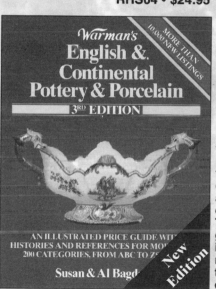
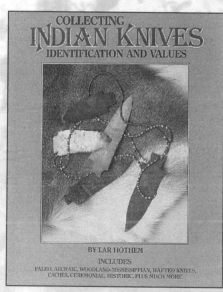